T NION
TO SEMIO

The Routledge Companion to Semiotics provides the ideal introduction to semiotics, containing engaging essays from an impressive range of international leaders in the field.

Topics covered include:

- the history, development and uses of semiotics
- key theorists, including Saussure, Peirce and Sebeok
- crucial and contemporary topics such as biosemiotics, sociosemiotics and semioethics
- the semiotics of media and culture, nature and cognition.

Featuring an extended glossary of key terms and thinkers as well as suggestions for further reading, this is an invaluable reference guide for students of semiotics at all levels.

Paul Cobley is Reader in Communications at London Metropolitan University. His publications include *Introducing Semiotics* (with Litza Jansz); *The American Thriller: Generic Innovation and Social Change in the 1970s*; *Narrative*; and, as editor, *The Communication Theory Reader*; *The Routledge Companion to Semiotics and Linguistics*; a *Communication Theories* (4 vols); and *Realism for the 21st Century: A John Deely Reader*.

WITHDRAWN

Also available from Routledge

Semiotics: The Basics (Second Edition)
Daniel Chandler
978–0–415–36375–4

Language: The Basics (Second Edition)
R.L. Trask
978–0–415–34019–9

Communication, Cultural and Media Studies: The Key Concepts (Third Edition)
John Hartley
978–0–415–26889–9

Language and Linguistics: The Key Concepts (Second Edition)
R.L. Trask
978–0–415–41359–6

Psycholinguistics: The Key Concepts
John Field
978–0–415–25891–3

Cultural Theory: The Key Concepts (Second Edition)
Andrew Edgar and Peter Sedgwick
978–0–415–39939–5

The Routledge Companion to Translation Studies
Jeremy Munday
978–0–415–39641–7

The Routledge Companion to Semiotics

Edited by
Paul Cobley

LIS LIBRARY
Date 13/5
Fund H
Order No 2111408
University of Chester

LONDON AND NEW YORK

First published 2010
by Routledge
2 Park Square, Milton Park, Abingdon, Oxon OX14 4RN

Simultaneously published in the USA and Canada
by Routledge
270 Madison Ave, New York, NY 10016

Routledge is an imprint of the Taylor & Francis Group, an informa business

© 2010 Paul Cobley for selection and editorial matter; individual
contributors their contribution

Typeset in Times New Roman by Book Now Ltd, London
Printed and bound in Great Britain by TJ International Ltd, Padstow, Cornwall

All rights reserved. No part of this book may be reprinted or reproduced or utilised in any form or by any electronic, mechanical, or other means, now known or hereafter invented, including photocopying and recording, or in any information storage or retrieval system, without permission in writing from the publishers.

British Library Cataloguing in Publication Data
A catalogue record for this book is available from the British Library

Library of Congress Cataloging in Publication Data
The Routledge companion to semiotics/edited by Paul Cobley.
p. cm.
1. Semiotics. I. Cobley, Paul, 1963–
P99.R643 2009
302.2—dc22
2009002260

ISBN10: 0–415–44072–6 (hbk)
ISBN10: 0–415–44073–4 (pbk)
ISBN10: 0–203–87415–3 (ebk)

ISBN13: 978–0–415–44072–1 (hbk)
ISBN13: 978–0–415–44073–8 (pbk)
ISBN13: 978–0–203–87415–8 (ebk)

To the memory of
Thomas A. Sebeok
'Facts do not convince me. Theories do'

Contents

Contributors

Initials of authors who contribute to Part II appear after each entry.

Myrdene Anderson is Associate Professor of Anthropology and Linguistics at Purdue University, West Lafayette, Indiana. Her publications include *On Semiotic Modeling* (co-edited); *Refiguring Debris – Becoming Unbecoming, Unbecoming Becoming* (co-edited); and *Cultural Shaping of Violence*. (**MA**)

Edna Andrews is Professor of Linguistics and Cultural Anthropology, and Director of the Duke Center for Slavic, Eurasian and East European Studies (CSEEES), Duke University, North Carolina. Her monographs include *Conversations with Lotman: Cultural Semiotics in Language, Literature and Cognition*; *The Semantics of Suffixation in Russian*; *About Sintetizm, Mathematics and Other Things . . . Zamiatin's novel* WE; and *Markedness Theory: The Union of Asymmetry and Semiosis in Language*. (**EA**)

Eugen Baer is Dean and Professor of Philosophy at Hobart and William Smith Colleges in Geneva, New York. His publications include *Semiotic Approaches to Psychotherapy* and *Medical Semiotics*. (**EB**)

Merja Bauters is a lecturer and researcher at Helsinki University and Helsinki Metropolia University of Applied Sciences and president of the international semiotic association UMWEB. Her publications include *Changes in Beer Labels and Their Meaning: A Holistic Approach to Semiosic Process*; and *Semiotics from S to S* (co-edited). (**MB**)

Søren Brier is Professor in the Semiotics of Information, Cognition and Communication Sciences in the Department of International Culture and Communication Studies at Copenhagen Business School. He has written six books in Danish and one in English, the latter being *Cybersemiotics: Why Information Is Not Enough*. His articles include 'Nature and machine'; 'Biosemiotics'; 'The Peircean paradigm for biosemiotics'; and 'Bateson and Peirce on the pattern that connects and the sacred'. He is the founder and editor of the interdisciplinary quarterly journal *Cybernetics & Human Knowing*, fellow of the American Society for Cybernetics and has been awarded The Warren McCulloch Medal. (**SB**)

Peer Bundgaard is an associate professor and PhD in General Semiotics at the University of Aarhus. His research interests include cognitive linguistics and phenomenology of language, as well as aesthetic semiotics. His recent publications include *Kunst – semiotiske beskrivelse af æstetisk betydning og oplevelse*; 'The ideal scaffolding of language – E. Husserl's fourth logical investigation in the light of cognitive linguistics'; 'The grammar of aesthetic intuition'; and, as editor, *Kognitiv Semiotik* (with Frederik Stjernfelt). (**PB**)

Sara Cannizzaro is a lecturer at London Metropolitan University. Her research is in the field of systems theory and biosemiotics and her publications include 'On logic and differentiation: Principles of life' and '"The Line of Beauty": On natural forms and abduction'. (**SC**)

Rocco Capozzi is Professor of Contemporary Italian Literature, semiotics and literary theories at the University of Toronto. He is the author of *Bernari. Tra fantasia e realtà*; *Scrittori, critici e industria culturale*; and *Leggere* Il Nome della Rosa *e l'intertestualità*. He is also the editor of *A Homage to Moravia*; *Scrittori e le poetiche letterarie in Italia*; *Reading Eco*; and *Italo Calvino Lightness and Multiplicity*. (**RC**)

Bruce Clarke is Professor of Literature and Science at Texas Tech University. His publications include *Energy Forms: Allegory and Science in the Era of Classical Thermodynamics*; *Posthuman Metamorphosis: Narrative and Systems*; and (with Mark Hansen) *Emergence and Embodiment: New Essays in Second-Order Systems Theory*. With Manuela Rossini, he is currently preparing the *Routledge Companion to Literature and Science*. (**BC**)

Paul Cobley is Reader in Communications at London Metropolitan University. His publications include *Introducing Semiotics* (with Litza Jansz); *Narrative*; *The American Thriller: Generic Innovation and Social Change in the 1970s*; and, as editor, *The Communication Theory Reader*; *Communication Theories* (4 vols); *The Routledge Companion to Semiotics and Linguistics*; and *Realism for the 21st Century: A John Deely Reader*. (**PC**)

Nikolas Coupland is Professor and Research Director of the Centre for Language and Communication Research at Cardiff University. His books include *Metalanguage: Social and Ideological Perspectives* (with Adam Jaworski and Dariusz Galasinski); *Style: Language, Variation and Identity*; *The Discourse Reader* (second edition, with Adam Jaworski); and *The New Sociolinguistics Reader* (with Adam Jaworski). He is currently editing *The Blackwell Handbook of Language and Globalisation*. (**NC**)

Marcel Danesi is a professor in the Department of Anthropology, University of Toronto. Among his recent books are *The Quest for Meaning: A Guide to Semiotic Theory and Practice*; *Problem-Solving in Mathematics: A Semiotic*

Perspective for Educators and Teachers; *Language, Society and Culture: Introducing Anthropological Linguistics*; *Why it Sells: Decoding the Meanings of Brand Names, Logos, Ads, and Other Marketing and Advertising Ploys*; *Popular Culture: Introductory Perspectives*; *X-Rated: The Power of Mythic Symbolism in Popular Culture*; and *Dictionary of Media and Communications* (edited). He is also editor-in-chief of *Semiotica*. (**MD**)

John Deely is a Full Professor of Philosophy at the University of St Thomas in Houston, Texas. His books include *Basics of Semiotics*; *New Beginnings*; *The Human Use of Signs: Elements of Anthroposemiosis*; *Four Ages of Understanding: The First Postmodern Survey of Philosophy from the Ancient Times to the Turn of the Twenty-first Century*; *Intentionality and Semiotics*; and *Augustine and Poinsot, Descartes and Poinsot*, among others (**JD**)

Claus Emmeche is an associate professor and centre director at the Center for the Philosophy of Nature and Science Studies at the University of Copenhagen. His publications include *Genes, Information, and Semiosis* (with Charbel Niño El-Hani and João Queiroz); *Constructing and Explaining Emergence in Artificial Life*; and *On the Biosemiotics of Embodiment and Our Human Cyborg Nature*. (**CE**)

Donald Favareau is an assistant professor in the University Scholars Programme at the National University of Singapore. His recent publications include chapters in *Introduction to Biosemiotics: The New Biological Synthesis*; *Biosemiotics in Transdisciplinary Contexts*; and *A Legacy for Living Systems: Gregory Bateson as Precursor to Biosemiotics*. He is vice-president of the International Society for Biosemiotic Studies and the editor of the anthology *Essential Readings in Biosemiotics*. (**DF**)

Roy Harris is Emeritus Professor of General Linguistics at the University of Oxford. His publications include *The Language Makers*; *The Language Myth*; *The Language Machine*; *The Language Connection*; and *Signs, Language and Communication*. His translation of Saussure's *Cours de linguistique générale* was awarded the Scott Moncrieff prize. (**RH**)

Anne Hénault, ENS (École Normale Supérieure, Paris), is Professor of Sciences of Language at the University of Paris (Doctoral School of Paris-Sorbonne). She has published, *inter alia*, *Le Pouvoir comme Passion* (which includes a debate between Algirdas J. Greimas and Paul Ricoeur); *Histoire de la Sémiotique*; and, both as editor and author, *Questions de Sémiotique*. She started, together with A. J. Greimas, *Actes Sémiotiques* in order to circulate the working papers of the Paris School. She is director of the series *Formes Sémiotiques*. (**AH**)

Jesper Hoffmeyer is an associate professor in the Department of Molecular Biology, University of Copenhagen. His publications include *Biosemiotics. An*

Examination into the Signs of Life and the Life of Signs and, as editor, *A Legacy of Living Systems: Gregory Bateson as Precursor to Biosemiotics*.

Nathan Houser is Professor Emeritus of Philosophy at Indiana University in Indianapolis (IUPUI). He has served as director of the Peirce Edition Project and the Institute for American Thought and as president of the Charles S. Peirce Society and the Semiotic Society of America. From 1993 to 2009 he was general editor for the Indianapolis critical edition of Peirce's writings, he co-edited the two-volume *Essential Peirce* and *Studies in the Logic of Charles Sanders Peirce* and is the author of many articles on Peirce's logic and semiotics. (**NH**)

Robert Innis is a professor in the Department of Philosophy at the University of Massachusetts, Lowell. His books include *Karl Bühler: Semiotic Foundations of Language Theory*; *Consciousness and the Play of Signs*; *Pragmatism and the Forms of Sense: Language, Perception, Technics*; and *Susanne Langer in Focus: The Symbolic Mind*. (**RI**)

Adam Jaworski is Professor at the Centre for Language and Communication Research, Cardiff University. His books include *The Discourse Reader*; *The New Sociolinguistics Reader*; (both with Nikolas Coupland); *Semiotic Landscapes: Language, Image, Space*; and *Tourism Discourse: Language and Global Mobility*; (both with Crispin Thurlow). (**AJ**)

Adam Kendon studied biology and psychology at Cambridge and Oxford. At present affiliated to the University of Pennsylvania and recently with the University of Naples 'Orientale' in Naples and the University of Calabria, he studies gesture as a component of communication in face-to-face interaction. He published a critical English edition of Andrea de Jorio's 1832 treatise on Neapolitan gesture in 2000 and, in 2004, a book entitled *Gesture: Visible Action as Utterance*. (**AK**)

Gunther R. Kress is Professor of Education/English at the Institute of Education, University of London. His publications include *Language as Ideology* and *Social Semiotics* (both with Robert Hodge); *Reading Images*: *The Grammar of Visual Design* (with Theo van Leeuwen); *Before Writing*; *Early Spelling*; and *Multimodal Teaching and Learning* and *Multimodality*. (**GRK**)

Kalevi Kull is Professor in Biosemiotics at the University of Tartu, Estonia. His publications include *Lectures in Theoretical Biology* (co-editor, 2 vols); a special volume of *Semiotica* about Jakob von Uexküll (editor); *Imagining Nature: Practices of Cosmology and Identity* (co-editor); and papers about the recognition concept of species, semiotic aspects of evolution, history and theory of biosemiotics, and ecosemiotics. (**KK**)

Richard Lanigan is University Distinguished Scholar and Professor of Communicology (Emeritus), Southern Illinois University. He is Director and Fellow of the International Communicology Institute, Washington, DC. He has twice been a Senior Fulbright Fellow (China 1996, Canada 2007) and is a Fellow of the International Academy for Intercultural Research. He is vice-president of the International Association for Semiotic Studies. His books include *Speaking and Semiology*; *The Human Science of Communicology*; and *Speech Act Phenomenology*. (**RL**)

Svend Erik Larsen is Professor of Comparative Literature at Aarhus University, Denmark. His semiotic publications include *Sémiologie littéraire*; *Signs in Use*; *Actualité de Brøndal* (editor); and *Gärten und Parks* (editor). (**SEL**)

David Machin works in the School of Journalism, Media and Cultural Studies, Cardiff University. His books include *Global Media Discourse*, co-authored with Theo van Leeuwen; *Introduction to Multimodal Analysis*; and *News Production: Theory and Practice*, co-authored with Sarah Niblock. His most recent book is on multimodality, titled *Analysing Popular Music,* along with an edited collection on *Media Audiences* with Barrie Gunter. He has published numerous articles in reviewed journals especially in the field of visual communication and discourse analysis. (**DMac**)

Giovanni Manetti is Professor of Semiotics and History of Semiotics at Siena University (Italy). His publications include *L'enunciazione. Dalla svolta comunicativa ai nuovi media*; *Specchio delle mie brame. Dodici anni di spot televisivi*; *Theories of the Sign in Classical Antiquity*; *Sport e giochi nell'antichità classica*; *Grammatica dell'arguzia* (with Patrizia Violi); and, as editor, *Animali, angeli, macchine. Come comunicano e come pensano* (with A. Prato); *Il contagio e i suoi simboli* (2 vols); *Semiotica: testi esemplari. Storia, teoria, pratica, proposte* (with P. Bertetti); *Forme della testualità. Teorie, modelli, storia, e prospettive* (with P. Bertetti); *Signs and Signification* (with H. S. Gill, 2 vols); *Knowledge through Signs. Ancient Semiotic Theories and Practices*; and *Signs of Antiquity/Antiquity of Signs*.

Timo Maran is Senior Research Fellow in Semiotics at Tartu University. His publications include *Mimikri semiootika* [*Semiotics of Mimicry*]; and, as editor, *Readings in Zoosemiotics* (with Dario Martinelli and Aleksei Turovski); *Eesti looduskultuur* [*Estonian Culture of Nature*] (with Kadri Tüür). (**TM**)

Dario Martinelli is Docent of Musicology and Semiotics at the University of Helsinki. His publications include *How Musical is a Whale? Towards a Theory of Zoomusicology*; *Zoosemiotics: Proposals for a Handbook*; *Of Birds, Whales and Other Musicians: Introduction to Zoomusicology*; and, as editor, *Semiotics from S to S*; *Music, Senses, Body*; and *Stili, Stilemi, Stilismi.* He is editor-in-chief of *IF – Journal of Italo-Finnish Studies*. (**DMar**)

Floyd Merrell is Professor of Semiotics and Spanish American Cultural and Literary Studies at Purdue University, West Lafayette, Indiana. His publications include *Unthinking Thinking: Jorge Luis Borges, Mathematics, and the 'New Physics'*; *Peirce, Signs, and Meaning*; *Signs Grow*; *Sensing Semiosis*; *Simplicity and Complexity*; *Tasking Textuality*; *Complementing Latin American Borders*; *Capoeira and Candomblé*; and *Processing Cultural Meaning*. (**FM**)

Paul Perron is Professor of French and Principal of University College, University of Toronto. His publications include *A. J. Greimas and Narrative Cognition* and *Analyzing Cultures* (with M. Danesi); *Balzac: Sémiotique du personnage romanesque*; and *Semiotics and the Modern Quebec Novel*. (**PP**)

Susan Petrilli is Professor of Philosophy and Theory of Languages at the University of Bari, Department of Linguistic Practices and Text Analysis. Her monographs include: *Significs, semiotica, significazione*; *Materia segnica e interpretazione. Figure e prospettive*; *Che cosa significa significare? Itinerari nello studio dei segni*; *Su Victoria Welby. Significs e filosofia del linguaggio*; *Teoria dei segni e del linguaggio*; *Percorsi della semiotica*; *Signifying and Understanding. Reading the Works of Victoria Welby and the Significs Movement*; and *Sign Crossroads in Global Perspective. Semiotics and Responsibilities*. In 2008 she was nominated 7th Thomas A. Sebeok Fellow of the Semiotic Society of America. (**SP**)

Augusto Ponzio is Full Professor of Philosophy of Language and General Linguistics at the University of Bari. He is the author of numerous books, including *I segni tra globalità e infinità. Per la critica della comunicazione globale*; *Elogio dell'infunzionale*; *Semiotica e dialettica*; *The Dialogic Nature of the Sign*; *La cifrematica dell'ascolto*; *Fuori luogo. L'esorbitante nella riproduzione dell'identico*; *Linguistica generale, scrittura letteraria e traduzione*; *A mente. Processi cognitivi e formazione linguistica*; *Linguaggio, lavoro e mercato globale. Rileggendo Rossi-Landi*; and *La dissidenza cifrematica*. (**AP**)

Anti Randviir is Senior Researcher at the Department of Semiotics, University of Tartu. His publications include *Mapping the World: Towards a Sociosemiotic Approach to Culture*; *Sociosemiotica* (co-edited); 'Spatialization of knowledge: Cartographic roots of globalization'; 'On spatiality in Tartu–Moscow cultural semiotics: The semiotic subject'; and 'Semiotization: What, where, how?'. He is also the editor of the journal *Acta Semiotica Estica*. (**AR**)

Raphael Salkie is Professor of Language Studies at the University of Brighton. His publications include *The Chomsky Update* and *Text and Discourse Analysis*, as well as 'Modals and prototypes: English and German in contrast'; 'Where is contrastive linguistics?'; and '*Will*: Tense or modal or both?'. (**RS**)

Peter J. Schulz is Professor of Communication Theories and Health Communication at the School of Communication Sciences and director of the Institute of Communication and Health, University of Lugano. He is the author of five books and of more than sixty journal articles, as well as the editor of five books (including *Communication Theories*, 4 vols). (**PJS**)

Thomas A. Sebeok (1920–2001) was Distinguished Professor Emeritus of Linguistics and Semiotics and Senior Fellow in the School of Information Sciences at Indiana University. As well as the being the major figure in the development of semiotics, along with Peirce and Saussure, he served as the General Editor of the *Encyclopedic Dictionary of Semiotics* (2nd edn, Vols 1–3, 1994), and was co-editor of *Semiotics: A Handbook on the Sign-Theoretic Foundations of Nature and Culture* (Vols 1–2, 1997; Vol. 3, 2002). (**TAS**)

Kathryn Staiano-Ross is a medical anthropologist. Her publications include *Interpreting Signs of Illness: A Case Study in Medical Semiotics*; *Tales from a Forgotten Place* (with Bismark Ranguy); and a number of articles published in *Semiotica* on the subjects of medical semiotics and biocultural semiotics. (**KSR**)

Pippa Stein (1955–2008) was an English teacher–educator at the University of the Witwatersrand, Johannesburg. She was the author of *Multimodal Pedagogies in Diverse Classrooms: Rights, Representations and Resources* and co-author of *English Studies in Africa*. She published in the *TESOL Quarterly* and the *Harvard Educational Review*. (**PS**)

Frederik Stjernfelt is a professor at the Center for Semiotics at Aarhus University. He is the editor of the periodical *KRITIK* and a critic at *Weekendavisen*. His publications include *Diagrammatology. An Investigation on the Borderline of Phenomenology, Ontology, and Semiotics*, as well as numerous papers in international journals and several books in Danish.

William C. Stokoe (1919–2000) was Professor Emeritus of Gallaudet University, Washington, DC. He taught language and culture there and investigated and described American Sign Language, giving that name to a language denied language status for millennia. His publications included *Sign Language Structure*; *A Dictionary of ASL*; *Gesture and the Nature of Language* (with David Armstrong and Sherman Wilcox); and *Language in Hand*. (**WCS**)

Mihály Szívós is Senior Researcher at the Hungarian Academy of Sciences. His publications include 'Introduction: The concept of emergence in philosophical and semiotic context'; 'Quelques aspects sémiotiques du savoir tacite'; and 'Le rôle des motifs socratiques et platoniciens dans la structure et la genèse du Neveu de Rameau de Diderot'. (**MS**)

Eero Tarasti is a professor at the University of Helsinki and is current president of the IASS. His books include *Myth and Music*; *A Theory of Musical Semiotics*; *Existential Semiotics*; and *Signs of Music*. **(ET)**

Peeter Torop is Professor of the Department of Semiotics at the University of Tartu, President of the Estonian Semiotics Association and co-editor of *Sign Systems Studies*. His major publications include *Total Translation*; *Dostoevsky: History and Ideology*; *Signs of Culture*; *Russian Text (19th Century) and Antiguity*; 'Tartu School as school'; 'The position of translation in translation studies'; 'Semiotics, Anthropology and the Analysability of Culture' and 'Translation as Communication and Auto-communication' (PT).

Jef Verschueren is Professor of Linguistics and Dean of the Faculty of Arts at the University of Antwerp. He is the founder and secretary-general of the International Pragmatics Association. His publications include *Handbook of Pragmatics* (co-edited with Jan-Ola Östman *et al.*, now also available online); *Debating Diversity* (co-authored with Jan Blommaert); and *Understanding Pragmatics*. **(JV)**

Sherman Wilcox is currently Associate Dean, College of Arts & Sciences, and Professor of Linguistics, University of New Mexico. His publications include *The Gestural Origin of Language* (with David Armstrong); *Learning to See: Teaching American Sign Language as a Second Language* (with Phyllis Wilcox); and *Gesture and the Nature of Language* (with David Armstrong and William Stokoe). Dr Wilcox specializes in the linguistic study of signed languages and the interface between gesture and language. **(SW)**

Acknowledgements

As editor it falls to me to write this section of the volume. However, what I would like to acknowledge is that this book is wholly a collective venture. It could never have come about without the cooperation of an international community of scholars in semiotics, many of them good friends (with me and one another). All the scholars whose endeavour is to be found in this volume have been a pleasure to work with. It is hoped that their dedication to knowledge and its dissemination, as well as the friendly spirit of collaboration in which the work was carried out, are reflected in this book.

There are some individuals whose names are not represented in this book who have equally been part of its collective authorship, principally David Avital who commissioned the volume. Katherine Ong later took up David's post at Taylor & Francis. Richard Appignanesi, a visionary in publishing and elsewhere, first dreamed up the idea of a 'companion' to semiotics back in the mid-1990s and incited what was to become *The Routledge Companion to Semiotics and Linguistics* in 2001. But, in the end, the truth of the matter is that this book would not be in your hands if it were not for the support and forebearance of three people: Alison Ronald, Stan Ronald Cobley and Elsie Ronald Cobley.

Finally, the usual disclaimer: although this book is a collective venture, it should be pointed out that any mistakes within its pages are not to be attributed to contributors. From first to last, I was assigned the task of preventing errors.

Paul Cobley

Using this book

The Routledge Companion to Semiotics presents up-to-date information on the key questions within its subject area. It is designed to allow the reader to navigate the subject with ease, through cross-referencing within the volume and by means of indications for further enquiry.

The book is divided into two parts. Part I, 'Understanding semiotics', consists of an introduction and ten short chapters. Each of these chapters broadly addresses key themes in contemporary semiotics. Part II, 'Key themes and major figures in semiotics', consists of a dictionary of semiotics, containing a wealth of information on terms used in the subject area as well as biographical entries on influential individuals.

Cross-referencing

The cross-referencing procedure takes place throughout the volume. Any topic or name which has an entry in Part II of the volume will, on its initial appearance, be printed in **bold** type. This is the case for the chapters in Part I as it is for the entries in Part II. On those occasions when an entry does not explicitly mention a name or topic which nevertheless bears some relevant further information on the entry, it will be followed by '*See also*' with the cross-reference printed in Capitals.

Cross-referencing from entries in Part II of the volume to chapters in Part I of the volume will occasionally take place. To avoid confusion, references to chapters in Part I are indicated by giving the author's name in underlined type; for example, <u>Hoffmeyer</u> or <u>Deely</u> or <u>Petrilli and Ponzio</u>, and so on. Despite the cross-referencing in the volume, both Part I and Part II can, of course, be used on their own terms: as a free-standing collection of essays or as a far-reaching dictionary of semiotics.

The identity of the author of each entry in Part II is indicated by bold initials at the end of the entry (see, also, the notes on contributors).

Further reading

Each of the chapters in Part I of the volume is followed by five recommendations for further reading.

Further reading recommendations continue into Part II. The entries in this section are of three different sizes (small, medium and large). Large entries such as **code** are followed by three recommendations for further reading; medium-sized entries such as **arbitrariness** are followed by one recommendation for further reading; and the smaller entries such as **pragmaticism** have none.

Bibliographical references

When reference is made to a published work, for example in the following fashion, 'Halliday's linguistic work has culminated in his extensive description of English in functional terms (1985)' or 'However, most sentences can only be understood against a set of background assumptions which effectively define a context (Searle 1978)', the bibliographic reference for the work is to be found in the References at the end of the volume and not at the end of the specific chapter or entry. Note, however, that Recommendations for further reading are not reproduced in the References at the end of the volume.

One peculiarity of the subject area must be mentioned in respect of bibliographical references to semiotics' major founding figures. In Peirce scholarship it has been customary to refer to the standard edition of his works, the eight-volume *Collected Papers*, which usually appears in bibliographies as follows:

> Peirce, C. S. (1931–1935; 1958) *Collected Papers of Charles Sanders Peirce*, Vols 1–6 ed. C. Hartshorne and P. Weiss; Vols 7 and 8 ed. A. Burks, Cambridge, MA: Harvard University Press.

However, when scholars make reference to the *Collected Papers* they invariably use a short-hand method which consists of naming the number of the volume and the number of the section within the volume; thus, 'The symbol is the sign "in consequence of a habit (which term I use as including a natural disposition)" (4.531).' To make matters slightly easier and to help prevent any confusion in the process of cross-referencing, this book will retain the numbering of volume and section but will designate the *Collected Papers* by the initials, *CP*: thus, 'The symbol is the sign "in consequence of a habit (which term I use as including a natural disposition)" (*CP* 4.531).'

Note that not all of Peirce's work appears in the *Collected Papers* and that much of his work is also published elsewhere: this includes original places of publication (for example, journals such as *The Monist*), the chronological edition of his writings currently being published by the Peirce Edition Project, as well as other, shorter collections of Peirce's essays, notes and letters. The other major publications containing Peirce's writings are referenced as follows:

> Peirce, C. S. (1975–1988) *Charles Sanders Peirce: Contributions to the Nation*, 4 vols, ed. K. L. Ketner and J. E. Cook, Lubbock, TX: Texas Tech University Press.
> Referenced by volume and page, for example *CN* 3: 124.

Peirce, C. S. (1982–) *The Writings of Charles S. Peirce: A Chronological Edition*, ed. Peirce Edition Project, Vols 1–6, Bloomington, IN: Indiana University Press. Referenced by volume and page, for example *W* 2: 49.

Peirce, C. S. (1839–1914) *The Charles S. Peirce Papers*. Manuscript Collection in the Houghton Library, Cambridge, MA: Harvard University.

Manuscript numbers of the Houghton Library Collection of Peirce's papers refer to the Richard Robin arrangement. The Robin Catalogue numbers are prefixed either with *MS* (sometimes *R*) or *L*, depending on whether they are ordinary writings or letters. The letters manuscripts are in a separate section in the Robin Catalogue and are numbered separately.

Peirce Edition Project (eds) (1998) *The Essential Peirce*, Vol. 2, Bloomington, IN: Indiana University Press.
Referenced by volume and page, for example *EP* 2: 28.

Semiotic discussion of Saussure's work usually refers to his *Cours de linguistique générale*, published in three major editions since 1916:

Saussure, F. de (1916, 1922, 1972) *Cours de linguistique générale*, Paris: Payot. Referenced as *CLG* with page number.

The preferred English translation of Saussure's *Cours* is:

Saussure, F. de (1983) *Course in General Linguistics*, trans. R. Harris, London: Duckworth.
Referenced in the usual date and page style

(although an earlier translation by Wade Baskin – McGraw-Hill, 1959 – exists and introduced some misleading translations which are still in use in semiotics).

The other editions of Saussure's writings used by scholars and referenced in this volume are:

Saussure, F. de (1967–1974) *Cours de linguistique générale*, edition critique, Vols 1 and 2, ed. R. Engler, Wiesbaden: Harrassowitz.
Referenced as *CLG/E* with page number.

Saussure, F. de (2002) *Ecrits de linguistique générale*, ed. R. Engler and S. Bouquet, Paris: Gallimard.
Referenced as *ELG* with page number.

Saussure, F. de (1986) *Le leggende germaniche*, ed. A. Marinetti and M. Meli, Este: Zielo.
Referenced as *LEG* with page number.

The majority of the works of Sebeok were published directly into English and are relatively unproblematic. However, many of Sebeok's writings – including those specifically on semiotics from 1963 onwards – are published in numerous places as well as in his own collections. Sebeok was so prolific as an editor and general convener of the work of others that it is sometimes difficult to keep track of publications and activities, particularly his work in linguistics and Finno-Ugric studies. The following bibliographies are helpful:

Deely, J. (ed.) (1995) *Thomas A. Sebeok Bibliography 1942–1995*, fascicle 15 in the Arcada Bibliographica Virorum Eruditorum of Gyula Décsy, Bloomington, IN: Eurolingua.

Umiker-Sebeok, J. (2003) 'Thomas A. Sebeok: A bibliography of his writings', *Semiotica*, 147(1/4): 11–73.

the latter being necessarily more complete.

Relation of this book to *The Routledge Companion to Semiotics and Linguistics*

Whether you are standing in a bookstore and pondering whether to buy this or if you are using this book in a library, a brief word is necessary about the relation of this volume to its predecessor. This is *not* a new edition of *The Routledge Companion to Semiotics and Linguistics* (2001). It is a very different book. First, it is strictly focused on semiotics whereas the previous book was designed to give an overview of the relation of semiotics and post-Chomskyan linguistics. Second, it has ten new essays plus a new introduction. Third, while Part II has kept a few entries from the previous book, the majority have been excluded and replaced by many more entries which give a clearer picture of the breadth of contemporary semiotics. The newness of the book is a testimony to the publisher's confidence in the readership as well as its desire to produce a volume that is focused and innovative.

Part I

Understanding semiotics

Introduction

Paul Cobley

What is semiotics?

With a book like this, the reader has every right to ask, 'What is **semiotics**?' Furthermore, s/he is entitled to a straight answer. The usual one that is offered is that semiotics is the study of the **sign** – full stop. That might satisfy some readers; but, immediately, one gets into all sorts of technicalities about what constitutes a sign and then questions about the consequences. Some of these technicalities are covered in portions of the book that follow. But they are not appropriate for getting this book started.

Thomas A. **Sebeok**, who, along with **Peirce** and **Saussure**, has been the key figure in the development of semiotics, preferred another definition. When speaking to the media or to lay persons he stated simply that semiotics is the study of the difference between illusion and reality. As with so many things, he was right. Moreover, he was right for two reasons to do with the recent history of semiotics. First, the most well-known version of semiotics, which experienced immense popularity in Western intellectual circles from the late 1960s to the early 1970s, was the Saussure-influenced mix of **structuralism** and **semiology** which swept through the humanities and the social sciences along with Marxism and psychoanalysis. Derived especially from **Barthes** (as well as **Lévi-Strauss**, **Greimas** and **Jakobson**), semiology promised to reveal the semiosic machinations behind all manner of contemporary and historical phenomena, albeit phenomena that were 'man-made', within 'culture' and seemingly susceptible to an analysis in terms of **glottocentrism** (that is, in terms of their features which resembled the human attribute of verbal **language**). Often based on variants of the analysis in Barthes' 1957 book *Mythologies*, which exposed the bourgeois myths that suffused the unconsidered trifles of popular culture, Barthes had actually publicly abandoned this approach as too facile by as early as 1971. Yet, the association of sign study with the exposure of illusion was already fixed.

The second reason that Sebeok's definition is correct has to do with the much more far-ranging ambitions of contemporary semiotics, by which is meant the semiotics – not semiology – which followed Barthes' abandonment of myth criticism and is associated with the doctrines of Peirce, Sebeok and, to a considerable extent, with Jakob von **Uexküll**. To be sure, this semiotics is very much concerned with 'culture' and the definition of what it is to be human; but it does not stop at culture's boundaries, nor does it countenance the theoretical short-cut whereby *Homo sapiens sapiens* is taken as divorced from its environment and its heritage in nature. In short, semiotics is the study of the sign wherever signs are to be found – perhaps, even, in places where humans have not yet set foot. At first sight, this looks rather limiting, a closing of the case: in sum, the stultifying notion that everything, everywhere is to be considered as a sign. If semiotics was simply that notion, then it would be sterile indeed. But seeing semiotics as the study of the difference between reality and illusion, once more, is a much different matter. A sign, as Peirce is especially keen to point out, is for someone or something; as such, there are signs which function as signs for *us* (or for others) and things beyond signs. The notion of **Umwelt**, from von Uexküll, which is crucial for contemporary semiotics, suggests that all species live in a 'world' that is constructed out of their own signs, the latter being the result of their own sign-making and receiving capacities. (A fly, for example, has a much different sensory apparatus for making/receiving signs than does the human.) Beyond those capacities of **semiosis** (sign action) there is a world – the 'real world', in one sense – which cannot be reached. Yet, while it is true that within a species' Umwelt there are all manner of possibilities of illusion – through misinterpretation of signs, through overlooking of signs and through signs not being 100 per cent adequate representations of reality – the testimony that an Umwelt is a fairly good guide to reality is offered by the survival of the species within a given Umwelt. If an Umwelt offered an irredeemably faulty grasp of reality, then that species would not survive. The study of the vicissitudes of signs in different Umwelten, including that of the human, and how such study sheds light on the human Umwelt – that is what contemporary semiotics is.

Does this mean that the study of human signs now has to proceed with an awareness of signs elsewhere in the **semiosphere**, in other Umwelten? The answer to this is, on one level, yes. Of course, there are plenty of instances of semiotics – some of them very good – which proceed without reference to any forms of signification outside of **anthroposemiosis**. Some of these are even by authors that know that there is signification outside of anthroposemiosis. However, to know that human **communication** and semiosis are characterized not just by verbal expression but also by the faculty of the nonverbal offers the opportunity of enriching the understanding not just of communication but also of cognition. To know that the faculty of the nonverbal is shared with animals and plants offers opportunities to any analysis where nonverbality is in any way a factor. To know that organisms have an ineffable number of sign processes taking place *within* them – **endosemiosis** – changes how one might understand human and other cognition, as well as human and other communication. Furthermore, to know that disciplines such as ethology (the study of animal communication), biology and aspects of the other sciences have light to shed on communication is of paramount importance not just because it encourages interdisciplinarity but because it promotes a more comprehensive knowledge. Biological and physical processes involve semioses, in the same broad way that culture does, that are often dismissed as mere metaphors. All the disciplines in the human and social sciences involve tracking sign processes, despite not necessarily avowing these processes as such. All are committed in principle to distinguishing reality from illusion. Effectively, then, semiotics is concerned with the matters that all the other disciplines either take for granted, dismiss or neglect.

So, this is semiotics and what this book is about – an enduring enquiry into the boundaries of illusion and reality, a practice of interrogating signs which has borne fruit from the pre-Socratics to the present. Semiotics as a field (within which other disciplines variously operate) has only really existed for around a century. Semiotics as a discipline – with a small degree of institutionalization in a period during which traditional disciplines have been increasingly specialized and fiercely protective – has only gained prominence in the last sixty years. How can it be stated that semiotics has both a long and short lineage in the history of ideas?

A brief word on the history of semiotics

A fair amount, in different ways, has been written on the history of semiotics. **Deely**'s *Four Ages of Understanding* (2001a) offers a comprehensive overview and much more, including a complete revaluation of the history of philosophy. Meanwhile, Favareau (2007) provides an excellent and incisive analytic history of the means by which traditional attempts to deal with the entire panoply of signification have been transmuted into today's concerns, with repressions and amplifications in the history of ideas. In the face of such contributions to the field, no more than a very cursory sketch can be offered here for the purposes of orientation. Further information is offered in the major essays in Part I as well as in many of the entries that make up Part II. What is notable, perhaps, is that any major discipline which finds itself in the position of being able to trace its own noble lineage and demonstrate that that lineage is still being realized is clearly in a healthy condition.

As Sebeok was repeatedly motivated to mention, semiotics derives from pre-Socratic thought. First, this entails a philosophy which is concerned with how the entire cosmos operates – the earth, its inhabitants and the elements – rather than just the interactions that constitute the polis. As is the case in the present, semiotics tends to address the bigger picture and sometimes arouses suspicion for this from those currents of thought that are fixated on shifts in power relations between humans as the whole of intellectual concern. However, the more direct link of semiotics to pre-Socratic thought is through the figure of **Hippocrates** and his (followers') corpus. As with the later ancient medic **Galen**, Hippocrates did not just assemble a huge list of universal symptoms with the same aetiologies in Cos as in Libya, but actually developed a full-blown science of symptomatology concerned not just with diagnosis but also prognosis (Sebeok 2001a). The first relied on the physical signs of the illness on the patient's body, along with the signs s/he emitted through groans, gestures or attempted vocal elucidation. Already, here, semiotics' recognition of the body as a container of signs, humans' repertoire of verbal and **nonverbal communication**, the systematicity of signs, and the dissemination of signs throughout nature was in place. In addition to this, the ancient medics' concern not just with the brute **index**ical reality of symptoms (and, sometimes, their **icon**icity and **symbol**icity), but with projecting the course of an illness, was, at the same time, a prefigurement of modern science and an anticipation of semiotics after Peirce.

It would be easy to read the subsequent history of semiotics through the refracting lens of Peirce. Yet, the temptation to do so is understandable because Peirce was so well versed in traditions of logic and semiotics. Moreover, it is often assumed in various areas of thought – partly because of the Dark Ages in Europe, partly for other complicated reasons to do with the historiography of ideas – that relatively little of importance went on between the work of the classical Greek period and the rediscovery of **Aristotle** that immediately preceded the Renaissance and the birth of the modern age. Although, in respect of the logic that suffuses semiotics, Deely (1982: 197) suggests of the development of Stoic tradition informing Aristotle's logic (see Manetti, this volume) that 'up to very recent times, in the post-classical civilizations of Europe the works of Aristotle in logic really provide the main backdrop against which logical development took place', his work, as emblematic of contemporary semiotics, has been devoted to opening up the lineages closed by intellectual history. Thus, Boethius (*c*. 480–524) and his near contemporary St **Augustine** (354–430) should now be understood as providing, in some ways, the template for thinking the sign in the much neglected tradition of the Latin Age. Both provided early suggestions that the sign was not a matter which could be considered either solely of nature or solely of culture. The contexts in which they delivered their theses on these issues could not be more different from those to be witnessed in the contemporary academy. However, they provide the lineage to today's semiotics.

Peirce, with some limitations, knew the work of scholasticism and the Latin thinkers rather well. For the Latins, the perspective on signs emanating from the teachings of St Thomas **Aquinas** – later called **Thomism** – was paramount and the subject of numerous exigeses. Most important of all of these latter, without a doubt, is that of John (sometimes 'Jean' or 'João') **Poinsot** (also cited on occasion as 'John of St Thomas'). Poinsot's writings, especially his *Tractatus de Signis* (1632), appearing nearly sixty years before **Locke** coined the term 'semiotics', offer in a number of ways the possibility of developing a proper semiotic **consciousness** even before the work of Peirce. The chief contribution of Poinsot is his specific realist foregrounding of the sign as the object of study to illuminate mind-dependent and mind-independent being. The overwhelming impediment to a semiotic consciousness in modern thought has been the prominence in such thought of the Kantian idealist notion of the 'ding an sich', the entity that is unknowable (i.e. totally mind-independent being). Yet, coming immediately before Descartes and the moderns, Poinsot's Thomism offered the means to overcome this impasse by demonstrating how cultural reality in the human species is the *locus* where the differences between mind-independent and mind-dependent being become knowable and distinguishable (see Deely 2005a: 76).

An iceberg's tip protrudes into experience as an ***object*** (a mind-dependent entity); moreover, it is, as such, a *thing* (mind-independent); but, above all, as is known from the popular phrase, the tip is a *sign* that there is much more below (Deely 1994a: 144). An important corollary of this is that whatever is beneath the tip of the iceberg cannot be *approached* as a thing. It is possible that experience could make it an object but, even then, through the sensations it provokes, the feelings about them and its consequence, it is only available as a sign. It is simultaneously of the order of mind-independent and mind-dependent being, and it would be foolish to bracket off one or the other in an attempt to render it as either solely object or thing. Hence Peirce's statement that 'to try to peel off signs & get down to the real thing is like trying to peel an onion and get down to the onion itself' (see Brent 1993: 300, n. 84).

Poinsot is, therefore, a pivotal figure in the history of semiotics, although, along with the other Latin thinkers, and aside from his recovery by contemporary semiotics, he has been almost completely written out of the history of ideas in favour of the much more convenient belief that between 1350 and 1650 – effectively between **William of Ockham** and Descartes – nothing happened. Yet the Latin thinkers should not be disregarded; crucially, for semiotics, their project was not fixated on twentieth-century preoccupations such as logic and the polis, but considered 'psychology' and the investigation of living things: that is to say **zoosemiotics** as well as **anthroposemiotics**. This conception of philosophy's task also characterized the work of Peirce, a commitment to **realism** (see Deely, this volume), **phenomenology** (or 'phaneroscopy' – see Houser, this volume) and a conception of the sign which is universally applicable rather than being confined to human **discourse**. As Houser demonstrates in his essay for this volume, Peirce was both a pre-Socratic in his bearing, committed to understanding the universe, as well as anti-Cartesian, not believing that thought was fully separable from the body. His theory of signs is often noted for its *triadic* character (**representamen**, object, **interpretant**), distinguishing it not just from Saussure but also from the mainstream of sign theory prior to Poinsot. It is based on another triad of categories of the universe (**firstness**, **secondness**, **thirdness**) and can be investigated in terms of qualities of signhood, relation to object and relation to users. (These would later be transformed by Charles **Morris** into the division of semiotics which actually set the agenda for linguistics in the latter part of the twentieth century: syntactics, **semantics** and **pragmatics**.) That Peirce was serious about systematizing sign types and that he was comprehensive in his approach is testified by his letter to Lady **Welby**, late in life, revealing that he had recognized ten basic types of signs and 59,049 different classes of signs in all (Peirce 1966: 407 – see Houser, this volume, for a discussion of the ten sign types).

Peirce's expansive sign theory has afforded much room for development in semiotics. His prefiguring of the syntactic/semantics/pragmatics, as well as his separation of the sign types in relation to objects – icon, index, symbol – have provided inspiration for a semiotics of culture still in development. The same has been true for a broad-based 'semiotics of nature' which has been more appreciative still, adopting Peirce's insight into order and **habit** (a tendency which is to be seen right across nature, not just in humans) as well as his concept of mind as not just a human phenomenon (see Hoffmeyer, this volume). Peirce saw semiotics as logic, with an illustrious lineage (see Deely 1982); as such, Peirce's semiotics is 'cognition-friendly' as Bundgaard and stjernfelt state (this volume). It envisages cognitive and communicative processes in a number of different sign types and, thus, furthermore, allows the possibility of **translation** between different sign systems. What it does *not* do is to posit verbal expression as the master sign system through which all other semiosis and cognition is either filtered or judged. In the semiology deriving from Saussurean thinkers, however, this kind of glottocentrism has been customary.

The immense success and fashionable ascent of semiology noted above initially brought the notion of broad sign study to the attention of the public and the academy in the latter half of the twentieth century. Semiology, of course, was inspired by the work of the Swiss linguist Ferdinand de Saussure, whose *Cours de linguistique générale* (1916) predicted the growth of a general science of signs that might be possible if his principles were followed. In the latter part of the twentieth century, Saussure's call was taken up by semiologists (for example, Barthes 1973a; Guiraud 1975) who confined their analyses to a limited range of cultural artefacts which might be susceptible to elucidation using broadly linguistic principles. However, while semiology prospered in Anglophone academia, it embodied a very partial view of the Saussurean project and, furthermore, in its extrapolation from short passages in the *Cours*, a limited view of the import of Saussure's *oeuvre* (see Hénault, this volume).

Semiology was not disseminated in a vacuum, of course; it developed during a period in which much of human life was being posited, here and there, as 'constructed in discourse'. As noted earlier, Barthes' *Mythologies* provided an agenda for systematically analysing and rejecting the superstructural products of capitalism. This derived from Saussure's separation of two sides of a linguistic sign into a) a 'sound pattern' in the mind which represented sensory impressions of sound outside the mind; plus b) a 'concept' consisting of an abstract formulation of phenomena in the world such as 'house', 'white', 'see' and so forth (1983: 65ff., 101ff.). Saussure referred to these as ***signifiant*** and ***signifié***, respectively, and the first principle regarding their connection that he emphasized was its **arbitrariness** (1983: 65ff., 101ff.). Saussure's *Cours* was first translated into English in 1959 and *signifiant*, *signifié* and *signe* were rendered as 'signifier', 'signified' and 'sign'. The first item gave the impression to English natives that the *signifiant* was anything that did the work of signifying or, to put it another way, a sign – precisely the formulation that Saussure wanted to avoid. The term for the *signifié*, at the same time, seemed to be anything that was the object of signification. At a stroke, Saussure's conception of the sign was lost and versions of semiology were given free rein to look at all manner of cultural artefacts as if they embodied a *signifié/signifiant* relationship. The matter was compounded by the currency of

Barthes' influential primer, *Elements of Semiology*, translated into English in 1967. In order to enable semiology to be extended beyond linguistic signs, Barthes effected a slippage from Saussure, suggesting that 'the signifier [*signifiant*] can, too, be relayed by a certain matter . . . the substance of the signifier is always material (sounds, objects, images)' (1967a: 47). Barthes is not shy about the reasons for this un-Saussurean assertion: it was made so that the matter of all signs, including those in mixed systems, could be considered in the same way (1967a: 47). Not only was there an encouragement to focus on those sign systems that were dominated by verbal modes, then, semiology also insisted that even nonverbal modes were susceptible to analysis based on the principles of Saussurean linguistics. In all cases, however, the sign systems to be analysed were human in origin.

Curiously, however, semiological principles have often been given the name 'semiotics', largely because the anthropocentric endeavours of semiologists were brought together with those of semioticians for the formation of the International Association for Semiotic Studies (**IASS**) in 1969. The very localized study of the *linguistic* sign, a sign type used by humans alone, is only one component of the study of the sign in general. The very human phenomenon of language is just one aspect of semiosis throughout the universe. Put this way, language looks very small compared to the array of signs engendered by all interactions between living cells. Moreover, the issue of what is living is crucial: many semioticians of the major, Peircean tradition, influenced by Sebeok (1994: 6), see semiosis as the 'criterial attribute of life' and, consequently, conceive signs in a 'global semiotics'. Sebeok, building on the work of his teacher Charles Morris, as well as the sign theory of Peirce, carved out the study of non-human semiosis originally with his work in zoosemiotics (1963). Superseding this has been a fully fledged **biosemiotics** (Sebeok and Umiker-Sebeok 1992; Barbieri 2007), in which it is recognized that not just a semiotics of human communication is needed, but, in addition to zoosemiotics, a semiotics of plants ('phytosemiotics'), of fungi ('mycosemiotics') and of the 3.5 billion-year-old global prokaryotic communication network within and between different bacterial cells ('microsemiotics, cytosemiotics'). Indeed, contemporary semiotics recognizes that the human, while s/he is a sapient user of signs, is not just a discursive entity: in fact, the human is a mass of signs enacting message transfer nonverbally within the body ('endosemiosis' – the neural **code**, the genetic code, the metabolic code, etc.).

Partly as a result of growing interest in Peirce and the major tradition, in addition to the decline of much of the Saussurean perspective outside circles where serious sign study is conducted, semiotics 'superseded' semiology despite, in its pre-Socratic origins, pre-dating it. Far from being a de-politicization of sign study – the idea, once more, that 'everything is a sign' – and a withdrawing from the putative political dimension of '**discourse**' and 'language', semiotics heralds a major paradigm shift in relation to many political matters but, especially, in relation to **ethics** (see Petrilli and Ponzio, this volume). What contemporary semiotics demonstrates, bluntly, is that interventions for change at the level of discourse alone are the equivalent of a gnat biting an elephant. While the glottocentrism of the influence of the 'linguistic turn' in Western intellectual life has attempted to paper over this fact, semiotics does offer the opportunity for the reconceptualization of the place of human affairs on the planet, by placing humans as thoroughly semiotic entities within a vast environment of semiosis. As such, it allows an alternative to the stalemate experienced in the prisonhouse of language.

Semiotic theory and analysis

The benefits of semiotics that are universally acknowledged are that it presents a *theory* of significatory processes, communicative and non-communicative; and that is has promoted a **synchronic** awareness of the universe by which *analysis* might proceed. Such a synchronic perspective did not develop alone: the same kind of broad investigation of phenomena and a theoretical approach to knowledge over a **diachronic** and solely empirical approach can be seen in the work of Propp, the young Jakobson and **Russian Formalism**; **Ogden**, **Richards**, Empson and Leavis in Britain; the New Criticism, Innis, McLuhan and Frye in North America; the structuralists in France; the slightly older Jakobson and the Prague Linguistic Circle (**Prague School**) in Czechoslovakia; the Copenhagen School in Denmark; and the early Tartu–Moscow semiotics of **Lotman** and his colleagues. Parallel with especially the latter was the movement in **cybernetics**, communication theory and **systems theory** in the United States from the late 1940s onwards, featuring Wiener, Shannon and Weaver, **Bateson**, von Foerster, Jakobson (again) and, convening like Mercury, the young Sebeok.

If one takes the example of literature and the arts, frequently the touchstone and testing ground of a nascent semiotics in the post-war period, it becomes clear how the synchronic approach represents a major shift in thinking. Quite simply, the previous questions about artefacts – Why is it great? What does it say? What is its value? How does it betray the talent of its producer? How might I be spiritually enriched by it? – were supplanted by the blunt and exclusive question: How does it work? On the one hand, this fostered formalist analysis which, to some, seemed excessively dry after the years of criticism that allowed art and literature to stand in for a moral gymnasium. On the other hand, it helped to dismantle the artificialities of the high culture/low culture edifice, replacing opportunities to demonstrate good 'breeding' and cultural capital with the demand to theorize the mechanisms of culture.

Although there was no possibility of going back to old ways, despite their continued existence in pockets of anachronistic activity (e.g. arts pages of newspapers), critiques of semiotics and the synchronic perspective as sterile formalism took the tack that readers, audiences, consumers and users of signs had been left out of the equation. Whether it was perceived as an evacuation of psychology, politics or social determinants, the focus on the '**text**' in cultural analysis – or individual signs or sign systems without context or environment – was seen to be blinkered. Which, of course, it was. The semiological variant of semiotics thus became the whipping boy for all manner of disciplines that wished to demonstrate that they were moving forward and getting on with empirical research irrespective of theory. Media and cultural studies, where semiotics had first found a welcome in the Anglophone academy, was particularly guilty in this respect.

What is laughable about the making of semiotics into such a straw man is that it was a case of mistaken identity. Semiotics proper has never left out the sign user (or audience or reader or consumer); in fact, Peirce's definition of the sign is something that stands for something else in some capacity for *someone* (or some organism). It could never leave out the user. Indeed, the recovery of the heritage of sign study in contemporary semiotics, especially Poinsot and Peirce, precisely foregrounds issues to do with the user of sign and the context in which use takes place. For example, one of the features of biosemiotics which makes it so 'outrageous' is the fact that it countenances a subject in nature or, at least, agentive action which subtends the traffic in signs. Recognizing signs in nature is one thing; that has a long heritage in the sciences. Yet, suggesting that those signs are 'minded' (see Hoffmeyer, this volume) is, on the one hand, heretical to the life sciences, which have repeatedly approached the idea through metaphors, and, on the other, is not noticed in the human sciences which has stood for so long on its own side of the 'two cultures' (Snow 1993). Things are changing, however. In the wake of cultural studies' eschewing of science because it does not live up to unrealistic expectations of so-called objectivity, science has been rediscovered in other areas of the humanities, be it neo-Darwinism and evolutionary psychology or complexity and **emergence**. One field of endeavour with a similar recent trajectory to semiotics is cognitive science (see Bundgaard and Stjernfelt, this volume). Thus, now the question of any phenomena studied by semiotics is not so much 'how does it work?' but rather interrogation to find answers to 'what is the role of emotion in this phenomenon?', 'what processes of cognition does it entail?', 'what kind of system generates this phenomenon and what is its relation to its environment?' and 'what is the larger place in nature that this phenomenon occupies?'. These questions are implicit in much contemporary semiotics after biosemiotics and explicit in specific enterprises such as **modelling systems theory**.

The essays that follow in this book attempt to provide the background for understanding contemporary semiotic theory and analysis. Giovanni Manetti's overview of ancient semiotics, from Mesopotamian divination to Augustine, gives a sense of the presence of the sign in classical thinking and also a sense of the very different contexts in which one has to look in order to find semiotics before the twentieth century. Fundamental in a slightly different way is Jesper Hoffmeyer's essay on semiotics of nature which shows how understanding nature as semiotic is the crucial first step to coming to terms with human embeddedness in the web of life. In truth, it's a 'resemiotization', as he shows; but the 're' in this instance connotes a greater awareness or the development of what, after Deely, has been called a 'semiotic consciousness' (above). If humans are to know where they stand in nature then they are compelled to know how their own world is constituted, as well as that of other species. Kalevi Kull's essay shows how contemporary semiotics offers the means to realize this.

Peirce's semiotics, as has been noted, identifies many different sign types and suggests that there is the possibility of translation between different sign systems. His sign types facilitate understanding of human communication as more than just a verbal affair; they also allow an understanding of cognition as being made of and 'more than words'. Bundgaard and Stjernfelt focus on diagrammatic thinking and **image schemas** in their essay, producing new insights from the fusion of Peircean semiotics and cognitive science. In the essay on realism and epistemology that follows, John Deely shows that the thinking that takes 'realism' as that which is 'most realistic' is not really in tune with semiotics. Rather, he shows, realism in semiotics – for reasons that are not far removed from the arguments of Bundgaard and Stjernfelt – involves both mind-dependent and mind-independent being. Meanwhile, in the most concise and yet rewardingly catholic presentations of Peirce's semiotics that one is likely to witness, Nathan Houser's essay which follows takes in Peirce's logic, his evolutionary philosophy, his systematicity, his **pragmatism**, his threefold division of signs, his decalogue, his speculative grammar, his critic, his speculative **rhetoric**, his mathematics, but, above all, his phenomenology (or 'phaneroscopy'). Houser's essay shows how Peirce set an example for today's semiotics of communication and cognition by being a phenomenologist, an experimental scientist, and a semiotician.

The field of anthroposemiotics and cultural semiotics has changed immeasurably in the last couple of decades, along with the developments in the semiotics of nature and cognition. Anne Hénault tracks the influence of Saussure in her essay on his heritage. This has been done before in numerous commentaries, of considerable vintage, on structuralism and semiology. Yet, Hénault's account is up to date and differs from all of these in that she shows that the work of the Greimas school evolved well beyond putative Saussurean principles to spearhead investigations into emotion and affect from the 1980s onwards. Furthermore, the 'mainstream' version of Saussure relies on selective reading of the *Cours*; a broader, incisive Saussure is recognized beyond the pages of the text with which he is most associated. Cultural – and even 'social' – semiotics has tended to be associated with the Saussurean paradigm, albeit often tenuously, up till the present. Randviir and Cobley's essay on **sociosemiotics** attempts to show the tangled lineage and wide (geographical) diffusion of semiotic thinking on 'the social'. Yet, more than 'the social', perhaps, semiotics has found a home in the study of media and culture – whether the guardians of such study desired it or not. Marcel Danesi's excellent account of the 'semiotization' of media and popular culture study suggests that the process was going on well before semiotics became momentarily *de rigeur* in those areas.

Finally, the essay of Petrilli and Ponzio deals with ethics. As one of the key topics in contemporary semiotics, they show how humans, the semiotic animal, have 'responsibility' arising from awareness of signs. With the peppering of 'must' across their text, Petrilli and Ponzio demonstrate that semiotics is not short of political commitment.

1
Ancient semiotics

Giovanni Manetti

Since its birth merely decades ago, modern **semiotics** has been undertaking a search for its origins. What was really at stake was a search for the identity of the discipline, a search that was expected to be conducted through a critical evaluation of the operative concepts already employed. A comparison between the modern notions of semiotics and those which marked the beginnings of the discipline was, and is, indeed, considered also a valid way to see the former established on a solid basis. But we must be ready to accept that the comparison between the modern concepts of semiotics – and mostly the concept of '**sign**' – and those notions which marked the beginnings of semiotics might lead to a radical change in the current paradigm.

The aim here, therefore, is to investigate both semiotic practices from their origins (as divination and medicine) and the theoretical considerations of the sign which were developed in the ancient world and which have come down to us through the literary, philosophical, medical, historical and **rhetoric**al tradition. We might thus rediscover a thread which may be traced through the classical world from its origins to the fourth century AD, revealing a conception of the sign which is significantly different from that proposed in the twentieth century.

An investigation of the way in which classical antiquity treated and developed considerations of the sign will enable us to discover that, not only is there no homologization of the different types of sign (linguistic and non-linguistic ones) according to the yardstick of the linguistic sign (as in Saussure's theory), but that the two theories (the semantic theory of **language** and the theory of the non-linguistic sign) proceeded rather in parallel, without ever being interconnected. Furthermore, those practices in which signs were foregrounded and which have come down to us through tradition (medicine, divination, detection), as well as classical theories, are based on a conception of the sign which works from *inference* or *implication* ($p \supset q$) rather than *equivalence* (**signifier ≈ signified**).

Mesopotamian divination

We can first find a foregrounded use of signs in Mesopotamian divinatory tablets from the third millennium BCE. The most significant aspect of Mesopotamian divination is that it is centred precisely on a distinctive and individual notion of the sign, which is a scheme of inferential reasoning that allows particular conclusions to be drawn from particular facts. The kind of sign model adopted by Mesopotamian divination is very close to what has come down to us from Greek thought at the height of its semiotic maturity: the model of implication that allows us to infer something hidden or non-present from something perceptible or present ('if *p*, then *q*'). For example: 'If a man has curly hair on his shoulders – women will love him' or 'If on the day of its disappearance the moon lingers in the sky (instead of disappearing all at once) – there will be drought and famine in the country'. Thanks to numerous divinatory tracts which have come down to us, we can form a fairly clear idea of this structure of the sign. The tracts consist of lengthy lists of complex propositions, each made up of a protasis and an apodosis. The protasis is introduced by the expression *summa* (the equivalent of the conjunction 'if') and has the verb in the present or past tense. This is the 'omen', that is, the ominous sign which is to be interpreted. The apodosis usually has the verb in the future tense and forms the 'oracle', that which is indicated or revealed by the interpretation of the sign. The examples of Mesopotamian divination enable us to make two immediate observations on the semiotic mechanism which they contain.

First, the structure of the sign is expressed in terms of the relationship between propositions and not between individual lexical units or between a 'signifier' [***signifiant***] and a 'signified' [***signifié***] as in the Saussurean model. This results in the fact that nonverbal signs and events immediately take on predominant importance in that they can be best expressed in the form of a proposition.

Second, the relationship between the protasis and the apodosis within each sign is an implicative relationship (as we saw before), but it is to be noted that I use 'implicative' to mean a still fairly generic inference. Within the **Stoic** school, where an analogous inferential model is used, as we shall see later, interest will be centred on the attempt to define in a formal way the implicative link which characterizes the sign, and divergences of thought will fuel a long and complex debate.

Greek divination

In contrast with the case of Mesopotamian divination, and as a direct consequence of the oral nature of Greek culture, *inspirational divination* formed the dominant divinatory model in ancient Greece. Inspirational divination is the form of divination in which the god speaks to humanity through a prophet who is selected as his or her voice, as in the famous example of oracle divination practised by the Pythia at Delphi. It is thus hardly by chance that in ancient Greece there was no formation and constant presence of a priestly class specializing in the interpretation of both writing and divinatory signs as was, in contrast, the case in Mesopotamia.

However, divination forms the first homogeneous area of ancient Greek culture in which it is possible to talk about the use of signs. The term *semeion*, which we encounter for the first time in this field, is a generic term which indicates a divinatory sign of any kind, including an oracular response, which is usually a verbal **text**.

The sign (which is the instrument through which the knowledge of the future or of a hidden past is obtained) comes not from the human sphere but from the higher, more numinous, sphere of the divine. The sign is the instrument of mediation between the total knowledge of the gods and the more limited knowledge of humankind. It is also the area in which divine knowledge erupts into the human sphere.

But the language of the gods is not the same as the language of the mortals. The words contained in the oracular response are human only insofar as they contain human sounds: they fail to produce meaning when the **code** of human verbal language is applied to them. This lack of equivalence in the expression of knowledge content separates humanity from the gods. However, there is also a more radical difference in the very modality of the knowledge: gods rule time by means of a simultaneous 'sight' of past, present and future; divine omniscience stems precisely from the possession of panoptic vision. Apollo, according to Pindar's expression, has 'the glance that knows all things' (*Pyth.* III, 29). Mortals, in contrast, can see only the present, while the other dimensions of time remain inaccessible to them, except through the mediation of the gods. Access may be achieved through visions which must then be translated into words. Nonetheless, the message of the vision becomes blurred in the very process of **translation**. This is why the divinatory sign is enigmatic, obscure and practically incomprehensible.

Greek medicine

The other major area of operation of semiotically oriented thought which precedes and is, to a large extent, independent of strictly philosophical research is Greek medicine. In this field may be seen not only the integral presence of semiosic processes but also the first real theoretical constructs around the sign and inference. Later, when semiotic theorizing passed directly into the field of philosophy and rhetoric, many traces of its medical origins remained. These may be seen first of all in the examples used to illustrate the sign both by philosophers and writers of treatises of rhetoric (examples which were often taken from medicine and sometimes from physiognomy). More significant traces remained in the choice of a formal **logic**al model of the sign in the form 'if *p*, then *q*', which was, as we have seen, the model used in divination and which was taken over into medicine with different contents but the same form.

Early Greek medicine produced an extremely rich documentation, the chief source of which is the *Corpus Hippocraticum*, a large collection of very varied texts which illustrate medical theory and practice during the fifth and fourth centuries BCE.

In contrast with doctors of today, who read signs in connection with the diagnosis of illness, early Greek doctors used signs in connection with the prognosis. There is an entire treatise of the *C.H.*, the *Prognostic*, which is dedicated to precisely this function. Prognosis is elaborated by signs not only as prediction of future events concerning the ill individual, but also involves elements of knowledge pertaining to both the present and the past. For the doctor must be able to describe also those symptoms and general facts which the patients omit to mention. This formula, with a threefold reference to past, present and future, is found elsewhere in the *C.H.*, for example in *Epidemics I* (and it is also found as a phrase which defines medicine in Plato's *Laches*, 198d), prompting us to set up a parallel with the similar formula used to identify the process of divination.

Nevertheless, even if, on the one hand, we can find common elements between medicine and divination, on the other, many of the treatises in the *C.H.* are fiercely emphatic in stressing the distance and differences between these two areas. The author of *Prorrhetic II* (Ch. I) is harsh in his criticism of bad doctors, stating that their miraculous predictions place them on a level with soothsayers, and he proudly offers his own method in contrast with the divinatory inference (*manteuein*), a method based on human signs (*semeia*) and on conjecture (*tekmairesthai*).

The concept of *semeion* ('sign', 'symptom') is one of the central concepts in the *C.H.*. The formal structure which is used to introduce the sign is relatively constant in that it implies its use in an inferential scheme of the type $p \supset q$. In linguistic terms, p and q are often represented by a complex proposition, i.e. a sequence of propositions, the linking of which forms a hypothetical period.

In general, as Vegetti (1976: 49) puts it, the inferential procedure (or *logismos*) begins with a process which is essentially 'abductive'. The individual phenomenon which the doctor observes is hypothesized as a case of some general rule. In other words, the *hekaston* ('singular phenomenon'), which is in itself insignificant, is thought of as a *semeion*, a sign which refers to a system from which it receives meaning. The first, ascending, movement of the construction of a system of reference is followed by a second, descending, movement of verification. If the hypothesized system is valid and works, it can be proved by applying it to other cases. The sign is thus transformed in a sort of *tekmerion* ('the proof') and the method becomes deductive.

Plato (427–347 bce)

The great Greek cultural tradition concerning signs and language finds in Plato its first true heir. However, in Plato we cannot yet find a theory of the sign completely separated from the theory of language, as it is the case with **Aristotle** and the later schools of philosophy. On the contrary, certain aspects of Plato's theory of language had an important semiotic character. Beside and independently of this aspect, in works of Plato we can find a use of semiotic terms (such as *semeion*) in relation to different domains: the domain of divination (*The Republic*, 382; *Timaeus*, 71a–72b; *Phaedrus*, 244b–c); the domain of writing (*Phaedrus*, 247c–276a; *The Sophist*, 262a, where the noun is defined as a 'vocal sign', *semeion tes phones*); and the domain of psychological facts such as memory, where the mind is described as a waxen tablet on which signs produced by the perception (*ton aistheseon semeia*) are imprinted (*Theaetetus*, 191a–195b).

The linguistic sign is seen in the Platonic dialogues concerning language (especially *Cratylus* and *The Sophist*) as *deloma*, 'revelation', of a non-perceptible object (this can be either the 'meaning' or the 'essence' of the object in question). The main concern of the major work on language, *Cratylus*, is the 'correctness of the nouns' in relation to their application to the things. This problem is present from the beginning of the **dialogue** in the form of a debate between Cratylus and Hermogenes, who choose Socrates as judge. Basically, Cratylus adopts what we might term a 'naturalistic' position, while Hermogenes defends a 'conventionalist' position, particularly in relation to 'naming' at the dawn of language. As usual, Socrates is the mouthpiece for Plato's opinions, and the motives for his negation of the other positions in the debate can be traced back to the general conception of philosophical method which Plato advocates. If either Cratylus or Hermogenes were right, dialectic as a method for attaining knowledge would be impossible. Indeed dialectic is threatened by both the 'subjectivism' of Hermogenes and by the 'total iconism' of Cratylus.

The solution proposed by Socrates is that the name is a 'revelation' (*deloma*), but the responsibility for this revelation is shifted from the relationship of resemblance between the name and the thing to the two factors acting together: the use (*ethos*) and the relationship between users of a name (*xyntheke* or 'convention'). However, Socrates does not substitute a conception whereby semiosis occurs through resemblance with a simple conventionalist conception. For him, the ideal situation remains that in which names are images which reproduce the essence of the object they name. It is rather the limits of **natural language** which make recourse to agreement and subsequent convention necessary (435a–c). This is the point at which some commentators have identified a compromise between the conventionalism of Hermogenes and the naturalism of Cratylus.

In the final lines of the dialogue there is also a shifting of the function assigned to the linguistic sign, whereby we can see an accentuation of the communicative function over the cognitive function. Language is not a sufficiently valid tool for attainment of knowledge of reality. Such knowledge requires a much more direct path, such as the recourse to things themselves. However, language can be seen as an excellent tool for the effective accomplishment of human **communication**.

Aristotle (384–322 bce)

In Aristotle's work we find a theory that has had a lasting influence on the history of semiotic thought. The first important factor in Aristotle's consideration of the question relating to signs is the separation, and consequent separate treatment, of the theory of language from the theory of the sign (that is, properly non-verbal sign). This may seem surprising to modern scholars and merits careful attention, precisely because modern semiotic theories assume a priori that the terms which make up verbal language are 'signs'. Indeed, according to one particular brand of structuralism, they are the signs *par excellence*, and many scholars have actually gone so far as to propose that the terms of verbal language can provide a model for all other types of sign. On the contrary, Aristotle distinguishes the elements which go to make up a theory of language with the name *symbola*, while the other elements of a theory of nonverbal signs he terms *semeia* or *tekmeria*.

The theory of nonverbal signs in fact forms part of the theory of **syllogism** and has both logical and epistemological features of interest. The nonverbal sign lies at the centre of the problem of how knowledge is acquired, whereas the linguistic symbol is principally connected to the problem of relationships between linguistic expressions, conceptual abstractions and states of the world. Aristotle sets out his theory of the linguistic symbol in *De Interpretatione*, expressing it in a model made up of three terms: a) *spoken sounds*, which are 'symbols' of the b) *affections of the soul*, which are themselves images of c) external *things* (Arist., *De Int.*, 16a, 3–8; trans. Ackrill 1963). It must be stated, first of all, that the appearance here of the term *semeia* apparently as a synonym of *symbola* should not be taken to mean that the two expressions are interchangeable. In this passage, Aristotle is using the term *semeion* to mean that the existence of sounds and letters can be considered the *evidence* (or the *clue*) of the parallel existence of affections of the soul.

For Aristotle, the theory of sign (specifically, nonverbal sign), completely distinct from the theory of language, may be located at the point of intersection between logic and rhetoric. Signs are dealt with therefore both in *Prior Analytics* and *Rhetoric*. The idea of sign simultaneously has two fundamental aspects. First of all it has an epistemological and ontological interest in that it is an instrument of knowledge which serves to guide the attention of knowing subjects to operate the passage from one fact to another. Equally important, however, is the strictly logical nature of the sign, stemming from the fact that it has a formal mechanism which regulates its function.

The general definition of the sign (*semeion*) is given in *Prior Analitics* (II, 70a, 7–9). The idea of the sign proposed by Aristotle in this passage involves the setting up of a relationship of implication between two things or two facts of the world, such as the fact, for example, that 'this woman has given birth' (*p*), a fact that implies a second fact: 'this woman has milk in her breasts' (*q*). The sign may be seen to coincide with the *second* term of implication, and therefore Aristotle's definition should be read as saying that '*q* is the sign of *p*'. In other words, the sign involves an inference from the consequent to the antecedent in an implicative relationship.

Aristotle develops the theory of reasoning by what follows in the *Sophistici Elenchi* (167b, 1–8). Conceived in this way, the sign can lead to misleading conclusions, as when someone, having observed once that the ground was wet after it had rained, concluded that, in general, if the ground is wet, then it has rained. Another example involves properties rather than events: if someone, having discovered that honey had the property of being yellow, concludes that you can know something is honey from its being yellow; in this case there would be the risk of mistaking gall for honey.

In order to establish a typology of signs, Aristotle proceeds first of all to show that there are three different ways in which the syllogism can use the premise expressed by a sign, each way corresponding to the possible position of the middle term in the different figure. In this way it is possible to have inferences which start from a sign in the first, second or third figure of the syllogism.

The sign appearing in the first figure of the syllogism is called by Aristotle *tekmerion*, i.e. 'necessary' or 'irrefutable' sign, in the sense that it leads to a necessarily true conclusion, as shown in the example 'If a woman has milk in her breasts, then she has given birth'. Here 'having milk' is both a consequence of having given birth and a sign that a woman has given birth; moreover the sign is the middle term in the syllogistic scheme.

The signs appearing within syllogisms in the second and third figure are called *semeia* and are refutable, even if they turn out to be true, as shown by the examples 'If a woman is pale, then she is pregnant' (in the second figure, establishing a relationship 'from the universal to the particular') and 'If Pittacus is good, all the wise men are good' (in the third figure, establishing a relationship 'from the particular to the universal').

The Stoics

Like Aristotle, the Stoics focused their research on two very distinct areas of thought. First of all we can find elements of semiotic interest in their theory of language, which involves an analysis of the relationship between language, thought and reality; and then also in their theory of the propositional 'sign', which is related to their theory of logical inference.

The semiotico-linguistic theory of the Stoics has its roots and develops within the terms of an ontology centred on the idea of 'particular', which is seen as a material object with definite shape, features that are defined as the sufficient and necessary condition for its existence.

The need for a theory of meaning stems precisely from the problem involved in identification of 'particular' and is connected to a theory of perception. The Stoics believed that images (*phantasiai*) produced in the mind by external objects gave rise to true perception if they reproduced the exact configurations of those objects. One of the ways of identifying a 'particular' is by identifying it linguistically. Thus A's ability to communicate with B that he or she is talking about X, and B's ability to indicate to A that the reference has been understood, is fundamental.

In a crucial passage concerning a conflict of opinions about truth, Sextus Empiricus presents the basic outline of the Stoic theory of language:

> Such, then, was the first disagreement about Truth; but there was another controversy, and in this some placed truth and falsity in the thing signified (*to semainomenon*), others in the sound (*phone*), others in the motion of

> intellect. The champions of the first opinion were the Stoics who said that 'three things are linked together, the thing signified (*to semainomenon*), and the thing signifying (*semainon*) and the thing existing (*to tynchanon*)'. And of these the thing signifying is the sound (for example, the word 'Dion'); and the thing signified is the actual state of affairs (*auto to pragma*) indicated by the spoken word and which we grasp as existing in dependence on (*paryphistamenon*) our intellect, but which the barbarians do not understand although they hear the sound; the thing existing is the external real object, that is, Dion himself. Of these, two are bodies, that is the sound and the existing thing; one is incorporeal, namely the thing signified and expressible (*lekton*), and this is true or false.
>
> (*Against the Logicians*, II, 11–12)

It has to be noted that here the terms 'signifier' [***signifiant***] (*semainon*) and 'signified' [***signifié***] (*semainomenon* or *lekton*) are used (as they are in **Saussure**'s theory), but not the term 'sign'. As in Aristotle, the idea of 'sign' (*semeion*) belongs to a different, non-linguistic, sphere of the theory.

The term first called *semainomenon*, then *lekton*, represents a unique case. The notion expressed by the term *lekton* is normally interpreted as the statement which an utterance makes with respect to some object. In this case, the more appropriate translation of *lekton* would be 'what is said', as such an expression covers both the notion of 'judgement' and that of 'state of affairs signified by a word or set of words' (Long 1971: 77).

In a passage from Seneca (*Epistulae Morales*, 117, 13) we can find a triadic scheme of signification analogous to that given by Sextus, but using a proposition ('Cato walks'), where Sextus had used only a name ('Dion'). Seneca draws attention to the distinction between the object of reference, which is a material object – in this case, Cato – and the assertion about this object ('Cato walks'), which is an incorporeal. This assertion is the *lekton*, and Seneca proposes three different Latin translations of the term: *enuntiatum* ('utterance'), *effatum* ('affirmation') and *dictum* ('assertion'). It is easier to see how the predicate 'true' or 'false' can be applied to Seneca's example, a proposition, than to the example used by Sextus Empiricus.

For the Stoics, signs (*semeia*) are above all *lekta* in that they are made up of propositions. Nonetheless, the fact that signs are *lekta* is revealing, given the need which the Stoics felt to translate the nonverbal signs into linguistic terms.

A very important point to be noted is that, while the Stoics consider the sign from the same point of view as Aristotle, the logical setting in which they place it is totally different. It is generally agreed that Aristotle uses a logic of classes for his syllogism, while the Stoics introduce propositional logic. The effect of their innovation is that attention is shifted (i) from the substance to events, with respect to the ontological point of view; (ii) from nouns/adjectives, which function as the predicate, to propositions, with respect to linguistic expression.

In post-Aristotelian schools of philosophy, the position of the sign changes radically. Inference from signs moves out from its beginning in rhetoric and dialectic to science in general and reaches the highest levels of philosophy. In the framework of science the sign must furnish a true and reliable knowledge. So, the most widely chosen parameter for the classification of signs is the probative force of the argument based on the sign or the cogency of the logical link between the two propositions of the conditional in which the sign can be reconstructed. In Aristotle – as we have seen – this leads to the distinction between a high degree of probative force characterizing the sign-inference which can be reconstructed in a first figure syllogism (*tekmerion*), and the low degree of certainty distinguishing sign-inferences which can be reconstructed in a second or third figure syllogism (*semeia*). In Hellenistic times classification resulted in two main dichotomies (the second of which has sometimes been interpreted as a subdivision of the second term of the first dichotomy):

1 The opposition between 'commemorative sign' and 'indicative sign': a commemorative sign (*hypomnestikon semeion*) is something observed in conjunction with what it signifies, as smoke observed in conjunction with fire (Sext. Emp., *Against the Logicians*, II, 152; *Outlines of Pyrrhonism*, II, 100). The indicative sign (*endeiktikon semeion*) is not something observed in conjunction with what it signifies, because the thing signified is inobservable, but it 'signifies that whereof it is a sign by its own particular nature and constitution, just as, for instance, the bodily motions are signs of the soul' (Sext. Emp., *Outlines of Pyrrhonism*, II, 101) or as when blushing is a sign of shame (Sext. Emp., *Against the Logicians*, II, 173);
2 The opposition between particular sign and general sign: the particular (or peculiar) sign (*idion semeion*) is one which is cogent in that it cannot exist except together with the thing signified (*On Signs*, I, 1–19; XIV, 2–11); the general (or common) sign (*koinon semeion*) can exist whether the unperceived object exists or not (ibid.); general signs do not necessitate their designata, because they can each indicate any of a number of possible objects, as when a yawn could be the common sign of tiredness or of boredom.

Epicurus (341–271 bce)

Epicurus, as the Stoics, sees the sign as representing the standard procedure for the passage from the known to the unknown. Indeed one of the key points of Epicurean epistemology was the semiotic principle of making conjectures about facts which are by nature imperceptible to the senses from visible phenomena. The fundamental elements of Epicurean physics (that is, the existence of atoms and of the void, the forms and reasons for celestial phenomena) are established by means of semiotic inferences which start from perceptible phenomena.

Epicurus rejected the deductive reasoning typical of Aristotle and the Stoics, judging it to be empty and devoid of use, but he accepted and believed in the importance of analogic inference. The central problem then became how to establish the criterion to check if and within what limits these judgements could be considered reliable or unreliable (that is, true or false) and to establish the basis on which to pronounce whether or not certain assertions indeed correspond to the facts which they describe. The notion of the 'truth criterion' thus comes to the fore, and this provides the framework within which both the theory of semiotic inference and the theory of language were developed. According to what Diogenes Laërtius records (X, 31) there is not a unique criterion, but many. So Epicurus considered truth criteria to be: perceptions (*aistheseis*), affections (*pathe*), preconceptions or anticipations (*prolepseis*) and immediate evidence or clear vision (*enargeia*, mentioned in the *Letter to Herodotus*, 82). The truth criteria are functional to a theory of semiotic inference, as they tend to establish basic truths regarding perceptible objects, which in turn form a starting point from which to make inferences about the things which are not accessible through sense perception.

1 Preconception has a decisive role in perceptive inference, as Diogenes Laërtius shows (as well as in the theory of language). According to Epicurus, it is only through the possession of the general concept of 'human being' that one can decide whether what one sees is a particular occurrence of this concept. Preconceptions also constitute a necessary condition of language and operate both on the level of decodification and on the level of codification. First of all, the act of uttering a name brings to the mind of a listener an image or a concept, an underlying entity (*hypotetagmenon*) of that name, which is derived from preconception (Diogenes Laërtius, X, 33). In addition, a speaker must have a preconception of what he or she intends to express, otherwise it would be impossible to say anything.

   If preconceptions then form the basis for all concepts, a theory of the linguistic sign begins to take shape which is very different from that usually attributed to the Epicureans by Sextus Empiricus (*Against the Logicians*, II, 13; 258) and Plutarch (*Adversus Colotem*, 1119f.). The centrality of preconception in the Epicurean theory of language is also shown by the fact that it can be identified also with the 'basic' or 'primary' meaning (*proton ennoema*) mentioned in the *Letter to Herodotus* (37–38), a meaning which stands apart from all other meanings which can be considered to be derived from it.

2 Preconceptions, as well as perceptions (*aistheseis*), are considered by Epicurus as the two kinds of tools for the investigator, and they must exist prior to any investigation (*Letter to Herodotus*, 37–38). Their function is to be used as signs in order to infer (*semeiosometha*) two kinds of things: (i) what is expected to be observed (*to prosmenon*, 'what is waiting'); and (ii) what is non-evident (*adela*).

   In Epicurus' works we can find a lot of examples of a thoroughly empirical reasoning where 'phenomena' are used as 'signs' of what is non-evident.

They can be divided into two kinds: one kind concerns the use of analogy to show that an unobservable entity is similar to a phenomenon (for example, in the *Letter to Herodotus*, 58–59, Epicurus says that atoms have minimal parts just like perceptible objects); the other kind concerns comparisons that show in how many ways something unobservable resembles what is observable (for example, in the *Letter to Pythocles*, 96, Epicurus uses comparisons showing that the eclipses of the moon or sun can happen in several ways just as it happens in deprivations of light in observed bodies).

Philodemus (*c.* 110–*c.* 40 or 35 bce)

After Epicurus, the theory of the sign was widely developed by later Epicureans. A first-century bce treatise, the *Peri semeion kai semeioseon* (*On Signs and Semiotic Inferences*) by Philodemus, demonstrates the depth and range which theory of the sign reached in the Epicurean school. The treatise is not a systematic exposition of the Epicurean theory of the sign, rather it records (in four distinct parts) the polemic which raged between the Epicureans and an opposing philosophical school that for some scholars is represented by the Stoics (De Lacy and De Lacy 1978; Sedley 1982), for others by the Academics (Asmis 1996), for some others it is impossible to be determined (Barnes 1988).

The discussion of inference by signs at the centre of debate in *On Signs* involves a host of important elements from semiotics, logic and epistemology, which are variously intertwined, as are the positions of the contenders in the debate. In one of the most interesting aspects of his contribution on this subject, Jonathan Barnes (1988) has shown that it is possible to take the various phases of the prolonged debate on signs between the Epicureans and their opponents and to consider each one separately. There are basically six distinct phases, as follows (and as alluded to in VII, 5–7): (i) an account of the theory of Epicurean inference by signs; (ii) the objections to this theory advanced by their opponents; (iii) the responses of the Epicureans to these objections; (iv) the technical objections of Dionysius to the Epicurean responses; (v) the counter-objections to Dionysius made by Zeno of Sidon, Philodemus's teacher; and (vi) Philodemus's own version of Zeno's approach. Even though this exact sequence, with its precise cast of characters, applies only to the first of the four parts of *On Signs*, its inventory of positions and counterpositions is valid for the entire treatise.

1 The Epicureans described in *On Signs* retained the inference from signs, or *semeiosis*, a procedure that leads us from a sign to what it means, that is from the known to the unknown, from the evident to the non-evident. We infer from objects of a certain kind that are a part of our experience, to objects of the same kind that are situated, temporarily or permanently, outside of our experience. The general form that semiotic inference assumes among the Epicureans is the following (Barnes 1988: 97): 'Since all the Ks in our experience are F, Ks elsewhere/everywhere are F.' Examples of the

Epicurean semiotic inference reported in *On Signs* are: 'Since men in our experience are mortal, so too are all men' (II, 26–28 = Ch. 5); 'Since living beings in our experience are mortal, so too are all living beings that can be in Britain' (V, 34–36 = Ch. 7). The examples illustrate the basis that Epicureans intended to furnish in order to make the inference cogent. Indeed, the Epicureans considered it necessary that extensive research and evaluation of the evidence be achieved.

2 Opposition to Philodemus was based on the idea that an inference must be based not on similarity, but rather on *anaskeué*, a term which had been translated into English as 'contraposition' (De Lacy and De Lacy 1978), but which is now better translated as 'elimination' (Sedley 1982: 244 and *passim*; Asmis 1996: 155 and *passim*) or as 'rebuttal' (Barnes 1988: 98 and *passim*). Barnes (1988: 100) asks the question how the *anaskeué* could supply, or seem to supply, a method of semiotic inference. One of the possibilities is that it roughly corresponds to what modern philosophers call 'inference to the best explanation'. We can suppose that, in relation to a conditional of the type 'if *p*, then *q*', there is an inference of the type 'since *p*, then *q*': the inference would be valid insofar as the corresponding conditional holds due to the method of elimination.

The opponents, proposing the *anaskeué* ('elimination'), did not present a real method of inference, but a criterion of validity of a conditional. The Epicureans, at the same level, elaborated instead on a criterion of validity of the conditional that they defined as *adianoesia* ('inconceivability'), of which we find an illustration in Philodemus's *On Signs* (XII, 14–31 = Ch. 17), and consisting in the fact that, given a certain conditional like 'If Plato is a man, Socrates is also a man', it is impossible to conceive that the first is or is not of a certain character and the second is or is not of such a character.

Latin rhetoric

In the passage from the Greek world into the Roman world, the semiotic paradigm moved away from the field of philosophy, in the strict sense, into the area of judicial rhetoric, where it assumed a central position. In contrast to the Greeks, the Romans were more interested in matters which tended principally to the pragmatic, and, although they recognized and appreciated the potentiality of the semiotic paradigm, they immediately channelled it into what were for them the more attractive ends of political and judicial debate, a debate which was conducted with instruments supplied by rhetoric. In Cicero, as with the other Roman writers on the subject, rhetoric no longer occupies second place after logic, but, in contrast, it is philosophy as a whole which becomes an ancillary science whose role is to contribute towards the making of a fine orator.

The consideration of signs rests at the heart of *inventio*, that is, the part of **discourse** where proofs must be found to convince the court of the guilt or innocence of the accused. In rhetoric, proofs have a special force; they start off from reasoning and become part of the procedure used to convince (*fidem facere*). It seems right to acknowledge a certain positive achievement which rhetoric accomplished in its attempt to classify the different degrees of probatory strength and the different argumentative powers of proofs or clues. Different writers had their own diverse views on how this classification system should be drawn up, and rarely did one coincide with the others any more than very partially, for example Cornificius (the supposed author of *Rhetorica ad Herennium*), Cicero and Quintilian.

Augustine (ad 354–430)

The most important semiotic figure of the late antiquity is **Augustine**. With him the two theories (of the sign and of the language) are first unified, for Augustine considers linguistic expressions to be fully signs (*De Magistro*, II, 3), in particular 'commemorative signs' (XI, 37). If this is the case, Augustine is making a move which is symmetrical with, but opposite to, Saussure's: Augustine unifies the two theories and the two classes of signs, making non-linguistic signs the model class, whereas in Saussure's theory the two classes of signs are unified under the model of linguistic sign.

The central importance of semio-linguistic matters in Augustine's works derives principally from his reading of the Stoics, as his early work *De Dialectica* (ad 387) demonstrates. This work summarizes many of the Stoic semiotic themes, including the principle that knowledge is, on a simple level, knowledge gained by means of signs.

But there are three important departures in Augustine's thought from that of the Stoics. The first is that he – for the first time in the ancient world – includes in the category of *signa* not only nonverbal signs, such as **gestures**, military insignia, fanfares, mime, etc., but also the expressions of spoken language (*De Magistro*, IV–IX).

The second important point of divergence between Augustine and the Stoics is that Augustine identifies the individual linguistic expression, that is the *verbum* ('word'), as the element in which signifier and signified are united, and considers this unification to be a sign of something else. In contrast, the Stoics had identified the utterance as the point of conjunction between the signifier [***signifiant***] (*semainon*) and the signified [***signifié***] (*semainomenon*).

The third important difference between Augustine and the Stoics is that, whereas the Stoics had formulated a theory of language centred on signification, Augustine proposes instead a theory of linguistic sign which has a psychological and communicative nature: the signifieds are to be found in the mind of the speaker and pass into the mind of the hearer.

In earlier theories of language, the relationship between linguistic expressions and their contents was conceived of as a *relation of equivalence*. There was an epistemological motivation for this view and it concerned the possibility of working directly on language, in the same way as on an object of reality, since language was understood to be a system for representation of reality (even though inevitably mediated through the mind). In contrast, Augustine conceives of the relationship between a sign and the thing referred to as a *relation of inference*, thanks to which the first term, by the mere fact of existing, enables the passage to knowledge of the second term.

For Augustine the meaning of a sign can be established or expressed by means of other signs, such as by using synonyms, by pointing at something with the finger, by using imitative gestures, or by means of ostensive gestures (*De Magistro*, 2, 7). Here a semantic conception very similar to **Peirce**'s '**unlimited semiosis**' can be seen at work.

A consequence of this fact is that Augustine has to deal with the problem of taking a firm position on the question of whether or not language provides, in itself and by its very nature, information about the things it signifies. Augustine's conclusion about the relationship between sign and object is that one must first have knowledge of the object of reference to be able to say that a word is a sign of this object. It is the knowledge of the thing which is responsible for the presence of the sign rather than vice versa. This solution has clear Platonic overtones, and to this may be linked the equally Platonic-inspired statement that knowledge of things is more important than knowledge of signs (*De Magistro*, 9).

A further important aspect of Augustine's work is the presence of various classifications of signs which appear most notably in *De Doctrina Christiana* (AD 397, with later additions) but which also feature in other works. The first interesting relationship in Augustine's classification is that between *res* ('things') and *signa*. Although the world is basically thus divided into things and signs, Augustine sees this distinction as functional and relative rather than ontological. Signs are also types of *res* (thing), and it is quite possible to take as a sign a *res* which had previously not been endowed with this status. It is in the framework of this classification that Augustine gives his fundamental definition of the sign: 'The sign is something which above and beyond the impression it produces on the senses on its own account, makes something else come to mind' (*De Doctrina Christiana*, II, I. 1).

The second interesting classification is that which is made according to the channel of perception employed. Augustine lists signs perceived through sight (nodding and shaking the head, gestures, bodily movements of actors, flags, military insignia and letters), smell, taste and touch. Particular importance is attributed to signs perceived through the sense of hearing. They include the basically aesthetic signs produced by musical instruments, the essentially communicative signs produced by military fanfares and trumpets, and of course words, defined as having 'the most important position among human beings for the expression of thoughts of all kinds which anyone wants to convey' (*De Doctrina Christiana*, II, III. 4).

Finally, perhaps the most important classification of the signs is that which opposes *signa naturalia* to *signa data*. The first type, that of the *signa naturalia*, includes '[signs which] without any intention or desire of signifying, make us aware of something beyond themselves, as for example, smoke which signifies fire' (*De Doctrina Christiana*, II, I. 2). Other examples of this type of sign are animal tracks and facial expressions which reveal, unintentionally, irritation or pleasure.

In Augustine's perspective the *signa data*, the signs of the second type, are more interesting, for this category includes Scriptural signs. They are defined as '[signs which] all living creatures make, one to another, to show, as much as they can, the motion of their spirit, that is, everything that they feel and think' (*De Doctrina Christiana*, II, II. 3). The prime examples of this type of sign are human linguistic signs, that is, words. But Augustine also includes animal sounds in this category, as, for example, the sounds the cock uses to inform the hen that he has found food. In this respect there is a very marked difference between Augustine and Aristotle, who placed animal noises among natural signs (*De Interpretatione*, 16a). *Signa data* are to be understood as 'intentional signs' (Jackson 1969: 14) and it is precisely the intentional nature of animal noises which causes Augustine to include them in this category.

From the past toward the future

One of the most important points that we can observe after having reviewed the history of semiotics from its origins is that there is a continuity between the ancient theories of sign and the contemporary line of cognitive semiotics, as represented by Peirce, Morris and the scholars who are now following their path. On the contrary, there is a profound fracture between the ancient semiotic theories and the Saussurean semiotic line.

In effect, the model of sign proposed by Saussure, based on equivalence, possesses characteristics that were not present in the ancient model: (i) it is substantially a linguistic model, and therefore does not function well for signs other than linguistic ones; (ii) it presupposes a type of **semantics** in the form of a 'dictionary' (Haiman 1980: 329ff.) that analyses the content of a sign utilizing a system of semantic features without taking into account the communicative contexts and circumstances (Eco 1984: 106ff.); and (iii) it presupposes a notion of language as a code which puts into a biunivocal relation elements of expression with elements of content, in a manner that is substantially closed.

The consequence of this weakness of the notion of sign based on equivalence is that some semiotic schools have abandoned the notion of sign as being not pertinent, considering it too superficial for a semiotic analysis. Contrary to this conclusion, however, the notion of sign can still be useful if we abandon the equative model, recovering, in the process, the ancient form of the semiotic model based on inference. This form is better adapted to operate with the modern semantic in the 'encyclopedia' form, as opposed to the idea of signs as components of a dictionary (Eco 1984: 106–134). An 'encyclopedia' semantics considers also the linguistic sign as functioning according to the inference model, because it connects every sign with a hypothetical plurality of contexts and circumstances. In fact, languages, as has been understood for many years, are not codes but much more complex systems, and the inferential model of signs makes it possible to master this complexity.

Thus, research on ancient semiotic notions goes further than pure historical reconstruction, learned and philological; rather, they are the bearers of a modern proposal.

Further reading

Deely, J. (1982) *Introducing Semiotic: Its History and Doctrine*, Bloomington, IN: Indiana University Press.

Deely, J. (2001) *Four Ages of Understanding. The First Postmodern Survey of Philosophy from Ancient Times to the Turn of the 21st Century*, Toronto: University of Toronto Press.

Manetti, G. (ed.) (1988) 'Signs of antiquity/antiquity of signs', *Versus,* 50/51.

Manetti, G. (1993) *Theories of the Sign in Classical Antiquity*, Bloomington, IN: Indiana University Press.

Manetti, G. (ed.) (1996) *Knowledge through Signs. Ancient Semiotic Theories and Practices*, Turnhout, Belgium: Brepols.

2

Semiotics of nature

Jesper Hoffmeyer

Setting the scene

The conception of nature as fundamentally semiotic is certainly not new; what *is* new, rather, is the nearly unanimous repression of this conception by learned society. The German-American philosopher Hans Jonas has pointed to the strange fact that our conception of nature has undergone a 180-degree inversion in the course of human history (Jonas 2001 [1966]). Originally, life was conceived as the uncontested principle inherent to everything, and the idea of non-life was simply unimaginable (as, accordingly, was the idea of an entity distinct from the body, the soul). Now, thousands of years later, non-life or inanimate nature has come to stand as the uncontested prime ontological entity. The deepest challenge to the scientific conception of nature now comes from the undeniable fact that some **object**s in the world are living creatures. For how can bodies be anything but chemistry? Isn't DNA, a purely chemical substance, the ultimate ruler of living systems?

Only at the midpoint in this grand historical movement did we get dualism, the idea that *soma* and *sema* represent equally inescapable but incompatible dimensions (substances, properties or whatever) of our world. Intellectually, dualism was based upon a quite natural but nonetheless unsubstantiated argument: since matter without spirit seems widespread in the world, there might equally well be spirit without matter. The main problem with this argument is not that spirit without matter remains an unobservable and thus basically speculative entity. The main problem is that it is not obvious what the matter–spirit distinction is all about. The idea of passive matter as ruled by natural laws (or the heavenly ruler) has long ago lost its credibility. The modern scientific world cannot easily be reduced to this far-fetched classical ideal (cf. Ulanowicz 2008, 2009). Instead modern conceptions of physical nature make ample space for the vision of the world as an emergent process in which those peculiar things we call living systems and their bodies might well have evolved as genuinely semiotic creatures (Kauffman 2000; Kauffman and Clayton 2005; Deacon and Sherman 2008).

Mainstream science regards **emergence** theories with great scepticism, fearing, one may suppose, that such theories are smuggling in supernatural intervention through the back door. There is a deep irony to this suspicion, for the ontology of natural law, i.e. the belief, held by most scientists, that the laws of physics describe all possible behaviours, is itself basically dependent on

Christian metaphysics. It seemed obvious to late-medieval Christian thinkers such as Thomas **Aquinas** that God would not, in his benevolence, have created nature as an unruly and lawless place. And this belief of course is the one idea that originally made natural science possible in the first place, for without an orderly universe there would be no natural laws for science to study. So, sharply put: the heresy of emergence theories seems to be none other than its rejection of the Christian metaphysics which justifies the ontology of natural law.

Emergentist theories turn the question of the apparent orderliness of our world upside down by suggesting that nature is basically indeterminate and that the lawful behaviours we nevertheless observe in our world have emerged in an evolutionary process. The sporadic existence in natural systems of order (lawful and predictable behaviour[1]) is therefore the very problem that science must explain. This was exactly the position that Charles **Peirce** recommended so many years ago, when he said:

> Uniformities are precisely the kind of fact that need to be accounted for. That a pitched coin should sometimes turn up heads and sometimes tails calls for no particular explanation; but if it shows heads every time, we wish to know how this result has been brought about. *Law is par excellence the thing which wants a reason.* Now the only possible way of accounting for the laws of nature and the uniformity in general is to suppose them results of evolution. This supposes them not to be absolute, not to be obeyed precisely. It makes an element of indeterminacy, spontaneity, or absolute chance in nature.
>
> (*CP* 6: 12–13) (italics added)

Adopting an emergentist conception of the world automatically opens up the study of non-deterministic processes and this implies that there is no longer any logical need for an outright rejection of the reality of human experiential worlds or free will. Science may not be a good tool for analysing the content of human experiential worlds, but it does allow such worlds to exist. And biology, furthermore, should feel compelled to produce theories to explain what the evolutionary advantages could possibly be of possessing this capacity for experiencing the world and not just for behaving in it. It was precisely the need to confront this challenge that led me – and others I suppose – to explore the potentials of a semiotic approach to the study of life on Earth.

The semiotic approach to the study of the biological world does not only break with the ontology of natural law. It also claims that from the moment **semiosis** first began to manifest itself in the first living units, or cells, a new dynamic principle was now superimposed upon the already established dynamics of emergence as exhibited by complex chemical systems. From now on what happened to living entities would be greatly influenced by an interpretative activity that is free in the

[1] Contrary to the idealized systems of classical physics we learned about at school, real natural systems (like, for example, living things or tornadoes) are generally complex and obey so-called chaos dynamics which for all practical purposes put them beyond reach of predictability and deterministic analysis.

sense of being underdetermined by physical lawfulness. Essentially this implies that the well-known efficient causality of physics has become superposed by *semiotic causality*, the bringing about of effects by semiotic interactions. Translated to biology this means that cells would now engage in intentional activities: their activities would not simply refer to the outer world but would do so only in a contextual setting of their internal self-referential system (the genomic system). Living entities became intentional systems – subjects in a sense – because they had established channels for an integration of other-reference (through surface receptors) with self-reference (Hoffmeyer 1998a). At first they were of course only marginally intentional but this new dynamic principle, semiosis, would have a self-perpetuating logic to it, so that *semiotic freedom* (see below) started to grow. And this growth may well be the inner core of organic evolution.

Semiotization of nature

Twentieth-century life science experienced a profound, although rather unnoticed, trend towards a semiotization of nature. An early expression of this trend was the ethology of Jakob von **Uexküll** (1864–1944), who in the 1920s developed his *Umweltsforschung*, i.e. research into the Umwelt, the latter being a term Uexküll introduced to refer to the phenomenal worlds of organisms, the worlds around animals as they themselves perceive them (see Kull, this volume).

In 1973 ethology became canonized through the awarding of the Nobel Prize in Physiology and Medicine to be shared among Konrad Lorenz and fellow ethologists Karl von Frisch and Nicolas Tinbergen. Lorenz clearly stated the debt of ethology to the early work of Jakob von Uexküll,[2] but the recognition of ethology as a proper scientific discipline nevertheless was obtained only because Lorenz turned his attention away from the Uexküllian Umwelt. The question of how animals *conceive* their surroundings was replaced in ethology by the question of animal *behaviour*, which was then described to a large extent as the result of *inborn instincts*. And so, instead of seeking a proximal explanation of behaviour from the specific Umwelt of the animal, ethology devoted itself to the study of more distal explanations based on genetic dispositions such as instincts and, ultimately, on natural selection.

A major breakthrough in our understanding of the semiotic character of life was the establishment in 1953 of the Watson–Crick double-helix model of DNA and the subsequent deciphering of the genetic **code**. While up to this point the semiotic understanding of nature had been concerned mainly with communicative processes between organisms, termed ***exosemiosis*** by Sebeok (Sebeok 1979a), it now became clear that semiotic processes were also prevalent at the biochemical level (***endosemiosis***). In 1973 the linguist Roman **Jakobson**

[2] Ethology 'certainly owes more to his [Uexküll's] teaching than to any other school of behavior study' said Lorenz (Lorenz 1971, cited in Sebeok 2001b: 72).

pointed out that the genetic code shared several properties with human **language** and that both were based on a double-articulation principle (Jakobson 1973; Emmeche and Hoffmeyer 1991). Due to its reductionist inclination, however, mainstream biology did not at the time – and still does not – apply a semiotic terminology (an exception to this is Florkin 1974[3]).

The biochemist Eugene Yates has pointed to the strange shift in vocabulary which gradually took place in biochemistry in the wake of the recognition of the genetic code (Yates 1985). It seems as if modern biochemistry cannot be taught – or even thought – without using communicational terms such as 'recognition', 'high-fidelity', 'messenger-RNA', 'signalling', 'presenting' or even 'chaperones'. Such terms pop up from every page of modern textbooks in biochemistry in spite of the fact that they clearly have nothing to do with the physicalist universe to which such books are dedicated. As Yates rightly remarks: 'There is no more substance in the modern biological statement that "genes direct development" than there is in the statement "balloons rise by levity"'(Yates 1985: 348).

Biochemists, of course, do not normally suppose that macromolecules or cells 'recognize', 'send messages' or 'present peptides at their surfaces' in the normal sense of these words, and if accused of sloppy use of terms they would claim that such language is only short-hand talk for complicated processes that might in the end be described in decent scientific vocabulary based on information theory and natural selection. There are, however, serious reasons to suspect that this is not the case. Natural selection presupposes competition between individual organisms, but in the absence of the alleged 'pseudo'-semiotic functions we are talking about here, there could be no functional cells or organisms in the first place and therefore no natural selection. Natural selection simply presupposes an intentionality – a 'striving' to use Darwin's own term – that is not accounted for.

It will not help either to answer the objection by reference to information theory. For many kinds of processes, such as DNA methylation or RNA editing, are now known to interfere with the supposed deterministic control exerted by the 'information' carried in the DNA. But more than anything else the recent finding, that small nucleic acid sequences of 20–24 nucleotides, so-called microRNAs, play a key role in gene regulation, has signalled a major shift away from the classical view of the gene. Approximately 500 different microRNAs have now been identified in human cells, and it is believed that as much as a third or more of our all our genes are prone to regulation by microRNA. Genetic information therefore does not 'determine' anything in the strict sense of this word, rather it 'specifies'. But a specification is no innocent thing when seen in the light of normal scientific ontology, for the meaning of a specification depends on a process of interpretation (Sterelny and Griffiths 1999). Natural

[3] Florkin unfortunately built his semiotic approach upon a Saussurean conception of semiotics that takes human language as the primary model for semiosic activity. Later biosemiotics has taken its inspiration from a Peircean conception where human language is seen as one very peculiar instantiation of a much broader semiotics pertaining to evolution at large.

selection therefore depends – as Darwin well knew – upon the interpretative activity of organisms, and strictly speaking it is not, of course, nature in all abstractness that selects. The selective agency must instead be exerted by some definite entity, and this entity is the lineage.[4] It is the lineage – seen as a historical and transgenerational subject[5] – that acts as the selective agent via its overall reproductive patterns. By virtue of the genetic specifications carried forward from generation to generation by individual organisms, the lineage maintains – and continuously updates – a selective memory (the momentary pool of genomes) of its past that in most cases will be a suitable tool for producing individuals capable of dealing with the future. This agential aspect of natural selection, however, is never admitted in the standard account of this process, and the sustained use of this spontaneous semiotic terminology in modern biology and biochemistry cannot therefore be excused by reference to natural selection.

Increasingly through the twentieth century biology had been forced by its own development to reach out for semiotic tools of explanation, but soon such tools were stripped of their genuine semiotic content and reduced to passive parameters in the dyadic schemes of efficient causality. The semiotic dimension was reached out for because of its heuristic potentials, but at the same time it had to be rejected because of its implicit incongruity with the prevailing ontological belief system of modern biology. Biology cannot have it both ways, though, and its continued need for semiotic terms to make the life-world understandable seems to indicate that it should drop its Newtonian ballast rather than continue to reject the reality of natural semiosis.

Three steps of semiotic emergence

While the semiotic nature of living systems seems hard to deny, it does not feel equally obvious to most observers that the non-living world would require description in semiotic terms. But the distinction of the world into two domains, an asemiotic non-biological domain and a semiotic biological domain respectively, raises the troublesome question of how semiosis could ever have evolved in an asemiotic universe. From the point of view of evolutionary philosophy the solution to this puzzle might be to see semioticity itself as an emergent phenomenon. Thus at the most macroscopic and inclusive level we would have what John **Deely** has called a ***physiosemiosis***,[6] 'an activity ... replete with the objective causality whereby the physical interaction of existing things is channeled toward a future different from what obtains at the time of the

[4] The word *lineage* here is used in the conventional sense of a succession of ancestors and descendants in a population, parents and offspring. The lineage is the population as evolving unit.

[5] The *lineage* is a *historical subject* and has a kind of *collective agency* as such, since its destiny as a temporal integrative structure is continuously influenced by the collectivity of interactions of its single units with their environments – much in the same way that multicellular organisms are integrative structures interacting with their surroundings via the activity of individual cells.

[6] As discussed below I have reservations towards the use of this particular term.

affected interaction' (Deely 1990: 30; see also Matsuno and Salthe 1995). As Deely observes, this would be a process 'whereby first stars and then planetary systems develop out of a more primitive atomic or molecular "dust" but these systems in turn give rise to conditions under which further complexifications of atomic structure becomes possible' (ibid.). This may be taken as a modern way of expressing the Peircean 'law of mind', i.e. nature's general tendency to acquire '**habit**s' or – as we would say today – regularities. Through the early evolution on our planet such regularities would have gradually served to produce more and more predictability, and finally, as this process had advanced far enough, systems arose that could proliferate by taking advantage of this increased predictability. Such systems were the first living systems which nourished themselves by means of a newly invented ability to anticipate, i.e. to interpret regularities in their surroundings as **sign**s pointing to important configurations of future situations. At first such anticipatory activities would have played out at a very simple level, as when a bacterium 'chooses' to swim upstream in a gradient of nourishment rather than tumbling around waiting for the nutrients to reach it, but little by little the advantages of this talent for anticipation would have favoured any improvement of the talent that might accidentally appear, and thus would have started the ongoing tendency of evolution to create systems with ever more semiotic freedom or *interpretance*, defined as the capacity of a system (a cell, organism, species, etc.) to distinguish relevant sensible parameters in its surroundings or its own interior states and use them to produce signification and meaning.[7] An increase in semiotic freedom implies an increased capacity for responding to a variety of signs through the formation of (locally) 'meaningful' interpretants. Since semiotic freedom allows a system to 'read' many sorts of 'cues' in the surroundings, it will tend to have beneficial effects upon fitness.

In the evolutionary cosmology suggested here the early universe is seen as essentially indeterminate and as in a deep sense perfused with proto-semiosic activity. By the term proto-semiosic activity I refer to what is nowadays called self-organizing processes, which in Peircean terminology would be 'habit-taking'.[8] In principle habit-taking may be seen as the most basic or general form of an **interpretant**, and in this sense the term physiosemiosis would indeed be a suitable way of characterizing this proto-semiosic activity. I hesitate however to use this term because it may so easily be misunderstood to imply that sign use did indeed take place in this early universe, and I would argue strongly against such

[7] Originally I defined this concept as 'the depth of meaning that an individual or species is capable of communicating' (Hoffmeyer 1992: 109; 1996), but the essence of this ability is interpretation rather than communication, although the two aspects are of course closely connected.

[8] The term self-organization has become standard in complexity research in spite of the inherent philosophical ambiguities connected to the use of the term 'self' as discussed by Alicia Juarrero (1999). That the self-organizing property of the early universe comes close to semiosis, since it presupposes a concept of molecular measuring processes, can be seen in Stuart Kauffman's important book *Investigations* (2000) (and further discussed in Hoffmeyer 2008a).

a conception. However, this proto-semiosic activity would cause a gradual formation of ordered configurations of processes and thereby produce a growing deviation from equiprobability or, in other words, a growing predictability. Under the particular physical conditions that reigned on planet Earth (and possibly a great number of other locations in our universe) this growth paved the way for the appearance of a new kind of semiosic activity, biosemiosis. While *proto-semiosic activity* refers to a profound general trend of the early universe, *biosemiosis* may be seen as a radical potentiation of this trend brought about by the creation of concrete semiotic agents, first – as we shall see – historical agents, lineages, and later in evolution individual organisms. Stanley Salthe's *specification hierarchy* expresses a related conception (Salthe 1993, 2007). The appearance on our planet of biosemiosis, in short, opened a new agenda for the evolutionary process by providing entities with the agential property that is presupposed for Darwinian 'striving' and thus for natural selection. At primitive levels the semiotic freedom of agents is still very low, and a bacterium for instance cannot itself choose to *not* swim upstream in a nutrient gradient. Therefore, at this stage of evolution, semiotic freedom is primarily exhibited at the level of the lineage (the evolving species).[9] Only later, with the evolution of brained animals, would emerge a more advanced stage of biosemiosis, in which the semiosic activity is no longer a species property but also, and importantly so, an organismic property.

The emergence of this individualization of semiotic freedom initiated a fundamental change in the dynamics of the evolutionary process. Patterns of interactive behaviour now became increasingly regulated or released by semiotic means, and this induced a new kind of flexibility upon inter- and intraspecific interactions. Innovations more and more would depend on semiotically organized cooperative patterns at all levels from single cells and tissues to organisms and species and, in the end, whole ecological settings.

Very late in organic evolution a further potentiation of semiosic activity took place through the appearance of human beings that from the first beginnings were embedded in a linguistic *Lebenswelt*, based on the particular ability of this species to understand symbolic linguistic referencing (Deacon 1997). This kind of semiosis has been called *anthroposemiosis*, but since the semiotic freedom of *Homo sapiens* is so much more obvious than the semiotic freedom of animals or plants, anthroposemiosis has until recently been conceived as the only kind of semiosis on our planet. Due, not least, to the indefatigable efforts of the late Thomas Sebeok, it has now gradually become accepted that human semiotic capacity is only one – although radical – further refinement of a biosemiotic capacity that has unfolded itself on Earth through nearly 4 billion years (Sebeok

[9] Even at this level one cannot rule out individual semiotic freedom right away, though. A bacterium is a hugely complex and well-tuned system of proteins and other components and although learning processes probably do not directly play a role at this level the bacterium is capable of changing its behaviour by the active uptake of foreign DNA from bacteriophages.

1979a; Sebeok and Umiker-Sebeok 1992). The semiosic difference between the human animal and other living systems is staggering indeed, but, as John Deely has repeatedly pointed out, by far the most important dimension of this difference is that humans know the difference between signs and things, while animals do not (Deely 2001a). Quoting Jacques Maritain's pithy statement 'Whoever does not love truth is not a human being!' Deely elegantly makes the point thus:

> The ability to be concerned with the truth is unique to the rational animal, predicated on the species-specifically human awareness of the objective world under the guise of being, transforming from the outset the animal Umwelt of objects ready-to-hand into an objective 'life-world' of things present-at-hand, able to be investigated for what they are, the Lebenswelt of semiotic animals.
>
> (Deely 2007a: 80)

(Where the term 'semiotic animal' is reserved in Deely for the human animal.)

In biology the question of the origin of life has mostly been posed in chemical terms, while the semiotic revolution embedded in this process has been overlooked. Building upon the important ideas of Stuart Kauffman (Kauffman 1993, 2000), I have suggested that this process presupposed the following four steps: *first*, the formation through membrane building of an asymmetry between an inside and an outside in an autocatalytically closed system, a protocell; *second*, an exchange of chemical substances (a proto-communication) between individual units in swarms of such protocells; *third*, creation of a *self-referential* mechanism: a redescription of important constituents (proteins) of the protocell in a digital code such as RNA or DNA; and *fourth*, the transformation of the outer membrane to become an interface linking the interior and the exterior. In modern cells millions of glycoprotein receptors at the surface of the cell membrane take care of this function, exerting a selective channelling of signs across the cell membrane. Through an elaborate 'signal transduction' system inside the cell events from the outside are connected to appropriate targets inside the cell and nucleus (Bruni 2007). Only through the completion of this fourth step has the protocell reached the stage of a living unit, a genuine cell:

> Only then does the system's understanding of its environment matter to the system, and this is how the logic of the Möbius strip becomes realized *in actu*: relevant parts of the environment become internalized as an 'inside exterior', a phenomenal world or perceptual model, the Umwelt.
>
> (Hoffmeyer 1998a: 40)

This, then, is the decisive step in the evolutionary process of attaining true semiotic competence, i.e. the competence to make meaningful distinctions in space-time where formerly there were only differences. The semiotic looping of organism and environment into each other through the activity at their interface, the closed membrane, lies at the root of the strange future-directedness or 'intentionality' of life, its Darwinian 'striving' towards growth and multiplication. The result of this process is an integration of the self-referential system (in DNA) and the other-referential system (connected to the activity of surface receptors), and I have suggested this as a biosemiotic definition of life: *a stable integration of a self-referential digitally coded system into an other-referential analogically coded system* (Hoffmeyer 1998b).

The semiotic nature

Let us consider a few cases to illustrate the remarkable semiogenic propensity of living systems. The phenomenon I want to discuss here has been called semethic interaction (from the Greek, *semeion* = sign + *ethos* = habit; Hoffmeyer 1994). Semethic interaction occurs when a regular behaviour or habit of one organism or species is interpreted as a sign by some other individuals (conspecific or alter-specific) and is reacted upon through the release of yet other regular behaviours or habits.

The bird that lures the predator away from the nest by pretending it has a broken wing – and then flies away as soon as the predator has been led astray – is an obvious example of a partner in a game of semethic interaction. And, in fact, at least two cases of semethic interaction are involved here: first, the predator has perceived (genetically or by experience) that clumsy behaviour signifies an easy catch. The bird's behaviour is therefore (mis)interpreted as a sign for an easy catch. This is a very simple semiotic process, where a nearly law-like (and clearly non-semiotic) relation (of one certain physical state to another – i.e. clumsiness with vulnerability) serves as a signifying regularity, or sign, for the predator (Hoffmeyer 2008a). Now, however, the bird takes advantage of a much less safe relation, the relation between a sign and its interpretant. By pretending to have a broken wing, the bird can 'count on' (and again, this may or may not be a genetically fixed interpretant) the predator to misjudge the situation. In other words, the success of this strategy counts on a false interpretative act in the predator. That the predator will misinterpret the bird's behaviour may be a safe assumption – seen from our view – but it is hardly a law-like necessity. Clearly the act of pretending in this case has to be well executed. In this way, then, semethic-interaction patterns are built upon other semethic-interaction patterns in chains or webs of increasing sophistication. And gradually, due to the multiform character of semethic interactions, the species of this world have become woven into a fine-meshed global web of semiotic relations. I find it very likely that these semiotic relations, more than anything else, are responsible for the ongoing stability of Earth's ecological and biogeographical patterns.

An interesting case of semethic interaction that connects the animal and plant kingdoms is exhibited by parasitic wasps (*Cotesia marginiventris*) that lay their eggs in caterpillars. When a caterpillar munches on the leaves of a corn seedling, a component present in the oral saliva of the larva induces the formation of a signal that spreads to the whole plant. This signal causes the corn seedling to emit a volatile compound, a terpenoid, which is carried off with the wind. Eventually, the terpenoid arrives at the antennae of female wasps and is interpreted as a sign for oviposition, prompting the wasps to fly upstream towards the source of the terpenoid. Upon detecting the caterpillars, the wasps lay their eggs in the young larvae, one egg in each, and a couple of days later the eggs hatch and the parasitoid starts eating up the interior of the caterpillar. Ten days after oviposition, the parasitoid emerges from the caterpillar and spins itself a silky cocoon, leaving the host larva to die.

Seen from outside, what happens here is that the wasp and the corn plant have common, if opposite, interests in the caterpillar and have each worked out a cooperative way of satisfying those interests by actively sharing a small part of the semiosphere.[10] Or, more concretely, a habit (the emission of a terpenoid by the corn plant when leaves are munched upon by caterpillars) has become a sign for the wasp, leading it to a suitable opportunity for oviposition. But should this wasp have any natural enemies, this very same successful oviposition mechanism might yet serve as a perfect habit for that enemy to exploit, building up even more layers of semethic interaction upon semethic interaction.

A creeping example of semethic interaction is exhibited by the fungus *Enthomophtora muscae*, which infects and kills ordinary house flies. In addition to killing the flies, however, the parasite also causes dead females to develop a set of special traits, 'such as distended abdomens, that acts as sexual attractants to the male flies . . . that are subsequently infected and killed by the fungal parasite' (Moeller 1993; cited in Sterelny and Griffiths 1999: 72). In this case a peculiar regularity pertaining to the mating **semiotics** of house flies has become enlisted to serve the food strategy of the fungus. A similarly case, discussed by Stephen Jay Gould, concerns parasitic barnacles of the crustacean *Rhizocephala*, which completely take over behavioural control in the crabs that they parasitize. The parasites suspend the crab's internal moult cycle (which might otherwise allow the crab to shed the parasite) and successively transform the brood care behaviours of the crabs in such a way that they will start nursing the parasitic

[10] I have defined the semiosphere as 'a sphere like the atmosphere, hydrosphere, or biosphere that permeates these spheres from their innermost to outermost reaches and consists of communication: sound, scent, movement, colours, forms, electrical fields, various waves, chemical signals, touch, and so forth – in short, the signs of life' (Hoffmeyer 1996: 46). The concept was originally introduced by the Russian-Estonian semiotician Yuri **Lotman**, who explicitly used it in comparison to Vernadsky's idea of the biosphere. For Lotman (2000 [1990]: 125), the semiosphere remained a cultural concept: 'The unit of semiosis, the smallest functioning mechanism, is not the separate language but the whole semiotic space in question. This is the space we term the semiosphere. The semiosphere is the result and the condition for the development of culture; we justify our term by analogy with the biosphere, as Vernadsky defined it.' For more details about the origin of these terms, see Sebeok (1999). John Deely accepts my use of the word semiosphere and suggests '*signosphere* as a term more appropriate for the narrower designation of semiosphere in Lotman's sense, leaving the broader coinage and usage to Hoffmeyer's credit' (Deely 2001a: 629).

eggs instead of their own (Gould 1996: 15–16). Again we see that habits are dangerous: the habits of one species become the point of attack (the interpretant) for another species.

Semethic interactions may, in some cases, be very complex and involve several species. This is, for instance, often the case in *plant signalling*, where plants that have been damaged by insect attacks emit signals that are received by undamaged conspecifics. Undamaged fava beans (*Vicia fabea*), for instance, immediately started attracting aphid parasites (*Aphidus ervi*) after having been grown in a sterilized nutrient medium in which aphid-infected fava beans had previously grown (Bruin and Dicke 2001). The damaged beans had thus managed to signal their predicament through the medium to the undamaged beans, which then immediately started to attract aphid *parasites*, although no aphids were, of course, available for parasites to find.

The complexity of these relationships is further increased by the intervention of non-conspecific plants that may gain advantage from the density of freely available parasitoids (insects whose larvae live as parasites that eventually kill their hosts) and it is therefore conceivable that these non-conspecific plants themselves may develop sensitivity to the volatile signal molecules. Bruin and Dicke (2001), reviewing a series of examples on this kind of **communication**, also advance the speculation that signals might be transferred by direct contact between the roots of neighbouring plants, or even through the fungal bridges (*ectomycorrhiza*) between them.

The normal case of semethic interaction concerns the interplay between two or more organisms, but abiotic regularities may also be used as a substrate for the semiogenic inventiveness of living systems, as we can observe in migratory birds that find their way across continents – or between them – by interpreting stellar configurations by night, or in dung beetles that forage by reading the polarization patterns of moonlight.

It should be noticed that semethic interaction is by no means exclusive just to the organismic level but may also take place at levels other than the organismic. This is for instance seen in so-called nest cooing in ring doves. Before a female ring dove lays her eggs, she and her mate go through a series of courtship displays. As courtship proceeds, hormonal changes in the female trigger the growth of follicles in her ovaries, each of which eventually bursts to release an egg. Recent experiments have shown that, if a female dove is operationally hindered in making the so-called 'nest coo', she will not be able to ovulate, despite enthusiastic courting by males. In control experiments, tape recordings of nest coos were played to females with no males present. Now follicles began to grow. The conclusion is simple: female doves that coo during courtship are not (only) cooing at the male – they are cooing at their own ovaries, to trigger the release of eggs. In this case, we saw that the physiological timing of ovulation had become scaffolded by habits of vocalization during courtship, since the brain of the dove apparently had evolved to interpret the body's own cooing behaviour as a sign for the initiation of ovulation (Hoffmeyer 1998b).

The ring dove example is only one of probably millions, but it highlights how the subtlety of synchronizations and chemical communication that must be reciprocally tuned between organisms involved in social behaviour is stunning – yet scientists at present are only scratching the surface of this new area of biosemiotic study.

Minding nature

Mainstream science has taught us to see nature as essentially soulless and silly. Descartes' old metaphor of nature as clockwork was in a later century replaced by the metaphor of nature as a steam engine, and in our days the preferred metaphor has become that of a computer. But even a computer is a silly machine, of course, and nobody takes much pleasure from tormenting machines while cruelty towards animals is quite common. Modern science has devoted much energy to developing tools for a healthy management of our natural resources, but this honourable endeavour risks being tacitly undermined by the implicit disrespect for nature of the scientific ontology.

A semiotic view of nature on the contrary immediately appeals to our feelings of relatedness or belonging. We all instinctively recognize mammals and birds as semiotic agents like ourselves, and although we may perhaps doubt that simpler life forms such as invertebrates, plants or fungi are genuinely semiotic agents we unthinkingly categorize them as teleological beings in their own right. It actually takes sophisticated computers to fool us into believing that non-living things are alive. One should not underestimate this aspect of our view of nature. It is no coincidence that the book that more than anything else contributed to raising a worldwide concern for the environmental question forty years ago was entitled *Silent Spring*. Rachel Carson's best-seller from 1962 described how the spread of man-made pesticides to every corner of the planet threatened to extinguish a huge number of bird species – and with them also, the existence in our world of bird song (Carson 1962). This last relation may have been the crucial one, for it was not the de-semiotized image of nature drawn up by university ecologists talking of energy flows or biotopes that had the potential to mobilize whole populations to a defence of ecological diversity – rather, it was the fear of losing the semiotic diversity and pleasure of nature, as epitomized by bird song, that got people off their chairs and into action. An important message is to be drawn from this, and it is one that should not be brushed aside as naïve or sentimental. The insignificant fungi that takes care of the degradation of pine needles may, for all we know, have a greater importance for the well-being of a pine forest than do all of its birds and mammals – but if people did not value pine forests in and of themselves, the conservation of pine plantations would be left strictly to those with economic concerns. If, however, in addition to the concerns for sustainability that supposedly will be met in a functional democratic society, we also want to take responsibility for the species diversity of natural systems for the sake of semiotic diversity itself, then it will be important for us to accustom our understanding of, and thinking about, natural systems in terms that will allow us to *experience* its richness, its swarming profusion of communicative activity (Hoffmeyer 2008a).

The full extent of our human embeddedness in the web of life will only come true when we adopt a view of nature as semiotic. Even the simplest living systems have a capacity to learn, and our own hugely larger capacity in that respect is thus no free-floating ability given to only one species on Earth. In fact learning may be seen as a distinctive mark separating life from non-life. That learning is essential for living systems immediately explains a characteristic feature shared by all living creatures: that life takes time. Learning usually induces a rather definite sequence of steps upon an organism in the sense that something must be learned before something else can possibly be learned and, since learning (even in humans) is a motoric as well as a mental process, learning entails we are firmly tied by natural constraints: it simply takes 18 years for a child to grow up, and although this process of socialization is of course highly influenced by social forces it also embraces millions, or even billions, of biological adjustments and calibrations spanning the whole scale from individual cellular determinations[11] to immuno-endocrinological developments and somato-psychological adaptations.[12] One might even suggest that the general semiotics of learning must play the same role in the life-world as the second law of thermodynamics does in the physical world. The semiotics of learning describes a general condition that must necessarily be obeyed by all living systems in much the same way that the second law of thermodynamics describes a constraint that no physical system (and, by implication, no biological system) can escape.

As Gregory **Bateson** saw, and before him Charles Peirce, it is essential that the concept of mind is not identified narrowly with the concept of the human mind. Mind, in Peirce's and Bateson's understanding, cannot be the exclusive property of human beings – lest they would be miracles on Earth – but must be a property pertaining to our world as such. Human mind, then, would be a peculiar instantiation of this more general mind. Bateson made an admirable approach to a scientific description of the phenomenon of mind as understood in this more general sense, but his lack of a semiotic approach may have prevented him from going all the way (Cashman 2008). Nevertheless he did make us see that 'Mind and Nature' forms 'a Necessary Unity' to quote the title of his book from 1979 (Bateson 1979) and his contribution thereby in many respects paved the way for the development of a semiotics of nature (Hoffmeyer 2008b).

Bateson understood that the epistemological error he saw expressed in the scientific rejection – or perhaps rather ignorance – of the idea of nature as *minded*, was a deeper source for the ecological disasters brought about by modern scientifically based production methods. The resemiotization of nature described in this chapter has aimed to transcend this error. Seeing nature as

[11] Increasing, for instance, the number of specialized cells in a tissue or fixating synaptic connections in the brain.

[12] Such as, for instance, voice adaptations in the course of male puberty.

fundamentally semiotic gives us an instrument for capturing mind from its enclosures in the brains of human beings and putting it back where it belongs, in nature at large. In this process we hope to have established the means for *minding nature* both as *it is* and as *we treat it*.

Acknowledgements

I am grateful to Donald Favareau for critical comments on the draft version of this manuscript.

Further reading

Bateson, G. (1979) *Mind and Nature. A Necessary Unity*, New York: Bantam Books.

Emmeche, C. and Hoffmeyer, J. (1991) 'From language to nature: The semiotic metaphor in biology', *Semiotica*, 84: 1–42.

Hoffmeyer, J. (2008) *Biosemiotics. An Examination into the Signs of Life and the Life of Signs*, Scranton, PA: University of Scranton Press.

Hoffmeyer, J. (ed.) (2008) *A Legacy for Living Systems: Gregory Bateson as Precursor to Biosemiotics*, Dordrecht: Springer.

Kauffman, S. and Clayton, P. (2005) 'On emergence, agency, and organization', *Biology and Philosophy*, 21: 501–521.

3

Umwelt and modelling

Kalevi Kull

Introduction

Semiotics is a study of semioses, or **sign** processes. Since any sign is about something, it follows that semiotics includes a study of all forms of awareness both conscious and non-conscious. Since being aware always assumes memory as its necessary component, and vice versa, since memory always stores information about something, we can also say that semiotics extends to all processes where memory is involved. As far as all living systems, including all cells, have at least some sort of memory, the life processes that make use of it should be studied on the basis of semiotics (Emmeche *et al.* 2002).

Umwelt[1] is the self-centred world of an organism – the world in which an organism lives, the one that it recognizes and makes. This concept was introduced as a scientific matter by Jakob von **Uexküll** (1864–1944) and became widely used and further developed in semiotics, anthropology, philosophy and elsewhere, especially since the late 1970s (Sebeok 1979b; Ingold 2000; Deely 2001a; etc.).[2]

As **Sebeok** has pointed out in regard to the scientific use of the term 'Umwelt', 'the closest equivalent in English is manifestly "model"' (Sebeok 2001c: 75). Description of somebody's Umwelt will mean the demonstration of how the organism (via its *Innenwelt*) maps the world, and what, for that organism, the **meanings** of the **objects** are within it. Therefore, semiosic systems are simultaneously ***modelling*** systems, as was emphasized already in the 1960s by the Tartu–Moscow School (Lotman 1967; Levchenko and Salupere 1999). Anderson and Merrell (1991a: 4) argue that 'signs, especially those of diagrams, metaphors, and images – hypoicons (*CP* 2.276) – are themselves models, and semiosis constitutes modeling, par excellence'. Modelling systems include both

[1] Umwelt |_ u mvɛ lt| (plural Umwelten |-t(ə)n|) – this word of German origin is now a word of English vocabulary, according to the British English version of the *New Oxford American Dictionary* (currently as a built-in software component in Apple computers). Initially, the word 'Umwelt' was constructed as a neologism by the Danish-German poet Jens Immanuel Baggesen in 1800, and became common in German, among other things due to its usage by Johann Wolfgang Goethe (see Sutrop 2001; Chien 2007). While denoting 'environment' in contemporary everyday German, it is a technical term in academic English-language usage.

[2] Some English translations of Uexküll's works have also appeared in the journal *Semiotica* (Uexküll 1982, 1992, 2001a, 2001b); special volumes devoted to Uexküll were published in *Semiotica*, Vol. 134 (2001), and *Sign Systems Studies*, Vol. 32 (2004). See also Hoffmeyer (1996); Kull (2001); Sharov (2001) and Lotman (2003).

organismal and cultural systems. Thus, semiotics can be thought of as a 'modeling of modeling' (Anderson and Merrell 1991a: 4).

Accordingly, this chapter has to deal with the current understanding of a most fundamental problem – what and which are the worlds of other organisms, and what are the ways to get knowledge about these worlds, on the basis of a semiotic approach. Umwelt, as **Deely** (2001b: 125) mentions, 'has become in fact a technical term within semiotics, and is also destined . . . to become a term of general use in philosophy and intellectual culture'. An important point here is that Umwelt is a characteristic feature of each living organism of any species. Concomitantly, the concept of Umwelt conjoins the biological and human sciences into the one field of semiotics. This will mean a non-Modern (*sensu* Deely 2001a) approach to living systems, which has also been well characterized by Robert Rosen, when he stated that 'what is important in biology is not how we see the systems which are interacting, but how they see each other' (Rosen *et al.* 1979: 87).

Uexküll's concept of Umwelt

The Uexküllian concept of Umwelt appeared first in Jakob von Uexküll's work of 1907, in which he also introduced several additional terms, like 'subjective biology', 'subjective anatomy' (under which he describes 'local signs'), and 'subjective physiology'. After using the term in subsequent years (Uexküll 1909, 1910), there was still a period of hesitation on his part when he said that his term 'Umwelt' was often misused, and he replaced it by 'Merkwelt' (Uexküll 1912, 1913a). Nevertheless, this change was a temporary one, and in his following works the concept of Umwelt finds its central place (Uexküll 1913b, 1922; etc.).

The Umwelt concept has a root in Johannes Müller's (a leading German physiologist, 1801–1858) observation on qualitative separation or energetic detachment of neural activity patterns from the nature and patterns of influences on sensory organs. According to an understanding within some areas of biosemiotics nowadays (e.g. Barbieri 2007), this relationship can be characterized as a **code**-relation – or simply, relation – as different from the relationships that are deducible from universal physico-chemical laws. In such a way, Müller's rule of specific neural energy can be reinterpreted as an example or a special case of an appearance of sign-relation, or information as such.

Uexküll saw as a major task of his scientific approach to describe the multispecies community of organisms on the basis of relations between Umwelten of different species of organisms; in order to achieve this task, he concentrated on the experimental study of Umwelten of particular species and carried on comparative studies. The programme of research, which he designed in his methodological and theoretical work (Uexküll 1913a, 1928), was carried out experimentally in his Institute for Umwelt-Research (*Institut für Umweltforschung*) in Hamburg from 1925 onwards (Rüting 2004; Mildenberger 2007).

The objects of one Umwelt may not at all coincide with the objects of another Umwelt. However, in functionally important cases, the relations work in unison and the distinctions made are in a good correspondence. The distinctions an organism draws are individual, but due to the similarity of body plan of the individuals of the same species, and of the environment they live in, the Umwelten of conspecifics may be quite similar. In simple Umwelten, like the ones of a tick or a snail, there are very few objects, whereas the Umwelten of birds and mammals are usually very rich. For instance, many birds distinguish more colours and have better spatial orientation than humans; at the same time, though, their sense of smell is almost absent. The objects in an Umwelt have a bearing on the behaviour of the organism, because objects, as components of signs, are (by definition) meaningful.

Uexküll was especially interested in the relations the organisms have between each other and with the objects they distinguish. He has described these as contrapuntal, using a concept from music as a model. For instance,

> In its role as a counterpoint, the shell's dwelling-quality in the snail's Umwelt and its dwelling-quality in the hermit crab's Umwelt are mutually interchangeable, the implication being that each one of the two qualities, although not identical with the other, can nevertheless be adapted by one of nature's composition to become the other, because they share the same meaning.
>
> Meaning in nature's score serves as a connecting link, or rather as a bridge, and takes the place of harmony in a musical score; it joins two of nature's factors.
>
> (Uexküll 1982: 64)

Another important point that Uexküll makes concerns the understanding of evolution:

> The Umwelten were certainly less complicated at the outset of the world drama than later. However, each meaning-carrier was always confronted with a meaning-receiver, even in those earlier Umwelten. Meaning ruled them all. Meaning tied changing organs to a changing medium. Meaning connected food and the destroyer of food, enemy and prey, and above all, male and female in astonishing variations. In every case an advance occurred, but never progress in the sense of the survival of the fittest; never selection of the superior one, through an unplanned, furious struggle for existence. Instead a melody prevailed, embracing both life and death.
>
> (Uexküll 1982: 69–70)[3]

Here, Uexküll emphasizes the dominance of **synchronic** relations over **diachronic**. Both in the course of the ontogenetic development of an organism, and in the formation of interorganismal relations, as well as organisms' relations with

[3] It is interesting to note that Juri Lotman had an analogous view on the absence of progress when he wrote about the development of cultures (see Lotman 2000).

LIBRARY, UNIVERSITY OF CHESTER

the objects in their Umwelten, the relations arise on the basis of meaning well before any evolutionary event (in the sense of irreversible genetic changes) would take place, 'provided that enough adaptive material is at hand' (Uexküll 1982: 75). Indeed, there is a considerable degree of 'adaptive material', since every living organism has an ability to adjust itself to the meanings it meets via differential expression of its organic capacities (including the changes in gene expression patterns). This resonates well with the 'epigenetic' tradition in biological thought, as expressed already by Karl Ernst von Baer, a predecessor of Uexküll, and later by James Mark Baldwin, as well as more recently by Eva Jablonka, Scott Gilbert, Terrence Deacon, and many others (see Hoffmeyer and Kull 2003).[4]

The dominance of ontogenetic and communicative processes over the phylogenetic, and the development of harmonious (optimal) networks of relations prior to the evolutionary changes, means, in biology, a radical generalization of the theory of evolution. In this post-Darwinist theory, neo-Darwinism (including sociobiology) merely amounts to a degenerate special case.[5]

The importance of the shift in evolutionary theory that is made by the Umwelt approach becomes even more visible if attention is shifted from the 'awareness' side of Umwelt to its 'manufacturing' side. Organisms *make* the world. Umwelt does not mean just a recognition of objects in the world, nor is it confined to remembering (including all forms of memory) – it is just as much a *manufacturing* of the world. The objects are not only sensed and perceived, or represented and imagined; the objects are also *produced*.

The concept of niche-construction (for instance as described by Odling-Smee *et al.* 2003) has begun the process of approaching this matter, albeit within the framework of neo-Darwinism; but it has not realized how radically fundamental this feature of any Umwelt is. Organisms not only work out the **habit**s, the rules or relations, they also *validate* them.[6]

Umwelt and the functional cycle

The process that creates and builds an Umwelt is the functional cycle (*Funktionskreis*, according to Uexküll 1928). The functional cycle is the whole of discrete and combined sensory and action processes. Both of these include a code (at the very least). A *sensory code* is a correspondence between a signal or a thing (which can be perceived and represented as an object) and certain processes (i.e. the sensory organs, brain) in the organism. An *action code* is a correspondence between the latter (the sensory organs) and the action (motor) organs of the organism. The sensory code concerns *Merkzeichen* (sensory signs), the action code concerns *Wirkzeichen* (motor signs). The functional cycle

[4] See also Strauss (2003).

[5] See Kull (2000).

[6] In order to express this relationship between sensory and effectory parts of the functional cycle, Uexküll used the terms *Merkwelt*, *Merkzeichen*, *Merkmal*, and *Wirkwelt*, *Wirkzeichen*, *Wirkmal* – the latter being a neologism.

in its entirety is both what works on the basis of habits (= codes) and what changes the habits, including the creating of new habits.

According to Uexküll (1973: 150), the functional cycles build the self-centred world of any animal. The functional cycles of the organisms are bridged (both intraorganismally and interorganismally), forming together the functional world of living beings. Moreover, the functional cycle of any animal can be divided into sectors. Uexküll distinguished between the functional cycles of medium, food, enemy, and sex (Uexküll 1973: 151–153; 1982: 33).

The work of the functional cycle includes 1) anticipation of the perceptual cue, 2) perception, 3) working out a relation between the perception and action (either just executing a habit, or using representation, or modelling anew), and 4) action (operation). 'Because the effector cue that is assigned to the meaning-carrier [= object] extinguishes in every case the perceptual cue that caused the operation, each behaviour is ended [i.e. has some meaningful "conclusion"], no matter how varied it may be' (Uexküll 1982: 31).

Different species may have very different functional cycles, which entails the species-specific Umwelten or objective worlds. For example, a flower stem is transformed as: a) it is picked by a girl to make it an ornamental object, b) it becomes a 'path' for the ant that walks along it, c) it is building material for the cicada-larva that pierces it, and d) it constitutes wholesome fodder for the grazing cow.

It is important to notice that the concept of the functional cycle was conclusively formulated[7] well before the concept of feedback became known and mathematically studied in cybernetics. Despite that, the functional cycle is richer than the concept of feedback, because it also includes the aspect of anticipation (later included into the concept of 'feed-forward' by Rosen 1999). Martin Krampen thus rightly identifies the functional cycle with **semiosis**, and classifies its description as a model of semiosis (Krampen 1997).

Modelling, and modelling modelling

Sebeok (2001c: 3) reminds us that 'The phenomenon that distinguishes life forms from inanimate objects is *semiosis*. This can be defined simply as the instinctive capacity of all living organisms to produce and understand *signs*.' And further (Sebeok 2001c: 156), '*semiosis* [is the] capacity of a species to produce and comprehend the specific types of models it requires for processing and codifying perceptual input in its own way'. 'All, and only, living entities incorporate a species-specific model (Umwelt) of their universe' (Sebeok 2000: 89). Adding to these programmatic statements, Claus **Emmeche** (1998: 11) has

[7] In its early version, Uexküll described this principle in his work on neuromotor regulation – as a basic mechanism of rhythms in animals – known as Uexküll's law (Uexküll 1904; see also Lagerspetz 2001). Soon after, he introduced the concept of 'functional body plans' (extensively studied in his work of 1909). The term 'functional cycle' (*Funktionskreis*) appeared in his article of 1919 (pp. 144–145) and in the first edition of *Theoretische Biologie* (1920: 116–117), but in a considerably developed final form in the second edition of the latter (1928; p. 105 presents its classic scheme; see also Kull 2001: 7).

defined life as a 'functional interpretation of signs in self-organized material code-systems making their own Umwelten'.

Similarly, Robert Rosen, concluding his major work *Life Itself*, writes in the final paragraph of the book: 'We began this discussion with the question, What is life? We ended with the answer: Life is the manifestation of a certain kind of (relational) model. A particular material system is *living* if it realizes this model' (Rosen 1999: 254). If we were to use the concept of model in a most broad sense, then we could also say: life is the process of modelling *sensu lato*. If Umwelt is a product of modelling, then the process of modelling an Umwelt turns out to be a modelling of modelling.

Since life necessarily creates and uses memory, it is possible to define life (any form of it) as a process of inheritance of relations.[8] Relations (or codes) can be generally seen as functional cycles – based on relations, or set out by them. Functional cycles are simultaneously the general mechanisms of intentionality (interpreted in the broadest sense): the mechanisms of needs which arise during the identification of anything absent. Thus, another definition of life can be formulated – life is a process of inheritance of needs.

It requires some analysis to demonstrate that a sign indeed is about a) what *is*, b) what *is not*, and c) what *is possible*. If a recognition process occurs, this means that a distinction is made 1) between what is *recognized* (e.g. a *G*) and all else. The ability to recognize (the *G*) will simultaneously mean an ability to *distinguish* 2) between the existence and absence of *G*. Therefore, together with the *arbitrariness* of the distinction made (between the arbitrarily chosen *G* and all else), it will also lead to a *non-arbitrary* distinction between the existence and absence (of *G*). Of course, there can be (and certainly will be) errors, deceptions, lying, but these are no more than errors, deceptions, lying.

Thus, to a certain extent, each sign (= sign process) is a modelling. It models, on the one hand, via the inclusion of an organism's experience, which is built into the organism's individual structure. On the other hand, the existence of the object in the sign makes the model correspond to the object. Relatedness to experience makes the sign (and its meaning) plural, whereas relatedness to an object makes it one (singular). However, any object turns out to be plural, as far as it is related to many signs.[9] The latter is particularly important: all (semiotic) objects are fundamentally plural, as different from its complementary counterpart, the (physical) thing, which is single.

Semiotics as an academic discipline, as a field of research with an aim to understand semiosis in its diverse manifestations, cannot escape modelling – this is our tool. But since this is also our object, it cannot be restricted to isolated analysis of the mechanism of sign functions alone; it cannot be just formal or decontextualized. In addition to requiring a context, it should be said that any

---

[8] This holds also for language: language is also an inheritance system – this is a process of (social) inheritance of propositional relations.

[9] Cf. 'Each thing is as many signs as there are grounds for distinct interpretations' (Short 1986: 106).

object studied by semiotics, being by its very nature plural, can never have a complete description. This is in distinct contrast to physics, for which a model of a thing can be close-to-complete, at least in principle. Therefore it is conceivable that some parts of physics can reach final conclusions, or can build an exact model. This may never happen for semiotics – chemical reactions *per se* might be identical, but life is not. Semiotic modelling is thus revealed to be based on qualitative relations and qualitative methods. Quantitative description can reveal next to nothing about the modelling process. Thus, semiotics goes beyond science, but it also includes it.[10]

Describing qualitative diversity and plurality requires the 'complementarity principle', a consideration of how phenomena relate, contextually, to other phenomena. Physics (the study of things) can be done without regard to complementarity; semiotics (the study of meaning-infused objects) cannot. The relationship of physics and semiotics, as we can see, is not symmetrical.

The matter may be illustrated by considering semiotics as **translation**: how the signs of one system may be understood through the signs of another. Of course, it needs to be borne in mind that translation always includes non-translatability.[11] The translations that semiotics is concerned with are invariably of an unusual type. In the case of semiotics of culture, there is a translation from one human sign system to another, both of which may be connected by common roots in **language**. But only a small number of sign systems are rooted in the species-specific human phenomenon of language. The ability to make translations from the sign system of an insect to that of a human, or – even more challenging – from one of a fungus, requires comprehensive contextual investigation of the modelling process. There are no verbs, nor nouns, in these sign systems.[12]

The common meaning of the word 'model' characterizes well the two complementary sides of model and modelling (and of a functional cycle) – being on the one side a means of recognition and understanding, and on the other side anything that is made. Yet, it also indicates the profound complexity that is encountered in the attempt to understand modelling processes.

Vegetative, animal, and cultural Umwelten

Umwelt, as a general characteristic of all living beings, is not only individual, but it also varies considerably in its type between different forms of living systems. A most general typology would distinguish between three major types of Umwelten: vegetative (non-spatial and non-temporal – solely **icon**ic), animal (spatial and non-temporal – exclusively iconic and **index**ical), and cultural (simultaneously spatial and temporal – iconic-indexical-**symbol**ic).

[10] See also Ponzio (2001a) and Kull *et al.* (2008).

[11] See, e.g., Lotman (2000).

[12] On translation between Umwelten, see Kull and Torop (2003).

A history of this typology goes back, for instance, to the classical distinction between *anima vegetativa*, *anima sensitiva*, and *anima rationale*. Already the doctrine of Thomas **Aquinas** included the view that, in the first stage of embryonic development, the vital principle has merely vegetative powers; then a sensitive soul comes into being, and still later this is replaced by the perfect rational soul.

More recently, Jablonka *et al.* (1998) have distinguished between four major inheritance systems: epigenetic, genetic, behavioural, and lingual. As based on different types of memory, this typology has to be in a certain correspondence with a semiotic classification.[13] Since epigenetic and genetic memory are both features of almost any cell, and since these are always found together (an exception would mean the complete lack or non-activity of the chromosomes), these two may concern one and the same memory system. Thus, we arrive at the same three classes as described below.

Here, we follow a **Peirce**an-like triadic classification. However, this has to be taken as a model, whereas the development of a more specific typology is evidently an empirical problem. Accordingly, the main types of Umwelten, as distinguished on the basis of different types of semiosis involved, may be separated by certain semiotic thresholds.[14]

Biosemiotic approaches have argued, with Thomas A. Sebeok as the leading proponent, that the lower semiotic threshold must be placed close to the appearence of living cells. This is not totally without problems. On closer examination, semiotic thresholds on closer look are really *threshold zones*. The lower, or primary, threshold includes the appearance of a whole set of features, including memory, self-replication, inside–outside distinction, codes, etc., which evidently appear somewhat interdependently, but not exactly at the same time; hence the idea of a 'zone'.

The two main secondary threshold zones lay probably between a) vegetative and animal life (the indexical threshold zone), and b) animal and human life (the symbolic threshold zone).

Tertiary semiotic thresholds may have a bearing, for example, on the appearence of eukaryotic cells (or sex), of emotions, etc. The only way to find out about this requires a combination of semiotic modelling with empirical studies.

Vegetative Umwelt

All cells have some specialized enzymes in their outer membrane that selectively recognize substances in the environment and convey the signal into the cytoplasm. These are signal transduction systems which make a code-based mapping; this means that an enzyme that has an affinity to a certain molecule (the signal) *A* at its outer end (at the active site) relates that *A* to an entirely different molecule *B* in the inner side of the membrane (at another active site of the

[13] For further details see Kull (2005).

[14] The concept of semiotic threshold has been introduced by Eco (1976: 19–22).

enzyme with the specific affinity to *B*). The molecule *A* outside of the cell which is in this way put into a correspondence to a molecule *B* inside the cell may have no chemical relationship whatsoever with molecule *B*; this is not a chemical reaction between *A* and *B*, despite the fact that both the *A* reaction with the enzyme and the *B* reaction with the enzyme are chemical; this is because the relation between *A* and *B* is based on the link between two active sites of the enzymes which is beyond mere chemical determination – since it has to be remembered. The link is made of a polycondensate chain of amino acids in the enzyme molecule: the particular chain or sequence which is like it is not due to chemical, but due to historical reasons. The sequence is kept stable via its reproduction with the help of DNA, the sequence of which, in a memory function, is regularly used to renew the membrane enzymes. The same sequence cannot be repeatedly formed on the basis of chemical affinity between any adjacent amino acid in the chain, because there are many possible adjacent amino acids which all perfectly fit, and therefore the chain that would have been rebuilt in this, chemical, way would never repeat the sequence in the earlier chain (due to the immense number of possible, chemically equal combinations). In the living cells the enzyme structures are remembered, and due to this, *A* is not only a molecule with its chemical relationships; *A* turns out to be in a code-relation and therefore becomes a sign-vehicle, a signal.

Many cells also have light-sensitive enzymes that may not just transfer the energy assimilated, but can convey the sensed environmental change to the other systems in the cell via a code-based sequence of events.

Living cells have several ways to act. This includes the changes in permeability of the membrane for certain substances, the changes in production or conversion of some structures, and various types of movement, amoeboid or flagelloid or cilioid. These actions can entail feedback via the recognition of a change in the environment by the sensory enzymes in the membrane.

Thus, the cell has the full set of components of a functional cycle. This is not just a sequence of chemically determined events that happen to have a cyclic form of process. In the case of a living cell, the relations between the signal received and the action followed can be related to the third – for instance to the lack or excess of something in the cell that could be regulated by the appropriate action in proper conditions sensed by the membrane enzyme. This is a memory-based triadic relation. A recognized absence of something (of a substrate, of a condition, of Other) is what drives the living process – the semiosis – of any cell, of any organism.

If there is a functional cycle, then there is an Umwelt. However, in the case of a cell, this consists of points without a picture, or a territory without a space. This is because a cell evidently has no means to distinguish between the patterns of the signals, thus it cannot categorize distances, angles, or shapes. Consequently, the Umwelt of a cell is a set of objects without spatial dimensions. Despite this fact, what the cell possesses can be enough to recognize another cell, so that a resulting movement or stopping or differentiation could lead to a formation of tissues or swarms of cells or relatively stable cohabitation with a certain other type of cells. It also enables them to perform some logical operations that ensure finding of food, or of symbiosis, or keeping away from other cells, for instance.

As a simple example, the functional cycle may work (performing a logical operation) as follows:

Reception	Action
T	*F*
F	*T*

Where, on the side of reception, *T* is the recognition of a decomposable substrate, and *F* is its absence; and, on the side of action, *F* is immobility of flagella, and *T* is a movement of flagella leading to a displacement of the cell. Resulting behaviour makes the cell move until it touches a suitable substrate, then stop until the substrate is consumed; after that the cell will move again until it will meet another site with a substrate to consume. In the case of a different operation, where the receptors will distinguish between the contact with a non-similar cell (*T*) and all else (*F*), the following operation would lead to an escape from the alien cells:

Reception	Action
T	*T*
F	*F*

In this way, a cell is capable of entering into various relations with the objects around it.

All organisms are supplied with many functional cycles that enable vegetative relations. These are generally responsible for categorization or speciation, and for the simple forms of search, selection, swarming, spreading, etc. Vegetative relations are just correspondences, or relations, of pure recognition only, which means these are exclusively iconic. Even the simple Umwelt of a tick – if we are confined to the description provided by Uexküll – may not include more than vegetative relations.

Relations – code-relations – are not deterministic in the physical sense, because, as they are not simply bound to physical law, they have exceptions, they are fallible, errors happen. However, in the case of vegetative semiosis, it is not yet anything as sophisticated as deception (that would require an animal sign system with its indexical relations), nor lying (which would require any form of language, the usage of true symbols) that takes place. Nevertheless, vegetative relations are sufficient for the biosphere (*sensu* Vernadsky) to be created.

In order to recognize correlations or linkages of causal relationships, which would mean a truly indexical relation, an ability to associate what has not been associated earlier is probably required, which is already the feature of a more complex, animal semiosis.

Animal Umwelt

The indexical semiotic threshold zone is probably the one where the capacity for associative learning arises. It obviously requires either a central nervous system or an immune system that can recode the relation between sensory and motor organs according to the correlations learned.

The existence of mobile connections between different receptors of the same organism which are further connected to its motor effectors may enable, in addition to putting an object into a correspondence with a form in the memory, a comparison between the objects an organism can recognize and, accordingly, the establishment of new relations between the different objects. This is usually accompanied, as a requirement, by the existence of multicellular receptors and the neural tissue that connects the receptors with effectors, making use of sensory and motor categorizations. This form of the functional cycle may then establish the relations of distance and angle which will allow the mapping of space. Such a cognitive mapping of space results in an effective capacity of orientation, evident in the behaviour of many animal species.

Indexes, in this sense, are relations built on icons, as described by Deacon (1997). At this stage, 'animals communicate and are aware of their surroundings, but not of their surroundings as surroundings, of their Umwelt *as* an Umwelt' (Bains 2001: 159).

Cultural (lingual) Umwelt

Terrence Deacon has thoroughly described (in his book *The Symbolic Species*, 1997) the mechanisms that had to evolve for human language to appear. He calls it the 'symbolic threshold', which means the point at which the origin of symbols can be found.[15]

Humans can be aware 'of their Umwelt *as* an Umwelt or objective world grasped as a whole in relation to itself, which requires a distinction of objects from things and relations from both' (Bains 2001: 159). According to Deleuze and Guattari, this transforms Umwelt into a *Welt*, or – according to Deely (recalling Heidegger) – into a *Lebenswelt*. For to Deleuze and Guattari (1988), the threshold from animal to human Umwelt would mean a deterritorialization of signs. What we will see with the appearance of language is the 'creation' of time.

The appearance of language becomes possible due to the appearance of signs that signify a relation itself. Such is, for instance, the sign 'and' whose object is

[15] If we were to use a more complex Peircean model, then this threshold can be put into correspondence with other types of signs. According to Frederik Stjernfelt (2007), the origin of human language was attendant on the appearance of hypostatic abstraction.

just a relation, a free relation-as-such, a relation that can be universally built between anything and which is independent of the items between which it is the relation. These signs of relation can be called ‘syntactic signs’, and it is in this sense that Sebeok assigns syntax characteristic status for human language (e.g. Sebeok 1996: 108). The syntactic aspect can be distinguished in any sign system, but syntactic signs are a characteristic feature of language alone; they are absent in animal and vegetative sign systems.

Symbols, as the relations built upon indexes, can move (indexical) maps, can reorder and rearrange them, can put them into asymmetrical sequences. This is necessary in order to create the phenomenon of time. That is, to create histories and biographies out of what might only be the present indexical signs. Any Umwelt that has in itself its past and future and is able safely to distinguish between them and to use the differing time representations differently is likely to possess, also, an exploratory and predictive advantage. Thus conscious purpose, with all its benefits and problems, becomes possible, as the whole diversity of culture, previously thought to be semiotics' only domain, with its recognition of tragedy and joy.

Modelling systems

The area where modelling has been most self-evidently insistent is the species-specifically human phenomenon of culture. Sebeok has considered the Umwelt as the ‘primary modelling system’, drawing on the concept of ‘modelling system’, itself introduced into semiotics by the Tartu–Moscow semiotics school. As head of that school, Lotman gave a brief definition of model: it is ‘an analogue of an object of cognition, replacing it in the process of cognition’ (Lotman 1967: 130). He also adds that

> model is different from a sign as such by not simply replacing a denotat, but replacing it usefully in the process of cognition or ordering. Therefore, while in a natural language the relation of language to a denotat is historico-conventional, the relation of a model to an object is manifested by the structure of a modelling system. In this sense only one type of signs – *the iconic signs* – can be equalized to models.
>
> (Lotman 1967: 131)

V. V. Ivanov (1981: 20) adds: ‘Semiotics deals with the scientific (particularly linguistic and cybernetic) models as special cases of the sign (semiotic) models.’ A modelling system is further defined as

> a structure of elements and rules for combining them that is in a state of a fixed analogy to the entire sphere of an object of knowledge, insight or ordering. Therefore a modelling system can be regarded as a language.
>
> (Lotman 1967: 130; see also Lotman 1977a)

Within modelling systems as 'languages', primary and secondary ones were distinguished: 'Systems that have a natural language as their basis and that acquire supplementary superstructures, thus creating languages of a second level, can appropriately be called secondary modelling systems' (Lotman 1967: 131).[16]

Sebeok – after distinguishing between language in a narrow sense (as acquired specifically by humans) and other sign systems – made a necessary statement that human language (including both verbal language and nonverbal sign-language) cannot be the primary modelling system. Indeed, what distinguishes humans from other species in terms of **communication** is, for Sebeok (2001d), the possession of a verbal *and* a nonverbal faculty. Thus he proposed to rename the primary modelling systems (previously synonymous with the verbal faculty alone) the secondary and the secondary ones (previously associated with 'culture') the tertiary (Sebeok 1991a: 57–58; 1994: 124–127; cf. Sebeok and Danesi 2000).

Lotman had stated that 'there is no doubt that any sign system (including a secondary) can be regarded as a certain type of language. ... Any sign system in principle can be studied using linguistic methods' (1965).[17] At that time, for Lotman and his colleagues, the field of semiotics did not extend beyond human culture, which means that the lower semiotic threshold (however not much discussed) was assumed to be where human culture starts. Taking this into account, we can state that their distinction concerned just primary and secondary linguistic modelling systems. The distinction introduced by Sebeok between the linguistic (human, both verbal and nonverbal) and other (non-human, nonverbal) sign systems turns out to be a far deeper difference than the one between the primary and secondary linguistic sign systems. Therefore, the latter should not be renamed secondary and tertiary, because the distinction within the linguistic sign systems belongs to a different (subordinate) rank. Thus it is reasonable to stay with using the original terms primary and secondary for the specifically human sign systems, simply adding that these both belong to the linguistic sign systems, which create the Umwelten that are very different from the animal and, far more, from the vegetative sign systems, despite the latter both taking part in the formation of culture, and obligatory for its understanding.

Indeed, as Sebeok (2001b: 159) has observed:

> The present terminological requirement to subsume a semiotics of culture, or just plain semiotics, under . . . biosemiotics, might have been obviated decades earlier. As things are going now, the boundaries between the two are already crumbling, giving way to a unified doctrine of signs embedded in a vast, comprehensive life science.

---

[16] This distinction has already been described in the introductory text 'From the editors' in *Trudy po znakovym sistemam* (*Sign Systems Studies*) 2: 6 (1965). See also Levchenko and Salupere (1999).

[17] 'From the editors', in *Trudy po znakovym sistemam* (*Sign Systems Studies*) 2: 6 (1965).

Further reading

Emmeche, C. (2001) 'Does a robot have an Umwelt? Reflections on the qualitative biosemiotics of Jakob von Uexküll', *Semiotica*, 134(1/4): 653–693.

Krampen, M. (1997) 'Models of semiosis', in R. Posner *et al.* (eds), *Semiotics: A Handbook on the Sign-Theoretic Foundations of Nature and Culture*, Vol. 1, Berlin: Walter de, Gruyter, pp. 247–287.

Rosen, R. (1999) *Essays on Life Itself*, New York: Columbia University Press.

Sebeok, T. A. (1991) *A Sign is Just a Sign*, Bloomington, IN: Indiana University Press, pp. 49–58.

Uexküll, J. von (1982 [1940]) 'The theory of meaning', *Semiotica*, 42(1): 25–82.

4
Logic and cognition

Peer Bundgaard and Frederik Stjernfelt

The present essay aims to explicate a key area of contemporary **semiotics** by laying bare the importance assigned to schematic representations in recent theories of meaning: so-called morphodynamic semiotics and **cognitive linguistics**. It suggests and gives evidence for the existence of a prelinguistic level of meaning organization on which categorization and conceptualization is founded, and it shows how this level supports different sorts of inferences. Where, previously, much **sign** theory had relied on a conception of meaning as generated by a system independently of cognitive factors such as perception, action, etc., and of logical factors such as reasoning, truth, etc., the ideas underpinning the theory of schemata suggest a new basis for meaning. This basis can be developed in interaction with the reactualization of **Peirce**'s semiotics and the crucial role it assigns to diagrams in cognition and theoretical reasoning.

Preamble

The combination of logic and cognition in semiotics goes without saying, since in one tradition semiotics is the study of how we humans, when thinking and reasoning, make use of, communicate, perceive and interpret signs and make inferences on the basis of these interpretations. In this, Peircean, view semiotics is the inquiry which lays bare how logical reasoning takes place in sign use, both in single inferences and in the scientific quest for knowledge in general.

However, in another, 'continental', tradition cognition and logic pertain to two realms which, from a scientific perspective, are heterogeneous: cognition belonging to psychology and its investigations into the empirical mental and psychophysical processes supporting human meaning making, as opposed to logic, now rephrased 'semiotics' proper, as the science which aims at establishing the formal tenets and internal scaffolding of meaning, freed from all psychology, context, concrete meaning intentions, actual manners of reasoning, etc. Roughly speaking, this latter position characterizes European semiotics from its roots in **Husserl**ian **phenomenology** and structural linguistics – take, for instance, Algirdas Julien Greimas and the so-called Paris School of Semiotics (Greimas 1987). Here, the **meaning** system is self-contained, with its own intrinsic principles of organization, meaning generating rules, correlations between the deep structures of meaning and the significant surface phenomena, etc.; thus, semiotic investigations can be and should be conducted in isolation, as it were, independently of other sciences and their findings (here, mainly psychology, philosophy of mind and philosophy of **language**). In short, semiotics, just like structural linguistics and the subsequent formal, generative and transformational branches of linguistics, is concerned with the formal properties of its **object** (meaning and how it is generated), not with cognition: the properties of meaning making and the pragmatic constraints on human meaning making.

Meaning and schemas in morphodynamic semiotics

Now, if the splitting of cognition and the logic of meaning characterizes continental semiotics in its origin and heyday (as crystallized in Greimas and Courtés 1979), from the mid-1980s a process of convergence was initiated. The ground for this convergence had been prepared by the French mathematicians René Thom's (1972, 1983) and Jean Petitot's (1992, 1995, 2004) groundbreaking contributions to linguistics and semiotics. Thom's hypothesis, and Petitot's further elaboration and refinement of it, is that there exist fundamental constraints on the construction of meaning which are not modular constraints, i.e. constraints stemming from the self-contained formal 'meaning system' (say, as it was defined in classical Greimasian semiotics independently of other systems such as perception and action). Rather, the constraints identified by Thom stem from mathematical topology and facilitate the mapping onto structural properties of the environment. They thus provide the structure of action and perception systems, in which meaning making – or semiosis – takes place.

Key to this approach is the concept of *schema*. Roughly speaking, Thom defines schemas as abstract representations of elementary spatio-temporal interactions between entities. In fact, he brings the argument a step further, in that in his view schemas are not only skeletal representations, they are the structural scaffolding of things themselves which may be extracted through perception. Now, what does '*elementary* interactions between spatio-temporal elements' mean? Well, it means that they are recurrent across different domains of experience, and, of course, that they display the same structural characteristics across these domain differences: a simple example of this would be one entity's 'inclusion' in some other entity, an abstract representation which then would make out the core meaning of all sorts of different verbal predications – say, to *capture*, *swallow*, *eat*, *integrate*, *enter*, etc. Another example could be the passage of an entity from one position to another, a transmission schema, which again constitutes the structural foundation of a long series of verbal predications, which aside from referring to the abstract schema specify it in different respects – say, *send* (object A from position X to position Y), *give*, *receive*, etc. (cf. Thom 1983 and the articles within it from the beginning of the 1970s for the first introduction to this hypothesis).

What is new – at least from a modern semiotic point of view – about this theory? Well, first, it displaces the origin or focus of semiosis: meaning is not defined as the outcome of certain abstract symbol manipulating processes, nor of some symbolic meaning generative device, but is something captured already in perception: in perception of events and their core interactional structure. Or, as Thom himself puts it,

> As a consequence, can we not agree that the factors of phenomenological invariance, which create in the observer the feeling of meaning, come from *real* properties of the objects of the external world and the *objective* presence of formal entities linked to those objects, which we call 'bearers of meaning'?
>
> (Thom 1983: 169)

Next, interaction with the environment is based on a limited set of primitive, so-called archetypical schemas: as represented in the human being, these are first and foremost the cognitive counterpart to the invariant structures of the environment or the recurrent patterns of experience. In this respect they are claimed to play a linking function between man and environment: our full-blown representations are founded on these skeleton representations and hook up with the world by virtue of them. What is more, the fundamental schemas are in fact not only considered to be sheer templates available for event categorization, they are also claimed to be syntactic constituent structures, i.e. they serve a semantic binding function: when we use a given verb, say *give*, *hand*, *send*, etc., the verb will not only refer to a specific sort of action, but also evoke a schema consisting of a SENDER-pos tion (abstractedly understood), an OBJECT-position, a TRAJECTORY-position and a RECEIVER-position; these positions function as semantic roles when represented in the mind, and the schema therefore functions as a syntactic gestalt, a configurational structure. When it is activated, it will be activated with all its semantic roles and therefore call for completion in terms of a particular kind of action and the particular elements instantiating the different semantic roles.

Seen retrospectively, the implications for semiotics of René Thom's topological linguistics and Jean Petitot's initial developments of it are primarily epistemological: that is to say they champion and seem to justify the rejection of the traditional approach to meaning as a modular phenomenon, generated by a modular system, independently of perception, action, etc. Thom and Petitot address the crucial issue concerning the relation between perceived types of invariance in the environment and mental representations, and redefine meaning as a not exclusively – in fact, far from exclusively – linguistic phenomenon: rather, linguistic meaning is a rearticulation of prelinguistic meaning structures. In short, it brings the world back into **semantics**, as the English philosopher Barry Smith (1993) once put it. However, it does not, for that matter, provide semioticians and linguists with many, nor with sufficiently elaborated, tools for description. To this end, its schemas are far too coarse grained and the exclusive focus on the interactional schemas is far too restricted.

Image schemas, scripts and frames in cognitive linguistics

Now, more or less parallel with, but independently of, the above, a similarly schema-driven approach to human meaning making developed, mainly in the United States. It is today known as cognitive linguistics and is represented by linguists, philosophers, psychologists and cognitive scientists such as Leonard Talmy (2000), Ronald Langacker (1987–1991), George Lakoff (1987), Mark Johnson (1987), Gilles Fauconnier and Mark Turner (2002), Jean Mandler (1992, 2005), Eve Sweetser (1990), etc. Key tenets of this programme are a couple of the assumptions which also constitute the cornerstone of the Thom–Petitot approach:

1. Language and cognition at large are not modal systems, they are not self-contained; they have developed along with and under the influence of other systems such as the perception and the action system.
2. Linguistic structure is grounded on a prelinguistic schematic structure, so-called schemas or **image schemas** (Johnson 1987; Mandler 1992, 2005); these schemas or abstract mental representations are acquired through perception and are as such cognitive counterparts to recurrent patterns of experience (more or less as in Thom) or they are acquired through bodily interaction with the environment: such schemas (as we shall see in somewhat more detail below) play a crucial role both in the organization of perceptual information (categorization and manner of experiencing a '**referent** scene') and at a linguistic level as a core semantic structure.

Now, in contradistinction to previous approaches, cognitive linguistics supplies detailed, subtle and systematic descriptions of the relation between perception and language, that is between the way in which a given referent scene (that is, the objective situation referred to) has been experienced and the way in which this mode of experience is specified in language. (It is obviously crucial to give a satisfying account of this correlation if one champions the claim to the effect that meaning is not exclusively a linguistic phenomenon.) The notion of image schemata has a rich philosophical background including **Kant**'s definition of schemata as figures making possible the meeting between perception and intuition on the one hand and understanding and concepts on the other hand – as well as the notion in Gestalt theory where gestalts are structured wholes of perception, action and environment organization. In the following we shall introduce three aspects of image schemas. First, their origin in perception and action. Second, their cognitive function as regards categorization and conceptualization. Third, their logical import, that is to say the fact that they, in various ways, also constitute the basis for basic forms of reasoning – that is, they support inferences.

The psychology of image schemas: When and how are they acquired?

As to the origin of image schemas, Jean Mandler (1992, 2005) provides exhaustive evidence for the fact that infants' acquisition of concepts in general, for example the concept of 'animacy', is based on a limited number of primitive image schemas. Already from the age of three months they perform distinctions based on pattern recognition: as regards animacy, they are capable of distinguishing between mechanical and biological movement; and they, of course, perform such distinctions across different types of experiences (for example, they recognize incorrect biological movement whoever enacts it). Between four and six months, the core image schema of biological versus mechanical movement is supplemented with yet another essential moment: namely, the distinction between self motion and caused motion (the former being the distinctive feature of biological movement). The cognitive reality of this schema for core causality is attested by the fact that infants do consider designs (of a Henri Michotte sort – Michotte 1963; see also Scholl and Tremoulet 2000) involving plain 'billiard ball causality', where one sphere is seen to move toward and hit another which then itself moves, as perfectly normal. Yet they dishabituate from, or react against, the same set-up whenever there is either a temporal or spatial gap between the movements of the two spheres. The simple hypothesis is, of course, that infants categorize an event in terms of its correspondence or match with an image schema, so that whenever a *fit* obtains between the structural make-up of an experienced event – captured by the cognitive mechanism Mandler calls 'Perceptual Meaning Analysis' – and the acquired image schema (e.g. the schema for 'launching'), then experience is categorically speaking felicitous; the inverse, of course, being the case for the *mis*fit.

A decisive stage in the acquisition of the concept of animacy consists in the formation of a schema for goal-oriented behaviour and thus the recognition of purposeful movement. The experiment in Figure 4.1 (Gergely *et al.* 1995; here we have used Scholl and Tremoulet's diagram) seems to provide evidence for the fact that nine–twelve-month-old infants do possess a 'shortest-path-to-goal' schema and thus assess the purposefulness of an action with respect to its conformity with such a schema.

In short, infants already engage in the process of capturing the structural design properties of events and objects. They do so by the cognitive mechanism of Mandler's Perceptual Meaning Analysis. What are, then, the fundamental properties of this cognitive processing device (which must, by the way, be

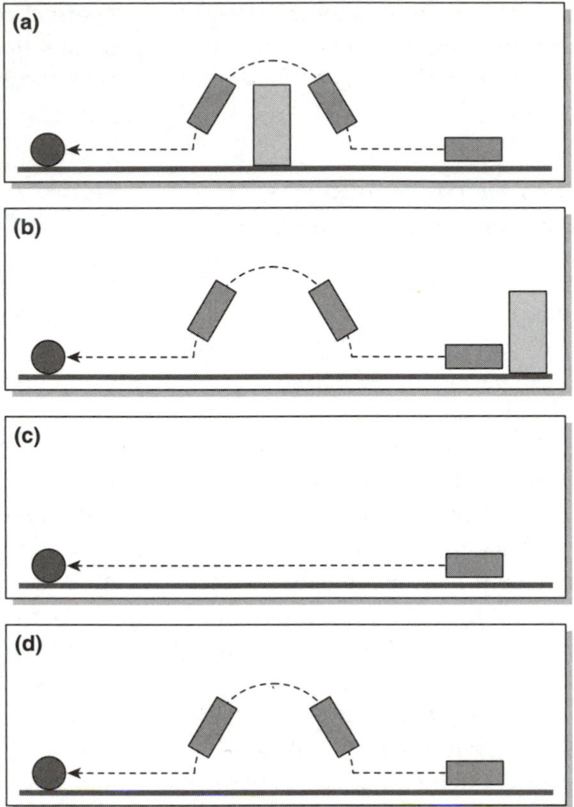

Figure 4.1 Nine- and twelve-month-old infants were familiarized with a movie showing either scenario (a) or (b). In (a) an oblong figure approaches an obstacle and jumps over the obstacle to join the circle; (b) shows the same action but with the obstacle moved to one side. After familiarization the infants were tested by being shown (c) and (d). When confronted with cases (c) and (d) where the obstacle had been removed, infants that had been familiarized with (a) dishabituate from (d), i.e. show astonishment (look longer at (d) than at (c)), even though the movement is identical with the one they were habituated to. They recognize the movement in (c) as normal, i.e. the most direct way of reaching a goal. Infants familiarized with (b) did not manifest this behaviour. This seems to suggest that infants reason and assess on the basis of an abstract. (From Scholl and Tremoulet 2000.)

presupposed by any theory which defends a claim to the effect that abstract, structural information can be grasped through perception)?

1 It is a spontaneous, attentive process which operates on perceptual information.
2 It is clearly preverbal, since performed by infants (even very young infants).
3 It recognizes and extracts invariant structure from the referent scenes.
4 It generalizes across particularities of different perceptual inputs.
5 It leads to the constitution of abstract representations which contain the skeleton structure common to different referent scenes.
6 This perceptual skeleton structure is what we understand by image schema.

As we have already seen, infants grasp and thus categorize events or relations in the environment by means of image schemas; image schemas are furthermore used to shape our experiences, i.e. they are used in the conceptualization of referent scenes; and they are finally mental devices supporting reasoning and inferences. So far we have only accounted for the fact that image schemas support concept formation and categorization. We have not commented on how such schemas are actively used in experience as tools for conceptualization, nor have we shown how humans use them to think or reason (although the Gergely experiment shows how infants assess the congruity of an action with respect to its conformity with a rational or adequate 'shortest-path-to-goal' schema). We shall now attempt to come to grips with these essential properties of schemas.

The phenomenology of image schemas: How do they shape our experiences?

A common supposition in cognitive linguistics and cognitive semiotics is thus that humans acquire an inventory of fundamental images through perception or bodily interaction with the environment. The origin of image schemas, however, is multiple, and a plurality of other possible sources must be mentioned: inborn brain structures (giving us, e.g., the image schema of a face), a priori structures (giving us, e.g., simple arithmetic, geometry, topology, etc.) and language and culture (selecting and combining image schemas while strengthening some and suppressing others). Once they are deployed, they are of course available for use; they may, as we have seen, then facilitate smooth and efficient categorization of spatio-temporal interactions between elements in terms of causality, purpose, wholes, etc. Schemas can not only be used in the categorical comprehension of the world, but also, as it were, in the intentional apprehension of it: in fact, whenever we perceive or experience a scene, a situation (what in phenomenological terms Husserl (1973 [1939]) called a *Sachlage*), we organize this situation, by distributing our attention to alight on certain and not other of its elements, profiling *this* and *not that* aspect of it, paying attention to this part and not that part of it, etc. The result of the way in which we have organized the referent scene is the object of experience proper (Husserl called it the state of affairs, the *Sachverhalt*). Image schemas play a crucial role in the organization of the referent scene and thus the constitution of the experienced object: it is by and large possible to show how the semiotic scaffolding of an object of experience is relative to the image schemas applied to the referent scene (and specified by certain linguistic expressions); image schemas which are, in turn, applied according to the experiencer's or the speaker's intentional focus. This is particularly clear in cases of alternate schematizations; that is to say, cases where the same situation or the same object is referred to in two or more different ways. Consider:

1a He went over the field
1b He went through the field

2a The boat is on the sea
2b The boat is in the sea

3a I jog together with him
3b I jog along with him

As Talmy (2000, 2005) has remarked, in 1a, by virtue of the schematic meaning of 'over', the field is conceptualized as a sheer surface, with all other properties abstracted away, whereas in 1b it is rather conceptualized as a container-like entity which partially covers the agent (i.e. the vegetation of the field is more profiled). In 2a, the sea is conceptualized as a surface, in 2b as a container, with focus on the fact that the boat is partially immersed in the water, which suggests a proximal viewpoint in 2b and a distal viewpoint in 2a (from where material properties of the water, waves, viscosity, etc. are not perceivable). And, finally, in 3a 'together' suggests that 'I' and 'he' are 'co-equal' (Talmy 2005: 220) participants in the activity, whereas in 3b 'along' qualifies one of the participants ('him') as the main participant, and 'I' as ancillary with respect to him.

Examples like the above are legion. They all point to the fact that meaning organization takes place already in perception, that the structure of the perceived scene can be determined in image schematic terms (or in its simplest version in terms of figure-ground segregation as in 'Peter has hit Paul' versus 'Paul has been hit by Peter'), and that this structure can be suitably expressed in language. In fact, Talmy claims that a whole subsystem of language – composed by the so-called closed word classes – is specialized in specifying the structure of the cognitive representation evoked by a given sentence or complex expression.

We are therefore now in a position where we can refine in some small measure the determination of the cognitive import of image schemas. The nice match between language and perception is an image schematic fit: the structures we make use of in our experience of the world are also the structures that make out the semantic core level of language. Language does refer to things in the world, and real properties in the world, but it does so through the schemas (and concepts) by means of which these things and properties have been intended.

Schemas and logic: How schemas support inferences and reasoning

As regards the schematic foundation of reasoning, arguably image schemas (as well as other more fleshy types of schemata, as we shall see) support inferences of different sorts, some very simple, others more subtle. As suggested above, it seems reasonable to consider the kind of cognitive reactions infants manifest when confronted with incongruous patterns of interactions (see Figure 4.1) as examples of inferences supported by image schemas. The referent scene is indeed assessed in terms of a schema for purposeful action (cf. Csibra *et al.* 2003 for more experimental evidence).

Now, it may be fruitful, however, to distinguish this sort of reasoning which concerns the fit or the misfit between an acquired schematic representation and the spatio-temporal structure of a referent scene, from reasoning and inferences directly based on the schema itself. Epitomes of such inferences are those based on the container-schema. Consider the schema of containment (which is one of the most fundamental, primitive and pervasively used schemas, probably due to early experience of our bodies as containers). A container-schema consists of an interior, a boundary and a relation to an exterior. Things are either inside or outside the container. From this a basic logic of transitivity can be derived: A is a container-schema, and X is in A. B is a container-schema, and if A is in B, then X is in B:

[A [X]], [B [A[X]]] => [B[X]]

This can be considered (as Lakoff 1988 claims) as the intuitive basis for *modus ponens*: if all As are Bs, and X is an A, the X is a B.

Everyday cognition offers, however, many other types of inferences, whose content is, say, more fluid and the extension more vaguely defined than in the above example. These are cases where the speaker's meaning intention should be inferred from the way in which he has activated a given schema. Consider classical examples of implicature:

4a He is a Republican, but he is smart
4b They are married but they don't live together

In both cases 'and' could, of course, be used with exactly the same truth value as 'but', but it would not imply the same thing: namely the fact that the speaker to some vaguely defined extent considers there to be some sort of incongruity between what is to the left and what is to the right of 'but'. In a nutshell, 'but' has a plain schematic meaning: whatever is to the left and right of it are considered to clash in some respect. This schema supports and guides the inferences we are likely to make about the speaker's attitude to what he is talking about.

Still, schemas need not be abstract as in the case of 'but', or purely topological (i.e. structures between positions in space) like in the case of the container-schema. They may very well be skeleton-like, but nevertheless contingent on cultural phenomena. This is evidently the case for Schank and Abelson's 'scripts' (Schank and Abelson 1977), i.e. the abstract representation of a complex event in terms of its constitutive elements, its sub-events, and the order of the latter. Most of us possess a restaurant-script canonically composed of sub-events like: 1) Entering the restaurant, finding a seat; 2) waiter brings menu card; 3) ordering; 4) eating; 5) paying. Now importantly, all the sub-events are systematically correlated to each other and to the whole they are part of so that whenever only one of them is mentioned the whole script is activated and the full restaurant scene is evoked. This obviously supports inferences based on minimal linguistic cues:

5a They got in, ate, left a tip, and went home.
5b They sat down, read the menu card, ate, and went home.
5c They sat down, asked the waiter for advice, ate, and went home.

In none of the above sentences is the restaurant explicitly mentioned; in all of them, however, the representation of it is clearly evoked.

The activation of scripts by one or a few of its constituent parts shares an essential property with schemas of the 'but' sort: they also specify the speaker's intentional relation to what s/he is speaking about. Indeed, since any constituent element triggers the full representation, the one which is chosen specifies, willy-nilly, how the speaker distributed his/her attention on the scene: we can infer the speaker's intentional attitude to the referent object from the way in which s/he activates the scripts. Consider a cousin to Schank and Abelson's script, namely Charles Fillmore's 'frame' (Fillmore 2006 [1982]): just as with 'script', it is defined as a complex semantic whole consisting of systematically correlated concepts so that you cannot understand one of them without understanding the whole structure it is a part of (the difference is just that frames do not imply any intrinsic temporal order of sub-events). Consider the classical 'commercial frame', consisting of a 'buyer', a 'seller', 'goods' and 'money'. Many different verbs can activate such a frame; all of them, however, will profile certain relations, thus endowing them with particular salience relative to the speaker's intentional focus. Thus, 'buy' profiles the buyer-role and the goods-role; 'sell' profiles the seller-role and the goods-role; 'purchase' profiles the money-role and the goods-role, etc.

Even though an example like the above is simple and does not seem to yield very interesting distinctions, two things should be observed. First, it is not because it is simple that it is trivial: it is a non-trivial fact – systematically explainable in terms of how schemas, scripts and frames are activated – that perspective, point of view and intentional attitude can be linguistically specified. Second, it is indeed easy to give simple, but nevertheless both remarkable and powerful, examples of how even worn-out frames, such as the 'commercial frame', can be instantiated so as to produce strong semantic effects. Consider the following **dialogue** from Cormac McCarthy's *No Country for Old Men*. Two policemen talk about the drugs they have found on a crime scene:

> He handed the transponder unit to the sheriff.
> What am I supposed to do with this?
> It's Maverick County property. Crime scene evidence.
> The sheriff shook his head. Dope, he said.
> Dope.

They sell that shit to schoolkids.
It's worse than that.
How's that?
Schoolkids buy it.

(Cormac McCarthy, *No Country for Old Men*, p. 194)

The point being, of course, that adults' selling of illegal substances or otherwise trying to pervert children for the purpose of personal gain is wicked but, alas, well known and, statistically speaking, expectable: it is part of the prototypical adult-frame. Whereas the fact that children actively desire and purchase the very thing which will pervert their nature is not expectable: it is not part of the prototypical child-frame.

A partial conclusion: up till now we have accounted for the role played by image schemas and other types of schemas such as scripts and frame in cognition and language. We have, very roughly, tried to account for their *ontology*, i.e. what they are: abstract structures which may inhere in representations which often are counterparts to recurrently experienced spatio-temporal structures in the environment. We have developed the *psychology* of schemas in the sense that we have accounted for the way in which such representations emerge in the (infant's) mind, through Perceptual Meaning Analysis or through bodily interaction with the world. Next, we accounted for what could be called the *phenomenology* of schemas, in the sense that we have shown how they structure our experiences, shape our conceptualizations and specify our intentional focus. Finally we have developed elements of a *logic* of schematic reasoning with particular focus on how schemas support inferences in everyday cognition and linguistic meaning construction.

In doing so, we have tried to establish the affinities between recent developments in continental semiotics and cognitive linguistics, which stem from these two research programmes' independent discovery of the schematic basis of meaning, their claim to the effect that language is not a self-contained modulary system, but should be examined in correlation with other cognitive systems, and that meaning construction in language, as well as other higher order cognitive skills such as categorization, conceptualization and inference, have a prelinguistic basis. We shall now turn to Charles Sanders Peirce whose thinking in many respects is at the root of the above research programmes, both as regards the importance of iconicity in symbolic thinking and as regards the schematic (or as he says, diagrammatic) foundation of everyday, as well as theoretical, inferences.

Peirce: Diagrammatic reasoning

The actual cognitive developments in semiotics may be located in an overall framework of Peirce's logic and semiotics. Modern semiotics was institutionalized during the late 1960s with the establishment of the central periodical *Semiotica*, as well as the **IASS** (International Association of Semiotic Studies).

At that time, the major semiotic current was **structuralism**, predominantly in its French versions – a current which emphasized the autonomous, modular study of meaning structures as mentioned above in relation to the school of Greimas. Despite the virtues of this tradition, it gradually appeared that it entailed a series of basic problems:

1 The arbitrarity hypothesis – that all signs are conventional through and through – made it difficult to understand signs involving iconic components – pictures, photographs, films, but also maps, diagrams, graphs, algebra, logic.
2 The idea that semiotic systems formed autonomous wholes made it difficult to understand the **communication** between such systems, e.g. between cultures, subcultures, scientific paradigms, world views, languages, etc. – in short, it had a tendency to lead to relativism.
3 The emphasis on language as the central example of a semiotic system made structuralism prone to what has been called linguistic imperialism – it tended to understand all other sorts of semiotic phenomena, logic, pictures, cultures, etc., in terms of linguistic concepts which were in many cases insufficient for the task.

The attempt at overcoming these shortcomings led to semiotics' movement towards cognitive linguistics and cognitive semantics as charted above – and it also led to a renewed interest and reinterpretation of the other central source of modern semiotics besides **Saussure**an structuralism: Charles Peirce's **pragmatism**.

By contrast with structuralism, Peirce's philosophy sees no distinction between semiotics and logic: rather, semiotics *is* logic, both taken in its narrow sense as the study of truth-preserving inferences by means of signs, and in the broader sense as the study of the development of the sciences by means of basic pragmatic principles. In 1883, Peirce developed the one-dimensional 'symbolic' semiotic notation for logic which – with small modifications by Schröder, Peano, and Russell – is still in use today. Furthermore, around the turn of the century, Peirce developed alternative semiotic representations of logic, this time a two-dimensional, more iconic representation which he claimed was in some senses heuristically superior to his older notation: the so-called Existential Graphs (which form exact equivalents to propositional logic and predicate logic as well as outlines of modal logic, temporal logic, speech act logic, etc.). By the same token, Peirce's semiotics is – again, unlike structuralism – intensively involved with perception and action. This semiotics is built on a conception of perception in which general structures are already present in perception and are not subsequently added to it by the mind – a conception in which perception in itself already forms a first piece of logical inference. As to action, Peirce's pragmatism is based on the connection of meaning to action – to Peirce, the meaning of a claim is the same thing as the conceived set of action consequences of that claim (cf. his famous 'pragmatic principle' in 'How to make our ideas clear', Peirce 1992a: 124). Action thus forms the control, weeding out false semiotic presumptions – most clearly in the scientific experiment, a specifically refined and focused piece of action. As a result, Peirce's semiotics is a 'cognition-friendly' semiotics: it frames semiotic processes as being basically processes of logical inferences connecting perception and action, and in the wider perspective such processes are interlinked so as to form sciences and thus facilitate the unique growth of human knowledge in history. Peirce's semiotics thus spans the range from logic, through perception, action and cognition, to science and theory of science. And thus his well-known truth-concept claims that the truth is what the scientific community converges upon in the long run – provided it adheres to basic pragmatist principles.

All in all, a Peircean semiotics 'cures', as it were, the central fatal deficits of structuralist semiotics – it includes iconic signs at a basic level; by taking logic, perception and action as the basic semiotic phenomena, it makes it possible to see how different semiotic systems may communicate; and by thus making a plural semiotics comprising different representation systems, it avoids the pitfalls of linguistic imperialism and the ensuing ideas of being trapped in 'the prisonhouse of language'. The rapid renewal of interest in Peirce during semiotic scholarship of recent decades is undoubtedly connected to these possibilities of avoiding some of the irrationalist consequences of 'the linguistic turn' and constructing a realist, rationalist, pluralist and 'cognition-friendly' semiotics. Peirce's semiotics, however, has also, on some of its more detailed levels, an amazing possibility for connecting with actual developments in cognitive linguistics and semantics, most notably around the concept of 'schema' – the analogous concept in Peirce's doctrine being that of 'diagram'.

This claim requires the introduction of a specific subset of Peirce's semiotics. As is well known, one of his distinctions between sign aspects is the triad **icon–index–symbol**, concerned with how a sign connects to its referent or object. Icons refer to their object by means of similarity (e.g. a picture, a map or a graph); indices refer by means of their actual connection to their object (smoke as the sign for fire; the pointing finger as the sign for the object pointed to); symbols refer by means of a **habit** (most words in a language, road signs, etc.; *EP* 1: 273–274). It is very important here that sufficiently complicated signs – that is, most signs we meet – contain several of these three aspects. The footprint on the beach is an icon because it is in certain respects similar to the foot that made it; but it is also an index because it is *caused* by that foot. The road sign showing two children walking with their bags is both an icon – depicting, by means of similarity, these children; a symbol – referring to schoolchildren in general; and an index – the sign being caused by the proximity of a school. Iconicity is taken as the most basic level of meaning providing the basis of all sorts of predicates in semiotic systems: icons *describe* (aspects of) the objects they refer to; indices provide the basis for *locating* the objects described in time and space (by means of causes, pointing arrows, proper names and demonstratives in language, etc.), and symbols provide the possibility of generalizing these simple semiotic devices to cover general cases – like the habit we learn of interpreting the two children in the road sign as not two particular individuals, but rather schoolchildren as such.

Peirce's central concept of diagrams forms a subspecies of icons. Among signs which are predominantly iconic – Peirce calls them 'hypoicons' – he distinguishes 'images', 'diagrams' and 'metaphors'. The former are icons using simple shapes, properties, forms, colours, tones, etc. – like the crescent shape as a sign for the moon. The diagrams are complex icons which analyse their object into a skeletal set of interconnected parts. The metaphors map such diagram signs onto other domains, such as the tree diagram mapped upon family structure to give the metaphor of an 'ancestral tree'. Peirce explicitly remarks how this diagram concept is the heir to Kant's schema concept: in Kant, the diagram unites intuition and understanding; in Peirce, iconicity and symbolicity. A completely pure diagram, it is true, needs no symbolicity; but a diagram only becomes functional when it is accompanied by a symbolic instruction of what the diagram refers to and which rules should pertain to our understanding of the relation between its parts. Peirce's diagram concept refers to a whole doctrine of 'diagrammatical reasoning' in the mature Peirce's semiotics and it may be developed so as to furnish the overall philosophical meta-concept of all the different schema-concepts of cognitive semiotics (scripts, frames, body schemas, perception and action schemas, image schemas, models, etc.). At the same time, diagrams form the prerequisite to deductive reasoning; thus diagrams constitute the link between formal logic on the one hand with the cognitive capacity for making logic inferences on the other hand. The most thorough presentation of the diagram doctrine can be found in a paper nicknamed 'PAP' (in Peirce 1976, 316ff. a further investigation; can be found in Stjernfelt 2007).

Let us here highlight Peirce's description of diagrams. First of all, diagrams are *types*. The diagram is not identical to the printed diagram token on the paper or the computer screen. Rather, we perform a whole series of abstracting and idealizing operations when reading such a diagram. We know that the side of the triangle is infinitely thin and completely straight even if no such line could ever be drawn on paper or screen. We know that the triangle we contemplate in some sense has no colour, even if all drawings must have some particular colour. In short, we idealize the diagram token in order to access the diagram type – by means of a whole bunch of symbolic directives, implicit or explicit. This is why Peirce can say that the diagram makes possible the direct observation of universal structures. Most importantly, he describes the possibility of thought experiments using the diagram – diagrammatical reasoning. This is connected to the basic similarity of icons – another way of describing this similarity to Peirce is to say that icons are signs which may be manipulated so as to make evident aspects of their objects which were not immediately present in the construction recipe for the sign. This idea comes to the fore in diagrams. Here, the example of a map is most instructive. Given a topographical map, a series of different diagram experiments are possible. A map of New York State, for instance, facilitates the experiment of determining the road distance between New York City and Buffalo. You take the ruler, partition the road into approximately rectilinear pieces, measure them and calculate the sum, say 11.6 cm. Now you divide by the scale of the map (most often printed in some corner of it, providing parts of the symbolic framing of the diagram) and you get an approximate measure of the distance between the two cities, say 480 kilometres. This small, everyday diagram experiment thus generates information about the object – Northeastern USA – by the manipulation of the diagram sign. Moreover, this information was never before explicitly present in the sign – it having been constructed by geodesic triangulation or stylized aerial photography or both. Thus, diagrammatical reasoning – or, inference using schemata – is a basic process of cognition in Peirce, placing diagrams or schemata centre stage in Peirce's logic and in a Peircean theory of cognition.

Diagrams are not only figures in the above sense – as in cognitive linguistics and semiotics, they also comprise cognitive schemata which we use economically to guide perception, thought and action. This becomes evident when we look at the extension of the diagram category in Peirce's semiotics. The prototypical diagrams are, of course, figures in geometry textbooks, maps, graphs, construction diagrams, and the like. But Peirce's basic definition of diagrams widely enlarges the category from this basis. Most importantly, seemingly non-iconic representation devices like formal languages, logic, algebra, etc., are shown to contain an ineradicable diagrammatical iconicity for the simple reason that they make possible diagrammatical reasoning, giving access to new information about their object. The equation '$x + 2 = 4$' is thus a diagram, because it may be manipulated (using the basic rules of arithmetic serving as the symbolic framing of the diagram) to give the result '$x = 2$'. Of course, the single signs 'x', '+', '2', '=' and '4' are symbols, but the whole algebraic proposition '$x + 2 = 4$' is a diagrammatical icon which may be used for diagrammatical inference. This is why Peirce's diagram doctrine entails two sweeping claims:

1 all deductive reasoning takes place by the manipulation of diagrams; and, correlatively,
2 mathematics as such is based on diagram manipulation.

Deductive reasoning in logic (e.g. *modus ponens*), everyday language (all Germans are Europeans), everyday perception (this chair is closer than this table), action (I must dribble around this full back in order to get a kick at the goal), planning (we must reserve a table at the busy restaurant) – all such pieces of reasoning depend on quick diagram manipulations – or schematic reasonings – in the mind. Moreover, the diagrams used, most often implicitly, in such everyday pieces of cognition, possess a mathematical core. This is why the mathematical approach of Thom and Petitot in the first part of this chapter could easily accommodate the more empirical approach of cognitive semiotics and cognitive linguistics. Simple cognitive schemata are built from simple topology, arithmetic and geometry, which, in turn, are clothed with domain-specific knowledge and constraints from the specific field of life in which we use these schemata. Thus – just like Thom, Petitot and cognitive semiotics – Peirce places cognitive diagrams (schemata) at the most basic level of cognition and action, facilitating, in turn, the construction of very different semiotic systems (vision, to a large extent inborn and inherent in the visual system; verbality, to a large extent learned and cultural specific; gesture, pictures, singing, etc.).

The role of such diagrams in the broader context of pragmatic activity, everyday inference and scientific developments is indicated by Peirce's doctrine of logical inference types and their pragmatic use. Peirce distinguishes the argument types of **abduction**, **deduction** and **induction**. The former concerns qualified guesses – or what is often nowadays referred to as 'inference to the best explanation'. In abduction, an explanation is sought to account for some unexpected event or phenomenon – and all hypotheses which entail this unexplained fact are possible explanations. You find a key in the road – possible abductions comprise:

1 a UFO landed nearby and placed the key in order to lure you to stop so you can be caught for an extraterrestrial breeding programme;
2 the key just happens to materialize there by spontaneous generation;
3 somebody lost it;
4 ... and infinitely many more abduction possibilities.

Thus, abductions come in many different sorts and qualities, and it is an important cognitive filter to be able to focus upon the most plausible, relevant hypothesis in a given case. Once such a hypothesis has been selected, deduction takes over. The hypothesis chosen – take number (1) – has an ideal, diagrammatical structure, and this hypothesis may now be subjected to deductive investigation, disregarding whether it is true or not. If the key has, in fact, been placed there by a UFO, it follows that such a vehicle must have left physical traces (ET footprints, fuel exhaustion, a burnt spot in the grass, green slime, etc.). This deduction is a diagram manipulation based on the general, ideal diagrammatical knowledge we have about the behaviour of material objects. After this deductive diagram experiment, induction enters the stage: can we, by investigating the area around the key, searching for traces, taking soil samples, etc., find any indication of the recent presence of small, green men and their vehicle? If not, induction tells us that hypothesis (1) must be discarded, and another abductive hypothesis may be chosen for further ideal, deductive and empirical, inductive scrutiny. The overall syntax of all sorts of investigation, thus, follows the order of abduction–deduction–induction – forming a cognitive trial-and-error circle where the inductive result leads to the discarding of the original abduction or to the possible refinement of it. In this overall semiotic theory of a pragmatist epistemology, the second phase, that of logic, deduction and diagram experiment, forms the locus of reasoning with schemata.

Thus, the actual reinterpretation of Peirce makes possible the integrated understanding of all the different current schema concepts in cognitive linguistics and semiotics – as well as the connection of them in a broader perspective including logic, action, perception, philosophy of mathematics and philosophy of science. The fertile development in the many detailed empirical studies of cognitive semantics and of cognitive semiotics may thus be integrated and advanced in the fertile reinterpretation and further development of Peircean semiotics.

Further reading

Bundgaard, P. F. (2004) 'The ideal scaffolding of language: Husserl's fourth Logical Investigation in the light of cognitive linguistics', *Phenomenology and the Cognitive Sciences*, 3 (1): 49–80.

Bundgaard, P., Østergaard, S. and Stjernfelt, F. (2006) 'Water proof fire stations? Conceptual schemata and cognitive operations involved in compound constructions', *Semiotica*, 161(1/4): 363–393.

Houser, N., Roberts, D. D. and van Evra, J. (eds) (1997) *Studies in the Logic of Charles Sanders Peirce*, Bloomington, IN: Indiana University Press.

Peirce, C. S. (1992) *Reasoning and the Logic of Things*, ed. K. L. Ketner and H. Putnam, Cambridge, MA: Harvard University Press.

Stjernfelt, F. (2007) *Diagrammatology. An Investigation on the Borderlines of Phenomenology, Ontology, and Semiotics*, Dordrecht: Springer Verlag.

5
Realism and epistemology

John Deely

'In **semiotics**, we must,' counselled Thomas A. **Sebeok** (1991b: 2), 'think of ourselves as both working within a tradition that changes over time and trying to grasp things as they "really are"'; in this effort, Sebeok counselled further (ibid.), so-called 'epistemology' can provide no more than 'the midmost target'. The aim of this essay is to show why, and to do so by showing how **semiosis**, the action of **sign**s, provides a path – the only path – whereon we find the means 'to reveal the substratal illusion underlying reality and to search for the reality that may, after all, lurk behind that illusion' (Sebeok 1985a: 21).

Sebeok's counsel

It is not, most assuredly, that we had to await the coming upon the intellectual scene of semiotics in order to know that there is a difference between truth and illusion. This difference in principle, however confused in fact upon various occasions of attempts to distinguish the two, has been clear to human animals from the dawn of their difference from the brute animals in being able to grasp more than what reduces back to sensations within perception. So notice that I do not say that *semiotics* provides the path whereon the distinction between reality and illusion becomes explicable theoretically, but rather that *semiosis*, which semiotics studies, provides the path. For the human animal depends upon the action of signs in everything that it comes to know, from the first stirrings of external sense to the highest reaches of understanding, and every point – the realm of sense perception – in between.

Thus Sebeok's counsel in this matter of '**realism**' and 'epistemology', again as he himself put it (Sebeok 1985a: 21), is no more than an 'abductive assignment' which it is 'the privilege of future generations to pursue'. Neither 'realism' nor 'epistemology' are semiotic terms, but are rather, as we shall see, in their main sense today 'children of the modern mainstream development of philosophy'. Precisely this development with its speculative sub-developments – the mainstream modern developments in philosophy overall – semiotics begins by transcending, at least insofar as semiotics succeeds in discerning and achieving the standpoint proper to and distinctive of the study of the action of signs.

In pursuing our abductive assignment toward the future, accordingly, we need to have a sense or grasp of both of what defines *modernity* in the matters before us (realism and epistemology), and of what (in sharp contrast) is the '*tradition of semiotics*' – that is, not only 'where semiotics is today', but how it got there, and where it is going ('how we got where we're going', as one author summarily put it (Gannon 1991) in discussing the situation in psychology at the end of the twentieth century). We need to have an awareness of the *trajectory of semiotic development* – without (of course) any pretension of a knowledge or prophecy *in detail* of the future – against the backdrop of philosophical modernity. And it is precisely this backdrop that requires us to demonstrate how semiotics provides a convincing alternative to what we might call 'the Kantian dilemma'. This dilemma, to tell the truth, is the very definition of modernity in philosophy, inasmuch as **Kant** (1781, 1787) succeeded to make his grand synthesis of the two main traditions of modern philosophy (namely, Rationalism after Descartes, esp. 1628, 1637 and 1641 (1985a, b, c); and Empiricism after **Locke**, 1690) which, on any account, defined the mainstream modern development as a revolt against the 'Scholastic realism' of Latin times which, in 1633, came a cropper over the trial of Galileo for the heresy of teaching that it is the earth that moves relative to the sun, and not the other way around.

'Realism' in philosophy and semiotics

Alain Rey – upon whom Sebeok based his limitation of epistemology to no more than semiotics' 'midmost target' – remarked that if we survey 'the specific objects of the history of semiotics',[1]

> we can observe in passing that *they are subsumed under the entire class of linguistic products*, and that they deal either with man in society, or with other objects, when and only when signs and semiosis are considered as essential, causal or explanatory for any of these objects *with no distinction between ontology and epistemology.*
>
> (Rey 1984: 91, italics added)

I have italicized the key points here. Let us examine them in turn.

'The entire class of linguistic products'

Linguistic **communication** is not **language**, and not all communication is linguistic. 'Language' is the biologically underdetermined feature of the human Innenwelt: this is 'language in the root sense'.[2] Language in this root sense is the

[1] On the other hand – and this may have been the motivation for Sebeok's point – Rey had observed earlier (p. 87) that while 'the objects of scientific research may be, or may not be, semiotic', by contrast, '*any* epistemological effort has a semiotic character, and all the sciences can be relevant in this regard'.

[2] This distinction between language in the root sense as a biological *adaptation* and language in the subsequent sense of linguistic communication as a species-specifically human *exaptation* was originally drawn in semiotics by Sebeok in 1984 (see also 1985b, c). The distinction was the key (see Deely 2007b) to Sebeok's making of J. von **Uexküll**'s Innenwelt 'the primary modelling system', displacing Yuri **Lotman**'s 'language' (i.e. Sebeok's linguistic communication) to the level rather of 'secondary modelling system'.

species-specifically human *adaptation* which is at the base of the distinction between sense perception as common to all higher animals and human understanding as able to go beyond perception in the consideration of **objects**, whether 'real' or not, which cannot be directly instantiated in sense-perceptible material structures, 'objects which range all the way from God and angels to relations as irreducible to the subjective divisions of being and suprasubjective respecting those divisions. What is commonly called 'language' – spoken, gestured or written words used to communicate – is in fact an *exaptation* of language via triadic relations as at once suprasubjective and imperceptible *for the purpose* of communicating about some aspect or aspects of the objective world of the human animal, the human **Umwelt** (or 'Lebenswelt', as the human Umwelt is sometimes called to highlight its linguistic features absent from the Umwelt of animals without understanding in its difference from perception).

Thus 'language' is a phenomenon of anthroposemiosis, sharply in contrast with *animal communication* as a feature generically of zoosemiosis which, as such, does not require understanding (i.e. language in the root sense as a biologically underdetermined **modelling** system or Innenwelt). Precisely the confusion of '*language*' in the species-specifically human sense of *linguistic communication* with '*language*' in the sense of purely zoosemiotic communicative exchanges, vocal or visual, among animals, human or not, is at the root of the ill-conceived 'teaching language to apes' (or dolphins, etc.) experiments of the late twentieth century. Public funding of these experiments was effectively ended after Sebeok and Rosenthal's 1981 session of the New York Academy of Sciences.[3]

In terms of semiotics, Jacques Maritain best summarized the matter in his observation that all animals make use of signs but only human animals are able to know that there are signs (see Maritain 1956; Deely 1986 and 2002). The reason is that the being which constitutes any sensible object as a 'sign' is precisely, as **Poinsot** first and **Peirce** later pointed out, a triadic relation uniting three terms, of which we *call* a 'sign' that term in the foreground position of representing

The cultural dimension of the human Umwelt (as Lebenswelt, i.e. as transformed by linguistic communication, Lotman's 'secondary modelling system') thus becomes, in Sebeok's theory, a 'tertiary modelling system', establishing anthroposemiosis in its outward visible differences from zoosemiosis, this latter – zoosemiosis – creating an Umwelt *equally based on communication*, often vocal as well as visual, but never *linguistic* communication (see Sebeok, ed., 1963 and 1977; Sebeok and Ramsay, eds, 1969; Sebeok and Umiker-Sebeok 1981; Sebeok 1988a). This was a remarkable series of intellectual moves, having the net effect of demonstrating the centrality to semiotics of the late-nineteenth–early-twentieth-century developments centred at Tartu University, Estonia, first in von Uexküll's 'Umwelt-Forschung', then in Lotman's 'modelling system' strategy for organizing semiotic inquiry. These twin developments, stemming alike and not coincidentally from Tartu University as housing the de facto oldest centre of semiotic studies on today's earth, are synthesized by Sebeok as the foundation for the global development of anthroposemiotics in the twenty-first century.

[3] See also the numerous related books and articles in Sebeok's extensive bibliography (available through Deely, ed., 1995, and Umiker-Sebeok 2003), esp. perhaps Sebeok 1978, and Sebeok and Umiker-Sebeok 1981, *inter multa alia*.

another than itself to or for some third term only because it serves within the triadic relation constituting the 'proper being' of the sign (as sign) as the *vehicle of the conveyance* of the signified (whence Peirce suggested that we *call* it more properly a '**representamen**' or 'sign-vehicle'). Thus *all* signs, *strictly* speaking, consist in triadic relations, whereas what we commonly call 'signs' are rather sign-vehicles supporting and occupying a particular role under or 'within' that relation. But since relations as such cannot be sensed directly but only understood, and it is just this capacity for becoming aware of objectivities not directly instantiable as material objects accessible to sense that distinguishes human understanding, it follows that only human animals, over and above making use of signs, are able to know that there are signs.

The suprasubjectivity of triadic relations, thus, explains why objects signified need not exist in order to be signified and public as objects. For every object (in contradistinction to things which are what they are independently of being known) yet has the advantage of owing *its* being to the triadic relation which the object as object directly *terminates* suprasubjectively as significate, just as the sign as vehicle of that signification owes *its* being to the triadic relation, too, but by virtue of occupying *a different position under that relation* (namely, the foreground position of 'standing for another') than does either the significate or the interpretant. Whence nothing prevents what is an object from *also* being a thing, an independent physical reality, but nothing requires that, either. And of course, what occupies the position of sign-vehicle in one set of circumstances may well occupy the position of object under changed circumstances; and similarly for the third term of the triadic relation, the one to or for whom the sign as vehicle conveys the object as signified, which Peirce named the '**interpretant**' (insofar as it need not always be 'mental', i.e. a psychological state of some animal organism). What is interpretant one time can become sign-vehicle or object-signified at another time, in the unending 'spiral of semiosis' out of which experience is constituted and which lies at the core of the 'growth of **symbols**'.

In linguistic communication the vocal sounds (or visible **gestures** or marks) whereby we manifest our thoughts or opinions or deceptions to others, then, are but the vehicles employed by unique animals to convey significates which may or may not be things – 'unique' in that the animals in question are able to manipulate the sign-vehicles precisely as distinct from and independent of the 'realities' of the physical and social environments (the objective world or Umwelt) within which the sign-vehicles of linguistic communication are put into play. Being able to deal with relations as such in their imperceptible but suprasubjective being, and hence with objects in their being as terminus of relations in principle distinct from the being of things existing subjectively and even from the being of relations existing intersubjectively, is precisely what makes linguistic communication as an anthroposemiotic phenomenon distinct from generically zoosemiotic communications. Just as all animals make use of signs and sometimes with an intent to deceive, so also human animals, with one difference. Using a variant of Maritain's formula cited above, we can say that, while all animals make use of signs sometimes to deceive, only human animals are able to lie. For while to lie is to deceive, deception is not the same as lying, for *lying* presupposes an awareness of the difference between *objects as objects* and *objects as things*, combined with the deliberate intention to present what is not a thing as if it were.

Deception is a pure form of behaviour generically zoosemiosic; *lying* is a form of behaviour species-specifically anthroposemiosic, grounded in the distinctively human ability to manipulate relations in their pure suprasubjective being as relations – to objectify the terms of relations *as if* they were things (which they are only *sometimes*), something that is not possible within a **consciousness** that is tied wholly to objects as directly instantiable within sense perception. Thus lying, just as language in the sense of linguistic communication as species-specifically anthroposemiosic, is dependent upon a consciousness which is able to grasp signs in their proper being as triadic relations, and not merely in their being as vehicles of signification, 'representamens', as Peirce put it.

This process whereby the human animal becomes aware of signs, thus, while hardly 'metasemiotic' (an oxymoronic impossibility, as can be shown,[4] inasmuch as all of human understanding depends upon signs), is yet '*metasemiosic*', that is to say, semiosis become aware of itself. Human animals, in their unique capacity for understanding objects not directly reducible to or instantiable within sense perception, are thus best defined as *semiotic animals*. Like all animals, semiotic animals – human animals – interact through their bodies with the surrounding bodies of the environment in the having of sensations, which are then interpreted perceptually in terms of what in the surroundings is to be sought (+), what avoided (–), and what safely ignored (Ø), to constitute the animal's 'objective world' or Umwelt, human animals no less than other animals. But as capable of metasemiosis through grasping relations imperceptible as such, human animals add to their objective world a relation of *self-identity in the very objects* (the process has been spelled out in Deely 2007a), thus severing the exclusive link of object to organism in opening the way to investigate what these same objects are *even apart from* their +, –, Ø relations to us. Precisely this investigation extends the human control over its surroundings, but eventually reveals also the *interdependency of all life forms* upon communication, and the *dependency of some communications* upon semiosis.

Hence does the human animal, in becoming aware of signs, become through metasemiosis first a *semiotic* animal and then, with the growing awareness of interdependency that semiotics brings, also a *semioethic* animal – an animal aware of becoming *responsible*, like it or not, for the *consequences* of its actions. This responsibility is not just 'an individual matter' but is rather a species-specific

[4] And has been shown in detail (*ab esse ad posse valet illatio*): see 'Todorov's Howler', Section 14.3 in Deely 2009.

property or consequence of metasemiosis, of being a 'semiotic animal' in relation to the biosphere as itself a semiosic whole. Semiosis thus constitutes a total trajectory within the being and non-being alike of things, leading the human animal first to a species-specifically unique theoretical knowledge giving humans more and more control over things, and then leading further, by inevitable extension, to a species-specifically unique *practical* knowledge which yields more and more *responsibility* of human animals that goes beyond the merely human world to the whole of the natural world with which the human world is semiosically, inextricably, entangled.[5]

We are now in a position, perhaps, to appreciate why linguistic semiosis, while far from being the whole of semiosis or even wholly independent as a species of semiosis,[6] is nevertheless the principal tool whereby metasemiosis advances in developing our understanding of the omnipresent role of signs in human experience and our understanding of that larger universe of which we are but a part, albeit the part wherein signs become conscious of themselves and perfuse the universe insofar as the universe comes to be understood wherever and to whatever extent the universe does become understood.

Linguistic products semiotically handled thus become, not, as some linguists and Analytic philosophers would have it, a whole conceptualizable unto itself (see the criticisms of Analytic philosophy in Todorov 1977 and Deely 2006b), but *an interface*, a perceptually diaphanous network of not-necessarily-real relations intervening as such (i.e. as indifferent to being real or unreal in the constancy of their suprasubjectivity) between specifically human language users (semiotic animals) and the layered manifolds of experience – the universe 'perfused with signs' – they seek to understand (see Deely 1982: Part II, esp. as summarized in Tables III and IV, pp. 119 and 121, respectively). Experience cannot be reduced to language any more than objects can be reduced to things, but language stands out among the illimitably other systems of sign in being the one that comes closest to the coextensivity of communication with being that relations enable and portend. Hence the importance of this first point, 'the class of linguistic products', as we set out to manifest.

[5] Precisely this is the trajectory from semiotics to semioethics, which I have not space to go into here, beyond pointing out that it was not Kant but Thomas **Aquinas** who first described its nature (*c.* 1266: *Summa* q. 79 art. 11 *sed contra*). Because human understanding is not divided within itself, speculative understanding of what it engenders is also the responsibility for whatever we do about that which we come to understand. See Petrilli and Ponzio 2003; Petrilli 2004; Deely 2004, 2006a, 2008a; Deely *et al.* 2005; etc.

[6] This was the mistake made by Saussure in his original proposal that the doctrine of signs be treated 'semiologically', and in a different way by the Analytic philosophers with their attempt to make of language (rather than a system of signs among and dependent upon other systems of signs only beginning with zoosemiotic systems) an autonomous object of analysis. Consider Dummett's attempt (1973: 466) to define 'realism' in the terms of Analytic philosophy compatible at once with Kantian epistemology and the view of language as an autonomous system: 'The fundamental tenet of realism is that any sentence on which a fully specific sense has been conferred has a determinate truth-value independently of our actual capacity to decide what that truth-value is.'

'With no distinction between ontology and epistemology'

Let us turn to Rey's second point, that semiotic analysis in principle cuts below the distinction between epistemology and ontology. In this respect semiotics is not simply 'premodern' ('ancient' or 'medieval'). On the contrary, it is determinately and distinctively *postmodern*. Epistemology and ontology, but especially *epistemology*, is 'an offspring of philosophical modernity' in the most invidious sense, to wit, the sense in which philosophical modernity goes the Kantian route of severing '*things*' (what exists *often* prior to, but *always* independently of, our mental representations, whether self-representations or other-representations[7]) from '*knowability*'.

Claus Emmeche famously observed (1994: 126) that 'we now view sign phenomena as occurring everywhere in nature, including those domains where humans have never set foot'. Well, where humans 'have never set foot' there are indeed phenomena, including semiosic phenomena, but there is neither epistemology nor ontology, for these belong to that subclass of phenomena which presuppose rather than antecede the human mind. Emmeche at the time was thinking of biosemiotics; but the 'domains where humans have never set foot' extend well beyond the realm of biosemiosis, reaching outward to the stars, backward to the beginnings of the universe, and forwards to the end of the present universe. We cannot take up here the questions of phytosemiosis and, even more broadly, physiosemiosis; but we can at least get clear about the meaning of 'realism'.

'Realism'

Realism became in modernity above all a state of mind, one in which its possessor is convinced that 'the way things are' is the way he or she *thinks* things are.[8] If the 'realist' is a Kantian, therefore, paradoxically, he or she is supremely confident that 'the way things are' is as *unknowable*. And the Kantian – following, after all, Kant himself with his 'only possible proof' of a world external to our realm of representations (Kant 1787: Preface 34–35, text 245ff.) – has no alternative to offer to solipsism, the world of 'monads without windows', of a human consciousness where nothing enters from without or exits from within. The Kantian has embraced a synthesis of Rationalism and Empiricism made on the basis of the *assumption common to Descartes as the founder of Rationalism and Locke as the founder of Empiricism*, to wit, the assumption that our mind

[7] And it makes a great difference which, as Poinsot may well have been first systematically to point out, inasmuch as we confront in this distinction the whole difference between sign as manifesting an object and object as presupposing sign: see Poinsot 1632: *Tractatus de Signis*, Book I, Question 1, 116/14–117/17.

[8] Hence the joke derived from Peter Gay (1966: 27) that a 'realist' is one who detects error by finding opinions differing from his or her own: see Deely 2001a: 741, n. 9. All this amounts to an incognizant conflation of philosophy with logic.

has no direct access to anything other than mental representations formed by its own activity in response to stimuli as such unknowable precisely because not formed by our own mind.[9]

Realism did not start out as a state of mind before all else, nor, with the advent of semiotics, can it so remain. But let us trace the main outline. As a philosophical doctrine, 'realism' bespeaks the claim that the human animal is capable of coming to know the structures of being as they obtain independently of our knowledge – in short, that it is possible for the human animal to reach a knowledge of 'things in themselves'.

In ancient Greek thought, 'realism' found its most startling expression in the doctrine of Plato that universal ideas exist not as psychological states (the modern meaning of 'ideas') but as finite-mind-independent *exemplars* of everything particular which can be seen or touched falling short of universality. Thus Plato – in this he had predecessors, to be sure, but none his equal – distinguished 'reality' as knowable only to intellect from 'appearances' as anything accessible to sensation or perception. Much later in the Latin Age theologians would identify Plato's Ideas with the divine exemplars used by God in the creation of the world, a construction which fitted well with the view prevalent in both Greek and Latin times that the 'essences' of things are unchanging, that only individuals come and go, not species.

Aristotle rejected **Plato**'s view, insisting that the world of sensible, material objects is itself a *part* and not a mere *shadow* of 'reality'. He developed the view that universals as universals exist only as intellectual concepts in the human mind, but precisely as normally applicable to individuals existing in the world of material and sensible things objectified in perception and understanding. In the Latin Age Aquinas took up the line of thinking Aristotle opposed to Platonism and gave it more precise form, holding that the intellect abstracts from particulars commonalities and sometimes essential commonalities. These abstractions become in the intellect concepts providing the basis or ground for relations to the numerous particulars existing in the physical environment terminating, as embodying in particular ways, the very commonalities that within the animal mind found the suprasubjective relations of apprehension. Hence the famous Latin definition of the universal as '*id quod natum est praedicari de*

[9] No one is scandalized by anything they remain unaware of. It was not Hume's denial of realism that scandalized Kant, it was his denial of the causal necessities upon which science relies. Like Locke before him, Kant quite missed the point that would open the way to the doctrine of signs, while continuing to insist that the fork in the road to take was the one leading nowhere. The 'turn to the senses' with Locke is now followed by the 'transcendental turn' with Kant, to be followed by the 'linguistic turn' with Rorty (after Wittgenstein) – all leading to the same destination: a self locked alone in a casket of consciousness, a bubble in time whose only way out is to burst. The modern situation in philosophy may be compared to a game of baseball: with the work of Descartes as 'home plate', Locke sets up first base with the 'turn to ideas of sensation'; Kant makes it to second base with the 'transcendental turn'; and Wittgenstein to third base with the 'linguistic turn'. Players who go to bat in the game may strike out, or get as far as first, second or third; but even if they hit a home run and round all the bases, they still wind up where they began.

pluribus' – that which is born in the mind to make possible **discourse** about the many things to which as termini a given concept supports a relation.

In this way the medievals distinguished Platonic realism as 'extreme', Aristotelian realism as 'moderate'. Opposed to both these 'realisms' was **nominalism**, the view that there exist apart from concepts only particulars, so that words which convey more than particularity are empty noises, 'vocal farts', in the crude expression (*flatus vocis*) of medieval thinkers, signifying nothing real. Later on in the Latin Age some attempted to distinguish nominalism as just described from *conceptualism* as the view that words conveying more than particularity are sign-vehicles only for thoughts, not for things. Peirce rightly dismissed this distinction between nominalism and conceptualism as 'but another example of that loose and slapdash style of thinking' that made nominalism possible in the first place, 'conceptualism' being 'itself an example in the very matter to which nominalism relates' (Peirce 1909: *CP* 1.27). For it turns out that the chasm between realism of any variety and nominalism of every variety is determined by the affirmation (realism) or denial (nominalism) of *relation* as a mode of being obtaining not merely in comparisons made within thought but also in the physical world as a connection *between* the subjectivities of individual existents ('substances' in Aristotle's sense, 'monads' in Leibniz's sense – but now endowed with windows, i.e. in the eventuality of relations being 'real' as belonging to the order of mind-independent being as well as to the order of mind-dependent being).

The ancient Greek and medieval Latin debates took a crucial turn in the work of Aquinas, with his attempt to identify what distinguishes human understanding from the sense perception generically common to higher animals. When Aristotle spoke of 'reality' he seems to have meant precisely what exists in relation to us, yes, but exists more fundamentally independently of any relations to us – the physical environment of rocks and plants and animals and stars, etc. This reality he labelled το ον or 'being', and it is what the Latins would call *ens reale*, mind-independent being.

But in Aquinas the *first meaning* of 'being', rather, is as the name identifying the distinctive object of understanding in its difference from perception; and *this* notion of 'being' emphatically does not reduce to το ον as *ens reale*. We noted above that, in classifying objects of perception as +, –, Ø, the animal has an awareness which includes things of the physical environment but always as wrapped in relations created by the animal's own awareness or 'mind' and expressive precisely of the animal's *interest in* these 'objects of sense'. The human animal, however, able to manipulate relations in their difference from related things, adds to the objective world (the Umwelt) of the brute animal the mind-dependent relation of objects-as-identical-with-themselves. This unique feature of anthroposemiosis thereby severs the exclusive link of perceived objects to the interests of the animal, thus enabling those very same objects of perceptual awareness to appear not only as something to be sought, avoided or safely ignored, but further as *things in their own right* apart from the question of the animal's interest. The objects of animal perception *seen in this uniquely anthroposemiotic light* Aquinas labels *ens primum cognitum*, 'being as the distinctive object of intellectual apprehension'.

In the course of experience, Aquinas goes on to say, the human animal is forced to introduce into this notion of being as the first of intellectual conceptions the first of intellectual distinctions, namely, recognition within objects experienced of the difference between aspects which reduce to human experience of them (such as the being of state officials) and aspects which do not so reduce (such as the being of biological organisms). The aspects which *do not* reduce to our experience of them Aquinas terms *ens reale*; the aspects which *do* reduce to our experience of them he terms *non ens*, alternatively *ens rationis*. Precisely here, with this notion of *ens primum cognitum* as including *non ens*, do we encounter the difference between 'reality' as *hardcore* and 'reality' as *socially constructed*. Notice, in particular, that *non ens* and *ens reale* are *equally objective*. It was a great mistake of the late-modern Thomistic revival ('Neothomism') to conceive of *ens rationis* as psychological subjectivity, *ens reale* as the 'external world' of modern philosophy. (Even Peirce fell into this misinterpretation.)

Consider the difference between a cloud and a flag. Both have a dimension of *ens reale*, indeed, but the cloud has a relation to rain that is itself in the order of *ens reale*, i.e. it would survive the demise of all humans, whereas the flag has a relation to country that could not survive the demise of all humans. So the objects of sense perception as common to higher animals are *always public in principle* (at least within the species aware of them) but never pure *ens reale*. These objects always involve whatever is necessary of *non ens*, *ens rationis*, of 'purely objective reality', to enable the animal to evaluate those objects in relation to its own interests. When human understanding adds to these same objects the relation of self-identity ('every being is what it is') it sees them as objects which are also things with their own identity, where the brute animal sees only objects in relation to itself. But the human animal then further learns that 'things' are not always what appears: for 'things' strictly are what they are *whether or not* cognized, but the 'things' of animal experience are not simply what they are whether or not cognized but are rather a *mixture* of *ens reale* with *non ens* – that is to say, a mixture of what does and what does not reduce to our perception of them.

Both aspects of objectivity, the *ens reale* aspects and the *ens rationis* aspects (*non ens* comparatively to the order of *ens reale*, but public and objective no less than are the *ens reale* aspects of objects), are equally located within the Umwelt, the public and objective world of the animal. But the *non ens* features (such as the being of a senator, the boundary of a civil state, etc.) are *purely* objective, whereas the *ens reale* features are subjective (i.e. physically existent) *as well as* objective. The *non ens* features are not subjective, they are not psychological. The Innenwelt is comprised of psychological states, yes, both cognitive (concepts) and cathectic (emotions); but not the Umwelt. The Umwelt is objective through and through, because the Umwelt comprises the *termination* of the relations suprasubjectively *founded* on the psychological states of the Innenwelt, the animal modelling system. When this modelling system contains a biologically underdetermined element, as in the case of the human animal, then the Umwelt is not only a *public* world respecting animals of the same or sufficiently overlapping species, the Umwelt becomes also *open* to the infinite. For in becoming aware (thanks to the addition to objects of the mind-dependent relation of self-identity) of the difference between objects as such and objects as things, and in being able to separate apprehensively relations as such (always suprasubjective, only sometimes intersubjective) and related things, the human animal is able to become aware of the action of signs suprasubjectively uniting within triadic relations both *ens rationis* and *non ens*. *Ens reale* pertains to objects which have a subjective being sustained within a network of intersubjective relations; *ens reale* pertains to objects lacking their own subjectivity yet attached within awareness to the subjectivity of other objects and sustained no less suprasubjectively and in a public way by the relations – the semiotic web – that we call 'experience' wherein the two orders are intertwined in the constitution of integral objectivity, the Umwelt as a whole.

We see thus how semiosis forms a path 'leading everywhere in nature', even where nothing exists independently of finite mind! But semiosis seen in this light stands in sharp contrast to the mainstream modern view of knowledge as 'epistemology' developed under the rubric of 'critical philosophy' in and after Kant down to the establishment of late-modern Analytic philosophy as the dying breath of the modern era of intellectual culture.

'Ontology' and 'epistemology'

Perhaps no two terms better capture the mainstream modern development of philosophy than these two terms, 'ontology' and 'epistemology', though especially the latter. The term 'epistemology' traces back to a coinage by Louis Ferrier (Ferrier 1854: 48)[10] to name 'the theory or science of the method or grounds of knowledge'. 'Ontology', by contrast, is also a modern term, though early modern, dating back at least to Gideon Harvey (1663: I. II. i. 18), where it is proposed as 'the most proper designation' for what Aristotle called 'First Philosophy' and the Latins termed 'Metaphysics', to wit, 'the science or study of being; that branch of metaphysics concerned with the nature or essence of being or existence'.

So the trap was laid. Philosophy had always concerned itself with knowing *being*, but *knowing* is presupposed to *knowing being*. So ontology perforce presupposes epistemology. But when we study epistemology in the modern context, what we discover is that there can be no ontology properly speaking, for there is

[10] The *Oxford English Dictionary* (2nd edn, 1989) traces the term to Ferrier, but gives the date as 1856. I have followed rather Owens 1992: 25, n. 1.

no way that the mind can bridge the gap between *phenomena* as the appearances the mind constructs for itself under the stimulus of something behind and beyond the appearances which the mind has no way whatever to reach.

The conclusion is unacceptable to common sense, but so much the worse for common sense. There is not a one of the moderns who did not resist the conclusion that the mind wholly makes whatever it is that the mind can directly know; nor is there a one of the moderns who, working logically from the modern assumption that it is self-representations made by the mind that constitute the appearances comprising the human Umwelt, could avoid the conclusion. Late in the game, referring to the 1956 article by Hudson purporting to show 'Why we cannot witness or observe what goes on "in our heads"', Russell commented (1959: 26) that 'What I maintain is that we *can* witness or observe what goes on in our heads, and that we cannot witness or observe anything else at all', adding later wistfully that 'those – and I fear they are the majority – in whom the human affections are stronger than the desire for logical economy, will, no doubt, not share my desire to render solipsism scientifically satisfactory' (1959: 105; this is later in the book cited, but is a quotation from an earlier paper of 1914).

Kant was surely the first in philosophy's long history, having delivered his 'only possible proof of the external world', to think that he could claim the title of 'realism' for the view that the world of being as it is in itself is unknowable! But having made the claim, he was not to want for followers. After all, if 'realism' is the claim to know 'the way things are', and 'the way things are' is *unknowable*, then it could be argued, as Coleridge put it in 1817 (Coleridge 1817: 127), that the modern mainstream view that epistemology shows the limits of human knowledge to be contained within its own self-representations, or the truth of idealism, *is* realism: 'It is only so far idealism, as it is at the same time, and on that very account, the truest and most binding realism.'

Lalande summarized the modern mainstream development on this score by observing that 'Idealism stands in opposition to ontological realism or, in a single word, to ontology' (Lalande 1947: 422 ['L'idéalisme s'oppose ainsi au réalisme ontologique, ou en un seul mot à l'ontologie']), and culminates in 'the epistemological paradox', to wit, that science 'cannot attain a complete explication of its object without making its object to vanish' [la science 'ne saurait atteindre à l'explication complète sans faire évanouir son objet'].

'Realism' as more than a state of mind and more than a return to premodern views

The reduction of realism to a state of mind, and the epistemological paradox that follows upon that reduction, is precisely what defined philosophy in its distinctive modern mainstream development. Prior to the modern 'turn to the subject', in the psychological sense of subjectivity, 'realism' was the doctrine that things as they are in themselves are knowable if investigated properly, with the further qualification, after Aristotle, that these 'knowable things' constitute the material objects of our surroundings as well as whatever their existence can be shown to implicate. In this Aristotelian line of development – and after all that line spans nearly the whole of ancient Greek philosophy as well as the last six centuries of the medieval or Latin Age – 'realism' meant the capacity of the human mind to come to know the structures of being which obtain independently of our consideration of them.

Aristotle, as we saw, simply called the fulfilment of this human cognitive capacity το ον; but the Latins distinguished it from *ens rationis* and called it rather *ens reale*. This was the knowledge at which the Scholastics aimed, and so did the early moderns (cf. Deely 1982), but with rather different methods, quite successful in the line of ideoscopic science after Galileo, quite disastrous in the line of cœnoscopic science after Descartes (see Deely 2001a: Chs 11–13; 2008). In fact, so complete was the debacle on the side of the modern mainstream philosophical development, that what Aristotle called το ον and the Latins distinguished as *ens reale* Kant placed 'under erasure', where it remained right down to Derrida and Foucault among us.

Bringing *ens reale* out from under erasure was the principal – almost the sole – objective of the Neothomist movement over the late nineteenth and twentieth centuries, which was not without its successes. Peirce considered 'Scholastic realism' as a recovery of the Latin Age to be *essential* to but *not sufficient* for the doctrine of signs or semiotics, for the very good reason that much of the everyday reality of semiotic animals does not fit with that hardcore definition of 'reality'. Much, very much indeed, of the actual realities with which we deal, from governments to school requirements, are not at all hardwired into the physical universe but are very much social constructs, public and obligatory, indeed, but socially constructed nonetheless.

Now all animals are realists in just the sense that Kant ruled humans could not be, because Kant failed to distinguish sensation prescissively considered (as reducible to a Secondness within genuine Thirdness) from perception as an interpretive act with the irreducible character of Thirdness. So humans, too, are 'realists', just because they are *animals* and have to eat and find shelter.

But being a realist in practice and being a realist in theory are not the same; and many are the individuals who live their lives in deviance from the way they think they should. So it is not enough that a thinker should *want* or *strongly desire* to be a 'realist' in philosophy. For that, he or she has to show in the first place *how a theoretical access to* ens reale *is possible.*

But even that prerequisite is not enough for semiotics, or for a postmodern epoch in philosophy. To settle for that would be to fall into the Neothomist fallacy that the highest achievements of philosophy lie simply in the past. For just as signs transcend the distinction between *ens reale* and *ens rationis*, so do they transcend the distinction between the theoretical and the practical. Semiosis, in short, at its highest point as 'metasemiosis' (in those animals able to become aware of the being of signs as irreducibly triadic, necessarily suprasubjective relations), deals preoccupatively neither with *ens reale* objectified nor with *ens rationis* objectified, but extensively with what we saw Aquinas pinpoint above as *ens primum cognitum*: being prior to, or rather, as inclusive of, all distinctions within and beyond things subjectively and intersubjectively constituting the physical world, the 'environment' of natural being. So, beyond any showing of how theoretical access to *ens reale* is possible, we need further a showing of how 'realities' socially constructed ('*non ens*') are yet public and non-psychological.

Semiotics, as the knowledge developed on the basis of awareness of the action of signs, distinguishes itself within the history of philosophy by being the first theory able to come to terms with the public existence of objects even when the objects in question turn out sometimes not to exist anywhere else at all than in the Umwelt – the Lebenswelt – of semiotic animals. That is why, as **Eco** famously said, semiotics is the study of everything that can be used to lie. But what turns out surprisingly is that lying and succeeding sometimes to tell the truth both depend on exactly the same processes of semiosis that semiotics takes as its subject matter! Semiotics achieves at the philosophical level, or cœnoscopically, exactly that transcendence of traditional speculative and practical philosophy that Aquinas was able to achieve in the middle ages only by founding a 'new science' (then new) of 'theology' as *sacra doctrina* (see Deely 2001a: 259–261, esp. 261, n. 28). But of course, unlike theology, semiotics does not require a sectarian religious commitment to determine its basic standpoint.[11] Semiotics recovers the 'Scholastic realism' of the Latins, but it does not (like Neothomism) simply *go back* to that achievement. On the contrary, semiotics goes forward, beyond modernity, with the theoretical ability in place to explain *both* hardcore *and* socially constructed 'reality' as a public phenomenon always suprasubjective (even though only sometimes intersubjective) because of the difference in principle (though only sometimes in fact) between *objects* as terminus of relations and *things* as normally independent of being in relation to a finite consciousness.

So 'realism', in philosophy, has usually meant the theoretical ability of thought to attain to a knowledge of *ens reale*. But, in semiotics, realism has a broader sense. Semiotic realism embraces our ability to know not only such 'hardcore realities' as the movement of the earth around the sun, objective appearances to the contrary notwithstanding (an achievement which presupposes the distinction within human understanding of things from objects), but also to construct such social realities as the border between Texas and Oklahoma or between Canada and the United States, or the Royal Family of England, the 'European Union', etc.

'Reality' as a semiotic phenomenon

In other words, 'semiotic reality' is not a fixed but a shifting boundary, and semiosis is precisely the reason why socially constructed realities are possible and

[11] In a later work (Deely 2003a: 100–112), I developed this point at some length, but considerable work remains to be done, for this is a point that goes right to the heart of semiotics, and explains its necessary further development as semioethics.

natural realities are knowable. Thus semiotics is considerably different from, say (as we noted above), twentieth-century Neothomism, which thought that it would be enough to vindicate realism to go back to the medieval account of knowledge as notably found in the work of Thomas Aquinas or Duns **Scotus**. Like the late-modern 'new scholasticisms', semiotics recovers Scholastic realism; but, unlike those retrospective developments, that recovery is not a final destination but only 'a midmost target', like epistemology itself in the modern sense – or ontology, for that matter. Semiotics establishes a framework for human knowledge that is not *ad hoc* but is *inherently* interdisciplinary and transdisciplinary. The reason is that by the action of signs human understanding establishes disciplinary boundaries in the first place, and by that same action understanding sees also how to *cross* those boundaries, redrawing them when necessary as knowledge advances, and realizing at every step that experience is a web of sign relations, and finite knowledge at every point is dependent upon that web.

But semiosis, note carefully, is far from confined to the sphere of human understanding. Indeed semiosis both makes possible in the first place and sustains that sphere by involving it, enmeshing it, in a tangle of triadic relations both genuine and degenerate which bids fair to explain how *the future* influences the present and rearranges the relevance of the past to such a degree that there is reason to think that semiosis may prove to be the proper name for what has heretofore more confusedly been called rather the general process of 'evolution', the process whereby the universe has passed from a lifeless state to one capable of sustaining life, and from one capable of sustaining life to one wherein semiosis has managed to become aware of itself in creating responsibilities for life on the part of semiotic animals. The story has only begun.

Further reading

Deely, J. (2002) *What Distinguishes Human Understanding?*, South Bend, IN: St Augustine's Press.

Deely, J. (2008) *Descartes and Poinsot. The Crossroad of Signs and Ideas*, Scranton, PA: University of Scranton Press.

Maritain, J. (1986) 'Language and the theory of the sign', in J. Deely, B. Williams and F. Kruse (eds), *Frontiers in Semiotics*, Bloomington, IN: Indiana University Press.

Petrilli, S. and Ponzio, A. (2003) *Semioetica*, Rome: Meltemi.

Todorov, T. (1977) 'The birth of occidental semiotics', in R.W. Bailey, L. Matejka and P. Steiner (eds), *The Sign*, Ann Arbor, MI: Michigan Slavic Publications.

6

PEIRCE, PHENOMENOLOGY AND SEMIOTICS

NATHAN HOUSER

Semiotics (or semeiotics) is a field of research that began in earnest with the innovative thought of Charles Sanders **Peirce** but that only began to be explored within mainstream disciplines in the late 1930s (for the history of **sign** theory and precursors to Peirce's semiotics see Deely 2001a). At the opening of the twentieth century, Josiah Royce at Harvard, and a few philosophers in Europe, gave some attention to Peirce's theory of signs, but it was in the 1930s and 40s that the Unity of Science philosophers, largely at the urging of Charles **Morris**, recognized the importance of the systematic study of signs and of sign relations and, through Morris's influence on Carnap, incorporated a limited form of Peirce's tripartite science into philosophy with their famous trilogy: syntactics, **semantics** and **pragmatics**. But semiotics, as a complete science, soon became marginalized and largely abandoned by philosophy and it survived by finding refuge in linguistics and in the interdisciplinary research programme founded by Morris's student, Thomas A. **Sebeok**. During the last generation, with the weakening of the hegemony of Analytic philosophy, semiotics has shown evidence of returning to philosophy and other established disciplines; this is especially true in Europe and South America. It remains to be seen if semiotics will survive as an interdisciplinary field of research as Sebeok believed it should be, or if it will evolve into a discipline in its own right, as seems to be happening with informatics, or if it will devolve into a variety of discipline-specific programmes.

Charles Peirce was among the most informed logicians of his time, with respect to history as well as theory and technique, and there have been few logicians from any time who have surpassed him. Peirce was convinced that the mission of logic ought to be the study of representation, inference and argument, and that it should make classifications and establish norms within these areas. Logic should not be supposed to be the foundation for mathematics but, on the contrary, a beneficiary of mathematics insofar as it borrows from mathematics its formal structures and relational models. Logic, Peirce claimed, is the science of representation, broadly speaking, a normative science co-extensive with formal semiotics. Technically speaking, the subjects for logical analysis are signs and sign-operations. One of the principal realms of sign activity, or **semiosis** (semeiosis), is human thought; but semiosis prevails wherever there is life and there is some reason to believe that even the laws of nature are semiotic products. Peirce is well known for his claim that all thought is in signs and that minds should be regarded as systems of signs. Thus logic in Peirce's broad sense, as semiotics, may provide the best framework for the philosophy of mind, the philosophy of **language** and **communication**, and for the theory of information processing at all levels.

In the spirit of the pre-Socratic philosophers, Peirce sought to understand the universe both broadly and deeply – 'philosophy seeks to explain the universe at large, and to show what there is intelligible or reasonable in it' (*CP* 4.375) – and his evolutionary thinking led him even to question the process by which the universe developed out of the 'original' chaos, under the increasing constraints of evolving laws, toward a rational system growing ever less arbitrary. Peirce speculated that the three elements active in the world are chance, law and **habit**-taking, and he came to associate these three elements with his famous categories: *firstness*, *secondness* and *thirdness*. At the basic level, *firstness* is that which is as it is independently of anything else, *secondness* is that which is as it is in relation to something else, and *thirdness* is that which is as it is as mediate between two others. Peirce regarded these categories as complete and ubiquitous; they provided a useful structure for approaching every discipline or field of study, though in a cascade of forms.

As this suggests, Peirce was a systematic philosopher in the style of some of the great architectonic thinkers that dominate the family tree of philosophy, in particular **Aristotle**, **Kant** and **Hegel**. He believed, with August Comte, that it was possible to classify the vast array of sciences and areas of study by reference to relations of theory dependence that systematically separate them. Peirce had studied the principles of classification under the great naturalist Louis Agassiz, and he approached the problem of classifying the sciences as a scientific problem in its own right.

But Peirce was also a devoted pragmatist, the first to develop and promote pragmatism as an alternative to the Cartesian 'platform' for philosophy, and he was thoroughly anti-foundationalist in his epistemology. Although he believed that it was unlikely that the vast edifice of human knowledge, however fallible and intertwined, was not layered or structured in some principled way that could be uncovered by assiduous probing, he was thoroughly opposed to the view that there was a logical structure to it that could enable one to deductively justify substantive claims made in one discipline by appeal to principles from a grounding discipline. Peirce was a thoroughgoing evolutionist who emphasized growth and process and who rejected absolutism of all sorts: 'There is no conceivable fulfillment of any rational life except progress towards further fulfillment' (*CN* 3: 124).

Over the course of his more than fifty productive years, Peirce worked out a number of different classifications, but in his mature classification we find that mathematics is the most fundamental science, the only science independent of all others, and that following mathematics comes philosophy which is divided into three branches: (in order of dependency) **phenomenology**, normative science and metaphysics. Peirce's categories make their appearance in each of these parts of philosophy. In attending to the universal elements of phenomena in their immediate phenomenal character, phenomenology treats of phenomena in their firstness. Here the categories appear as fundamental categories of experience (or **consciousness**). In attending to the laws of the relation of phenomena to ends, normative science treats of phenomena in their secondness. The three normative sciences – aesthetics, **ethics**, logic (semiotics) – were associated with three kinds of goodness: aesthetical goodness (aesthetics considers 'those things whose ends are to embody qualities of feeling'), ethical goodness (ethics considers 'those things whose ends lie in action') and logical goodness (logic considers 'those things whose end is to represent something'). The three normative sciences are followed by metaphysics, the third and last branch of philosophy. The general task of metaphysics is 'to study the most general features of reality and real **objects**'. In attempting to comprehend the reality of phenomena, that is, in treating of phenomena as representing something that is inherently mind-independent, metaphysics treats of phenomena in their thirdness. After philosophy come the special sciences, physics and psychics, and these are followed by the sciences of review and the practical sciences. Logic (semiotics), we find, is the third of the three normative sciences (in order of dependency), preceded by aesthetics and ethics (Houser and Kloesel 1992).

Peirce's semiotics is a general and formal theory of signs. It is general in the sense that it applies to any kind of sign. It is formal in the same sense that cognitive science is formal; its subject is signs and sign activity whether in humans, or animals, or machines, or anything else. Peirce's semiotics is a normative, not a descriptive, science (this distinguishes it from the mainstream of **Saussure**an semiology). As far as Peirce's theory goes, it is not relevant to ask what sort of thing may instantiate the sign activity in question. In practice, however, Peirce does generally relate his sign analyses to actual sign user types, usually (but not always) persons. Semiotics divides into three branches. The first, speculative grammar, deals with signs as such, focusing on the necessary and sufficient conditions for signhood or, as Peirce says, what is requisite for representation of any kind. Speculative grammar deals mainly with syntax. The second branch, often simply called critic, deals with the relations of signs to the objects that they represent. The focus of critic is on semantic questions. The third branch of Peirce's semiotics is speculative **rhetoric**, which deals with the relations of signs to their users (or to the effects of the signs). The focus of this branch is on the pragmatic and rhetorical aspects of semiosis.

This division of labour in logic, or semiotics, is obviously related to Peirce's triadic theory of representation in which any sign is said to be in a triadic relation with an object and an interpretant. The first division focuses on the sign as such. The second division, building on the results of the first, focuses the reference of signs to objects. The third division, building on the results of the two preceding divisions, focuses on the interpretation of signs or on the effects of signs on interpreters. There is an interesting resemblance between these divisions of semiotics and the Morris–Carnap triad: syntax, semantics and pragmatics – but there are also important differences.

In Peirce's view, every sign is in a special kind of triadic relation with the object that it represents and with what he calls its '**interpretant**', the effect the sign has on its user or interpreter. Every interpretant is related to its object through the mediation of a sign: thus, Peirce's denial of intuition. Intuition, for Peirce, technically speaking, involves a direct dyadic relation between an interpretant and its object; somehow we just know something about an object (a person, a state of affairs, whatever) without the intervention of a sign. According to Peirce, we can have direct dyadic experience of external objects but not *intellectual* experience; we cannot *know* directly. Intellectual experience is always triadic – sign mediated. There is one sense in which Peirce's semiotic theory provides the benefits generally supposed to depend on intuition. Our powers of **abduction**, given our attunement to nature through centuries of evolutionary development and selection, endow us with a natural inclination for guessing correctly – for forming true hypotheses, at least when vital concerns are at issue. But this Peircean 'intuition' is semiotic through and through; it bears the Peircean sign of the three. The semiotic triad (object–sign–interpretant) belongs to the category Peirce calls 'thirdness' and is what, in his view, constitutes mind; signs are the medium for thought or, as he says, all thought is in signs. We can summarize Peirce's position by saying that minds are *sign systems* and that thought is *sign action*.

It is difficult to form a working conception of Peirce's semiotics without going a bit deeper into the first branch of semiotics where sign structures and types are elaborated. Bearing in mind that anything can be a sign as long as it mediates between its object and an interpretant, we can make some useful distinctions by considering a sign's ground (its nature in itself), how the sign relates to its object, and how the sign is represented in its interpretant. In themselves, signs may be either qualities, facts or laws (or conventions). Accordingly, signs may be identified, in this respect, as qualisigns, sinsigns or legisigns. A sign may relate to its object by virtue of similarity – by sharing the qualitative features it represents its object to have. Or a sign might connect with its object as a matter of fact by being in a causal relation with its object (as when lightning signifies impending thunder or when an object is signified by pointing at it). Or a sign might connect with its object by an agreement or through practice (as when words are used to signify their objects). Accordingly, signs may be identified, in this respect, as **icon**s, indices or **symbol**s. Finally, signs might be represented in their interpretants as signs of possibility (a term, for example), as signs of fact (a proposition) or as signs of reason (an argument, where the premises signify the conclusion as following logically). Accordingly, signs may be identified, in this respect, as rhemes, as dicent signs or as arguments. These three trichotomies can be usefully represented in Table 6.1. Since every sign will fit into one of the alternatives for each of the three trichotomies, we can use these distinctions to isolate different classes of signs.

Perhaps it is evident that Peirce's categories inform all of these triadic divisions; that the rows descend from firstness to thirdness and the columns move right from firstness to thirdness. Bearing in mind that higher categories

Table 6.1 Threefold division of signs

The sign's ground (the nature of the sign in itself)	QUALISIGN	SINSIGN	LEGISIGN
The sign's relation to its object	ICON	INDEX	SYMBOL
How the sign is represented in its interpretant	RHEME	DICENT	ARGUMENT

can involve components from lower categories, but not vice versa, we can use Table 6.1 to work up a list of ten classes of signs. For example, a sign which in itself is a quality, say the colour red, is a qualisign occupying the place of firstness within the first trichotomy and, as a firstness, it cannot be related to an object except at the level of firstness; nor can it be represented in its interpretant except as a sign of firstness. Thus the colour red, as a sign, must belong to the class of rhematic, iconic, qualisigns. We will adhere to Peirce's constraints on how to identify sign classes if we move straight up the table or to the right, remembering that each class will only occupy one place in each trichotomy. Following out this method we can easily identify these ten classes (I include examples, though with the caveat that some may be disputable):

1	rhematic iconic qualisigns	(a paint chip as a sign of its colour)
2	rhematic iconic sinsigns	(a happy face with reference to a given happening)
3	rhematic iconic legisigns	('English' as a sign of a word written in English)
4	rhematic indexical sinsigns	('Watch out!' as a sign of present danger)
5	rhematic indexical legisigns	(proper names, at least in their baptismal use)
6	rhematic symbolic legisigns	(ordinary words by themselves)
7	dicent indexical sinsigns	(a weathervane in standard use)
8	dicent indexical legisigns	('the winner' referring to winner of a specific competition)
9	dicent symbolic legisigns	(a declarative proposition: 'The cat is on the mat.')
10	argumentive symbolic legisigns	(the sentence: 'Socrates, in being a man, is mortal.')

This classification of signs is based on Peirce's least complex rendering of the fundamental sign relation as a triadic relation between an object, sign and interpretant. In his late work on semiotics, Peirce analysed the sign relation more deeply and developed a more complex account of signs as a relation involving two kinds of objects, one immediate (the object as the sign represents it) and one dynamic (the external object that determines the sign), and three kinds of interpretants, one immediate (the interpretant as represented by the sign), one dynamic (the actual effect produced by the sign) and a final interpretant (the habit that exhausts the function of the sign). This more complex account of the sign yields ten divisions (trichotomies) and sixty-six classes (Peirce Edition Project 1998: 483–491). One of the most difficult problems in Peirce's theory of signs is to work out an adequate account of his two objects and three interpretants and his expanded classification of signs. Perhaps in our present state of understanding of language and of semiosis there is no need for such complexity but when sixty-six classes of signs can be distinguished, albeit with much difficulty, it is clear that a far less specific classification must create ambiguities (see Houser 1992).

Scholars who treat Peirce's theory of signs often appeal to underlying mathematical models and relational structures to illustrate and explain the semiotic structures and relations that provide the basis for Peirce's semiotics. This is reasonable because mathematics is the least dependent of the sciences, according to Peirce's classification, and the less independent sciences naturally will appeal to mathematics for general principles. But, as pointed out above, it is phenomenology (or 'phaneroscopy', as Peirce came to prefer) that comes next in the order of principal dependency after mathematics. Then comes the normative sciences, first aesthetics, then ethics, and only then semiotics. So a complete study of the structures, relations and principles that inform semiotics would require separate studies of each of these intermediate sciences and a consideration of what semiotics incorporates from each one.

Phenomenology, especially, must take its place beside mathematics as a supporting science for Peirce's semiotics. Almost from the beginning of his career, Peirce held that, 'whenever we think, we have present to the consciousness some feeling, image, conception, or other representation, which serves as a sign' (Houser and Kloesel 1992: 38). Here Peirce turned from the standard account of thinking as some kind of awareness of ideas in the mind, what Quine called 'the idea idea' (Quine 1961: 48), to an externalist view of thinking as semiosis where every thought (sign) is 'directed' toward its object. This view is similar to that of Franz Brentano, who held that mental phenomena always exhibit intentionality or directedness toward an object (Brentano 1874). This may be said to be a semiotic turn anticipatory of the later and much heralded linguistic turn. It was this line of thinking that led Peirce to his view that we can only know ourselves as objects of signs and, further, that persons in their fundamental natures are indeed signs (Houser and Kloesel 1992: Chs 2 and 3).

In his early treatment of semiotics, Peirce focused mainly on what he would later call 'intellectual signs', linguistic signs traditionally divided into terms, propositions and arguments. This focus encouraged Peirce to look to mathematics for logical structures and relations more than to phenomenology. But as Peirce extended his treatment of semiotics to cover a more comprehensive account of experience, in particular what he would call the universe of feeling, phenomenology took a more dominant place in his account. By 1892, when he wrote 'Man's Glassy Essence' for *The Monist*, Peirce had come to regard the substrate of feeling as basic for the formation of signs and, therefore, of thought (Houser and Kloesel 1992).

According to Peirce, phenomenology is 'the study which observes the different elements that occur in whatever . . . real or fictitious we can experience, feel, conceive, talk about, etc. and makes out the characters of the different classes of such elements' (*MS* 326: 34). The task of phenomenology is to disclose the fundamental structure of experience where experience, as the subject matter of phenomenology, is conceived of very broadly. Peirce's work in phenomenology is not well known by comparison with that of his contemporary, Edmund Husserl, yet his reputation is growing as the second great phenomenologist of the early twentieth century. Although the phenomenologies of Peirce and Husserl were independently formulated and are very different, Herbert Spiegelberg has identified four important parallels (Spiegelberg 1957):

1 The programme of a fresh approach by way of intuitive inspection and description of the immediately given, an approach free from preconceived theories.
2 The deliberate disregard, in so doing, of questions of reality or unreality.
3 The insistence upon the radical differences between phenomenology and psychology.
4 The claim that such a phenomenology would be a rigorous science, basic not only for philosophy but even for logic.

In addition to these parallels, Charles Dougherty has argued that the phenomenologies of Peirce and Husserl have two common roots: 'the recognition of the mind's active collaboration in the process of knowing' and 'the use of a method for the imaginative separation of non-independent parts of any given whole' which Husserl referred to as 'boundless free variation' and Peirce called 'prescission' (Dougherty 1980).

Prescission is the critical, really defining, technique of Peirce's phenomenology. It is a technique for separating elements or features of what is present in experience. The present or given in experience, the object of study for phenomenology, is the phaneron (taken from the Greek word πηανερον, meaning manifest) – accordingly, Peirce came to call phenomenology 'phaneroscopy'. Peirce uses 'phaneron' to mean 'all that is present to the mind in any sense or in any way whatever, regardless of whether it be fact or figment' (*CP* 8.213).

Prescission is only one of three techniques for separating elements of the phaneron. Peirce calls the other forms of separation 'dissociation' and 'discrimination'. Dissociation is 'the consciousness of the one thing without the necessary simultaneous consciousness of the other' (*CP* 1.549). We can only dissociate elements of the phaneron which can actually appear separately in experience. Thus, for example, we can dissociate red from blue, but not space from colour, colour from space, nor red from colour. This is the strongest kind of phaneroscopic separation. Discrimination, on the other hand, is the weakest. 'Discrimination has to do merely with the senses of terms, and only draws a distinction in meaning' (*CP* 1.549). Whenever elements of the phaneron are represented by terms that are fully distinct in meaning, they can be discriminated. Thus we can discriminate red from blue, space from colour and colour from space, but not red from colour. Prescission is intermediate between dissociation and discrimination with respect to strength of separability. Prescission is based on our ability to *attend* to one element while we *neglect* another (*CP* 1.549). For prescissive separation it is not enough that we can discriminate between elements, for it is possible to discriminate even when we cannot really suppose that the discriminated elements could ever appear separately in consciousness. Yet prescission is weaker than dissociation, for we do not require of prescission that the prescinded elements actually be separable in experience, but only that we can suppose that they are separable in some possible universe (*CP* 1.549n). Thus we can prescind red from blue, and space from colour, but not colour from space nor red from colour. Obviously prescission is not a reciprocal process.

Peirce chose prescission over the other techniques for separating elements of the phaneron because it was the most objective, or neutral, approach. Peirce developed his phenomenology in an effort to find a grounded theoretical foothold for semiotics (and for the rest of philosophy) and for the empirical sciences. To provide an empirical base for the subsequent sciences, not merely a formal foundation as is provided by mathematics, phenomenology could not concern itself with the epistemological or ontological status of elements of the phaneron, nor with the actual capacities and limitations of our mental faculties. What Peirce sought from phenomenology was a set of universal categories *of experience*; categories which, unlike the categories of mathematics, would have material content. The material, or empirical, content of the phenomenological categories derives from the fact that they are distilled from the phaneron itself. Only prescission could yield the objective universal categories Peirce sought. Discrimination depends on how we assign meaning to elements of the phaneron and, therefore, cannot be pre-semiotic; furthermore, by distinguishing elements of the phaneron that cannot be imagined or supposed separately from one another, discrimination cannot yield categories that meet Peirce's criterion of objectivity. Discriminations are not grounded in purely experienced (objective) differences but in distinctions of meaning. Dissociation, on the other hand, depends on how elements of the phaneron *really* can be separated in experience and, therefore, cannot be completely pre-psychological: 'it is doubtful whether a person who is not devoid of the sense of sight can separate space from colour by dissociation, or, at any rate, not without great difficulty' (*CP* 1.549n). Furthermore, the demand of dissociation that the elements it distinguishes really be separable seems to be a denial of the criterion of universality. Only prescission, which depends neither on the meanings of terms nor on the actual separability of the elements of our experience, but only on their *supposed* separability, can yield the foundation Peirce sought. Only by prescission can we make distinctions between elements universally present without basing those distinctions on differences of meaning. Prescission, therefore, provides the chief tool for phenomenology in its pursuit of objective universal categories to ground all less abstract sciences. Nevertheless, prescission is not the only special technique of phenomenology.

From mathematics the phenomenologist imports the technique of hypostatic abstraction to provide a means for ascending to the generality necessary for a list of universal categories. By hypostatic abstraction we derive substantive abstract singular terms from predicate expressions or, as in mathematics, numerical expressions used adjectivally (first, second and third become firstness, secondness and thirdness). (See Houser 1989 for further discussion.)

Peirce's phenomenological investigations were carried out over many years and resulted in many different, though generally overlapping, classifications of the elements of experience. The higher, more general, classifications all contain three classes. In 1866, for example, Peirce identified feelings, efforts and notions (elements of information) as the three classes of elements of conscious experience (*W* 1: 491). In 1891 he identified feeling-qualities, reactions and the consciousness of habit-taking (*MS* 1099: 9). In 1898 he isolated immediate consciousness (feeling-quality), the sense of reaction (exertion and the shock of experience) and the consciousness of habit-formation (learning/association of ideas) (*MS* 445: 12–13). In 1902, Peirce admitted that 'the question of names and other terminology for [his phenomenological categories] still somewhat perplexes me', but that he was inclined to call them flavour, reaction and mediation (*L* 75: 605). In December 1909, in a letter to William James, Peirce classified consciousness into qualisense, molition and the recognition of habit. Molition, Peirce said, is 'volition minus all desire and purpose, the mere consciousness of *exertion* of any kind' (*CP* 8.303). Notwithstanding minor differences, it seems clear that his years of phenomenological investigations led Peirce to conclude that there are three general classes of elements (or, as Peirce says, 'ingredients') in every phaneron: elements of feeling, 'the unanalyzed total impression made by any manifold not thought of as actual fact, but simply as a quality. . .' (*CP* 8.329); elements of reaction (a sense of exertion or opposition); and elements of habituation or learning in which we sense that other elements of the phaneron are connected or brought together (Peirce sometimes calls this element 'representation' or 'thought'). Peirce coined new words for these three universal classes of consciousness:

> There are no other forms of consciousness except . . . Feeling, Altersense, and Medisense. They form a sort of system. Feeling is the momentarily present contents of consciousness taken in its pristine simplicity, apart from anything else. It is consciousness in its first state, and might be called *primisense. Altersense* is the consciousness of a directly present other or second, withstanding us. *Medisense* is the consciousness of a thirdness, or medium between primisense and altersense, leading from the former to the latter. It is the consciousness of a process of bringing to mind. Feeling, or *primisense*, is the consciousness of firstness; altersense is [the] consciousness of otherness or secondness; medisense is the consciousness of means or thirdness.
>
> (*MS* 1107: 18)

Here Peirce refers to firstness, secondness and thirdness in the context of phenomenology, and it is not too difficult to imagine how he might have reached those conceptions. From his classification of the elements of the phaneron into primisense, altersense and medisense (feeling, reaction, thought) he prescinded the independent categories: quale, relation and sign. Every feeling necessarily involves a quality; altersense, the sense of reaction, necessarily involves, or depends upon, relation or opposition; and it is a well-known thesis of Peirce's that all thought is dependent on signs – that all thought is in signs (*CP* 5.250–253). By prescinding from our conception of a sign, we discover that all signs involve (contain) both relations and qualia and thus are *third* to them; relations, on the other hand, are independent of signs but are dependent on qualia and therefore are *second* to qualia; qualia, however, are independent of both relations and signs and, thus, are *first.* (It should be noted that qualia, relations and signs, in the present context, are elements of the phaneron and are thus instantiated – we are dealing with material relations – which explains why we can say that relations are dependent on (contain) **qualia**, something we could not say of relations in a mathematical, or strictly formal, context.) By hypostatic abstraction we can now ascend to the generality of our ever more familiar set of categories: firstness, secondness and thirdness. These, then, are the categories reached by the phenomenologist who follows Peirce, and they are offered as a foundation upon which to build philosophy and the special sciences. They are the same categories reached by a mathematical analysis of fundamental relations except that as mathematical categories they are without empirical content. Peirce's categories constitute an important link between the a priori world of mathematics and the contingent world of experience, at which juncture we find the ground of phenomenology. (The precise relationship between mathematics and phenomenology still needs to be worked out; see Houser 1989 for further discussion.)

Firstness, secondness and thirdness are highly abstract universal categories of experience which provide the key to the structure of the phaneron (and, thus, of experience). Perhaps this is easiest to see when we regard firstness, secondness and thirdness as levels of dependency, as expressed above. Some elements of the phaneron are independent; these are elements of firstness. Other elements are dependent only on another element; these are elements of secondness. Still other elements of the phaneron are dependent on two elements between which they somehow mediate; these are elements of thirdness. According to Peirce, these three classes of elements comprise the whole of the phaneron. At this level of abstraction the phenomenological categories appear as characters, or qualities, of elements of the phaneron. They are the phenomenological categories in their firstness. As qualia, relations and signs, the categories appear as facts. In this form the categories appear in their secondness. As feeling, reaction and thought, the categories appear as signs. In this way the categories appear in their thirdness. This structural account of the phaneron can be represented in Table 6.2.

These three forms of appearing are described by Peirce as three universes of experience. Insofar as it is the job of the phenomenologist to distil from the phaneron, by prescission and hypostatic abstraction, the most fundamental, most general, set of universal categories, that work is concluded with the abstraction of firstness, secondness and thirdness.

Table 6.2 Structure of the phaneron

Universal categories (form of firstness)	FIRSTNESS	SECONDNESS	THIRDNESS
Universal categories (form of secondness)	QUALIA (facts of firstness)	RELATIONS (facts of secondness)	SIGNS (facts of thirdness)
Universal categories (form of thirdness)	FEELING (signs of firstness)	REACTION (signs of secondness)	THOUGHT (signs of thirdness)

As a young man, Peirce's metaphysics was more idealistic in the traditional sense than it would be in his later years. Initially he only recognized the universe of signs, or of thirdness, as real. But as his thought matured, Peirce came to recognize that reality extended also to the universe of facts (secondness) and the universe of feeling (firstness). We live in a complex world where feelings, facts and signs are intertwined but where, in order to understand who we are and what there is, we must find ways to 'separate' and investigate these universes as independently as possible. To investigate the universe of feeling, in Peirce's sense, we turn to the phenomenologist. To investigate the universe of facts, we turn to the experimental scientist. To investigate the universe of signs, we turn to the semiotician. Or so we would if Peirce were followed. Peirce was all three: a phenomenologist, an experimental scientist and a semiotician, and in his later years his work in these areas would inform a complex and unique metaphysics that is yet to be fully comprehended.

Peirce would come to speculate that 'in the beginning' there was a timeless and indescribable chaos but that it is best understood as a chaos of feeling and disconnected 'happenings'. Somehow, perhaps through some kind of proto-sympathy, repetitions began to occur and incipient habits arose. Chance still reigned supreme. But as habits grew stronger laws evolved and chance began to give way to rational organization. Chance will never be eradicated, unless the universe grinds to a halt, and sympathy will never cease to be a force, but as the universe of feeling becomes more domesticated it influences the course of events more and more through reason than through sympathy. Semiosis is what makes this transition to rational action possible. The universe of feeling, through the phaneron, stimulates the growth of perceptive faculties. The crucial and astonishing moment that makes perception possible is the abductive moment when a judgement is made on an otherwise innocent phaneron (we may say, here, a sense experience). This is *the* semiotic moment, the remarkable introduction of **text** (really anything understood to be a sign) into experience and the beginning of intelligence. Peirce would argue in his later years that this view of intelligence, as a natural development where thought serves the function of situating semiosis-capable organisms (or entities) to have a better than chance advantage in their environments, brings his phenomenology and semiotics into harmony with his pragmatism. It remains to be seen how these themes will play themselves out in the third and least developed branch of Peirce's semiotics, speculative rhetoric, as it receives more attention (Bergman 2004).

Further reading

Dougherty, C. J. (1980) 'The common root of Husserl's and Peirce's phenomenologies', *The New Scholasticism*, 54: 305–325.

Ketner, K. L. and Kloessel, C. J. W. (eds) (1986) *Peirce, Semeiotic, and Pragmatism: Essays by Max H. Fisch*, Bloomington, IN: Indiana University Press.

Peirce, C. S. (1931–1935; 1958) *Collected Papers of Charles Sanders Peirce*, Vols 1–6 ed. C. Hartshorne and P. Weiss; Vols 7 and 8 ed. A. Burks, Cambridge, MA: Harvard University Press.

Peirce, C. S. (1998) *The Essential Peirce: Selected Philosophical Writings*, Vol. 2, ed. Peirce Edition Project, Bloomington, IN: Indiana University Press.

Spiegelberg, H. (1957) 'Husserl's and Peirce's phenomenologies: Coincidence or interaction?', *Philosophy and Phenomenological Research*, 17: 164–185.

7
The Saussurean heritage

Anne Hénault

Saussure (1857–1913) is the scientist, who, educated in sciences (mathematics and physics) as well as in philology and in the linguistics of his time, thought it necessary to transform this discipline into a hard science, by giving it a really rational basis. Linguistics, which had started to come together with the works of von **Humboldt**, Rémusat, de Chézy, Bopp, Steinthal amongst other authorities, could not, according to Saussure, constitute a rigorous and specific knowledge about **language**, expression and circulation of codified **meaning**s unless an axiomatic approach was settled:

> From the outset, we differ from the theoreticians who think that the point is to give an idea of the phenomenon of language or from those, already less numerous who endeavour to fix the operations of the linguist within these phenomena. Indeed, our point of view is that the knowledge of a phenomenon, or an operation of the mind, requires the previous definition of a term, whatever; not a definition at random, that can always be given of a relative term with regard to other relative terms, eternally running round in a vicious circle, but a consistent definition, starting at a given point from a base which I would not consider absolute, but explicitly chosen as an irreducible basis for us and central for the system. To imagine that in linguistics one can do without such an healthy mathematical logic, under the pretext that language is something concrete that 'becomes' and not something 'abstract' that 'is', represents to my mind a deep error.[1]

---

[1] Long quotations are offered in the original French in the footnotes, as here. All English renderings of extracts from the *Cours de linguistique générale* are from Harris' 1983 translation, hereafter cited as Saussure (1983), with the original French coming from *Cours de linguistique générale* (*CLG* 1916, 1922, 1972). Quotes are also taken from the critical edition of the *Cours de linguistique générale* (*CLG/E* 1967–1974), rendered in English by the author. Likewise, English renderings from Saussure's *Ecrits de linguistique générale* (*ELG* 2002) are those of the author.

Short quotations appear in English and, in brackets, in French in the main text.

> Nous différons, depuis le principe, des théoriciens qui pensent qu'il s'agit de donner une idée des phénomènes du langage, ou de ceux, déjà plus rares, qui cherchent à fixer les opérations du linguiste au milieu de ces phénomènes. Notre point de vue est en effet que la connaissance d'un phénomène ou d'une opération de l'esprit suppose préalablement la définition d'un terme quelconque; non pas la définition de hasard qu'on peut toujours donner d'un terme relatif par rapport à d'autres termes relatifs, en tournant éternellement dans un cercle vicieux, mais la définition conséquente qui part à un endroit quelconque d'une base, je ne dis pas absolue, mais choisie expressément comme base irréductible pour nous, et centrale de tout le système. S'imaginer qu'on pourra se passer en linguistique de cette saine logique mathématique, sous prétexte que la langue est une chose concrète qui 'devient' et non une chose abstraite qui 'est', est, à ce que je crois, une erreur profonde.
>
> (*ELG*, p. 34)

In those days, when David Hilbert was developing an axiomatic method, Saussure had the intuition to systematize or even to 'mathematicize' the relational interplays, which characterize 'la **langue**' and subtend the speech: 'The day will come, when it will be recognised that [the values and] quantities of language and their relationship are regularly expressible in their fundamental nature by mathematical forms';[2] or, again: 'Each sort of linguistic unit represents a relation and a phenomenon is also a relation. Therefore everything is relation. The units are not phonic, they are created by the mind . . . All phenomena are relations between relations.'[3]

He could envision the moment when it would be possible to transcribe the calculus of meanings into formalized languages that could be completely detached from verbal languages and that would also escape their slipperiness: 'Some day, there will be a special and very interesting book to be written about the role of the word as the main disturber of the science of words.'[4]

Here again, such an approach is perhaps in a random accordance (the so-called 'air du temps') with epistemological propositions that are its contemporary, for instance Peano's work on formalized languages. In the same way, for the next generation, the works of Hans Reichenbach were to provide A. J. **Greimas** with examples of a rigorous grasp of meaning outside of verbal language and were to encourage him towards what he called 'symbolic language' (hence, for instance, Greimas' famous algebraic schematizations of narratives).

Such a theory of knowledge was to overturn the whole of linguistics and to throw it into a frenetic search for structures (that was going to end up, for a limited period, with the excesses of structuralist mechanicism). The debates surrounding this new orientation and its key terms were the most eagerly disseminated linguistic research between the years 1960 and 1980 and the story behind these debates is well known. Therefore, here we will concentrate on the strictly semiologic aspect of Saussure's research and will also explain why it is no longer possible, today, to split the personality of Ferdinand de Saussure into several contradictory fragments as was frequently the practice during the heyday of structuralism. The very progress in the publishing of Saussure's manuscripts and in the corresponding semiotic research allows us today to acknowledge the strong coherence of the totality of his cutting-edge thinking and shows that the same theoretical project is at work in what came to us from the real *Cours de linguistique générale* (*CLG*) and from his studies on anagrams and on Germanic legends.

---

[2] 'Il arrivera un jour (. . .) où l'on reconnaîtra que les [valeurs et] quantités du langage et leurs rapports sont régulièrement exprimables dans leur nature fondamentale par des formes mathématiques' (*CLG/E*, I, n. 10, p. 22).

[3] 'Toute espèce d'unité linguistique représente un rapport, et un phénomène aussi est un rapport. Donc tout est rapport. Les unités ne sont pas phoniques, elles sont créées par la pensée . . . Tous les phénomènes sont des rapports entre des rapports' (*CLG* 1908–1909).

[4] 'Il y aura un jour un livre spécial et très intéressant à écrire sur le rôle du mot comme principal perturbateur de la science des mots' (*CLG/E*, IV, 3281, p. 5).

Chronologically speaking, the Saussurean heritage first was exploited with the development of linguistics, then, second, by the debut of **semiotics**: the first results of Saussurean linguistics, as is well known, brought researchers like **Barthes** and Greimas to the intuition of a broader scientific project, encompassing linguistics, and which would be explicitly subtended by the really rational bases for which Saussure had called. Such researchers envisioned the semiological project as a consequence of Saussure's global theoretical approach, even if the then published *Cours* had very few references to semiotics, in contrast with the unpublished manuscripts of Saussure, which do develop this new concept.

The onus today is to show how the semiological (or semiotic) approach imposed itself in order to conceive the phenomenon 'Langue' as a whole, seizable and analysable as such, but also, at the same time, as a component of a wider whole towards whose definition it would contribute. And to explain, at the same time, how the pyramid of descriptive languages to which this semiotic hypothesis gave birth embodied precisely the type of cognitive operations which build and guarantee, authentically, the scientific nature of a large number of human sciences.

We will then discuss how, from this largely implicit – and at least unpublished – theorization, Saussure's direct heirs (**Hjelmslev** and Uldall in Denmark) and their followers (Greimas and Barthes in France) have been able to begin discovering certain constants of **signification**. Finally, we will consider how the publications that are now representative of Saussure's work on textuality (anagrams or old legends) provide greater theoretical depth and significant breadth to what we hitherto knew about his views.

Some preliminary questions

There has been much confusion attendant on the interpretation of the 'cohesion' of Saussure's thought; from the outset we should eliminate some of these confusions including the very common ones about *semiotics* or ***semiology***.

For Saussure, the evolution of language is merely change and alteration on the backdrop of an abstract and logical continuity. Under the pressure of the intense research to which they have been subjected, the meanings of certain terms in his manuscripts have evolved and have even split into antagonistic or complementary notions. Such is the case of 'semiology' exclusively used in the *Cours* and in all Saussure's handwritten notes, though the word 'semiotics' had existed already in French since the sixteenth century. Semiotics indicated the set of corporeal **sign**s that allow a physician to diagnose a state of health or illness. Nowadays, after several mutations by which even the terminological choices of **Benveniste** have been abolished (cf. the two articles – 'La forme et le sens du langage', 1967, and 'Sémiologie de la langue', 1974 – in Benveniste 1967, 1974), 'semiology', in the theorized definition given by Saussure, has turned into 'semiotics' whilst 'semiology' indicates a less formal analytical practice, more composite, more intuitive, linked to considerations concerning extra-linguistic references. Hence, in our contemporary studies, the substitution of the term 'semiotics' for that of 'semiology' is common.

Theory or philosophy of language

One has only to sketch a comparison of Saussure's work with that of his American contemporary, C. S. **Peirce** (1839–1914), also presented as one of the founding fathers of semiotics, to observe that the works of these two pioneers who never met are in opposition as much as 'Theory of language and signification' and 'Philosophy of inference and deduction' are. Peirce elaborates a philosophical system comparable to the great classical systems of **Kant**, **Hegel** and Schopenhauer. The type of abstraction he aims for, and which he attains, belongs to the realm of philosophy. All the notions he posits are thought out with the same realistic and substantial investment as the categories of **Aristotle**'s Metaphysics. These notions receive an 'ontological' definition: they exist, and they are. In contrast, Saussure's problematics display a totally rational schematism with no ontology, a formal thinking that is neither nominalist nor realist. This attitude constitutes a radical break with the millennial philosophy of language subjacent to the various traditional grammars. This break, well ahead of its time, from the point of view of the aesthetics of knowledge, can only be compared to the 'transmental' experiments undertaken, in the same period, by Russian painting (Kandinski, Rozanova, Popova or Malevitch). We will return to this precise idea of 'theory' when the time comes to specify some of the characteristics of semiotics considered as a science.

The irreductible polysemy of the notion of 'semiology' for Saussure and his heirs

For Saussure, this term concentrates the most intense reflexive activity and, as can be foreseen, its significations split according to the points of view under consideration. We will limit ourselves here in distinguishing three major meanings of this term and therefore three successive aspects under which we will examine this notion:

- On the one hand, semiology is the universal competency with which the living being is endowed to elaborate expression. It does look as if Saussure only attributes this competency to the human species, given that he conceives language as 'what happens when mankind attempts to signify its thinking through a necessary convention'.[5] For generations of researchers who have been exposed to phenomenology (from R. Ruyer to our times, including A. J. Greimas and R. Chambon), alternatively, the semiologic competency (alias semiotics) is not exclusive to human beings. They share

[5] 'Ce qui se produit lorsque l'homme essaie de signifier sa pensée au moyen d'une convention nécessaire' (*CLG/E*, IV, 3342).

it, to various degrees, with the entire living realm. Greimas liked to say that the dog is a great semiotician.

- On the other hand, 'semiotics' designates the various products of this competency, i.e. the different languages that circulate amongst living beings. With mankind, this competency takes on extremely varied forms. This is liable to generate numerous distinct semiologies, and, in this case, a 'semiology' (une sémiotique) is a particular language, as in 'The particular semiology called "language"'.[6] However, Saussure also mentions 'general semiology' (D 222, ibid.) and thus indicates the vast ensemble of which each semiology (each language, alias each semiotic) is but a particular implementation. As we are about to see, this notion of 'general semiology' plays a key role for Saussure's theory: it is essential for the constitution of semiotics as a science, as, *mutatis mutandis*, the invention of the 'zero' for mathematics.
- Finally, 'semiotics' (for contemporary researchers) must also be understood as the science of all the various particular semiologies and/or that of general semiotics as well as the study of the ability for language, which generates these various semiotics.

To sum things up, in Saussure's thinking a sentence such as 'Man is a born semiotician' could be understood as:

- 'Man is an animal which could not survive without expressing and exchanging significations.' Or
- 'Man has the capacity to create various means of expression; he elaborates significations through all sorts of semiotics which have it in common to be articulate, codified and systematized (to various degrees, however). Amongst these semiotics, verbal language is the most articulate.' Or, finally, as
- 'Man intends to construct a rational knowledge, called "semiotics", which is a science of the different languages at his disposal.'

Saussure's 'semiology'

'Semiology' as universal competence of the living being

In a certain sense, Saussure takes verbal language for granted. For him there is a kind of self-evidence of language as an institution that he never challenges in its genesis, its acquisition, or in its concrete aspect and in its expressive function. The question of the faculty of language only occurs twice in the *CLG*. Its clearest occurrence is noted by Constantin (Komatsu, *Le cahier de Constantin*, as cited in Saussure 1993: 276): 'For us, language will be the social product the existence of which allows the individuals to exercise the faculty of language.'[7]

[6] 'La sémiologie particulière dite langage' (N 10 in Godel 1957: 275).

[7] 'La langue sera pour nous le produit social dont l'existence permet à l'individu d'exercer la faculté de langage.'

Through his family background as well as his own inclinations Saussure was born into the learned linguistics of his day, to which many of his youthful 'memories' bear witness. On the other hand, he had a totally different experience of significations, through the work he dedicated to anagrams and old German legends. Obviously, when he devoted lengthy studies to a corpus, Saussure was extending what were common practices in his century: Auguste Comte, for instance, had shown great interest in anagrams, and the Romanist philologists (Gaston Pâris) and many Germanists were analysing the ancient legends spread around by the oral tradition of the entire Indo-European world. But, in revisiting this field, according to those radically formal and relational orientations that are his own, Saussure laid himself open to a semiological experience of a new sort. He discovered that, with man, the production of meaning does not depend only on the prison of words but is constantly on the point of springing up from nowhere, from the gathering of two straws or three feathers, as from some non-existent beings, evoked by a storyteller or shaped in clay (statues, figurines, any modelling). He, thus, had to take into account the fact that the transmission of meaning is not necessarily attached to the verbal expression as such, an experience, which led to the broadening of semiotic enquiry.

'Semiology' as the necessary foundation of the theory of language

As he was working on the *Cours*, Saussure's thinking reached a bedrock of 'delimitations' which began to bring forth the specificity of the domain of language while establishing some unarguable 'truths'. What is the status of such operations of thought? They deal with the initial statements from which one must start in order to 'lay out the foundations of the edifice' and find 'the foundations of language'.[8] Thus Saussure had a clear perception of the two kinds of competence he needed to muster in order to endow linguistics with the hypothetico-deductive method which guarantees its scientificity. He had to continue to be the expert linguist, heir to the various European schools he had followed. At the same time he had to adopt the behaviour of an epistemologist familiar with 'hard' science. In his own eyes, only a true epistemological commitment was liable to establish a system of language out of the mass of facts already observed and collected.

Here are some of the initial statements, starting points for an acceptable theoretical path:

1 'In a language there are only differences, *and no positive terms*' (Saussure 1983: 118) ('Dans la langue, il n'y a que des *différences* sans termes positifs', *CLG*, 166).

[8] 'Tracer les bases de l'édifice' and to discover 'les fondements du langage' (*CLG/E*, IV, 43).

2 'A language constitutes a system' (Saussure 1983: 73) ('La langue est un *système*', *CLG*, 107).
3 '*The linguistic sign is arbitrary*' (Saussure 1983: 67) ('*Le signe linguistique est arbitraire*', *CLG*, 100).
4 'Linguistic phenomena always present two complementary facets, each depending on the other' (Saussure 1983: 8) ('Le phénomène linguistique présente perpétuellement *deux faces* qui se correspondent et dont l'une ne vaut que par l'autre', *CLG*, 23).

It may be observed that these statements do not apply only to natural languages but, in fact, to all systems of signification. These various statements specify the field of language in general and thus place linguistics in a mental whole of which it is but a particular component. With the result that one can embrace linguistics in its totality (just as when one looks, from a distant and external point of view, at a geographical zone it becomes possible to embrace this zone as a whole, be it a given country or a continent). It is only once the phenomenon 'language' is thus apprehended as a whole that its 'internal order' of 'la langue' can be discerned as a unitary system.

Thus the statements we have just listed function as 'a good generalization', rigorously delimited and, for that very reason, discriminating for the field of language. The next operations consist in exploring the specific properties of the various languages inasmuch as they relate to each other, hence establishing operators of individualization for each one of them. For example, one of the very obvious specificities of the semiotic 'verbal language' is its *linear* dimension which allows for a temporal deployment. In contrast, visual language is necessarily planar or n-dimensional. A verbal semiotic is also by necessity *arbitrary*, whereas a pictographic semiotic may appear partially *motivated*, because it appears to resemble. Thus, progressively, by alternate operations of generalizations and differentiations, operating concepts build up, leading to a formal method for the analysis of significations.

An extremely detailed presentation of the way these sequences of statements guarantee the soundness of semiotic work is to be found in Pariente (1973). The rationality of this work proceeds from the establishment of a rigorous hierarchy of inferences and implications, and this first step leads to the formulation of fundamental concepts and to the constitution of a **metalanguage** as reliable as the language of mathematics or logic, as well as rigorously specific and adequate to the object 'language'.

Let us give the floor to Saussure himself who sums up, as follows, his practice, his 'faire', in 1894: 'The two things, a good generalization on language which can interest anybody or a sound method assigned to comparative grammar for precise everyday operations, are in fact one and the same.'[9]

---

[9] 'Les deux choses, une bonne généralisation sur le langage, qui peut intéresser qui que ce soit, ou une saine méthode à proposer à la grammaire comparée pour les opérations précises de chaque jour sont en réalité la même chose' (*CLG/E*, IV, 3297).

Semiotics as a scientific discipline

Semiotics as social psychology

The phrase 'sémiologie, partie de la psychologie sociale' (Godel 1957: 275) is frequently to be found in Saussure's manuscripts, and this, in the *CLG*, becomes the 'prediction' so often quoted:

> It is therefore possible to conceive of a science *which studies the role of signs as part of social life*. It would form part of social psychology, and hence of general psychology. We shall call it '*semiology*' (from the Greek *séméion*, 'sign').[10]

This formulation is disturbing because all Saussure's declarations and what has been possible to infer from his work is that there is nothing psychological about his linguistics. How is one supposed to understand this idea of 'psychologie sociale' which is nonetheless at the heart of the definition of his scientific endeavour? We have developed elsewhere an answer to this enigma (Hénault 1996: 9–54). In short, in his thinking, on the 'carte forcée', on the constraints that the social dimension of the 'langue' places upon individuals and, especially, on the factors of linguistic change that no individual can change, Saussure represents the social mass made of all the speaking individuals as a 'weightiness', active through its mass alone, and subject to another 'weightiness' – the time factor. None of these actors is endowed with an individualized psychology and, if there is continuous creation in language, it acts more like a series of glacial deposits: 'Of these vast moraines to be seen on the edge of our glaciers, picture a prodigious accumulation of things borne down over the centuries.'[11] However, these relations of uncertainty, linked to the disorder inflicted by the passage of time and by the speaking mass, are recaptured at a less superficial level by a sort of logical fibrillation of the language: 'All the logical features of the language depend or can depend on immutable data that the accidents of time or the geographical place do not explain.'[12]

This 'logic face of *langue*' is made up of the deep constants which are a sort of particular reason, specific to the linguistic field, a linguistic rationalism (in a meaning akin to Bachelard's 'electric rationalism', designating the sum of the regular occurrences and laws of the physics of electricity). This linguistic

[10] 'On peut concevoir une science qui étudie la vie des signes au sein de la vie sociale; elle formerait une partie de la psychologie sociale et par conséquent de la psychologie générale; nous la nommerons sémiologie (du Grec séméion, "signe")' (*CLG*, 33).

[11] 'De ces grandes moraines qu'on voit au bord de nos glaciers, tableau d'un prodigieux amas de choses charriées à travers les siècles' (Première conférence à l'Université de Genève, 1891, *CLG/E*, IV, 3281, p. 5).

[12] 'Toute la face logique de la langue dépend ou peut dépendre de données immuables que les accidents du temps ou du lieu géographique n' atteignment pas' (Notes pour *le Cours* III, 1910–1911; *ELG*, 306).

rationalism, also described by Saussure as describing 'the forces operating permanently and universally in all languages' (Saussure 1983: 6) ('ces forces qui sont en jeu d'une manière permanente et universelle dans toutes les langues' (*CLG*, 20), can be considered as an expression of the 'esprit collectif'. It is therefore in this area that we might seek what Saussure means by 'psychologie sociale'. The task assigned to the social psychology called semiotics would be to bring to light the constant and universal relations that subtend significations and allow them to take shape.

Theory of signs taken separately or theory of the planes of signifying and signified

The first Saussurean readers – convinced by the examples in the editions of the *Cours* by Bally and Sechehaye (1916) and Tullio de Mauro (1972) and, in particular, by the famous oval-enclosed binaries (p. 99) with the superposition of a tree and the word 'arbour' or the French word 'arbre' and the Latin word 'arbor' – have portrayed Saussure as the 'Sign guy', the man who advocates analysis of isolated signs. A. J. Greimas (1917–1992) used to explain frequently that the first of his own contributions to the theorizations of signification had been to break the straitjacket of the dimension-sign, supposedly imposed by Saussure, to consider all dimensions of systems of significations and of the two planes of the signifying (or expression) and the signified (or content), and to describe them in their full extent. In reality, Greimas himself, very early on, had suspected that the first publishers of the *Cours* had insisted on the idea of the sign taken in isolation, because they maintained a conception of language as nomenclature (i.e. like a list of signs, each sign associated with its referent and fundamentally separated from the other signs) which is precisely what Saussure had aimed to overturn. In 1984, in still unpublished conversations with the present author, A. J. Greimas indicated, however, that he thought he had perceived in the metaphors of the 'Royaume flottant' and of the sheet of paper an explicitly planar conception of the approach to 'sounds' and 'ideas': 'So, we can envisage the linguistic phenomenon in its entirety – the language, that is – as a series of adjoining subdivisions simultaneously imprinted both on the plane of vague, amorphous thought (A), and on the equally featureless plane of sound (B)' (Saussure 1983: 110). (Here a schema shows two undulating surfaces: the more or less parallel waves are segmented by parallel dotted lines.)

> The characteristic role of a language in relation to thought is not to supply the material phonetic means by which ideas may be expressed. It is to act as intermediary between thought and sound, in such a way that the combination of both necessarily produces a mutually complementary delimitation of units.
>
> (Saussure 1983: 110)

And some lines further on, the junction of these two 'indefinite planes' is described as 'the coupling of the mind with phonic matter'.[13]

None of this has prevented the proliferation of so-called Saussurean theories of the sign taken in isolation, approaches which, from the point of view of theoretical semiotics, are so many dead ends. Umberto **Eco** acknowledges this fact in *A Theory of Semiotics* (1976: 12): the semiotic universe is not made up of *signs* but of '*semiotic functions*', a term that Saussure would not have taken exception to.

Dichotomies or dualities

Chapter III of the *CLG* opens with the enumeration of some of these dualities constantly called upon by Saussure to demonstrate the character of language, so difficult to apprehend. For example, this formulation that has already been quoted: 'linguistic phenomena always present two complementary facets, each depending on the other'[14] (Saussure 1983: 8).

With a very literary mind, Jakobson named Saussure as the great revealer of linguistic antinomies. He saw this as a sort of character trait and felt free to reproach Saussure for his perpetual dual thinking, calling him 'the great doubter who always saw the two sides of the problem' (1939: 237).

The earliest commentators on these dualities, of this perpetually dual thinking, insisted on its antithetic aspect and radicalized the contrasts to the point of turning them into contradictions. The dichotomies became unmanageable antinomies and semiological thought was, in an act of flagrant abuse, made rigid. The publication of larger proportions of the handwritten notes left by Saussure, on the other hand, has enabled the demonstration of how, for instance, far from being totally hampered by the discontinuist binarism of structuralist thought, his theory is conceived of evolution and gradualism in many fields. This can be constantly witnessed in the recently published *Ecrits*.

Theorematic aspect of the theory

What is the exact meaning that Saussure gave to the word 'theory'? A short note in his own hand leaves no room for doubt:

> Baudouin de Courtenay and Kruszewski have got closer than anyone to a theoretical view of language, without departing from purely linguistic

[13] 'Nous pouvons nous représenter le fait linguistique dans son ensemble, c'est-à-dire la langue, comme une série de subdivisions contiguës, dessinées à la fois sur le plan indéfini des idées confuses et sur celui non moins indéterminé des sons'; 'Le rôle caractéristique de la langue vis-à-vis de la pensée n'est pas de créer un moyen phonique matériel pour l'expression des idées, mais de servir d'intermédiaire entre la pensée et le son, dans des conditions telles que leur union aboutit nécessairement à des délimitations réciproques d'unités'; 'l'accouplement de la pensée avec la matière phonique' (*CLG*, 155–156).

[14] 'Le phénomène linguistique présente perpétuellement deux faces qui se correspondent et dont l'une ne vaut que par l'autre' (*CLG*, 23).

> considerations. Most western scholars anyway ignore them. The American Whitney, whom I revere, has never said a word on these same subjects that was not right, but like for all the others, it does not occur to him that language needs a systematic.[15]
>
> (cited by Godel 1957: 51)

On the one hand, his praise of these two Russian researchers impugns any proposition that does not stem from the very technicity of linguistics; thus understood, scientific thinking leads to the apprehension of regularities that have been *discovered*. There is no longer a case for formulating arguments that have merely been *invented*. On the other hand, his reservations about the erudite work of Whitney show that, for Saussure, a theory cannot be construed without a 'system' which allows the results that have been obtained to contribute to the elucidation of similar cases.

Without such a systematic approach, the gathering of facts does not result in the construction of cumulative knowledge. Thus one can see that Saussure intends to constitute a theory which would provide foundations for a theory of language, and which would eventually be modelized or formalized in the same way as 'hard' sciences. For him, the word 'theory' does not carry the speculative meaning intended by a literary mind; it takes on the meaning to be found in expressions such as 'Theory of Relativity' or 'Theory of Electricity'. For scientific theories, the establishment of observables that specify the area of knowledge which is in the process of formation does not proceed from that immediate common sense which is supposed to drive ordinary life. It requires lengthy preliminary work, identical to the founding movement of a new science about to emerge. There is no doubt that Saussure hoped that some of the findings of linguistics would attain the status of scientific laws in the sense understood by his friend, the epistemologist from Geneva, Naville. In fact Saussure considered that there were two ways of treating the facts of language, one scientific alias 'Theorematic', the linguistics of language and the other, which attained a weak theoretical level, dealing with speech. Sometimes known as 'Stylistique', the linguistics of speech were confined to a mere practise of observations and classifications:

> Stylistics . . . seeks its object above all in the observation of what is spoken, in the living forms of language, recorded or not in a text . . . It is not a normative science edicting rules. It claims and is correct in claiming to be a science of pure observation, registering facts and classifying them.[16]

---

[15] 'Baudouin de Courtenay et Kruszewski ont été plus près que personne d'une vue théorique de la langue, cela sans sortir de considérations linguistiques pures; ils sont d'ailleurs ignorés de la généralité des savants occidentaux. L'Américain Whitney, que je révère, n'a jamais dit un seul mot sur les mêmes sujets qui ne fût juste, mais comme tous les autres, il ne songe pas que la langue ait besoin d'une systématique.'

[16] 'La stylistique . . . voit avant tout son objet dans l'observation de ce qui est parlé, dans les formes de langage vivantes, consignées ou non dans un texte . . . Elle n'est pas une science normative édictant des règles. Elle prétend et a droit de prétendre être une science de pure observation, consignant les faits et les classant' ('Rapport sur la création d'une chaire de linguistique', in *ELG*, 2002: 209).

> Whereas for linguistics of 'langue', short working notes show themselves to be far more exacting, as here, under the title 'Laws': 'Laws: The universal laws of language [which are imperative] (theorematic)'.[17]

What is the purpose of this theory? 'a) to describe all known languages and record their history . . .; b) to determine the forces operating permanently and universally in all languages, and to formulate general laws which account for all particular linguistic phenomena historically attested; c) to delimit and define linguistics itself' (Saussure 1983: 6). Which, in Saussure's authentic manuscripts, is formulated as follows:

> Some recurrent truths . . . Let us not speak of axioms, principles or propositions. They are [merely, and] in the pure etymological sense, aphorisms, delimitations, [but] limits in between which, wherever we start from, the truth is to be found.[18]

An expanding Saussurean heritage

The Ecole de Paris: The (discontinuist) standard theory

Under the impulse of the Lithuanian-born French researcher A. J. Greimas, a largely international group of researchers which used to meet in Paris, and was thus known as the 'Ecole de Paris', elaborated, between 1956 and 1980, what appears as a theory of signification, rigorously inherited from Saussurean tenets. The most representative works of this semiotic current are *Sémiotique structurale*, *Maupassant* and *Sémiotique, dictionnaire raisonné de la théorie du langage*, a manifesto published in the form of a dictionary. These publications advertise the coherence and the analytical power of a systematic of which Greimas had an intuition in the 1950s and from which he never departed: that is, starting from the base of the indefinable and first strivings for definition, selected according to Saussure's own criteria, making explicit the relational system that Saussure considered the only possible path leading to rigorous definitions in matter of language. The name of *metalanguage* applies to the entirety of biunivocal and interdefined concepts (avoiding the confusion of common language) thus brought to light. Amongst the models and concepts, let us take note of the following: *semic analysis*, *narrative schema*, *constitutional model*

[17] '"Langue" tandis que pour la linguistique de la langue, de brèves notes de travail stipulent une tout autre exigence, comme ici, sous le titre "Lois" "Lois: 1 Les lois universelles de la langue [qui sont impératives] (théorématique)"' (*CLG/E*, IV, 3310, 8).

[18] 'a) faire la description et l'histoire de toutes les langues . . . ; b) chercher les forces qui sont en jeu d'une manière permanente et universelle dans toutes les langues et dégager les lois générales auxquelles on peut ramener tous les phénomènes particuliers de l'histoire; c) se délimiter et se définir soi-même' (*CLG*, 20). 'Quelques vérités qui se retrouvent . . . Ne parlons ni d'axiome, ni de principes, ni de thèses. Ce sont [simplement et] au pur sens étymologique des aphorismes, des délimitations. . . . [mais] des limites entre lesquelles se retrouve constamment la vérité, d'où que l'on parte' (*CLG/E*, N 19, IV, 42).

(alias *semiotic square*), *modalities* and *generative trajectory*, which have led to numerous demonstrative analyses in visual semiotics as well as in other semiotics (auditive and musical, tactile or gustatory) in many fields of social life.

New phenomenological and continuist perspectives in general semiotics

The first works of the Ecole de Paris inspired by Saussurean tenets mainly concerned the analysis of tales, as narrativity appeared to be the very form of the verbal expression of the transformations that human action brings to (or inflicts on) the world. Binarism proved to be perfectly adequate to rationally segment narrative sequences as well as the inversions of contents that that entailed. When it is the task to programme an action for a clearly formulated objective, one deals mainly with rather cerebral and generally 'clear and distinct' (Descartes) significations. Binarism was precisely this.

Then, from the 1980s onwards, this same Ecole de Paris moved towards a continuist epistemology, closer to the sensitive and/or affective apprehension of experienced meanings. The attempt was to handle 'less cerebral' significations in order to account for that portion of meaning which is experienced closest to the body.

Thus it seemed that semiotics was therefore under the obligation to square the circle: that is, to conceive procedures that would analyse a continuum of feelings which, taken, problematically, on their own, were unstable in the first place. Could not analysis simply be confined to the process of segmenting? Half a century of research has allowed for experimentation with a theory and a method that Saussure discovered without having the time to explicate its various articulations but whose orientations he managed nonetheless to impose enduringly. This happens to be particularly clear with his work on legends.

The semiological teachings of ancient legends

A certain number of works have recently thrown light on the analyses that Saussure himself devoted to the old legends taken from the Germanic tradition (cf. especially, Arrivé 2002, 2007; Kim 1993). Through them one can now follow, as if in a running commentary, a storm in Ferdinand de Saussure's brain, an authentic problem of semiotic epistemology experienced under Saussure's pen. Let us give a much-accelerated account of the discoveries made by Michel Arrivé from the short notes dealing with these Germanic legends (Arrivé 2007).

Starting point: an enigma

In the *Cours de linguistique générale*, as in all the manuscripts that deal with the linguistic sign, Saussure never explicitly refers to semiosis of legends, and the other sign systems that are quoted as semiologies alternative to language are always very close to verbal language. In contrast, in the work on legends, proven to have been undertaken at the same time as the study of language and linguistic sign, there are abundant references to the *Cours de linguistique générale.* Why?

The semiologic unit of the legend (either the character, the geographical location or the historical period) is not arbitrary like the linguistic sign. From the beginning, it is motivated by onomastics, history and geography. One can frequently retrace and prove that these units have a referential origin and, therefore, a precisely limited meaning. As such, the unit is not a semiological sign. This is how Saussure first describes the unit of legendary meaning.

Later on, Saussure manages to convince himself of the fact that there comes a moment in the evolution of the great legends when the mythical character is totally detached from his origin and from all initial referential charge. The character then becomes an empty form, an 'inexistent being' like a letter in the alphabet or like a word. Such a form is then liable to enter into the open *combinatoire* that bestows on language its infinite creativity. It attains the same degree of plasticity as the linguistic sign, it has turned into a real semiological sign, liable to be loaded with meaning and value by anybody searching for the specific expression conveyed by the ancient legends. Thus, a new area of meaning with a very particular texture and colouring is placed at the disposal of the 'Corps Social'. This new semiotic reaches areas of meaning other than those of the linguistic sign, as is exactly the case for musical or visual semiotics.

The area of meaning specific to the semiosis of legends could be described as the mental space for dreams of love, heroism and glory, or even secret identifications with legendary characters. The object 'mythical person' is both an 'inexistent being' (Saussure's expression) and a possible prop for our affections:

> As one can see, the incapacity to maintain a certain identity should not be attributed to the effects of Time – such is the remarkable error committed by those who deal with signs – but is placed beforehand within the being that one cherishes and observes as an organism though it is no more than a fleeting combination of two or three ideas . . . The association – that we sometimes cherish – is but a soap bubble.[19]

Thus the legend generates an affective and very intimate sort of meaning, it is an autonomous semiology and, exactly as with verbal language, it goes through incalculable changes and modifications in the course of time (*LEG*, 31): 'What philosophers and logicians have missed here is that, from the moment a system of symbols is independent from the designated objects, it is prone, for its part, to suffer displacements that the logician is unable to calculate.'[20]

[19] 'Comme on le voit, l'incapacité à maintenir une identité certaine ne doit pas être mise sur le compte des effets du Temps – c'est là l'erreur remarquable de ceux qui s'occupent des signes – mais est déposée d'avance dans l'être que l'on choye et observe comme un organisme, alors qu'il n'est que la combinaison fuyante de deux ou trois idées . . . L'association – que nous chérissons parfois – n'est qu'une bulle de savon' (*LEG*, 192).

[20] 'Ce qui a échappé ici, aux philosophes et aux logiciens, c'est que, du moment qu'un système de symboles est indépendant des objets désignés, il était sujet à subir, pour sa part, par le fait du temps, des déplacements non calculables pour le logicien' (*ELG*, 20).

Hence we witness, almost 'live', the birth of another idea of semiotics in the mind of Saussure. *Not only*, any more, is there the *logical cum grammatical* semiology that is the necessary foundation for proposing the limits between which is brought into play the entire system of relations empty of meaning that serves to describe the abstract system of 'la langue' (language), *but also* a *sensitive and affective* semiology that intends to take into account feelings as truer to life and the experience of meaning at the affective level. In this moment of improbable synthesis that is one of the most respected aspects of Saussure's thinking, we witness the point that all semiotic schools have reached today: all have, at the same time, but following very different paths, set their agendas, for their research, on the question of instinct, emotions and passions.

The work on legends introduces Saussure's reflection on some textual workings that he considers *because they are not literary* and because, for this reason, they present units of meaning which are not set ('figées'), but, on the contrary, totally subject to the pressure of the 'masse parlante' that moves them around like it moves the meaning and the value of everything, in language.

The contradiction between the referential and motivated aspect of the mythical character and the necessarily arbitrary nature of the real sign disappears here in order to bring in, at a deeper and more theoretical level of understanding, a 'linguistication' of the mythical character which becomes available for just about any signification. Thanks to this exigency of thought, 'semiotics' is not only an all-embracing logical concept that enables the theory to function. It is also a process whose beginning and evolution Saussure is capable of experiencing and seeing with his own eyes: one cannot imagine *the* origin of language, but one can, however, witness at each moment the appearance of new semioses assumed by the *Corps Social*.

It is therefore thanks to this extremely honest work on his own systematicity that Saussure loses nothing of what he perceives in the universe of the living, in the living functioning of semiosis. In *CLG/E*, 2780 B, one finds the expression 'the living units beneath the word' ('les unites vivantes au-dessous du mot') and this is in relation to the infinite plasticity of true semiotics. He thus attains stronger and more anticipatory views than, say, Hjelmslev, who did not share this mental flexibility and open-mindedness which bring together the hazards of concrete observation and the most open experiences with ongoing theoretical commitments. The solution of the enigma which the legends present rests upon two major criteria, in constant demand in order to distinguish what is 'semiotic' and what is not:

- A real semiotic constantly evolves under the double and combined influence of time and of society.
- True semiotics should be able to take into account any signification.

One will have observed that Saussure (*ELG*, 20) dismisses unnamed 'philosophers and logicians' so as to claim his scientific autonomy and so render autonomous the field of knowledge that he calls into existence, the field of the rational analysis of emergence and creation of meaning in all its forms. Our last quotation of Saussure will not surprise by the gravity it takes on here:

> The nobleness of legend as of language stems from the fact that both – set to make use of elements brought before them and bearing random meanings – bring them together and continuously draw from them a fresh meaning. A solemn law stands which one might be well advised to ponder before reaching the conclusion that this conception of legend is incorrect: nowhere do we witness the flowering of something that is not the combination of inert elements and nowhere do we see that matter be anything but the continuous food that thought digests, ordains, commands, unable however to do without.[21]

Saussure's theory is difficult and its editing and translation has promoted misunderstandings of all sorts. Nonetheless the entire semiotic field is making progress, in an astonishing harmony with Saussure's *Ecrits*. Thus, components like these works on the legends, which had practically seemed aberrant to his contemporaries, now appear liable to be the most fecund in that they reinvent the phenomenological experience of meaning and that they raise, with the utmost pointedness, some major questions such as: How come meaning is constantly renewed from any kind of material? How should we rationalize our perceptions and put together all heterogeneous units in analysis? On the one hand, we deal with the clear and distinct minimal units (syntactic items and phonological, morphological or semic components of words) of the linguistic level. On the other hand, we handle enigmatically (narratively or otherwise) modelized macro-units like **text**s and enormous ensembles of texts (corpus) considered as one single unit of meaning. We reduce them to some singular 'whole of signification' ('un Tout de signification') and, in between, mysterious middle-sized units such as emotional expressions or legendary characters, plus spaces (for instance, Pompeii, for Freud's Gradiva) and remote or future times, which may become semiotic because they are permeated by some vague scents of the collective unconscious.

Universal negativity, which, for Saussure, is the founding operation of language – with his strictly formal, differential and oppositional definition of all the elements of language never credited with the slightest positive element – is not to be interpreted as a 'pulsion de mort' (a death drive) and destruction like mainly literary minds may be led to believe. Saussurean negativity is but the

[21] 'Ce qui fait la noblesse de la légende comme de la langue, c'est que condamnées, l'une comme l'autre, à ne se servir que d'éléments apportés devant elles et d'un sens quelconque, elles les réunissent et en tirent continuellement un sens nouveau. Une loi grave préside qu'on ferait bien de méditer avant de conclure à la fausseté de cette conception de la légende: nous ne voyons nulle par fleurir une chose qui ne soit la combinaison d'éléments inertes et nous ne voyons nulle part que la matière soit autre chose que l'aliment continuel que la pensée digère, ordonne, commande mais sans pouvoir s'en passer' (*LEG*, 307).

abstract mental mechanism (at the same degree of abstraction as negative numbers in mathematics), which allows, on the contrary – as we have just seen with the metaphor taken from food (supra, *LEG*, 307) – the perpetual surge, the perpetual renewal of meaning.

Further reading

Arrivé, M. (2007) *A la recherche de Ferdinand Saussure*, Paris: PUF.

Cahiers Ferdinand de Saussure, *passim*, Geneva: Droz.

Saussure, F. de (1967–1974) *Cours de linguistique générale*, edition critique, Vols 1 and 2, ed. R. Engler, Wiesbaden: Harrassowitz.

Saussure, F. de (1983) *Course in General Linguistics*, trans. R. Harris, London: Duckworth.

Saussure, F. de (1986) *Le leggende germaniche*, ed. A. Marinetti and M. Meli, Este: Zielo.

8

Sociosemiotics

Anti Randviir and Paul Cobley

Definition

Sociosemiotics – sometimes 'social **semiotics**' – clearly stands in relation to '**semiotics**', a term that is itself infrequently defined with any great rigour. Furthermore, it also has a close relationship with different kinds of applied semiotics (cf. Pelc 1997) and their attempts to reconfigure **sign** study as the appropriate means for closely studying the phenomena of everyday life. Amongst the very few explicit definitions of sociosemiotics is that of Gottdiener and Lagopoulos who state, simply, that 'sociosemiotics is materialistic analysis of ideology in everyday life' (Gottdiener and Lagopoulos and Lagopoulos 1986: 14). This definition, however, may be open to accusations that it is 'too materialistic' in the sense that in semiotic analysis it is impossible to escape from everyday life and the consummation of signs at the stage of data collection (see, for example, Danesi and Perron 1999: 293ff.). Nor is it easy to escape from the necessarily pragmatic angle of semiotic studies (see, for example, Morris 1971: 43–54) in which the 'context', embedded in sign use, should be an important guide to interpretation. Stressing ideology may have also encouraged Gottdiener and Lagopoulos to distinguish sociosemiotics from so-called 'mainstream semiotics' by associating the former exclusively with the analysis of connotative signification connected with ideological systems. Yet, one would be hard pressed to find a cultural phenomenon in which denotative aspects were deprived of connotative **code**s.

Frequently, sociosemiotics is left undefined, despite the fact that it appears in the titles of numerous publications (e.g. Halliday 1978; Hodge and Kress 1988; Alter 1991; Flynn 1991; Riggins 1994; Jensen 1995). Clearly, it must at least be a matter of a critical sign study which is aware of the specific and strategic ways in which signs are deployed in social formations. The opposites of this definition are probably implicit: that is, first, study of signs in nature (as if nature did not feature 'sociality') and sign study in social formations which is *not* aware of the specific/strategic deployment of signs (a straw man for some versions of sociosemiotics which deplores the supposed apolitical nature of some semiotics). In various ways, a good paradigm is provided by the evolution of **language** study in the twentieth century, especially in relation to anthropology. Influential here, but by no means watertight, has been the **Sapir–Whorf hypothesis**. Along with his student Benjamin Lee **Whorf**, the linguist Edward

Sapir pursued the argument that, in brief, the language one speaks influences the way one thinks. Concomitantly, the thought processes of one culture are separated off from another by virtue of the language in which each 'thinks' and conceives the world. The idea was principally derived from the huge differences Whorf perceived between European languages and native American languages like Hopi (Carroll 1956). The idea of linguistic relativism (Gumperz and Levinson 1996; Lee 1996), in which language is seen to be responsible for many key cultural differences, clearly chimes with social-specific uses of signs.

Indirectly, then, the Sapir–Whorf hypothesis influenced the development of **sociolinguistics** and, in turn, this influenced part of the development of sociosemiotics. Coupland and Jaworski's list of sociolinguistic principles is illustrative of some of the imperatives that would be passed on to a full-blown sociosemiotics (Coupland and Jaworski 1997: 1–2):

- How are forms of speech and patterns of **communication** distributed across time and space?
- How do individuals and social groups define themselves in and through language?
- How do communities differ in the 'ways of speaking' they have adopted?
- What are typical patterns in multilingual people's use of languages?
- How is language involved in social conflicts and tensions?
- Do our attitudes to language reflect and perpetuate social divisions and discrimination, and could a better understanding of language in society alleviate those problems?
- Is there a sociolinguistic theory of language use?
- What are the most efficient, and defensible, ways of collecting language data?
- What are the implications of qualitative and quantitative methods of sociolinguistic research?
- What are the relationships between researchers, 'subjects' and data?

As can be seen, the list not only identifies the interface of signs and the 'social', it also implicates methodology in the relationship. Furthermore, that methodology is itself a hybrid, derived from various disciplines within the human sciences.

Thus, if sociosemiotics is to be understood as a term – despite the fact that, even as a loosely recognized term, it is able to unite an array of formidable scholars – it is worth mentioning what is involved in any attempt to outline its boundaries. To do this, it would be necessary to briefly consider the development of the humanities, especially as these converge, criss-cross and diverge during the tense period at the turn of the nineteenth and twentieth centuries. In this perspective, special attention would have to be paid to (cultural) anthropology, semiology and **semiotics**, early sociology and other social sciences. The first step, though, would involve an examination of different 'subsemiotic trends' in the context of the contemporary state of semiotics in order to distinguish the grounds for the (re)creation of a (new) field of sociosemiotics.

Sociosemiotics, contemporary semiotics and subsemiotics

Although semiotics, for a long period, saw its founding fathers as Charles S. **Peirce** and Ferdinand de **Saussure**, a perspective associated with the latter – **semiology** – was most successful in entering the **consciousness** of various disciplines. Semiological figures such as **Barthes** and representatives of **post-structuralism** were thought to represent contemporary semiotics on their own. This mistaking of Saussureanism for semiotics in general, or the *pars pro toto* error, is now well known (see, for example, Singer 1984: 42).

The confusion of semiotics/semiology as conflated or antagonistic is further compounded in the case of sociosemiotics. Saussure's understanding of the sign, clearly evinced in the *Course in General Linguistics*, is based on the unity of 'concept' and 'sound-image' in the mind. Peirce, on the other hand, has a more materialist understanding of the sign as exemplified in the '**object**' component of his triad. For some anthropologically oriented contributors to the general field of sociosemiotics, this was potentially a boon. Put simply, the sign could be demonstrated to have a clear efficacy in everyday life and material culture. Yet, oddly enough, sociosemiotic investigations still managed to flourish as 'materialist' studies using the semiological tradition, often in blissful and hubristic ignorance of Peircean semiotics. Barthes' highly influential primer on Saussure, translated into English in 1967 as *Elements of Semiology*, re-presented the Saussurean *signifiant* as a material entity, a substance in the circulation of signs.

One important branch of sociosemiotics which relied on Barthesian semiology, among other things, was the Anglo-Australian tradition of 'social semiotics'. Drawing, too, on the work of **Halliday**, general sociolinguistics and, later, Foucault and contemporary studies of the media, this tradition gained enormous influence in Northern Europe, North America and Australasia, especially, augmenting a burgeoning field of **discourse** theory which includes a plethora of robust journals (*Discourse and Society*, *Social Semiotics*, *Discourse Studies*, etc.) and subdivisions such as '**Critical Discourse Analysis**' (CDA).

Yet, the separation and the conflation of semiotics/semiology are, at least in one sense, misguided. Human signs and semiosis are located in the mind, and concepts and sound-images are in connection, on the one hand, with sociocultural sign systems in terms of expression and, on the other hand, with either *concrete* or *abstract* referents, such that they are always implicated in the semiotic reality of a community. The tension of different regimes of semiosis really arises from relations between sociocultural reality and institutionalized sign systems on the one hand, and the internalized relations and individual applications of signs on the other.

The third major figure in semiotics with Saussure and Peirce, although aligned most closely with the latter, has produced work which proposes to solve the problem of different regimes of semiosis and different realities. Thomas A. Sebeok's career has consisted not just of his publishing and teaching ventures. His massive project of promoting disciplines and bringing together its representatives is well known and well documented. This included bringing together workers in the field of **Chomsky**an linguistics and sociolinguistics, as well as his work in convening biosemiotics and an impressive array of textual semiotics. Semiotics redefined by Sebeok made it necessary to understand that human affairs are only a small part of what semiotics' proper object is. Drawing on the work of the Estonian-born German theoretical biologist Jakob von **Uexküll** and the Tartu–Moscow School of semiotics, Sebeok (1988b) identified three levels of **modelling** that amounted to a schematization of different kinds of semiosis and, possibly, the different semiotics needed to treat them. Hence, Sebeok encouraged specialism in semiotics: partly because he understood that academic endeavour has an aptitude for proceeding in this way, but also because subsemiotic branches – one would include sociosemiotics among them – were crucial to the work of semiotics as a whole.

Yet, to complicate matters, subsemiotic branches of study have a longer prehistory than the theoretical formalization of modelling systems. Thus, the main way in which subsemiotic branches of research have emerged is through the logic of information channels (e.g. the optical channel – see Landwehr 1997; the acoustic channel – see Strube and Lazarus 1997; the tactile channel – see Heuer 1997, etc.). Also terms like 'visual semiotics', 'semiotics of space' and the like similarly point at the possibility of differentiating between objects on the basis of the channels of human perception by which the world is turned into signs. However, it is doubtful that these channels can be actually studied separately (see, for example, Krampen 1997). Furthermore, different areas of semiosis have been articulated that lead to, and are included in, the cultural processes of anthroposemiosis: microsemiosis, mycosemiosis, phytosemiosis and zoosemiosis (see Wuketis 1997). So, the problem arises once more that sociosemiotics is always embedded in 'general' semiotics.

One area where levels and processes of interaction brought forward in sign creation and exchange has been considered is in late twentieth-century communication study. The *processual stages* of sign exchange as communication have been articulated by those influenced by the classical model of communication found in Shannon and Weaver (1949). While such processual models can principally be traced back to Saussure's sketch of oral speech, other types of communication models centre on the *functions of interaction* as presented by Roman Jakobson (1960). Yet others focus on perceptions and events (Gerbner 1956) or on particular occupational communication (Westley and MacLean 1957). On numerous occasions, Sebeok argued that semiotics in general and communication theory are the same thing. Certainly, as Dan Sperber argues, there were many in the 1940s and 1950s who believed in and sought a unified science of communication based on semiotics, cybernetics and information theory (1979: 48). In light of this, it might be perceived that sociosemiotics is the equivalent to a more sociologically orientated communication, an approach which is sub-semiotic ('signs in society') and whose methodology is defined by its objects ('signs in society', again). There is some truth in this; however, it is not the end of the matter since sociosemiotics' sources, influences and correspondences are also located elsewhere than sociology.

Sources and correspondences

Apart from those areas mentioned already (notably, sociology, sociolinguistics and communication theory), it should be noted that sociosemiotics has its sources and correspondences in the following areas: cultural anthropology (Kluckhohn 1961; Goodenough 1980; Keesing 1972, 1974; Rosaldo 1993), cultural semiotics (Shukman 1984; Randviir 2004), sociology and the social sciences (Kavolis 1995; Nikolaenko 1983; Ruesch 1972), Marxism (Ponzio 1989a; Rossi-Landi 1986a, 1986b, 1990), **pragmatics** (Verschueren 1999; Davis 1991; Morris 1938), **pragmaticism** (Peirce 1998a [1906]; cf. Schutz 1967 and Garfinkel 1967), as well as constructionism (see Gergen and Gergen 2003; Gergen 1985; Potter and Wetherell 1987) and the linguistic turn (Rorty 1967). Let us comment on each.

Cultural anthropology

In attempting to define the content of 'culture' for contemporary semiotic analysis, it is difficult to avoid commenting on the development of cultural anthropology during the twentieth century. The expanding range of cultural anthropology is related to the way in which sociosemiotics (as well as mid-twentieth-century semiotics, generally) found its objects. European cultural anthropology had roots in early sociology and Saussurean semiology that are revealed in structural anthropology. Furthermore, principles of semiology, **structuralism** and formalism are evident in the parallel development of cultural semiotics. Semiology is important both for structural anthropology (cf. Leach 1976) and for cultural semiotics (cf. Lucid 1977), since it has directed culture studies toward the analysis of sign systems as cognitive social systems. A gradually increasing emphasis on the description of cultural phenomena as the outcome of individually (or communally) articulated social sign systems led to the burgeoning currency of schools in cultural analysis associated with cognitive trends in cultural anthropology. Thus, there was a steady movement from the late nineteenth-century description of cultures as sets of artefacts organized according to cultural patterns toward the interpretation of cultures as ideational systems (Geertz 1993). This means that cultures were no longer understood to be 'made' only at the metalevel, through the organization of relations between cultural phenomena in scientific discourse. Indeed, while cultures could be viewed as 'theories' in Kluckhohn's sense (Kluckhohn 1961), throughout the development of the humanities there has been an increased attention to cultures as abstractions existing at the level of the cultural object. This has been characteristic of schools analysing cultures as ideational or semiotic systems.

Sociocultural systems are reflective systems and the overt behaviour revealed in cultural traits depends on the covert behaviour directed by cognitive structures such as image schemata, values, behavioural schemes, etc. Thus, the aim of understanding cultures has been to describe them as systems of knowledge, intersemiotic sign systems and reflective systems. In the fashion of the cognitive anthropologist Ward Goodenough, cultures can be seen as sets of decision standards, intellectual forms, perception models, models of relating, interpretation models, preference ratings and organizational patterns (see, for example, Goodenough 1961, 1980, 1981). For a unified cultural anthropology, these cognitive structures would converge into sociocultural systems defined as systems that 'represent the social realizations or enactments of ideational designs-for-living in particular environments' (Keesing 1974: 82).

An important feature of the development of the humanities has been the widening of the scope of culture study by new methods, a process which is not unconnected to the development of semiotics. Rosaldo presents an understanding of the development of ethnographic and social thought as having its roots in the epoch of 'the Lone Ethnographer' deeply immersed in fieldwork, the results of which were used by armchair theorists as information storehouses. The period of the Lone Ethnographer, according to Rosaldo, was followed by the classic period lasting, in anthropology, from approximately 1921 to 1971; this was characterized by the objectivist research programme which viewed society as a system and culture as a coherent set of patterns: 'Phenomena that could not be regarded as systems or patterns appeared to be unanalyzable; they were regarded as exceptions, ambiguities, or irregularities' (Rosaldo 1993: 32). Similarly, as Kluckhohn pointed out, the sudden expansion of the range of objects for culture analysis took place in tandem with the arrival of new methods allowing explanations of diverse phenomena supposedly outside the mainstream domain of culture, e.g. psychoanalysis (Kluckhohn 1961).

On the other hand, categorization of certain phenomena as not representative of a cultural system would principally allow descriptions of given systems by way of a principle of negation. This is not dissimilar to the predilection of both psychoanalysis and poststructuralism for the 'marginal' as a repository of meaning by which to understand the mainstream. From this perspective, exceptions, ambiguities and irregularities gain specific significance for the analysis of both the object-level (the so-called 'wastebasket method') and the metalevel. Discussions in cultural anthropology about the range of objects for the study of culture and society have been of great value for the social and human sciences. Whereas one can find fault in Western scholarship for its 'primitivization' of certain cultures and societies until at least the turn of the nineteenth and twentieth centuries, extending the range of research objects was of crucial importance in placing Western cultures and societies under the anthropological microscope. In a critical vein, Marcus and Fischer (1986: 20) have labelled this the 'salvage motif' of ethnography.

Until the beginning of the twentieth century, indigenous *cultures* were taken as research objects for Western humanitarian scholarship. So-called 'primitive' cultures tended to be described as *cultural groups* rather than *societies*. The Western population which lived in *societies* was deemed, at the same time, too elaborate to study. Complex developments in Western civilization at the object-level (industrialization, inventions and discoveries that brought technology, medicine and natural science to a level which inspired confidence – modernity) induced new attitudes at the metalevel: *society* became a proper object of study alongside *culture*. Yet, more far-reaching still has been the self-reflexivity of anthropologists later in the twentieth century (e.g. Clifford 1988; Marcus and Fischer 1986). What became apparent to cultural anthropology was not only that the phenomena studied in culture are *semiotic* in their bearing, but that the way in which investigation of such phenomena took place was by partaking of procedures which were as equally semiotic (or, in a more limiting way, discursive) as the phenomena under question:

> The primary data of ethnographic analysis consist of informants' statements about the code and records of their speech behaviour . . . All available data, including behavioural records, the ethnographer's intuitions and speech behaviour, provide evidence from which an underlying cultural code can be inferred, and against which descriptions can be tested.
>
> (Keesing 1972: 301)

What anthropology came to realize, partly influenced by sociosemiotics-orientated ethnographers such as Hymes, was that it was dealing not so much with the subject and object, but with the triplet of object, researcher and informant. This has been a pretty salient point within the perspective of sociosemiotics.

Cultural semiotics

While Western cultural anthropology widened its objects of analysis and adopted a more interpretative bent, sociosemiotics also drew inspiration from work carried out in more constricting circumstances. Indeed, it may have been such circumstances that prevented cultural semiotics as developed by the Tartu–Moscow School from being overly transparent, despite the clarity and breadth of its principal theses (Uspenskij *et al.* 1973). What is central, however, is the conceptual floating of the elementary notions of **metalanguage** (see Levchenko and Salupere 1999). Cultural semiotics as a discipline developed in the context of a totalitarian regime, involving also other, explicitly political spheres. Under totalitarian conditions it was largely impossible to present the kind of breadth to approaching research objects that might have been achieved in less constraining regimes. Whereas it might be possible to openly promote philology or literature studies, it was simply not possible to promulgate semiotics as an individual field of scholarship with an identifiable structure and featuring the usual academic paraphernalia such as research projects, monographs and textbooks. Any monolithic semiotic paradigm having to do with the analysis of society and culture would sooner or later have to get involved in the examination of power and ideology, social and cultural structure and political developments. Scholarship via articles (as in the case of *Sign Systems Studies*, the oldest journal of semiotics in the world) was fruitful but prevented the development of a unified metalanguage even by members of the same school of scholarship. Of course, this is not uncharacteristic of textbooks and anthologies in different disciplines that have developed in free societies and in the tradition of long-term institutionalization (e.g. psychology, sociology). Yet, in those cases, variation at least worked within a certain established framework; adjustments and innovations served to make the paradigmatic and methodological boundaries of a discipline continuous and more exact. The circumstances of cultural semiotics' gestation forced it to be wary of social and political structures when it might have been self-reflexively defining its parameters and methodologies (see, for example, Cherednichenko 2000).

Problems in terminology and methodology that concern the definition and study of cultural phenomena under the label of cultural semiotics are, on the other hand, related not only to the unfavourable political environment in which the Tartu–Moscow semiotic school was to operate, but also to the relatively complicated and rapid development of the social sciences and humanities in general. The evolution of cultural semiotics represents an interesting dynamism in which multiple scholarly traditions were involved. Distinctions can be made between the several predecessors of cultural semiotics according to certain political and geographic, and possibly also linguistic, factors. There is an added complexity to the case, of course, in that the representatives of cultural semiotics were largely isolated from trends in scholarship that directly pertained to their study at the object and metalevels (e.g. Western cultural studies, cultural anthropology, etc.). Thus 'structuralism' in relation to the Tartu–Moscow School cannot be really considered on the same terms as, say, the French tradition. Nevertheless, French structuralism, Tartu–Moscow cultural semiotics and (American) cultural anthropology could be said to be at least analogous in their *ideals* and range of objects, and prefigure the *principal* methodological standpoints of sociosemiotics. The main importance (if not appeal) of cultural semiotics probably consists of individual notions and concepts that can be used to describe semiotic systems, while, at the same time, the multiplication of these ideas sometimes renders cultural semiotics confusingly diverse. It features descriptive concepts familiar to most of sociosemiotics, such as textuality, intertextuality, code, secondary modelling systems and so forth; but it lacks a consistent, unified methodology for the study of sociocultural phenomena. One problem which seems to have prevented cultural semiotics from metamorphosing into a fully fledged sociosemiotics is the generality of its objects of analysis (e.g. 'semiosphere'; cf. Randviir 2004: 67–70). Sociosemiotic studies – particularly the successful ones – have seemed to benefit from their insistence on specificity of objects, a quality shared with disciplines within the social sciences.

Sociology, the social sciences and social psychology

As with cultural anthropology, the seemingly straightforward discovery that humans are semiotic beings has had a profound impact on the whole topic of empiricism in all walks of scholarship. If human semiotic systems filter human semiotic reality in communication, then human cognition is, to a large extent, defined through language and language-based sign systems. If the human's perceptual abilities have been shaped by those very systems, then, what is called 'reality' *is always inevitably mediated and arbitrated*. This does not lie at odds with the biosemiotic paradigm convened by Sebeok, by way of von Uexküll, in which the human **Umwelt** consists of the unique combination of verbality and nonverbality. Yet, the realization of the semiotic determination of the human relation to 'reality' is part and parcel of a pragmaticist understanding that has penetrated into various fields from linguistics to sociology.

Thus, the disciplines commonly regarded as 'hard' or devoted to the research of the physical and chemical features of the Earth gain the position of being speculative, if not hypothetical. They attempt to characterize the human and his/her reflective abilities rather than those structures and phenomena that cannot be switched into the chain of communication (cf. Russell 1948: Chs 3 and 7). Mead seconds this: 'The whole tendency of the natural sciences, as exhibited especially in physics and chemistry, is to replace the objects of immediate experience by hypothetical objects which lie beyond the range of possible experience' (Mead 1938: 291).

Sociosemiotics, as part of the social sciences, can be seen, therefore, as the empirical paradigm *par excellence*. Its objects and its empiricism are rooted in the mediatedness of physical and sociocultural reality and, while studying the mediation of these realms in communication, such study does go as far as possible in its search for 'objective empirical reality'.

'Sociosemiotics' implies sociality, but must simultaneously entail reference to the pragmatic aspect of semiotic studies which orientates semiotics to the social sciences (and effects methodological control as one of its most important facets). On the other hand, the sociality of semiotics indicates the role of sociosemiotics as a metadiscipline in the sense that sociosemiotics can serve as a methodological toolkit enabling researchers to outline the boundaries of any study of sociocultural phenomena and sign systems. The fact that 'social behaviour' or 'sign systems' can be and are metaphorically found in extremely wide areas concerning both living and inorganic systems does not – from the viewpoint of sociosemiotics – guarantee their semiotic essence or features. The scientific analysis of social behaviour 'must survive direct tests, if practicable, or any tests of derived propositions no matter what their domain' (Nicholson 1983: 79). The recent extension of semiotic vocabulary to the whole biosphere has been fruitful but not without risk: namely, the animation and anthropomorphization of species and phenomena which are ultimately outside the scope of human understanding and frequently outside the parameters of testing in terms semiotically and communicationally graspable by the perceptive and cognitive powers of *Homo sapiens*.

Understanding human environments as (semiotically) constructed, or at least accessible via signs, has led to a common conception of the 'whole' of research objects. Whilst the expressions used for the holistic web of mutually dependent and connected objects of study are often pretty diverse, they represent very similar treatments of humans, culture and society. Consider: 'social world' (Schutz 1967), 'social system' (Parsons 1952), 'culture' (Kluckhohn 1961), '*Lebenswelt*' (Garfinkel 1967), 'semiosphere' (Lotman 1984), 'mundane reason' (Pollner 1987), 'semiotic reality' (Merrell 1992), even the '**semiotic self**' (Wiley 1994) or 'signifying order' (Danesi 1998). These notions indicate that despite the disintegration of the social and human sciences into diverse 'individual disciplines' which happened alongside socio- and geo-political developments attendant on the end of the Second World War, the study of 'social structure(s)' always tends to be 'functional' in one sense. In the discussion above, certain types of objects (gender, media, etc.) frequently associated with 'sociosemiotics' were mentioned. The features of the analysis of culture and society outlined here suggest that, through the process of socialization, social structures become functional in respect to the metalevel. Ideological fluctuations that spotlight certain developments in society and culture (e.g. feminism, the emergence of transvestism, actualization of (in)differences between races, social groups, sex-roles, etc.) can – and have – lead to insular fields of research. The sociosemiotic understanding of the study of culture and society, however, calls for the holistic complex perspective that some scholars have striven for in the last hundred years.

Marxism

It is well known that Marxist ideas have been quite popularly 'semiotized' in Continental and even in Anglo-American semiotic circles (some of the most well known include Lefebvre 1968, Althusser 1975 and, the most explicitly semiotic in orientation and knowledge, Rossi-Landi 1990; see, also, *Zeitschrift für Semiotik* 1988 and Ponzio 1989a). Semiotized Marxism has sometimes been studied as 'structural' Marxism (e.g. Benton 1984); it has also been associated with the analysis of dynamism between culture and society as holistic units, and labelled as belonging to the social systemic approach to culture in cultural sociology (see Kavolis 1995: 4–6). Of course, it is not difficult to discern meaningfulness in any system of (human) communication, be that communication accomplished either by immaterial or material sign-vehicles. The semiotic nature of material phenomena is evident in communication systems in Marxist terms, but just as well in anthropological analysis or in the study of material culture (for example, early study of the Kula ring; Mauss 1969; Malinowski 1999). It is also detectable in any material phenomena forming the context for communication and everyday life (see, for example, Riggins 1994). Furthermore, the material environment that both forms, and is formed by, sociality does follow a certain logic that is grounded in semiotic considerations (see, for example, Gottdiener 1985; Hillier and Hanson 1993; Lefebvre 1991).

Rossi-Landi asserts that 'Karl Marx made a remarkable contribution to the study of symbolism in general and to the theory of social communication' although he qualifies this by adding that 'he made it in a most indirect way' (Rossi-Landi 1986a: 482; cf. Ponzio 2001b). Too mechanistic a relation between Marxism and semiotics presents fairly obvious perils. In particular, it might promote a search for the *true meanings behind the appearances*, the return of the Era of the Lone Ethnographer (Rosaldo 1993: 32) and so-called armchair scholarship. Such work has had its influence, indeed an enormous one. Identified chiefly with the 'myth criticism' of Roland Barthes, designed to expose the naturalizing influence of bourgeois culture (with **connotation** being the foremost bourgeois weapon), this perspective still has a hold in areas where international semiotics is insufficiently well known. Such a hold has been superseded; indeed, Barthes' *Mythologies* (1973a), with its undermining of the tenets of 1950s French cultural artefacts, was effectively laid to rest by Barthes in 1971 when he lamented how facile 'myth criticism' had become in the intervening years, calling, instead, for a more comprehensive 'semioclasm' (1977a). Notwithstanding this, Barthes' semiotized Marxism is still widely taught and *Mythologies* remains a popular paperback book. This is largely because it is undeniable that signs do have connotations and that they are enforced connotations. But, as with structuralism, the 'actual meanings' revealed in work from this perspective are invariably just as arbitrary as those enforced by bourgeois culture.

Semiotized Marxism has informed sociosemiotics by being forthright in drawing attention to the existence of a very strong relation of ideology and culture, even though that relation is not quite as it first seemed. The other major bequest from semiotized Marxism to sociosemiotics is the argument that all sign systems are, in one way or another, material. Lévi-Strauss's (1978) treatment of homologies between settlement space, social structure, cooking and world view constitutes an early example of both the close relation of ideology and culture *plus* the materiality of sign systems. To some extent, this kind of reasoning has cemented the relation of structuralism with the study of symbolic discourse in the Marxist sense, in turn giving an impression of the proximity of semiotics and Marxism (e.g. de George and de George 1972; cf. 'materialistic semiotics' in Rossi-Landi 1986b; Ponzio 1989a: 394–396; cf. Heim 1983). Sign *systems* (if not the individual sign) can be understood as material even in Saussure's division of the sign process into three levels: psychological, physiological and physical (Saussure 1983: 11–17). Sign systems are often materialized in normative and/or descriptive grammars; this is not unconnected to the understanding of sign systems as formal or informal institutions (cf. Ruesch 1972: 277–298). Rossi-Landi, speaking of a Marxist semiotics, sums up, also, sociosemiotics:

> The program, then, is that of a semiotics founded on social reality, on the actual ways in which members of the human race interact among themselves and with the rest of the living and inanimate world. Such an approach cannot examine sign systems apart from the other social processes with which they are functioning all along. It cannot make everything rest on signs by themselves.
>
> (Rossi-Landi 1986b: 486)

This offers a seductive definition of sociosemiotics as a matter of analysing signs and revealing their embeddedness in relation to 'non-signs' (inescapably important forces such as the relations of production and the exercise of power through institutions). This might lead to the conclusion that sociosemiotics is simply semiotized Marxism, were it not for the simple fact that the relation of signs to non-signs always already renders the latter as signs. Sociosemiotics, then, is not merely the study of the relation of signs to non-signs, nor is it sign study plus context.

Pragmatics

The 'relation to' context in sociosemiotics is mostly a matter of its pragmatic heritage, especially the initial division of linguistics made by one of semiotics' key conveners. The semiotician Charles **Morris**, in an influential formulation, suggested that the study of language could be split into syntactics (the study of the relation of signs to other signs), **semantics** (the study of the relationships of signs to their objects) and **pragmatics** (the study of the relationships of signs to their interpreters or users) (Morris 1938). Taking the third of these, the project of pragmatics has frequently been thought to be devoted to series of topics or categories in linguistics such as propositions and 'principles' in speech, interactive implicatures, deixis, politeness, speaker roles, 'speech acts' and 'context'. Many of these interests overlap with sociolinguistics and, for some, pragmatics is a part of sociolinguistics in the same way as **discourse analysis** or **CDA** are (e.g. Coupland and Jaworski 2001). Verschueren (1999, 2001) argues that pragmatics appears to have no real object of study and that, in truth, it is more sensible to treat it as a 'perspective'. What this perspective focuses on, for Verschueren, is choice, variation and adaptation, a set of phenomena which actually allies pragmatics to Anglo-Australian sociosemiotics in particular, especially in respect of the latter's systemic-functionalist heritage. What Verschueren calls for, then, is an understanding of pragmatics as an interdisciplinary perspective comprising the study of cognition, society and culture.

Sociosemiotics is not so much a matter of signs plus non-signs, then; nor is it a matter of signs plus context. Rather, its principles and methods of analysis, across all its schools, either wittingly or unwittingly, are a matter of relations between signs and sign users, the latter of which are thoroughly semiotized by virtue of their existence in a comprehensively semiotic environment, observed by analysts of signs who inhabit an analogously semiotic environment.

Pragmaticism

Having made these general statements about the relation of sociosemiotics and the pragmatic perspective it is necessary, nevertheless, to make one qualification regarding an intellectual tradition that has been important for semiotics. 'Pragmaticism', as is well known, was introduced by Peirce in his later writings to distinguish his concept of pragmatism from those of James and others. In 1905, he wrote:

> No doubt, Pragmaticism makes thought ultimately apply to action exclusively – to conceived action. But between admitting that and either saying that it makes thought, in the sense of the purport of symbols, to consist in acts, or saying that the true ultimate purpose of thinking is action, there is much the same difference as there is between saying that the artist-painter's living art is applied to dabbing paint upon canvas, and saying that that art-life consists in dabbing paint, or that its ultimate aim is dabbing paint. Pragmaticism makes thinking consist in the living inferential metaboly of symbols whose purport lies in conditional general resolutions to act.
>
> (*CP* 5.402, n. 3, 1906)

With this perspective on action considered, and if the human's world is semiotically created and maintained, then the metalevel must concentrate on the study of methods people use to build the sociocultural environment. Ultimately, one could argue, pragmaticism gave rise to ethnomethodology (Garfinkel 1967), and in more particular ways, through so-called *verstehen*-methodology (Schutz 1967), also to studies of the resolution of social situations under the conceptions of **Conversation Analysis** (Sacks 1992) and discourse analysis (originating with **Harris** 1952). Discourse analysis constantly brings sociocultural studies back to notions of representation. Although it developed separately from ethnomethodology, 'discourse analysis', particularly in its later developments, is similar in its aims to Conversation Analysis. Works in discourse analysis share a commitment to the general idea that meaning and social roles are produced in interaction. Similarly to pragmaticism, forms of communication between humans are not simply a matter of attempting to 'reflect' the world; rather, they are forms of social action.

In addition to its roots in pragmaticism, the social constructionist position of much discourse analysis can be traced back to **Vološinov**, another key figure for sociosemiotics in different ways, whose 1920s critique of Saussure and Marr in *Marxism and the Philosophy of Language* (1973) emphasized at length that verbal communication is much more a matter of what people want to get out of a situation than a matter of pure information exchange. In this respect, there is a clear line forward to discourse analysis generally and Conversation Analysis specifically as well as more emphatically constructionist methodologies still, such as discursive psychology (e.g. Potter and Wetherell 1987). The idea that words *do* things rather than merely describing things, of course, was the focus of the celebrated discussion in **Austin**'s *How To Do Things with Words* (1962), an intervention whose broad influence in the world of communication and sign study is not to be underestimated (see Cobley 2006a).

What might be the central dilemma of sociosemiotics, then, is the extent to which it is pulled towards a conception of 'signs in relation to non-signs' and/or 'signs and action versus signs *as* action'. Many would not wish to subscribe to the extreme constructionist position that everything is 'constructed in discourse', an outgrowth of the much vaunted 'linguistic turn' (Rorty 1967); however, equally, it is the case that there is a recognition of the semiotic nature of the environment in which humans find themselves and through which they make observations. Metaphors such as 'language' or '**text**' have been heuristic extrapolation devices serving sociosemiotics. As with the machinery of science, designed to capture phenomena which it has hitherto been impossible to observe, it is never guaranteed that machinery provides the observer with meaning or meaningfulness, as opposed to mere physical information (see Russell 1948; Pelc 1992: 33). Thus a vital distinction has to be made between the existence of an entity as a sign, on the one hand, and the existence of something as being interpretable as a sign, on the other (see Pelc 1992: 26). In short, what is understood by the 'sign' has direct impact on what can be studied under the general label of 'culture' or 'society'.

Sociosemiotic terms

The difficulties of establishing what exactly a sign is are most manifest in sociosemiotics' insistence on a fairly uniform repertoire of combinations of signs and the (sometimes considerable) differences between schools in approaching them. The main examples of combinations of signs and sign functioning repeatedly employed by schools of sociosemiotics can be listed as follows:

social structure
representation
dialogue
the other
multimodality
discourse
motivation (in signs and in combinations of signs)
identity
genre (routinization of communicational forms).

The list might be extended but it would be difficult to shorten it. Above all, though, even more than a relation of signs to 'non-signs', what this list implies is a set of terms in which signs are subject to social forces (which may be semiotic in themselves) or 'signs in society'. That is, the compound of individual, society, sign systems and sociocultural reality.

Unsurprisingly, the concept of the 'self-in-society' is also implied in these terms. In this light, 'self-in-society' as a concern of sociosemiotics has developed out of a number of binaries which characterized the early social sciences. These were the oppositions of:

- developed cultures versus primitive cultures
- developed specimens of the human race versus others
- societies, or social orders, or civilized orders, versus cultures, or cultural orders
- processes versus structures
- consciously intentional versus instinctive
- rational thought, or reflection, versus unconscious motivation, or natural programme
- human emotions versus ritualistic routine
- sign-based behaviour versus signal-based behaviour.

Most of the first elements in each of these oppositions have been a matter for philosophy; yet, they have been adjusted to a metalevel when considered in the frame of the self and society. At the same time, it is possible to see these oppositions within the frame of an overarching opposition – tackled at length in more recent semiotics – that of humanity versus the animal kingdom; although, clearly, this overarching opposition also partakes of that social science staple between developed cultures/societies and individuals versus primitive cultures and individuals.

The relation of animal and human worlds in understanding the development of the self in sociosemiotics is worth commenting on here. Much of the groundwork on modern theory of the self was laid down by Cooley (1902, 1909, 1918) and, in turn, Mead's treatment of the self as a dynamic process resulting from social communication (1907, 1913, 1922, 1930) was comprehensively based on Cooley. There is little difficulty in recruiting Mead into the ranks of (socio)semioticians (cf. Wiley 1994 and, especially, Kilpinen 2000). If Saussure's placing of 'semiology' amongst social or general psychology, or Peirce's equation of semiotics and logic, is taken into account, not to mention Mead's adoption of Peirce's triadic logic and his influence on Morris (see Mead 1934, 1938), Mead's position in semiotics is further strengthened. Understanding the self as a product of social communication, Mead relates to the paradigm of the Frankfurt School and the topic of socialization and the social construction of reality (Berger and Luckmann 1972 [1966]). However, in his social behaviourism, Mead's position is close to that of Morris, which is far from 'common behaviourism', since the *social* in this case concerns the behaviour of the self in the mind. Mead realized that humans as *biological* beings live in the world(s) of sign systems, and modelling takes place already on the level of perception, since perceptual objects are results of interaction between man and his environment (Mead 1938: 81). Sebeok's discussion of modelling after the Tartu–Moscow School (Sebeok 1988b), a discussion which ultimately crystallized **Modelling Systems Theory** and **biosemiotics**, clearly developed out of this tradition. Moreover, Sebeok was a student of Morris and thus at least indirectly acquainted with Mead. As has been mentioned, the theory of *Umwelt* (Uexküll 1982) is crucial here. Yet, while sociosemiotic studies have not always adopted this term, they have, in Mead's wake, figured the self in relation to some key processes or entities which determine the self's 'social reality' (as opposed to any 'individual reality' that may be perceived to exist independently).

As a result, it is possible to draw up a list of the key entities which make up the concerns of sociosemiotics in its discussions of the self's relation to/ constitution by social reality:

organization
intentionality
exchange
communication
interaction-communication
process-structure
praxis
agency
socialization
culture (and multiculturalism)
ideology
institution
modernity
globalization.

This is not an exhaustive list, by any means. But it should offer an idea of the ways in which the issues of sign combinations and fundamental sociocultural oppositions produce a concern with a fairly specific set of entities or processes. To put it another way, it gives a sense of what are the foremost preoccupations in the discussion of signs in relation to the supposed 'non-signs' of the social.

The place(s) of sociosemiotics

We have been able only to offer a sketch of the place of sociosemiotics in contemporary semiotics and its embeddedness in a longer tradition of research in the social sciences. For a flavour of sociosemiotics in action, one has to scrutinize individual instances of research in addition to theory, be it discussions of social placement of toys, discourse, ideological currents in public communication, instances of collective memory, the many facets of globalization, gender biases, the uses and abuses of space, statements about the nature of practice in any field, and so forth (see Cobley and Randviir 2009). We have tried to trace the lineage and parameters of a set of symbolic rules and procedures that make up sociosemiotics; but a field as vibrant as this also comprises various personages – journal or book series editors, professional organizations, compilers of widely used reference material, conference organizers, leaders of important research centres or 'schools', popular lecturers, and so forth – and, typically, these are located in specific areas around the globe and in specific institutions whose work and interactions determine a domain (see Sebeok 2001b: 163–164). These include the 'Anglo-Australian school', the 'Bari school', the 'Finnish school', Tartu sociosemiotics, the 'Greek school' centred in Thessaloniki, the 'Vienna school', as well as contributions beyond these schools. Some of the participants may not recognize themselves as part of a school. Also, some members of the Anglo-Australian school, say, may be neither in Australia nor the UK (for more, see Cobley and Randviir 2009).

Yet, what we can say about the place of sociosemiotics is that it is not fixed (in one space or discipline), nor is it transient (in the sense that it is likely to go away). In this it is like semiotics in general. Yet, whereas observers, however mistakenly, might see in various manifestations of sign study the scrutiny of more or less interesting relations between and within phenomena brought to light by harmless drudges, sociosemiotics is inexorably tied to the quotidian realities of social life. Such realities are part of semiosis in all its glory; although sociosemiotics has made it a central task not to shrink from exposing their disturbing ugliness and oppressive potential.

Further reading

Berger, P. L. and Luckmann, T. (1972 [1966]) *The Social Construction of Reality: A Treatise in the Sociology of Knowledge*, Harmondsworth: Penguin Books.

Cobley, P. and Randviir, A. (eds) (2009) *Sociosemiotica*, special issue of *Semiotica*, 173 (1/2): 134.

Kilpinen, E. (2000) *The Enormous Fly-Wheel of Society: Pragmatism's Habitual Conception of Action and Social Theory*, Department of Sociology, University of Helsinki: Research Report no. 235.

Mead, G. H. (1934) *Mind, Self, and Society*, ed., with introduction, by C. W. Morris, Chicago: University of Chicago Press.

Riggins, S. H. (ed.) (1994) *The Socialness of Things: Essays in the Sociosemiotics of Objects*, Berlin: Mouton de Gruyter.

9

SEMIOTICS OF MEDIA AND CULTURE

MARCEL DANESI

INTRODUCTION

The overarching aim of **semiotics** is to study **semiosis** (the production and comprehension of **signs**) as it manifests itself in human and non-human spheres. The general study of semiosis comes today under the rubric of ***biosemiotics***, whereas the study of human semiosis, in specific cultural contexts, comes instead under the rubric of *cultural semiotics* (Posner *et al*. 1997–2004). As a cultural science, the latter discipline has proven itself to be particularly well suited as a framework for analysing the signs, **texts**, and signifying practices used by the contemporary mass media.

The semiotic purview envisions human cultures as networks of intertwining sign systems. Cumulatively, these comprise the ***semiosphere*** – a concept originating in the work of the late Estonian-based Russian semiotician Jurij **Lotman** (1922–1993). The semiosphere regulates and enhances human cognition in tandem (Lotman 2000). In this theoretical framework, specific cultures are seen to be both cognitively constraining, in that they impose upon individuals born into them already-fixed sign systems, which will largely determine how they come to understand the world around them; and liberating, because they also provide the signifying resources by which individuals can construct new signs and systems at will. Particularly interesting is the role of mass communications media in the semiosphere. There is, in fact, a general 'semiotic law of media', so to speak, implicit in the Lotmanian approach to the study of culture – namely, as the media change, so too do the sign systems of culture. Studying the implications of this 'law' is a primary aim of *media semiotics*, one of the contemporary offshoots of cultural semiotics. Although the analysis of media and contemporary culture goes back at least to the late 1930s, a full-fledged media semiotics did not surface until the mid-1950s, becoming a major discipline in the 1990s (Jensen 1995; Bignell 1997; Nöth 1997; Danesi 2002). Media semiotics interweaves insights and findings from other disciplines in order to gain understanding of all aspects of 'mediated signification', as the use and interpretation of media-based signs and texts is called.

THE EMERGENCE OF MEDIA STUDIES

The academic study of the media and their effects on individuals and cultures was motivated by a media event that became itself a headline story – the 1938 radio broadcast of the *War of the Worlds* in the United States. The programme's creator, actor and director Orson Welles, had simply recast H. G. Wells' novel about interplanetary invasion as a radio drama simulating the style of a news broadcast, with a series of 'on-the-spot' news reports describing the landing of Martian spaceships in the New Jersey area. An announcer would remind the radio audience, from time to time, that the show was fictional. Even so, many listeners became panicky, believing Martians had actually invaded the Earth. The police and the army were notified by concerned citizens. The reaction took Welles by surprise, since he did not expect that people would take the show seriously. In retrospect, the event perfectly exemplified what French philosopher Jean **Baudrillard** (1983) called, years later, the *simulacrum* effect, whereby the media representations and reality evolve into simulacra of each other, thus blurring the distinction between the two.

The radio broadcast motivated the first psychological study of the media by Hadley Cantril of Princeton University. Cantril (2005) wanted to ascertain why some listeners believed the fake reports and others not. After interviewing 135 subjects, Cantril's research team came to the conclusion that the key element was level of education – better-educated listeners were more capable of recognizing the broadcast as fiction than less-educated ones. The study opened the door to a host of similar studies, leading to what is now called Hypodermic Needle Theory (HNT). The main contention of the theory is that media directly affect mental processes in a way that is analogous to how the contents of an injecting hypodermic needle affect bodily processes. Starting in the late 1940s, a new set of findings showed, however, that media had little or no direct impact on people, but rather, that people got out of media content what they were already inclined to get. In a 1948 study, titled *The People's Choice*, American sociologist Paul Lazarsfeld (1901–1976) and his co-researchers found, for instance, that the media had virtually no ability to change people's minds about how they would vote in an election. People simply extracted from newspapers or radio broadcasts only the views that fitted their preconceptions, ignoring the others. In 1956, Lazarsfeld and Elihu Katz (b. 1926) found, moreover, that media audiences constituted interpretive communities guided by opinion leaders (Katz and Lazarsfeld 1956). So, in contrast to HNT, which portrays media textuality as a one-step flow reaching a homogeneous audience directly, Lazarsfeld and Katz portray it instead as a two-step flow, in which the first step is through the opinion leader, who takes in media content, interprets it, and then passes it on to group members (the second step):

Flow Theory cannot explain, however, the power of visual media to affect people directly. This was brought out dramatically by another well-known media episode – the Kennedy–Nixon TV debate, which turned the 1960 election around in favour of Kennedy. People who heard the debate on radio maintained that Nixon had won it, coming across as the better candidate; those who watched it on television claimed the opposite. Nixon looked dishevelled and apprehensive on television; Kennedy looked self-assured, idealistic, and vibrant, a veritable 'president of the future'. Kennedy went on to win the election and a society-wide debate emerged on the persuasive effects of media images.

By the early 1950s, the academic study of media started to branch out in several new directions. One of these involved the analysis of the relation among three spheres – mass communications technologies, media content, and cultural evolution. The leader in this field was the Canadian communications theorist Marshall McLuhan (1911–1980) who claimed that the three were interconnected (McLuhan 1951, 1962, 1964). McLuhan never really coined a term for his theory. However, the term *Convergence Theory*, as used today to refer to the integration of technologies with cultural forms and evolutionary tendencies (Negroponte 1995), would seem to be an appropriate one to characterize McLuhan's overall perspective retrospectively. Also originating in McLuhan's work is the idea of mediation, or the notion that media influence text construction and interpretation. Mediation is the likely reason why the MediaSphere (as it is called in McLuhan studies) has largely replaced the traditional religious sphere in shaping signification. It is relevant to note in this regard that, as John Morrish (1999: 83) points out, the term *icon* has been used to describe visually impressive celebrities such as Madonna: 'At first, people probably were aware of the sacrilegious irony of this use given her name. But that soon faded and is now used broadly.' The term has been applied retrospectively to describe past celebrities who have become virtually akin to religious figures – Elvis Presley, Marilyn Monroe, James Dean, and so on.

McLuhan was also among the first to realize that changes in media (like changes in signs) leads to changes in social structure and in knowledge systems. For example, the move away from pictographic to alphabetic writing around 1000 BCE was, he suggested, the first great cultural paradigm shift of human history. Ancient cuneiform writing, for instance, allowed the Sumerians to develop a great civilization; papyrus and hieroglyphics transformed Egyptian society into an advanced culture; the alphabet spurred the ancient Greeks on to make extraordinary advances in science, technology, and the arts; the alphabet also made it possible for the Romans to develop an effective system of government; the printing press facilitated the dissemination of knowledge broadly and widely, paving the way for the European Renaissance, the Protestant Reformation, and the Enlightenment; radio, movies, and television brought about the rise of a global pop culture in the twentieth century; and the Internet and the World Wide Web ushered in McLuhan's 'global village' as the twentieth century came to a close (McLuhan 1962, 1964).

Proto-semiotic approaches

In summary, McLuhan's approach to media analysis can be characterized as 'proto-semiotic', since it was based on two essentially semiotic notions, even though he never directly used the term semiotics (or even alluded to it) in his work:

1 the notion that mass communications technologies allow humans to extend themselves cognitively and socially; and
2 the notion that the dominant media used to communicate in a society in a specific historical epoch affect the content of the messages communicated (mediation).

The claim that media are extensions of human beings is a concept that parallels Charles **Peirce**'s contention that signs are extensions of sensory and intellectual processes. In effect, signs are tools – things (real or imaginary) that extend some sensory, physical, or intellectual capacity. An axe extends the power of the human hand to break wood; the wheel of the human foot to cover great distances; the computer of the human brain to organize and process information; and so on. Media are also tools, extending the ability of humans to communicate with each other better (and further) than they can with the voice or hands.

The intrinsic interconnection between mass communications technologies and cultural evolution became, in the 1950s, a fertile area of study, as a consequence of McLuhan's crucial insights. The American **communication** theorist Wilbur Schramm (1907–1987) provided a common terminology for studying this connection, elaborating on previous work by the telecommunications engineer Claude Shannon (1948) – a terminology that continues to be used today. The notions of encoder and decoder are central to Schramm's overall conception – the *encoder* is the component (human or electronic) converting a message into a form that can be transmitted through an appropriate channel; the *decoder* reverses the encoding process so that the message can be received and understood successfully. Schramm's model came to be called, logically, the *Sender–Message–Channel–Receiver* model, or SMCR for short (Schramm 1954; cf. Berlo 1960).

An elaboration of the model, based on the notion of ***code***, was put forward by George Gerbner (1919–2005) in 1956, bringing media studies more and more into the semiotic domain. For Gerbner a code is anything that is used to create messages in a socially meaningful way. The relations between the sexes in, say, a television sitcom, or the features that make a hero superhuman in adventure movies, are based on codes that have a socio-historical origin. Codes are sign systems – collections of signs that cohere with each other in historically determined ways. There are three general features that define codes and their relation to media (Danesi 2007). The first one can be called *representationality*. This implies simply that codes are used to stand for – *represent* – something, wittingly or unwittingly. The representation, moreover, will vary according to medium. The news on television will be represented in a more visual and condensed fashion (given the visual nature of the television medium) than it will in print, which is less condensed, allowing for more reflection on content. The second feature is *interpretability*. This implies that messages can be understood successfully only by anyone who is familiar with the codes used to construct them (or which underlie them). The third is *contextualization*. This implies that message interpretation is affected by the context in which it occurs.

The concept of code entered media and culture studies in the early 1950s, finding many applications. It was used, early on, by the late social critic Raymond Williams (1921–1988), who argued that mediated spectacles are self-perpetuating because of their ability to adapt to changes in social codes (Williams 1950). In Williams' writings it is often impossible to distinguish between code and culture. Williams called the mainstream form of culture in place at any given time a *dominant* interpretive code. He saw in this code *residual* tendencies from previous codes, including non-dominant ones, and *emergent* tendencies, which point to the future. It is in tapping into the latter that media industries beget their power to change and thus perpetuate themselves.

Roland Barthes

The French semiotician Roland **Barthes** (1915–1980) became (to the best of my knowledge) the first one to apply semiotic theory directly to media and culture in his now classic 1957 book *Mythologies* (Lavers 1982; Culler 1983; Moriarty 1991; Cobley 2006b). Like the early theorists of the Frankfurt Institute for Social Research (founded at the University of Frankfurt in 1922 to study the impact of modern technology and capitalism on modern societies), Barthes came to view mediated culture as a 'bastard form of mass culture' beset by 'humiliated repetition' and thus by a constant mania for 'new books, new programmes, new films, news items, but always the same meaning' (Barthes 1975a: 24). His main contention was, in fact, that the subtexts in media spectacles were invariably recyclings of previous texts and especially mythological ones. This is presumably what he meant by a 'bastard form of culture'. His 1957 book escaped the attention of the Anglo-American world of academia at first, perhaps due to the time-lag in getting the book translated and to the perception at the time that its purview may have been restricted to the semiotic analysis of French media culture or, at the very least, to a French-based interpretation of media. But since the mid-1960s, it has become a point of reference for any meaningful study of the modern media and their relation to pop culture.

Mythologies signals, in effect, the start of media semiotics proper, bringing out the importance of studying media texts (spectacles, movies, consumer products, etc.) in terms of how they recycle mythological or second-order (connotative) meanings. A photograph in a newspaper, for example, does not simply capture a fact or event directly. It takes on social **connotation** through the way it is shown, where it is placed in the newspaper layout, and how captions annotate its subtextual meaning. The photograph of a cat on a stool, when viewed without a caption, lends itself to many interpretive possibilities. However, if the caption *Looking for a Companion* were added to it, then the primary interpretation that the photo would elicit is that of an appeal for pet adoption. Barthes' book also demonstrated clearly how media and pop culture texts are assembled, namely through a technique that can be designated *textual pastiche*. The idea is to mix things together, borrowing especially from other texts. Pastiche seems, in fact, to characterize everything in pop culture, from early vaudeville performances to *The Simpsons*. The former was literally made up of a hodgepodge of acts, ranging from skits to acrobatic acts; the latter uses diverse themes and personages from different levels of culture in the same episode, creating an overall effect similar to the collage in painting.

Barthes claimed that a large part of the emotional allure of media culture spectacles is due to the fact that they are based on a pastiche of unconscious mythic texts and meanings. To distinguish between the original myths and their contemporary versions, Barthes designated the latter *mythologies*. In early Hollywood westerns, for instance, the heroes and villains were contemporary reconstructions of the ancient mythic heroes and their opponents. Because of the unconscious power of myth, it is little wonder to find that early Hollywood cowboys such as Roy Rogers, John Wayne, Hopalong Cassidy, and the Lone Ranger have become cultural icons, symbolizing virtue, heroism, and righteousness above and beyond the movie scripts. Hollywood has broken away from this mythology in recent times, but the tradition of the maverick cowboy loner hero fighting for justice remains a central mythic image even in contemporary cowboy narratives.

Basic concepts

Following on Barthes' coat-tails in the early 1970s was another French scholar, the sociologist Jean Baudrillard (1929–2007), who came to be well known for his studies of media image-making and of the simulacrum effect (discussed briefly above). Among Baudrillard's many other interesting ideas, perhaps the one most discussed is that in consumerist societies media representations are made not to fulfil a need, but to create it (Baudrillard 1973). Like many Marxist critics of American capitalist culture, Baudrillard saw media culture as a kind of 'culture industry', churning out popular texts for instant consumption, in the same way that factories churn out products. This portrayal of media culture actually took shape in the Frankfurt School (mentioned above), and continues to enjoy widespread popularity among various media schools. Essentially, culture industry theory sees media texts as being controlled by those in power in order to ensure consent by the masses, rather than using overt forms of coercion. Today, this theory has morphed into so-called *hegemony* theory – a concept going back to Italian Marxist Antonio Gramsci (1891–1937). Those who espouse this theory are generally highly pessimistic about the possibility of genuine culture under modern capitalism, condemning media culture as a form of propaganda designed to indoctrinate the masses and disguise social inequalities.

One of the more interesting contemporary versions of hegemony theory is the one associated with the writings of the American linguist Noam **Chomsky**

(b. 1928). Chomsky has always claimed that those who control the funding and ownership of the media, including the government in power, pressurize the media to select and present news coverage in ways that are favourable to them. In such a model, the contemporary mass media are seen as nothing more than a propaganda arm of the government and of capitalist interests. The mainstream media are thus seen as complicit in the 'manufacturing of consent', selecting the topics to be printed or broadcast, establishing the character of the concerns to be expressed, determining the ways in which issues are to be framed, and filtering out any information assessed to be contradictory (Chomsky and Herman 1988). Examples used to support this view include American TV coverage of recent wars, from the Vietnam War to the War on Terror (in Afghanistan and Iraq), in which it is transparently obvious that the government in power has the ability to influence how the media present stories. The end result is a media propaganda system that espouses an elemental form of patriotism and the benevolence of power brokers and the institutions that they head. Like the Frankfurt scholars, propaganda theorists do not seem to believe that common people can tell the difference between truth and manipulation. The solution they offer is to ensure that access to the public media is an open and democratic process. Such access is, in fact, becoming a reality because of the Internet, where basically anyone can post an opinion and garner an international audience for it.

The semiotic approach to media and pop culture has, since the 1970s, become a focal one, not only within cultural semiotics proper, but also across media disciplines. Take, for example, the notions of code and text. Already in the early period, scholars such as Gerbner and Lazarsfeld (above) argued that the whole array of spectacles delivered by the media was socially coded – that is, structured to support or reinforce existing norms. For example, the over-representation of deviancy and violence in movies and on TV crime programmes was designed, by and large, to warn people about the dangers these pose to the social order and, thus, to evoke their condemnation, not justification. The subtext in these programmes is respect for law and order. The textual representations themselves constitute divine justice dramas, so to speak, in which the criminals will ultimately pay for their sins. In the 1970s, British cultural theorist Stuart Hall (b. 1932) also approached the study of media from the standpoint of text theory. Hall argued that people do not absorb media texts passively, but rather read them in one of three ways (Hall 1977). A *preferred* reading is the one that the makers intended to convey with their text. A *negotiated* reading is the one that involves some negotiation or compromise with the text's intended meaning. And an *oppositional* reading is one that is in opposition to what the makers of the text had intended. A simple way to understand the difference between the three types of readings is to consider a comedian who has just told a joke on stage. If the audience laughs unreservedly, then the joke has produced the preferred reading. If only some of the audience laughs, possibly with some reservation, while others chuckle or sneer, then the joke has brought about a negotiated reading. Finally, if the audience reacts negatively to the joke, then it has produced an oppositional reading.

A semiotic concept that has found special fertile ground in the study of media is that of *opposition* – a notion that goes right back to Ferdinand de **Saussure** (1857–1913), a founder of modern semiotics (Saussure 1916). This implies that we do not perceive meaning-bearing differences in absolute ways, but rather in relational terms. For example, if we were to think of *day*, its opposite, *night*, would invariably crop up in our mind. Essentially, the notion of opposition allows media analysts to flesh out the hidden meanings built into texts. Take, for example, the differences that are associated with the *white-versus-black* opposition. The former connotes positive values, while the latter connotes negative ones. This opposition manifests itself symbolically in all kinds of media texts. In early Hollywood cowboy movies, many heroes wore white hats and villains black ones. Interestingly, the poles of an opposition, such as this one, can be turned around, so to speak, to bring out the same pattern of connotative nuances even more forcefully. This is why the *Zorro* character of television and movie fame wears black, as did several Hollywood western heroes of the past (such as *Lash LaRue*).

Although the idea of opposition originated with **Aristotle** as a principle of logical structure (Hjelmslev 1939, 1959; Benveniste 1946), and even though it was used explicitly by Saussure, it became the basis of semiotic and linguistic method only after the Prague School linguists gave it a formal treatment in the 1930s (Trubetzkoy 1936, 1939; Jakobson 1939). Along with Gestalt psychologists (Ogden 1932), the Prague School linguists saw opposition as a pivotal technique for examining levels of **language**. Within linguistics and semiotics, the concept of opposition has always been seen essentially as an analytical tool for identifying minimal contrasts, such as phonemic ones. This implies, basically, that a sound such as /p/ can replace other consonants, such as /w/ or /b/, to make English words – *pin*-versus-*win*-versus-*bin*. Opposition allows us to identify the phonemes of a language through a derived technique called the *commutation test*, which consists in comparing sounds in minimal pairs (two words that are alike in all respects except one), in order to see if a difference in meaning results (*sip*-versus-*zip*, *sing*-versus-*zing*, etc.). If the commutation produces a difference in meaning, the two sounds can be assigned phonemic status. The commutation test has been used extensively in media studies. In the domain of advertising, for instance, it consists in changing an image or word in an ad, removing it and replacing it with another one, in order to see what kind of reaction it generates.

The Prague School linguists realized early on that extending opposition beyond the study of minimal contrasts within language was fraught with problems. In 1957, the psychologists Osgood, Suci, and Tannenbaum showed that the technique could be expanded. They called their version the *semantic differential*. It consists in posing a series of opposition-based questions to subjects about certain concepts – *Is X good or bad? Should Y be weak or strong?*

etc. Subjects are subsequently asked to rate a concept on a seven-point scale, with the two end points constituting the oppositional poles. The ratings are then collected and analysed statistically. Use of the semantic differential has shown that the range of interpretations of concepts is not a matter of subjectivity, but rather, a matter of culturally based interpretation. In other words, subject ratings are semiotically constrained by culture: for example, the word *noise* turns out to be a highly emotional concept for the Japanese, who rate it consistently at the ends of the oppositions presented to them; whereas it is a fairly neutral one for Americans, who tend to rate it in the mid-ranges of the same scales.

The semantic differential is not, clearly, a radical break from opposition theory. It simply indicates that interpretive gradations might exist in binary oppositions that are culture-specific. The semiotician Algirdas J. **Greimas** also entered the debate on opposition theory, introducing the notion of the *semiotic square*, which involves two sets of oppositions forming a square arrangement (Greimas 1987). Given a sign s_1 (for example, *rich*), Greimas claimed that we understand its meaning by opposing it to its contradictory $-s_1$ (*not rich*), its contrary s_2 (*poor*), and its contradictory $-s_2$ (*not poor*) in tandem. Greimas' technique seems to have borne particularly useful results in the analysis of narrative media texts. It is beyond the purpose here to delve into the merits of the semiotic square. Suffice it to say that, along with the semantic differential, it suggests that there may be levels and scales of opposition that determine how we interpret signs and texts. In the same time frame, anthropologist Claude **Lévi-Strauss** (1977a) showed that pairs of oppositions often cohere into sets. In analysing kinship systems, he found that the elementary unit of kinship was made up of a set of four oppositions: *brother*-versus-*sister*, *husband*-versus-*wife*, *father*-versus-*son*, and *mother's brother*-versus-*sister's son*. Lévi-Strauss suggested that similar sets characterized units in other cultural systems.

In sum, the opposition structure of media texts can be binary, as are phonemic oppositions in language (*black*-versus-*white*); it can be four-part, as are some semantic distinctions (*rich–not rich–poor–not poor*); it can be graduated, as the semantic differential technique has shown with respect to cultural concepts; or it can be set-based, as Lévi-Strauss discovered. These types of opposition are not mutually exclusive, as some have argued in the past. They are, in effect, complementary. The type of opposition that applies in any context of analysis, therefore, depends on what system (language, kinship, etc.) or subsystem (phonemic, semantic, etc.) is involved. Barthes had implicitly adopted the notion of opposition in his *Mythologies*, arguing that basic mythic oppositions (*father*-versus-*son*, *good*-versus-*evil*, *male*-versus-*female*, *youth*-versus-*elder*, etc.) are built into media texts and spectacles, from wrestling matches to blockbuster movies.

Poststructuralism and beyond

The notion of opposition comes under the general methodological rubric of ***structuralism***. In media studies, it was initially called the *semiological* method, which is the term used by Saussure to designate the study of signs and the one used by Barthes in his groundbreaking work on media. The structuralists explained 'non-oppositional' meaning phenomena, from metaphor to irony, as substitutions or combinations of oppositional features. There is much merit in such an approach. However, it is beyond the scope of the present discussion. Suffice it to say that it raised some fundamental questions around the middle part of the twentieth century. Taking his cue from other scholars (such as Louis **Hjelmslev** and Emile **Benveniste**), Barthes was among the first to react to structuralism in its rigid dimensions, introducing the notion of second-order connotation and, thus, the idea that readers, not implicit textual structures, are the ones who determine what a text means.

A major problem with structuralism was the question of the psychic function of the two poles in a binary opposition. Which of the two is the cognitively more salient one? To answer this question, the Prague School linguists introduced the notion of *markedness* (Tiersma 1982; Eckman *et al.* 1983; Andrews 1990; Battistella 1990; Corbett 1991). To grasp what this means, consider a simple grammatical example. In Italian the masculine gender is classified as the *unmarked* one when referring to people, whereas the feminine one is *marked* specifically for the feminine sex. So, for example, the masculine plural form of a noun such as *turisti* ('tourists') refers (non-specifically) to any person, male or female; whereas the feminine plural form, *turiste*, is marked, referring only to females. Markedness theory raises some fundamental questions about the relation of oppositions, such as the *masculine*-versus-*feminine* one, and society. The fact that the unmarked form in Italian is the masculine gender, as it was (and often still is) in English, is a cue that, Italian society is historically male-centred, leading to speculation that, in societies (or communities) where the masculine gender is the unmarked form, it is the men who tend to be in charge of social processes (family lineage patterns, surnaming patterns in marriage, etc.); while in societies (or communities) where the feminine gender is the unmarked form, the women are typically the ones in charge. Research has tended to bear this out, suggesting that grammatical structure mirrors social structure. As King (1991: 2) aptly puts it, in societies where the masculine is the unmarked form in grammar, 'men have traditionally been the political leaders, the most acclaimed writers, the grammarians, and the dictionary makers, and it is their world view that is encoded in language'.

In media semiotics, this notion initially provided a kind of useful **discourse** for explaining the content of various media texts. For example, in early 1950s TV sitcoms the *fatherhood*-versus-*motherhood* opposition clearly reflected the existing social view of fatherhood as unmarked and, thus, socially crucial. This was evident even in the titles of the sitcoms (for example, *Father Knows Best*). Motherhood was portrayed instead as complementary and even supplementary to fatherhood in the representation of the family. There were some exceptions to this (for instance, *I Love Lucy*), but by and large fatherhood was depicted as the primary pole in the opposition. As society changed, so too did the nature of the opposition. It literally came to be 'deconstructed', as emerging semiotic models of the media emphasized as far back as the early 1970s (see Danesi 2002). Starting with *All in the Family*, the *fatherhood*-versus-*motherhood* opposition was being deconstructed and markedness relations altered. By the 1980s, the whole construct was parodied in sitcoms such as *Married with Children* and *The Simpsons*.

In effect, the early use of opposition theory in media analysis may have itself opened up the debate that ensued on structuralism. The problem was seen as being particularly pronounced in the case of conceptual oppositions such as *male*-versus-*female* and *self*-versus-*other*. Which of the two is the marked pole? Clearly, this question raises deep issues about structural analysis. Out of this frame of questioning, **poststructuralism** emerged in the 1960s, a movement associated at first with the late French philosophers Michel Foucault (1926–1984) and Jacques Derrida (1930–2004), who bluntly refuted the classic notions of Saussurean structuralism (Foucault 1972; Derrida 1976). Arguably, the central idea that set off this movement was that oppositions do not encode reality, but rather construct it. According to Derrida all sign systems are self-referential – signs refer to other signs, which refer to still other signs, and so on ad infinitum. Thus, what appears stable and logical turns out to be illogical and paradoxical. Many semioticians have severely criticized this radical stance of poststructuralism. However, as Nesselroth (2007: 442) has remarked, Derrida's perspective has nevertheless been useful to semiotics as a whole because it portrayed signification as 'a process that constantly decenters fixed meanings and puts into question the ontological status of language (both written and spoken) and of communication in general'.

From many points of view, poststructuralism is really nothing more than structuralism expanded to include a few radical ideas (at least for Saussurean theory). One of these is logocentrism – the view that all human knowledge is constructed by linguistic categories. It is also claimed by poststructuralists that this very same logocentrism characterizes semiotic practices themselves, rendering them virtually useless. Derrida maintained, in essence, that linguistic forms encode 'ideologies', not 'realities'. And because written language is the fundamental condition of knowledge-producing enterprises, such as science, philosophy, and semiotics (of course), these end up reflecting nothing more than the writing practices used to articulate them (Nesselroth 2007). In actual fact, there is nothing particularly radical in the poststructuralist position, because the same kind of questions asked by poststructuralists were implicit within structuralism itself. Already in the 1920s, **Jakobson** and Trubetzkoy started probing the relativity of language oppositions in the light of their social and psychological functions. Basing their ideas in part on the work of German psychologist Karl **Bühler** (1879–1963), they posited three main functions of language – the cognitive, the expressive, and the conative (or instrumental). The cognitive function refers to the employment of language for the transmission of factual information; the expressive to the fact that language allows the speaker (or writer) to convey mood or attitude; and the conative to the use of language to influence the persons being addressed or to bring about some practical effect via communication. A number of Prague School scholars even suggested that these three functions correlated in many languages, at least partly, with social categories.

Poststructuralism has had several interesting applications to the study of the media. One of these is its claim that all texts have **rhetoric**al structure. Roland Barthes, as we saw, portrayed media texts as rhetorical, consisting of two levels: the *linguistic* and the *mythical*. The former implies that there is a denotative or referential meaning to a text that presents itself at first reading. But, at the mythical level, it invariably triggers a chain reaction of unconscious connotative (rhetorical) meanings. The meaning of a media text, thus, oscillates back and forth between the linguistic (denotative) and rhetorical (mythic) levels. As a simple example, consider the word *Sonata* as used to name a certain car model. At the linguistic level, it denotes the name of a specific automobile. However, at a rhetorical level it connotes classic aesthetic qualities associated with 'sonata form' in classical music. All media texts can be read in this way, as Barthes showed.

Another contribution of poststructuralism to media semiotics is its focus on the importance of agency in the whole process of interpretation, thus validating empirical work in media studies on the ability of audiences to select from texts what they expect to get from them. In a fundamental move, media semiotics and media studies generally have discovered, in a roundabout way, Charles Peirce's notion of the ***interpretant***, which is essentially a process of potentially infinite semiosis – that is, the process of deciphering what something 'stands for'. The Peircean approach to semiosis has become a dominant one in current media semiotics, defining its current zeitgeist. It has been particularly useful in explaining the ways in which certain texts are designed to produce semiosis. A common technique in Peircean-based media semiotics is to identify how iconicity shapes the form and content of texts – iconicity being the primary force in semiosis. Iconic brand names and logos, for example, dominate the marketing scene – *Splash* (detergent) evokes what is done with the product through sound imitation ('splashing'); the *Polo* logo, which represents the sport of polo visually with a horse and a rider dressed in polo garb; etc.

The above discussion is not meant to imply that structuralist techniques are no longer used in media semiotics. The technique of opposition, for example, continues to have widespread utilization, in a *prima facie* sense. Like archetype theory in Jungian psychology, which started rather simply as a way of understanding the recurrence of symbols and rituals in cultures across the world, opposition theory is still useful in showing how certain notions relate to each other throughout the human intellectual landscape. And, of course, the concept of mythic code is still a primary one. Consider the case of the *Star Wars* set of six movies (1977–2005), which recycle many elements of Greek myth. The set is divided into individual episodes, released in a sequence that starts in *medias res* with the fourth episode being the first one put out. Homer's *Iliad* is structured in this manner. The unifying theme of all the episodes is the universal struggle between Good (the Rebel Alliance) and Evil (the tyrannical Empire) – one of Lévi-Strauss's basic mythic oppositions. The saga reverberates, in fact, with other ancient mythic oppositions and themes (Danesi 2007):

youth-versus-*old age*
nature-versus-*technology* (*culture*)
democracy-versus-*totalitarianism* (*Jedi*-versus-*the Sith*)
common folk-versus-*autocracy* (*rebels*-versus-*the Empire*)
freedom-versus-*tyranny*
father-versus-*son*
and so on.

There is one more emerging and growing trend within media semiotics and media studies generally that requires some commentary. Known as *Carnival Theory*, and inspired by the work of the Russian social critic Mikhail **Bakhtin**, it asserts that media texts are emotionally powerful because they are part of profane symbolism – a transgressive symbolism that actually validates social norms (Bakhtin 1981, 1993). In effect, we come to understand the role of those norms through a mockery of them. This would explain why media texts and pop culture do not pose (and never have posed) any serious subversive political challenge to the moral and ethical status quo. Flappers, punks, goths, gangsta rappers, Alice Cooper, Kiss, Eminem, Marilyn Manson, strippers, porn stars, and all the other 'usual transgression suspects' are, according to this theory, modern-day carnival mockers who take it upon themselves to deride, confuse, and parody authority figures and sacred symbols, bringing everything down to an earthy, crude level of theatrical performance. They constitute the marked end of the *sacred*-versus-*profane* opposition.

Carnival Theory asserts that media mockery institutes a vital **dialogue** in society at large. It is an oppositional dialogue, pitting the sacred against the profane in a systematic gridlock, manifesting itself in the theatrical and narrative arts, from docudramas and sitcoms to rock concerts and social networking websites. Carnival is part of popular and folkloristic traditions that aim to critique traditional mores and idealized social rituals, bringing out the raw, unmediated links between domains of behaviour that are normally kept very separate. Carnivalesque **genre**s satirize the lofty words of poets, scholars, and others. They are intended to fly in the face of the official, sacred world – the world of judges, lawyers, politicians, churchmen, and the like. Modern-day examples on television are *The Simpsons* and *South Park*. The 'media carnival', as it is now sometimes called, is the context in which distinct common voices can be heard, and where they will flourish through 'polyphonic' expression, as Bakhtin called it. People attending a carnival do not merely make up an anonymous crowd. Rather, they feel part of a communal body, sharing a unique sense of time and space. Through costumes and masks, individuals take on a new identity and, as a consequence, renew themselves spiritually in the process.

The transgressive antics of the latest pop musician, fashion model, movie star, or cult figure are, in this framework, manifestations of an unconscious profane instinct that seeks expression in symbolic-carnivalesque ways.

Concluding remarks

Perhaps in no other medium is the carnivalesque nature of the human psyche more manifest today than it is online. From YouTube sites that parody pop culture spectacles (a kind of parody of the parodies), to sites promoting 'indie culture', the Internet is fast becoming the primary platform for enacting the carnivalesque within us. It is thus little wonder that the focus of media semiotics, as Mazzali-Lurati (2007) has suggested, will be turning more and more to online culture. The Internet is leading to a redefinition of the roles of the author and the reader of a text. The 'popular' in pop culture is now taking on a literal meaning, as readers interact with authors, scholars, artists, and others in determining how they will ultimately be informed, engaged, or entertained. One area of particular interest is that of how the new technologies are shaping codes and traditional sign systems. One of the most conspicuous features of online communication is miniaturization, as evident in the constant production of compressed forms (abbreviations of words and phrases, acronyms, etc.) in the language used in chatrooms and other virtual linguistic communities. Is this a new linguistic phenomenon responding to new technologies? Is it spreading to language generally? What does this foretell for the future of writing, given that there are few, if any, corrective forces at work in cyberspace? Will media texts become reshaped as a consequence? As mentioned at the start of this discussion, media semiotics can provide relevant insights into the interconnection between technology and culture, perhaps like no other discipline can.

Many are concerned about cyberspace and its influence on true culture and on the human psyche. As a result, some are prepared to take interventionist action. There is nothing new here. As Stan Cohen (1972) observed in his study of mods and rockers, many new trends tend to be perceived with 'moral panic', that is, as indicative of a decline in morality and traditional values. As it turns out, however, as these lose their impact, blending silently into the larger cultural mainstream or disappearing altogether, the moral panic also evanesces. The idea that mass media culture is detrimental to human beings ignores not only history, but also the fact that people can discriminate between levels of culture. Moreover, history also teaches us that interventionism has never worked. Prohibition did not work. Censorship does not work and can even backfire. As Peter Blecha (2004) has documented, some of the most famous songs of Billie Holiday, Elvis Presley, Woody Guthrie, The Beatles, The Rolling Stones, Jimi Hendrix, Frank Zappa, The Sex Pistols, Patti Smith, Public Enemy, Ice-T, 2 Live Crew, Nirvana, Bruce Springsteen, Eminem, The Dixie Chicks, and many more, were either censored or stifled in some way at the start. But all this did was to make them even more popular than they otherwise would have been. Even if it were possible in a consumerist culture to control the contents of media texts, this would invariably prove to be counterproductive. The answer is to become aware of the meanings that are generated by pop culture representations. When the human mind is aware of these, it will be better able to fend off any undesirable effects that they may cause. That is where media semiotics has proved itself to be the most useful.

Further reading

Albertazzi, D. and Cobley, P. (eds) (2009) *The Media: An Introduction*, 3rd edn, Harlow: Pearson.

Deely, J. (2004) *Why Semiotics?*, Ottawa: Legas Press.

Lechte, J. (1994) *Fifty Key Contemporary Thinkers*, London: Routledge.

Newbold, C., Boyd-Barrett, O. and Van Den Bulck, H. (eds) (2002) *The Media Book*, London: Arnold.

van Leeuwen, T. (2005) *Introducing Social Semiotics*, London: Routledge.

10

Semioethics

Susan Petrilli and Augusto Ponzio

Semioethics as diagnostic without patients

'Semioethics' is a neologism which has its origins in the early 1980s with 'ethosemiotics', and was introduced by us as the title of one of our Italian books in 2003 (*Semioetica*). We propose the term 'semioethics' (Ponzio and Petrilli 2003; Deely *et al.* 2005) to name an approach or attitude we deem necessary today more than ever before in the context of **globalization**. Semioethics is not intended as a discipline in its own right, but as a perspective, an orientation in the study of **signs**. By 'semioethics' we understand the propensity in **semiotics** to recover its ancient vocation as 'semeiotics' (or symptomatology), which focuses on symptoms. A major issue for semioethics is 'care for life' in a global perspective (Sebeok 2001b), according to which **semiosis** and life converge (Ponzio and Petrilli 2001, 2005). This global perspective is made ever more urgent by growing interference in planetary **communication,** between the historical-social and biological spheres, between the cultural and natural spheres, and between the **semiosphere** (**Lotman**) and the biosphere.

The origin of semiotics may be identified in symptomatology, following **Sebeok** (who contextualizes the general science of signs in a tradition of thought that originated with **Hippocrates** (*c.* 460–377 BCE) and was developed by **Galen** (*c.* 129–200)). The connection between semiotics and **medical semiotics** is also examined by Eugen Baer (1988: 37–99). But Rudolph Kleinpaul in *Sprache ohne Worte* (1972 [1888]: 103) had already indicated Hippocrates as 'der Vater und Meister aller Semiotik', the father and master of all semiotics. Symptomatology became a branch of medicine characterized by a threefold temporal orientation according to Galen who recovered the teachings of Hippocrates (*praeteritorum cognitio*, *praesentium inspectio*, *futurorum providentia*): towards the past (anamnesis), the present (diagnostics), the future (prognosis). Apart from acquiring knowledge about its origins, to relate semiotics to the branch of medicine that studies symptoms implies recovery of the ethical instance of semiotic studies. The ethical instance is explicit in the Hippocratic oath. This is not just a question of professional ethics, it does not concern the physician solely in the role of physician. Instead, the whole person in one's daily activity is involved (see Hippocrates, *Decorum*, VII, and *Precepta*, VI). Hippocrates prescribed that the physician should help citizens and foreigners alike and, if necessary, without payment. For wherever there is love for a human being, he said, there is also love for art. Galen too observed the inseparability of science and ethics.

To relate semiotics to ancient medical semeiotics or symptomatology means to recover the ancient *vocation* of 'semeiotics' (symptomatology) for the health of life. And given that semiosis and life converge, as is repeatedly attested in the *oeuvre* of Sebeok – life globally over the entire planet – the ancient vocation for the health of life, as practised by 'semeiotics', is a vocation for the general science of signs. From this perspective semiotics is also 'semioethics'.

We have stated that the major issue for semioethics is 'care for life' in a global perspective according to which semiosis and life converge. It is important to specify that *to care for* is different from *to cure*, *to treat*. The semiotician who focuses on symptoms because s/he has semiosis, that is, life at heart, is not a physician, nor a general practitioner or specialist. S/he does not prescribe treatments, cures, drugs. On the contrary, s/he disputes widespread medicalization in our society (on this topic, see Szasz 2001 and Verdiglione 1997). The semiotician does not use the paradigm normal/abnormal, healthy/ill. His/her attention for symptoms bears a certain resemblance to Freudian analysis, given that in both cases interpretation plays a central role and the aptitude for listening to the other is a decisive factor. Here it is not a question of medical auscultation: to listen to the other is not to auscultate. And if semiotic analysis of symptoms is similar to Freudian analysis, it shares nothing with psychiatry, with psychiatrized psychoanalysis, with psychiatric patients, psychiatric treatment, use of drugs, and sundry concoctions, with the psychiatrization of human life.

Victoria, Lady **Welby** writes:

> It is unfortunate that custom decrees the limitation of the term diagnosis to the pathological field. It would be difficult to find a better one for that power of 'knowing through', which a training in Significs would carry. We must be brought up to take for granted that we are diagnosts, that we are to cultivate to the utmost the power to see real distinctions and to read the signs, however faint, which reveal sense and meaning. Diagnostic may be called the typical process of Significs . . .
>
> (Welby 1983 [1903]: 51)

Analogously, diagnostic can be associated with the semioethic attitude of semiotics. However, semioethics draws inspiration precisely from Welby's significs and its focus on sense, signification and significance, as well as from Charles S. **Peirce**'s interest in **ethics** (mostly neglected by the Peirceans), and from Charles **Morris**'s connection between signs and values, signification and significance, semiotics and axiology (see Morris 1964). By contrast with a strictly cognitive, descriptive and ideologically neutral approach as it has largely characterized semiotic studies, semiotics today must recover the axiological dimension of human semiosis. This ethical bent of semiotics also results from a reading (especially in Ponzio's interpretation) of texts by Emmanuel **Levinas** and Mikhail M. **Bakhtin**.

What interests semioethics in the **anthroposemiotic** sphere is the human individual in her/his concrete singularity and inevitable interrelation with others. Semioethics starts from the assumption that the human individual in her/his concrete singularity, whatever the object of study, and however specialized the analysis concerning her/him, cannot disregard her/his involvement without alibis in the destiny of others. In this sense, the symptoms studied by semioethics are always social, but at the same time they are always specified singularly, according to one's singular relations with others, the world and oneself. Consequently, each idea, wish, sentiment, value, interest, need, exigency, evil or good, examined by semioethics as a symptom, is embodied, expressed by words, the singular word, the embodied word, that is, by voice. Semioethics carefully listens to voices. This implies the capacity for *listening* and *dialogical interrelation.* **Dialogue** is not a condition we concede out of generosity towards another, rather it is structural to life itself, a condition for life to flourish (Ponzio 1993, 2006a; Cobley 2007a). Singularity, the uniqueness of each one of us, implies otherness, and otherness implies dialogism.

THE DESTINY OF SEMIOSIS OR LIFE

Semioethics is also an answer to the question regarding the destiny of semiosis, proposed by Sebeok (1991a). The intention is to evidence the responsibility of semiotics towards semiosis, consequently proposing that Sebeok's 'global semiotics', which is founded in the general science of signs as conceived by Peirce, now be developed in terms of 'semioethics'. This is a far cry from dominant trends in twentieth-century semiotics that reduce the study of signs, verbal and nonverbal, to a question of message exchange viewed separately from historico-social relations of production processes, and from the relation between signs and values. On several occasions we have noted the inadequacy of such trends which imply a view of the human subject reduced to mere exchange value.

Semioethics stresses the 'unifying function of semiotics', identifying three aspects of this function: the 'descriptive–explanatory', the 'methodological' and the 'ethical'. Semiotics must not only describe and explain signs, it must also search for methods of inquiry and knowledge acquisition, and furthermore make proposals relative to human behaviour and social programming. As the general science of signs, it is obvious that semiotics must overcome parochial specialism; that is, any form of separatism among the sciences. The ethical aspect of semiotics is projectual and should include proposals for the critical orientation of human practice generally, covering all aspects of life from the biological to the sociocultural, and paying attention to reconnect that which is considered and experienced as separate. The terms we have introduced to designate the ethical trend in semiotics include 'ethosemiotics', 'telo' or 'teleosemiotics' (from 'telos' = end), and most recently 'semioethics' (Petrilli and Ponzio 2005: 562).

The capacity for criticism, social awareness and responsible behaviour must be central themes in semiotic studies intending to interrogate not only the sense of science, but the sense of life for man. Developing Sebeok's standpoint and proceeding beyond him, semioethics evidences the ethical implications of global semiotics and their importance for education, particularly for the comprehensive and critical interpretation of communication under present-day conditions; that is, communication in globalization, global communication.

Semioethics draws on Sebeok's criticism of anthropocentric and glottocentric semiotic theory and practice identifying a major shortcoming in 'semiology', the science that only turns its attention to 'signes au sein de la vie sociale' ['signs as part of social life'] (Saussure 1916: 26), and among these only studies intentional signs. Furthermore, semiology is based on the verbal paradigm and is vitiated by the *pars pro toto* error – that is, it mistakes the part (human signs and in particular verbal signs) for the whole (all possible signs, human and non-human). The general science of signs cannot be limited to the study of communication in culture, and to claim that semiology thus conceived is the general science of signs is a mystification. When the general science of signs chooses the term 'semiotics' for itself, it distances itself from semiology and its errors. Sebeok tags the semiologic conception the 'minor tradition' and promotes instead what he calls the 'major tradition' as represented by John **Locke** and Peirce and by the early writings on signs and symptoms by the ancient medics. Insofar as it signifies, the entire universe enters Sebeok's 'global semiotics' (Sebeok 2001a). The human being is thus a sign in a universe of signs. Semiotics is the place where the 'life sciences' and the 'sign sciences' converge, which implies that *signs* and *life* converge, indeed, according to Sebeok semiosis, is the criterial attribute of life. It follows that a biosemiotic perspective is necessary for an adequate understanding of communicative behaviour.

As regards the critique of the *pars pro toto* error and the detotalizing method, we believe that Sebeok's approach is emblematic and fundamental to semioethics. He appropriately introduced the expression 'global semiotics' to indicate the expansiveness of sign studies, which he described as potentially unlimited by boundaries of any sort. With his global semiotics Sebeok takes his place in a semiotic horizon delineated by Peirce, Charles Morris and Roman Jakobson, evidencing the limits of approaches to sign studies based on the error of exchanging the part for the whole (see Sebeok 1998a, 2001b, c; Deely 1995; Ponzio and Petrilli 2000, 2002; Petrilli and Ponzio 2001, 2005). 'Global semiotics' indicates a new trend in semiotics which has been evolving since the 1960s.

In the context of global communication understood as converging with life, dialogism is not reduced to the exchange of rejoinders among interlocutors but indicates the permanent condition of intercorporeal involvement and reciprocal implication among bodies and signs throughout the semiosic universe. The vital condition of biosemiosic dialogism is a necessary condition for the emergence of more specialized forms of dialogue in the sphere of human semiosis. For example, Bakhtin (1984 [1963]) distinguishes between 'formal dialogue' and 'substantial dialogue'. From a biosemiotic perspective ***modelling***, *communication* and *dialogue* presuppose each other and together form the foundation and condition of possibility for life to flourish in its multiplicity and specificities, including the human, over the entire planet. In such a global framework communication cannot be simply understood in terms of message transmission from emitter to receiver, though this is one of its possible manifestations. Far more pervasively, communication coincides with semiosis, therefore with life, and presupposes the universal condition of dialogical interrelatedness and interdependency among signs forming the great biosemiosic network that is life over the planet.

Theorization of the relation between '**interpretant** signs' and 'interpreted signs' in terms of dialogism, active participation and otherness is a central topic in semioethics. Interrelation between the level of sign interpretation and the ideological level of **discourse** is another major focus in semioethics according to which **language** and ideology cannot be separated. Indeed, research on the relation between semiotics and ideology, such as that conducted by Ferruccio **Rossi-Landi** and Adam **Schaff**, is particularly important given that this relation is inseparable from the relation between signs and values – including linguistic, economical, ethical and aesthetical values. Besides, contrary to the dualism established by Noam **Chomsky** between 'experience' and 'competence', semioethics – in line with modern conceptions after **Kant** – presupposes a general semiotics that describes experience as a series of interpretive operations, including inferential processes of the Peircean abductive type. Through interpretive operations the subject completes, organizes and relates data which otherwise are fragmentary and partial. As such, experience is innovative and qualitatively superior by contrast with original input. Semioethics bases its view of experience and competence on a dialogic theory of signs, interpretation and inference (see Ponzio 2006b).

Today's social-economic world is the world of 'global communication', to understand which calls for an approach that is just as global, an approach that 'global semiotics' associated with 'semioethics' is capable of providing. The world today is characterized by a new computer-driven Industrial Revolution, by global free markets, and thus by the pervasiveness of communication throughout the entire production cycle (production, exchange, consumption). Communication is exploited by capitalism for profit. But what characterizes our world in the phase of globalization is its destructive potential at a planetary level. The risk of destruction for life throughout the entire planet today is increasing. If semiosis and therefore life is to continue, risks must be identified and communicated to others (especially the younger generations). We need a sense of global responsibility, just as global as the social system that is overwhelming us. This means to understand the connection between communication and life, as Sebeok's 'global semiotics' or 'semiotics of life' teaches us. His planetary perspective lays the conditions for an approach to contemporaneity that is capable of transcending the limits of contemporaneity itself, which from a semioethical perspective is the condition for the assumption of responsibility without alibis.

In a world governed by the logic of production and market exchange where everything is liable to commodification, humanity is faced with the threat of desensitization towards the signs of unfunctionality and ambivalency: from the signs forming the body to the seemingly futile signs of phatic communication with others. Capitalism in globalization is imposing ecological conditions that are rendering communication between self and body, self and the environment, ever more difficult and distorted (see Ponzio and Petrilli 2000; Sebeok *et al.* 2001). If we are to improve the quality of life, it will be necessary to recover these signs and their sense for life. As part of this project, a task for semioethics from the perspective of narrativity is to reconnect rational world views to myth, legend, fable and all other forms of popular tradition that focus on the relation of human beings to the world around them. The principal function of the semiotics of life, the ethical, is rich with implications for human behaviour: the signs of life that we cannot read, do not want to read or no longer know how to read must be fully recovered in their importance and relevance to the health of humanity and of life globally.

From a global semiotic perspective human semiosis is only one special sphere of sign activity interconnected with all other spheres of semiosis forming the great sign network. Studies in **biosemiotics** evidence how this sign network converges with life in its multiplicity of different forms proliferating over the entire planet. Semiotic studies must account for all terrestrial biological systems, from the sphere of molecular mechanisms at the lower limit, to a hypothetical entity at the upper limit christened 'Gaia', which is Greek for 'Mother Earth' – a term introduced by scientists in the late 1970s to designate the entire terrestrial ecosystem that encompasses the interactive activities of the multitudinous life forms on Earth. As Sebeok stated, alluding to the fantastic worlds of *Gulliver's Travels*, semiosis spreads over the Lilliputian world of molecular genetics and virology and through Gulliver's man-size world, and finally to the world of Brobdingnag, of Gaia, our gigantic bio-geo-chemical ecosystem.

Well before the advent of global communication in today's capitalist and globalized society, that is, before the worldwide spread of the communication network thanks to progress in artificial intelligence, technology and support from the global market in socio-economic terms, global communication was already a fact of life. From a biosemiosic perspective, global communication characterizes the evolution of life from its origins, and is a fact of life we cannot ignore, if life, including the human, is to continue flourishing globally as inscribed in the very nature of sign activity. Human communication is part of a global biosemiosic network where all life forms are interrelated and interdependent upon all others. Instead, global communication understood in terms of today's global socio-economic system investing social reproduction in all its phases (production, circulation and consumption), in other words, global communication understood as the expression of corporate-led capitalist globalization, is neither inevitable nor desirable – indeed it even threatens to destroy life on earth as we know it, as denounced by its oft devastating effects over the entire planet.

Out of place, out of identity, u-topos

With respect to social roles, human rights, individual identities and their internal and external indifference as established by the order of dominant discourse regulated by the logic of identity and equal exchange, semioethics is specifically interested in the other. This other is not the other understood as means but as end, not the other understood in terms of relative otherness, but absolute otherness, the other for its value in itself, in its unfunctionality, improductivity, in its right to absolute otherness and excess, in its difference unindifferent to the other of others, the other as the 'play of musement' (an expression introduced by Peirce and reproposed by Sebeok as the title of his 1981 book). The concept of 'fuori luogo' (Ponzio 2007), 'hors lieu', 'out of place', 'exo-topos', 'u-topos', indicates the singularity of each one of us, the self which cannot be reduced to the I, to the individual, to identity (see Petrilli *et al.* 2001). The singularity of each one of us, of self by contrast with I, is inevitably involved in the relation with others, in a relation without alibis, without substitutes. In this sense self is unique, incomparable, irreducibly other. 'U-topos' with respect to role, position, function, community, belonging, identity. 'Out of place' means to be exposed, to find oneself in a position of exposition, vulnerability, without shelter, protection, justification, without excuses, without a way out, without alibis (Lat. *alibi* = somewhere, another place). Out of place means out of genre, not to belong, it implies an existence, an interrelation, an involvement in the life of others apart from the role of subject and its identity, apart from the individual's affiliation to a **genre**, a set, an agglomerate, a community. Out of place implies out of the places of discourse, apart from judgement, definition, stereotypes, predication of being, apart from the claim of closing with the other. To listen to the voice of the other 'out of place' – as in the case of the Levinasian 'hors sujet', 'otherwise than being' – implies a return to the word that listens and makes a gift of time to the other and for the other. Out of place is the place of encounter with the other, of unlimited responsibility for the other, unlimited answerability to the other.

To take care of life in the sphere of human semiosis, semioethics investigates the 'properly human' outside the space, time and values of the already made world. The properly human refers to a dimension where interhuman relations cannot be reduced to the category of identity, to relations among predefined subjects and objects, or to relations of exchange, equality, functionality, productivity, self-interest. Semioethics explores the possibility of response in a dimension beyond given being, what Levinas (1974) calls 'otherwise than being'. By contrast with 'being otherwise', the expression 'otherwise than being' indicates the outside with respect to the already given world, to the world as it is. The allusion is to the capacity for earthly transcendence beyond the already given world, to a dimension of sense that is other with respect to the sense of this world as it is. By contrast with the humanism of identity, another form of humanism is possible based on the logic of otherness, the humanism of **alterity** (Levinas 1972).

What responsibility?

Why does each human being have to be responsible for semiosis or life over the whole planet? This question is central to semioethics. In ethics this question does not necessarily require an answer. To be responsible for life on the planet is a moral principle, a categorical imperative. But from the semioethic perspective an answer is required, because with semioethics we are in the field of scientific research, of reasonable argumentation, explication, interpretation. As a biological organism the human being flourishes in the great biosemiosic network interconnectedly with other biological organisms populating the biosphere. All life forms are endowed with a capacity for ***modelling***, which determines *world view*, *communication* and *dialogism*. Following Sebeok, we can embrace the hypothesis that the human modelling system is endowed with a species-specific capacity for 'metasemiosis', 'semiotics', 'language' or 'writing'. Here we understand 'writing' as 'writing *ante litteram*', *ante verba*, before speech, an a priori, characterized by *syntactics*, and not as transcription or translation of oral verbal signs into written verbal signs. These terms designate the human modelling capacity, which precedes and is the condition for human communication through verbal and nonverbal signs.

On the basis of this species-specific characteristic, the human being is described as a 'semiotic animal' – in Deely *et al.* (2005) – an animal capable not only of semiosis, but also of *semiotics*, that is, of using signs to reflect on signs, therefore capable of being fully aware, of acting in full awareness. It should be clear by now that the expression 'semiotics' refers both to the *specificity of human semiosis* and to the general *science of signs*. According to the first meaning, semiotics relates to the specific human capacity for *metasemiosis*. In the world of life which converges with semiosis, human semiosis is characterized as metasemiosis – that is, as the possibility of reflecting on signs. We can approach signs as objects of interpretation undistinguished from our response to them. But we can also approach signs in such a way as to suspend our responses to them, laying the conditions for deliberation. Human semiosis, anthroposemiosis, presents itself as *semiotic*. That *Homo* is a rational animal means that s/he is a semiotic animal. This implies that the human being is a unique animal, that is, an animal capable of responsibility for the health of semiosis, for life, over the entire planet.

As *semiotic animals* human beings are capable of a global view on life and communication: consequently, the question is, 'What is our responsibility towards life and the universe in its globality?'

As a capacity exclusive to human beings, semiotics provides the key to a full understanding of why and in what sense each human being is responsible for semiosis or life over the entire planet. Semiotics or metasemiosis, understood as the capacity to reflect upon signs, is connected with responsibility: as the only existing semiotic animal, the human being is capable of accounting for self. Therefore, the human being is subject *to* and subject *of* responsibility. As a semiotic animal the human being is endowed with the capacity to suspend action and deliberate, with a capacity for critical thinking and conscious awareness. Therefore, by contrast with other animals, the human being is invested bio-semiosically and phylogenetically with a unique capacity for taking responsibility, for making choices and taking standpoints, for creative intervention upon the course of semiosis throughout the biosphere. This means to say that human beings are endowed with a capacity to care for semiosis, for life, in its joyous and dialogical multiplicity. In this sense the 'semiotic animal' is also a 'semioethic animal'. As the specificity of human semiosis, 'semiotics' is a condition for responsible and open living. This implies the capacity for *listening*.

But the responsibility of the semiotician – that is, the person who practises the semiotic science – is even greater. In fact, if semiotics understood as metasemiosis is specific to each human being, semiotics understood as a science is specific to the semiotician and presents itself as *metasemiotics*, by comparison with semiotics understood in the former of the two senses. We may claim that if each human being is a semiotic animal, a *metasemiosical animal*, the semiotician is a *metasemiotical animal.* Consequently, the metasemiotician is doubly responsible. More than anybody else, the semiotician must not only account for self and for others, but as a global semiotician s/he must also account for life over the entire planet.

A TRIDIMENSIONAL SEMIOTIC ANIMAL

Semiotics is a *critical* science in the sense that it investigates its own conditions of possibility in Kant's sense, but not only this. Semiotics is a critical science also in the sense that it interrogates the human world today on the assumption that it is not the *only* possible world, that this world has not been established *definitively*, once and for all, by some conservative ideology. Instead, critical semiotics looks at the world as a possible world, one among many possible worlds, therefore as a world subject to *confutation*.

As global semiotics, or metasemiotics, as critical semiotics in the double sense mentioned, *semiotics must concern itself with life over the planet* – not only in cognitive terms, but also in the pragmatic. That is why semiotics must *care for life*. From this point of view, semiotics must recover its relation with symptomatology, with diagnostics. And this is not only a question of history, of remembering the origins. Far more radically we are signalling a question of the *ideologic-programmatic order* for the health of semiosis and the future of globalization by contrast to a globalized world tending towards its own destruction. This is the aim of making a diagnosis and prognosis of our world. From this perspective, semiotics is *listening*, it is oriented to listening. Semiotics today must listen to the symptoms of today's globalized world and identify the different expressions of unease and disease – in social relations, international relations, in the life of single individuals, in the environment, in life generally over the entire planet.

This is the reason why when we say that each human being is a semiotic animal we understand, with Ferruccio Rossi-Landi, that s/he is *wholly semiotic*: 'l'uomo, quale animale semiotico, è semiotico per intero' ['man, as a semiotic animal, is wholly semiotic'] (Rossi-Landi 1978: 217; new edition 2005: 347); this entails men and women of course, man in general, or better, as we prefer, each single human being (on this terminological question, see Rossi-Landi 1985; new edition 2006: xii–xiii). *Wholly semiotic animal*, because the semiotic animal involves all semiotic dimensions, the syntactic, the semantic and the pragmatic (see Morris 1938); from this point of view, the semiotic animal is a semiotically tridimensional animal.

From the point of view of semiotics, to disregard the pragmatic dimension which is closely related to values and ideologies is not scientifically possible. Nor can semiotics itself claim to be ideologically neutral. When semiotics claims to be merely descriptive and instrumental, it is precisely then that it works for the perfect running of communication as it presents itself today, that is, in the form of communication-production, thereby contributing to preserving relations founded on power and exploitation and the relative conditions of alienation and false conscience.

The wholly semiotic and therefore tridimensional semiotic animal as such is different from **Cassirer**'s 'symbolic animal' (see Cassirer 1944). The symbolic animal is devoid of the pragmatic dimension and is understood in accordance with the Kantian dualism of cognitive reason and practical reason. Cassirer's symbolic animal reflects the limits of critique in the Kantian sense, that is, of the Kantian investigation on the conditions of possibility of the human world. But this world is not subject to criticism in the sense that it is not questioned, it is not susceptible to confutation, it is not open to otherwise than being. In addition to this, Cassirer's symbolic animal belongs to traditional humanism in its neo-Kantian formulation, that is, the humanism of identity which Heidegger, in the famous 1929 debate with Cassirer in Davos, totally demolished. Emmanuel Levinas was present at this debate and was so deeply *affected* by it that he then wrote three essays on this question (between 1964 and 1970), now collected in *Humanisme de l'autre homme* [*Humanism of the Other Man*] (1972), a real milestone on the pathway to semioethics.

Semioethics and humanism of otherness

Semioethics may be considered as working towards a new form of humanism, inseparable from the question of otherness. This also emerges from its commitment at the level of **pragmatics** and its focus on the relation between signs, values and behaviour. Another important characteristic is the intention to transcend separatism among the sciences insisting on the interrelation between the human sciences, the historical-social sciences and the natural, logico-mathematical sciences. Also, semioethics evidences the condition of interconnectedness between the problem of humanism and the question of alterity.

The new form of humanism we are proposing is the humanism of otherness, following in particular Levinas, author of *Humanisme de l'autre homme*. So far the claim to human rights has been mostly oriented by the logic of identity, leaving aside the rights of the other. Said differently, the expression 'human rights' is mostly oriented in the direction of the humanism of identity and tends to refer to one's own rights, the rights of identity, of the I, forgetting the rights of the other. In other words, the very concept of 'human rights' thus conceived tends to leave aside the rights of the other. On the contrary, from the perspective of our concern for life, human and non-human, over the entire planet, for the health of semiosis generally, for the development of communication not only in strictly cultural terms but also in far broader biosemiosical terms, the tendency to leave out the rights of the other from what is understood by human rights must quickly be counteracted by the humanism of otherness, where the rights of the other are the first to be recognized. Our allusion here is not just to the rights of the other *beyond self*, but also to the self's very own other, to the other *of self*. Indeed, the I characteristically removes, suffocates and segregates otherness, which it tends to sacrifice to the cause of identity. But developed on the basis of the sacrifice and extromission of otherness, identity is fictitious, such that all efforts to maintain or recover it are destined to fail.

Semiotics contributes to the humanism of otherness by evidencing the extension and consistency of the sign network connecting every human being to every other on both a synchronic and diachronic level. The worldwide spread of the communication network means that a communication system is progressively being developed on a planetary level. As such, this phenomenon is susceptible to analysis in synchronic terms. Furthermore, given that the destiny of the human species in its wholeness is implied in all events, behaviours and decisions made by the single individual, in the destiny of the individual from its remotest to its most recent and closest manifestations, involving the past and the evolutionary future, on both the biological and the historico-social levels and vice versa, diachronic investigations, staggering to say the least for diversity, are also just as necessary.

This sign network concerns the semiosphere as constructed by humankind, a sphere inclusive of culture, its signs, symbols, artefacts, etc. But global semiotics teaches us that the semiosphere is far broader than the sphere of human culture. Indeed, it converges with the great biosphere if we accept Sebeok's axiom that semiosis and life converge. The semio(bio)sphere forms the habitat of humanity, the matrix whence we sprang and the stage upon which we are destined to act.

Semiotics has the merit of demonstrating that whatever is human involves signs. Indeed, it implies more than this: viewed from a global semiotic perspective, we now know that whatever is simply alive involves signs. And this is as far as cognitive semiotics and global semiotics reach. But semioethics pushes this awareness even further by relating semiosis to values and by focusing on the question of responsibility, of radical, inescapable responsibility inscribed in our bodies insofar as we are 'semiotic animals', on the human capacity for responsibility for life over the entire planet. Semioethics develops our awareness of the extension of the semiosic network in the direction of ethics; from a semioethic perspective the question of responsibility cannot be escaped at the most radical level (that of defining commitments and values).

This perspective leads us to interpret the sign behaviour of humanity in the light of the hypothesis that, if all of the human involves signs, all signs, in turn, are human. However, this humanistic commitment does not mean to reassert (monologic) identity yet again, nor to propose yet another form of anthropocentrism. On the contrary, this humanistic commitment implies a radical operation of decentralization and detotalization, nothing less than a Copernican revolution. As Victoria Welby would say, 'geocentrism' must be superseded, then also 'heliocentrism', until we approximate a truly 'cosmic' perspective (see Welby 1983 and Petrilli 1998a), where global semiotics and semioethics intersect. The attainment or approximation of such a perspective is an integral part of our ultimate end, hence a point where global semiotics and 'semioethics' intersect. As observed, otherness more than anything else is at stake in the question of human responsibility and therefore of humanism as we are now describing it. However, otherness in the present context of discourse is other with respect to that which has been commonly acknowledged in the past: otherness does not only allude to the otherness of our neighbour or even of another person at a distance – though today relatively so given the worldwide expansion of the communication network. Otherness also implies our relation to living beings most distant from us in genetic terms. Indeed, in the present context a special task for semioethics is to expose the illusoriness of the claim to the status of indifferent differences (see Ponzio 1995a).

Reformulating a famous saying by Terence ('*homo sum: umani nihil a me alienum puto*'), Roman Jakobson (1960) asserts that: '*linguista sum: linguistici nihil a me alienum puto*'. This commitment on the part of the semiotician to all that is linguistic, indeed, endowed with sign value (not only relatively to anthroposemiosis nor just to zoosemiosis, but to the whole semiobiosphere), should not only be understood in a cognitive sense but also in the ethical. And this commitment alludes to concern not only in the sense of 'being concerned with...', but also in the sense of 'being concerned for . . .' and 'taking care of . . .'. Viewed in such a perspective, concern for the other and care for the other imply a capacity for responsibility without limitations in terms of belonging, proximity or community, a capacity which is not exclusive to the 'linguist' or 'semiotician'. Developing Jakobson's statement, we could claim that it is not as professional linguists or semioticians but more significantly as human beings that no sign is '*a me alienum*'; leaving the first part of Terence's saying unmodified, '*homo sum*', we may continue with the statement that as humans not only are we *semiosic animals* (like all other animals), but we are also *semiotic animals*, and in this sense humans are unique with respect to the rest of the animal kingdom. Consequently nothing semiosical, including the biosphere and the evolutionary cosmos whence it sprang, '*a me alienum puto*'.

Semioethics does not have a programme to propose with intended aims and practices, nor a decalogue, nor a formula to apply more or less sincerely, therefore more or less hypocritically. From this point of view, semioethics contrasts with stereotypes as much as with norms and ideology. Semioethics offers a critique of stereotypes, norms and ideology, of the different types of value as characterized, for example, by Charles Morris in *Signification and Significance* (1964; think of his triad 'operative value', 'conceived value' and 'object value' and subordinate tripartition 'detachment', 'dominance' and 'dependence').

Semioethics implies the exquisitely human capacity for critique. Its special vocation is to evidence sign networks where it seemed there were none (cf. Cobley 2007b), bringing to light and evaluating connections, implications and involvement which cannot be escaped, where it seemed there were only net separations, boundaries and distances with their relative alibis. Alibis serve to safeguard responsibility in a limited sense, therefore they safeguard the individual conscience, which readily presents itself as a 'clean conscience'. The component 'telos' in the expression 'telosemiotics' does not indicate some external value or pre-established end, an ultimate end, a *summum bonum* outside the sign network. Rather, it indicates the telos of semiosis itself understood as an orientation beyond the totality, beyond the closure of totality, the capacity for detotalization, for transcendence beyond a given entity, a given being, infinite semiosis, movement towards infinity, desire of the other.

Further reading

Deely, J., Petrilli, S. and Ponzio, A. (2005) *The Semiotic Animal*, Ottawa: Legas.

Petrilli, S. (ed.) (2004) *Ideology, Logic, and Dialogue in Semioethic Perspective*, special issue of *Semiotica*, 148(1/4): 1–9.

Sebeok, T. A. (2001) *Global Semiotics*, Bloomington, IN: Indiana University Press.

Sebeok, T. A., Petrilli, S. and Ponzio, A. (2001) *Semiotica dell'io*, Rome: Meltemi.

Welby, V. (2009) *Signifying and Understanding: Reading the Works of Victoria Welby and the Significs Movement*, ed. and intro. S. Petrilli, Berlin: Mouton de Gruyter.

Part II

Key themes and major figures in semiotics

A

Abduction Abduction is the inferential process by which hypotheses are framed. It is the process of inference by which the rule that explains the fact is hypothesized through a relation of similarity (**icon**ic relation) to that fact. This rule that acts as the general premise may be taken from a field of **discourse** that is close to or distant from that to which the fact belongs, or it may be invented *ex novo*. If the conclusion is confirmed, it retroacts on the rule and convalidates it (ab- or retro-duction). Such retroactive procedure makes abductive inference risky, exposing it to the possibility of error. At the same time, however, if the hypothesis is correct, the abduction is innovative, inventive and sometimes even surprising (cf. Bonfantini 1987).

According to **Peirce**:

> Abduction is the process of forming an explanatory hypothesis. It is the only logical operation which introduces any new idea; for induction does nothing but determine a value, and deduction merely evolves the necessary consequences of a pure hypothesis.
>
> **Deduction** proves that something *must be*; **Induction** shows that something *actually is* operative; Abduction merely suggests that something *may be*.
>
> (*CP* 5.172)

The relation between the premises and the conclusion may be considered in terms of the relation between what we may call, respectively, interpreted **sign**s and **interpretant** signs. In induction, the relation between premises and conclusion is determined by **habit** and is of the **symbol**ic type. In deduction it is **index**ical, the conclusion being a necessary derivation from the premises. In abduction, the relation between premises and conclusion is iconic, that is, it is a relation of reciprocal autonomy. This makes for a high degree of inventiveness together with a high risk margin for error. Abductive processes are highly dialogic and generate responses of the most risky, inventive and creative order. To claim that abductive argumentative procedures are risky is to say that they are mainly tentative and hypothetical, leaving only a minimal margin to convention (symbolicity) and mechanical necessity (indexicality). Abductive inferential processes engender sign processes at the highest levels of otherness and dialogicality.

The degree of dialogicality (cf. Ponzio 1985, 1990a) in the relation between interpreted and interpretant is minimal in deduction: here, once the premises are accepted, the conclusion is obligatory. Induction is also characterized by unilinear inferential processes: identity and repetition dominate, though the relation between the premises and the conclusion is no longer obligatory. In contrast, the relationship in abduction between the argumentative parts is dialogic in a substantial sense. In fact, very high degrees of dialogicality are attained and the higher, the more inventive becomes reasoning.

Abductions are empowered by **metaphor**s in simulation processes used to produce models, inferences, inventions and projects. The close relationship between abductive inference and verisimilitude is determined by the fact that, as demonstrated by **Welby**, 'one of the most splendid of all our intellectual instruments' is the 'image or the figure' (Welby 1985a [1911]: 13; cf. also Petrilli 1986, 1995a, 1998b). Given the close relationship among abduction, icon and simulation, the problem is not to eliminate figurative or metaphorical discourse to the advantage of so-called literal discourse, but to identify and eliminate inadequate images that mystify relations among things and distort our reasoning. As Welby states, 'We need a linguistic oculist to restore lost focussing power, to bring our images back to reality by some normalizing kind of lens' (Welby [1911] 1985a: 16). (**SP**)

See also DIALOGUE.

FURTHER READING

Peirce, C. S. (1955) 'Abduction and induction', in J. Buchler (ed.), *Philosophical Writings of Peirce*, New York: Dover.

Peirce, C. S. (1992) 'Types of reasoning', in K. L. Ketner (ed.), *Reasoning and the Logic of Things: The Cambridge Conferences Lectures of 1898*, Cambridge, MA: Harvard University Press.

Sebeok, T. A. and Umiker-Sebeok, J. (1980) *'You Know My Method': A Juxtaposition of Charles S. Peirce and Sherlock Holmes*, Bloomington, IN: Gaslight.

ACCENT From a semiotic viewpoint, the concept of accent is particularly relevant not as a graphic signal to denote a stress, a stressed syllable, nor as pronunciation, as in the expression 'he speaks with an American accent', nor as a tone of voice, e.g. an angry tone. Considered semiotically, the accent is not merely a graphic or acoustic device, nor does it solely concern verbal signs. Insofar as it is engendered among individuals and is created within a social milieu, the accent refers to the evaluative accentuation present in human verbal and nonverbal **sign**s. The verbal sign, both oral and written, is a sign in a strong sense, not just a signal, but is endowed with plasticity of **meaning** which enables it to respond to different ideological perspectives and different senses. By virtue of such qualities, the verbal sign above all not only has a **theme** and meaning in the referential, or content, sense of these words, but also a value judgement, a specific evaluative accent. There is no such thing as a word, especially a word used in actual speech, whether written or oral, which does not have an accent in terms of evaluative intonation (cf. Ponzio 1980a, 1992). Through a passage from Dostoevsky's *Diary of a Writer*, which analyses the conversation of a band of six tipsy artisans, **Vološinov** (1973 [1929]: 103) shows how evaluations, thoughts, feelings and even trains of reasoning can be expressed merely by using the same noun with an accent that is different each time. (**AP**)

Alterity Alterity (or otherness) indicates the existence of something on its own account, autonomously, independent of the I's initiative, volition, **consciousness**, recognition. Alterity is a synonym of materiality understood as objectivity. The world of physical objects is other with respect to the I. One's own body, the body of each and every one of us, is other in its autonomy from volition and consciousness.

But the most other of all is the other person in his/her irreducibility, refractoriness to the I. Assassination is proof of the other's resistance and of the I's checkmate, his/her powerlessness. Of course we also have 'relative alterity' which **Peirce** classifies as **secondness**, but this is the alterity of the I, in one's roles (of a father relative to his child, a student relative to his teacher, a husband relative to his wife, etc.). But the alterity of the other as other is 'absolute alterity'.

Consequently, when a question of absolute and non-relative alterity arises (cf. Levinas 1961, 1974; Ponzio 1996, 1998a), the otherness of the other person can neither be reduced to the communitary 'We' of Heidegger's *Mitsein* (*being-with*), nor to the Subject–Object relation of Sartre's *being-for*. Alterity is located inside the subject, the I, in the heart itself of the subject, without being englobed by the latter. For this reason the subject cannot become a closed totality but is continually exposed to **dialogue**, is itself a dialogue, a relation between self and other. Contrary to Sartre and **Hegel**, the self of 'being conscious of oneself' does not coincide with consciousness nor does it presuppose it; rather, it is pre-existent to consciousness and is connected to it by a relation of alterity. The other is inseparable from the ego, the I, the Self (*Même* as intended by Emmanuel **Levinas**), but cannot be included within the totality of the ego. The other is necessary to the constitution of the ego and its world, but at the same time it is a constitutive impediment to the integrity and definitive closure of the I and of the world.

The relation to the other – as authors like Charles S. Peirce, Victoria **Welby**, Mikhail **Bakhtin**, Charles **Morris** and Levinas teach us – is a relation of excess, surplus, of escape from objectivating thought, it is release from the subject–object relation; on a linguistic level it produces internal dialogization of the word, the impossibility of ever being an integral word (cf. Bakhtin 1984 [1963]; Vološinov 1973 [1929]). (**AP**)

Further reading

Levinas, E. (1989) 'Time and the other', in S. Hand (ed.), *The Levinas Reader*, Oxford: Blackwell.

American structuralism Linguistics in America developed in a distinctive way in the late nineteenth and early twentieth centuries. A great deal of energy was spent on recording and classifying the indigenous **language**s of America, and linguists therefore looked for rigorous methods of collecting and analysing data. This involved a deliberate effort to break away from preconceptions based on European languages, and to treat each language in its own terms. The focus was on the sounds and the word structure of each language, as these were regarded as concrete and replicable; information about sentence structure was felt to be less dependable, and the **meaning** and use of language were seen as hard to catalogue reliably and were often given less attention.

Although it would be misleading to talk of a 'school', an emphasis on observable elements of structure underpinned much of the work during this period. It has been fashionable for many years to highlight the theoretical inadequacy of structuralist linguistics, but its descriptive achievements were enormous and reflect the great intellectual labour and pioneering dedication that gave rise to them. (**RS**)

See also Bloomfield, Harris *and* Sapir.

FURTHER READING

Fought, J. G. (1994) 'American structuralism', in R. Asher and J. Simpson (eds), *The Encyclopedia of Language and Linguistics*, Vol. 1, Oxford: Pergamon Press, pp. 97–106.

Anthroposemiosis *see* **Anthroposemiotics**

Anthroposemiotics 'Anthroposemiotics' is a name for the study of the human use of **sign**s. It is one of the recent branches on the tree of terms that has grown out of Charles S. **Peirce**'s original coinage of the term '**semiosis**' to name the action of signs. This usage was suggested to Peirce (Fisch 1986a) by reading Philodemus (i.54–40 BCE). Thus, the study of semiosis gives rise to the branch of knowledge that Peirce followed **Locke** in calling '**semiotics**', or 'the doctrine of signs'. So, just as semiotics is the name for the general study of the action of signs (or semiosis), so anthroposemiotics is the name for the specific study of the human use of signs (or anthroposemiosis). The other main branches on this tree of terms, to wit, **zoosemiotics** (the study of the communicative behaviour of animals that do not have **language**), phytosemiotics (the study of communicative behaviours in plants) and physiosemiotics (study of communicative behaviours in the physical universe at large), have all been tied to specific authors of the twentieth century (see Deely 2001a: Ch. 15); but precise authorship of the term 'anthroposemiotics' has, curiously, so far not been identified.

The first work devoted exclusively to the subject of anthroposemiotics (Deely 1994a) concentrated on the species-specifically distinctive features of anthroposemiosis. But the field is actually much broader than such a study would suggest, inasmuch as all the other systems of signs that are found outside the human species are also found at play, in one manner or another, within the human species, and so form a part, even if not the species-specifically distinctive part, of anthroposemiosis. In this way 'anthroposemiotics' may be said to revive within the doctrine of signs the ancient **Stoic** notion of the human being ('anthropos') as the microcosm wherein is summarized and concentrated all that is to be found in the cosmos or universe at large. So the field opened up under the designation of anthroposemiotics actually is vast, subsuming all the traditional studies of human life and culture but under a new focus or perspective, namely, the attempt to appreciate the role of the sign in making possible all that is distinctively human in the realms of life, action and knowledge. The traditional humanities, art, medicine, technology – all can be grouped under the heading of 'anthroposemiotics'.

The reworking of traditional ideas of the human being under this perspective will eventually require nothing less than an encyclopedia wherein the traditional materials of the human sciences can be presented as they have been rethought in the perspective proper to the doctrine of signs. Such an enterprise will have the advantage from the outset of overcoming the split between 'human' and 'natural' sciences (*Naturwissenschaften* und *Geisteswissenschaften*) by virtue of the perspective proper to the sign, recognized to be, from its earliest systematization (Poinsot 1632), superior to the division between nature and culture, because inclusive of both. From the standpoint of anthroposemiotics, culture itself is a part of nature, albeit a species-specifically distinctive part, every bit as much as the human body. (**JD**)

See also Biosemiotics *and* Stoics and Epicureans.

Further reading

Deely, J. (1990) *Basics of Semiotics*, Bloomington, IN: Indiana University Press.

Nöth, W. (1990) *A Handbook of Semiotics*, Bloomington, IN: Indiana University Press.

Sebeok, T. A. (1985) *Contributions to the Doctrine of Signs*, with Foreword by B. Williams, Lanham, MD: University Press of America.

Aquinas Thomas Aquinas (1224/26?–1274) was to the medieval Latin Age what Plato and **Aristotle** were to the ancient Greek epoch of philosophy, to wit, the thinker whose work set the standard for agreements and disagreements over the Latin centuries after him. As regards semiotic, Aquinas proved to be a transition figure from **Augustine**'s definition of sign, which applied only to material objects of perception, to the forging of a more general understanding which included percepts and concepts as essentially signs by reason of representing always objects *other* than themselves. Though **Scotus** after Aquinas would be the first thematically to focus on the notion of concepts as signs, and also anticipated **Peirce**'s distinction between ***interpretant*** and *interpreter*, along with the dynamics of signs as a system, it would not be till the early seventeenth-century *Treatise on Signs* of John **Poinsot** (1632), writing as a follower of and commentator upon Aquinas's scattered discussion of signs, that the general notion of signs as having their being in relations triadic in character would become fully established (only to be forgotten by modern philosophy which turned attention elsewhere, opening the period **Sebeok** calls 'cryptosemiotics' wherein the approach to knowledge called 'epistemology' eclipsed and pushed underground the Latin development in which the work of Aquinas had been pivotal to the development of an initial semiotic **consciousness**) (Deely 2006c). Never himself focused thematically on sign as a question of systematic pursuit, thus, yet Aquinas left a corpus of writings both vast and treating of problems central to the eventual formation of a systematic doctrine of signs. This trail of tantalizing suggestions semiotically to be pursued runs from Aquinas's earliest writings (1254) to those of his last days (1273). Three hundred and fifty-eight years after Aquinas's death, Poinsot, as 'the latest and the most mature of the geniuses who explained St Thomas' (Maritain 1955: vi), follows exactly that trail to find that it leads to the demonstration of the existence of a unified subject matter for semiotic inquiry. **(JD)**

Further reading

Deely, J. (2004) 'The role of Thomas Aquinas in the development of semiotic consciousness', *Semiotica*, 152(1/4): 75–139.

Arbitrariness 'Arbitrariness of the sign' is an expression that designates the non-founded, unmotivated relation, uniting, in the constitution of the sign, the plane of the **signifier** and the plane of the **signified**: 'The link that unites the signifier to the signifying is arbitrary' (Saussure 1983: 67–68). It is not a philosophical debate concerning the link between the object and the name but truly a 'linguistic principle' given, as such, according to which a signifier, for example 'tree', is not linked to the signified 'tree' by any internal or 'natural' relation. What is the importance of this principle? Clearly, 'no one challenges the principle of arbitrariness', writes **Saussure** (Saussure 1983: 67–68). However, in the eyes of Saussure, those who see **language** as a convention incur the reproach he addressed to Whitney – none the less a conventionalist – of 'not having been thorough enough'.

The manuscript sources for the *Course in General Linguistics* mention a 'radically' arbitrary link. This means that there is no causal relation between the signified and its signifier, and especially that there is no signified prior to the semiotic act, i.e. the *semiosis*, which constitutes the sign. On the contrary, it is precisely this arbitrary link that, as it gives birth to the created sign, creates correlatively the signifier and the signified. This principle, which, more than a hundred years after it was formulated, still appears paradoxical and anti-intuitive, lays in reality the foundation of the autonomy of language considered as form. Indeed, the Saussurean conception of language is that of an immanent structural organization, dominating speaking subjects who are thereby subject to its rule as a necessity: 'Mass is linked to language (*la **langue***) as it is' (Saussure 1983: 70). The establishment of a relation in between the plane of the signified and the plane of the signifier in no case rests on pre-established divisions and adjustments of these planes, implemented in relation to an immediate reality to be described. The establishment of this relation is 'radically arbitrary' as it rests exclusively on the totality of all the other relations presently in play in the system-language, with no privileged attachment of any single word to the extra-linguistic reality. The task of linguistics, for Saussure, is to describe this immanent system. It is up to other disciplines, amongst them philosophy, to raise questions about the adequacy of a given linguistic expression to the data of concrete experience. (**AH**)

See also SAUSSURE *and* VALUE.

FURTHER READING

Saussure, F. de (1983) *Course in General Linguistics*, trans. R. Harris, London: Duckworth, pp. 65–70.

ARGUMENT A set of interdependent statements or beliefs where some, the premises, support a conclusion. In **Peirce**'s semiotics an argument is a sign of a lawful relation between premises and conclusion. There are three types of inference, or passage from premises to conclusion, depending on the argument form: deduction, or certain reasoning, induction, where general conclusions are drawn from select cases, and abduction, or intelligent guessing. (**NH**)

See also DICENT *and* RHEME.

ARISTOTLE Greek philosopher (384–322 BCE), one of the most respected authorities of the ancient world, and often referred to throughout the European Middle Ages simply as 'the philosopher'. A pupil of Plato, he lectured on topics ranging from metaphysics and poetics to politics and biology. Although he left no work specifically devoted to the study of **language**s or **grammar** or etymology (as modern scholars understand those subjects), he laid the foundations of Western logic. Logic is arguably what he saw as the analysis of language at the level of abstraction necessary to make tenable generalizations about it. It is sometimes said that Western logic would have taken quite a different shape if Aristotle had spoken some other language than Greek. (**RH**)

AUGUSTINE Christian saint and theologian (354–430), bishop of Hippo in North Africa. He is generally regarded as perpetuating the **Stoic** theory of **sign**s, and in particular as championing the distinction between natural and conventional signs, but his interest in these matters was dictated by his religious convictions and problems involving interpretation of the sacraments and the scriptures rather than by anything else. The same is true of Augustine's pronouncements on translation, where his underlying motivation was to justify the early Church's use of Latin versions of the Bible. He held that it was possible for words to share the same **meaning** in spite of belonging to different **language**s. Augustine's account of how he learned his native language as a child was taken by **Wittgenstein** as typifying a common but extremely naïve view of how language works. (**RH**)

See also STOICS AND EPICUREANS.

AUSTIN John Langshaw Austin (1911–1960) was Professor of Philosophy at

Oxford University, where he was one of the prominent figures in a tradition known as the Oxford school of '**ordinary language philosophy**'. The tenets of this tradition, as well as Austin's personal style, are captured nicely in the formulation of his philosophical goal as an attempt to discover

> the distinctions men [*sic*] have found worth drawing, and the connections they have found worth making, in the lifetimes of many generations: these surely are likely to be more numerous, more sound, since they have stood up to the long test of the survival of the fittest, and more subtle, at least in all ordinary and reasonably practical matters, than any of you and I are likely to think up in our armchairs of an afternoon – the most favoured alternative method.
>
> (Austin 1957: 24)

It is from this angle that Austin approached a wide range of traditional philosophical topics, such as the problem of **truth**, knowledge and **meaning**, or the problem of free will. His **language**-based philosophical method was presented as an antidote against a more popular logical empiricism.

His most influential and lasting contribution was made in the philosophy of language, where, not surprisingly, his method and object are made to merge. In *How To Do Things with Words*, the William James Lectures delivered at Harvard University in 1955, published posthumously in 1962, Austin dwells on the observation of language as a form of action. Whenever something is *said*, something is *done by* or *in* saying it. From this point of view he questions the distinction between **constative** utterances such as 'It is raining outside' (in which something is *said*, and which are either true or false) and **performatives** such as 'I name this ship the Queen Elizabeth' or 'I apologize' (in which something is *done*, and which may be happy or unhappy depending on whether a number of conditions are fulfilled, e.g. in relation to the identity of the speaker who may or may not be the appointed person to christen the ship or his/her intentions which may or may not be appropriate to the act of apologizing). He observes that also constatives are subject to criteria of felicity unrelated to truth or falsity (e.g. 'All John's children are bald' is neither true nor false in a context in which John does not have any children). Conversely, performatives are liable to a dimension of criticism closely related to truth and falsity (e.g. 'I declare you guilty' may be a verdict that was reached properly and in good faith; yet it matters whether the verdict was just or not). Thus rejecting the distinction, Austin then introduced a three-fold conceptual framework to capture different aspects involved in every type of utterance: the **locution** (the act *of* saying something with a specific phonetic and grammatical form and with a specific meaning), the **illocution** (the act performed *in* saying something, such as asserting, promising or ordering) and the **perlocution** (the act performed *by* saying something, such as persuading, deceiving or frightening). This framework became the basis of **speech act** theory, as developed further by John Searle and as adopted by numerous linguists from the 1960s onwards. (**JV**)

Further reading

Austin, J. L. (1961) *Philosophical Papers*, Oxford: Oxford University Press.

Austin, J. L. (1962) *How To Do Things with Words*, ed. J. O. Urmson, Oxford: Oxford University Press. (Second revised edition, 1975, ed. J. O. Urmson and M. Sbisà, Cambridge, MA: Harvard University Press.)

Warnock, G. J. (1989) *J. L. Austin*, London: Routledge and Kegan Paul.

Autopoiesis The concept of autopoietic system is crucial to Niklas Luhmann's theory of the social as **communication**. The concept was originally invented by the Chilean professor of biology Humberto Maturana, and his student Francisco Varela, as a definition of life. Autopoiesis means self-creating or self-producing. It is a process whereby a living system – such as a cell – produces its and own organization and maintains and constitutes itself in a spatial environment. The living system's components participate recursively in the same network of productions that produced them. Thus such self-organizing systems are *operationally closed* at the level of organization and the system's basic distinction is between itself and the environment. There is no flow of information from the environment into the system in this bioconstructivist theory. All irritations are perceived as perturbations or noise with a possible destructive effect. Regular disturbances create a *structural coupling*, which is a systematic change in the inner organization with the purpose of conserving the system's organization against the persistent disturbances in its drift in evolution and history. Thus its reaction may look like a causal stimuli–response reaction in information, but it is not. It is the autopoietic character of living systems that makes it possible for them to conserve structural couplings in the form of stable cognitive constructions of objects. Thus 'to live is to know'. Computers are not autopoietic and therefore have no cognition and communication as such.

Luhmann also understood psychological and social–communicative systems as autopoietic. Contrary to the biological system working the medium of life, these operate in the medium of meaning. The psyche is a silent closed system of perception, emotions, thinking and volitions. It is not a self and it does not communicate. *Only communication communicates*. Luhmann views social systems as communicative autopoietic systems with human bodies and minds as their environment. (**SB**)

See also Cybersemiotics.

Further reading

Luhmann, N. (1995) *Social Systems*, Stanford, CA: Stanford University Press.

B

Bakhtin Mikhail Mikhailovich Bakhtin (Örel 1895–Moscow 1975), a Russian philosopher. He met Pavel N. Medvedev (1891–1938) and Valentin N. **Vološinov** (1884/5–1936) in Vitebsk in 1920 and established relations of friendship and collaboration with them. Together they formed the 'Bakhtin Circle' with the participation of the musicologist I. I. Sollertinskij, the biologist I. I. Kanaev, the writers K. K. Vaginov and D. I. Kharms, the Indologist M. I. Tubianskij and the poet N. A. Kljuev. Even if only on an ideal level, Bakhtin's brother Nikolaj (1894–1950) may also be considered as a member of the 'Circle' (cf. Ponzio, 'Presentazione. Un autore dalla parte dell'eroe', in N. Bakhtin 1998: 7–13). (Having left Russia in 1918 Nikolaj eventually settled in England, where at the University of Birmingham he founded the Department of Linguistics in 1946. He died there four years later.)

During the 1920s Bakhtin's work interconnected so closely with that of his collaborators that it is difficult to distinguish between them. This would seem to confirm his thesis of the 'semi-other' character of 'one's own word', in spite of the critics who insist on establishing ownership and authorship. Bakhtin played a significant role in writing Vološinov's two books *Freudianism: A Critical Sketch* (1927) and *Marxism and the Philosophy of Language* (1929) as well as *The Formal Method in Literary Scholarship* (1985 [1928]), signed by P. N. Medvedev. He also contributed to various articles published by the same 'authors' between 1925 and 1930, as well as to Kanaev's article 'Contemporary Vitalism' (1926). And even when the 'Circle' broke down under Stalinist oppression, with Medvedev's assassination and Vološinov's death, the 'voices' of its various members were still heard in uninterrupted **dialogue** with Bakhtin who persevered in his research until his death in 1975.

Problems of Dostoevsky's Art was published in 1929, followed by a long silence broken only in 1963 when at last a much expanded edition appeared under the title *Problems of Dostoevsky's Poetics*. With Stalinism at its worst, in fact, Bakhtin had been banished from official culture and exiled to Kustanaj. In 1965 he published his monograph *Rabelais and His World*. A collection of his writings in Russian originally appeared in 1975 and another in 1979, followed by editions of his unpublished writings or re-editions of published works by himself and his circle (cf. in English, Bakhtin 1981, 1986, 1990). Since then numerous monographs have been dedicated to his thought (Clark and Holquist 1984; Holquist 1990; Morson and Emerson 1989, 1990; Ponzio 1980b, 1992, 1998b; Todorov 1981).

Evaluated as 'critique', in a literary as well as philosophical sense after **Kant** and **Marx**, Bakhtin's fundamental contribution to 'philosophy of **language**' or 'metalinguistics' consists in his *critique of dialogic reason*. He privileged the term 'metalinguistics' for his particular approach to the study of **sign**, utterance, **text**, **discourse**, **genre** and relations between literary writing and nonverbal expressions in popular culture, as in the signs of carnival. Bakhtin's critique of dialogic reason focuses on the concept of *responsibility without alibis*, a non-conventional responsibility, but which concerns existential 'architectonics' in its relation with the I, with the world and with others and which as such cannot be transferred. Dialogue is for Bakhtin an embodied, intercorporeal, expression of the involvement of one's body, which is only illusorily individual, separate and autonomous. The adequate image of the body is that of the 'grotesque body' (see Bakhtin 1993 [1965]) which finds expression in popular culture, in the vulgar language of the public place and above all in the masks of carnival. This is the body *in its vital and indissoluble relation with the world and with the body of others*. With the shift in focus from identity (whether individual, as in the case of **consciousness** or self, or collective, as in a community, historical language, or cultural system at large) to **alterity** – a sort of Copernican revolution – Bakhtinian critique of dialogic reason not only questions the general orientation of Western philosophy, but also the tendencies dominating over the culture engendering it. (**AP**)

FURTHER READING

Bakhtin, M. M. (1981) *The Dialogic Imagination: Four Essays*, trans. C. Emerson and M. Holquist, Austin, TX: University of Texas Press.

Bakhtin, M. M. (1984) *Problems of Dostoevsky's Poetics*, trans. C. Emerson, Minneapolis, MN: University of Minnesota Press.

Bakhtin, M. M. (1984 [1965]) *Rabelais and His World*, trans. H. Iswolsky, Bloomington, IN: Indiana University Press.

BARTHES Roland Barthes (Cherbourg 1915–Paris 1980), French semiotician, literary theorist, critic of the mediocrity of literary criticism and of ideology, writer and painter. In 1947 he began publishing an analysis of Albert Camus's 'Blank writing' ('*écriture blanche*') in the journal *Combat*. As a French **language** teacher in Alexandria (Egypt), he met **Greimas** and took an interest in **Saussure**, **Hjelmslev** and **Jakobson** while continuing his studies in literature and theatre, focusing especially on Brecht and the historian Michelet.

He settled in Paris in 1950, after which *Le degré zéro de l'écriture* was published in 1953, followed by *Michelet par lui-même* in 1954. His interest in semiology, literature and the *nouveau roman* (Robbe-Grillet, Butor, etc.) dovetails with his critique of mass culture ideology. *Mythologies* (1957) testifies to such interests: Barthes focuses on 'everyday objects', from automobiles to products in plastic, detergents and potato chips, considered through categories taken from authoritative authors such as Saussure, Hjelmslev and **Marx**. *Système de la Mode* (1967b; written between 1957 and 1963) belongs to the same context.

It studies the relation between verbal and nonverbal semiotic systems in women's attire as illustrated in fashion magazines, which also led his attention to fashion as spoken (as a mode of speaking) (*la mode parlée*), without which images are nothing.

In *Éléments de sémiologie* (1964a) the relation between verbal signs and nonverbal signs is central. The linguistics of the linguists must be abandoned, he argues, to employ a far broader concept of language as a practice that models and organizes **discourse** fields. On leaving aside the limited view of linguistics as conceived by the linguist (an analogous critique was conducted by **Morris** 1946), it becomes evident that 'human language is more than the pattern of **signification**: it is its very foundation', and that it is necessary 'to reverse Saussure's formula and assert that semiology is a part of linguistics' (Barthes 1967a: 8). Another 'shift' produced by this essay is the transition from a *sémiologie de communication* (Saussure, Buyssens, Prieto, Mounin) to a *semiotics of signification*, according to which signs are not only those produced intentionally to communicate (but also, for example, symptoms in **medical semiotics**, or 'dreaming' according to Freud). These studies in general semiotics, which have concrete application, include 'L'introduction à l'analyse structurale des récits' (1966a).

The 'transgressive character of semiotics' is also present in Barthes' contributions to literary analysis such as *Sur Racine* (1963), *Essais critiques* (1964b), *Critique et vérité* (1966b), *S/Z* (1970a), *L'Empire des signes* (1970b), *Sade, Fourier, Loyola* (1971), *Le plaisir du texte* (1973b) and *Fragments d'un discours amoureux* (1977b). Here his interest in literature goes together with his interest in signification and for what, in an essay of 1975 ('L'obvie et l'obtus', now in Barthes 1982), he calls the 'third sense', *the semiotics of significance*, whose object is not the message (semiotics of **communication**), nor the symbol in the Freudian sense (semiotics of signification), but the ***text*** or *writing*, that is, the maximum opening of sense which characterizes especially literary writing (cf. Ponzio 1995b; Marrone, 'Introduzione', in Barthes 1998: ix–xxxv). But the filmic, the pictorial, the musical (*Image–Music–Text*, 1977c), the photographic (cf. *La chambre claire*, 1980) also achieve significance. Owing to the interdependency between the readerly (*lisible*) text and the writerly (*scriptible*) text of the writer (*scripteur*, *écrivant*), which instead is present to a lesser degree in the text of the *non-literary author* (*écrivant*), the reader assumes a role of co-authorship and therefore participates dialogically in the constitution of sense.

From 1962 to 1967 Barthes taught sociology of signs, **symbol**s and representations at the École Pratique des Hautes Études en Sciences Sociales. In 1967 he was called to the Collège de France. His inaugural *Leçon* at the Collège (1977d) attributes to literary writing a subversive character thanks to the shift operated by significance: it enables the *écrivant* to say without identifying with the subject-author and therefore to escape the order of discourse which the speaker reproduces when he obeys ***langue***. (**AP**)

Further reading

Barthes, R. (1967) *Elements of Semiology*, trans. A. Lavers and C. Smith, London: Cape.

Barthes, R. (1974) *S/Z*, trans. R. Howard, New York: Hill and Wang.

Barthes, R. (1977) *Image–Music–Text*, ed. and trans. S. Heath, London: Fontana/Collins.

Bateson Gregory Bateson (1904–1980), a British anthropologist, social scientist and **cybernetic communication** theoretician, worked in a transdisciplinary and holistic frame. He was one of the original members of the core group of the Macy Conferences (1942–1953) with Warren McCulloch, John von Neumann, Kurt Lewin, Norbert Wiener, as well as Heinz von Foerster, and took part in the creation of cybernetic theory. Bateson's major project was to explain the relation of mind and nature – or mind in nature – from a modern scientific basis, avoiding the metaphysical dualism of Descartes as well as the mechanicism of Laplace. Bateson provided a new delimitation of the concept of information: 'In fact what we mean by information – the elementary unit of information – is a difference which makes a difference' (1973: 428). For Bateson, the elementary, cybernetic system with its messages in circuits is the simplest mental unit, even when the total system does not include living organisms. Mind is synonymous with a cybernetic system that is comprised of a total, self-correcting unit that prepares information. Mind is immanent in this wholeness, because mind is essentially the informational and logical pattern that connects everything through its virtual recursive dynamics of differences and logical types. He sees life and mind as coexisting in an ecological and evolutionary dynamic, integrating the whole biosphere. For Bateson, mind cannot exist without matter; meanwhile, matter without mind *can* exist, but it is inaccessible. Matter and energy are imbued with informational circular processes of differences creating 'patterns that connect'. Cybernetic science, which is also a science of **codes**, is seen as the key to such a deep non-mystical knowledge of the relation between humans, mind, ecology, living systems and evolution through a recursively dynamic of logical types. His theory of the double-bind further connected communication theory and psychiatry. (**SB**)

See also Cybersemiotics.

Further reading

Bateson, G. (1979) *Mind and Nature: A Necessary Unity*, New York: Bantam Books.

Baudrillard Jean Baudrillard (1929–2007), French social theorist. The early Baudrillard saw society as organized around conspicuous consumption and the lavish display of commodities by means of which one could acquire identity, prestige and status in the community. Baudrillard made efforts to combine Saussurean semiological theory in terms of a 'critique of the political economy of the sign' with a **Marx**ist critique of capitalism (Baudrillard 1975, 1981). For the later Baudrillard, labour is no longer a force of production but has itself become just another **sign** among signs. Production is nothing more than the consumerist system of signs referring to themselves (Baudrillard 1983a, b, 1988, 1995).

Baudrillard's mass media have generated an inundation of images and signs, the consequence of which is a 'simulation world', which erases the age-old distinction between the 'real' and the 'imaginary'. The privileged domains of modernity – science, philosophy, labour, private enterprise, social programmes and, above all, theory – are sucked up by a whirlwind of vacuous **signifier**s and into a 'black hole'. The age-old cherished illusions of the referential sign vanish, as signs and their objects implode into mere disembodied signs. Consequently, the commodities of contemporary 'postmodern' culture organized around conspicuous consumption have lost their value as material goods. Like signs in **Saussure**'s differential system of **language**, they take on **value** according to their relations with all other sign-commodities in the entire system. Everything is flattened to the same level, that of signifiers existing in contiguous relationship with other signifiers, the totality of which composes a vast tautological system. Individuals become nothing more than socially invented agents of needs. Each individual becomes tantamount to any and all individuals. The individual, like any given sign-commodity, is equal to no more than any and all other sign-commodities of the same name and value.

Three 'orders of simulation', Baudrillard writes, have culminated in our mind-numbing, complex, 'postmodern' social life: 1) the order of the counterfeit (the natural law of value) which coincides with the rise of modernity, when *simulacra* implied power and social relations; 2) the final stage of the Industrial Revolution, when serial production and automation (based on the commercial law of value) opened the door to infinite reproducibility, and machines began to take their place alongside humans; and 3) our present cybernetic society, when models began to take precedence over things, and since models are signs, signs now began to exercise the full force of their hegemony. This third order simulation is obsessively binary or dyadic in nature – which is to be expected, for after all Baudrillard's own model is indelibly Saussurean. Language, genetics and social organization are analogous and governed by a binary logic underlying social models and **code**s controlling institutional and everyday life. In contrast to classical theories of social control, Baudrillard's theory *prima facie* appears radically indeterminate: everything resembles 'a Brownian movement of particles or the calculation of probabilities'. Signs and modes of representation rather than representation itself come to constitute 'reality'. Signs become mere atoms: lonely, hermetic signs making up a new type of social order. They become charged with **meaning** only in relation to, and take their rightful place in the language of, the media with respect merely to other signs in the entire interwoven, variegated, labyrinthine tapestry. Signs have no destiny other than that of floating in an undefinable, reference-less space of their own making. **(FM)**

See also BINARISM.

FURTHER READING

Baudrillard, J. (1975) *The Mirror of Production*, trans. M. Poster, St Louis, MO: Telos.
Baudrillard, J. (1981) *For a Critique of the Political Economy of the Sign*, trans. C. Levin, St Louis, MO: Telos.
Gane, M. (ed.) (1993) *Baudrillard Live: Selected Interviews*, London: Routledge.

BENVENISTE Emile Benveniste (Cairo 1902–Paris 1976) was a French linguist and defining figure in the thought of post-war France and beyond. Educated at the Sorbonne by **Saussure**'s student, Antoine Meillet, Benveniste went on to teach at the Collège de France from 1937 until 1969. Although Benveniste was never granted the celebrity afforded to many of his contemporaries, he was still a major force across disciplines in academic circles. J. G. Merquior reports: 'I still recall how we were awestruck as we passed by the door of his office on the way to **Lévi-Strauss**'s crowded seminar' (1986: 15). Furthermore, it is clear that Benveniste is the father of **poststructuralism**, his work from the late 1930s onwards paving the way for the critiques of **structuralism** offered by the likes of Derrida, Lacan, **Kristeva**, the later **Barthes**, **Baudrillard** and assorted Anglo-American theorists in studies of film, literature and philosophy (see Easthope 1988).

Benveniste's work mainly took place within the field of Indo-European **language**s, but it was probably the collection of his essays, *Problèmes de linguistique générale* (1966; translated into English in 1971), which lent his insights greater currency. The essays in the volume were short, highly focused and closely argued. They ranged from a penetrating critique of Saussure's principle of arbitrariness in the **sign**, 'The nature of the linguistic sign', through a consideration of the general role of prepositions, 'The sublogical system of prepositions in Latin', to his essay on the 'third person' as a 'non-person', 'The nature of pronouns'. Despite the minute reasoning behind each of these essays, they all ask the larger questions which force a fundamental re-orientation of post-Saussurean general linguistics. Even more than the work of **Jakobson**, these essays are concerned with the consequences of the phenomenon known as 'Subjectivity in language' (the title of essay number 21 in the volume).

In this light, it is easy to see how Benveniste so influenced poststructuralists. 'It is in and through language that man constitutes himself as *subject*,' he writes, 'because language alone establishes the concept of "ego" in reality, in *its* reality which is that of being' (1971: 224). For Benveniste, the separation of *I* and *you* in **dialogue** was crucial to the category of *person* because it is the means by which the individual sets him/herself up as a subject in **discourse**. The personal pronouns are just one, albeit most important, means by which each speaker appropriates a language; **deixis** is another means, demanding that **meaning** can only be realized with reference to the instance of discourse in which the deictic category appears. As such, language creates the designation of person; but it also contributes to the human understanding of such supposedly autonomous phenomena as time and space.

Yet the subject is not only made possible by language in Benveniste's theory; in a development which makes his work congenial to some variants of psychoanalysis, the subject is fundamentally split in relation to the linguistic capacity. Benveniste identifies two sides of any use of language: he calls these *énoncé* and *énonciation*. The *énoncé* is simple enough: it is the statement or content of the particular instance of language, what is being said. The *énonciation*, on the other hand, is the *act* of utterance and presupposes a speaker and a listener. The two can be recognized when separated in this abstract way but, in practice, they are always entangled. In a room containing a large group of people, one person might whisper to those within earshot that one of the group who is out of earshot has very bad body odour. The *énoncé* will be about a person who smells, but the *énonciation* will be a whisper. Yet the one is caught up in and necessitated by the other: the personal remark is made all the more personal by the *sotto voce* rendering of it.

The subject of this dynamic in language cannot help being pulled in two ways. There will be the rendering of him/herself as a subject represented in the use of pronouns such as *I* (*énoncé*); but there will also be that other 'I' who does the rendering (*énonciation*). The dilemma, here, is made clear in such paradoxical constructions as 'I am lying', in which the subject speaking *must* be separate from the subject represented in the instance of discourse.

Benveniste's writings on subjectivity and language found a ready welcome in poststructuralist and psychoanalytical circles. However, his work is more wide-ranging than this fact allows and his essays in general linguistics are worth repeated readings, especially as they so frequently coincide with **ordinary language philosophy**, **pragmatics**, the work of **Morris** and **semiotics**. Benveniste's contribution to international semiotics is now well known. After retiring from the Collège de France he became President of the **IASS**, an organization that, with others, he had initiated. He died in tragic circumstances in 1976. (**PC**)

Further reading

Benveniste, E. (1971) *Problems in General Linguistics*, trans. M. E. Meek, Coral Gables, FL: University of Miami Press.

Benveniste, E. (1973) *Indo-European Language and Society*, trans. E. Palmer, London: Faber.

Lotringer, S. and Gora, T. (eds) (1981) *Polyphonic Linguistics: The Many Voices of Emile Benveniste* (Special Supplement, *Semiotica*).

Berkeley George Berkeley (1685–1753). Second of the three most influential British empiricists: **Locke**, Berkeley and Hume. On the assumption that only sensations can be experienced, and that nothing can be sensed but ideas, Berkeley concluded that only mind and ideas exist. He claimed that we can only have ideas of ideas, not of objects out of mind, and he denied that we can have abstract general ideas. We can distinguish real experience from imagination by its greater vividness and by the continuity that characterizes reality. But Berkeley held that 'to be is to be perceived', so the connectedness of the ideas that constitutes reality depends on continual perception. This Berkeley attributed to God. So Berkeley accepted the reality of ordinary experience but denied that there is an external world that causes sensations and is the source of the continuity we experience. Charles S. **Peirce** argued that this was a sham **realism**, and that Berkeley belongs in the **nominalist** tradition. However, Peirce was impressed with Berkeley's proto-pragmatic idea that thoughts are **sign**s and his rejection of material objects that can have no sensible effects. Hume, a more sceptical empiricist, denied mind along with matter and admitted only impressions and ideas. (**NH**)

FURTHER READING

Warnock, G. J. (1953) *Berkeley*, Harmondsworth: Penguin.

BINARISM In linguistics, the assumption is that contrasts may be analysed in terms of binary oppositions or choices. Thus, in **phonology**, for example, consonants may be classified in terms of the opposition between 'voiced' and 'voiceless'; or in **grammar**, number specified by reference to the opposition between 'singular' and 'plural'. The logical basis of binarism is negation, i.e. the proposition 'not *p*' as opposed to '*p*'. Thus binarism is often associated with the assumption that one member of the pair is 'marked' (i.e. plus or positive) and the other 'unmarked' (i.e. negative or lacking the feature in question). Binary analyses may be controversial for at least two reasons. One is that they tend to provide a straitjacket into which more subtle and elaborate kinds of linguistic contrast have to be forced. The other is that although binarism poses as an analytic methodology it is in effect an a priori theory about universals of linguistic structure and lacks any well-argued foundation.

In **semiotics** and cultural studies generally binarism has had a bad press because the insistence on such oppositions ('good' versus 'bad', 'scientific' versus 'unscientific', 'democratic' versus 'undemocratic', etc.) is seen as a way of inculcating those values favoured by current establishments and suppressing dissidence or alternative views. (**RH**)

BIOSEMIOTICS Throughout Western history, most semiotic theories and their applications have focused on messages, whether verbal or not, in circulation among human beings, generally within their cultural setting. This kind of semiotic inquiry – characterized as anthropocentric and logocentric – has been the rule since ancient times, with the partial exception of iatric semiotics (symptomatology, diagnostics, or the like), practised and written about by physicians such as **Hippocrates** of Cos (*c.* 430 BCE) or **Galen** of Pergamon (129–*c.* 200), as well as their innumerable modern successors, notably **Thure von Uexküll**, MD (1908–2004), who regards biosemiotics as an underlying exemplar for all psychosomatic medicine. Indeed, the ultimate cradle of biosemiotics rests, if tacitly, in antique medicine.

Step by hesitant step, the scope of traditional semiotics has widened immensely since the 1920s, or, to put it the other way around, 'normal' **semiotics** gradually became embedded and submerged in the far vaster domain of what the Italian medical oncologist Giorgio Prodi (1928–1987) came to denominate 'nature semiotics' (1988). The study of biological **codes** is nowadays more commonly designated *biosemiotics* – a term independently coined in recent decades in the USA and elsewhere – which harks back to the work of **Jakob von Uexküll**'s (1864–1944) now classic work, *Theoretische Biologie* (1920, et seq.). Biosemiotics presupposes the axiomatic identity of the **semiosphere** with the biosphere.

Uexküll called his subject matter ***Umwelt****lehre*, the study of phenomenal self-worlds, perhaps best rendered as unique models of each subject's universe. Every subject is the constructor of its 'significant surround', each wrapped according to its equipment of perceptual organs – which order perceptual **sign**s into perceptual cues; and effector organs – which are parts of the operational world of the subject, signs for the changes which the effector evokes in the object through which the perceptual cue is extinguished. A so-called functional cycle links parts of the environment with the internal model of a living being via its perceptual organs and effector organs, coordinated with the medium in which the animal manoeuvres (e.g. fin/water, wing/air, foot/path, mouth/food, weapon/enemy, or the like). Such networks are made up of signs accessible only to the encoding subject; they remain 'noise' for all others.

The Swiss psychologist, and founder of zoo biology, Heini **Hediger** (1908–1992), influenced by Jakob von Uexküll's theories, studied animal flight responses, the precepts of taming and training of captive animals in the wild as well as in zoo and circus environments, and the domestication of household pets and farm animals. He was chiefly responsible for working out, by strictly empirical biosemiotic routines, concepts of individual and social space in applications to animals of many kinds. These were later applied by others to humans and further developed under such labels as '**proxemics**'.

While Uexküll tested various animal species singly – say, the tick in search of mammalian blood – Hediger often investigated them in their dyadic interdependence with other species, signally so with *Homo sapiens* (famously including interactions of the 'Clever Hans phenomenon' kind). Later, reflections on animal **semiosis** (dubbed '**zoosemiotics**') were extended by other scholars to plants ('phytosemiotics'), fungi ('mycosemiotics') and, importantly, to the global prokaryotic **communication** network within and between different bacterial cells evolved three and a half billion years ago ('microsemiotics', 'cytosemiotics').

The body of any living entity consists of an intricate web of semioses; the term '**endosemiosis**' refers to trains of sign transmission inside the organism. The messages that are transmitted include information about the **meaning** of processes in one system of the body (cells, tissues, organs or organ systems) for other systems as well as for the integrative regulation devices (especially the brain) and such control systems as the immune **code** (crucially capable of distinguishing self from non-self). Among the other fundamental endosemiotic codes are the genetic code, the metabolic code and the neural code. (**TAS**)

See also ANTHROPOSEMIOTICS.

FURTHER READING

Hoffmeyer, J. (1996) *Signs of Meaning in the Universe*, Bloomington, IN: Indiana University Press.

Hoffmeyer, J. (2008) *Biosemiotics: An Examination into the Signs of Life and the Life of Signs*, Scranton, PA: University of Scranton Press.

Markoš, A. (2002) *Readers of the Book of Life: Contextualizing Developmental Evolutionary Biology*, Oxford: Oxford University Press.

BIRDWHISTELL Ray Lee Birdwhistell (1918–1994) introduced '**kinesics**', the study of body motion as a **communication** system in human interaction. Born in Cincinnati, Ohio, he remained deeply attached to Kentucky, his parental home. He gained a PhD in anthropology from the University of Chicago in 1951 for a study of socialization in rural Kentucky. While at Chicago he became acquainted with Margaret Mead and Gregory **Bateson**. Their influence on one another was mutual and considerable. In 1956 he was involved with Bateson in the 'Natural History of an Interview' project at the Center for Advanced Study in the Behavioral Sciences in Palo Alto. Begun on the initiative of linguists and psychiatrists, this was the first attempt ever to examine face-to-face interaction as a multimodal communication process in which microanalyses of sound-synchronized films of interactions were undertaken. It laid the foundations for Birdwhistell's fundamental ideas about the nature of kinesics and communication. Birdwhistell taught at the University of Toronto, the University of Louisville, Kentucky, and the University of Buffalo, New York. He directed the Project on Human Communication at the Eastern Pennsylvania Psychiatric Institute in Philadelphia, and was Professor in the Annenberg School of Communications, University of Pennsylvania. He was a charismatic teacher and had a wide influence on several generations of students. (**AK**)

FURTHER READING

Kendon, A. and Sigman, S. J. (1996) 'Ray L. Birdwhistell (1918–1994): Commemorative essay', *Semiotica*, 112: 231–261.

BLENDING/CONCEPTUAL INTEGRATION Gilles Fauconnier and Mark Turner's theory of conceptual integration or blending captures the nature of a pervasive and fundamental mode of cognitive processing. It characterizes human meaning construction in terms of continuous online combinations of representational contents (*mental spaces*) with each their organizing structure. Contrary to metaphorical mappings, the most interesting blends (double scope blends) are not asymmetrical, but genuine conflations. Moreover, the result of the conceptual integration, the blend, contains meaning which cannot be inferred from either of the input spaces: the incompetence asserted in 'this surgeon is a butcher' is not a property inherent in butchers and mapped onto surgeons; it thus emerges in the blend. Blending has been attested as a fundamental mental operation in various domains such as grammar, **language** use, visual art, literary art, reasoning, mathematics, etc. (**PB**)

Bloomfield Leonard Bloomfield (1887–1949) was a major pioneer in modern linguistics, and a leading figure in **American structuralism**. After doctoral research on the history of the Germanic **languages**, he went on to do important work on native American and Austronesian languages. His book *Language* (1933) expertly synthesized much of what was known in linguistics at the time, and is still well worth reading. Bloomfield worked hard to establish linguistics as an independent subject and played a prominent role in setting up the Linguistic Society of America in 1924. He wrote introductory textbooks on Dutch and Russian as well as many academic papers.

The epitome of the cautious scholar, Bloomfield refused to make claims that were not backed up by painstaking observation and analysis. He was unwilling to use the **meaning** of words and sentences as the basis for grammatical analysis, as he was not convinced that meaning could be described scientifically. He did not, however, ignore meaning altogether: the later chapters of *Language* discuss meaning and change of meaning extensively. (**RS**)

See also Sapir.

Further reading

Hall, R. (1987) *Leonard Bloomfield: Essays on His Life and Work*, Amsterdam: John Benjamins.

Boas Franz Boas (1858–1942), born in Germany of Jewish parentage, first studied physics and geography there before turning to anthropology. Following his first Arctic expeditions, he relocated to the United States in 1887. He became involved with the Chicago World's Fair (1892–1894), the Jessup North Pacific Expedition (1897–1902) and major museums. Between 1896 and 1936 he taught anthropology at Columbia University, training the first generation of professionals. His ethnographic research focused on the North West coast of North America.

Boas integrated time (historicity) and space (context) in **language**, culture and biology, thus contesting the then deterministic, reductionistic conflation of race and culture (Williams 1996). He distrusted the presumption of 'progress' and the unilineal, orthogenetic cultural evolutionism of his day (Boas 1963 [1911]). Boas' 'culture' was a loose conjunction of relationships (Stocking 1966). The **Sapir–Whorf hypothesis** – concerning the interplay between language, culture and cognition – was co-formulated by one of his students. Boas' recognition of oral language as both means for data collection and as substance for analysis itself contributed to the mission of structural linguistics.

Boas' innovative commitment to intensive ethnographic data collection rather than nomothetic generalizations, to longitudinal studies and to training of native investigators set the stage for substantive theory-building in later twentieth-century anthropology (Goldschmidt 1959; Stocking 1996). (**MA**)

See also American structuralism.

FURTHER READING

Stocking, Jr, G. W. (ed.) (1996) Volksgeist *as Method and Ethic: Essays on Boasian Ethnography and the German Anthropological Tradition* (History of Anthropology, Vol. 8), Madison, WI: University of Wisconsin Press.

BOUISSAC Paul Bouissac (b. 1934), French semiotician based in Toronto, who has been a major researcher, theorist and convenor of **semiotics**. He taught at the University of Toronto's Department of French between 1962 and 1999 where he set up the legendary International Summer Institutes for Semiotic and Structural Studies in the 1980s. He also founded and edited the groundbreaking publication *Semiotic Review of Books* before passing on the editorship and launching the rigorous and vibrant web resource, www.semioticon.com (which includes the Semiotic Institute Online, international reports and other regular features of interest to semioticians). Bouissac has made a lasting contribution to semiotic theory in his *La mesure des gestes: Prolegomenes à la sémiotique gestuelle* (1973) and numerous articles. He has also contributed to defining the field through his editing of the *Encyclopedia of Semiotics* (1998). However, he is possibly best known for his research into the circus (he ran a one-ring circus in the 1960s), especially *Circus and Culture: A Semiotic Approach* (1976), which he continues as Emeritus Professor. This is in addition to the projects in semiotics by others that he has been instrumental in encouraging over the years through his various acts of convening. Like his fellow semioticians Umberto **Eco** and Eero **Tarasti**, he has also published fiction (e.g. *Les demoiselles*, 1970, and *Strip-tease de Madame Bovary*, 2004). (**PC**)

BRÉAL Michel Bréal (1832–1915) introduced historical comparative **grammar** in France. Having studied with Franz Bopp, his initial inspiration was the German tradition. However, from the very beginning Bréal stressed that the approach to linguistic evolution as a 'natural' science should be enriched with reference to a human and cultural dimension. In his seminal work *Essai de sémantique* (1897) he moves from linguistic form to function and **meaning**, intrigued in particular by functional distinctions that are not given directly by the form and by the role of human intelligence in filling those gaps in the process of interpretation. Bréal thus became one of the founding fathers of present-day **semantics** (and maybe a cognitive linguist *avant la lettre*), defined in his words as 'a science of **signification**'. He believed firmly in the complementarity between the science of **language** and philology as an ingredient of historical research. In his meaning-oriented approach to language change and development, or the evolution of signification, the concept of human volition is the key. (**JV**)

FURTHER READING

Bréal, M. (1995) *De la grammaire comparée à la sémantique: Textes de Michel Bréal publiés entre 1864 et 1898*, ed. P. Desmet and P. Swiggers, Leuven: Peeters.

BÜHLER Karl Bühler (1879–1963), a German psychologist and linguist, was the founder and director of the Institute of Psychology at the University of Vienna (1922–1938). Bühler's term for **semiotics** was 'sematology'. He is best known as a pioneering advocate of the **sign** character of **language**. The focal point of all linguistic analysis is the speech event (*Sprechereignis*) which takes place in two fields: an **index** field (*Zeigfeld*), constituted by **deixis**, and a **symbol** field (*Symbolfeld*), constituted by signs with conceptual content. Language signs have three functions: as symptoms they express inner states of speakers, as signals they give directions to hearers, and as symbols they represent states of affairs in the world. Following **Humboldt**, Bühler believed that each language had its own world view (*Weltansicht*). Like Mead, he was a strong advocate of the social matrix of **meaning** and the primacy of action. His theory of metaphor paved the way to developments in **cognitive linguistics**. With his organon model of language as **communication** between senders and receivers he anticipated **biosemiotic** studies of cell and animal communication through effector signs and receptor signs. Major works are *Ausdruckstheorie* (1933) and *Sprachtheorie* (1934). The latter has been translated into English (Bühler 1990). (**EB**)

Further reading

Innis, R. (1982) *Karl Bühler: Semiotic Foundations of Language Theory*, New York: Plenum Press.

C

Cassirer Ernst Cassirer (1874–1945), a German philosopher and historian of ideas, formulated a programme for philosophy that turned it into a 'philosophy of symbolic forms', developed at great length in his trilogy by that name, and that led to a semiotics of cultural forms, culminating in his summary volume, *An Essay on Man*. This meant for Cassirer that philosophy was to study all the ways that meaning was embodied and appeared in human life. Cassirer saw that meaning was expressed on multiple levels and that the levels were to be distinguished by how close the sign and its meaning were connected. Such a way of thinking allowed him to distinguish *expression*, *representation* and *pure signification* as the three matrices or frames in which human meaning making occurred. Expression joined the sign and its meaning in the closest, inseparable fashion, giving us a realm of 'symbolic pregnance'. Representation, exemplified first and foremost in natural **language**s, while wedded to intuition and labile perceptual and imaginal structures, is more flexible. It is the main reason that there is linguistic relativity, that is, alternative ways of interpreting the continuum of experience and making alternative, but not totally arbitrary, cuts in it. Pure signification 'frees' itself from its material and perceptual substrates so that the play of signs can focus on a world of pure relations. The main exemplifications of these frames of meaning are myth, language and science, the subjects of his *Philosophy of Symbolic Forms* (1953–1957 [1923–1929]).

Cassirer had practically universal interests and he offers a powerful model for semiotic research. He was interested in the foundations of science (*Substance and Function*, 1923 [1910]), the importance of the German humanistic tradition for philosophy (*Freiheit und Form*, 1916), the semiotic analysis of technology ('Form und technik', 1930), the semiotic implications and roots of the Fascist myth of the state (*The Myth of the State*, 1946), and of the symbolic structures exemplified in the totality of cultural forms (*An Essay on Man*, 1944). (**RI**)

Further reading

Cassirer, E. (1998) *The Philosophy of Symbolic Forms*, 4 vols, New Haven: Yale University Press.

Chomsky Noam Chomsky (b. 1928) is an American linguist and political campaigner. Born in Philadelphia, Chomsky had nearly dropped out of university when he met Zellig **Harris** through a shared interest in left-libertarian Jewish politics. Harris encouraged Chomsky to study linguistics, and soon Chomsky won a fellowship at Harvard University. In 1955 he moved to the Massachusetts Institute of Technology (MIT) in Boston, where he has been based ever since.

Chomsky put forward a new approach to the study of **language**, though he has often said that his work is a development of ideas that were commonplace in the Renaissance and the Enlightenment. His starting point was profound dissatisfaction with the structuralist linguistics (see **American structuralism**) that flourished in America in the first half of the twentieth century. His forceful critiques of structuralism (Chomsky 1964) and the behaviourist psychology with which it was linked (Chomsky 1959) helped to build his reputation, though they also aroused enormous hostility which has continued to this day.

The structuralists' emphasis on observable data had led them to regard a language as a set of utterances: thus the English language was everything that speakers of English said and wrote, taken as a whole. Chomsky had two practical objections to this view of language. First, this set is potentially infinite, and therefore, although it can be specified mathematically, it does not exist in the real world (in the same way that the set of positive integers does not exist in the real world). Second, this set includes errors, repetitions, false starts and similar things that linguists typically ignore when they describe a language.

A more fundamental objection to structuralism, in Chomsky's view, was that it failed to capture the common-sense view of a language, which is tacitly assumed by all linguists. What speakers of a language have in common (and what a **grammar** of that language tries to describe) is a system of knowledge in their minds. Chomsky dismissed arguments by philosophers that knowledge is not something that can be investigated scientifically: on the contrary, he argued, if this knowledge exists in our minds, it must have a more tangible reality than a 'language' in the structuralist sense. In some way, the knowledge must have a physical existence in the neural circuits of the human brain. The term 'knowledge' is just an abstract way of referring to this part of our brains. This abstraction is just as legitimate as any abstract procedure in science: physicists, for instance, constantly use abstract models of the universe (involving perfectly straight lines, notions like 'points' which have location but no magnitude, and so on). The question is whether insight and understanding can be gained by using abstract models: condemning all abstraction out of hand is simply unscientific dogma.

Chomsky went on to argue that some aspects of this linguistic knowledge are innate, that is, they result from human genetic programming rather than being learned from experience. The main aim of his research programme is to specify these genetic properties of language, which he calls **Universal Grammar**. **(RS)**

Further reading

Chomsky, N. (1996) *Powers and Prospects*, London: Pluto Press.

Cook, V. and Newson, M. (1996) *Chomsky's Universal Grammar: An Introduction*, 2nd edn, Oxford: Blackwell.

Salkie, R. (1990) *The Chomsky Update: Linguistics and Politics*, London: Unwin Hyman.

Clever Hans Clever Hans was a horse that belonged to a German schoolteacher Wilhelm von Osten and in the 1890s became famous for its cognitive skills. The horse was believed to understand German and be capable of giving correct answers to questions involving arithmetic calculations, time and the calendar. People asked questions verbally; Clever Hans gave answers by tapping with its hoof. In 1907 psychologist Oskar Pfungst conducted a study of the horse's cognitive skills. The study revealed that Clever Hans was able to give correct answers only if it could see its master or questioner, and only if the person him/herself knew the right answer. The conclusion was that the horse observed and followed the minute changes in the human face and gestures.

The story initiated the concept of the Clever Hans phenomenon (also Clever Hans effect, Clever Hans fallacy) that denotes the effect of a researcher's expectations on the results of the research conducted with animals (Sebeok 1981b: 162–167). The Clever Hans phenomenon stands also for the reports of other 'thinking animals' (mostly cats, dogs and apes): both popular stories and results of scientific research that have their roots in the over-interpretation and anthropomorphization of animal behaviour. To rule out the possibility of the researcher's impact, blind tests are suggested where even the observer does not know the right solution.

There is, however, also a positive interpretation of Clever Hans's story. The horse's accomplishment was in the transposition of information from one sign system to another. Small changes in the human face were indiscernible to humans themselves, whereas hoof taps were clearly audible. The mistake of the humans was in not recognizing the source of knowledge, but that does not discredit the communicative skills of the horse. As such, the story falls in the same category with other cases where animals make hidden information available to humans, for example dogs that search for chemical substances or elephants that warn their owners against earthquakes. (**TM**)

Further reading

Sebeok, T. A. (1981) *The Play of Musement*, Advances in Semiotics, Bloomington, IN: Indiana University Press.

Closed text Before the appearance of Umberto **Eco**'s essays on the aesthetics of the open work (*Opera aperta*, 1962; *The Open Work*, 1989), it was generally assumed that there were no such things as completely open or closed **texts** (especially literary ones). Such a distinction today takes into consideration Eco's definition of what constitutes openness and consequently considers as closed any text that sets clear constraints on the reader's possible interpretations. In short, the author has intentionally constructed (if it is possible) a text as a fixed system, completed, with no ambiguities or implications, and with no operative choices or open-ended possible readings.

This must not be confused with the notions of 'limits' that are outlined in Eco's *The Limits of Interpretation* (1990), where the same author, who with his notions of 'open work' may have been partly responsible for having shifted the authority on the possible **meaning**s foreseen by an author, first to the text and then to the reader (as we see with deconstructionists), nearly three decades later insists that, even though there may not be a set number of possible interpretations of a text, most certainly one cannot make a text say what it has no intention of saying.

Unlike scientific texts, it is difficult to conceive that literary works could have only one possible level of reading/interpretation. By closed texts it is assumed that we are referring to a text structured in such a way that not only does it not elicit a reader's inventiveness or his free play of interpretive cooperation in finding possible meanings/conclusions, but that it actually regulates our reading by pointing to specific messages, or pieces of information, that the author wishes to convey. A closed text is exhausted by its reading because it does not call for mental or psychological interaction with the author. In general, closed texts are associated with conveying information and messages rather than meaning and cultural awareness. (**RC**)

See also OPEN TEXT.

FURTHER READING

Eco, U. (1979) *The Role of the Reader: Explorations in the Semiotics of Texts*, Bloomington, IN: Indiana University Press.

CODE Communication is classically described as an exchange of **meaning**s that are represented by **sign**s. Coding is the process of representing meanings systematically. Communicators can be said to encode their meanings into particular sequences of signs (e.g. strings of sounds, marks on paper, or visible gestures); recipients can be said to decode such meanings from the sign sequences they receive.

A code itself is therefore the set or system of rules and correspondences which link signs to meanings. Potentially, any one meaning can be represented by any sign, arbitrarily chosen. As **Saussure** indicated, there is no inherent link between the meaning of the word 'ox' and the shape of that word (phonetic or graphic) in English, or between that meaning and the French word 'bœuf'. The only general requirement is that the coding rules are known and followed by the relevant community of code users.

The coding of meaning in human **language**s is multi-dimensional. **Jakobson** distinguished **paradigmatic** from **syntagmatic** dimensions of linguistic organization, as underlying coding principles. That is, the coding conventions of any human language need to specify paradigms from which meaningful signs have to be chosen, to fill our specific 'slots' in a sequence of signs. An example is choosing a noun from a set of possible nouns, to convey a selected meaning. The conventions also require language users to build chains of 'syntagms', according to specified combination rules. For example, some types of modifiers must appear before others in English ('large' must appear before 'steel' in 'a large steel bridge'). At the level of word morphology (the construction of words out of meaningful parts), adjectives are quite regularly formed by adding certain suffixes to verbs in English – 'watch-able', 'kiss-able'. Similarly, verbs are formed by adding suffixes to nouns or adjectives – 'item-ize', 'regular-ize'. But grammatical and lexical coding rules of this sort must be accompanied by further rules for representing grammatical sequences in speech, writing or some other medium. For example, in standard English pronunciation the suffix morpheme '-able' is coded as the neutral vowel called 'schwa' plus 'b' plus 'l'. The suffix '-ize' is coded as the sound sequence 'ai' (the diphthong) plus 'z' (the voiced sibilant).

Coded realizations of meanings can themselves be re-coded. For example, speech is often seen as the primary code for a human language, with conventional written (orthographic) forms as secondary or overlaid representations. In turn, written forms of a language can be re-coded into binary digital strings to be stored and exchanged in computing applications. Earlier technology allowed written languages to be re-coded and transmitted as Morse code. Morse code or digitized written English can be further re-coded by rules that encrypt it – that is, render it unintelligible to everyone who does not have access to the decoding rules.

Non-linguistic representation also involves coding. Music and pictures, for example, have their own means of representing **semantic** information and semantic relations. **Kress** and van Leeuwen give the example that some meanings conveyed by locative prepositions in English are realized in pictures by the formal characteristics that create the contrast between foreground and background (1996: 44). Gestural communication is coded, although for most people only a relatively small range of **gesture** signs will have firmly agreed, specific significance within a community. Sticking out one's tongue might denote mild deprecation of a target person, whereas distending one's cheek with one's tongue might have no codified meaning. It might signify that the speaker has a particle of food lodged between two teeth, but nothing of focused, interactional significance. Turning the palms of one's hands upwards while speaking might suggest that the speaker is dismayed, or uncertain, but these meanings are not strictly codified. A clear exception is gestural signing among hard-of-hearing users, where the level of formal specification is the same as with spoken or written codes. We must therefore distinguish between formal and informal coding, and degrees of codification.

Sociocultural norms and conventions can, rather generally, be thought of as codes, such as dress codes, politeness codes and institutional codes of practice. Once again the implication is that communities of people will agree on rules prescribing (and outlawing) sets of behaviours in specific circumstances, such as revealing more of their bodies on beaches than in churches. Codes of etiquette can prescribe event sequences (syntagms) too, such as what one eats first at a formal dinner, or the coordinated timing of drinking a toast. Cultural and sub-cultural groups may in fact be defined by their shared adherence to codes of this sort. Outside of anthropological analyses, or reflexive commentaries in cultural narratives, cultural codes will generally be tacit understandings rather than explicitly codified rules, but no less influential and constraining for that.

While the notion of coding is therefore a core one for **semiotics**, it nevertheless risks oversimplifying some facets of communication. Culturally endorsed associations between forms or **signifier**s and **signified** meanings are rarely as neat as the coding model implies they are. In the case of human language, meanings can rarely be defined as the precise denotata of specific words or expressions. Certainly across cultural groups, there can be a significant variation between the meanings of apparently equivalent forms. Even in Saussure's example of 'ox' and 'bœuf', this is clearly the case. These words do not encode identical meanings in English and French. Benjamin Lee **Whorf**'s principle of linguistic relativity points out how social realities are categorized differently by different communities. The implication is that coding, even linguistic coding, is a more active and variable process than is often assumed.

A further, fundamental point is that we should not overstate the extent to which human communication is accurately to be described as a sequence of encoding and decoding operations. Studies of discourse processing, such as Sperber and Wilson in their work on **relevance theory**, argue convincingly that meaning making is more of an inferential process than a coding process. That is, speakers do not simply encode meanings which listeners, who share an understanding of the code, can directly recover. Rather, speakers deploy signs on the understanding that listeners will find them relevant. The precise relevance, however, remains to be established through the active search procedures listeners activate. The direction and result of inference cannot be guaranteed by speakers in advance. Meanings are not 'there to be discovered', coded into utterances, as much as they are actively constructed by listeners on every occasion of social interaction. (**NC** and **AJ**)

See also GESTURE *and* SPEECH COMMUNITY.

FURTHER READING

Geertz, C. (1993) 'Thick description', in *The Interpretation of Cultures*, London: HarperCollins.

Kress, G. R. and van Leeuwen, T. (2006) *Reading Images: The Grammar of Visual Design*, 2nd edn, London: Routledge.

Sperber, D. and Wilson, D. (1995) *Relevance: Communication and Cognition*, 2nd edn, Oxford: Blackwell.

CODE-DUALITY ***see*** **HOFFMEYER**

COGNITIVE LINGUISTICS The word 'cognitive' means 'having to do with thinking', so cognitive linguistics can be understood broadly as the study of **language** in connection with thought. This connection can, however, be understood in several different ways.

Chomsky describes his approach to linguistics as forming part of what he calls the 'cognitive revolution' which took place around the middle of the last century. For Chomsky, the central feature of this revolution was a new belief that knowledge was amenable to scientific investigation. Linguistic knowledge is only one type of knowledge, but it can be studied empirically and hypotheses can be formulated about the structure of linguistic knowledge in the human mind. Chomsky distinguishes knowledge of a particular language, which is described by a **generative grammar** of that language, from knowledge of language in general, which is covered by **Universal Grammar**.

Linguistics is thus in Chomsky's view part of cognitive psychology, but it employs methods which look very different from those usually used by psychologists. Despite its cognitive foundations Chomsky's methods are strictly linguistic, though the hypotheses put forward are influenced by their cognitive foundations: the development known as principles and parameters theory is a clear example. Chomsky has nothing to say about how linguistic knowledge is used: in other words, he does not try to link language with the active process of thinking.

Other linguists have tried to explore the relationship between thinking and language, and would see their work as part of cognitive science. The assumption behind this work is that human beings are essentially machines, and that the functioning of the human mind can be described in the same way as the functioning of a computer (note that Chomsky is not committed to this assumption, which he explicitly rejects). Computers are machines that process information, and cognitive scientists have tried to analyse language in the same way. One aim has been to program computers to understand and use language, an aim that has had only partial success up to now.

A third strand of research is called cognitive grammar, and is committed to the view that the structure of language is strongly influenced by the way the mind works (another assumption that Chomsky rejects). The key names in cognitive grammar include Ronald Langacker and George **Lakoff**, and they regard grammar as essentially 'symbolic', its role being to structure and symbolize the conceptual content of language. Unlike Chomsky, cognitive grammarians refuse to make a sharp distinction between linguistic knowledge and other types of knowledge. Their work in semantics tries to look at **meaning** in a broad perspective, going beyond simple dictionary-type definitions of words and attempting to identify the whole range of mental experience associated with words and sentences when they are used in specific contexts.

Cognitive linguistics thus covers a number of frameworks, with radically different assumptions about the relationship between language and the mind. What they have in common is the belief that an exclusive concern with language is less useful than research which links language and other aspects of human experience: but the nature of that link remains contentious. (**RS**)

Further reading

Johnson-Laird, P. (1993) *The Computer and the Mind: An Introduction to Cognitive Science*, 2nd edn, London: Collins.

Langacker, R. (1986) 'An introduction to cognitive grammar', *Cognitive Science*, 10: 1–40.

Salkie, R. (1990) *The Chomsky Update: Linguistics and Politics*, London: Unwin Hyman.

Cognitive semantics *see* **Lakoff**

Cohesion The category of 'cohesion' deals with the formal elements and principles which make a collection of sentences into a **text**. These range from pro(noun or sentence) forms such as 'these' (at the beginning of this sentence), 'this' (as in the preceding two words) and 'therefore'; text-organizing elements such as 'however'; the repetition and/or substitution of lexical elements to form lexical chains; to the uses of **syntax** to fit a sentence (or part of a sentence – as in this parenthesis just now) to its specific place in the unfolding text. (**GRK**)

COMMUNICATION The Latin root of 'communication' – *communicare* – means 'to share' or 'to be in relation with' and is related to the words 'common', 'commune' and 'community', suggesting an act of 'bringing together'. The notion of communication has been present and debated in the West from pre-Socratic times. **Hippocrates** and his followers, for example, produced a corpus of symptoms, 'bringing together' the **sign**s of a disease or ailment with the disease itself for the purposes of diagnosis and prognosis. In contemporary **semiotics**, however, it is considered that a fundamental form of communication is to be found in the semioses that occur between cells (see **semiotic self**).

The understanding of communication in the twentieth century has generally proceeded from the flow of

Sender → Message → Receiver

For Shannon and Weaver (1949), famously, an information source with a message uses a transmitter to produce a signal, which is received by a receiver, which delivers a concomitant message to a destination. At the interface of the sent signal and the received signal is likely to be 'noise'. Such 'noise' might corrupt the implicit integrity of the message as a product during the process of transmission, the prime example being several conflicting signals in the same channel at once.

Observing developments in media in the twentieth century, 'Medium theorists' stressed that media are, in the phrase made famous by the Canadian communication theorist Marshall McLuhan, 'extensions' of humans. Like tools, media extend the capabilities of humans to reach out into a broader world of communication and interaction. However, as a corollary of this, the media transform humans' apprehension of the world and produce a **consciousness** that is tied to particular modes of communication, for example orality and literacy. As such, all the major media of communication have entailed 'paradigm shifts in cultural evolution' (Danesi 2002).

In the West, the bias towards understanding communication in terms of media has been notable and longstanding: classic works of Greek philosophy set the agenda, largely because they were produced at the transition between oral and literate societies. Oral communication, because it could not store information in the same ways and amounts as writing, evolved mnemonic, often poetic, devices to pass on traditions and cultural practices, such as **dialogue**s or narratives of human action to be retold in relatively small public gatherings of people. Communication, in this formulation, was necessarily a locally situated process. Literate societies, on the other hand, involved communication resulting in a 'product' to be stored, distributed and used as a reference for scientific analysis, critique and political organization. After 1450, the introduction of print – like orality and literacy, another 'extension' – has been seen as crucial in defining communication because of the ways it facilitated widespread communication of messages that might be deemed educational or seditious, ultimately enabling confrontation (as in the Reformation) as well as specialization (sciences building on the Renaissance), and promoted a more private, individual communication centred on the self. With the emergence in the twentieth century of new communications technologies – in particular, photography, film, radio and television – a fully fledged 'communication theory' consolidated the definition of communication as embodied in media.

Yet, developing alongside institutionalized communication theory, semiotics shed further light on communication because of its focus on signs *as* signs, whether they are part of communication in films or novels, the expressions of animals, or the messages that pass between organisms or cells. The nonverbal signs that are exchanged between animals *communicate*, of course, as do the verbal and nonverbal signs passed between humans. Frequently, because of the **glottocentrism** enshrined in investigations into communication, nonverbal messages are not recognized, ignored or repressed, even when the focus of study is human message transfer. It is hardly surprising, then, that in addition to the neglect of **nonverbal communication** in humans and animals the nonverbal signs that occur in components of organisms or plants receive little or no attention in communication theory. The concept of intrahuman and interspecies – as well as interhuman – message transfer amounts to a major re-orientation of the understanding of communication, one in which human affairs constitute only a small part of communication in general.

Furthermore, while definitions of communication often assume successful contact and interaction, semiotics has been concerned to pay close attention to non-communication (or mis-communication). This includes ambiguity, misunderstanding, lying, cheating, deception and unconscious and wilful self-deception. The famous case of '**Clever Hans**', involving a horse whose abilities 'proved' that animals could think and speak, but in fact was responding to a number of nonverbal cues emitted by his 'interlocutor', illustrates well the vicissitudes of communication (Sebeok and Rosenthal 1981). Similarly, the overvaluing of verbal communication has tended to encourage neglect of nonverbal communication, a fact well understood by magicians and others practised in deception. Lying is also central to communication, particularly as lies are often necessary to the project of human interaction (Ekman 2001). Nor is this exclusively a matter of human communication. In the animal world, too, lying is widespread (Sebeok 1986a). Indeed, the reliance of communication on signs to substitute for something else which 'does not necessarily have to exist or to actually be somewhere at the moment that a sign stands in for it' (Eco 1976: 7) suggests the fraternity of communication with lying. (**PC**)

FURTHER READING

Cherry, C. (1966) *On Human Communication: A Review, a Survey and a Criticism*, Cambridge, MA: MIT Press.

Cobley, P. (ed.) (2006) *Communication Theories*, 4 vols, London: Routledge.

Sebeok, T. A. (1991) 'Communication', in *A Sign is Just a Sign*, Bloomington, IN: Indiana University Press.

COMPETENCE A person's knowledge of a particular **language**, as opposed to **performance**, the actual use of a language in concrete situations. Someone who is competent in a language can normally speak and understand the language, but disability such as deafness may permanently impair or prevent some aspects of performance, and other factors (emotion, background noise, food in the mouth, etc.) may temporarily obstruct performance. It is a person's competence in a language which makes their use of that language possible, and which is fundamental in linguistics.

When we say 'the English language', then, we normally mean 'the particular system of linguistic knowledge that certain people have acquired, called English'. Dictionaries and **grammar**s of English aim to describe this competence accurately and explicitly, leaving aside performance factors as irrelevant. The distinction between competence and performance is very similar to **Saussure**'s separation of ***langue*** and ***parole***, though Saussure puts more emphasis on the shared, social aspects of *langue*. It has sometimes been said that competence is mysterious and that only performance is concrete and observable: **Chomsky** argues, however, that competence is a straightforward notion and that explaining performance may be impossible in principle. (**RS**)

FURTHER READING

Chomsky, N. (1965) *Aspects of the Theory of Syntax*, Cambridge, MA: MIT Press.

CONATIVE One of the six fundamental functions given in the **Jakobson**ian **speech act**, determined by the addressee factor of the speech act. When the focus of the utterance is on the addressee, more salient forms of the conative function occur phonemically, grammatically or syntactically. Examples include vocative case and the imperative mood. (**EA**)

CONNOTATION A putative 'second-order **meaning**', often a 'cultural' one, complementing **denotation**. An apple is called 'green' because that is its colour when it is unripe. When 'green' is used of a person because he or she is unripe/immature, it has been used as a metaphor; it has been extended beyond its core meaning. Such uses lead to a 'penumbra' around the word, indicating its connotations. The distinction between denotation and connotation is especially associated with the work of **Barthes** and **Hjelmslev**. (**GRK**)

CONSCIOUSNESS Consciousness is a quality of mind that includes self-awareness, subjectivity, perception, feelings and conscious will. It is the quality of 'how it feels like to be you or me' and therefore also the ability for empathy and mutual understanding through **communication**. It also produces existentiality and therefore questions like: 'Who am I?', 'What is the purpose of life?', 'What is right and what is wrong?' Consciousness also contains the intentionality of perception, semiosis and thinking. The role and necessity of consciousness in communication and language is highly debated. Do you need to be aware in order to communicate? In much cybernetic information science, communication – as the transfer of information – is the basic process independent of any awareness or even life. Many linguistic theories see the generative rules of language as buried deep underneath conscious awareness. We do not speak with **language**, language speaks with us. Wittgenstein, for example, considered us to be living within language. It is said that we do not know what we mean before we have heard what we are saying. Normally, speaking is a flow where we do not consciously plan our sentences before we speak; but still we do produce them from an intention of expressing something within our awareness. On the other hand, there is also general agreement that it is language that creates the human self-aware type of consciousness that sets us apart from other animals. We are an animal 'infected' with language and thereby culture, an artificial product and therefore linguistic cyborgs. Still we also know that we can use our consciousness to control language especially when we write it down and read from a manuscript. We can also plan speech in our own deliberations 'inside' our consciousness. It is also clear that the meaning of words comes from our conscious experiences and interpretations of perception and our general ability to make sense of experiences. (**SB**)

See also CYBERSEMIOTICS, MODELLING SYSTEMS THEORY, QUALIA *and* Petrilli and Ponzio.

FURTHER READING

Slatev, J. and Menary, R. (eds) (2008) 'Consciousness and language', *Journal of Consciousness Studies*, 15(6).

CONSTATIVE In the contrast constative–**performative**, the term 'constative' is used to describe declarative utterances or statements which can be said to be true or false. It was because of their dimension of truth or falsity that constatives formed the focus of attention for most philosophers of **language** before the advent of **speech act** theory. J. L. **Austin** showed, however, that just like performatives a constative or statement of fact can also be 'infelicitous' in ways unrelated to truth. For instance, 'All John's children are bald' violates the presupposition that John has children if pronounced in a context where John does not, in fact, have children. Similarly, 'The cat is on the mat' violates the implication that the speaker believes the cat to be on the mat if stated by someone who does not in fact hold such a belief. Finally, 'All the guests are French' entails that it is not the case that 'Some of the guests are not French' and would violate this entailment if followed by that second statement. (**JV**)

FURTHER READING

Austin, J. L. (1963 [1958]) 'Performative–constative', in C. E. Caton (ed.), *Philosophy and Ordinary Language*, Urbana, IL: University of Illinois Press, pp. 22–54.

CONVERSATION ANALYSIS The origins and much of current practice in Conversation Analysis (CA) reside in the sociological approach to **language** and **communication** known as ethnomethodology (Garfinkel 1974). Ethnomethodology means studying the link between what social actors 'do' in interaction and what they 'know' about interaction. **Social structure** is a form of order, and that order is partly achieved through talk, which is itself structured and orderly. Social actors have common-sense knowledge about what it is they are doing interactionally in performing specific activities and in jointly achieving communicative coherence. Making this knowledge about ordinary, everyday affairs explicit, and in this way finding an understanding of how society is organized and how it functions, is ethnomethodology's main concern (Garfinkel 1967; Turner 1974; Heritage 1984).

Following this line of inquiry, CA views language as a form of social action and aims, in particular, to discover and describe how the organization of social interaction makes manifest and reinforces the structures of social organization and social institutions (see, e.g., Boden and Zimmerman 1991; Drew and Heritage 1992).

Hutchby and Wooffit, who point out that 'talk in interaction' is now commonly preferred to the designation 'conversation', define CA as follows:

> CA is the study of recorded, naturally occurring talk-in-interaction . . . Principally it is to discover how participants understand and respond to one another in their turns at talk, with a central focus being on how sequences of interaction are generated. To put it another way, the objective of CA is to uncover the tacit reasoning procedures and sociolinguistic competencies underlying the production and interpretation of talk in organized sequences of interaction.
>
> (Hutchby and Wooffit 1998: 14)

As this statement implies, the emphasis in CA, in contrast to earlier ethnomethod ological concerns, has shifted away from the patterns of 'knowing' *per se* towards discovering the structures of talk which produce and reproduce patterns of social action. At least, structures of talk are studied as the best evidence of social actors' practical knowledge about them.

One central CA concept is preference, the idea that, at specific points in conversation, certain types of utterances will be more favoured than others (e.g. the socially preferred response to an invitation is acceptance, not rejection). Other conversational features which CA has focused on include: openings and closings of conversations; adjacency pairs (i.e. paired utterances of the type summons–answer, greeting–greeting, compliment–compliment response, etc.); topic management and topic shift; conversational repairs; showing agreement and disagreement; introducing bad news and processes of troubles-telling; and (probably most centrally) mechanisms of turn-taking.

In their seminal paper, Sacks *et al.* (1974) suggested a list of guiding principles for the organization of turn-taking in conversation (in English). They observed that the central principle which speakers follow in taking turns is to avoid gaps and overlaps in conversation. Although gaps do of course occur, they are brief. Another common feature of conversational turns is that, usually, one party speaks at a time. In order to facilitate turn-taking, which usually takes place in 'the transition relevance places' (Sacks *et al.* 1974), speakers observe a number of conventionalized principles. For example, speakers follow well-established scripts, as in service encounters, in which speaker roles are clearly delineated. They fill in appropriate 'slots' in discourse structure, e.g. second part utterances in adjacency pairs, and they anticipate completion of an utterance on the basis of a perceived completion of a grammatical unit (a clause or a sentence). Speakers themselves may signal their willingness to give up the floor in favour of another speaker (who can be 'nominated' by the current speaker only). They can do this by directing their gaze towards the next speaker and employing characteristic gesturing patterns synchronizing with the final words. They may alter pitch, speak more softly, lengthen the last syllable or use stereotyped discourse markers (e.g. *you know* or *that's it*). (**NC** and **AJ**)

Further reading

Hutchby, I. and Wooffitt, R. (1998) *Conversation Analysis*, Cambridge: Polity Press.

Schegloff, E. A., Ochs, E. and Thompson, S. A. (1996) 'Introduction', in E. Ochs, E. A. Schegloff and S. A. Thompson (eds), *Interaction and Grammar*, Cambridge: Cambridge University Press.

Ten Have, P. (1999) *How to Do Conversation Analysis*, London: Sage.

Critical Discourse Analysis Critical Discourse Analysis (CDA) is a strand of critical linguistics comprising a loose set of tools and techniques for analysing the linguistic choices contained in texts allowing the analyst to reveal the broader discourses that are signified by them. These **discourse**s are treated as models defining events, actors and sequences of action. CDA seeks to reveal what kinds of social relations of power are present in texts and the kinds of inequalities and interests they seek to perpetuate, generate or legitimate. It is criticized for its form of analysis that abstracts texts from broader production and reception contexts. (**DMac**)

See also Discourse analysis, Sociolinguistics *and* Sociosemiotics.

Further reading

van Leeuwen, T. (2008) *Discourse and Practice: New Tools for Critical Discourse Analysis*, New York: Oxford University Press.

Cybernetics 'Cybernetics' was defined by the mathematician Norbert Wiener, in the title of one of its founding books (Wiener 1961 [1941]), as 'the science of control and **communication**, in the animal and the machine', a definition seen as foundational by one of cybernetics' developers, Ross Ashby (1957: 1). The etymological derivation of cybernetics stems from the Greek *kybernetes*, pilot, steersman. Cybernetics is a theory of the behaviour of machines, organisms and organizations. It does not ask 'what *is* this thing?' but '*what does it do*?' Cybernetics is concerned with scientific investigation of systemic processes of a highly varied nature, including such phenomena as regulation, information processing, information storage, adaptation, self-organization, self-reproduction and strategic behaviour.

Cybernetics started by being closely associated in many ways with physics, but it depends in no essential way on the laws of physics nor on the properties of matter. Cybernetics deals with all forms of behaviour insofar as they are regular, or determinate, or reproducible. The materiality is irrelevant, and so is the adherence or not to the ordinary laws of physics. Cybernetics has its own foundations as, first, a science of self-regulating and equilibrating systems. Cybernetic systems are goal-seeking systems, like thermostats, physiological regulation of body temperature, automatic steering devices, and economic and political processes. These were studied under a general mathematical model of deviation-counteracting feedback networks. Systems that are open to energy but closed to information and with control-systems that are information tight, as the governor on a steam engine, were the primary objects of study. Because numerous systems in the living, social and technological world may be understood in this way, cybernetics cuts across many traditional disciplinary boundaries and thus developed a metadisciplinary **language** of information and goal-oriented self-organized behaviour through negative feedback that works on differences and uses feedback/feed forward mechanisms to home in on the target. Thus we see the new information concept's interaction with the idea of the von Neumann computer, based on the concept of the bit carrying the information in computing. The research programs of artificial intelligence and machine translation of human language, game and decision theory are among other things developed on this basis. These are also the subject areas where the limited definitions of cognition, intelligence, language and communication have become obvious because they lack the theory of signification that **Peirce**an **semiotics** offers.

Applications of cybernetics are found in computer and information sciences, and in the natural, social and communicative sciences, and cybernetics has been fairly compatible with **structuralist** semiotics and, therefore, to some extent influential in the French tradition. Within the general cybernetic approach theoretical fields such as systems theory and communication theory – combined and further developed by Niklas Luhmann – have developed. Thus, cybernetics, like semiotics, has been concerned with flows of distinctions and their consequences. Semiotics shares with cybernetics the aim of understanding communicative systems in relation to their environment. From the 1950s – particularly as a result of **Sebeok**'s early collaboration, contact and interest with cybernetics' key figures (including Wiener, von Foerster, **Bateson**,

Wilden and Meystel) as well as the cybernetic theory of culture developed by **Lotman** and his collaborators in the late 1950s and early 1960s – the two fields have pursued broadly similar objectives. Their points of convergence are to be found, especially, in **Umwelt** theory, **cybersemiotics** and **modelling systems theory**. 'Second order cybernetics' investigates cybernetics with the awareness that the investigator and the investigation are, in fact, part of the system (see von Foerster 1980), making the observation itself a cybernetic system. Accordingly, it seeks to account for this often in a radical constructivist form often using the theory of **autopoiesis** of Maturana and Varela. (**SB**)

See also BATESON, BAUDRILLARD, CONSCIOUSNESS, POSTHUMANISM, QUALIA *and* UEXKÜLL, J.

FURTHER READING

Ashby, W. R. (1956) *An Introduction to Cybernetics*, London: Chapman & Hall (now available electronically at: http://pespmc1.vub.ac.be/books/IntroCyb.pdf).

Foerster, H. von (1974) *Cybernetics of Cybernetics*, Urbana, IL: University of Illinois Press.

A set of classic/seminal cybernetics papers are available on the Web at Principia Cybernetica: http://pespmc1.vub.ac.be/LIBRAPAP.html

CYBERSEMIOTICS Transdisciplinary science framework, developed by Søren Brier (editor of the interdisciplinary journal *Cybernetics & Human Knowing*), that integrates **biosemiotics** with the cybernetic information science of Norbert Wiener and Gregory **Bateson** as well as the second order **cybernetics** of Heinz von Foerster and Niklas Luhmann's autopoietic theory of society as **communication**. In the making of a transdisciplinary theory of signification and communication encompassing living, human, social and mechanical systems, **semiotics** is in competition with the information processing paradigm of cognitive science that is based on systems and cybernetics. Life can – from a chemical point of view – be explained as auto-catalytic, autonomous, autopoietic and systemic; but that does not say much about how individual awareness appears in the nervous system and how it feels to be a living being. Brier found it necessary to add a semiotic foundation in order to encompass both nature and machine in a theory of **signification**, cognition and communication that encompasses the sciences and technology as well as the humanities' aspect of communication in order to include signification and interpretation. As **Peirce**'s semiotics is distinguished by dealing systematically with non-intentional signs of the body and of nature at large, it has become the main source for semiotic contemplations of the similarities and differences of sign types of inorganic nature, signs of living systems (biosemiotics), and the cultural and linguistic signs of humans living together in a society. The cybersemiotic approach integrates a semiotized version of Luhmann's triple autopoietic theory of communication combined with pragmatic theories of embodied social meaning. Combining this with a general systems theory of **emergence**, self-organization and closure/**autopoiesis**, it is an explicit theory of how the inner world of the organism is constituted in **semiosis** as a material discursive system through evolutionary development. (**PC**)

See also CONSCIOUSNESS *and* CYBERNETICS.

FURTHER READING

Brier, S. (2008) *Cybersemiotics: Why Information Is Not Enough*, Toronto: University of Toronto Press.

D

Damasio Antonio R. Damasio (b. 1944) is a renowned neurologist and neuroscientist. He has opened a new era in neurobiology of the mind. Damasio's approach is grounded in understanding of neural systems that serve memory, **language**, emotion and decision-making. He has argued heavily against the Cartesian division of body and mind. Damasio's main claims are that *affect* (comprising *emotions* and *feelings of emotions*) has an essential and important role in all human reflections, problem-solving and learning, and that there is a crucial distinction between emotions and feelings. Damasio also developed the idea of 'somatic markers'. His inspirational sources, James and Spinoza, are evident in his books *Descartes' Error* (1994), *The Feeling of What Happens* (1999) and *Looking for Spinoza* (2003), which have gained considerable cross-disciplinary interest. (**MB**)

Danesi Marcel Danesi (b. 1943), prolific semiotician based at the University of Toronto. Also a scholar of the Italian **language**, **Vico**, media, **cognitive linguistics**, a specialist on **metaphor** and well versed in mathematics, Danesi's key interest has been **semiotics**. In addition to running the most successful undergraduate semiotics course in the world, he has been a key contributor to research and theory in the field. His works on linguistics, particularly influenced by Langacker and **Lakoff**, have made contributions to semiotics as a whole. His textbook publications have also helped to define the field in the last few decades. His collaborations with **Sebeok** generated **modelling systems theory**, a perspective and mode of praxis which promises to make a lasting contribution to sign study. Since 2004, Danesi has been editor-in-chief of the journal *Semiotica*. (**PC**)

Deacon Terrence Deacon (b. 1950) is an American neuroscientist and biological anthropologist whose research is directed at understanding the nature and evolution of human cognition and **communication**. The author of over seventy scientific publications on evolutionary biology, Deacon is best known for his 1997 book *The Symbolic Species: The Co-evolution of Language and the Brain*, which applies a **Peirce**an **semiotic** approach to the question of **language** evolution. Drawing on findings from anthropology, linguistics and comparative neuroanatomy, as well as from his own laboratory research in cellular and molecular biology, Deacon carefully delineates how the **icon**ic and **indexi**cal sign-processing abilities of other species are a necessary but not sufficient stepping-stone to the eventual evolution of self-consciously **symbol**ic human language use and that human brains and minds evolved their unique characteristics in response to the special demands imposed by symbolic communication. His book *Homunculus: Evolution, Information, and the Emergence of Consciousness* expands on the arguments about evolutionary **semiosis** presented in *The Symbolic Species* by explicating the kinds of self-organizing dynamics that would be necessary for the even prior evolution of physical chemistry into 'semio-chemistry' (DNA), and with it, the biological basis of reference. Such an explication, if successful, would establish a much needed explanatory bridge from the scientific findings of classic information theory and physics to the meaning-making processes of semiosis. **(DF)**

Further reading

Deacon, T. (1997) *The Symbolic Species: The Co-evolution of Language and the Brain*, New York: W.W. Norton.

Deacon, T. (2009) *Homunculus: Evolution, Information, and the Emergence of Consciousness*, New York: W.W. Norton.

Sherman, J. and Deacon, T. (2007) 'Teleology for the perplexed: How matter began to matter', *Zygon*, 42(4): 873–901.

Deduction Deduction is an inferential process with ***abduction*** and ***induction***. According to Charles S. **Peirce** (*CP* 5.172), deduction merely evolves the necessary consequences of a pure hypothesis. It proves that something must be. **Aristotle**'s definition of the **syllogism** coincides with the definition of deduction. Deduction is a necessary, inevitable derivation of a conclusion from the premises (major and minor premises). The perfect syllogism is the perfect deduction, the inference in which the premises already contain that which is necessary to the conclusion (*Analytica priora* I, 1, 24 b 17ff. and 24 b 23). If, with Peirce, we consider the relation between premises and conclusion in terms of the triadic relation between what may be called 'interpreted' (which includes sign and object) and '**interpretant**', then we can claim that in deduction this relation is **index**ical, the conclusion being a necessary derivation from the premises. **Sign**s and **argument**s (Peirce) are formally dialogical given that both are the result of a **dialogue** between 'interpreteds' and 'interpretants', according to varying degrees of dialogicality. In semiotic terms the relationship between interpreteds and interpretants results in signs which – on a scale ranging from a maximum degree of monologism to a maximum degree of dialogicality, otherness and creativity – are (prevalently) 'indexical', '**symbol**ic' or '**icon**ic'; in terms of logic the relationship between interpreteds (premises) and interpretants (conclusions) results in arguments or inferences of the 'deductive', 'inductive' or 'abductive' type. The varying balance in indexicality, symbolicity and iconicity in any given sign situation, whether or not formally a dialogue, involves variations in the degree of otherness and dialogicality which regulates the relationship between the interpretant (conclusion) and the interpreted (premise) of an argument: in deduction indexicality prevails, in induction symbolicity, in abduction iconicity. Therefore, argumentative value can also be measured in terms of the degree of substantial dialogicality. **(SP)**

FURTHER READING

Peirce, C. S. (1998) 'Deduction, induction and hypothesis', in *Chance, Love and Logic: Philosophical Essays*, ed. M. Cohen, Lincoln, NE: Bison Books.

DEELY While **Peirce** is acknowledged as the greatest American philosopher, John Deely (b. 1942), in his wake, is arguably the most important *living* American philosopher and is the leading philosopher in **semiotics**. An authority on the work of Peirce and a major figure in both contemporary semiotics, Scholastic realism, Thomism and, more broadly, Catholic philosophy, Deely's thinking has demonstrated how awareness of **signs** has heralded a new, genuinely 'postmodern' epoch in the history of human thought. 'Postmodern' here means 'after the modern' rather than the fashionable intellectual and publishing movement emanating mainly from Paris and associated with the academic trend of **poststructuralism** from the 1960s onwards (the postmoderns 'falsely so called' – Deely 2003b). Deely's writing on signs calls for a thoroughgoing superseding of the 'modern', proposing an understanding of humans as the 'semiotic animal' to replace the modern definition as 'res cogitans' (see Deely 2005a).

The crucial feature of Deely's philosophy is his insistence on **realism**, as opposed to **nominalism**, as the means to apprehend the world. Effectively, Deely could be said to track the development of a '**pragmaticist**' realism, following Peirce. So, Deely's work would seem to pertain to questions of knowledge – how humans come to know (realism) and how they remember (or repeatedly forget) what they might know (the history of premodern, modern and postmodern thought; cf. Deely 1985, 1988). Such an agenda is not far removed from that of any phenomenologically orientated thinker of the last hundred years. Except Deely is very suspicious of the term epistemology and its deployment in philosophy and in thinking in general (see Deely).

Deely's early articles focused on the problems that the idea of evolution posed for conceptions of what it is to be human. This concern runs through all of his work, including his most recent discussions of the human as the animal possessing a semiotic **consciousness**. Important to this is the concept of ***Umwelt***, the 'objective' world of any animal. Customarily, 'objective' implies phenomena completely separate and closed off from the vagaries of subjects' apprehensions. Deely, however, demonstrates that the world that seems to be wholly independent of humans – 'objective' – can never be such. Things exist; but **objects** are 'what the things become once experienced' (1994a: 11), bearing in mind also that experience takes place through a physical, sensory modality. In this sense, even such entities as unicorns or the minotaur can be considered objects *embodied* in the physical marks of a text or contours of a statue. Objects are thus sometimes identical with things and can even 'present themselves "as if" they were simply things' (1994a: 18). Likewise, signs seem to be just objects of experience – the light from a candle, the scent of a rose, the shining metal of a gun; but a sign also signifies *beyond* *itself*. In order for it to do so, a sign must be: not just a physical thing; not just an experienced object; but experienced as 'doubly related' (Deely 1994a: 22), standing for something else in some respect or capacity (or, for short: in a context).

As Deely repeatedly attests, this perspective on signs is not new. It is derived from the work of the Latin scholars, especially the *Tractatus de Signis* (1632) of John **Poinsot** which Deely rescued from consignment by historiographical partiality to mere footnote status. What is frequently considered the sign – the 'relation' between some **ground** and some terminus – is shown by Deely, through Poinsot, to be false. The real relation that constitutes the sign consists of ground, terminus and 'relation' as a triad. Furthermore, Poinsot delineates the functions of signs in relation to objects. As such, the relation of representation must differ from that of signification simply because an object can represent another and also represent itself, whereas it would be a contradiction for a sign to be a sign of itself.

Deely's work has been most closely concerned with the definition of signs. However, it also ranges over analytic concerns in the history of philosophy (for example, 'relation' and 'intentionality') as well as the general history and historiography of ideas. Many see the pinnacle of Deely's writing in his 2001 book, *Four Ages of Understanding*. However, unlike many scholars who produce a single landmark work, Deely has repeatedly published books and articles that have broken new ground. The former include *Introducing Semiotic* (1982 – an extension of his groundbreaking 1981 article, 'The relation of logic to semiotics'), *The Human Use of Signs* (1994a), *New Beginnings* (1994b), *Intentionality and Semiotics* (2007a) and, of course, the best-selling *Basics of Semiotics* (1990). (**PC**)

See also ETHICS, SEBEOK *and* UEXKÜLL, J and Deely.

FURTHER READING

Cobley, P. (2009) *Realism for the 21st Century: A John Deely Reader*, Scranton, PA: University of Scranton Press.

Deely, J. (1990) *Basics of Semiotics*, Bloomington, IN: Indiana University Press.

Deely, J. (2001) *Four Ages of Understanding. The First Postmodern Survey of Philosophy from Ancient Times to the Turn of the 21st Century*, Toronto: University of Toronto Press.

DEEP STRUCTURE In early versions of **generative grammar** the level of analysis before any transformations have applied. It was argued that the semantic component operated on deep structures. For instance, a sentence like *Ruby hopes to arrive on time* would have a deep structure of the form *Ruby hopes [Ruby arrives on time]*. This analysis makes it clear that it is Ruby who will arrive, even though *to arrive* has no subject next to it as verbs normally do. A transformation called Equivalent Noun Phrase Deletion (*equi*) deleted the second occurrence of *Ruby*, and changed *arrives* into *to arrive*.

Although popular outside mainstream generative grammar, this conception of deep structure was quickly abandoned by specialists, for various empirical and theoretical reasons. What remains is the notion that a sentence can be represented in a series of abstract ways, with rules linking the different levels of representation. (**RS**)

See also SURFACE STRUCTURE.

FURTHER READING

Chomsky, N. (1965) *Aspects of the Theory of Syntax*, Cambridge, MA: MIT Press.

DEIXIS Words which pick out features of the speech situation are called deictic words or are said to have the property of deixis, a Greek word for 'pointing'. They include *I* and *you* (referring to the speaker and hearer), *here* and *this* (referring to the place where the speaking occurs) and *now* (referring to the time of speaking). Deictic words are sometimes called 'shifters' (especially after Jespersen and **Jakobson**). (**RS**)

DENOTATION The term rests on a theory of **language** in which words are the names of phenomena in the world, and language is stable, so that relations of word to object are fixed. If **connotation** is the realm of cultural **meanings**, then denotation is the phenomenon of 'pure' naming, theoretically devoid of culture's influence. Denotation names the appropriate relation of word to phenomenon; 'green', for example, names a specific area of the colour spectrum. (**GRK**)

See also CONNOTATION.

DENOTATUM 'Where what is referred to actually exists as referred to the object of reference is a denotatum' (Morris 1938: 5). For example, if the **sign** 'unicorn' refers to what it designates considering it as existent in the world of mythology, that sign has a denotatum since it exists in that world. If, on the other hand, the sign 'unicorn' refers to what it designates considering it as existent in the world of zoology, that sign does not have a denotatum since it does not exist in that world. In this case the sign has a designatum or a **significatum**, as **Morris** (1946) was later to call it, but it does not have a denotatum. 'It thus becomes clear that, while every sign has a designatum, not every sign has a denotatum.' Morris's distinction between designatum and denotatum avoids misunderstandings as regards the **referent**. In the triangular diagram of the sign proposed by **Ogden** and **Richards** (1923) the referent is always foreseen and forms one of the three apexes. On the contrary, in other **semantic** theories (cf. Eco 1976, 1984), the referent is eliminated given that what the sign refers to does not always exist as referred to by the sign, in which case the designatum is not taken into account.

As demonstrated by Augusto **Ponzio** (1981a, 1990b, 1997; Ponzio *et al.* 1985), the sign always has a referent, or in Morris's terminology, a designatum, and if this referent exists as referred to by the sign, it also has a denotatum: the referent of 'Cheshire cat' in Lewis Carroll's *Alice in Wonderland* is a designatum as well as a denotatum; 'God' has a referent both as a designatum and denotatum for the believer, whereas in the proposition 'God does not exist', 'God' has a referent (otherwise the proposition would not make sense), but only as a designatum and not as a denotatum. (**SP**)

DESIGNATUM ***see*** **DENOTATUM** ***and*** **SIGNIFICATUM**

Diachrony (Diachronic) The mainstream of linguistic thinking in the twentieth century was dominated by attempts to understand the interrelations of elements in a system, the relation of elements in structures and the relation between the system and the structures. It might be said to be **synchronic** in its orientation. Linguistic work in the preceding century, by contrast, had been concerned with changes in systems (in **languages**, in 'families' of languages), the tracing of such changes, and the establishing of 'laws' that might be discovered underlying such changes. 'Grimm's Law', for instance, explained the link between voiceless plosive sounds – /p/, /t/, /k/ – and their equivalent fricatives, showing the relation between English *nut* and German *Nuss*. This was typical of a diachronic approach.

Major effort had gone into two areas in particular, the sound systems of (families of) languages, and the semantic changes of words. This work established beyond question the relatedness of groups of languages across Europe, the Middle East and the Indian subcontinent both over time and at particular periods (the relatedness of languages such as Italian, Portuguese, Spanish, Catalan, langue d'oc and Romanian, and their common derivation from Latin).

One of the central issues for **semiotics** in the coming decades will be to simultaneously consider diachrony and synchrony: to connect the micro-histories of social interactions with the relative stabilities of representational systems, so that history is always seen as present in structure. **(GRK)**

Dialect The term names systematic differences within one **language** in words and sounds, with less emphasis on **syntax**. In work deriving from nineteenth-century historical linguistics, dialect boundaries were established, as lines that can be drawn on a map showing the distribution of criterial words (e.g. 'the weakest member in a litter': 'runt'; or, in one German dialect, *Wurnagei*). On one side of the line the word is used, on the other it is not. Similar lines can be drawn for the sound systems of dialects (north of a line in England *France* is pronounced with a vowel sound as in *mat*, south of it with a sound as in *car*).

The distinction between what is a language and what is a dialect is always a political one (Fishman's dictum, for instance, that 'a language is a dialect with an army and a navy'). It rests on the state of affairs deriving from relative geographical stability of populations. Increasing mobility corrodes the integrity of (geographical and social) dialects. The mobility produced by the media and the advent of mass-literacy accelerates and deepens this process. Political power is often used to attempt to control, channel and direct these processes, suppressing dialects, or even promoting dialects to languages. **(GRK)**

See also Sociolinguistics.

Further reading

Chambers, J. K. and Trudgill, P. (1980) *Dialectology*, Cambridge: Cambridge University Press.

Dialogue External or internal **discourse** in which the word of the other, not necessarily in the second person, interferes with one's own word. It is also a discourse **genre**. Philosophers like Charles S. **Peirce** and Mikhail **Bakhtin** consider it as the modality itself of thought. For this reason, a distinction must be drawn between *substantial dialogicality* and purely formal *dialogicality*. Substantial dialogicality is not determined by the dialogic form of the text, *formal dialogicality*, but by the *degree of dialogicality* in that text which may or may not take the form of a dialogue. In other words, as shown by Augusto Ponzio (1994), substantial dialogicality is determined by the higher or lower degree of opening towards **alterity**.

Another distinction concerns verbal action, dialogue included, which from a pragmatic viewpoint may be considered as an end in itself, as carrying out an instrumental function, in which case it is a means to an end, or as determining and evaluating ends and means. On the basis of both distinctions, Bonfantini and **Ponzio** (1986) propose the following tripartite typology of dialogue:

1 *Dialogue as an end in itself*; in other words, conversation or entertainment dialogue. This type of dialogue refers to talking for the sake of talking, to dialogue with a **phatic** function, and may in turn be divided into:
   1.1 *conformative-repetitive dialogue*; and
   1.2 *diverting dialogue*.

An example of variant 1.1 is offered by certain forms of television **communication** which tends to be repetitive, obeying hyperdetermined compositional-instructional rules and just as hyperdetermined decoding processes.

2 *Dialogue functional to attainment*, which may in turn be divided into:
   2.1 *exchange dialogue*; and
   2.2 *competition dialogue*.
3 *Cooperative or reflective or investigative dialogue*. Using the degree of substantial dialogicality as the criterion for differentiation, this type of dialogue may be classified (on an increasing scale in the degree of dialogicality) as:
   3.1 *re-discovery and revelation dialogue*;
   3.2 *research and construction dialogue*; and
   3.3 *exploration and problematization dialogue* (on the relation between dialogue and truth, cf. Bonfantini *et al.* 1996).

Dialogue may be tied to the logic of identity or open to displacement towards alterity. The second case moves away from what has been classified as attainment dialogue, where interlocutors aim at achieving an end, therefore, at maintaining and reconfirming identity. Dialogue is of central importance in argumentative reasoning, which is reasoning that is not fixed in terms of defence and reproduction of identity but rather is open and available to otherness. Mikhail Bakhtin has highlighted how unilaterality, ossification and rectilinear dialectics derives from sclerotized dialogue. Monological, unilinear and totalizing dialectics is oriented towards a given synthesis and conclusion and as such calls for, as demonstrated by Ponzio (1993), a critique of dialogic reason. That is critique of the category of Identity which dominates over Western thought and praxis today. (**AP**)

FURTHER READING

Bakhtin, M. M. (1981) *The Dialogic Imagination: Four Essays*, trans. C. Emerson and M. Holquist, Austin, TX: University of Texas Press.

DICENT A word introduced by Charles S. **Peirce** for the second division of his trichotomy of **sign**s that concerns how they are interpreted. A dicent sign (or dicisign) is, or tends to be, interpreted as a sign of fact or actual existence. One of several kinds of dicent signs is the **proposition**, which combines a dicent element, tending to indicate the fact of the matter (subject), and a rhematic element, tending to describe it (predicate). **(NH)**

See also ARGUMENT *and* RHEME.

DISCOURSE The word is used in two distinct though connected senses. One points to a **meaning** such as 'extended stretch of **language**'; the other points to the social organization of contents in use. The former is characteristic of linguistically oriented work; the latter of socially focused approaches. There is often considerable overlap between the two.

The linguistic approach focuses on formal properties of stretches of language *above* the level of the sentence, for instance establishing frequencies of word use; of syntactic structures; of lexical collocations; of regularities of structures of the **text** itself; and of above-sentence level units in the text (topic structures; paragraphs; [elements of] scripts; **genre**s; turn-taking structures in spoken interactions, etc.).

The linguistically focused approach goes back to work by Zellig **Harris** who realized that certain problems of structuralist linguistics could not be solved by reference to the sentence alone, but had to be explained by relations across sentence boundaries. Inevitably this involved considerations of meaning, as well as the development by him of the formal concept of *transformation*.

In the socially focused approaches text (whether spoken or written) is the material site where socially produced meaning emerges. *Text* is the means of realizing non-material social meanings, in language or in other representational modes. *Discourse* is social; and text need not be linguistic.

In such approaches the social can be known only through its appearance in the text; the focus is on the social–discursive construction of the world. Broadly speaking, the aim is to discern and describe textual elements as indicators of social or social psychological entities such as *identity* and formations of identity (e.g. gendered identity); or *subjectivity*. The attempt is to uncover how discursive organization makes available – and suggests – particular 'inner' configurations which can form the basis of outwardly apparent entities such as what it is to be a 'proper' father, daughter, citizen, etc., and how it produces behaviours and structures which follow from such (inner) structures.

This work itself is influenced by the theories of Louis Althusser, for whom ideologies make appeals to individuals to assume certain positions; and to the theories of Michel Foucault, whose work showed the discursive constructions of potent social–historical categories. For Foucault such larger level constructs were produced in 'institutions' such as the legal system, the medical profession, the Church and Western science, which produced and projected statements which regulated the domain of their power.

One of the most extensive applications of this approach has been in the work of Edward Said, in particular in his book *Orientalism* (1978). Said shows how 'the West' has produced an all-encompassing discourse about 'the East', namely what it means to be 'oriental'. Work in a similar vein deals with issues of nationalism and racism. Approaches in which the linguistic/textual and the social–ideological are brought closely together are those of '**Critical Discourse Analysis**', in which linguistic and textual realization are seen as direct indicators of social–ideological organizations beyond them. **(GRK)**

See also DISCOURSE ANALYSIS.

FURTHER READING

Schiffrin, D. (1994) *Approaches to Discourse*, Oxford: Blackwell.

DISCOURSE ANALYSIS With the emergence of the term **discourse** as a major explanatory category in the humanities and social sciences from the 1970s onward (Foucault's inaugural lecture 'Orders of discourse' was delivered in 1959), discourse analysis became a term often fashionably used for any work that concerned itself with **text**s in any form. It may be best to reserve the term for accounts of regularities of various kinds which can be made to be apparent in texts, as signs of social (or social–psychological) organizations which are manifest in the text. These can be referred 'back' to institutions in which they originate. The approaches range from those which place more emphasis on linguistic/textual form to uncover the realization of social entities in discourse, to those which place emphasis on larger level structures of content often lexically manifested in a text. Discourse analysis is concerned equally with establishing the internal characteristics and constitutions of discourses; the relation of discourses with each other; and their social and psychological effects – in the constitution of subjectivities, identities, social orders, behaviours and practices. **(GRK)**

See also CONVERSATION ANALYSIS, DISCOURSE *and* HARRIS.

FURTHER READING

Coupland, N. and Jaworski, A. (eds) (2006) *The Discourse Reader*, 2nd edn., London: Routledge.

Gumperz, J. J. (ed.) (1982) *Language and Social Identity*, Cambridge: Cambridge University Press.

Lee, D. (1992) *Competing Discourses*, London: Longman.

DOUGLAS One of the most prolific of twentieth-century anthropologists, Mary Tew Douglas (1921–2007) was trained at Oxford University and did ethnography among the Lele of Congo. The titles of just a few of her (sometimes co-authored) books **index** the range of her contributions to British **structuralism**: *Purity and Danger* (1966); *Natural Symbols* (introducing group/grid analysis) (1970); *The World of Goods* (1979); and *Risk and Culture* (1982). **(MA)**

DUNS SCOTUS ***see*** **SCOTUS**

E

Eco The international scholar of **semiotics**, expert on aesthetics, sharp observer of mass media and cultural phenomena, and best-selling novelist (*The Name of the Rose*, 1980; *Foucault's Pendulum*, 1988; *The Island of the Day Before*, 1994; *Baudolino*, 2000; *The Mysterious Flame of Queen Loana*, 2004), Umberto Eco was born in Alessandria in 1932. He has attracted readers and critics around the world with every publication since his first polemical and innovative essay *The Open Work* (1989; *Opera aperta*, 1962).

Semioticians began to pay attention to Umberto Eco at the first international conference on semiotics, the **IASS** Congress in Milan, June 1974, where he was elected secretary of the association. In the preface to the Proceedings (*A Semiotic Landscape*, Eco and Chatman 1979), commenting on Roman **Jakobson**'s lecture, Eco suggests that the history of philosophy could be read in terms of semiotics. He pursued this suggestion at the second congress of the IASS, in Vienna (1979), with a lecture on 'Historiography of semiotics'. This remains a fundamental axiom that can be traced throughout Eco's writings from *A Theory of Semiotics* (1976) and *Semiotics and the Philosophy of Language* (1984), to *The Search for the Perfect Language* (1997), *Kant e l'ornitorinco* [1998] [*Kant and the Platypus,* 1999] and *Dall'albero al labirinto: Studi storici sul segno e l'interpretazione* (2007).

A student of philosophy and aesthetics under the guidance of L. Pareyson at the University of Turin, Eco's initial concerns with the production of signs and **communication** can be traced to his studies on media and popular culture in the early 1960s. His readings of Charles S. **Peirce** and Charles **Morris**, his collaboration with the eminent semiotician Thomas A. **Sebeok** and his enthusiasm for **Lotman**'s **sociosemiotics** fuelled his new concerns with **Barthes**' chains of **signifier**s, Peircean triadic relations between **sign** (**representamen**), **interpretant** and **object**, encyclopedia, **paradigmatic** structures, mechanisms of **abduction**, and the universe of intertextuality. This distancing from Saussurean **semiology**, Claude **Lévi-Strauss**' ontological **structuralism** (see in *The Open Work*, 'Series and Structure') and, in general, from binary relations between signifier and **signified**, or between sign, **code** and dictionary **semantics**, leads Eco to embrace the notion of a theoretically infinite semiosic process of interpretation of signs and **text**s.

Eco's notion of encyclopedia slowly becomes a reformulation of the spectrum of code in terms of Peirce's notion of **unlimited semiosis**. And like Peirce's view that 'a sign is something by knowing which we know something more' (*CP* 8.332), Eco places less importance on the **referent** and more on the mental processes that follow in the dynamics of our perception of all signs demonstrating that indeed a sign stands for another sign. From the late 1960s onwards Eco, convinced that cultural phenomena are systems of signs, switched his focus from semiotics of communication to semiotics of **signification**, and from sign production and signification to inferential processes in the mechanisms of semiosis.

La struttura assente [*The Absent Structure*] (1968) documents this transition as it also deals with code, structure and aesthetics, and it lies at the foundation of *A Theory of Semiotics* (1976 [1975]). In *Semiotics and the Philosophy of Language* (1984) Eco combines his observations on general theories with a history of semiotics as he continues to discuss sign, metaphor, symbol, frames, **denotation** versus **connotation**, and encyclopedia. In *Kant and the Platypus*, referring mainly to the works of **Kant** and Peirce, as he elaborates on semiotic issues of perception, categories, awareness, cultural experience, mental associations and interpretation, Eco revises some of his own earlier theoretical formulations, stressing that abduction is the key inferential process that regulates our activities of cognition, logic and interpretation.

Beginning with the essay *Segno* [*Sign*] (1973), Eco investigates the history of philosophy of **language** as he reconstructs the science of signs and the relationships between sign and thought from ancient writers (from Plato to St **Augustine**), to medieval times (**William of Ockham** and Bacon), through the seventeenth century (Hume, Wilkins and **Locke**), and to modern thinkers like Kant, Peirce and **Wittgenstein**. His historical research follows his belief that our perception and interpretation of signs are based on a series of inferences (abductions) which go beyond the linear relation of signifier and signified and that a sign does not follow the equation 'a = b' but rather the relation 'a' stands for '_' (Eco 1984).

Throughout his work Eco shows that semiotics, rather than a discipline or a theory, is an interdisciplinary field and an ongoing process of cognition based on the active intervention of our experience and encyclopedic competence (our overall culture). He also maintains that we often rely on ready-made 'frames' (scenes and fragments of our encyclopedia) for our inferences. In his essays, as in his fiction, readers can appreciate how Eco combines linguistics and cognitive sciences, and philosophy and literary theories, in order to demonstrate the interrelation of all signs. In so doing he adopts metaphors of libraries, labyrinths, rhizomes and of the encyclopedia for the interpretation of signs, texts and cultural events in general.

Eco's overwhelming interdisciplinary competence, combined with his talent for making witty observations and analogies, for recalling fascinating anecdotes and for exploiting intertextual echoes, make his theoretical and scientific essays always informative and as entertaining at the same time, as is his fiction. (**RC**)

See also Closed text *and* Open text.

FURTHER READING

Capozzi, R. (ed.) (1997) *Reading Eco: An Anthology*, Bloomington, IN: Indiana University Press.

Eco, U. (1976) *A Theory of Semiotics*, Bloomington, IN: Indiana University Press.

Eco, U. (2004) *Mouse or Rat? Translation as Negotiation*, London: Phoenix.

ECOSEMIOTICS The study of the interface of humans and their natural environment. It comprises the study of **communication** between humans and nature at large as well as the question of the **meaning** of the human ecosystem for humans. It also includes, in a broader sense, the relation of humans with other humans – although this is to be pursued through the perspective of **biosemiotics**, particularly the theory of **Umwelt** (as opposed to mainstream anthropology, sociology and so forth). The field was first explicitly suggested and named in 1998 by **Nöth** and has subsequently been further elucidated by **Kull** and others. (**PC**)

EMERGENCE The general semiotic concept of emergence indicates a process by which, in a given well-defined space, new sign systems and **codes** with new properties develop and survive. The transdisciplinary character of **semiotics** made necessary the elaboration of the problems of uneven development, its comprehensive semiotic interpretation. Emergence is a special case of development and in semiotics a decisive part of the evolution of **semiosis**. Semiotic results are more and more frequently used in different biological and social development theories; thus a semiotic elaboration of the concept of emergence has also been required with reference to its philosophical and biological interpretations.

The first philosophical description of emergence appeared in Fichte's philosophy, without the application of its concept. He formulated how a new individual being, with new properties, as an effect surpassing the common result of different causes, can emerge from the constellation of these causes. G. W. F. **Hegel** traced back the appearance of a new emergent being to the struggle between opposites. J. S. Mill already grasped 'emergent properties' as not being pure summations of causes in a constellation, but as the surpassing of causes. In his philosophical–biological book published in 1875, G. H. Lewes already used the concept of emergence. In the twentieth century emergence became an important concept of biology as well. The discovery of fundamental biological codes (DNA/RNA) and **biosemiotics** paved the way to the new semiotic interpretation of development and emergence. Research into the history of nature and palaeoanthropology made obvious that there were two very important scientific examples of emergent processes: the development of life on Earth and the formation of humans in it.

The four biosemiotic conditions of emergent processes are as follows:

- well-defined and saturated **sign-space** constituting the **sign-environment** of living beings in it;
- the relationship between the parts and the whole with the dominance of the latter;

- a hierarchy of signs;
- destruction of signs.

The concept of sign-environment is very close to **Hoffmeyer**'s concept of '**semiotic niche**'. The sign-environment continuously exerts effects on its living beings, transmitting simultaneously the influence of other sign systems, inspiring development towards complexity. Biosemiotic emergence is a special case of Jakob von **Uexküll**'s model describing **communication** between living beings and their environment. Living beings and their sign-environment constitute a whole that can only be disassembled with considerable losses suffered. The individuals of a species and their narrower environments are connected to each other by this entire sign-environment. New living beings move up in hierarchy and subordinate other living beings by integrating other sign systems, as well as by developing a more differentiated sign perception and processing system. As a consequence of emergent processes, the destruction of a part of subordinated sign systems always takes place because of the disappearance of living beings and their sign-environment.

With necessary modifications, the above-mentioned four conditions of emergence are also valid at the anthroposemiotic level. In society, interactions between human sign systems, intercultural effects, their conscious development and instrumentalization have a greater role in the launching of emergent processes resulting in more complex **codes**. **Sociosemiotic** emergence concludes historical periods and opens new ones. **(MS)**

FURTHER READING

Hoffmeyer, J. (2003) 'Semiotic aspects of biology: Biosemiotics', in R. Posner, K. Robering and T. A. Sebeok (eds), *Semiotics. A Handbook on the Sign-Theoretic Foundations of Nature and Culture*, Vol. 3, Berlin: Walter de Gruyter, pp. 2643–2666.

Nöth, W. (2000) *Handbuch der Semiotik*, 2nd edn, Stuttgart: Verlag J. B. Metzler.

Szívós, M. (2008) 'Introduction: The concept of emergence in philosophical and semiotic context', *Semiotica*, 171(1/4): 3–24.

EMIC ***see*** **PIKE**

EMMECHE Claus Emmeche (b. 1956), esteemed theoretical biologist, head of the Center for the Philosophy of Nature and Science Studies at the Faculty of Science, University of Copenhagen. A collaborator with Jesper **Hoffmeyer**, Emmeche is a biosemiotician and was an early theorist of artificial life. His 1994 book, *The Garden in the Machine*, outlines the problems involved in computer simulations of life processes. His work in general is concerned with the definition of (levels of) life and includes numerous articles in **biosemiotics** on **emergence**, **modelling**, complexity and genetic information. **(PC)**

ENDOSEMIOSIS The body of any living entity consists of a huge number of semioses; the term 'endosemiosis' refers to trains of **sign** transmission inside the organism. Messages transmitted within a living body include information about the **meaning** of processes in one system of the body (cells, tissues, organs or organ systems) for other systems, as well as for the integrative regulation devices (especially the brain). Bodies also contain endosemiotic **code**s, amongst which the most crucial, perhaps, is the **semiotic self**. Among the other fundamental endosemiotic codes are the genetic code, the metabolic code and the neural code. It follows that signs outside of bodies should be thought of in terms of *exo*semiosis. (**PC**)

Epicureans ***see*** **Stoics and Epicureans**

Ethics Ethics, from ancient times, named critical inquiry into human behaviour measured by criteria of 'right' and 'wrong'. In **Aristotle**, ethics was that branch of practical thought concerned with the criteria that proved the measure of right behaviour among human beings, including politics (human behaviour at the level of the state), family (which was called 'economics' in that ancient time) and individual behaviour (responsibility of the individual for what he or she does). 'Ethics' in this last sense, measure of individual responsibility, became the main focus in modern discussions of 'ethics'. With the discovery of **semiosis** as the action of signs upon which the whole of human knowledge depends, and the realization that this action of signs – in principle (though in fact 'slow by slow') – carries human understanding 'everywhere in nature' (Emmeche 1994: 126), **semiotics**, as the study of semiosis, has brought about a revolution in the understanding of ethics, a return to a generalized sense of 'human responsibility for behavioural consequences'. For just as semiotics has restored animal nature to modernity's 'thinking thing' (Deely 1990, 2004, 2005b; Deely *et al.* 2005), so also has semiotics revealed that the *consequences* of human action extend to *all of life on earth* by impacting the biosphere as such. With the discovery that not only individuals but species themselves 'come and go', and that human action accordingly impacts earthly life as a whole – its biodiversity, and its very continuation – a quite new general dimension of responsibility emerges (Deely 2005a) concerning human behaviour. Heretofore restricted to the cultural sphere and to individual behaviour in particular, ethics appears now in semiotic perspective as *human responsibility for the whole of life*. The name finding general acceptance in semiotics today for this realization of the broadened perspective of human responsibility, coined by Susan **Petrilli** and Augusto **Ponzio** (2003; see also Petrilli 2004), is 'semioethics'. (**JD**)

See also Petrilli and Ponzio.

Further reading

Deely, J. (2008) 'Evolution, semiosis, and ethics: Rethinking the context of natural law', in A. M. González (ed.), *Contemporary Perspectives on Natural Law*, Aldershot: Ashgate, pp. 413–442.

Etic ***see*** **Pike**

Existential semiotics Existential **semiotics** constitutes a new approach to the study of **sign**s, **signification** and **communication**. It has its roots, on the one hand, in classical semiotics to what can be called 'neosemiotics' and in the European philosophical tradition from **Kant**, **Hegel** and Kierkegaard to Karl Jaspers, Martin

Heidegger, Jean Paul Sartre, Simone de Beauvoir, Maurice Merleau-Ponty and Gabriel Marcel. However, this does not mean any return to 'existentialism' but simply rereading and reinterpreting the foundations of semiotics in the light of these philosophers.

On the epistemological and ontological level it establishes that semiosis takes place essentially between the *Dasein* (Being-There) – which is the world consisting of subjects and **objects** – and transcendence. In Dasein all theories of classical semiotics from **Peirce** and **Saussure**, to **Greimas**, **Lotman**, **Eco** and **Sebeok**, remain valid. Yet, in the light of transcendence, the basic categories of being, appearing and doing are redefined, with the origin of signs lying in their ability to 'transcend', to reach the sphere of virtuality in which such entities as values are supposed to dwell. Thus, values undergo a transformation from their virtual state when they are actualized in the Dasein, chosen by subjects, and then 'realized', i.e. when they exercise their impact on other subjects and objects. From the viewpoint of subjects again, 'transcendental' is anything which is absent but present in one's mind. The very notion of sign is a 'transcendental' entity since it is something which stands for something absent, *aliquid stat pro aliquot*. Every act of communication is also a transcendental act, transgressing the empty space between subject A and B in a **dialogue**. The subject reaches this realm via two acts, negation – whereby he encounters the Nothingness (le Néant) – and affirmation, i.e. the plenitude, universe full of meanings (the notion of the world soul by Emerson and Schelling, or pleroma by Vladimir Soloviev). Nevertheless the concept of transcendence is philosophico-conceptual; neither psychological nor anthropological, it mixes the Kantian modes of transcendental and transcendent. If the life of signs in Dasein is dominated by modalities – in the Greimassian sense – in transcendence they appear as metamodalities.

However, the transcendence can be reached only by metaphors. In Dasein the transcendence appears either vertically as signs, symbols and metaphors, or horizontally as *Erscheinen*, appearance. Thus signs as such belong to the sphere of appearance, *Schein*, in the sense of Kant as 'mere' Schein – compared to their 'truth' in transcendence, or as Shine, brilliance of signs and joy of their play, in the sense by Schiller. Ultimately entirely new sign categories stem from these standpoints when signs are determined in their traffic between Dasein and transcendence. Such new types are, e.g., presigns, actsigns, postsigns, endosigns, exosigns, transsigns, as-if-signs, phenosigns, genosigns, semiogerms (signs in their relationships to their **Umwelt**; see **Uexküll** and **biosemiotics**), and signs as moral acts (semioethics; see Petrilli and Ponzio), aesthetic choices and social practices, like sign in counter current leading to a theory of resistance, or postcolonial signs. The field of social and cultural applications of existential semiotics seems to be full of potential. (**ET**)

FURTHER READING

Tarasti, E. (2001) *Existential Semiotics*, Bloomington, IN: Indiana University Press.

Exosemiosis *see* Endosemiosis

Expression Expressions are the linguistic forms uttered in the performance of propositional acts (proper names, pronouns, nouns and noun phrases for referring, and grammatical predicates for predicating) or in the performance of **illocutionary** acts (typically complete sentences). It is in relation to these forms that '**meaning**' can be defined. Often (e.g. in Searle 1969) the link between expressions and meaning is formulated in a 'principle of expressibility' which holds that whatever can be meant can be said. **(JV)**

See also Propositions.

F

Field One of three linked terms (the other being **mode** and **tenor**) in the theory of **register**. Field describes the social practices which are the focus of a linguistic (inter)action, spoken or written: on what is, on who acts, who is involved, and on the attendant relevant circumstances. (**GRK**)

Firstness Firstness is the name given to one of the three categories of phenomena in the universe identified by Charles S. **Peirce**, the other two being **secondness** and **thirdness**. Firstness helps to explain logico-cognitive processes and therefore, at once, the formation of **sign**s. Analysed in terms of Peirce's typology of signs, firstness coincides with the sphere of **icon**icity. Something which presents itself as firstness, presence, 'suchness', pure quality is characterized by the relation of similarity (cf. *CP* 1.356–358). As demonstrated by **Petrilli** (1999a), firstness is also foreseen by Edmund **Husserl**'s **phenomenology** of perception and predicative judgement, though his terminology is different.

In *Erfahrung und Urteil* (1938) Husserl analyses 'passive predata' as they originally present themselves to perception by abstracting from all qualifications of the known, of familiarity with what affects us. His analyses reveal that similarity plays an important role at the level of indeterminate perception as well. In fact, if, by way of abstraction, we leave aside reference to the already known **object** which produces the sensation (secondness, **index**icality), and from familiarity through **habit** and convention, where what affects us exists as already given (thirdness, conventionality, **symbol**icity) and as already known in some respect even though it is unknown to us, we end up in pure chaos, as says Husserl, in a mere confusion of data. When colour is not perceived as the colour of a thing, of a surface, as a spot on an object, etc., but as pure quality, or, in Peirce's terminology, when we are in the sphere of firstness where something refers to nothing but itself and is significant in itself, this something eventually emerges as a unit through processes of *homogeneity*. As such it contrasts with something else, that is, with the heterogeneity of other data, for example red on white. Similarity at the level of primary iconism, that is, of the original, primitive phase in the formation of the sign as an icon, determines homogeneity which stands out against heterogeneity: 'homogeneity or similarity', says Husserl, is achieved to varying degrees through to complete homogeneity, to equality without differences. We could state that similarity is what makes the synthetic unification of firstness or primary iconism possible.

Primary association has nothing psychological about it. Here Husserl's anti-psychologism encounters Peirce's. Transcendental primary association is a condition of possibility for the constitution of the sign.

By virtue of the dimension of firstness, the dynamical object is not exhausted in the identity of the immediate object, but, as the **ground**, that is as the primary icon, it imposes itself on the **interpretant** over and over again (*immer wieder*, Husserl would say), as its irreducible otherness.

We may only reach this original level of firstness, of primary iconism, by way of abstraction. This involves either a *phenomenological reduction* of the *epoché*, according to Husserl; that is, bracketing the already given world and relative interpretive habits, or an artistic vision. As Maurice Merleau-Ponty shows in relation to Cézanne, painting is the search for the other constrasting habitual attitudes towards familiar objects and conventions.

The painting of Cézanne returns to a perceptual relation where the category of firstness, as understood by Peirce, dominates almost completely, 'à donner l'impression d'un ordre naissant, d'un objet en train d'apparaître, en train de s'agglomérer sous nos yeux' (Merleau-Ponty 1966: 25). And agglomeration occurs through associative processes based on similarity. (**SP**)

See also Representamen.

Further reading

Peirce, C. S. (1955) 'The principles of phenomenology', in J. Buchler (ed.), *Philosophical Writings of Peirce*, New York: Dover.

Peirce, C. S. (1958) 'Letter to Lady Welby, 12 October 1904', in P. Wiener (ed.), *Charles S. Peirce: Selected Writings*, New York: Dover.

Petrilli, S. (1999) 'About and beyond Peirce', *Semiotica*, 124(3/4): 299–376.

Firth John Rupert Firth (1890–1960), English linguist. Like **Halliday**, Bernstein and, later, **Kress**, he was to become associated with the colleges comprising the University of London, first at University College and then at the School of Oriental and African Studies where he was Professor of General Linguistics. He also spent nine years as a professor of English at the University of the Punjab. Scrutiny of his later papers from the 1950s in particular will reveal convincing reasons for his influence on the British tradition of **sociolinguistics**. While, as a linguist, he took the abstract nature of **synchrony** very seriously, he was most concerned with the **meaning** and import of utterances for **languages**' users. In this, his work follows a similar path to that of his student Halliday, and that of the Russian theorist **Vološinov**. Even more pointedly, however, he pursued his studies through examples of language use or text varieties specific to given situations, that is to say through **registers**. His focus on speech events was guided by many principles which have become virtually axiomatic of post-Hallidayan approaches to language and **communication**. One example of this might be Firth's particularly prescient formulations regarding the status of 'context' in relation to language use, made prior to the crystallization of both **pragmatics** and sociolinguistics. (**PC**)

Further reading

Firth, J. R. (1968) *Selected Papers of J. R. Firth, 1952–1959*, ed. F. R. Palmer, London: Routledge and Kegan Paul.

Force dynamics In Leonard Talmy's cognitive semantics, force dynamics designates the prelinguistic schematic system sustaining the representation of causal relations at large: i.e. how entities – whether physical, psychological or abstract – are construed to interact with respect to force. Human understanding of causation is based on a minimal structure involving two entities endowed with an intrinsic tendency to manifest a force: the focus of attention, called the 'agonist', and a correlated entity, the 'antagonist', whose force is exerted against the former. Force dynamics accommodates a wide diversity of causal predications in one coherent structural system, both within **language**, i.e. concerning the conceptual structures underlying the expression of causation in language, and across cognitive or symbolic domains: perception, naïve physics, narratives, etc. (**PB**)

G

Galen Galen of Pergamum (129–*c.* 215) was an eminent philosopher/physician, born in what is today Turkey of Greek parentage. He took as his primary subject the nature of the human body.

Galen is recognized as an important figure in the history of semiotics for his insistence that *semiotike* (the observation and classification of past and present signs for the purpose of revealing the underlying nature of a patient's condition and in order to prognosticate his/her future) was critical to effective medical practice. He has been referred to as the 'founder of clinical **semiotics**' and the 'first "scientific" semiotician' (Sebeok 2001a: 52).

Galen construed the symptom (*semeia*) as any sign of bodily disorder that was contrary to nature or, more specifically, to the patient's own nature. He believed that a comprehensive knowledge of the hidden causes of symptoms (here the term refers to both signs observed by the practitioner and complaints issued by the patient, though the patient's report was less credible) would lead to a systematic classification of diseases and a rational basis for allopathic treatment. He attempted to lay out just such a taxonomic structuring of symptoms, causes and diseases in several treatises. Galen thought it important, as **Hippocrates** had, to search for **sign**s in the patient's past (this he termed the mneumonic or anamnestic), though he gave this process less importance than observation and prognostication. He held that disease could be tracked to external or internal antecedent events or inherent conditions which resulted from an imbalance in the principal elements and humours of the body. Effective treatment was the mark of a valued practitioner, but accurate prognostication was of even greater value. Galen noted that he did not go about extolling the accuracy of his forecasts in order that other physicians/philosophers might not 'hate him even more' or call him a 'wizard or a prophet'.

While much of his work is directed to creating a rational basis for medical practice and encouraging experimentation, he also wrote extensively on pharmaceuticals and on anatomy, which he learned from attendance at the Alexandrian schools (where human dissection was still approved practice), from vivisectional experiments with animals, from surgical practice and from the treatment of wounds when he served as physician to the gladiators of Pergamum. In one treatise he records his delight at finding the body of a robber picked clean by birds lying along a roadside.

The high regard in which Galen was held and the systematic nature of his attempts to reveal the underlying causes of illness was so compelling (though largely incorrect, based upon a belief in humours and a body that was constituted of hot, cold, wet and dry) that Galenic medicine was adopted by Arab and Asian practitioners, circled the globe several hundred years later with European explorers and persisted as the orthodox in Western medicine for centuries. Many medical historians today believe the dominance of Galenic medicine/anatomy effectively stifled valuable work that yielded contrary results well into the middle of the second millennium.

Galen's longer lasting contribution is that he insisted all illness was of natural and not of supernatural origin and that practitioners must not attempt to apply broad medical knowledge to individual cases without respect for the uniqueness of the patient. He encouraged anatomical exploration and experimentation and is to be much credited for his refusal to treat psychical disease (what today we would term 'mental disorders') as significantly different from physical disease. (**KSR**)

See also MEDICAL SEMIOTICS.

FURTHER READING

Galen (1997) *Galen: Selected Works*, trans., Introduction and Notes by P. N. Singer, New York: Oxford University Press.

Johnston, I. (2006) *Galen: On Diseases and Symptoms*, New York: Cambridge University Press.

Sebeok, T. A. (2001) *Global Semiotics*, Bloomington, IN: Indiana University Press.

GENERATIVE GRAMMAR A description of a **language** which is formal and explicit: one which does not rely on the linguistic knowledge of the human being who reads or writes the **grammar**. Generative rules are a convenient notation for writing grammars. In mathematics a set is said to be generated by the rules which specify it: for instance, the rule 'include months of the year which end in *-ember*' generates the set {September, November, December}. In the same way, the rule 'put adjectives in front of nouns' generates a set of expressions including *nice meal*, *happy hour*, *fervent believer* and many others in English. For **Chomsky**, a generative grammar of a particular language is interesting if it is a step towards a theory of **Universal Grammar** for all languages. (**RS**)

GENERATIVE SEMANTICS A controversial tendency in linguistics which flourished in the USA in the late 1960s but gradually declined in influence. The disagreement began with a technical dispute about the nature of **deep structure**, which some linguists thought was unnecessary because it was simply the same as **meaning**. As the issues broadened, the emphasis in generative semantics was increasingly on questions of meaning rather than **syntax**, with many arguments put forward that meaning influenced grammatical form. Some generative semanticists claimed that the beliefs and presuppositions of speakers also had a role in **grammar**. Generative semantics was strongly opposed by **Chomsky** and led to a great deal of angry controversy, most of it now of purely historical interest. (**RS**)

See also LAKOFF.

FURTHER READING

Harris, R. A. (1993) *The Linguistics Wars*, New York: Oxford University Press.

Genre The term has a history reaching back to **Aristotle**, who named prominent literary forms and their textual characteristics. This usage has informed much of the debate in the intervening centuries, establishing the salient textual forms of literary production. Since the 1970s the term has enjoyed an enormous resurgence, in two distinct directions: in the description and naming of new and largely 'popular' forms (popular print fiction, and filmic texts; for instance, the 'Western'), and in the description of all textual production as conforming to regularities. In part, the popularity of the term is a recognition of the social and cultural origin of textual form, as a 'realization' of the features of the social environment in which it has been produced.

The theoretical interest dates back to the late 1970s and the early 1980s. Two strands are discernible: one in which the term genre is used as a near synonym for **text**, that is, genre describes all the relevant features which characterize text; the other treats genre as one of the constitutive categories of text, that is, it sees the text as the product of several distinct social factors.

Genre work of both kinds has been developed in Australia, in Canada and in the USA. Where genre is taken to equal text, emphasis tends to be placed on the overall shape and structure of the text. The narrative is a well-known instance. Or, in a job interview for instance, there are the opening welcoming remarks by the chair of the meeting; the introduction of members of the panel; the thanks to the applicant for attending the interview; the series of questions/answers in turn; the invitation by the chairing member to the interviewee to put questions to the panel; and the concluding remarks. These constitute a relatively stable structure, so much so that it is possible to prepare for, and to provide training in, 'interview techniques'. The structures are of relative stability only: job interviews in 2001 are very different from those in 1981.

Genre responds to the changing social structures, of which it is a realization. In genres power is not evenly or equitably distributed, so that the means for alteration are unequal and attended by unequal risk of sanctions. Genres make available specific 'positions' for its participants (e.g. the interviewer, the interviewee), which they may – given the constraints of power – simply adopt, may attempt to change, or may reject entirely.

There is some irony in the fact that the newly intense interest in genre comes at a time when the very constitution and stability of genres have come under the severest pressure. The current period is characterized much more by blurring of generic boundaries, by the dissolution and corrosion of stable types (the interview which becomes a 'chat', the advertisement which has become indistinguishably blended with the feature article), than by the (relative) stability of genres which had characterized the immediately preceding period. This is a reflection of the questions posed by new distributions of power in the contemporary period. (**GRK**)

Further reading

Altman, R. (1999) *Film/Genre*, London: BFI.

Bakhtin, M. M. (1986) *Speech Genres and Other Late Essays*, trans. V. McGee, ed. C. Emerson and M. Holquist, Austin, TX: University of Texas Press.

Kress, G. R. and van Leeuwen, T. (2006) *Reading Images: The Grammar of Visual Design*, 2nd edn, London: Routledge.

Gesture 'Gesture' usually refers to any visible bodily action expressing thought or feeling or that plays a role in symbolic action. Although it cannot be precisely defined, actions considered as 'gesture' are commonly regarded as 'voluntary', at least to a degree. Such actions range from the informal to the highly formalized. Included are the hand, head and face movements that often accompany speech; bodily actions employed to convey something when speech is impossible; codified forms such as the 'OK' gesture, 'thumbs up' gesture and 'V for victory' gesture; and handshakes, embraces, and the like, that play a role in greeting and other interaction rituals. The manual and facial actions of **sign languages** such as those found in communities of the deaf (primary sign languages) (e.g. Klima and Bellugi 1979) or in tribal communities such as certain groups of Australian Aborigines (Kendon 1988) or of Native Americans (alternate sign languages) (Mallery 1972 [1881]; Farnell 1995) are also part of 'gesture' but today often receive separate, specialized treatments. Also to be included are the complex gestural systems found in some dance traditions, especially in India; actions in religious ritual such as those performed by priests in celebrating mass or the mudras used in prayer in Tantric Buddhism.

The earliest systematic treatment of gesture in the West is by Quintilian (1924) who discussed it in his treatise on **rhetoric** from the first century. Gesture is discussed in books on courtly etiquette in the sixteenth century. In the seventeenth century many books on the art of gesture in rhetoric and in acting were published (Barnett 1987). Representative are Bonifacio's *L'arte dei cenni [Art of Signs]* (1616), Bulwer's *Chirologia* and *Chironomia* (1644), Austin's *Chironomia* (1806) and J. J. Engel's *Ideen zu einer Mimik* (1756). Gesture was of great interest to the philosophers of the French Enlightenment for what it might reveal about the original nature of language (Seigel 1969; Wells 1987). It was also seen as a possible basis for a universal language (Knowlsen 1965). In the nineteenth century, anthropologists such as Edward Tylor (1865) and Garrick Mallery (1972 [1881]) considered inquiries into gesture important for questions about language evolution.

Today, students of cognition and language examine the relationship between gesture and speech for what may be learned about the thought processes underlying the production of utterances. Gestures used simultaneously with speech are deemed to express aspects of **meaning** not manifest in words and reveal a fuller view of a speaker's conceptualizations (McNeill 1992). The study of the processes by which gestures can become conventionalized and systematized when used apart from speech, as in the elaborate gesture vocabularies found in some cultures (e.g. Southern Italy) or in language systems fashioned in gesture such as sign languages, provides insight into the origins and development of **symbol** formation and the organization and origin of language

(Armstrong *et al.* 1995). Gesture is also of interest to students of the history of the culture of everyday life, who study gestures and bodily expression in sculptures, paintings, prints, and the like, for the clues this can provide for an understanding of the expressive practices of the past (Bremmer and Roodenburg 1992). There is also interest in gesture in computer science, both in relation to attempts to develop computers that can respond to the gestures of users and in relation to the development of animated robots. (**AK**)

See also KINESICS.

FURTHER READING

Calbris, G. (1990) *Semiotics of French Gesture*, Bloomington, IN: Indiana University Press.

Kendon, A. (2004) *Gesture: Visible Action as Utterance*, Cambridge: Cambridge University Press.

McNeill, D. (1992) *Hand and Mind*, Chicago: Chicago University Press.

GLOBALIZATION The notion of 'globalization' can be understood in a double sense. *Globalization* in ordinary **language**, in the mass-medial version of the term, in economic, sociological and political terminology, refers to global **communication** in today's social reproduction system. It is connected with progress in technology and expansion of the market. But global communication in today's social reproduction system is only one aspect of the great web of communication formed by life over the planet Earth. In other words, globalization can also be understood in biosemiosic terms as globalism, a tendency that characterizes the evolution of life from its origins. Globalization was a fact of life well before the advent of global communication as understood in today's capitalist society. Globalization is understood reductively if identified with the characteristic phenomenon of modern society with its now wide-ranging (and mostly devastating) effects over the planet. Globalization in the biosemiosic sense is the structural condition provided by evolutionary development for the proliferation of life over the planet, in its multifarious and interconnected manifestations. As a specific sphere of life, anthroposemiosis is strictly interrelated with the other spheres – microsemiosis, phytosemiosis, mycosemiosis and zoosemiosis, all being specifications of biosemiosis. Together they form the global communication network that is the biosemiosphere. The *vital* challenge today for human beings – 'vital' in the sense of *crucial*, *essential*, but also in the sense that *it is a matter of life*, that *life is at stake* – is to reconcile economic globalization with global communication of life on the planet. This question concerns humans as unique 'semiotic animals', that is, capable of **sign**s of signs, reflection, conscious awareness; consequently as exclusively responsible for all life over the planet. (**SP**)

See also Petrilli and Ponzio.

FURTHER READING

Ponzio, A. and Petrilli, S. (2000) *Il sentire della comunicazione globalizzata*, Rome: Meltemi.

GLOTTOCENTRISM Bias, in analysis or any thinking about **sign**s, towards verbal **communication**. Frequently noted by **Sebeok**, such a bias is particularly evident in **structuralism** and **poststructuralism**, purporting to be derived from **Saussure**, thinking which often claims to identify and expose other biases such as 'phonocentrism', 'logocentrism', 'phallogocentrism' and 'ethnocentrism'. Where these biases pertain to differences of emphasis within the phenomena of culture and human interaction, glottocentrism draws attention to the fact that **semiosis** takes place also outside the world of humans, in the spheres of animals and plants as well as within organisms (**endosemiosis**). As such, glottocentrism is also a 'speciesism'. It is important to note that glottocentrism is frequently responsible for, in some considerations of signs, a repression of the fundamental non-verbal component of human **modelling**. (**PC**)

Goffman Erving Goffman (1922–1982), one of the pioneers in qualitative human science research who originated the concept of frame analysis and its research methodology. A frame is a schematic matrix of human behaviours that phenomenologically constitutes a conscious experience of the self that is recognizable by others. The titles of Goffman's books provide clear examples of a frame: *The Presentation of Self in Everyday Life* (1959); *Encounters* (1961a); *Asylums* (1961b); *Stigma* (1963a); *Behavior in Public Places* (1963b); *Interaction Ritual* (1967); *Strategic Interaction* (1969); *Relations in Public* (1971); *Frame Analysis: An Essay on the Organization of Experience* (1974); and *Gender Advertisements* (1978). Born in Canada, Goffman's 1945 BA degree is from the University of Toronto, but his 1949 MA and 1953 PhD are from the University of Chicago where he began his teaching career in the Division of Social Sciences. He subsequently worked for the National Institute of Mental Health in Bethesda, Maryland, before moving to the Sociology Department at the University of California at Berkeley. After one year there, he was promoted to Associate Professor in 1959, then to Professor in 1962. In 1968, he was appointed Benjamin Franklin Professor of Anthropology at the University of Pennsylvania in Philadelphia where he remained until his death. Goffman is a communicologist, although he never used that contemporary name for his work. Nonetheless, he devotes his major methodology book *Frame Analysis* (1974) to the approach of semiotic **phenomenology** which is the common theory and method of Communicology. He uses the first chapter of this book to take up the history of phenomenology from Edmund **Husserl**'s method of 'bracketing' to Alfred Schutz's phenomenology of 'typicality', and finally to the anthropologist Gregory **Bateson** (from whom he takes the notion of 'frame') and Jürgen Ruesch (from whom he takes the concept of '**communication** as interaction'). Thus, Goffman's frame analysis method consists of 1) description (bracketing, a 'token' focus on specific interactions called a *strip*), 2) reduction (a search for 'types' or typicality in strips where logic depicts a definition) and 3) interpretation (the analytic determination of the ***code*** or structural system that governs the 'tone' behaviour in its typicality). Type, token and tone are terms used by Charles S. **Peirce**, not Goffman. However, the Peircean terms help us explicate the logic of semiotic phenomenology adopted by Goffman. Goffman literally ends his book with an extensive quotation from the modern French semiotic phenomenologist Maurice Merleau-Ponty whose three-step method (description, reduction, interpretation) Goffman has mastered in all of his published research. Goffman's own theory and method is concise: 'There is a relation between person and role. But the relationship answers to the interactive system – to the frame – in which the role is performed and the self of the performer is glimpsed.' (**RL**)

Further reading

Goffman, E. (1974) *Frame Analysis: An Essay on the Organization of Experience*, Cambridge, MA: Harvard University Press.

Lanigan, R. L. (1990) 'Is Erving Goffman a phenomenologist?', in S. H. Riggins (ed.), *Beyond Goffman: Studies on Communication, Institution, and Social Interaction*, Berlin: Mouton de Gruyter.

Lemert, C. and Branaman, A. (eds) (1997) *The Goffman Reader*, Malden, MA: Blackwell.

Goodwin Charles Goodwin (b. 1943) is a linguistic anthropologist who has developed the concept of **multimodal semiotic fields** to denote the multiply embedded sign processes that are always at work in any given instance of human interpretation. Originally working within the discipline of **Conversation Analysis**, Goodwin's work has evolved beyond the examination of talk alone to include the study of the sequential organization of moment-to-moment body positioning, eye-gaze and manipulation of the artefacts of the material surround whereby **meaning** is co-constructed in human interaction. His work is devoted to discovering and explicating the fine-grained details of participant-fashioned semiotic resources and the essentially 'public' nature of **semiosis** *per se*. In all instances, Goodwin seeks to identify and explicate the many simultaneously available meaning-making resources that the interactants themselves are continually recognizing and manipulating in their acts of co-constructing communicative meaning. Goodwin's wife and frequent collaborator Marjorie Harness Goodwin conducts similar semiotic investigations into children's moment-to-moment co-construction of their **discourse** and play. (**DF**)

Further reading

Goodwin, C. (2000) 'Action and embodiment within situated human interaction', *Journal of Pragmatics*, 32: 1489–1522.

Goodwin, C. (2006) 'Human sociality as mutual orientation in a rich interactive environment: Multimodal utterances and pointing in aphasia', in N. Enfield and S. C. Levinson (eds), *Roots of Human Sociality*, London: Berg Press, pp. 96–125.

Goodwin, C. and Goodwin, M. H. (1996) 'Formulating planes: Seeing as a situated activity', in D. Middleton and Y. Engestrom (eds), *Cognition and Communication at Work*, Cambridge: Cambridge University Press, pp. 61–95.

Grammar The term 'grammar' has a range of definitions, all of which revolve around the process of systematization in **language**. Generally, grammar means the rules which are employed in the construction of language structures such as words or sentences (see **syntax**). These rules can, on the one hand, be the precise systems which have to be learnt as a child at school and which have been the subject of prescriptions since the teachings of the classical period, and through the 'general' grammar provided during the Enlightenment by the **Port-Royal** scholars. On the other hand, and increasingly following the work of **Chomsky**, the rules have been understood to constitute an 'internalized' capacity for language in humans. In this formulation, the capacity to observe certain syntactical rules is thought to be innate or contained within the genetic **code** passed down to successive generations of humans as a **Universal Grammar**. However, it should be remembered that post-Chomskyan linguistics also identifies rules in languages which are not innate but are sufficiently systematic to allow prescriptions to invariably be effective. Such **generative grammar**s make it possible to write textbooks describing the rules of national languages. Somewhat confusingly, such accounts are often themselves called a 'grammar'. **(PC)**

Further reading

Crystal, D. (1996) *Rediscover Grammar*, 2nd edn, Harlow: Longman.

Greimas Algirdas Julien Greimas (1917–1992) was a French semanticist and semiotician. Born in Russia, A. J. Greimas studied law in Kaunas (Lithuania) before enrolling at the University of Grenoble, France, where, before the Second World War, he focused on the **language** and literature of the Middle Ages. He obtained a first university degree with a specialization in Franco-Provencal dialectology. He enrolled for his military service in Lithuania in 1939 and escaped to France in 1944 when his country was invaded and occupied by the Soviets for the second time, after three years of German occupation (1941–1944). He enrolled at the Sorbonne University in Paris. There he obtained his State Doctorate in 1948 with a primary thesis on fashion in France in 1830, a lexicological study of the vocabulary of dress as depicted in the journals of the times, and a secondary thesis, based on the analysis of the various aspects of social life of this same period. Greimas taught the history of the French language at the University of Alexandria, Egypt, where he met Roland **Barthes**, before taking up appointments at the Universities of Ankara and Istanbul, Turkey, and Poitiers, France. He was elected to the École Pratique des Hautes Études in Paris in 1965, where he directed a yearly seminar in **semiotics** that attracted a large number of graduate students and professors from France and abroad. This seminar, which continues to be held today by his students and colleagues, subsequently evolved into the Paris School of Semiotics.

Greimas proposed an original method for **discourse analysis** that evolved over a thirty-year period. His starting point began with a profound dissatisfaction with the structural linguistics of the mid-century that studied only **phoneme**s (minimal sound units of every language) and morphemes (grammatical units that occur in the combination of phonemes). These grammatical units could generate an infinite number of sentences, the sentence remaining the largest unit of analysis. Such a molecular model did not permit the analysis of units beyond the sentence.

Greimas begins by positing the existence of a **semantic** universe that he defined as the sum of all possible **meaning**s that can be produced by the value systems of the entire culture of an ethno-linguistic community. As the semantic universe cannot possibly be conceived of in its entirety, Greimas was led to introduce the notion of semantic micro universe and discourse universe, as actualized in written, spoken or **icon**ic texts. To come to grips with the problem of **signification** or the production of meaning, Greimas had to transpose one level of language (the **text**) into another level of language (the metalanguage) and work out adequate techniques of transposition (Greimas 1987).

The descriptive procedures of narratology and the notion of narrativity are at the very base of Greimassian semiotics. His initial hypothesis is that meaning is only apprehensible if it is articulated or narrativized. Second, for him narrative structures can be perceived in other systems not necessarily dependent upon natural languages. This leads him to posit the existence of two levels of analysis and representation: a surface and a deep level, which forms a common trunk where narrativity is situated and organized anterior to its manifestation. The signification of a phenomenon does not therefore depend on the mode of its manifestation, but since it originates at the deep level it cuts through all forms of linguistic and non-linguistic manifestation. Greimas' semiotics, which is generative and transformational, goes through three phases of development. He begins by working out semiotics of action where subjects are defined in terms of their quest for objects, following a canonical narrative schema, which is a formal framework made up of three successive sequences: a mandate, an action and an evaluation. He then constructs a narrative grammar and works out a syntax of narrative programmes in which subjects are joined up with or separated from objects of value. In the second phase he works out a cognitive semiotics, where, in order to perform, subjects must be competent to do so. The subjects' competence is organized by means of a modal **grammar** that accounts for their existence and performance. This modal semiotics opens the way to the final phase that studies how passions modify actional and cognitive performance of subjects and how belief and knowledge modify the competence and performance of these very same subjects. The challenge ahead lies in working out adequate and necessary descriptive procedures not only of the modal but also of the aspectual features of cognitive and passional discourse: for example, aspects such as inchoativity (the beginning of an action), durativity (the unravelling of an action) and terminativity (the end of an action) that allow for the description of temporality as processes in texts. **(PP)**

FURTHER READING

Greimas, A. J. (1987) *On Meaning: Selected Writings in Semiotic Theory*, ed. and trans. P. Perron and F. Collins, Minneapolis, MN: University of Minnesota Press.

Perron, P. and Collins, F. (eds) (1989) *Greimassian Semiotics*, special issue of *New Literary History*, 20(3).

Schleifer, R. (1987) *A. J. Greimas and the Nature of Meaning*, Lincoln, NE: University of Nebraska Press.

GRICE A philosopher of **language**, H. Paul Grice (1926–1985) started his career in the tradition of **ordinary language philosophy** while working with **Austin** at Oxford in the 1940s and 1950s. With relatively few publications during his lifetime, he exerted an unparalleled influence on the theory of **meaning**. He introduced a distinction between 'natural' meaning (as in 'Clouds mean rain') and 'non-natural' meaning (or linguistic meaning). Though allowing for the existence of conventional meaning associated with linguistic expressions (some of which may be implicit rather than explicit, as when the expression 'the US President' logically implies that we are talking about 'a US President'), Grice devoted most of his attention to those types of non-natural meaning dependent on the utterer rather than on the structure of words and sentences; hence the term 'utterer's meaning' in contrast to 'sentence meaning' and 'word meaning' (Grice 1957, 1968, 1969). Utterer's meaning, which is occasion-specific in contrast to the 'timeless' sentence and word meaning, is further defined in terms of the speaker's intentions (without denying that some forms of meaning are simply expressed without being intended): utterer's meaning is the speaker's intention in the making of an utterance to produce an effect in the hearer by means of the hearer's recognition of the intention to produce that effect.

Observing that utterances, more often than not, mean more than what is literally said, Grice probes into implicit meaning beyond the realm of logical implications (Grice 1975, 1978, 1981). According to Grice, conversations are typically governed by a 'cooperative principle' which says: 'Make your conversational contribution such as is required, at the stage at which it occurs, by the accepted purpose and direction of the talk exchange in which you are engaged' (1975: 45). In keeping with this principle, a number of 'maxims of conversation' guide conversational interaction:

1 *The maxim of quantity*: (i) Make your contribution as informative as is required for the current purposes of the exchange. (ii) Do not make your contribution more informative than is required.
2 *The maxim of quality*: Try to make your contribution one that is true. (i) Do not say what you believe to be false. (ii) Do not say that for which you lack adequate evidence.
3 *The maxim of relation* (later called *relevance*): Be relevant.
4 *The maxim of manner*: Be perspicuous. (i) Avoid obscurity of expression. (ii) Avoid ambiguity. (iii) Be brief. (iv) Be orderly.

Assuming that these maxims are normally adhered to, utterances give rise to conventional or standard conversational implicatures: thus the statement 'It is raining outside' implicates, on the basis of the maxim of quality, that the speaker believes that it is raining outside (an implicature that reflects the sincerity condition of an assertive **speech act**). Often, however, the maxims are obviously broken. But since interlocutors are supposed to be cooperative, any obvious breach of a maxim will lead to further (non-conventional) conversational implicatures. Thus, in Grice's classical example, the response 'There's a garage round the corner' in response to 'I am out of petrol', because it does not adhere to the maxim of quantity, but because cooperativity is assumed, will implicate that the garage has petrol for sale and is open. (**JV**)

See also RULES *and* SEMANTICS.

FURTHER READING

Grice, H. P. (1989) *Studies in the Way of Words*, Cambridge, MA: Harvard University Press.

Leech, G. N. (1983) *Principles of Pragmatics*, London: Longman.

Levinson, S. C. (1983) *Pragmatics*, Cambridge: Cambridge University Press.

GROUND A term introduced by Charles S. **Peirce** to denote 'some respect or capacity' on the basis of which something becomes a **sign** or **representamen** (in other words, stands for something else, an object), thanks to another sign which serves as **interpretant**. In fact, the something which serves as a sign does not stand for the object in all respects but in reference to a particular respect or capacity or, as Peirce also says, 'in reference to a sort of idea' (*CP* 2.228). This is the fundamental idea that forms the ground of the representamen. Therefore, this something in its indeterminacy is gradually determined under a certain respect, thanks to which it becomes a sign for an interpretant. If, to recall an example made by Peirce, I say 'This stove is black', the immediate **object** 'stove' is assumed in a certain respect, its 'blackness', which is the ground of the interpretant (cf. *CP* 1.551). From the point of view of the phenomenology of perception (**Husserl**, Merleau-Ponty) the ground is something which was undifferentiated and is now differentiated in a certain respect, thereby becoming a sign for an interpretant. (**SP**)

H

Habit An acquired propensity or disposition to act in a regular way in familiar circumstances. Generally the result of repeated uniform reactions or responses, whether physical or intellectual, to events or experiences of the same kind. Instincts may be regarded as natural habits and in the cosmology of Charles S. **Peirce** and others even laws of nature are said to be habits. Habitual responses are usually made involuntarily, without reflection or conscious decision-making, and thus are not subject to immediate self-control; but habits can be intentionally changed by a controlled regimen of behaviour repatterning. The role of habit is of key importance in Peirce's philosophy. According to Peirce, beliefs are habits of action produced by inferential processes. He also held that the final effect of **semiosis**, which he called the final **interpretant**, is an intellectual habit, which, although not itself a sign, culminates in a process of intellectual refinement through adjustment to experience. This is a central tenet of Peirce's **pragmaticism**. **(NH)**

See also Ground, Icon, Index *and* Symbol.

Further reading

Peirce, C. S. (1905) 'What pragmatism is', and (1907) 'Pragmatism', in C. S. Peirce (1998) *The Essential Peirce: Selected Philosophical Writings*, Vol. 2, ed. Peirce Edition Project, Bloomington, IN: Indiana University Press, pp. 331–345 and 398–433.

Hall Edward Twitchell Hall (b. 1914), American anthropologist. In **semiotics**, Hall is possibly best known for his writings and research on **nonverbal communication** and **proxemics**. However, his interests are extraordinarily wide-ranging. In the 1930s he worked on Navajo and Hopi reservations, gaining his BA in Anthropology (University of Denver, 1936), MA in Anthropology (University of Arizona, 1938) and his PhD (Columbia, 1942), thereafter serving in the Philippines in the Second World War before returning to the University of Denver to head the Anthropology Department (1946–1948). Hall's experience during overseas service seems to have crystallized his interest in intercultural **communication** and cultural perceptions of space. He subsequently (1950–1995) became Director of the Foreign Service Institute of the US State Department's 'Point Four' training programme for technicians on overseas duty. Also in the early 1950s, Hall was associated with the Palo Alto School, an 'invisible university' interested in animal communication (see **zoosemiotics**), psychiatry, the family, **pragmatics** of communication, nonverbal communication and **cybernetics**. The School included Gregory **Bateson**, Margaret Mead, Ray **Birdwhistell**, Albert Scheflen, Erving

Goffman and Paul Watzlawick. Beginning, especially, with his 1959 book *The Silent Language*, Hall wrote a series of works which united his interests in intercultural communication in general, proxemics, cultural conceptions of space and architectural conceptions of space. In *The Hidden Dimension* (1966), for example, he considers the future of urban humans, projecting, with the help of proxemics and his own version of zoosemiotics, the potential advantages and disadvantages of species 'crowding' – in cities, for example.

His understanding of proxemics proceeded from a dialectic of humans' sensory apparatus (in effect, their **Umwelt**) and cultural coordinates and constraints (see **sociosemiotics**). In contemporary literature on nonverbal communication (so-called 'body language') the idea of 'body space' or 'personal space' is probably most often derived from Hall's elucidation of proxemics. The concept has close affinity with the ideas put forward by **Hediger** and **Sebeok**, particularly the latter's concept of the **semiotic self**.

Hall retired from his academic post in 1977, although his work has been celebrated in the field of intercultural communication ever since, whether it be for instrumental business purposes or for genuine production of new knowledge. (**PC**)

FURTHER READING

Hall, E. T. (1969 [1966]) *The Hidden Dimension*, New York: Anchor Books.

HALLIDAY The work of Michael Halliday (b. 1925) is the major contemporary alternative to the domination of linguistic thinking by **structuralist** approaches. While structuralists have focused on the **syntagmatic** plane, Halliday focuses predominantly on the **paradigmatic**. '**Meaning** is choice in context' is his re-statement of a major tenet of **Saussure**. It shapes the impact of his thinking: placing emphasis equally on the actor who makes choices from the resources of the linguistic system, and does so in palpably present contexts. In this there is more than an echo of **Marx** and Engels' 'Men make their own history but not in conditions of their own choosing'.

The system-structure theory of J. R. **Firth**, his teacher, shaped his early work, as in the seminal 'Categories of the theory of grammar' (1961), as have the functionalist approaches to **language** of the anthropologist Bronislaw **Malinowski**. The three functions which Halliday posits as inhering in every fully functioning semiotic system – the function to represent events and states of affairs in the world (the **ideational** function), the function to represent the social relations between participants in an interaction (the **interpersonal** function), and the function to represent a coherent account of the world of the message (the **textual** function) – are close echoes of Malinowski. His work is equally influenced by his close knowledge of Chinese gained during a stay in Beijing (1949–1951) as a student at that university. The notions of *theme*, of *mood* and of *transitivity*, as much as his work on the organization of (English) speech, in particular the place of intonation in English (as grammatical and textual), owe most to a perspective from within Chinese.

Three articles published between 1966 and 1968 (in the new *Journal of*

Linguistics), entitled 'Notes on transitivity and theme in English', marked a decisive move from the earlier equal emphasis on system and structure and their interrelation, to an emphasis on function: transitivity in the clause as the core of the *ideational function*; mood as the core of the *interpersonal function*; and theme as the core of the *textual function*. This also led to the description of the distinction, grammatically and textually, between language in its spoken and written forms. This is now commo place in most linguistic thinking, and has begun to replace the abstraction of *language-as-such*. A focus on the significance of the materiality of language (as of other representational systems) is a consequence of this move, and is likely to be one of the major developments in semiotic work in the coming decades.

Halliday's linguistic work has culminated in his extensive description of English in functional terms (1985). In this work the slogan of 'grammar as a resource for meaning' is documented, both in outlining the systems of choices available to members of the culture, and in the potential for the constant remaking of this resource through the normal use of (grammatical) metaphor. The **grammar** has had the most widespread application, whether in the development of parsing programmes in the new information technologies, or in the development of descriptions that enter into language and literacy curricula at any level. **(GRK)**

Further reading

Halliday, M. A. K. (1976) *Halliday: System and Function in Language, Selected Papers*, ed. G. Kress, Oxford: Oxford University Press.

Halliday, M. A. K. (1978) *Language as Social Semiotic*, London: Arnold.

Halliday, M. A. K. (1985) *An Introduction to Functional Grammar*, London: Arnold.

Harris Zellig Harris (1915–1992) was a leading exponent of structuralist linguistics (see **American structuralism**). Born in the Ukraine, he lived in Philadelphia for most of his life, where he taught linguistics at the University of Pennsylvania. Harris also spent much of his time at Mishmar Ha-emek, a kibbutz in Israel.

Harris is usually remembered nowadays for three things. First, his 1951 book *Methods in Structural Linguistics* is seen as the brilliant final statement of structuralism, just before **Chomsky**'s theories replaced it to become the dominant tendency in American linguistics. Leonard **Bloomfield** had allowed tests of sameness or difference in **meaning** to be used as a basis for grammatical statements, but Harris was committed to the principle that the distribution of linguistic elements was the only sound basis for grammatical analysis. The distribution of an element such as a morpheme or a word is simply the sum of the environments in which the element occurs (cf. Fought 1994: 103).

An example is the treatment of expressions like *give a damn* or *take no for an answer*, both of which normally only occur in the negative:

1 Frankly, my dear, I don't give a damn.

2 You don't take no for an answer when you've nothing to lose.

Rhett Butler could not have said **I give a damn*, and nor could Tom Robinson have sung **You take no for an answer* (the asterisk indicates that the sentence is not possible in English). Such expressions are found after *don't* in these examples, but they also occur after *hardly* (*I hardly give a damn*) and *never* (*You never take no for an answer*). Bloomfield would have said that these are all negative expressions, but for Harris it is the fact that the items occur nearby, not their meaning, which is the determining factor.

This method is sometimes dismissed as a convoluted way of arriving at grammatical analysis, since starting with meaning seems much simpler. Recent work in corpus linguistics by John Sinclair and others (cf. Sinclair 1991), however, is equally consistent in stressing distribution rather than meaning as a more reliable starting point for analysis.

Harris's second contribution is his influence on Chomsky: it was he who introduced Chomsky to linguistics, and his use of the term *transformation* foreshadows its later use in Chomsky's work.

Third, Harris coined the term '**discourse analysis**' and tried to extend structuralist methods to texts rather than just isolated sentences.

Harris continued to produce important and original work until late in his life (cf. Harris 1991), but his work was largely ignored except by a small group of close colleagues. This is a great pity: one only needs to read Harris's masterly paper on **Sapir** (Harris 1984 [1951]) to see that he had an outstanding mind. (**RS**)

Further reading

Harris, Z. (1984 [1951]) 'Review of *Selected Writings* by Edward Sapir (Berkeley, University of California Press, 1949)', *Language*, 27(3): 228–333. (Reprinted in K. Koerner (ed.) *Edward Sapir: Appraisals of His Life and Work*, Amsterdam: John Benjamins, 1984, pp. 69–114.)

Harris, Z. (1991) *A Theory of Language and Information*, Oxford: Clarendon Press.

Hiz, H. (1994) 'Harris, Zellig S.', in R. Asher and J. Simpson (eds), *The Encylopedia of Language and Linguistics*, Vol. 2, Oxford: Pergamon Press, pp. 1523–1524.

Hediger Heini Hediger (1908–1992) was a Swiss zoo-biologist, whose work had an enormous impact on zoosemiotics, particularly on the study of human–animal interaction (anthrozoosemiotics) (1965). His studies on proxemic, social and territorial aspects of animal behaviour resulted from a combination of J. von **Uexküll**'s **Umwelt**-theory and modern ethology. Hediger's work focused on the description of interpersonal distances used between animals, in social or generally interactional contexts (among other things, inspiring Edward **Hall**'s theories on social distance). A friend of Uexküll's and **Sebeok**'s, he was *elected* 'semiotician' by the latter, who wrote extensively about his work and his specific semiotic applications, particularly on the so-called **Clever Hans** effect (1981). (**DMar**)

See also Hall *and* Proxemics.

Further reading

Hediger, H. (1974) 'Communication, between man and animal', *Image Roche* (Basel), 62: 27–40.

Hegel Georg Wilhelm Friedrich Hegel (1770–1831), German idealist and one of the greatest systematic philosophers, known especially for his triadic dialectic method (thesis giving rise to antithesis and resolved in synthesis, which becomes thesis for new antithesis, and so on) and view that history embodies this dialectic as it evolves rationally toward an 'absolute idea'. Hegel's philosophy has been important in the development of Marxism and other European philosophies and influenced some of the classic American philosophers, especially Royce, Dewey and **Peirce** (in his later years). (**NH**)

Hermeneutics The term 'Hermeneutics' (from the Greek *hermeneuo*, 'translate' or 'interpret') designates the science and art of interpretation and understanding texts. Although hermeneutics can be traced back to ancient philosophy, namely to Plato and **Aristotle**, it developed particularly in the Middle Ages and the Reformation on two different paths: on one side, within the interpretation of biblical studies; on the other, in the field of philological studies. In both fields, hermeneutics pretended to be the study of general as well as specific rules that govern interpretation of the entire biblical text in respective to humanistic literature, where general rules refer to historical–cultural or contextual conditions of **text** understanding, while specific rules apply to the specific **genre** (symbolic, allegoric, etc.).

In the period of German romanticism and idealism, mainly starting with Friedrich Schleiermacher, hermeneutics developed more and more from a theory of text interpretation according to rules into a more general theory of the conditions of human understanding that underlie any text interpretation. Within this theory the assumption that each attempt to understand texts has to consider the implicit limitations of human understanding becomes relevant: instead of reaching at any time a conclusive, fully and definite understanding of a text, in the process of interpretation there always remains an undetected rest. Following Schleiermacher, Wilhelm Dilthey then built on the romantic version of hermeneutics, developing it in a general theory of how understanding takes place in the humanities in contrast to acquiring scientific knowledge in natural sciences: in the humanities it is based on a different ground of knowledge, that is how the world is given to us through symbolically mediated practices.

In his groundbreaking book *Wahrheit und Methode* (1994) Hans-Georg Gadamer, on the basis of Martin Heidegger's *Sein und Zeit* [*Being and Time*] (1962 [1927]), develops systematically the idea that any understanding of art, culture, historical texts and so on always is closely related to the specific world view, the subjectivity of interpreters. This assumption, then, is still at the very foundation of important contemporaneous discussion in the Anglo-American (Rorty and Davidson) as well as in the Continental context (Ricoeur, Apel, Derrida). (**PJS**)

Further reading

Bruns, G. (1992) *Hermeneutics. Ancient and Modern*, New Haven, CT: Yale University Press.

Gadamer, H.-G. (1994) *Truth and Method*, trans. J. Weinsheimer and D. G. Marshall, New York: Continuum.

Ricoeur, P. (1981) *Hermeneutics and the Human Sciences: Essays on Language, Action and Interpretation*, trans. J. B. Thompson, Cambridge: Cambridge University Press.

HETEROGLOSSIA For Mikhail **Bakhtin** the term 'heteroglossia' captured the fact that any society consists of groups of diverse constitution and interests. Their diversity gives rise to difference in **language** (-use) so that members of any society always speak with many diverse 'voices', which are in contestation in any utterance. Bakhtin's arguments about heteroglossia were demonstrated most spectacularly with reference to the novel form of narrative. (**GRK**)

HIPPOCRATES Hippocrates of Cos (*c.* 460 BCE–*c.* 366 BCE) was an influential physician and teacher who is known to us primarily through the writings of Plato, **Aristotle** and **Galen**. Hippocrates is often referred to as the 'father of medicine' and by some as the 'father of **semiotics**'. The work with which he has been credited is constituted of some sixty treatises on disease and its treatment known as the *Corpus Hippocraticum*. It is now well established that few if any of the treatises are attributable to Hippocrates himself. The *Corpus* more likely represents the collected body of knowledge about disease and the body produced over a period of a century or more by prominent Greek (and Sicilian) schools of medical thought and practice.

While the concept of the '**sign**' appears in earlier Greek writings and the notion of a disease that narrates its nature through bodily signs was well understood in all the world's medical traditions prior to the period of the Hippocratic writings, the *Corpus* moved the philosophical underpinnings of medicine decidedly away from the attribution of disease to supernatural causation and towards a more rigorous investigation of the patient's body and the patient's complaints in practical and secular terms. Such ideas were not entirely unique to Hippocrates and can be found in the earlier work of Greek physician/philosophers such as Empedocles and Alcmaeon.

In the *Corpus* we find the first systematic focus on the value of signs and symptoms in revealing the patient's state of health or disease. The medical practitioner is encouraged to carefully examine the 'visible' signs of illness – those signs that were to be seen 'on' the body of the patient – and the 'invisible' signs that lurked beneath the skin and were to be elicited using such techniques as the application of drugs or foods to force the body to secrete or excrete fluids that would better reveal the inner workings of the body. The *Corpus* urges the physician to consider all such symptoms and the course of these symptoms over time and to carefully note the patient's response to treatment. The physician was also directed to consider the patient's medical and social history, including his/her age, gender, diet, activities and personal **habit**s, and to consider the diseases and environmental factors found where the patient lived. Through such observations, the skilled practitioner learned those treatments that would cure specific diseases.

The *Corpus* contains treatises undoubtedly produced by different authors, is inconsistent and sometimes contradictory in its notions of causation, and can be shown to have been influenced by various earlier medical thinkers who held differing views of the body. Nevertheless, it is almost totally consistent in its emphasis on the body as a product of nature, disease as the result of natural causes, and the requirement that the physician carefully observe the patient's body and note its changes over the course of an illness.

The *Corpus* also provides us with the first evidence that physicians of the period were attempting to separate medicine from philosophy in their rejection of a priori philosophical notions that were untested and untestable in favour of observation and experience. In other words, the *Corpus* shows us the beginnings of a *semeiology* that was separate from philosophy. The term *semeiology* continues in modern (though infrequent) usage and refers to the process of diagnosis or the practice of differential diagnosis. (**KSR**)

See also Manetti.

FURTHER READING

Hippocrates (2007) *The Genuine Works of Hippocrates*, trans. F. Adams, New York: Kessinger Publishing.

Longrigg, J. (1998) *Greek Medicine: From the Heroic to the Hellenistic Age*, New York: Routledge.

Porter, R. (1997) *The Greatest Benefit to Mankind. A Medical History of Humanity*, London: W.W. Norton.

HJELMSLEV Louis Hjelmslev (1899–1965), Danish linguist and semiotician, Professor of Comparative Philology in Copenhagen (1937–1965), founder of the linguistic theory called glossematics. The glossematic project is an attempt to radicalize Ferdinand de **Saussure**'s claim (1916) that **language** is form not substance. This theoretical approach has been the emblem of the Copenhagen School of linguistics.

The essence of glossematics is contained in *Omkring sprogteoriens grundlæggelse* (English translation, *Prolegomena to a Theory of Language*, 1961 [1943]) and *Résumé of a Theory of Language* (1975). *Prolegomena* was intended to be the popular version of the theory, *Résumé* the strictly scientific presentation. Both were prepared simultaneously during the 1930s in collaboration with Hans-Jørgen Uldall (1907–1957), although his *Outline of Glossematics* (1957) shows essential differences to glossematics in its almost phenomenological approach. A series of Hjelmslev's seminal articles from the 1930s are reprinted in *Essais linguistiques* (1959) and *Essais linguistiques II* (1973). With Viggo Brøndal he founded the Cercle Linguistique de Copenhague (1931) as well as *Acta Linguistica Hafniensia* (1939–).

Hjelmslev's early works, *Principes de grammaire générale* (1928), *Études Baltiques* (1932) and the *La catégorie des cas* (1935–1937), are examples of a structural linguistics prior to glossematics. Here Hjelmslev, like the members of the **Prague School**, defined linguistic units from distinctive features, i.e. elements bound by formal properties. Glossematics, however, sets up definitions based solely on functions, i.e. element-independent relations. All linguistic elements are to be defined, and only to be defined, by their mutual relations, called their functions. The aim of the linguistic analysis is to transform features (like case, syntactical position, glottal stop, etc.) to functions.

Therefore, the linguistic object will be constituted by the method through which the rigorously immanent analysis is carried out: a procedure of dichotomic partitions of the material **text**. The units isolated in each step of the analysis are defined by their relation to other units, the units having no properties beyond this functional definition. The ultimate goal is to turn all linguistically relevant aspects of a text into constants, i.e. the two units in an interdependent relation or one of the units in a unilateral dependence. The structure of a given language phenomenon is the system of relations between the constants. The other units have a unilateral dependence and the simply co-occurrent units are the variables.

The basic linguistic units are called figurae. As they have no content except their function, it is an arbitrary choice what we call expression and what we call content. Together with the rigid immanency of the linguistic structure this radical consequence is the basis of the general semiotic influence of glossematics.

The **sign** is defined as a mutual interdependence between two planes, the expression plane and the content plane. The two interrelated forms, called the expression form and the content form, are the constants of the two planes. The variables of the two planes are the so-called expression substance and the content substance (the last one characterized only vaguely by Hjelmslev). These two substances are articulated by the respective forms so as to bring about a manifested sign in a specific expression substance (for example, the acoustic material of a natural language) and in a specific content substance (for example, the psychological content of a text). The variables have to be studied by other sciences than linguistics in order to acquire a formal status as constants if, and only if, these sciences follow the glossematic procedures, thereby becoming semiotic sciences.

The formal definition of the sign allows for an analysis of the content plane of the sign following the same basic principles as the analysis of the expression plane. This is the basis of structural semantics as carried out on glossematic grounds in most detail by Algirdas J. **Greimas** (1917–1992). The emphasis on pure form also implies that the expression substance is irrelevant for the principles of the analysis: glossematics is applicable to any sign system, also non-linguistic systems. The same goes for the content substance: any ideological or psychological contents are secondary to the formal principles that make them accessible as contents. Without the formal articulation they would not exist as contents, but as a chaotic unspecifiable substratum, called the purport, if they existed at all. Any formal sign system articulating substance on the two planes is called a semiotic.

As the sign is a formal unit, the sign itself as a whole can be a content form or an expression form. Thus, the signs of a given sign system may have the signs of another sign system, a so-called denotative semiotic, as their content plane, itself being a meta-semiotic (for instance, linguistics *vis-à-vis* **natural languages**). Or, they may have the signs of another sign system as their expression plane and thereby constituting a connotative semiotic (for instance, the **symbols** and **metaphors** of literary language). Hence, natural language only becomes the basic sign system when seen as a denotative semiotic, i.e. only when it is embedded in a hierarchy of semiotics. The ultimate goal for this progressive hierarchical stratification is to make a metasemiotic on a higher level transform the variables of the semiotics on the lower levels into constants. This perspective is the most wide-ranging semiotic perspective of glossematics. (**SEL**)

See also BARTHES, CONNOTATION *and* DENOTATION.

FURTHER READING

Caputo, C. and Galassi, R. (eds) (1985) 'Louis Hjelmslev: Linguistica, Semiotica, Epistemologia', *Il Protagora*, IV: 7–8.

Rasmussen, M. (ed.) (1993) *Louis Hjelmslev et la Sémiotique Contemporaine*, Travaux du Cercle Linguistique de Copenhague, XXIV, Copenhagen: Munksgaard.

Siertsema, B. (1954) *A Study of Glossematics*, The Hague: Martinus Nijhoff.

HOFFMEYER Jesper Hoffmeyer (b. 1942) is a Danish biologist, author and a leading pioneer in contemporary **biosemiotics**. As a student with a belief that the key to the mystery of life must hide in its chemistry, Hoffmeyer graduated as MSc in biochemistry at the University of Copenhagen, and went on a research grant to the Collège de France, Paris, 1966–1968. Back at the University of Copenhagen he became associate professor in biochemistry, 1972. In the 1970s, he engaged in studying the social embeddedness of science and wrote semi-popular books and articles on the philosophy of biology, in part as a non-reductionist response to Jacques Monod's materialist philosophy of nature, in part as a contribution to an ecologically informed macro-history of the energetic and technoscientific foundations of civilization. Both sides led Hoffmeyer, utilizing his academic freedom, to start a systematic reflection on the concepts of information, in their bio-ontological dimension as well as in their applied contexts related to the upcoming 'smart' bio- and information technologies of the 1980s that he analysed as dealing with genetic and cultural information, respectively. Searching for common functional principles governing bio- and infotechnologies, he conjectured that the kind of information they both handled could only be fully grasped through some theory dealing with meaning and interpretation of **coded** messages. Thus, in the late 1980s, Hoffmeyer was led to the semiotic traditions, in part through intermediate stations such as the polymaths Gregory **Bateson**, Michael Polanyi, Anthony Wilden, Howard Pattee and Peder Voetmann Christiansen. When finally connecting to Thomas **Sebeok** in the USA, Thure von **Uexküll** in Germany and Kalevi **Kull** in Tartu, Estonia, Hoffmeyer formulated a new programme for a scientific biology that would define life as a sign-based phenomenon. The first comprehensive essay outlining this theoretical vision of biosemiotics and its implication for a non-dualist understanding of the embodied self was his *Signs of Meaning in the Universe* (in Danish, *En snegl på vejen*, 1993). Since 2001, when the yearly 'Gatherings in Biosemiotics' began, Hoffmeyer has been a central figure in establishing biosemiotics as a scientific cross-disciplinary field, assembling scientists and scholars to investigate how the semiotic toolbox can inform current biological thinking, and how the findings of biology provide general semiotics with a firmer ground. In 2005 he was conferred with a Danish doctoral degree for his treatise *Biosemiotics* (see Hoffmeyer 2008a) that spells out a semiotics of living nature from the origin of life with its self-organizing code-duality in evolution and development, the complex endosemiosis in living bodies, the '**semiotic niche**s' in ecosystems, the self as an iconic absence, and the peculiarities of human semiosis, such as **language**. Hoffmeyer's contributions stand out as a visionary and detailed investigation of semiotic relations at the various levels of organization in living nature, sharing aspirations for a more integrative paradigm (coping with emergence, contexts and complexity) known as 'systems biology', but with a more relational conceptual grounding. **(CE)**

Further reading

Favareau, D. (2007) 'The evolutionary history of biosemiotics', in M. Barbieri (ed.), *Introduction to Biosemiotics. The New Biological Synthesis*, Dordrecht: Springer, pp. 1–67.

Hoffmeyer, J. (1996) *Signs of Meaning in the Universe*, Bloomington, IN: Indiana University Press.

Hoffmeyer, J. (2008) *Biosemiotics. An Examination into the Signs of Life and the Life of Signs*, Scranton, PA: University of Scranton Press.

Humboldt Wilhelm von Humboldt (1767–1835), Prussian diplomat and scholar, saw **language** as the key to understanding the human mind. He was acknowledged by many later linguists as an important influence. His magnum opus, *On the Kawi Language of the Island of Java*, was published posthumously (1836–1839). **(RH)**

Husserl ***see*** **Phenomenology**

I

IASS IASS is the acronym now most commonly used for the International Association for Semiotic Studies (a learned society alternatively identified as AIS, for Association Internationale de Semiotique). This organization, bilingual by constitutional provision, was created on 21–22 January 1969, by a group of like-minded individuals convened in Paris at the initiative of Emile **Benveniste**, of the College de France. Since its foundation, the Association proclaimed and has endeavoured to adhere to three principal aims: to promote semiotic researches in a scientific spirit; to advance global cooperation in this field; and to promote collaboration with local organizations worldwide.

The day-by-day governing body of the IASS is led by its officers, each of whom (excepting one, whose term is unlimited) may serve for up to two terms, usually of five years each. Emile Benveniste was elected as the first President in 1969, holding that office until his death in 1976. He was succeeded by Cesare Segre (Italy), Jerzy Pelc (Poland), Roland Posner (Germany) and Eero Tarasti (Finland). There are currently four Vice-Presidents: Adrián Gimate-Welsh (Mexico), Richard L. Lanigan (United States), Youzheng Li (China) and Jean-Claude Mbarga (Cameroon). (Earlier Vice-Presidents included Roman **Jakobson** and Yuri M. **Lotman**.) The first Secretary General was Julia **Kristeva** (France), succeeded upon her resignation by Umberto **Eco** (Italy); this position is currently held by José M. Paz Gago (Spain). The first Treasurer was Jacques Geninasca (Switzerland), succeeded by Gloria Withalm (Austria), a position now occupied by John **Deely** (United States) and Susan **Petrilli** (Italy). A ninth officer is Marcel **Danesi** (Canada), Editor-in-Chief of *Semiotica*.

The officers report to, and are in turn elected once every five years or so by, the members of the General Assembly with an Executive Committee, chosen from among (currently) thirty-eight different countries.

One of the Association's principal responsibilities has been the organization of periodic International Congresses, usually at five-year intervals: the First Congress, convened by Umberto Eco in Milan, was held in 1974, followed by others in Vienna (1979), Palermo (1984), Barcelona/ Perpignan (1989), Berkeley (1994), Guadalajara (1997), Dresden (1999), Lyon (2004), Helsinki (2007) and La Coruña (2009).

The other paramount IASS activity is the co-sponsorship with Mouton (formerly of The Hague, now Mouton de Gruyter, Berlin) of the 'flagship' publication of the IASS, *Semiotica*, established in 1969, now published in 2000 pages annually. By the end of

2009, this journal will have appeared in 175 volumes; an 800-page Index of Vols 1–100 was published in 1994, supplemented by a Finder List up to date through mid-1999. (**TAS** and **PC**)

FURTHER READING

Website of the IASS-AIS: http://filserver.arthist.lu.se/kultsem/AIS/IASS/

ICON One of three types of signs identified by Charles S. **Peirce**, the other two being **index** and **symbol**. The icon is characterized by a relation of similarity between the **sign** and its **object**. However, similarity alone will not suffice to determine an iconic sign. Twins look similar but are not signs of each other. My reflection in the mirror looks like me but is not an iconic sign. For iconic signs to obtain the effect of convention or **habit**, social practices or special functions must be added to similarity. Iconic similarity is a special kind of similarity: it is an abstraction on the basis of a convention, for it privileges given traits of similarity and not others. Similarity between one banknote and another worth $50 is no doubt a sign that the first banknote too is worth $50. But if similarity is complete to the point that the serial numbers of both banknotes are identical, we have a false banknote that cannot carry out a legitimate function as an iconic sign on the money market. All the same, as Peirce states, the icon is the most independent sign from both convention and causality/contiguity: 'An *icon* is a sign which would possess the character which renders it significant, even though its object had no existence; such as a lead-pencil streak as representing a geometrical line' (*CP* 2.304). (**SP**)

IDEATIONAL A term in **systemic functional grammar**, which assumes that any semiotic system must have the facility to communicate about states of affairs and events in the world. The ideational function indicates the salient participants, and the processes which relate them, usually seen as the 'content' of a sentence. (**GRK**)

See also INTERPERSONAL *and* TEXTUAL.

ILLOCUTION (ILLOCUTIONARY) In the terminological framework introduced by **Austin** (1962) to cope with the multi-functionality of all utterances (**locution**–illocution–**perlocution**), illocution refers to a type of act performed *in* saying something: asking or answering a question, giving a command or a warning, making a promise or a statement, and the like. The basic question is: in what way is a locution uttered on a given occasion of use? The answer to that question is an assessment of the function of what is said or its illocutionary force. Though the illocution is basically a functional category, it is not unrelated to aspects of form. Often there are clear markers of illocutionary force indicating devices such as **performative** verbs used in explicit performatives (e.g. *I promise to come tomorrow*), or the interrogative form marking a question or a negation (e.g. 'not' turning a promise into the refusal *I do not promise to come tomorrow*). In later versions of **speech act** theory (Searle 1976 onwards), the notion illocutionary point is introduced as one of the parameters along which classes of illocutionary acts can be distinguished: the point of an assertive is to represent a state of affairs; the point of a directive is to make the hearer do something; the point of a commissive is that the speaker commits him/herself to doing something; the point of an expressive is to express a psychological state; and the point of a declaration is to bring something about in the world. (**JV**)

FURTHER READING

Austin, J. L. (1962) *How To Do Things with Words*, ed. J. O. Urmson, Oxford: Oxford University Press. (2nd rev. edn, 1975, ed. J. O. Urmson and M. Sbisà, Cambridge, MA: Harvard University Press.)

IMAGE SCHEMAS In **cognitive linguistics** image schemas are entrenched preconceptual skeleton representations. They emerge from our bodily interaction with the world and capture the structural make-up and the outline of recurrent experiential patterns.

As semantic gestalts they play an essential role in conceptualization in that they structure human experience and therefore serve as links between perception and **language**. Since they apply across different domains, they are key to the understanding of meaning extension and metaphorical mapping. Thus *She is in love*, *She is in Paris* and *She is in the coffin* all specify a CONTAINMENT schema; whereas *She achieved her goal* and *She reached her destination* both activate the SOURCE–PATH–GOAL schema. (**PB**)

INDEX One of three types of sign identified by Charles S. **Peirce**, the other two being **icon** and **symbol**. The index is a sign that signifies its object by a relation of contiguity, causality or by some other physical connection. However, this relation also depends on a **habit** or convention. For example, the relation between hearing a knock at the door and someone on the other side of the door who wants to enter. Here convention plays its part in relating the knocking and the knocker, but contiguity/causality predominates to the point that we are surprised if we open the door and no-one is there. Types of index include:

1 *symptoms*, medical, psychological, of natural phenomena (actual contiguity + actual causality);
2 *clues*, natural phenomena, attitudes and inclinations (presumed contiguity + non-actual causality);
3 *traces*, physical or mental (non-actual contiguity + presumed causality).

'An *index*,' says Peirce, 'is a sign which would, at once, lose the character which makes it a sign if its object were removed, but would not lose that character if there were no interpretant' (*CP* 2.304). (**SP**)

INDUCTION Induction is an inferential process with ***abduction*** and ***deduction***. In induction, the relation between premises and conclusion is determined by **habit**. In terms of Charles S. **Peirce**'s typology of signs it is of the symbolic order. Both in abduction and induction, one is only inclined towards admitting that the conclusion be true, given that the premises can be accepted without the obligation of accepting the conclusion. Consequently, in induction, prediction, expectation and orientation towards the future weigh more on the argument than memory and the past. Contrary to deductive argument, induction offers the possibility of broadening belief by virtue of its opening towards the future, importance attached to the interpretant, and relation of the conclusion to the premises, which is not of mechanical dependence. All the same, inductive argument is simply repetitive and quantitative, given that its sphere of validity remains that of the fact, that is, of the totality of facts on the basis of which alone it can infer the future. According to **Aristotle**, induction (in Greek *epagogé*) is the method that leads from the particular to the universal (*Topicorum libri VIII*, I, 12, 105 a 11). Moreover he ascribes the discovery of this type of inference to Socrates (*Metaphysica*, XIII, 4, 1078 b 28). According to Aristotle, induction only demonstrates the mere fact and consequently has an insufficient demonstrative value. In post-Aristotelian philosophy, the **Epicureans** considered induction as the only method of valid inference, while the Stoics denied its argumentative value (Philodemus, *De signis*, III, 35). The Epicureans supported their position arguing that, until the conclusion is invalidated, inductive generalization is true. According to Peirce (*CP* 2.729) the pragmatic value of induction consists in its capacity for self-correction. In fact, the conclusion is not imposed by the premises and therefore is susceptible to modification. (**SP**)

FURTHER READING

Peirce, C. S. (1998) 'Deduction, induction and hypothesis', in *Chance, Love and Logic: Philosophical Essays*, ed. M. Cohen, Lincoln, NE: Bison Books.

INNENWELT ***see*** **UMWELT**

INTERCULTURAL COMMUNICATION ***see*** **COMMUNICATION, HALL** ***and*** **SOCIOSEMIOTICS**

INTERPERSONAL The interpersonal function deals with the organization and shape of (the clause in) **language** as a means of expressing the social relations between those engaged in **communication**. It is concerned with expression of both power and solidarity in social relations. (**GRK**)

See also IDEATIONAL *and* TEXTUAL.

INTERPRETANT The interpretant is a concept introduced by Charles S. **Peirce**'s **semiotics**. According to Peirce, **semiosis** is a triadic process whose components include **sign** (or **representamen**), **object** and interpretant.

> A *Sign*, or *Representamen*, is a First which stands in such a genuine triadic relation to a Second, called its Object, as to be capable of determining a Third, called its Interpretant, to assume the same triadic relation to its Object in which it stands itself to the same Object.
> (*CP* 2.274)

Therefore, the sign stands for something, its object, by which it is 'mediately determined' (*CP* 8.343), 'not in all respects, but in reference to a sort of idea' (*CP* 2.228). However, a sign can only do this if it determines the interpretant which is 'mediately determined by that object' (*CP* 8.343). 'A sign mediates between the *interpretant* sign and its object' insofar as the first is determined by its object under a certain respect or idea, or **ground**, and determines the interpretant 'in such a way as to bring the interpretant into a relation to the object, corresponding to its own relation to the object' (*CP* 8.332).

The interpretant of a sign is another sign which the first creates in the interpreter. This is 'an equivalent sign, or perhaps a more developed sign' (*CP* 2.228). Therefore the interpretant sign cannot be identical to the interpreted sign, it cannot be a repetition, precisely because it is *mediated*, interpretive and therefore always something new. With respect to the first sign, the interpretant is a *response*, and as such it inaugurates a new sign process, a new semiosis. In this sense it is a more developed sign. As a sign the interpretant determines another sign which acts, in turn, as an interpretant: therefore, the interpretant opens to new semioses, it develops the sign process, it is a new sign occurrence. Indeed, we may state that every time there is a sign occurrence, including the 'First Sign', we have a 'Third', something mediated, a response, an interpretive novelty, an interpretant. Consequently, a sign is constitutively an interpretant (cf. Petrilli 1998c: I.1). The fact that the interpretant (Third) is in turn a sign (First), and that the sign (First) is in turn an interpretant (is already a Third), places the sign in an open network of interpretants: this is the Peircean principle of infinite semiosis or endless series of interpretants (cf. *CP* 1.339).

Therefore the **meaning** of a sign is a response, an interpretant that calls for another response, another interpretant. This implies the dialogical nature of the sign and semiosis. A sign has its meaning in another sign which responds to it and which in turn is a sign if there is another sign to respond and interpret it, and so forth ad infinitum. In Augusto Ponzio's terminology (1985, 1990b) the 'First Sign' in the triadic relation of semiosis, the object that receives meaning, is the *interpreted*, and what confers meaning is the interpretant, which may be of two main types. The interpretant which enables recognition of the sign is an *interpretant of identification*, it is connected to the signal, **code** and sign system. The specific interpretant of a sign, that which interprets sense or actual meaning, is the *interpretant of answering comprehension*. This second type of interpretant does not limit itself to identifying the interpreted, but rather expresses its properly pragmatic meaning, installing with it a relation of involvement and participation: the interpretant responds to the interpreted and takes a stand towards it.

This dual conception of the interpretant is in line with Peirce's semiotics, which is inseparable from his **pragmatism**. In a letter of 1904 to Victoria **Welby**, Peirce wrote that, if we take a sign in a very broad sense, its interpretant is not necessarily a sign, since it might be an action or experience, or even just a feeling (cf. *CP* 8.332). Here sign is understood in a strict sense given that the interpretant as a response that signifies, that renders something significant and which therefore becomes a sign, cannot, in turn, be anything other than a sign occurrence, a semiosic act, even if an action or feeling. In any case, we are dealing with what we are calling an 'interpretant of answering comprehension', and therefore a sign. In line with his triadomania, instead, Peirce on classifying interpretants distinguishes among feelings, exertions and signs (*CP* 4.536). And in one of his manuscripts (*MS* 318), a part of which is published in *CP* 5.464–496 (cf. Short 1998), he also distinguishes among the emotional, the energetic and the logical interpretant. The latter together with the triad consisting of the 'immediate', 'dynamical' and 'final interpretant' are perhaps the two most famous triads among the many described by Peirce to classify the various aspects of the interpretant.

The relation between the sign and interpretant has consequences of a semiotic order for the typology of signs and of a logical order for the typology of inference and argument. Whether we have an **icon**, **index** or **symbol** depends on the way this relation is organized. And given that the relation between premises and conclusion is understood in terms of the relation among sign and interpretant, the triad **abduction**, **induction** and **deduction** also depends on it. (**SP**)

See also DIALOGUE, FIRSTNESS, SECONDNESS, THIRDNESS *and* UNLIMITED SEMIOSIS.

FURTHER READING

Merrell, F. (1993) 'Is meaning possible within indefinite semiosis?', *American Journal of Semiotics*, 10(3/4): 167–196.

Peirce, C. S. (1955) 'Logic as semiotic: The theory of signs', in J. Buchler (ed.), *Philosophical Writings of Peirce*, New York: Dover.

Peirce, C. S. (1992) 'Some consequences of four incapacities', in N. Houser and C. Kloesel (eds), *The Essential Peirce: Selected Philosophical Writings*, Vol. 1, Bloomington, IN: Indiana University Press, pp. 83–105.

J

Jakobson Roman Osipovič Jakobson (1896–1982). One of the most important contributors of the twentieth century to a scientific theory of **language** as a semiotic system. Graduate of the Lazarev Institute in 1914, Jakobson then enrolled in Moscow University. Co-founder of the Moscow Linguistics Circle in 1915, the St Petersburg OPOJAZ (Society for the Study of Poetic Language) and the Prague Linguistics Circle in 1926. His scholarship can be divided into his Moscow period (1915–1926), his Czechoslovak period (1926–1939) and his American period (1949–1982). Originally known as a representative of **Russian Formalism**, Jakobson became one of its major critics and, subsequently, a primary contributor to the **structuralist** paradigm. By 1957 Jakobson had become the first scholar to hold simultaneous chairs at both Harvard (specifically the Samuel Hazzard Cross Professor of Slavic Languages and Literatures) and the Massachusetts Institute of Technology. Other American affiliations include the Salk Institute for Biological Studies and a term as president of the Linguistic Society of America.

Jakobson was a major force in bringing Mikhail **Bakhtin** and Charles S. **Peirce** to the forefront of the American scholarly community devoted to literary studies and linguistics respectively. His theoretical contributions include a developed theory of invariance in the study of human language and semiotic systems, a re-evaluation of the Saussurean view of language, a sophisticated notion of relative autonomy, asymmetrical markedness relations and a multifaceted speech act model that continues to play a profound role in the **modelling** of human language. Some of Jakobson's most profound published contributions include *Remarques sur l'évolution phonologique du russe comparée à celle des autres langues slaves* (1929), 'Musikwissenschaft und Linguistic' (1932), 'Beitrag zur allgemeinen Kasuslehre' (1936), 'Signe zéro' (1939), *Preliminaries to Speech Analysis* (1952), 'Morfologičeskie nabljudenija nad slavjanskim skloneniem' (1958), 'Linguistics and Poetics' (1960) and 'Poetry of Grammar and Grammar of Poetry' (1961) (see Jakobson 1971–1985). **(EA)**

See also Prague School *and* Saussure.

Further reading

Jakobson, R. (1987) *Language in Literature*, ed. K. Pomorska and S. Rudy, Cambridge, MA: Belknap Press.

Jakobson, R. (1995) *On Language*, ed. L. R. Waugh and M. Monville-Burston, Cambridge, MA: Harvard University Press.

Waugh, L. R. (1998) 'Semiotics and language: The work of Roman Jakobson', in R. Kevelson (ed.), *Hi-Fives: A Trip to Semiotics*, New York: Peter Lang.

K

Kant Immanuel Kant (1724–1804), philosophical giant who changed the course of modern philosophy by asking the revolutionary question: 'How is synthetic a priori knowledge possible?' Kant answered that we should not presuppose that all knowledge arises from and conforms to objects of thought but, rather, that objects of thought conform to capacities for knowing or conditions of experience. This shift of view is known as Kant's Copernican revolution in philosophy. Since, according to Kant, space and time are forms of human sensibility and, therefore, necessary conditions of human experience, it follows a priori that all objects of possible experience will be situated in space and time. This is a transcendental deduction. A consequence of Kant's metaphysics is that we can only know objects as they appear (phenomena) not as they are in themselves (noumena or *Ding an sich*). This is Kant's transcendental idealism.

Kant also argued that human understanding presupposes, as a regulative principle, that nature is purposive. In his moral philosophy, Kant distinguishes between hypothetical imperatives, where action can only be understood in relation to human purposes, and categorical imperatives, where commands to action appeal to duty, not purpose. Kant's categorical imperative stated generally, 'Act only on the maxim which you can at the same time will to be a universal law', brings to mind the 'golden rule'. Charles S. **Peirce**, although much influenced by Kant, considered the view that the unity of thought depends on the nature of the human mind rather than on 'things in themselves' to be a form of **nominalism**. **(NH)**

Further reading

Körner, S. (1955) *Kant*, Harmondsworth: Penguin.

Kinesics Kinesics was introduced by **Birdwhistell** in 1952 to designate the study of body motion as **communication** in face-to-face interaction in which the actions of the face, head, hands and the whole body are viewed as culturally organized and learned by individuals as they become competent in the use of the unmediated communication systems of their culture. Kinesics was developed as part of an attempt to expand the scope of structural linguistic analytic techniques to cover all aspects of behaviour involved in face-to-face interaction. Birdwhistell proposed a terminology and conceptual framework paralleling that used in linguistics. The least discriminable unit of body motion effecting a contrast in **meaning** was called a *kineme* (analogous to **phoneme**). Kinemes combined into *kinemorphs* which in turn were proposed as components of *kinemorphic* *constructions*. Attempts to analyse body motion in these terms were rarely more than programmatic; however, the concept was highly influential in developing awareness of the importance of the role of visible bodily actions in communication. Today 'kinesics' may be found in English **language** dictionaries where it is defined as the study of how body movements convey meaning. It is also used to refer to those movements a person makes that are regarded as conveying meaning. (**AK**)

See also GESTURE, HALL *and* PROXEMICS.

FURTHER READING

Birdwhistell, R. L. (1970) *Kinesics and Context*, Philadelphia, PA: University of Pennsylvania Press.

KRESS Gunther Kress (b. 1942) has been central in forging social semiotics as a cutting-edge mode of investigating the diversity of representational production in contemporary reality. Social semiotics is founded on a social theory of the **sign** and claims that the relationship between the **signifier** and the **signified** is not arbitrary, but motivated. Not only this, Kress insists that there is a relationship of motivation between the world of the sign user and the signifier. This theory is based on the recognition that human beings produce signs as a result of their interested action as culturally and historically formed individuals within particular social contexts and relations of power. By placing human social and cultural environments at the centre of semiotic analysis, Kress emphasizes **meaning** making as unstable, transformative action which produces change both in the object being transformed and in the individual who is the agent of the transformation. Meaning making is a constant process of re-designing available resources for representation; thus the making of signs is not an act of imitation but of creativity and innovation.

Kress's work on multimodality decentres written **language** as the dominant mode of representation in a contemporary world which is increasingly privileging multiple modes of **communication**, particularly the visual mode. Kress has applied many of these ideas to rethinking language and literacy education in a global, plural society in which the representational resources of all people need to be harnessed for productive, social and humane futures. (**PS**)

See also HALLIDAY *and* MULTIMODALITY.

FURTHER READING

Kress, G. R. (2003) *Literacy in the New Media Age*, London: Routledge.

KRESS AND VAN LEEUWEN see KRESS

KRISTEVA Julia Kristeva, born in Bulgaria in 1941, has been working in Paris since 1966 as a semiotician, psychoanalyst, writer, literary theorist and critic. She is editor of the famous journal *Tel Quel* and teaches at Paris University VII as well as at Columbia University in New York. She has authored four novels, *Les samouraïs*, which mirrors French society, *Le vieil homme et les loups*, *Possessions* and *Murder in Byzantium*, and has written a trilogy, *La génie féminine*, devoted to

Hannah Arendt, Melanie Klein and Colette (the first volume of which has already appeared).

In her book *Le langage, cet inconnu* (1969a), Kristeva outlines the field of linguistics while pointing out its limits. These are traced to the history of linguistics and to its compromise with European culture, with phonocentrism, with the priority or exclusiveness accorded to the alphabetic script, etc. By taking into account the reflections on **language** offered by philosophy of language and **semiotics**, linguistics today has broadened its scope. At the same time, however, the epistemological paradigms adopted from the philosophical tradition at the birth of linguistics remain the same. Above all the notion of speaking *subject* is not called into question.

With her proposal of 'semanalysis' as formulated in *Semiotiké* (1969b), Kristeva had already attempted a sort of short circuit by connecting the linguistic and the semiotic approach to the psychoanalytic. She confronts the Cartesian ego and the transcendental ego of Husserlian phenomenology, the subject of utterance linguistics, with the dual subject as theorized by Freud and his concept of the unconscious. In Kristeva's perspective the unconscious implies describing signification as a heterogeneous process. This is best manifested in literary writing.

In *La révolution du langage poétique* (1974) Kristeva establishes a distinction between the *symbolic* and the *semiotic*. The symbolic designates language as it is defined by linguistics and its tradition, language in its normative usage. Semiotics refers to primary processes and to the pulsions that enter into contradiction with the symbolic. Literary writing is generated in the contradiction between the symbolic and the semiotic. Its value for semiotics, therefore, consists in its potential for exploring the experience of heterogeneity in signification processes.

Subsequently, Kristeva developed her distinction between the semiotic and the symbolic in a psychoanalytical framework. She analyses the heterogeneity of signification, which she also experiences directly in analytical practice, in her books *Pouvoirs de l'horreur: Essais sur l'abjection* (1980), *Histoires d'amour* (1985) and *Soleil noir: Dépression et mélancolie* (1987). But the questions of the speaking subject's identity and of heterogeneity of the **signification** process emerge just as well in situations of strangeness to language, analysed in *Étrangers à nous-mêmes* (1988).

The question of strangeness is also dealt with in one of her most recent works, *Le temps sensible: Proust et l'expérience littéraire* (1994). Kristeva also analyses the role played by strangeness (racial: the Jew; sexual: the homosexual) in Proust's *Recherche*. Literary writing can enrich our understanding of the outsider thanks to its dealings with heterogeneity in signification and with **alterity**. The more we recognize ourselves as strangers to ourselves, the more we are capable of greeting the strangeness of others. (**AP**)

Further reading

Kristeva, J. (1981) *Desire in Language: A Semiotic Approach to Literature and Art*, trans. T. Gora, A. Jardine and L. S. Roudiez, Oxford: Blackwell.

Kristeva, J. (1982) *Powers of Horror: An Essay on Abjection*, trans. L. S. Roudiez, New York: Columbia University Press.

Kristeva, J. (1984) *The Revolution in Poetic Language*, trans. M. Waller, New York: Columbia University Press.

KULL Kalevi Kull (b. 1952), biosemiotician and Head of the Department of Semiotics at the University of Tartu. He has been the editor since 1998 of *Sign Systems Studies*, the first ever **semiotics** journal (founded by **Lotman** in 1964), and since 1999 a co-editor of *Folia Baeriana*. He is the author of numerous articles as well as books and edited collections on theoretical biology and **biosemiotics** in English and Estonian. In addition, he edited the major 2001 special issue on Jakob von **Uexküll**. Originally a professor in Tartu's Institute of Zoology and Botany, he has done important work on ecology, such as his analysis of the sustainability features of 'wooded meadows' (Kull *et al.* 2003). Yet, his greatest influence in biosemiotics, supplementing his advocacy of perspectives from von Baer and Uexküll, is probably his institution of a 'post-Darwinist' theory of evolution as the backbone of biosemiotic thinking. Through his writings on the 'Baldwin effect' he has attempted to 'widen up evolutionary theory by putting explicit emphasis on the influence of mental processes in the broadest sense possible of this term, in other words as comprising semiotic interactions even at the cellular level' (Hoffmeyer and Kull 2003: 253). **(PC)**

See also BIOSEMIOTICS, ECOSEMIOTICS, EMMECHE, HOFFMEYER *and* NÖTH.

L

Labov The sociolinguistic work of William Labov (b. 1927) takes the relation between social and linguistic structures as the primary object of inquiry. This can be read in two ways. On the one hand, it establishes through precise empirical work – in the analysis of phonetic variation, and in quantitative documentation and evaluation of variation – the close co-variation of linguistic form and social structure. On the other hand, it can provide the theoretical basis and detailed description of the mechanisms of linguistic change. It may be most productive to see Labov's work as integrating sociolinguistic and historical inquiry by a single powerful assumption, namely that the 'correlations' which he has described are produced by social forces and processes; and that they are the same for the differences visible at the micro-level of **phonetics** as for the macro-level that come to constitute separate **language**s.

Labov's method was to isolate an element subject to significant variation within a linguistic community, for instance the *r* sound which follows a vowel (post-vocalic *r*) in New York English (as in bea*r*, pa*r*ty). He manufactured texts which differed in terms of this variable alone. This enabled him to establish its function as a marker of socio-economic position, and to describe how it functioned as a prestige-marker, correlating significantly with judgements about the speaker's socio-economic status, or about the status of an occasion of speaking (ranging from formal to casual).

Labov found consensus by all members of groups (in a socially stratified structure) on certain **meaning**s. These meanings were assigned on the basis purely of chosen markers. All groups related users of the prestige forms as possessing higher earning power; in terms of physical power ('good in a fight'), those who were of high socio-economic status tended to rate users of low-prestige forms highly, and higher than did those who themselves used the forms.

This procedure opened up what had previously been impressionistically understood as (linguistic) prejudice to quantitative description: making available a precise and new instrument for studying the mechanisms and processes of group formation, and the complex social–ideological meanings which sustain them. In microanalyses of this kind Labov could detect and describe evidence of ideological shifts and contradictions in group alliances, resistances by established groups to 'newcomers' – as for the residents of Martha's Vineyard who resented and rejected incoming 'outsiders' using hyper-corrected forms of the local **dialect**.

Labov's work has given rise to a large effort in linguistics: variation studies.

His assumption that the processes which operate on the micro-level are effective in the same way at the macro-level has enabled him to work in both (as in his work on language in the inner city, on verbal duelling, for instance). In some of his work the use of the framework of transformational **generative grammar** with its incompatible theoretical assumptions has led him into positions at odds with his foundational work, as in his enormously influential article 'The logic of nonstandard English' in which the attempt is made to erase, in the description, the difference between Black English and (White) middle-class forms. **(GRK)**

See also SOCIOLINGUISTICS.

FURTHER READING

Labov, W. (1972) 'The logic of nonstandard English', in P. P. Giglioli (ed.), *Language and Social Context*, Harmondsworth: Penguin.

Labov, W. (1972) *Sociolinguistic Patterns*, Philadelphia, PA: University of Pennsylvania Press.

Labov, W. (1994) *Principles of Linguistic Change*, Vol. 1, Oxford: Blackwell.

LAKOFF George Lakoff (b. 1941), Professor of Linguistics at the University of California at Berkeley since 1972, is a leading figure in the **cognitive linguistics** movement. Of particular importance to semiotics is his notion of *conceptual metaphor*, which he developed initially with philosopher Mark Johnson in their now classic 1980 book, *Metaphors We Live By*.

Consider the sentence 'That man is a snake'. In it there are two referents: 1) 'that man', called the *topic*; and 2) 'a snake', termed the *vehicle*. The linkage of the two creates a type of meaning, called the ***ground***, that is much more than the simple sum of the meanings of the two referents. Moreover, it is not the denotative meaning of the vehicle that is associated with the topic, but rather its connotative (cultural) meanings as a dangerous reptile. The question now becomes: Is there any psychological motivation for linking these two referents? The probable reason seems to be an unconscious perception that human personalities and animal behaviours are linked in some way. Lakoff and Johnson argued that such a sentence is, thus, really a token of a mental formula – *humans are animals* – that links an abstract concept (human personality) to the concrete traits we perceive in animals. Utterances of this type – 'John is a gorilla', 'Mary is a snail', etc. – are not, therefore, isolated examples of poetic fancy. Rather, they are specific *linguistic **metaphors*** manifesting the mental formula – a formula that Lakoff and Johnson call a *conceptual metaphor*.

Each of the two parts of the conceptual metaphor is called a *domain* – human personality is the *target domain* because it is the abstract concept (the 'target' of the conceptual metaphor); and animal behaviour is the *source domain* because it represents the concrete concepts that deliver the metaphor (the 'source' of the metaphorical concept). Take, for example, linguistic metaphors such as the ones below:

1 Those ideas are *circular*, leading us nowhere.
2 I don't see the *point* of that idea.

3 Her ideas are *central* to the entire discussion.
4 Their ideas are *diametrically* opposite.

The target domain inherent in these linguistic metaphors is 'ideas' and the source domain 'geometrical figures/relations'. The conceptual metaphor is, therefore: *ideas are geometrical figures/relations*. The choice of the latter to deliver the concept of ideas is due, in all likelihood, to the tradition of using geometry in mathematics and education to generate ideas and to train the mind to think logically. Such conceptual metaphors permeate everyday **language**. Lakoff and Johnson trace their psychological source to ***image schemas*** – mental outlines or images that are produced by our sensory experiences of locations, movements, shapes, substances, etc., as well as our experiences of social events and of cultural life in general. They are thought mediators, so to speak, that allow us to objectify our sensations and experiences with words in systematic ways.

Conceptual metaphors permeate cultural sign systems. The conceptual metaphor *people are animals*, for example, crops up in the names given to sports teams (*Chicago Bears*, *Detroit Tigers*, *Toronto Blue Jays*, *Denver Broncos*, etc.), in childhood narratives, in religious symbolism (Egyptian gods had animal heads, the main god of the Hindus is Ganesha the elephant, the godhead of the Aztecs was the green-plumed serpent Quetzalcoatl, and so on), in astrology to symbolize human character, and so on. We rarely detect the presence of conceptual metaphors in language and cultural practices such as these because they are largely unconscious forms of thought. (**MD**)

FURTHER READING

Lakoff, G. (1987) *Women, Fire, and Dangerous Things*, Chicago: University of Chicago Press.

Lakoff, G. and Johnson, M. (1980) *Metaphors We Live By*, Chicago: Chicago University Press.

Lakoff, G. and Johnson, M. (1999) *Philosophy in the Flesh: The Embodied Mind and Its Challenge to Western Thought*, New York: Basic Books.

LAKOFF AND JOHNSON ***see*** **LAKOFF**

LANDMARK ***see*** **TRAJECTOR/LANDMARK**

LANGAGE **Saussure**an technical term, not to be confused with ***langue***. According to the *Cours de linguistique générale*, *langage* is a human 'faculty', requiring for its exercise the establishment of a *langue* among the members of a community. (**RH**)

See also **PAROLE** *and* Hénault.

LANGER Susanne Langer (1895–1985) continued the semiotic turn in philosophy exemplified for her in the work of Ernst **Cassirer**. Langer saw that sign processes were equally at work at the lowest stratum of sentience and in the highest reaches of cultural forms. She pushed '**semiosis**' both 'up' and 'down'.

Her 'new key' in philosophy was 'symbolic transformation' of experience: philosophy was to study its conditions, points of origin and diverse logics. She argued that rationality was not limited to the 'discursive' domain but was extended and embodied in the realm of 'presentational symbols', such as art, ritual and myth, to which she devoted penetrating analyses. Her best-known works are *Philosophy in a New Key* (1990 [1942]) and *Feeling and Form* (1953). (**RI**)

FURTHER READING

Langer, S. K. (1990) *Philosophy in a New Key: A Study in the Symbolism of Reason, Rite and Art*, 3rd edn, Cambridge, MA: Harvard University Press.

LANGUAGE The term 'language' in common parlance has many possible **meaning**s but, most often, these are to do with verbal expression: national languages, **dialect**s, **accent**s, idioms, verbs, nouns, conjugation, and so forth. For **semiotics**, and particularly its semiological variants, this is also sometimes the case. However, it is a definition that lacks rigour and leads to confusion about the object under discussion. While language is now widely accepted to be central to the definition of what it is to be human, there is no consensus on what language actually is. The one point of agreement that does exist, however, is that English, Turkish, Chinese and American Sign Language (ASL), for example, are to be considered as languages; 'body language', music, animal **communication** systems and other semiotic devices like traffic signals, on the other hand, are not. Thomas A. **Sebeok** (2001d) warns against such misleading figures of speech. Moreover, the idea that the world is 'constructed in language', as derived from the **Sapir–Whorf hypothesis** and elsewhere, is multiply confusing in this respect.

Instead, contemporary semiotics proceeds from a conception of language as primarily a biological faculty of human **modelling**, the very constitution of the human **Umwelt**. This conception had already arisen in linguistics in the latter part of the twentieth century (see Augustyn 2009). Noam **Chomsky** and his co-workers posited an innate human propensity for language – more accurately, a **Universal Grammar** – which profoundly re-orientated linguistic study. Second, three key figures – Charles **Morris**, Roman **Jakobson** and Sebeok – two of whom were schooled in and contributed to modern linguistics, worked tirelessly to broaden the remit of sign study beyond the merely vocal. For all three, the sign theory of **Peirce**, itself a reformulation of the ancient doctrine of semiotics, was pivotal in their attempts to investigate the breadth of communication and **signification** and to define language.

Both the enterprises of Chomskyan linguistics and contemporary semiotics problematized the commonly utilized term 'language'. Chomsky's work presented a serious challenge to both common sense and academic understandings of language as a material phenomenon made up of words, sentences and so forth which facilitate human communication. After Chomsky it has become necessary to investigate the possibility that language is more adequately seen as a system of knowledge in the minds of humans.

Jakobson's studies of the **icon**ic and **index**ical qualities of vocal signs and his discussions of their role in certain speech disorders also challenged the frequently assumed **symbol**ic status of language. Terrence **Deacon** was later to extend some of these insights with an investigation, contributing to **biosemiotics**, which suggested humans share an iconic and indexical bearing with animals but that humans are quintessentially the 'symbolic species'. Even more important in approaching the elusive definition of language, perhaps, was the earlier work, led by biology, of Morris and Sebeok. In particular, the latter's investigations into animal communication – captured in the self-coined designation **zoosemiotics** – revealed a considerable amount about the *human* capacity for communication and signification. Contrary to the more credulous commentators on the attempts of experts to teach a limited repertoire of signs to captive primates, Sebeok's writings have repeatedly demonstrated the *exclusively human* propensity for what is to be understood as *language*.

What is known about early humans provides some important evidence for classifying 'language', 'communication' and 'speech'. It is thought that early hominids (*Homo habilis*, about two million years ago) harboured a language, **grammar** or modelling 'device' in their brains. *Homo erectus* (about one-and-a-half million years ago), with an increased brain size over his/her predecessor, also possessed the capacity, an as yet unrealized ability to learn a sophisticated human verbal communication system. However, verbal encoding and decoding abilities only came into use about 300,000 years ago with early *Homo sapiens*. Humans therefore possessed the capacity for *language* long before they started to implement it through *speech* for the purposes of verbal *communication*. Prior to the verbal form, *communication* would have taken place by nonverbal means, a means that humans continue to use and refine today (see Sebeok 1986b and 1988b; cf. Corballis 1999), and, in conjunction with the possession of **syntax**, constitutes language or the human Umwelt.

What had been clear to many linguists, at least from Wilhelm von **Humboldt** onwards, was that languages consist of a finite set of rules and a finite set of lexical items which together can, potentially, generate an infinite number of different word combinations. Even **Saussure** seems to subscribe to this idea in distinguishing ***langue*** from ***parole***, although his use of the word 'règle' certainly does not correspond to Chomsky's 'rule' and he does not formally present *langue* as a generative system. The product of applying the finite set is syntax or syntactic structure; yet even with the *seemingly* very social notion of generative 'rules' and their socially useful product, language resists being defined as a purely 'cultural' phenomenon in the sense of existing somehow separate from nature. Chomsky's contention is that at least some generative rules are inexorable in the same sense as rules of logic which humans are constrained to obey without even being aware that they know them. Hence 'rules' are not something that humans 'agree on' through social interaction.

The study of language cannot proceed through the dissection of human brains; linguistics, instead, has had to work backwards by examining actual language use in order to be able to theorize the constitution of the mental system which precedes it. Yet the problem remains: the search for a definition of language needs to take account of a human faculty which pre-exists its verbal manifestations. Organisms other than humans are not aided in their communication by the syntactic component; that faculty is, at root, a biological one specific to the species *Homo*. (**PC**)

See also **Sign languages** *and* Kull.

Further reading

Chomsky, N. (1972) *Language and Mind*, New York: Harcourt, Brace and World.

Deacon, T. (1997) *The Symbolic Species: The Co-evolution of Language and the Brain*, New York: W. W. Norton.

Sebeok, T. A. (1988) 'In what sense is language a primary modeling system?', in H. Broms and R. Kaufmann (eds), *Semiotics of Culture*, Helsinki: Arator.

Langue Saussurean technical term, not to be confused with ***langage***. According to the *Cours de linguistique générale, la langue* is 'a body of necessary conventions adopted by society to enable members of society to use their faculty of *langage*'. (**RH**)

See also **Parole** *and* Hénault.

Legisign Charles S. **Peirce**'s term for the third division of his trichotomy of the **grounds** of signs. A legisign is a **sign** which, in itself, is a general law or type. Conventional signs, such as words, are legisigns. Legisigns signify through replicas or tokens (instances of their application). There are different kinds of legisigns distinguished principally by whether their underlying objects are represented **icon**ically (as in diagrams), **index**ically (as in demonstrative pronouns) or **symbol**ically (as in common nouns, propositions or arguments). (**NH**)

See also **Argument**, **Dicent**, **Qualisign**, **Rheme** *and* **Sinsign**.

Levinas Emmanuel Levinas (Haunas 1906–Paris 1995), one of the most significant philosophers of the twentieth century, has profoundly contributed to semioticolinguistic problematics by dealing with the question of **alterity** in terms of the critique of ontology. His work represents an original contribution, alongside Hartman, Block, Heidegger, **Husserl**, Sartre, Merleau-Ponty and **Bakhtin**, to that multifaceted movement in philosophy concerned with the refoundation of ontology. Such refoundation contrasts with philosophies hegemonized by the logic of knowledge and reductively stated in epistemological terms. Levinas developed his thought in **dialogue** with Husserl and Heidegger whose works he was the first to introduce into France after having followed their courses in Freiburg between 1928 and 1929. (**AP**)

Further reading

Levinas, E. (1990) *The Levinas Reader*, ed. S. Hand, Oxford: Blackwell.

Lévi-Strauss **Structuralist** anthropologist Claude Lévi-Strauss – born in Brussels (of French parents) in November 1908 and still professionally active in his centenary year – has been associated with the University of Paris and College of France throughout most of his life. His earliest training there, from 1927 to 1932, was in philosophy and law. In 1934 he accepted a position in sociology at the University of São Paulo in Brazil, from which post he ventured on several field trips into the Amazon, intermittently between 1935 and 1938. From this background and in this crucible, fertile empirical fieldwork laid the foundation for a vast *œuvre* of ethnographic, ethnologic, and particularly theoretical, treatises. Anthropological **structuralism** took shape through Lévi-Strauss, but not without the integration of earlier and later influences in his life (**Marx**, **Kant**, Durkheim, Mauss, **Saussure**, **Jakobson**); he was also early to understand entropy in sociocultural systems.

At the outset of the Second World War, Lévi-Strauss lost an academic position due to the racial laws of the Vichy government. He relocated to the United States in 1941, holding a position at the New School for Social Research and serving, 1945–1947, as French cultural attaché. While in New York, he met Roman Jakobson, Franz **Boas** and innumerable other intellectuals from the USA and abroad (Sebeok 1991b). The contact with Jakobson and structural linguistics ignited Lévi-Strauss's intuitive handle on **synchronic** approaches to **language** and culture studies.

Lévi-Strauss's work until mid-century focused on kinship systems and marriage rules (e.g. 1949), while later he concentrated on belief systems embodied in myths and religion (e.g., his *Mythologiques* tetralogy 1969–1981 [1964–1971]). In both realms, his aim was the same – to reveal the abstract systems with their internal logics of relations, rendering coherent the often chaotic and seemingly arbitrary practices and beliefs at the level of social life (de Josseling de Jong 1952; Jenkins 1979).

Inspired by linguistics and especially **phonology**, Lévi-Strauss developed a methodology to elicit principles pertaining to universal systems of marriage alliance and of narrated myth. One such principle is reciprocity (1944), fed by exchange/circulation/**communication**, whereby the process has value over and beyond what is exchanged. Restricted and generalized exchange not only elucidates the circulation of goods, women and words, but goes further to explain the universal institution of incest prohibition. Proscription of sex and of marriage in the nuclear family and particular other entities leads to matrimonial alliances throughout the wider society; conversely, incest would extinguish reciprocity.

Lévi-Strauss abduced universal principles in abstract systems from empirical ethnographic observations and ethnological comparisons. His work is structural in its synchronic bias, and in its dissatisfaction with temporal (diffusionist and genealogical) explanations. History is relevant, but not because it is prior and certainly not because of authenticity claims. Between **diachronic** forms and between synchronic versions of cultural forms lie congruent transformational logics relying on the same intellectual techniques of analogy, homology, inversion, symmetry and redundancy.

Lévi-Strauss asserts that human mentality and human culture are molar, linked, universal, symbolic processes. A controversial thinker having immeasurable impact on contemporary intellectual thought, Lévi-Strauss has raised the bar for all of the human sciences. (**MA**)

See also DOUGLAS *and* PIKE.

FURTHER READING

Hénaff, M. (1998) *Claude Lévi-Strauss and the Making of Structural Anthropology*, trans. M. Baker, Minneapolis, MN: University of Minnesota Press.

Leach, E. R. (1970) *Lévi-Strauss*, London: Collins.

Rossi, I. (ed.) (1974) *The Unconscious in Culture: The Structuralism of Claude Lévi-Strauss in Perspective*, New York: E. P. Dutton.

LINGUISTIC SYSTEM In **structuralist** approaches, **language** is seen as a system of interrelated systems, arranged in a hierarchy of levels: the phonological system deals with regularities of sound; the grammatical system deals with regularities of form (both of elements such as words, and of structures); and the semantic system deals with elements and arrangements of **meaning**. (**GRK**)

LOCKE John Locke (1632–1704), English philosopher. By a tangled tale (L. J. Russell 1939; Sebeok 1971; Romeo 1977; Deely 1994b: Ch. 5, 2001a: Ch. 14), the word '**semiotics**' in English seems to derive as a transliteration from what would be the Latin ('semiotica') of the miscoined Greek term ΣΗΜΙΩΤΙΚΗ [*sic*] from the closing chapter of Locke's *Essay Concerning Human Understanding* of 1690. This original coinage Locke introduced to name what he also called 'the doctrine of signs', echoing the Latin expression 'doctrina signorum' widely circulated in the Latin university world of sixteenth-century Iberia, where, unknown to Locke, the idea had first been reduced to systematic foundations in the doctrine of triadic relation by John **Poinsot** (1632). Picked up by Charles S. **Peirce** as the nineteenth century reached its end, the term 'semiotics' gradually came into general usage over the course of the twentieth century, edging out its rival (**semiology**) as the term of popular culture for the new intellectual movement. In this way, to Locke has fallen the honour of naming the postmodern development that overthrew the modern epistemological paradigm (to which Locke himself in the main body of his *Essay* subscribed) in favour of, as Locke presciently put it, 'another sort of Logick and Critick, than what we have been hitherto acquainted with'. (**JD**)

FURTHER READING

Deely, J. (1978) 'What's in a name?', *Semiotica*, 22(1/2): 151–181.

LOCUTION (LOCUTIONARY) In the terminological framework introduced by **Austin** (1962) to cope with the multifunctionality of all utterances (locution–**illocution**–**perlocution**), 'locution' is reserved for the act *of* saying something. This always involves the act of uttering certain noises, i.e. a *phonetic act*. Further, it is always connected with the act of pronouncing certain words belonging to and as belonging to a particular vocabulary, and certain constructions belonging to and as belonging to a particular **grammar**, i.e. a **phatic** act. Moreover, 'saying something' is generally the performance of a phonetic and phatic act with a more or less definite sense and reference (together adding up to '**meaning**'), i.e. a *rhetic act*. In later versions of **speech act** theory (since Searle 1969) the term 'locution' is not in common use; it has generally been replaced by '**proposition**' (covering reference and predication, and leaving out the aspects of sound, vocabulary and grammar that were included by Austin). **(JV)**

Further reading

Austin, J. L. (1962) *How To Do Things with Words*, ed. J. O. Urmson, Oxford: Oxford University Press.

Lotman Juri (sometimes 'Yuri', or 'Jurij') Lotman (Petrograd 1922–Tartu 1993), scholar of literature and semiotician, co-founder of the Tartu–Moscow School. From 1939 to 1940 and 1946 to 1950 he studied at the Leningrad State University (1940–1945 in Soviet Army); from 1950 he was resident in Tartu and, from 1954, at the Tartu University (1960–1977 Head of the Department of Russian Literature, from 1963 professor). During the period 1968–1985 he was Vice President of the **IASS** (Terras 1985; Le Grand 1993).

Lotman's first explicitly 'semiotic' publication was 'Lectures on structural poetics' (1964) which formed the foundation to the series *Semeiotik: Sign Systems Studies*. Lotman's **semiotics** originated from distinguishing structure in **language** and texts (Lotman 1964, 1975), grounded by the notion of a '**modelling** system' as a structure of elements and their combinatory rules. The 'primary modelling system' is formed by **natural language** (cf. Sebeok 1988b), while 'secondary modelling systems' are *analogous* to language, or use language as material (literature, fine arts, music, film, myth, religion, etc.). In culture these systems function together, aspiring to autonomy on the one hand, creolizing on the other. Thus, 'cultural semiotics' became, for him, 'the study of the functional correlation of different **sign** systems' (Lotman *et al.* 1973).

Sign systems can be analysed individually, but their correlation is expressed best in the most important analytic unit – the **text** (Lotman 1976, 1977b). While culture 'is defined as a system of relationships established between man and the world' (Lotman and Uspenskij 1984; Lotman *et al.* 1985), the foundation of its description is a functional analogy between cerebral hemispheres, language, text and culture. From the primeval semiotic dualism – the splitting of the world in language and the doubling of the human in space – arises an asymmetric **binarism** of the minimal semiotic mechanism. Effectively, there is a division of systems into two main types: in 'discrete' systems (verbal, logical) the **sign** is basic and independent from behaviour; in 'continual' systems (**icon**ic, mythological) there are texts in which signs are depictive and connected with behaviour. In the first case language is created by signs, in the latter by the text. Thus text may simultaneously be a sign and one or more sign systems.

Understanding heterogeneity and coherence of text is inseparable from the notion of 'border'. The border segregates (guaranteeing structural cohesion) and unites (assuring dialogism with the extra-textual). Borders intertwining in time and space form a system of 'semiospheres' in a global semiosphere that is 'the result and the condition for the development of culture' (Sturrock 1991; Mandelker 1994; Deltcheva and Vlasov 1996; Lotman 2000 [1990]).

Lotman's semiotics is characterized by a firm connection with empirical material: analyses of text, literary history and biography (Shukman 1987). **(PT)**

See also Kull.

Further reading

Lotman, J. M. (2000 [1990]) *Universe of the Mind*, trans. A. Shukman, Bloomington, IN: Indiana University Press.

Lotman, J. M. (2009) *Culture and Explosion*, Berlin: Mouton de Gruyter.

Lotman, J. M. and Uspenskij, B. A. (1984) *The Semiotics of Russian Culture*, Ann Arbor, MI: Michigan Slavic Contributions 11.

M

Malinowski Bronislaw Malinowski, born in Poland in 1884 (died 1942), is one of the most influential founding British social anthropologists. From his work with the Trobriand Islanders of New Guinea he pioneered a set of principles for carrying out ethnographic fieldwork. He viewed that all societies should be understood as interconnected mutually functioning parts and, drawing on Freud, was able to show how beliefs such as magic were not primitive superstition but about individual psychology and also served an important social role. The publication of his fieldwork diaries in the 1960s, however, led to a critical debate about the nature of observing other cultures. His work was extremely influential in **sociosemiotics** circles from **Firth** onwards. **(DMac)**

See also Halliday.

Further reading

Malinowski, B. (1923) 'The problem of meaning in primitive languages', in C. K. Ogden and I. A. Richards (eds), *The Meaning of Meaning*, London: Routledge and Kegan Paul.

Marx Karl Marx (1818–1883). In the theoretical field as in politics 'Marxism' has interfered with an understanding of Marx's greatness as a thinker. Except for rare cases (such as **Vološinov/Bakhtin**, **Schaff** and **Rossi-Landi**), 'Marxist' theories of the sign and even 'Marxist linguistics' (an example is the 'Marxist linguistics' practised by N. Ja. Marr – see Marcellesi *et al.* 1978) have nothing to do with Marx's remarkable contribution to the study of **language** and social **communication**. It seems that Marx himself said: 'The only thing I can say is that I'm not a Marxist!' (see Enzensberger 1973: 456).

Marx suggests that 'From the start the "spirit" is afflicted with the course of being "burdened" with matter, which here makes its appearance in the form of agitated layers of air, sounds, in short, of language' (Marx and Engels 1968: 42). Language occupies a very important part of Marx's philosophy. His materialism is not mechanistic and accepts the historical dimension; it maintains a balance between 'natural' and 'social' factors in order to preserve continuity between human and non-human animals as well as to assess the qualitative leap that distinguishes what is species-specifically human from the rest of life on the planet. Language is the requisite for the passage from 'mere life' to **consciousness** and consequently to the organization of life. In other words, it is required for the move from **semiosis** to **semiotics**, from the mere passing of signs to the specific life of the human as a semiotic animal. Language is not one of several means of communication between the self and the other but the basis of the self and of one's relations, as self, with others. The possibility of 'having relations' and not merely of being in relation, which is a specifically human possibility, is founded on language.

> Language is as old as consciousness, language *is* practical consciousness that exists also for other men, and for that reason alone it exists for me personally as well … The animal does not 'have relations' … For the animal its relations do not exist as relations … Language is the immediate actuality of thought … Neither the thought, nor the language exist in an independent realm from life.
>
> (Marx and Engels 1968: 42, 503–504)

Marxian critique concentrates on deciphering the 'language of commodities' (Marx 1962: Vol. 1, Ch. 1), and on explaining the entire process of the functioning of such commodities as messages. In tandem with this, the critique of the fetishistic vision of commodities aims at demonstrating that the relation among commodities, and among commodities and values, are relations of communication among human beings and are all founded on social relations. **(AP)**

FURTHER READING

Marx, K. (1973) *Grundrisse: Foundations of the Critique of Political Economy*, trans. M. Nicolaus, Harmondsworth: Penguin.

Marx, K. and Engels, F. (1974) *Über Sprache, Stil und Übersetzung*, ed. K. Ruschiski and B. Retzlaff-Kresse, Berlin: Dietz.

Ponzio, A. (1989) 'Semiotics and Marxism', in T. A. Sebeok and J. Umiker-Sebeok (eds), *The Semiotic Web 1988*, Berlin: Mouton de Gruyter.

MEANING 'Meaning' is at issue whenever something can be said to be a *culturally established* **sign** of something else, whether linguistic as in 'The French word "neige" means snow' or non-linguistic as in 'A white flag means surrender'. Meaning generated in the use of signs may be intentional or non-intentional (though some scholars would recognize only the intentional variety, thus emphasizing the production side). It may be literal (where the link between the sign and what the sign stands for is explicit and fully conventional) or figurative or indirect (where further inferencing is required, even though a degree of conventionality is often involved as well, as in the case of figures of speech and indirect speech acts). It may be seen as 'timeless' (sentence meaning and word meaning) or as occasion-specific (in which case **Grice** would use the term 'utterer's meaning').

Various theories of meaning can be distinguished. A referential or denotational theory views the meaning of an **expression** as that which it stands for. A mentalist theory would relate the meaning of an expression to the ideas or concepts it is associated with in the mind of anyone understanding it. A behaviourist theory views the stimulus evoking an expression or the response evoked by it as its meaning. The meaning-is-use theory holds that the meaning of an expression is a function of the way(s) in which it is used. According to the verificationist theory, the meaning of an expression is determined by the verifiability of the propositions that contain it. And a truth-conditional theory defines meaning as the contribution made by an expression to the truth conditions of a sentence. (**JV**)

See also Bréal, Connotation, Denotation, Proposition, Referent, semantics, Signification, Speech act *and* Truth.

Further reading

Lyons, J. (1995) *Linguistic Semantics: An Introduction*, Cambridge: Cambridge University Press.

Medical semiotics The practice of healing is one of the world's oldest professions. The ability to recognize **sign**s of distress or injury existed well before the ancient Greeks. In that sense, all societies had and continue to practise a form of medical semiotics. Nevertheless, the term *semiotic* comes to us exclusively out of ancient Greek medical practice where *semiotike* stood for the process that professional physicians followed in evaluating signs of bodily disorder, understanding their cause, offering therapy where beneficial, and prognosticating the patient's future. Thus ***semiotics*** as developed by **Peirce** and others, *medical semiotics* as a subdiscipline of today's *semiotics*, and diagnostic practice in Western medical practice (sometimes referred to as *semeiology*) trace their origins to the same era.

The clinically produced, and professionally evaluated, sign is generally believed to be **index**ical. That is, the sign (e.g. an x-ray finding) is believed to be connected to its object within the body in a non-arbitrary manner. The x-ray image 'stands in' for some object which the physician cannot actually see. As indices, the signs produced by the body are typically considered to be semiotic phenomena, but have been of lesser interest to most semioticians because they are not thought to be culturally constructed and symbolic. Peirce spent little time dealing with the sign or symptom of bodily disorder.

However, there are several respects in which signs/symptoms of illness and the systems used to classify them yield productive information when subjected to semiotic analysis. Today, *medical semiotics* encompasses several approaches to the phenomena of illness and the body, some of it interfacing with ***biosemiotics*** and *ethnosemiotics*. Among the several assumptions which medical semioticians generally share are the beliefs that:

1 Every sign expressed on or within the body is a form of **communication**. The body consists not of static parts but constantly communicating cells and organs engaged in an exchange of messages within the organism and with the social and physical environment in which it exists. Medical semioticians recognize that even supposedly objective signs may be altered within the body in its relationship with its internal and external environments. Organs, cells and DNA transmit messages which may not be consistently interpreted and which appear in some respects to act with intention.

2 It is critical that we examine how healers know what they know and to what extent this knowledge is affected by events and beliefs beyond the biology of the body. The technologies that allow physicians to invade and explore the body are understood as a critical but sometimes suspect tool in the production of knowledge about the body.
3 Limitations are imposed by technology, economics, politics and belief systems upon the healer's and the patient's ability to generate and incorporate signs. The healer sees what he knows must exist. Signs and symptoms are categorized into illnesses that may or may not exist.
4 Patients are often assigned to specific categories of disease, deformity and defect in order to create for them a separate and undervalued identity.
5 The sign or symptom is always polysemous. That is, the sign is infinitely regressive, pointing back to events even beyond the patient's lifetime, and infinitely progressive, producing a multitude of interpretants over time.
6 A patient's signs (objectively produced clinical indications) and symptoms (subjectively produced by the patient) may bear little relationship to any internal event but are culturally/socially constructed narratives about the patient's life or about the society in which he/she lives, a manner of expressing what cannot otherwise be successfully and/or acceptably expressed.
7 Patients construct for themselves stories of illness separate from those narratives generated by the physician; they array signs, symptoms, events and relationships in order to coherently narrativize themselves. (**KSR**)

See also **Galen**, **Hippocrates**, **Polysemy** *and* Manetti.

Further reading

Baer, E. (1988) *Medical Semiotics*, Lanham, MD: University Press of America.

Nöth, W. (1990) *A Handbook of Semiotics*, Bloomington, IN: Indiana University Press.

Staiano, K. V. (1986) *Interpreting Signs of Illness: A Case Study in Medical Semiotics*, New York: Mouton de Gruyter.

Mental space Mental spaces are, according to Gilles Fauconnier, small representational entities which are constructed and combined while we talk and perceive. A mental space contains the elements actually represented in or referred to in thought, language and perception. It is therefore linked to online meaning construction. The mental space prompted by the expression 'hot potato' contains the meaning actually intended (the potato is hot versus spicy or something is delicate to handle), accessed by virtue of contextual cues as well as general structure: knowledge about potatoes, idiomatic expressions, etc. Human cognition is claimed to consist in setting up and linking mental spaces: thus, 'this lion is safe' is meaningful only against a standard mental space in which lions are represented as dangerous. Mental spaces are the key component of conceptual integration. (**PB**)

Metalanguage Generally defined as the use of **language** to speak of language. In the Jakobsonian speech act model (1960), metalanguage is represented in the metalingual function, an ever-present aspect of any linguistic event, which is determined by reference to the **code** itself. The metalingual function is particularly important in child language acquisition and in any form of second or third language acquisition. Manifestations of metalingual breakdown are discussed at length in **Jakobson**'s 'Two aspects of language and types of aphasic disturbances' (1956). Also relevant is Jakobson's discussion of the metalingual function in duplex linguistic structures in 'Shifters, verbal categories and the Russian verb' (1957). **(EA)**

See also DEIXIS, METAPHOR *and* METONYMY.

METAPHOR The discovery of metaphor is due to the Greek philosopher **Aristotle**, who coined the term – itself a metaphor (from the Greek *meta*, 'beyond', and *pherein*, 'to carry'). Aristotle saw metaphor as a product of proportional reasoning – an elaboration on literal **language**, not a systematic part of it. John **Locke** characterized it instead as a 'fault' of language in his *Essay Concerning Human Understanding* (1690).

Interest in metaphor as a cognitive phenomenon can be found in the writings of Friedrich Nietzsche, Giambattista **Vico** and, in more recent times, I. A. **Richards** and George **Lakoff** (among others). Richards is responsible for the terms used to name the parts of a metaphor today: in 'That idea is square', the subject is called the *topic* or *tenor* ('That idea') and the image used ('square') is called the *vehicle*. The meaning produced by the linkage is called the ***ground***. George Lakoff is responsible for showing that metaphorical language is a systematic part of semantics; not an idiomatic part. In semiotics, metaphor is seen as pivotal in guiding the interpretation of texts. **(MD)**

FURTHER READING

Danesi, M. (2004) *Poetic Logic: The Role of Metaphor in Thought, Language, and Culture*, Madison, WI: Atwood.

METONYMY In Jakobsonian theory, metonymy is no longer a mere 'figure of speech', but rather becomes one of the two defining axes of human **language**. Each linguistic act requires a selection from a set of pre-existing units and a combination of these units into more complex **syntagm**s. The axis of selection is primarily based on similarity relations, which are metaphoric in their essence, while the axis of combination is based on contiguity relations, which are metonymic. All forms of aphasia for **Jakobson** rest between these two extremes. Jakobson's contiguity aphasic disorders are defined primarily by the loss of metonymic relations. No manifestation of language of verbal art excludes metaphor and metonymy; however, one of the poles may be dominant (cf. Cubism and Eisenstein's cinematic art as examples of dominating metonymy). **(EA)**

MODE In the theory of **register**, mode refers to the channel of **communication** which is enacted in a speech **situation**. In a classroom, for example, the

field or the social practices which inform the linguistic interaction will be the general ethos or process of education. The **tenor** will be the power relations between the teacher who might be active in imparting information and the student who might rely on the teacher for this purpose. These role relationships will take place through the mode: the specific channel of pedagogic communication, typical forms of which include lectures, seminars, brainstorming, and so on. (**PC**)

See also **Halliday**.

Modelling A process by which something is performed or reproduced on the basis of a model or schema, whether ideal or real. For example, Plato's world of ideas is used as a model by the demiurge to create the empirical world. In **semiotics** models are based on a relation of similarity or isomorphism and are therefore associated to the **icon**ic sign as understood by **Peirce**. The concept of 'modelling' is present in the term 'patterning' as used by **Sapir** (1962 [1916]) to designate the original and specific organization of culture and **language**: *cultural patterning* and *linguistic patterning*. Among all social behaviours none is as dependent upon unconscious mechanisms as language. Unconscious patterning operates at all levels of **natural language**, phonological, **syntactic**, semantic and pragmatic. Natural language resists intervention by the individual and rationalization more than any other element in culture. However, it is also subject to transformation, but this is due to an internal 'drift' process. By comparison with all other cultural products, **natural language** is the most perfectly autarchic, unconscious and varied through internal 'drift' and for this reason it is the anthropologist's most important instrument for studies on the original patterning of culture.

'Modelling system' is used by the so-called Tartu–Moscow School. The expression 'primary modelling system' has been used since 1962 by A. A. Zaliznjak, V. V. Ivanov, and V. N. Toporov. In 1967 (English translation 1977a) Jurij M. **Lotman** specified that 'a modelling system can be regarded as a language'. 'Primary modelling system' is used to distinguish natural language from other semiotic systems. The expression 'secondary modelling system' is used by semioticians of the Tartu–Moscow School to denote human cultural systems other than natural language.

The concept of modelling as proposed by the Tartu–Moscow School comes very close to Sapir's. It confers upon language 'originariness' in modelling over other systems. As in Sapir, it involves the relativity of cultures with respect to such primary modelling and does not solve the problem of communicability among different languages and cultures, and of the multiplicity of languages, and still less the problem of language origin.

One way of developing and extending the Tartu conception is by connecting it to the biologist and semiotician Jakob von **Uexküll** and his concept of ***Umwelt***, translatable as 'model'. This approach is adopted by **Sebeok** (1988b) and Anderson and Merrell (1991b), who attribute the capacity for primary modelling to *language* as distinct from speech. Language is specifically designed to produce and organize world views, whereas speech is an adaptive derivation in *Homo* arising for communicative purposes. *Homo* evolved into *Homo sapiens sapiens* thanks to this modelling device and its species-specific properties, language. All animal species construct their own worlds in which things assume a given sense; the distinctive feature of the human species rests in its capacity for conferring an infinite number of different senses upon a limited set of elements and, therefore, for constructing a great plurality of different possible worlds. Speech, with its specific communicative function, appears only subsequently in the evolutionary process. The plurality of languages and 'linguistic creativity' (**Chomsky**) testify to the capacity of language, understood as a primary modelling device, for producing numerous possible worlds. On the contrary, verbal language and the natural languages in which it is differentiated are the expression of *secondary modelling* processes. (**AP**)

See also Kull.

FURTHER READING

Anderson, M. and Merrell, F. (eds) (1991) *On Semiotic Modeling*, Berlin: Mouton de Gruyter.

Sebeok, T. A. and Danesi, M. (2000) *The Forms of Meaning: Modeling Systems Theory and Semiotic Analysis*, Berlin: Mouton de Gruyter.

Zaliznjak, A. A. *et al.* (1977) 'Structural typological study of semiotic modeling systems', in D. P. Lucid (ed.), *Soviet Semiotics: An Anthology*, Baltimore, MD: Johns Hopkins University Press.

MODELLING SYSTEMS THEORY Modelling systems theory (MST) is a methodical study of human cultural systems developed by **Sebeok** and **Danesi** (2000). It elaborates the notion of modelling systems present in the work of Tartu Semiotics which emphasized the derivational character of cultures in relation to verbal **language**. Sebeok distinguished natural language as a prior, and therefore primary, modelling system to verbal language. The primary modelling system (PMS) can be defined as the instinctive ability to model the sensory properties of objects through iconic representational forms or denotata. Natural language or nonverbal language in humans includes **gesture**s, facial expressions, body posture, proximity, tone of voice, etc. In the secondary modelling system, reference to objects is made through indicative and **index**ical (extensional) forms or connotata. This is the realm of **syntax**-based models, such as verbal language – texts, but also media or technology in general. The tertiary modelling system is the capacity to further extend secondary models such that they acquire **symbol**ic values, constituting **paradigm**atic systems of symbols or annotata. This is the realm of **code**s, conventions and cultural structures, and it may include mathematics, literature and religions as well as such practices as veganism. Although particularly fit for understanding human cultural organization, MST can be used to grasp the nature of animals' models, for example the **icon**ic character of camouflage, the indexical function of the honeybee dance and the symbolic purpose of the bowerbird mating gift. As far as humans are concerned, Sebeok's innovation, an extension of Tartu thinking, lies in the positing of natural language – which, in an evolutionary frame, utilized **nonverbal communication** well over a million years before it utilized speech – as the infrastructure for all other human sign systems and as the engine of evolution. (**SC**)

See also Kull.

FURTHER READING

Sebeok, T. A. and Danesi, M. D. (2000) *The Forms of Meaning: Modeling Systems Theory and Semiotic Analysis*, Berlin: Mouton de Gruyter.

MORRIS, CHARLES Charles Morris (Denver, Colorado, 1901–Gainesville, Florida, 1979) studied engineering, biology, psychology and philosophy. After having finished his science degree in 1922, he completed a PhD in philosophy at the University of Chicago in 1925, where he taught from 1931 to 1958.

Morris's **semiotics** offers a general description of **sign** as embracing all that belongs to the world of life. He aimed at developing an approach to semiotics that could deal with all kinds of signs, and to this end he constructed his terminology within a distinctly biological framework, as emerges particularly from his book of 1946, *Signs, Language and Behavior*. For this reason Ferruccio **Rossi-Landi** – who as early as 1953 had authored the monograph *Charles Morris* – described Morris's research in terms of 'behavioristic biopsychology'.

But Morris's interest in biology coincided with the beginning of his studies on signs, or, as he said in the 1920s, 'symbolism'. His PhD dissertation *Symbolism and Reality* (*SR*), of 1925 (but published only in 1993), includes a chapter entitled 'Some psychological and biological considerations'. Therefore, the terms 'symbolism' and 'biology' appear very early in his work. Also, in the preface to *Six Theories of Mind* (1932), he states his intention to develop a general theory of symbolism on the conviction that the mind and the symbolic process are identifiable.

On describing semiotics as a 'science of behavior', Morris was not referring to a philosophical–psychological trend known as behaviourism, but rather to a 'science', a discipline yet to be developed, a 'field', to use his own terminology. Morris underlines that his behaviourism derived mainly from George H. Mead as well as from Edward Tolman and Clark L. Hull. From Otto Neurath he took the term 'behaviouristics' to name the science or field in question. And, indeed, differently to other behaviourists who apply psychology as developed in the study of rats to the study of men (as one of Morris's reviewers protested), these scholars attempted to develop a general theory of behaviour, a 'behaviouristics', says Morris, able to account for the behaviour of both men and rats, while at the same time accounting for their differences.

Charles S. **Peirce**'s **pragmatism** played an important role in the development of Morris's semiotics. This is evident in the monograph entitled *Logical Positivism, Pragmatism and Scientific Empiricism* (1937). In 1938, in addition to *Foundations of a Theory of Signs*, his groundbreaking contribution to the science of signs, Morris also published 'Scientific Empiricism' (both in the *International Encyclopedia of Unified Science*) as well as 'Peirce, Mead and Pragmatism' (*Philosophical Review*). In the latter Morris insists on the affinity between Peirce and Mead or between the original pragmatism of the former and the more recent version of the latter.

By comparison with *Foundations*, Morris in *Signs, Language and Behavior* (1946) consolidates the relation between biology, behaviourism and semiotics. His recourse to biology for semiotic terminology does not at all imply 'biologism', for there is no tendency to *reductionism* (the temptation of reducing a plurality of universes of **discourse** to only one, in this case the discourse of biology). From this point of view, his attitude was different from the reductionism of the logical empiricists or neo-positivists due to their explicitly physicalist orientation.

In *Signification and Significance* (1964), Morris develops his interest in values in addition to signs and indeed he establishes a close connection between semiotics and axiology. The word '**meaning**' has a dual meaning, not only the **semantic** (signification) but also the valuative (significance). At the same time, in this book Morris's semiotics confirms itself as an 'interdisciplinary enterprise' (ibid.: 1) focusing on signs in all their forms and manifestations, relatively to human and non-human animals, normal and pathological signs, linguistic and non-linguistic signs and personal and social signs. (**SP**)

FURTHER READING

Morris, C. (1938) *Foundations of the Theory of Signs*, Chicago: University of Chicago Press.

Morris, C. (1946) *Signs, Language and Behavior*, Englewood Cliffs, NJ: Prentice-Hall.

Morris, C. (1971) *Writings on the General Theory of Signs*, ed. T. A. Sebeok, The Hague: Mouton.

MORRIS, DESMOND Desmond John Morris (b. 1928) is a very popular sociobiologist, whose work has been influential in several fields, including zoosemiotics, and especially in the study of animal aesthetics (1963) and anthro-zoosemiotics (1969). A pupil of Niko Tinbergen, Morris started investigating chimpanzee drawings (Morris is himself a painter) in the late 1950s, successfully exhibiting a few apes' paintings *incognito*, making a point that – when assessed unbiasedly – animal art can stand the comparison with the human one. Later, his work focused on the animal components of human behaviour, resulting in his best-known (and most controversial) works, including *The Naked Ape* (1967). Morris is still active as a writer and TV personality. (**DMar**)

See also CLEVER HANS, HEDIGER *and* ZOOSEMIOTICS.

FURTHER READING

Morris, D. J. (1967) *The Naked Ape*, London: Jonathan Cape.

MOTIVATION *see* ARBITRARINESS

MUKAŘOVSKÝ Jan Mukařovský (1891–1975), one of the co-founders of the Prague Linguistics Circle (with R. **Jakobson**, N. Trubetzkoy, V. Mathesius, B. Havránek and S. Karcevskij) in 1926. His academic positions included a grammar school in Pilsen, a professorship at the University of Bratislava and, after 1937, a position as professor of aesthetics at Charles University. Scholarly works focus on the study of Czech poetics and the construction of a theory of structural aesthetics. Although

Mukařovský was the only member of the Prague Linguistics Circle who was not a linguist, he is considered by many to be one of its more influential members. Mukařovský's more notable works include *Príspevek k estetice ceského verse* (1923), 'O jazyce básnickém' (1982 [1940]) and *Kapitoly z ceské poetiky* (1948). Mukařovský became quite active in politics in post-war Czechoslovakia as a pro-Communist supporter and apparently abandoned his intellectual (structuralist) roots. **(EA)**

See also PRAGUE SCHOOL.

FURTHER READING

Mukařovský, J. (1979) *Aesthetic Function, Norm and Value as Social Facts*, trans. M. E. Suino, Ann Arbor, MI: University of Michigan Slavic Contributions.

MULTIMODAL SEMIOTIC FIELDS Multimodal semiotic fields is a concept developed by linguistic anthropologist Charles **Goodwin** to denote the multiply embedded sign processes that are always at work in any given instance of human interpretation. Originally working within the discipline of **Conversation Analysis**, Goodwin's work has evolved beyond the examination of talk alone to include the study of the sequential organization of moment-to-moment body positioning, eye-gaze and manipulation of the artefacts of the material surround whereby **meaning** is co-constructed in human interaction. Devoted to discovering and explicating the fine-grained details of these participant-fashioned semiotic resources and the essentially 'public' nature of **semiosis** *per se*, Goodwin conducted a decades-long study of the communicative interactions of an aphasiac man and his interlocutors, in addition to studies of workplace interaction in flight operation centres, courtrooms, archaeological excavations and surgical operating theatres. In all instances, Goodwin seeks to identify and explicate the many simultaneously available meaning-making resources that the interactants themselves are continually recognizing and manipulating in their acts of co-constructing communicative meaning. **(DF)**

See also MULTIMODALITY.

FURTHER READING

Goodwin, C. (2000) 'Action and embodiment within situated human interaction', *Journal of Pragmatics*, 32: 1489–1522.
Goodwin, C. (2006) 'Human sociality as mutual orientation in a rich interactive environment: Multimodal utterances and pointing in aphasia', in N. Enfield and S. C. Levinson (eds), *Roots of Human Sociality*, London: Berg Press, pp. 96–125.
Goodwin, C. and Goodwin, M. H. (1996) 'Formulating planes: Seeing as a situated activity', in D. Middleton and Y. Engestrom (eds), *Cognition and Communication at Work*, Cambridge: Cambridge University Press.

MULTIMODALITY A term introduced by **Halliday**an linguists from the mid-1990s who sought to expand the application of systemic functional linguistics (SFL) to the study of other communicative modes. This would advance linguistics from its 'monomodal' focus on **language** alone in an increasingly multimedia world. Non-linguistic modes of **communication**, such as images, sound and gesture, could be usefully characterized, like language, as made up of systems of choices with grammatical rules. Whereas traditional semiotic approaches to such communicative modes analysed individual signs and the way they connoted or symbolized, here the emphasis was on the way that signs worked in combinations.

There are two threads of multimodal approaches. A more direct SFL approach inspired by O'Toole (1994) in *The Language of Displayed Art* aimed to show how objects of art fulfilled Halliday's communicative functions for language, which are: communicate ideas and moods and have their own internal coherence. O'Toole analysed art by looking for the way that visual elements fulfil these functions. The less strictly SFL approach of **Kress** and van Leeuwen (1996) in *Reading Images* was additionally informed by the earlier semiotics of **Barthes** and the visual psychology of Arnheim, and was driven by their background in critical linguistics. Arguably in their best work they were more able to represent visual communication in its own terms and built their observations from the semiotic choices made by authors rather than simply seeking to force the visual into Halliday's functions.

Criticisms of multimodality centre around its lack of engagement with other theories of the visual and the imposing of a model of language on other phenomena. Others have argued that multimodal analysis is for the most part post hoc where examples are conveniently chosen that allow the models to be illustrated and which rely more on contextual knowledge than is acknowledged. (**DMac**)

FURTHER READING

Kress, G. R. and van Leeuwen, T. (2001) *Multimodal Discourse: The Modes and Media of Contemporary Communication*, London: Arnold.

Kress, G. R. and van Leeuwen, T. (2006) *Reading Images: The Grammar of Visual Design*, 2nd edn, London: Routledge.

O'Toole, M. (1994) *The Language of Displayed Art*, London: Continuum.

MUSICAL SEMIOTICS Major discipline situated at the crossroads of musicology and semiotics. Peopled by musicians and music scholars, linguists, anthropologists, semiotically oriented psychologists; literary scholars and natural scientists (psychologists, cognitive scientists, acousticians, computer specialists), the common denominator seems to be the belief that music is meaningful and signifying human – or animal – activity. The minimal prerequisite of musical semiotics has been reached when we say that music appears at least as two levels, the **signifier**, i.e. the physical, acoustic sound, and the **signified**, its meaning, value and content, and that these two levels are interlinked.

As an independent approach or even discipline, musical semiotics appeared perhaps for the first time in a congress held in Belgrad in 1973. Gino Stefani, Mario Baroni and Jaroslav Jiranek were active at this time. The first anthology and reader on the topic was *Fondements d'une sémiologie de la musique* (1976) by the French-Canadian Jean-Jacques Nattiez. Nattiez believed in a three-part model of musical semiosis consisting of poiesis, neutral level and aesthesis. He studied semiotically most varied musical phenomena from Debussy and Varèse to Wagner and Boulez, as well as inuit music.

Yet musical semiotics had its precursors in many academic traditions. In the United States Charles Seeger had got interested in semiotics as early as 1962. In Sweden, Ingman Bengtsson based his whole view on musicology on a model of 'chain of **communication**' in his *Musikvetenskap*. However, these figures remained solitary and were recognized only later.

In France a research project on Musical Signification was launched in 1984 in Paris, at the French Broadcasting company, with scholars such as Gino Stefani, François Delalande, Marcello Castellana, Luiz Heitor Correa de Azevedo, Costin Miereanu and Eero Tarasti. Soon the centre of the project became the Department of Musicology at the University of Helsinki. The project held international symposia in Helsinki, Imatra (at the International Semiotics Institute), Edinburgh, Bologna, Paris (twice), Rome and Aix en Provence, and international doctoral and postdoctoral seminars in Finland. The proceedings were systematically published in anthologies featuring works from some of the project's 500 members from all over the world.

Theoretically European musical semiotics developed in various directions, but **Greimas**sian studies were well represented, especially in France (Ivanka Stoianova, Marta Grabocz, Costin Miereanu, Nicolas Meeus, Bernard Vecchione, Christine Esclaplez and Jean-Marie Jacono). Tarasti's theories began with a strong **Lévi-Strauss**ian influence but steadily became more Greimassian. In the United Kingdom, Raymond Monelle started his career in musical semiotics under the auspices of the Musical Signification project; other scholars in the United Kingdom active in the field are Michael Spitzer, who has studied musical metaphors, the Mahler scholar Robert Samuels, David Pickett, conductor and Sibelius scholar, and Tom Pankhurst, who has applied Tarasti–Greimas models to Schenkerian-based musical analysis. In North America, the composer David Lidov promoted musical semiotics from Toronto, and has published books on both musical and general semiotics. The major figure in the United States, Robert S. Hatten, whose output focuses on the classical style, particularly Beethoven, has scrutinized tropes and metaphors and developed his theory towards the study of musical gestures. Other figures on the American scene include Leo Treitler, William Dougherty, Lew Rowell and Alexandra Pierce.

Internationally, musical semiotics has been recognized as one of the major approaches within general musicology as well as in semiotics. The study of musical signs reveals new sides in semiosis in general. It is also expanding to many neighbouring fields like philosophy (e.g. Daniel Charles in France), existential semiotics (Drina Hocevar in Helsinki), bio and zoomusicology (Dario Martinelli), vocal studies (Juan Miguel Martinez in Spain) and cognitive approaches (David Osmond-Smith, Lelio Camilleri, Mark Leman and Mark Reybrouk). **(ET)**

Further reading

Hatten, R. S. (2004) *Musical Meaning in Beethoven: Markedness, Correlation and Interpetation*, Bloomington, IN: Indiana University Press.

Monelle, R. (2000) *The Sense of Music*, Princeton, NJ: Princeton University Press.

Tarasti, E. (2002) *Signs of Music: A Guide to Musical Semiotics*, Berlin: Mouton de Gruyter.

N

Natural language The phrase 'natural **language**' distinguishes languages used in actual communities from languages that individuals or committees invent to promote international harmony (e.g. Esperanto), or to serve a special population (e.g. the Paget–Gorman Sign Language, and numerous American sign systems for educating deaf children). Applied to language in general, however, the adjective 'natural' carries various **connotations**.

In the tradition of Descartes and **Saussure**, some language scholars think that so arbitrary a system as language cannot have evolved naturally from other animals' **communication** (e.g. Chomsky 1957; Bickerton 1995). Others call language an instinct (e.g. Pinker 1994), implying its use is as natural as any other instinctive behaviour. But still others find evolutionary continuity by tracing language to **gestures**, the meaningful movements that higher primates make and humans interpret syntactically as well as semantically (Armstrong *et al.* 1995; Stokoe 2001b).

To the broad question 'Does language happen naturally?' the answer appears to be 'Yes, but only under certain conditions'. Natural or normal language acquisition requires both social interaction and functioning human physiology. Infants deaf from birth do not acquire a spoken language, at least not in the usual way. A review of many longitudinal studies of hearing and deaf children, in various language environments, finds that all children communicate gesturally for some months before they use the language others around them use (Volterra and Iverson 1995). Gestural communication appears to be a normal stage in an individual's acquisition of language – perhaps analogous to crawling before walking. (**WCS**)

See also Modelling *and* Sign languages.

Further reading

Armstrong, D. F., Stokoe, W. C. and Wilcox, S. E. (1995) *Gesture and the Nature of Language*, Cambridge: Cambridge University Press.

Neurosemiotics Neurosemiotics is the study of neuronal sign processes taking place in the central nervous system of organisms, especially the brain, where such processes are thought to enable and coordinate the semiotic accomplishments of *perception*, *representation*, *categorization* and the species-specific varieties of *cognition* that emerge therefrom. A still largely unrealized specialization within the larger project of *endosemiotics*, or the study of internal signalling processes in organisms, it shares with that project (and with the still larger umbrella project of **biosemiotics**) the conviction that such naturally occurring sign processes as neuronal *signalling* and **communication** must be examined in their fullness as signs *qua* signs, in addition to the in-depth examination of their chemical and electrical constitution that traditional neuroscience provides, but fails to examine in its semiotic aspects. Although an all but undeveloped undertaking as of this writing, a fully developed neurosemiotics would seek to empirically examine the ways in which individual and collective neuronal events 'stand for' something other than themselves, so as to engender the phenomena of understanding and thought. Given the inability of contemporary neuroscience to bridge the divide between the physical and the mental naturalistically, the future of development research projects such as neurosemiotics seems assured. (**DF**)

Further reading

Chernigovskaya, T. (1999) 'Neurosemiotic approach to cognitive functions', *Semiotica*, 127(1/4): 227–239.

Favareau, D. (2002) 'Constructing representema: On the neurosemiotics of self and vision', *Semiotics, Evolution, Energy and Development Journal*, 2(4): 3–24.

Roepstorff, A. (2004) 'Cellular neurosemiotics', in J. Schult (ed.), *Studien zur Theorie der Biologie*, Vol. 6, Berlin: Verlag für Wissenschaft und Bildung, pp. 133–154.

Nominalism The doctrine that whatever generality there is in the universe pertains to names and not to real things. Only particulars, or individuals, exist and universals, or generals, are merely creations of **language** for the purpose of referring to many things at once. In its most extreme form, nominalism takes the position that universals and abstract ideas do not exist in any sense except as empty names or words. This view does not necessarily imply that general terms are ineffectual or useless but only that they can always be reduced to expressions involving reference to nothing more than particulars or expressions that serve some logical purpose. On this view, universal terms of any kind are fictions. A more moderate form of nominalism, conceptualism, holds that while universals have no substantive existence they may have a subjective existence as mental concepts. Conceptualism is often regarded as a middle ground between nominalism and its principal opponent, Platonic **realism**.

The main arguments for nominalism emerged in the twelfth century with Roscellinus and Abelard and were further developed in the fourteenth century by **William of Ockham** in opposition to the realism of Duns **Scotus**. All of the main British empiricists were nominalists who, like Ockham, argued that general terms are in one way or another only linguistic contrivances for referring to many particulars at once. Following the widespread acceptance of evolutionary theory in biology, nominalism tended to merge with materialism to support a mechanistic physicalist reductionism of the sort advanced by Herbert Spencer in the latter part of the nineteenth century and, more recently, so successfully advocated by philosophers like Willard van Orman Quine and Wilfrid Sellars. In continuing to guard against what they believe to be the unnecessary multiplication of entities, modern nominalists deny reality to all sorts of abstract entities from laws and possible states to properties, sets and natural kinds. The denial that intentions and **qualia** are real and general is typical of contemporary nominalism.

With so many different abstract entities and generals now in the mix, there are many degrees and varieties of nominalism. Quine, for example, admits sets into his ontology, but otherwise only particulars. Although the traditional enemy of nominalism has been realism, some forms of realism are in fact quite compatible with nominalism. For example, what is now called external realism, the view that real things exist independently of all thought about them, is held by many contemporary nominalists. When nominalism is combined with external realism there is a tendency toward a Kantian isolation of fundamental reality from thought about it and to suppose that the principal content of thought is of linguistic or psychological origin. According to Charles S. **Peirce, Kant**'s view that all unity of thought depends upon the nature of the human mind, and does not belong to the 'thing in itself', is a form of nominalism.

Nominalism has significant ramifications for **ethics**, semiotics and other disciplines. Nominalist ethics concerns itself exclusively with the interests of individuals and is built up without any reference to efficacious purposes or to universal goods or rights. Nominalist semiotics rejects any robust distinction between types and tokens, a core feature of Peirce's semeiotic. (**NH**)

Further reading

Armstrong, D. M. (1978) *Universals and Scientific Realism*, 2 vols, Cambridge: Cambridge University Press.

Loux, M. J. (1998) 'Nominalism', *Routledge Encyclopedia of Philosophy*, London: Routledge.

Peirce, C. S. (1992) 'Some consequences of four incapacities' (1868), and 'Review of Fraser's *The Works of George Berkeley*' (1871), in *The Essential Peirce: Selected Philosophical Writings*, Vol. 1, ed. N. Houser and C. Kloesel, Bloomington, IN: Indiana University Press, pp. 83–105 and 28–55.

Nonverbal communication *see* **Communication, Gesture, Glottocentrism, Kinesics, Proxemics, Sign languages** *and* **Zoosemiotics**

Nöth Winfried Nöth (b. 1944), German semiotician operating out of Kassel and Saõ Paolo. Introduced the notion of **ecosemiotics** (1998, from his original 1996 article in German), as well as writing on the broad scope of **semiotics**, including **biosemiotics** and machine semiotics. He has also produced the most rigorous 'handbook' of semiotic research and theory (*Handbuch der Semiotik*, 1985 [translated into English, 1991], 2000). (**PC**)

O

Object Anything that can be sensed, reacted to or thought about, either directly or indirectly. Often limited to that which stands in some relation as separate from or other than something else, but sometimes extended to include real things in themselves (independently of their relations). When taken in the first sense, objects can be distinguished from subjects. Objects may be of an intellectual (mental) nature, e.g. Plato's conception of justice, or they may be natural (external), e.g. the hemlock that Socrates drank. Also, a goal or purpose; that for which action is taken. As a verb: to oppose or raise an objection. In the semeiotic of Charles S. **Peirce**, an object is anything that is represented in a **sign**. If the object of a sign is of the nature of a character, the sign's **interpretant** will be a feeling. If the object is an existential thing or event, the interpretant will be a resistance or reaction. If the object is a law, the interpretant will be a thought. According to Peirce, signs involve two kinds of objects: immediate objects, which are just what signs represent them to be, and dynamical objects, which are instrumental in the determination of their signs but are not immediately represented in them. Signs cannot express dynamical objects but can only indicate them and leave it to interpreters to find them by 'collateral experience' (Peirce 1998b: 498). (**NH**)

FURTHER READING

Réthoré, J. (ed.) (1993) *Variations sur l'objet*, special issue of *European Journal for Semiotic Studies*, 5(1/2).

Ockham *see* **William of Ockham**

Ogden Charles Kay Ogden (1889–1957) was unquestionably a polymath, known above all for his book with Ivor A. **Richards**, *The Meaning of Meaning* (1923). As a student at Cambridge University, Ogden was one of the founders of the Heretic Society for the discussion of problems concerning not only religion but also topics related to philosophy, art, science, etc. He worked as editor of the *Cambridge Magazine* and subsequently of *Psyche* (1923–1952), a journal of general and linguistic psychology. Among his various undertakings he founded the Orthological Institute and invented Basic English, an international **language** comprising 850 words for people with no knowledge of English.

The orientation and development of his research was significantly influenced by his relationship with Victoria, Lady **Welby** and Richards. The unpublished correspondence between Ogden and Welby (1910–1911) is of noteworthy interest from the viewpoint of the connection between Welby's **significs** and the conception of meaning proposed in the above-mentioned book by Ogden and Richards (cf. Gordon 1990;

Petrilli 1995b, 1998a, d). As a young university student Ogden was an enthusiastic promoter of significs and in 1911 he gave a paper for the Heretic Society on 'The progress of significs' (cf. Ogden 1994). In *The Meaning of Meaning* Ogden and Richards (1923) propose a triadic schema of the sign where interpretation and meaning emerge as relational processes, ensuing from the dynamic interaction between **sign** (or **representamen**), **interpretant** and **object**, or in the authors' terminology, between ***symbol***, *reference* and ***referent***. In this book, while the importance of Charles S. **Peirce** for **semiotics** is recognized with the insertion of a section devoted to him in the Appendix with which his ideas were introduced and made to circulate for the first time in England alongside the names of other important figures, Welby is mentioned but the significance of her contribution is not sufficiently acknowledged. (**SP**)

FURTHER READING

Gordon, T. W. (1991) 'The semiotics of C. K. Ogden', in T. A. Sebeok and J. Umiker-Sebeok (eds), *Recent Developments in Theory and History. The Semiotic Web 1990*, Berlin: Mouton de Gruyter, pp. 111–177.

ONOMATOPOEIA The process of forming a word based on the sound of what the word names. Examples in English are *cuckoo* and *hiss*. In other **languages** we find words like Hebrew *bak-buk*, 'bottle' (from the sound that liquid makes as it comes out), Shona (a Zimbabwean language) *vhuvhuta*, 'to blow like the wind', and German *knusprig*, 'crisp, crunchy'. (**RS**)

OPEN TEXT In 1962, *L'opera aperta* (*The Open Work*, 1989) found many readers disagreeing on the innovative and somewhat controversial proposals of Umberto **Eco**. Today the expression 'open work' has become such a popular expression that it does not always refer to the original views of the Italian semiotician and novelist.

Eco's 'poetic of the open work' was a reaction to Benedetto Croce's idealistic aesthetics on inspiration, form and content; it was also the result of having studied under the supervision of Luigi Pareyson whose philosophical teachings on aesthetics focused on how art is a cognitive experience and how it knows the world through its formal structures.

The Open Work precedes a number of theoretical concepts on the dialectics between author, **text** and reader that in the 1960s and 1970s were revolutionizing literary criticism; and it announces a number of strategies foreseen by authors who regard readers as possible collaborators in the genesis of their work. In his essays we can easily detect elements of **Barthes**' notion of 'readers as collaborators', of 'reader reception theories' popularized by Wolfgang Iser and Roman Ingarden, and of the new approaches to art and literature proposed by the avant-garde and experimental 'Gruppo 63' in Italy.

The reflections on aspects and degrees of 'openness' begin with references to the musical compositions of Berio, Pousseur and Stockhausen which give complete (interpretative) freedom to artists who wish to perform them. What follows is a variety of observations on such diverse forms of expression as Calder's mobiles, Baroque and Impressionist poetics, kitsch, Antonioni's movies, Mallarmé's poetry and Joyce's novels, in order to examine what is meant by an 'open' structure. The remarks about composers, artists, movie directors and audience are all implicitly linked to the views on open texts and readers.

The key words and expressions at the centre of 'openness' are ambiguity, discontinuity, possibility, plurivocal, indeterminancy, movement, on-going process, performance and free interplay. The underlining motif throughout the essays is that an open work does not suggest any conclusion or specific interpretation as it demands a free inventive response from the performer/reader.

An open work continuously transforms its **denotation**s in **connotation**s and its **signified**s in **signifier**s of other signifieds.

This process of decoding remains open and on-going, guaranteeing open readings of the text. With open works every reading/interpretation may explain a text but will not exhaust it because its inner laws are based on ambiguity (e.g. Joyce's *Finnegan's Wake*). Moreover, open texts are systems of relationships that emphasize the genesis of processes rather than messages. They also encourage an active collaboration with the author and invite a free play of associations that functions as divertissement and as an instrument of cognition. For Eco the openness of a work of art is the very condition of aesthetic pleasure and it is an epistemological metaphor of our society. Openness transcends historical parameters (an example might be the way that Dante's *Commedia*, though containing highly specific messages, is still pleasurable today) and allows a work to remain valid for a long time. (**RC**)

See also CLOSED TEXT.

FURTHER READING

Eco, U. (1989) *The Open Work*, trans. A. Cancogni, Cambridge, MA: Harvard University Press.

ORDINARY LANGUAGE PHILOSOPHY Ordinary **language** philosophy is often referred to as 'Oxford Philosophy' because it was largely developed by a group of philosophers working in Oxford (from the 1930s till the 1960s), including J. L. **Austin**, P. F. Strawson and H. P. **Grice** (who later moved to the USA). This tradition emerged against the background of earlier forms of analytical philosophy (beginning in the late nineteenth century) which represented a 'linguistic turn' in philosophy, paying explicit attention to the problem of knowledge in its relation to language, as influenced by or represented in the work of Frege, G. E. Moore, Russell, the early **Wittgenstein** and Carnap. In contrast to earlier analytical philosophy, ordinary language philosophy (to which the later Wittgenstein contributed strongly from Cambridge) shifted its concerns from reduction and reformulation to description and elucidation and switched from the language of science as its primary object to ordinary everyday language. In the context of this emphasis on actual language use, utterances also came to be viewed as forms of action, the basic observation that gave rise to **speech act** theory as first formulated by Austin and further developed by Searle. **(JV)**

FURTHER READING

Austin, J. L. (1961) *Philosophical Papers*, Oxford: Oxford University Press.

OTHERNESS *see* ALTERITY

P

Paradigm (Paradigmatic) Technical term in neo-Saussurean linguistics, but one which **Saussure** himself did not use. It often replaces Saussure's *série associative* ('associative series'), which is a set of signs linked by partial resemblances, either in form or in **meaning**. Saussure described such sets as being established 'in the memory' and the items thus associated as forming a 'mnemonic series'. Substituting paradigmatic for associative seems to place the emphasis rather on the notion (which Saussure discusses) of sets of items related by the possibilities of substitution in a particular position. The flexional paradigm familiar from Latin grammar (*dominus*, *dominum*, *domini*, etc.) is cited by Saussure as just one type of example of an associative series. (**RH**)

See also Syntagm.

Parole **Saussure**an technical term for the linguistic level at which individual **speech act**s occur. Two persons talking to each other constitute the minimum 'speech circuit' (*circuit de la parole*). The speech act (*acte de parole*) is entirely under the control of the individual, unlike *la* ***langue***. (**RH**)

Peirce Charles Sanders Peirce (Cambridge, MA, 1839–Milford, PA, 1914), an American scientist, historian of science, logician, mathematician and philosopher of international fame. He founded contemporary **semiotics**, a general theory of **sign**s which he equated with logic and the theory of inference, especially **abduction**, and later with **pragmatism**, or as he preferred, **pragmaticism**. Peirce graduated from Harvard College in 1859 and then received an MSc from Harvard University's newly founded Lawrence Scientific School in 1863. His thirty-one-year employment as a research scientist in the US Coast and Geodetic Survey ended in 1891. Apart from short-term lectureships in logic and philosophy of science at the Johns Hopkins University in Baltimore (1879–1884), at the Lowell Institute in Boston (1866), and at Harvard (1865, 1869–1870, 1903, 1907), as well as at private homes in Cambridge (1898 and in other years), Peirce worked in isolation, outside the academic community. He had difficulty publishing during his lifetime. A selection of published and unpublished writings were eventually prepared in the *Collected Papers*, the first of which appeared in 1931. But an anthology of his writings edited by M. R. Cohen and entitled *Chance, Love and Logic* had already been published in 1923. His works are now being organized chronologically into a thirty-volume critical edition under the general title *Writings of Charles S. Peirce: A Chronological Edition* (Indianapolis, IN: Peirce Edition Project), the first volume having appeared in 1982. In a letter to Victoria, Lady **Welby** (1837–1912) of 23 December 1908, Peirce, who was nearly seventy, conveys a sense of the inclusive scope of his semiotic perspective when he says:

> it has never been in my power to study anything – mathematics, ethics, metaphysics, gravitation, thermodynamics, optics, chemistry, comparative anatomy, astronomy, psychology, **phonetics**, economics, the history of science, whist, men and women, wine, metrology, except as a study of semeiotic.
>
> (in Hardwick 1977: 85–86)

As anticipated in a paper of 1905, 'Issues of pragmaticism' (Peirce 1998c [1905]), in Peirce's conception the entire universe, the universe of existents and the universe of our conceptual constructions about them, that wider universe we are accustomed to refer to as ***truth*** of which the universe of existents is only a part, 'all this universe is perfused with signs, if it is not composed exclusively of signs' (*CP* 5.448, n. 1).

While developing a general model of sign, Peirce was particularly interested in a theory of method. His research focused specifically on the sciences and therefore on the search for a scientific method. However, in the perspective of Peircean pragmatism, knowledge understood in terms of innovation and inventiveness is not conceived as a purely epistemic process. Knowledge presupposes ethical knowledge, responsiveness to the other, which the self listens to both as the other from self and as the other self: for there to be an interpreted sign, an **object** of interpretation, there must be an **interpretant**, even when we are dealing with cognitive signs in a strict sense. The sign as a sign is other; in other words it may be characterized as a sign because of its structural opening to the other and therefore as **dialogue** with the other. This implies that the sign's identity is grounded in the logic of **alterity**. Consequently, learning, knowledge, wisdom, understanding and sagacity in their various forms are situated in a sign situation which, in the last analysis, is given over to the other, is listening to the other. Cognitive identity is subject to the other and as such is continually put into crisis by the restlessness of signs that the appeal of the other inexorably provokes. Therefore, insofar as it is part of the sign network by virtue of which alone it earns its status as sign, the cognitive sign is placed and modelled in a context that is irreducibly ethical. **(SP)**

See also **ARGUMENT**, **DICENT**, **GROUND**, **HABIT**, **ICON**, **INDEX**, **LEGISIGN**, **QUALISIGN**, **REPRESENTAMEN**, **RHEME**, **SINSIGN**, **SYMBOL** *and* Houser.

FURTHER READING

Brent, J. (1998) *Charles Sanders Peirce: A Life*, rev. and enlarged edn, Bloomington, IN: Indiana University Press.

Peirce, C. S. (1998) *The Essential Peirce: Selected Philosophical Writings*, Vol. 2, ed. Peirce Edition Project, Bloomington, IN: Indiana University Press.

Peirce, C. S. (1992) *The Essential Peirce: Selected Philosophical Writings*, Vol. 1, ed. N. Houser and C. Kloesel, Bloomington, IN: Indiana University Press.

Performance The actual use of a **language** in concrete situations, as opposed to **competence**, the knowledge of a language. Although grammars and dictionaries describe competence, the study of performance is increasingly important, both for scientific reasons (sometimes performance has systematic features which do not directly reflect competence) and for practical reasons, since second language learners need help to perform authentically. (**RS**)

Performative In the contrast **constative**–performative, 'performative' refers to a category of utterances (such as 'I name this ship the Queen Elizabeth', 'I apologize', 'I welcome you', 'I advise you to do it') which do not just *say something* but which serve to *perform an action* (e.g. baptizing a ship, apologizing, welcoming or offering advice). Performatives cannot be said to be true or false (even if a dimension of **truth** may be involved, as when someone is judged to be guilty of a crime), but they are liable to a dimension of criticism based on criteria of 'felicity'. Thus 'I name this ship the Queen Elizabeth' is felicitous only if the speaker has the proper authority to baptize the ship (otherwise the act is 'null' or 'void'), or 'I apologize' is felicitous only if the speaker intends to express regret (otherwise the utterance is 'abused').

J. L. **Austin** (1962) introduced a distinction between *primary* and *explicit* performatives. In contrast to primary performatives (such as 'I'll come tomorrow'), explicit performatives (such as 'I promise to come tomorrow') contain an explicit indication of the act that is being performed, e.g. a performative verb used in the first person singular indicative active ('promise' in this case). Often the term 'performative utterance' is reserved for the narrower category of 'explicit performatives' (e.g. in Searle 1989). (**JV**)

See also Speech act.

Further reading

Verschueren, J. (1995) 'The conceptual basis of performativity', in M. Shibatani and S. Thompson (eds), *Essays in Semantics and Pragmatics*, Amsterdam: John Benjamins, pp. 299–321.

Perlocution (Perlocutionary) In the terminological framework introduced by **Austin** (1962) to cope with the multi-functionality of all utterances (**locution–illocution**–perlocution), perlocution is reserved for the act performed *by* saying something. In Austin's words:

> Saying something will often, or even normally, produce certain consequential effects upon the feelings, thoughts, or actions of the audience, or of the speaker, or of other persons: and it may be done with the design, intention, or purpose of producing them.
> (ibid.: 101)

Arguing that such consequential effects are not part of the **language** system or that they are too random, unstable and unpredictable to be handled as constitutive properties of types of speech acts, Searle (1969) decided to leave perlocutionary aspects largely undiscussed. Others have tried to preserve the role of the notion 'perlocution' in **speech act** theory by considering that all illocutionary act types must have certain effects that are typically associated with them even though their actual emergence is not predictable. Thus assertives are typically intended to inform an audience of a state of affairs, questions are typically intended to elicit answers and promises are typically intended to generate trust in the speaker's future course or action, just like directives are typically intended to make the hearer do something (which would even be regarded as their illocutionary point). (**JV**)

FURTHER READING

Austin, J. L. (1962) *How To Do Things with Words*, ed. J. O. Urmson, Oxford: Oxford University Press. (2nd rev. edn, 1975, ed. J. O. Urmson and M. Sbisà, Cambridge, MA: Harvard University Press.)

PETER OF SPAIN Peter of Spain (Petrus Hispanus) was born in Lisbon sometime before 1205. From 1220 to 1229 he studied at the University of Paris, a famous centre for studies in logic, philosophy and theology. He studied medicine in Salerno or Montpellier and graduated *c.* 1235. He had already written his *Summule logicales* or *Tractatus* (critical edn 1972), the work which gained him fame ('e Pietro Ispano/lo qual già luce in dodici libelli', Dante, *Paradise*, XII, 134–135), some years before, in the early 1230s, presumably while living in the north of Spain. He taught medicine at the University of Siena, from 1245 to 1250. In 1276 he became Pope under the name of John XXI. He continued his pursuit of scientific studies in an apartment equipped for the purpose built alongside the Papal Palace at Viterbo, where he met his tragic death in 1277 when the roof of his study collapsed in on him.

In the *Tractatus*, Peter of Spain systematized and explained logic as it had developed so far, in depth and with originality. He locates the **sign** within the complex process of **semiosis** identifying its fundamental aspects. His model of sign anticipated that of Charles S. **Peirce** (cf. Ponzio 1990c; Ponzio and Petrilli 1996). The correspondences that emerge are indicative of the orientation of the *Tractatus* and his anticipation of Peirce: *vox significativa* = **representamen**; *significatio* or *rapresentatio* = **interpretant**; *res significata* or *representata* = immediate **object**; *acceptio pro* = to stand for; and *aliquid* (the **referent** of *acceptio*) = dynamic object. This explains **Peirce**'s interest in Peter of Spain whom he cites on numerous occasions. (**AP**)

See also SEMIOTICS.

FURTHER READING

Ponzio, A. (1990) 'Meaning and referent in Peter of Spain', in *Man as a Sign*, trans., ed., intro. and appendices S. Petrilli, Berlin: Mouton de Gruyter.

PETRILLI Susan Petrilli (b. 1954), Australian–Italian semiotician based in the 'Bari School'. Theorist of semioethics, **dialogue**, global **communication** and **alterity**, she has also been instrumental in promoting her *maitres de penser*: **Peirce**, Charles **Morris**, **Sebeok**, **Rossi-Landi** and, especially, through formidable archival scholarship, Victoria, Lady **Welby**, whom Petrilli has reinstated as **semiotics**' 'founding mother'.

In general, Petrilli's work (in consonance with Sebeok) promotes a global (or 'holistic') semiotic perspective on phenomena, eschewing **glottocentrism** and monologism. She observes that **globalization** is commonly understood as a socio-economic phenomenon, but asserts that it is also a semiotic phenomenon with reference to the synthesis of Peircean sign theory, Bakhtinian dialogue and biosemiotics. Recently, drawing on the collaborative formulation of the idea of the 'semiotic animal' (see Deely *et al.* 2005), she presents an outline of 'semioethics' – an imperative that is not merely discursively constructed but, instead, is the result of the 'concrete' demands of the other (**Levinas**, as well as **Bakhtin**, is a key figure, here). Furthermore, for her, otherness is not just a matter of explicit requests from our co-habitants on earth; rather, it is thoroughly grounded in the sign, both in communication and non-communication.

One impediment to the realization of a 'true' dialogue has been the prevailing liberal notion of dialogue as the result of an initiative to be taken in discourse. Without announcing a programme, Petrilli shows that semioethics entails not just the constant demands of the other but, also, a perspective that reaches beyond the glottocentrism of liberal dialogue to embrace the semiosis of the entire **semiosphere**. Petrilli's semioethics delineates not just a 'limited responsibility' but an 'unlimited responsibility' to 'all of life throughout the entire planetary ecosystem, from which human life cannot be separated' (Petrilli and Ponzio 2005: 534).

Putting responsibility into practice in the sphere of intellectual life, Petrilli has been open to her fellow scholars, promoting collaborations, inviting participations, organizing conferences and colloquia and editing and co-editing numerous scholarly volumes and journals. Her publications include collaborations with Sebeok, Marcel **Danesi**, Jeff Bernard, John **Deely** and, most frequently, her Bari colleague, Augusto **Ponzio**. Her single-author publications include *Significs, semiotica, significazione* (1988), *Materia segnica e interpretazione. Figure e prospettive* (1995c), *Che cosa significa significare? Itinerari nello studio dei segni* (1996), *Su Victoria Welby. Significs e filosofia del linguaggio* (1998a), *Teoria dei segni e del linguaggio* (1998b), *Percorsi della semiotica* (2005), *Sign Crossroads in Global Perspective* (2008) and *Signifying and Understanding: Reading the Works of Victoria Welby and the Significs Movement* (2009).

In 2008, Petrilli was made the seventh Sebeok Fellow of the Semiotic Society of America. (**PC**)

See also Petrilli and Ponzio.

Further reading

Petrilli, S. (2008) *Eight essays on the theme 'Sign Crossroads in Global Perspective'*, Sebeok Fellow Special Issue of *The American Journal of Semiotics*, 24(4).

Petrilli, S. (2009) *Signifying and Understanding: Reading the Works of Victoria Welby and the Significs Movement*, Berlin: Mouton de Gruyter.

Petrilli, S. and Ponzio, A. (2005) *Semiotics Unbounded: Interpretative Routes through the Open Network of Signs*, Toronto: University of Toronto Press.

PHATIC One of the six fundamental functions given in the **Jakobson**ian **speech act**, determined by the contact factor of the speech act. When the main goal of the utterance is to initiate, terminate or check the channel of **communication**, the phatic function may dominate. The only function to be shared by humans and birds. (**EA**)

PHENOMENOLOGY Edmund Husserl's phenomenology is the study of **consciousness**, both as regards the nature of its acts and as the essence of the objects it intends.

Husserl's pathbreaking work, the *Logical Investigations* (2001 [1900–1901]), has deeply influenced linguistics and the theory of meaning throughout the twentieth century. It had immediate bearings on the development of structural linguistics in general and Roman **Jakobson**'s structuralist theory of **meaning** and **language** in particular (besides being a recurrent reference in Karl **Bühler**'s *Theory of Language*). In the *Fourth Investigation*, which aims at laying down a pure universal grammar, Husserl establishes language as a general abstract entity governed by ideal principles of meaning construction, sustaining any possible, empirical grammar. Husserl thus claims the existence and establishes the nature of the 'ideal scaffolding' inherent in and constitutive for language as such. This notion precedes both Ferdinand de **Saussure**'s concept of ***langue*** and Jakobson's definition of the object of linguistics in terms of a structured whole, governed by immanent laws, i.e. a systematic pattern of relations. The purely syntactical aspects of Husserl's outline of a universal grammar also appears to be a clear anticipation of Noam **Chomsky**'s universal linguistic **competence**.

Husserl's theory of parts and wholes, developed in the *Third Investigation*, and applied to language in the *Fourth*, constitutes the categorical grounds on which Jakobson develops his notion of structure within phenomenology: namely in terms of relations of mutual or unilateral dependency (cf. his phonological laws of implication).

Husserl did not only develop an objective phenomenology of language proper, but also a phenomenology of language use. Key to this analysis – developed in the *First* and partially in the *Fourth Investigations* – is the question of how linguistic structure is bound up with the structure of our mental acts. To the extent that language serves the function of expressing meaning intentions, or cognitive representations, it must be capable of faithfully specifying the structure of our experiences and the way in which we intend the objects of our experiences. In this respect, linguistic structure is founded on prelinguistic structure. Husserl thus considers language a cognitive subsystem characterized by its relations to other cognitive subsystems (notably vision) and the intentionality of consciousness in general. Consequently, an essential task – only very rudimentarily undertaken by Husserl himself – consists in systematically elucidating the way in which prelinguistic, intentional structures of experience are grammatically and semantically specified in language.

As regards this task, evidence for the actuality of Husserl's phenomenology of language is today given by ***cognitive linguistics***, i.e. the research programme in linguistics in which the foundation of language structure on preconceptual, perceptual or experiential structure is a pivotal claim. Key concepts in cognitive linguistics, such as **image schema** and **trajector/landmark**, are intended to capture the exact way in which linguistic semantics is bound up with mental acts and the structure of mental meaning construction.

Phenomenology of language marshals the idea that language reveals something essential about the mind; however, not because the mind is structured like a language, but on the contrary because language faithfully specifies the intentional, preconceptual, prelinguistic structures of the mind. Language is in this respect considered a window to the mind. (**PB**)

FURTHER READING

Bundgaard, P. F. (2004) 'The ideal scaffolding of language: Husserl's fourth *Logical Investigation* in the light of cognitive linguistics', *Phenomenology and the Cognitive Sciences*, 3(1): 49–80.

Husserl, E. (1973 [1939]) *Experience and Judgment*, Evanston, IL: Northwestern University Press.

Husserl, E. (2001 [1900–1901]) *Logical Investigations*, London: Routledge.

PHILOLOGY As distinguished from *linguistics*, the term philology is usually applied to a more traditional form of **language** study, based on texts (particularly of bygone periods). Comparative philolology in the nineteenth century established the relationships between languages of the Indo-European family before the emergence of modern linguistics. (**RH**)

PHONEME The fundamental unit of sound in any **language**. For **Saussure** and others, differences between phonemes are crucial in generating **value**. A simple example of this is the difference between the sounds in the words *tin* and *kin* in English. The distinction of the phonemes designated by *k* and *t* enables different **meaning**s to be engendered by each word. The study of such units is the subdomain of linguistics known as 'phonemics' (as opposed to **phonetics**). (**PC**)

PHONETICS The study of speech sounds: how they are produced by the organs of speech (articulatory phonetics), how they are perceived by the ear (auditory phonetics) and their physical properties (acoustic phonetics). Phoneticians have also developed systems for writing down the sounds of any **language**, the most widely used being the International Phonetic Alphabet (IPA). In IPA the word *phonetics* is written [fənetIks]. (**RS**)

See also PHONEME.

PHONOLOGY The study of the sounds and sound patterns of particular **languages**. Phonologists list the sounds that each language has (for instance, English has the sound *h* as in *hat*, but French does not), and how the sounds are structured (English *h* is only found at the beginning of a syllable). (**RS**)

PHYSIOSEMIOSIS *see* **SEMIOSIS**

PIKE Kenneth Lee Pike (1912–2000), a long-time contributor to the Summer Institute of Linguistics, remains best recognized for his coinage (1954) and defence (Headland *et al.* 1990) of the terms 'emic' (culture-bound) and 'etic' (culture-free), derived from 'phonemic' and 'phonetic', respectively, and for his adventurous deployment of metaphor in methodology and theory, e.g. 'particle, wave and field' (1959). An eclectic, Pike has published widely in all realms of linguistics. (**MA**)

Poinsot John Poinsot, contemporary with Galileo and Descartes, lived at a time of major revolution in intellectual culture. It was the moment in human history when *ideoscopy* – that is to say, science in the modern sense of specialized experimental discovery of new phenomena, in contrast to *cenoscopy* as the sort of science that is founded upon the common experience of all humans – began fully to take root, and gave rise to that period of intellectual euphoria called 'The Enlightenment', when it was possible to dream that the new sciences would eventually displace the whole of human knowledge as heretofore attained. But, as Peirce and other late moderns came to realize, ideoscopy presupposes cenoscopy; for if common experience has no independent validity as a source of knowledge, neither could the special experiences give any purchase on reality. Even special experience takes its origin from the senses and human understanding as initially unaided by instruments and mathematics! Poinsot was wholly a man of the cenoscopic past, but paradoxically, this very circumstance guaranteed his role in the future of thought beyond modernity (Sebeok 1982). For not only does ideoscopy depend upon cenoscopy, but the broadest and most fundamental of the cenoscopic sciences is precisely the doctrine of signs, or semiotics (Peirce 1998d [1908]; *CP* 8.342–379, *EP* 2: 478–483), a systematic demonstration of which Poinsot had the privilege first to work out. In showing that triadic relation provides the being common to all signs, Poinsot provided the first demonstration of a unified subject matter for semiotic inquiry. Eclipsed in his own day by the scientific work of Galileo and the philosophical work of Descartes (the former depending upon semiosis, but incognizantly; the latter blinding modern philosophy to the hard-won Latin achievement of semiotic **consciousness**), Poinsot nonetheless was historically the first to give thematic substance to Augustine's turn of the fifth-century proposal that sign be regarded as a mode of being transcending the differences between nature and culture. By this achievement, Poinsot established himself as a harbinger of *post*modernity in philosophy (Deely 1994b, d), to remain a figure of seminal importance long after the epistemologies inspired by Descartes would prove to entail the dead-end of solipsism. Poinsot performed this intellectual feat of establis ing semiotics as the doctrine of signs by seizing upon two earlier achievements, and combining them with the contemporary realization (Araújo 1617) that signs are irreducibly triadic. He seized first upon Boethius's translation of Aristotle's problem in distinguishing between substances as subjectivities requiring to be understood relative to their environment ('transcendental relatives'), on the one hand, and, on the other hand, *pure relations* ('ontological relatives') having being only as *suprasubjectively linking* the substantial subjectivities. Poinsot then seized upon **Aquinas**'s realization (1266: q. 28) that pure relations as identified by Aristotle, in transcending their subjective ground, are, among the modes of being which are mind-independent, *singularities*, for relations alone remain unaffected in their positive being when changed circumstances make them mind-dependent. Whence, as suprasubjective, relations ('ontological relatives', in contrast to the subjectivity of 'transcendental relatives') render **semiosis** as a transcendence of the limits of finite subjectivity possible in the first place, and constitute 'experience' as a tapestry or 'semiotic web' (Sebeok 1975) woven precisely from pure relations, linking subjectivities and objectivities alike because terminating at 'the other' than the knower grounding them. **(JD)**

FURTHER READING

Bains, P. (2006) *The Primacy of Semiosis. An Ontology of Relations*, Toronto: University of Toronto Press.

Deely, J. (2001) *Four Ages of Understanding. The First Postmodern Survey of Philosophy from Ancient Times to the End of the Twenty-First Century*, Toronto: University of Toronto Press.

Poinsot, J. (1632) *Tractatus de Signis*, subtitled *The Semiotic of John Poinsot*, arranged in bilingual format by J. Deely in consultation with R. A. Powell, 2nd edn, South Bend, IN: St Augustine's Press, 2010. First edition available also in electronic form, Charlottesville, VA: Intelex Corp., 1992.

POLITENESS A means of showing courtesy, deference, consideration and social position in **language**. Politeness can consist of key words added to a free-standing utterance such as 'please'. It can also consist of words already **coded** as polite forms, for example the formal second person *Lei* in Italian as opposed to the informal *tu*. Because of the contextual factors which politeness embodies so commonly and so acutely, the phenomenon has been the object of considerable scrutiny in **pragmatics**. **(PC)**

POLYSEMY (POLYSEMIC) Term introduced by Bréal (1897) to refer to the capacity of **signs** or **texts** to have numerous meanings. The word 'crack', for example, is an instance of **onomatopoeia** (an **icon** of a specific sound) both as a verb ('the fireworks began to crack') and as a noun ('a loud crack'). It is also a verb to do with breakage ('I decided to crack it open') and a noun ('the money fell into the crack'). It is a noun referring to sardonic remarks ('he made a crack about the prime minister's poor performance') or even as a verb designating the same ('he started to crack wise again'). In colloquial usage it refers to highly potent cocaine crystals ('crack'), to the join between the buttocks and, sometimes, to the vagina. In Ireland 'craic' (pronounced 'crack') often has a far more benign meaning to do with having a good time. These are just some of its possible decodings.

When extended to the level of larger texts and **discourse**, polysemy undoubtedly becomes more complex. In these cases, specific understandings of texts' potential meanings might be the result of a restriction of polysemy by **speech communities** or by the particular kinds of composition of texts (for example, a **closed text** or a text from a given **genre**). **(PC)**

See also ILLOCUTION, OPEN TEXT *and* UNLIMITED SEMIOSIS.

FURTHER READING

Eco, U. (1979) *The Role of the Reader: Explorations in the Semiotics of Texts*, Bloomington, IN: Indiana University Press.

PONZIO Augusto Ponzio (b. 1942), philosopher of language, linguist and semiotician at the University of Bari. Ponzio is a celebrated theorist, in particular of **dialogue**, **alterity**, subjectivity and global **communication**. He is well known for his collaborations and friendships with, as well as his presentations of the work of, **Schaff**, **Levinas**, **Barthes**, **Kristeva**, **Bakhtin**, **Sebeok** and **Rossi-Landi**. He has also written about **Peirce**, **Wittgenstein**, **Marx** and **Peter of Spain**. He has collaborated with numerous scholars including Julia Ponzio, Cosimo Caputo, Massimo Bonfantini and, especially, Susan **Petrilli**.

Despite his towering achievement in his many fields of interest, it is possible to argue that, at the very core of his thinking, there lies a single concept: dialogue not as an initiative but as a constant demand. It is a conception of dialogue which, in going beyond the liberal notion of meeting others halfway, negotiating and compromising, actually *opposes* such agentive programmes, recognizing in dialogue a compulsion and demand rather than self-identified goodwill. Such a framing of dialogue is to be found, too, of course, in Bakhtin; as Ponzio and Petrilli succinctly state:

> For Bakhtin, dialogue is not the result of an initiative we decide to take, but rather it is imposed, something to which one is subjected. Dialogue is not the result of opening towards the other, but of the impossibility of closing.
>
> (Ponzio and Petrilli 1998: 28)

Yet, it would be a mistake to imagine that dialogue after Ponzio is merely a gloss on Bakhtin and Levinas. And as Ponzio puts it, dialogue should not be seen in the service of mere self-affirmation:

> On the contrary, as formulated by Levinas, dialogue is passive witness to the impossibility of escape from the other; it is passive witness to the fact that the other cannot be eluded, to the condition of involvement with the other apart from initiative taken by the subject who is called to answer *to* the other and *for* the other. The 'I' is constitutionally, structurally dialogic in the sense that it testifies to the relation with otherness, whether the otherness of others or the otherness of self.
>
> (Ponzio 2006c: 11)

For Ponzio, then, dialogue provides the crucial means for addressing the communication–ontology relationship, especially in the phase of global communication.

What global communication has made clear is that, in touting the inclusiveness of capitalism, it has reached a crisis point in the latter's own palpable logic of exclusion. What capitalism represses – and it does so in many forms – is the very compulsion of dialogue that his work describes.

Taking his cue from Thomas A. Sebeok, Ponzio views **semiosis** in a 'global' perspective which is not fixated on **anthroposemiosis** alone, despite the fact that, in his formation 'communication-production', the profit-making imperative of global communication has assumed a crucial position and has become, potentially, disastrous for the planet. Where theory is concerned, Ponzio demonstrates that there is a need to adhere to the larger picture of semiosis. In *Semiotica dell'io* (Sebeok *et al.* 2001), inspired, principally, by Sebeok's observations on the **semiotic self**, Ponzio does not stop at mere societal observation. Rather, his 'depth' analysis sees sign processes at work across all practices and across all species, in the process of communication where dialogue is repeatedly stymied. Although he proceeds from the tyrannies of global communication and its inculcation in 'communication-production', he also identifies the general repression of dialogue in deriving from the denial of communication beyond the verbal.

Ponzio's critique of the category of 'Identity' (see Ponzio 2006c) demonstrates that 'care of the self' can only realistically proceed from a *dialogic* 'care of others', where 'others' must mean the entirety of the **semiosphere**. It is in this sense that Ponzio has been compelled to map the contours of a future semioethics. (**PC**)

See also ETHICS *and* Petrilli and Ponzio.

FURTHER READING

Ponzio, A. (1990) *Man as a Sign*, ed. S. Petrilli, Berlin: Mouton de Gruyter.

Ponzio, A. (1993) *Signs, Dialogue and Ideology*, ed. S. Petrilli, Amsterdam: John Benjamins.

Ponzio, A. (2007) *The Dialogic Nature of Sign*, Ottawa: Legas.

PORT-ROYAL Name of a famous educational Jansenist foundation in seventeenth-century France, where Antoine Arnauld (1612–1694) and Claude Lancelot (1615–1695) produced an innovative French **grammar**, the *Grammaire générale et raisonée* (1660), based on radical pedagogic principles. The 'rationality' of the method was based on the assumption that certain principles applied to all **language**s and that all languages could give expression to certain universal operations of the human mind. Arnauld and Pierre Nicole (1625–1695) co-authored an accompanying *Art de penser*, commonly referred to as 'The Port-Royal Logic'. These works are often taken to epitomize the thesis that the structure of thought determines the structure of linguistic expression. (For the opposite thesis, see **Saussure**.) (**RH**)

POSITIVISM The philosophical approach or movement, originating with Henri Comte de Saint-Simon (1760–1825) and Auguste Comte (1798–1857), which stressed the importance of basing knowledge on positive facts deriving from direct experience. Many features of the positivist programme can be found in the work of earlier empiricists, including Hume and **Kant**, but positivism distinguished itself by its strict adherence to the methods of the exact sciences and by its sharp hostility to metaphysics and religion.

The proponents of positivism (positivists) were strongly opposed to basing knowledge claims on speculative beliefs and insisted that no hypothesis can be admitted for serious consideration unless it is capable of verification by direct observation. Positivists were much enamoured with the successes of experimental science and were convinced that scientific method was the only route to truth for inquiry of any kind. The positivists wanted to remake philosophy and the social sciences in the image of the hard sciences.

Though hostile to traditional religion, positivism was promoted as a sort of secular religion, a religion of humanity. Human progress was described as the movement from a theological base, involving belief in the supernatural, through a metaphysical phase, involving much speculation and appeal to abstractions, to a final positive stage where metaphysical abstractions (e.g. final causes) are dismissed, and all knowledge is derived from experience and known scientific laws. As positivism developed after Comte, for example in the work of John Stuart Mill, Herbert Spencer and Ernst Mach, it ceased to be promoted as a secular religion, but it continued to be concerned with the advancement of society and the well-being of humankind. Positivists typically believed that the way to a better world is through mastery of nature, which can only be achieved through a sufficient increase in scientific knowledge.

Through related movements and programmes, positivism was spread throughout philosophy. In Vienna a group of philosophers known as the Vienna Circle expanded on the ideas of Ernst Mach to develop logical positivism. This version of positivism continued to be staunchly opposed to metaphysics, but focused mainly on the process of verification by which knowledge claims can be justified. The *Tractatus Logico-philosophicus* of Ludwig **Wittgenstein** was a key text for logical positivists, among whom could be counted Moritz Schlick, Otto Neurath, Felix Kaufmann, Herbert Feigl, Philipp Frank and Rudolf Carnap. Key members of the Vienna Circle emigrated to the United States in the early 1930s and, with Charles W. **Morris**, formed the Unity of Science Movement, dedicated to establishing a comprehensive empirical philosophy based on a rigorous scientific methodology guided by formal logic. Morris introduced semiotic principles to the members of this movement, in particular the important tripartite division of **semiotics** into syntactics, **semantics** and **pragmatics**. In psychology and the philosophy of psychology, behaviourism incorporated the main principles of positivism. Through these and other outgrowths, positivism exerted an enormous influence on analytical and linguistic philosophy in the twentieth century.

Pragmatism, too, with its emphasis on scientific method and on practical consequences, and with its mission to improve society, bears some resemblance to positivism. But pragmatists never wanted to dismiss metaphysics wholesale, hoping, rather, to purify it, and in other ways deviated from positivism. **Peirce** believed that positivism was fatally nominalistic and he noticed that its insistence on verification by direct observation precluded historical knowledge (Peirce 1984: 45, n. 8). Other pragmatists, in particular John Dewey, and many contemporary philosophers, object to the many dichotomous distinctions positivists espoused, for instance the distinction between metaphysics and science, facts and values, the analytic and the synthetic, and the verifiable and the non-verifiable. Recent philosophy has been, to a large extent, an undoing of the ill effects of positivism and a rethinking of its achievements. The international movement toward a Peircean brand of semiotics is largely a movement away from positivism. (**NH**)

Further reading

Ayer, A. J. (1946) *Language, Truth and Logic*, rev. edn, New York: Oxford University Press.

Kremer-Marietti, A. (1998) 'Comte, Isidore-Auguste-Marie-François-Xavier', *Routledge Encyclopedia of Philosophy*, London: Routledge.

Peirce, C. S. (1984) 'Critique of positivism' (1867–1868), in *Writings of Charles S. Peirce*, Vol. 2, ed. E. C. Moore, M. H. Fisch, *et al*., Bloomington, IN: Indiana University Press.

Posthumanism Posthumanism refers to a body of thought seeking to go beyond the legacies of humanism – its maskings of political, sexual, racial and species exclusions under discourses of universality. Posthumanism is the philosophical counterpart of the visionary notion of the *posthuman*, a conceptual trope conveying images of biotechnological or cybernetic systemic couplings, especially as these are taken to comprise an evolutionary vector beyond the human (sometimes called *transhumanism*). Posthumanism is also to be distinguished from *antihumanism*, a stance of negation or misanthropic rejection of humanist ideals more properly associated with modernist firebrands like Filippo Marinetti or Wyndham Lewis. From a semiotic perspective, the implication of posthumanism is that the production and processing of **semiosis** pervades the non-human cosmos as well as the human world.

As a philosophical idea, posthumanism elicits primary anticipatory strands of **poststructuralist** and postmodernist thought. Friedrich Nietzsche's *Übermensch* is perhaps the archetype of posthumanist figures. Michel Foucault echoes Nietzsche in his famous prediction at the end of *The Order of Things*, that 'man would be erased, like a face drawn in sand at the edge of the sea' (Foucault 1973: 387). This line of philosophical reflection on the evanescence or contingency of the humanist subject ranges from Donna Haraway's 'Cyborg Manifesto' to the work of Gilles Deleuze and Félix Guattari as that focuses on notions of becoming-other and heterogenesis.

While texts such as Robert Pepperell's *Posthuman Condition* (2002) lean to the technoid side of posthumanism, the recent work of Neil Badmington, Ivan Callus and Stefan Herbrechter has delineated a 'critical posthumanism' (Badmington 2007) that stresses the range of the concept beyond the cyborgian imaginary. For instance, Cary Wolfe presents an ethical posthumanism that rethinks the humanist rejection of non-human or animal subjectivity. Wolfe draws on Jacques Derrida and Niklas Luhmann to observe how, if pressed upon, the metaphysics of humanism self-deconstruct. In sum, posthumanism at its most productive is not the rejection but the deconstruction of humanism. (**BC**)

Further reading

Wolfe, C. (2009) *What is Posthumanism?*, Minneapolis, MN: University of Minnesota Press.

Poststructuralism (Poststructuralist) Definitions of poststructuralism are infrequently found: this is partly because the phenomenon described by the term is so nebulous; partly because, as an intellectual current, it is especially difficult to periodize; and partly because many of its proponents purport to eschew definitions. Undoubtedly, it has a relation to '**structuralism**', but it is an uneasy one.

While structuralism might be said to embody the notion of a system of **sign**s in which humans can collectively participate – derived from the 'functionalist' aspect of **Saussure**'s concept of ***langue*** – poststructuralism envisages a fundamentally different relation between signs and humans. Structuralist approaches to cultural phenomena benefited from analyses which often took signs isolated from their contexts as the object of discussion. Poststructuralism, by contrast, stresses not only how signs are related to other signs but also how the human subject always apprehends signs in the plural, in chains, as **discourse**. As Silverman insists, 'signification occurs only through discourse … discourse requires a subject and … the subject itself is an effect of discourse' (1983: vii). Put another way, **signification** is not embodied in the '**meaning**' of one sign but in a sign as it is related to other signs; signification also has to be related to the human or humans who use the signs at a given moment; and, crucially, the sign user is not outside the discourse, using it in a perfectly controlled way, but is instead caught up in it, to the extent where s/he is actually a product of that discourse. These propositions are virtually axiomatic, albeit in nuanced ways, for all the major poststructuralists: Lacan, Derrida, **Kristeva**, Foucault, **Baudrillard**, Deleuze and Guattari.

However, the immediate Saussurean roots of the poststructuralist perspective actually *pre-date* those currents of thought in the humanities called structuralism which became popular in France in the 1950s and 1960s and in parts of the Anglo-Saxon intellectual world in the 1970s and 1980s. The father of poststructuralism was the French linguist Emile **Benveniste**, whose writings of the 1940s made possible the critiques of Saussure and structuralism by Lacan in the late 1950s and Derrida in the 1960s.

Chiefly, Benveniste drew attention to some anomalies in Saussure's assertion of the *arbitrary* nature of the sign. That the sign was 'bipartite', made up of a ***signifié***, concept, and a ***signifiant***, sound image (frequently translated in a misleading way which has become the norm as '**signified**' and '**signifier**' – for a corrective, see Harris 1987 and <ins>Introduction</ins>, above, pp. 8–9), was accepted. However, Benveniste located the arbitrary nature in *signification*; that is, in the relation between the sign and the reality (or, to use other terms, **referent** or **object**). The relations in the Saussurean *sign*, both parts being mental, were rather to be seen as *necessary*: the sound image and the concept were so close as to be almost one.

What Benveniste showed was that *sign* and *signification* were highly susceptible to conflation. The knowledge that the word *cat* only refers to the feline quadruped in an arbitrary way is omnipresent because it is clear that there are other ways of referring to the animal in different national **language**s: *chat*, *gatto*, etc. But the sign used for this purpose is composed of a relationship so strong and so close that its arbitrary nature in referring to reality can only be revealed 'under the impassive regard of Sirius' (Benveniste 1971 [1939]: 44). In short, for the habitual user of the sign the way it refers *feels* unquestionably natural.

So, a linguistic sign might have **value** by virtue of its difference from other signs in a system (*langue*), and this might be recognized through abstract thought. But the existence of this foundation for arbitrariness in signification is customarily overlooked because of the close, necessary relations in the sign. As a result, humans are subject to a system which they ultimately know to be constructed and arbitrary; in order to take their place and communicate with others they have to subscribe to a representation of the world which, however much they might feel it to be natural, is actually constructed. To use a typical poststructuralist trope, the subject is 'always already' constituted by the system.

The reverberations of this reorientation of the sign were to be felt throughout the manifestations of poststructuralism. Notions such as 'deconstruction', 'the decentring of the subject', 'interpellation' and 'simulation' are all in some way derived from Benveniste's deflection of the aims of **semiology**.

Poststructuralism was never a movement recognized within its 'native' France (Easthope 1988: xxiii) and its success in parts of the Anglo-Saxon intellectual milieu was always unlikely to be mirrored within semiotics. On its home ground of **anthroposemiotics** the totalizing cultural pessimism which was characteristic of many brands of poststructuralism was already countered by the social semiotics which followed the work of **Halliday**. The very fundamentals of the latter, itself distantly related to the early critique of Saussure by **Vološinov** but largely based on empirical work, stressed conflict between sign systems and delineated a space for human resistance to pre-existing structures. On different grounds, poststructuralism was to fare even less well. The comprehensive version of the sign derived from **Peirce** which took hold outside of France and the United Kingdom in the closing decades of the twentieth century, coupled with the growing awareness of the importance of **biosemiotics**, only served to further reveal poststructuralism's semiological bias and anthropocentric limitations. (**PC**)

Further reading

Benveniste, E. (1971) *Problems in General Linguistics*, trans. M. E. Meek, Coral Gables, FL: University of Miami Press.

Derrida, J. (1976) *Of Grammatology*, trans. G. C. Spivak, Baltimore, MD: Johns Hopkins University Press.

Lacan, J. (1977) *Écrits: A Selection*, trans. A. Sheridan, London: Tavistock.

Pragmaticism The term 'pragmaticism' was introduced in 1905 by Charles S. **Peirce** to distinguish his own conception of **pragmatism** from that of William James and Ferdinand C. S. Schiller (*CP* 5.414–415). Peirce rejected the idea of 'Doing' as 'the Be-all and the End-all of life' (*CP* 5.429). Differently from vulgar pragmatism, meaning is a general law of conduct independent from the particular circumstances of action. As such, it is always general and communal. **(SP)**

Pragmatics In Charles **Morris**'s theory of **semiosis**, the pragmatical dimension of the functioning of **signs** pertains to 'the relation of signs to interpreters' (1938: 6) and the study of this dimension is called pragmatics. In linguistics, pragmatics has often been treated as a waste basket to which problems were referred that could not be dealt with in **syntax** and **semantics**. As a result, in part of the pragmatic literature, its domain looks like a random selection of topics, in particular: **deixis**, presuppositions, implicatures, **speech acts** and conversations (see Levinson 1983). It may be more useful, however, to go back to Morris's original definition and to view pragmatics as a general functional (i.e. cognitive, social and cultural) perspective on **language** and language use, aimed at the investigation of processes of dynamic and negotiated meaning generation in interaction. Language use is then viewed as a form of action with real-world consequences and firmly embedded in a context. **(JV)**

See also Austin, Constative, Grice, Illocution, Locution, Meaning, Performative, Perlocution *and* Relevance theory.

Further reading

Verschueren, J. (1999) *Understanding Pragmatics*, London: Edward Arnold/New York: Oxford University Press.

Pragmatism Pragmatism is a set of doctrines and methods elaborated by Charles S. **Peirce** and William James and continued above all by G. H. Mead, C. I. Lewis, Charles **Morris** and John Dewey. 'Pragmatism' makes its official entry into philosophical literature in 1898 when James held his conference 'Philosophical Conceptions and Practical Results', at G. H. Howinson's Berkeley Philosophical Union. But pragmatism was expounded for the first time in a series of six articles by Peirce, published in *Popular Science Monthly* between 1877 and 1878 in the series 'Illustrations of the Logic of Science' (cf. *CP* 5.358–387, 5.388–410, 2.645–660, 2.669–693, 6.395–427, 2.619–644). However, as a thought system it may be traced back to an original nucleus of three writings by Peirce of 1868 (*CP* 5.213–263, 264–317, 318–357), subsequently developed in his writings of 1877–1878. In his search for the origins, Peirce considers Nicholas St John Green as the 'grandfather' of pragmatism (implicitly reserving the title of 'father' for himself). The latter, in turn, evoked the Scot, Alexander Bain, author of *The Emotions and the Will* (1859), urging the importance of applying his definition of belief as 'that upon which a man is prepared to act' (*CP* 5.12).

In general, pragmatism re-evaluates the importance of action in cognitive processes in the light of discoveries in biology, psychology and sociology traceable to Charles Darwin. Chauncey Wright, who was a member of the 'Metaphysical Club', also recalled Darwin and it was in the meetings which took place between the end of 1871 and the beginning of 1872 in Cambridge, Massachusetts, that Peirce (cf. 'The Doctrine of Chances', *CP* 5.12) situated the birth of pragmatism. The

'Metaphysical Club' meetings were organized both in his and in James's study with the participation of scientists, theologians and lawyers. The influence of Darwinian biologism is obvious in Peirce's essay 'Fixation of Belief' (1877) where he states that logicality in regard to practical matters might result from the action of natural selection (cf. *CP* 5.366).

According to pragmatism, mind (or spirit or thought) is not a substance, as in Cartesian dualism, nor is it a process or act as understood by idealism, nor a set of relations as in classical empiricism, but rather it is a function exercised by verbal and nonverbal **sign**s. The study of signs and of verbal **language** in particular is therefore the condition for understanding mind (cf. Morris, *Six Theories of Mind*, 1932). Pragmatism is also a theory of meaning understood as the practical verifiability of the **truth** of an assertion. In 'How to Make our Ideas Clear' (1878), Peirce intended to demonstrate:

> how impossible it is that we should have an idea in our minds which relates to anything but conceived sensible effects of things … It appears, then, that the rule for attaining the third grade of clearness of apprehension is as follows: Consider what effects, that might conceivably have practical bearings, we conceive the object of our conception to have. Then, our conception of these effects is the whole of our conception of the object.
>
> (*CP* 5.401–402)

This aspect was taken up but significantly modified by James who transformed pragmatism into a theory of truth. James interpreted pragmatism in terms of instrumentality and, therefore, of the dependency of knowledge on the needs of action and emotions (*The Will to Believe*, 1897). For James that which has satisfying practical consequences is true. Consequently he emphasizes the practical value of religious faith, of the will to believe, of the reasons of the heart (cf. also James's *Pragmatism*, 1907). Dewey also insisted on this aspect which he vigorously developed into his own version of pragmatism denominated 'experimentalism' or 'instrumentalism'. In Italy, pragmatism was developed along Peircean lines by Giovanni **Vailati** and Mario Calderoni and along Jamesian lines by G. Papini and G. Prezzolini. Ferdinand C. S. Schiller (cf. *Studies in Humanism*, 1907) oriented his approach in James's direction asserting the relativity of knowledge to personal or social utility.

Peirce returned to pragmatism in his set of seven conference-lessons held at Harvard at the initiative of James (cf. *CP* 5.14–40, 5.180–212), in which he identified pragmatism with the logic of **abduction** and with the theory of inquiry and implicitly, therefore, with logic and **semiotics**. In his *Monist* articles of 1905 (*CP* 5.411–437, 5.438–463, 4.530–572), Peirce established his distance from pragmatism as conceived by James and Schiller, identifying his own position with the substitute term **pragmaticism**. **(SP)**

Further reading

Morris, C. (1937) *Logical Positivism, Pragmatism and Scientific Empiricism*, Paris: Hermann.

Murphy, J. P. (1990) *Pragmatism: From Peirce to Davidson*, Boulder, CO: Westview Press.

Peirce, C. S. (1907) 'Pragmatism', in Peirce (1998) *The Essential Peirce: Selected Philosophical Writings*, Vol. 2, ed. Peirce Edition Project, Bloomington, IN: Indiana University Press, pp. 398–433.

Prague School Originally known as the Prague Linguistics Circle (PLC), founded in 1926 by V. Mathesius, B. Havránek, J. **Mukařovský**, R. **Jakobson**, N. Trubetzkoy and S. Karcevskij. Dedicated to the study of Slavic languages and literature, poetics, **phonology** and morphology. According to Waugh and Monville-Burston (1990: 6), it was Jakobson who coined the term '**structuralism**' for the group. The first detailed presentation of the PLC programme occurred at the First International Congress of Slavists in 1929 in Prague. Also initiated in 1929 was the series *Travaux du Cercle Linguistique de Prague*. For a clear statement of the fundamental propositions of the PLC, see 'Thèses' (with Bally, Jakobson, Mathesius, Sechehaye and Trubetzkoy, originally presented April 1928 and reprinted in Toman 1995).

According to the official by-laws of the PLC (dated 1 December 1930, translated and reprinted in Toman 1995: 265), the primary purpose of the PLC 'is to work on the basis of functional-structural method toward progress in linguistic research'. Roman Jakobson was Vice-President of the PLC until 1939 when he was obliged to leave as the Nazis invaded Czechoslovakia. In post-war years, the membership of the PLC changed considerably, in particular due to the absence of Jakobson and Bogatyrëv and the death of Trubetzkoy and Mathesius. In some accounts, the PLC is said to have ceased to exist in 1939. However, Mukařovský and others continued to lecture and conduct research. The post-Soviet era witnessed a revival of the Prague School in the 1990s. **(EA)**

Further reading

Galan, F. W. (1985) *Historic Structures: The Prague School Project, 1828–1946*, Austin, TX: University of Texas Press.

Steiner, P. (ed.) (1982) *The Prague School: Selected Writings, 1929–1946*, Austin, TX: University of Texas Press.

Winner, T. G. (1995) 'Prague structuralism: Neglect and resulting fallacies', *Semiotica*, 105(3/4): 243–276.

Propositions Propositions differ from sentences and **speech act**s in that different sentences or speech acts (e.g. 'The cat is on the mat', 'Is the cat on the mat?' and 'Cat, on the mat!') may contain the same proposition, consisting of a *reference* (an **expression** identifying any thing, process, event or action) and a *predication* (what is 'predicated' or said about a thing, process, event or action identified by means of a referring expression). It is propositions, not sentences or speech acts, that are true or false. Assertive speech acts can nevertheless be said to be true or false because it is the nature of their **illocutionary** force to present a state of affairs as true or false. Thus one and the same sentence form (e.g. 'Napoleon was defeated at Waterloo') has different truth conditions associated with it, depending on the precise proposition it expresses (which will vary in relation to, for example, the reference of 'Napoleon' which may be the name of a historical figure or the speaker's dog). **(JV)**

See also MEANING.

FURTHER READING

Lyons, J. (1995) *Linguistic Semantics: An Introduction*, Cambridge: Cambridge University Press.

PROTOTYPICALITY As suggested by Eleanor Rosch's prototype theory, human understanding of a token's membership of a category is not defined in terms of necessary and sufficient conditions. Rather a category is considered as possessing a radial structure with prominent or salient members close to its core and gradually less representative members toward the periphery. Membership is therefore assessed in terms of prototypicality. A prototype of a category is a core instance which possesses most or all of the basic features of that category. Therefore a sparrow is experienced as a prototypical instance of the category BIRD, whereas an ostrich is a peripheral member. **(PB)**

PROXEMICS Where **kinesics** refers to bodily movement in **communication**, proxemics is concerned with communication derived from the distances and territorial occupation of communicating agents. As part of his investigations into **nonverbal communication**, the American anthropologist Edward T. **Hall** considered proxemics in the distance regulation and crowding **habit**s of animals, perceptions of spaces (including cultural phenomena such as cities) and in the complex interactions that make up the everyday life of contemporary humans (see, especially, Hall 1969). Proxemics has been of immense importance in environments such as zoos, circuses and wherever there is human interaction with other animals: it helps identify the line where an animal might feel under attack, dominated, vaguely intimidated or comfortable with the presence of another. It has obvious applications to human/human communication, too, since it allows a delineation of body space in interactions. Additionally, it may be instrumental in defining the **semiotic self** which **Sebeok** (1979c) sees as arising somewhere between the skin of an animal and a 'bubble' identified by **Hediger** as a non-material extension of the body. **(PC)**

See also BIOSEMIOTICS, BIRDWHISTELL *and* ZOOSEMIOTICS.

FURTHER READING

Hall, E. T. (1974) *Handbook for Proxemic Research*, New York: Society for the Anthropology of Visual Communication.

PSYCHOLINGUISTICS The study of **language** and the mind, or the psychology of language. The mechanisms for producing and understanding language are a central concern of psycholinguists. Another is the way language might be stored in the brain. Many experimental methods have been devised to investigate these matters: they include measuring the time it takes for people to understand or respond to speech that has been distorted in various ways, and observing the speech errors that people make in different circumstances.

Another important concern of psycholinguists is the acquisition of language by young people. Acquisition of all languages seems to follow regular stages: infants produce single words first, followed by two-word sequences and then longer utterances with the beginnings of **syntax**. Speech and language pathology are related areas that have an important practical dimension. They also raise difficult issues about the relationship between language and other aspects of the mind, such as memory, general intelligence and emotion. A young person who has difficulty in learning to talk, or who later is slow at learning to read at school, may have a purely linguistic problem; often, though, there may be a link with other psychological problems that a young person is experiencing. (**RS**)

Further reading

Garnham, A. (1989) *Psycholinguistics: Central Topics*, London: Routledge.

Q

Qualia The experiential and phenomenal properties or characters of perceptual and/or internal bodily experience as well as feelings and, to some, also desires and thoughts. They are most often considered physically and informationally unexplainable. In **Peirce**'s **semiotics** they are **sign**s: **qualisign**s, which are a part of **firstness** and need another sign in order to become manifest. As such they are a prerequisite for all cognition and **communication** and therefore the phenomenal mystery on which information, cognitive and communication sciences rest, including **cybernetics** of first and second order as well as Luhmann's autopoietic system theory and Spencer-Brown's law of forms. **(SB)**

See also Autopoiesis.

Qualisign Charles S. **Peirce**'s term for the first division of his trichotomy of the **ground**s of **sign**s. A qualisign is a sign which, in itself, is a quality, and is thus fit only to represent **object**s with which it bears some similarity or has something in common. A paint chip represents its own colour. All qualisigns are **icon**s and can only function when embodied. **(NH)**

See also Legisign *and* Sinsign.

R

Realism The Platonic doctrine that universals or essences exist independently of individuals which instantiate them. Realism in this sense is opposed to **nominalism**. In its extreme form, it supposes that there is some kind of Platonic realm where universals exist timelessly and that particulars are imperfect copies of their universal counterparts. **Aristotle**'s realism was more moderate. He reversed the Platonic doctrine and held that the fullest reality is found in existing particulars in which universals inhere. But he also attributed reality to universals. Those who accept this doctrine today champion the reality of natural classes and abstract entities and such 'univerals' as laws and properties (including moral properties) rather than 'Platonic forms'.

Another form of realism, external realism, opposes idealism. The principal intuition of those who accept this kind of realism is that the external world exists independently of thought about it – reality exists separately from **consciousness** or mental representations. Since, on this view, the world is how it is independently of what we believe about it, then whether or not what we believe is true or false will depend on whether it corresponds with the facts of the matter. External realists accept that there may be unknowables, facts that we have no human capacity for cognizing. In its extreme form, external realism tends to merge with nominalism, the view that, though the world is stocked with plenty of real things that are completely independent of what we think about them, our knowledge of the world cannot transcend its linguistic and psychological basis to meaningfully connect with 'things in themselves'. Michael Dummett has rounded out the modern form of external realism by further characterizing it as the view committed to the principle of excluded middle, and holding that, for any property, an object either must have that property or not. Any view that does not accept all of the assumptions of external realism is said to be anti-realism (Dummett 1978).

There are many other varieties of realism (or anti-realism). Internal realism, advocated by Hillary Putnam, denies that there are incognizables and rejects the correspondence theory of **truth** in favour of the view that truth must be understood, not as correspondence with the facts, but as the result of inquiry carried out long enough and in the right way (Putnam 1987). Scientific realism covers a wide variety of viewpoints including that scientific theories refer to real features of the world and, also, that a good and useful theory is not necessarily a true one.

Charles S. **Peirce** advocated a form of realism that resembles in some ways Putnam's internal realism, particularly in the view that truth must be understood in terms of the projected settlement of belief at the end of inquiry. But Peirce enriched the conception of realism by developing the position advocated by Duns **Scotus** that reality includes far more than the existent. Peirce identified three categories of reality: **qualia** or properties (**firstness**), facts or events (**secondness**), and types or laws (**thirdness**). The first and third categories are general, opposing Peirce to nominalism. It was Peirce's opinion that the 'battle' between nominalism and realism is one of the most crucial struggles in philosophy:

> Though the question of realism and nominalism has its roots in the technicalities of logic, its branches reach about our life. The question whether the *genus Homo* has any existence except as individuals, is the question whether there is anything of any more dignity, worth, and importance than individual happiness, individual aspirations, and individual life. Whether men really have anything in common, so that the *community* is to be considered as an end in itself, and if so, what the relative value of the two factors is, is the most fundamental practical question in regard to every institution the constitution of which we have it in our power to influence.
>
> (Peirce 1992c: 105)

In the fine arts, realism usually refers to styles and techniques that emphasize common conceptions or ordinary experience. (**NH**)

See also Deely *and* SEMIOTICS.

FURTHER READING

Armstrong, D. M. (1978) *Universals and Scientific Realism*, 2 vols, Cambridge: Cambridge University Press.

Haack, S. (1987) 'Realism', *Synthese*, 73: 275–299.

Peirce, C. S. (1992) 'Review of Fraser's *The Works of George Berkeley*' (1871), in *The Essential Peirce: Selected Philosophical Writings*, Vol. 1, ed. N. Houser and C. Kloesel, Bloomington, IN: Indiana University Press, pp. 83–105.

REFERENT Term commonly used to designate the thing in the world to which **sign**s refer. This consists of available things such as the real chair one is sitting on while one produces the sign, and unavailable things, for example Napoleon: 'in which case there may be a long list of sign-situations appearing in between the act and its referent: word – historian – contemporary record – eye-witness' (Ogden and Richards 1923: 11). In light of this definition certain similarities with the concepts of **Peirce** and certain dissimilarities with those of **Saussure** should be noted. Peirce's sign triad includes an **interpretant** and a **representamen** as well as an **object** which itself can be either immediate or, like a referent, dynamic – that is to say, existing in the world but not directly available at the same time and place as the sign. Saussure's dyadic sign, on the other hand, comprises a **signifier** and also a **signified**, the latter being a mental concept. In some accounts of **semiology**, the signified is confused with a referent or, more frequently, supplemented with the concept of referent as the entity that Saussure neglected. However, Saussure's *Cours* focuses on the relation in the sign between a mental sound pattern and a concept, not on the relation between linguistic signs and referents. (**PC**)

See also OGDEN, POSTSTRUCTURALISM, RICHARDS, SEMIOTICS *and* STRUCTURALISM.

FURTHER READING

Ogden, C. K. and Richards, I. A. (1923) *The Meaning of Meaning: A Study of the Influence of Language upon Thought and of the Science of Symbolism*, with supplementary essays by B. Malinowski and F. G. Crookshank, London: Routledge and Kegan Paul.

REGISTER (TEXT VARIETY) A term deriving from (neo-) **Firth**ian linguistics which focuses on the relation of **language** and its social environments, and its variations in response to changes in context and use. It sees language as a resource through which its users 1) represent 'what is going on' in the world: the **field** of a text; 2) the characteristics of the social relations between the participants in linguistic interaction: the **tenor** of a text; and 3) the organization and shaping of language in **communication**: the **mode** of the text.

Register names the textual configuration which results from the combined interaction of each of the variables of field, tenor and mode. There may be relative stabilities of social **situation**, giving rise to relatively stable registers (the 'sermon', for instance). In general, register theory assumes a constantly dynamic and fluid arrangement for language in use. Register theory has been hugely influential for a range of developments concerned with language for special purposes, for **genre** theory, and in language planning. (**GRK**)

See also SOCIOLINGUISTICS.

FURTHER READING

Halliday, M. A. K. (1978) *Language as Social Semiotic*, London: Edward Arnold.

REID Thomas Reid (1710–1796), Scottish philosopher. Reid stands out among moderns in proposing 'an essentially semiotic theory' of mind (Henle 1987: 156). Reid in effect argues for the priority of *cenoscopy* (what Reid called 'common sense' – knowledge that does not require new observations with instruments) over *idioscopy*, those studies depending upon specialized observations instrument-aided and mathematized. Rejecting the modern doctrine that ideas *are* objects, Reid made his case for direct knowledge of physical things so strong as to be unable to deal with fundamental differences between perceptual objects in their objective constitution through relations, and perceptual objects in what they have of a subjective constitution as things accessible in sensation. (**JD**)

RELEVANCE THEORY One of **Grice**'s maxims of conversation was the maxim of relation, 'Be relevant' (Grice 1975). Some of the other maxims could be quite sensibly reduced to this notion of relevance. For instance, the statement 'There's a garage round the corner' in response to 'I am out of petrol' violates the maxim of quantity: the explicit **meaning** of the answer is not enough to guarantee the satisfaction of the expressed need; therefore, assuming the speaker's co-operativity, the utterance implicates that the garage has petrol for sale and is open. In other words, the response would not be *relevant* unless those aspects of implicit meaning can be assumed. Sperber and Wilson's (1986) relevance theory makes this generalized notion of relevance into the overriding principle to formulate a theory of **communication** and cognition intended to explain utterance understanding.

Relevance theory bears specifically on so-called 'ostensive communication', i.e. communication that is intentional and overt in such a way that the speaker does not only intend to convey a specific meaning but is also engaged in efforts to help the hearer recognize this intention. Such forms of communication are said to be governed by a 'principle of relevance', which holds that 'Every act of ostensive communication communicates the presumption of its own optimal relevance' (ibid.: 158). In order for ostensive communication to be successful, an audience has to pay attention to the ostensive stimulus, and an audience will not pay attention unless the phenomenon to attend to seems relevant enough. In contrast to Grice's maxim, the principle of relevance is not formulated as a norm that can be adhered to or broken, but rather an exceptionless generalization about human cognition. Yet, the principle cannot guarantee that communication will always succeed. Success requires that the first accessible interpretation which a rational interlocutor selects as optimally relevant matches the intended one.

The theory of understanding based on these assumptions distinguishes between implicatures (of the Gricean type) and explicatures, which are the explicitly communicated **propositions** that (could have) replace(d) those implicatures. It further hypothesizes that a principle is involved according to which needless cognitive effort is avoided. For that reason, expressions carrying implicatures may have additional meanings that can be said to be 'weakly implicated'. Thus there has to be a reason why a speaker puts a hearer to extra effort in the interpretation process by not expressing him/herself explicitly. For instance, if a speaker responds 'I have to study for an exam' in reaction to an invitation to go to the movies, this implicates that he/she does not accept. But the speaker could have said so directly. In addition to this implicature, therefore, the presumption of relevance in relation to the principle of least cognitive effort would dictate that a number of 'weak implicatures' – not intended specifically in the same way as the identified implicature – have to be added to the interpretation: the speaker wants to convey that there are good reasons for not accepting the invitation; or he/she wants to communicate a state of mind. (**JV**)

See also RULES.

FURTHER READING

Blakemore, D. (1992) *Understanding Utterances: An Introduction to Pragmatics*, Oxford: Blackwell.

Rouchota, V. and Jucker, A. H. (eds) (1998) *Current Issues in Relevance Theory*, Amsterdam: John Benjamins.

Sperber, D. and Wilson, D. (1986) *Relevance: Communication and Cognition*, Oxford: Blackwell.

REPRESENTAMEN/SIGN A representamen conveys information about the **object** it represents. According to Charles S. **Peirce**, a representamen is a correlate in a triadic relation with an object and an **interpretant**. It determines the interpretant to stand in relation to the object as it does, so that the interpretant is mediately determined by the object. **Sign**s, which convey information to human minds, are the most familiar representamens, but perhaps not all representamens are signs. For example, a pathogen may be the representamen of some disease to an immune system without technically being a sign. Usually 'sign' is no longer restricted in this way and is used synonymously with 'representamen'. **(NH)**

RHEME Charles S. **Peirce**'s term for the first division of his trichotomy of **sign**s that concerns how they are interpreted. A rhematic sign (or rheme) is understood to represent its **object** in its characters and is thus interpreted as a sign of essence or possibility. Rhemes may be **icon**ic, **index**ical or **symbol**ic, but they are always understood as representing a qualitative possibility of some sort rather than a fact of the matter or a reason. Rhemes are often associated with grammatical terms or with open predicates. **(NH)**

See also ARGUMENT *and* DICENT.

RHETORIC The art of using **language**, or elements of language such as tropes (figures of speech), effectively or persuasively; thus the study of how to influence the thoughts, emotions or behaviour of others through the use of language. One of the three subjects of the Roman trivium: **grammar**, logic and rhetoric. Classically, the art of rhetoric was divided into five parts: invention, disposition, elocution (diction and style), memory (mnemonics) and action (delivery). In Charles S. **Peirce**'s semeiotic, speculative (theoretical or pure) rhetoric is the third branch, after speculative grammar and speculative critic. According to Peirce, speculative rhetoric is 'the science of the essential conditions under which a **sign** may determine an interpretant sign of itself and of whatever it signifies, or may, as a sign, bring about a physical result' (1998b: 326). Speculative rhetoric is the study of the necessary and sufficient conditions for the **communication** of information or of semeiotic content at any level of **semiosis** or information transfer, whether from person to person or even as a development of individual thought. Rhetoric is sometimes regarded as the imaginative or poetic use of language, that aspect of language that refuses to be limited to the rigorous demands of logic or rational discourse. In its most current sense rhetoric may be taken to be the general theory of linguistic expression or even the general theory of textuality. **(NH)**

See also GROUND, HABIT *and* INTERPRETANT.

FURTHER READING

Liszka, J. J. (1996) *A General Introduction to the Semeiotic of Charles Sanders Peirce*, Bloomington, IN: Indiana University Press (especially Ch. 4).

RICHARDS Ivor Armstrong Richards (1893–1979), literary theorist, linguist and cultural critic, taught at Cambridge and Harvard. Among his numerous books are *Principles of Literary Criticism* (1925), *Practical Criticism* (1929), *Coleridge on Imagination* (1935), *The Philosophy of Rhetoric* (1936), *How to Read a Page* (1942), *Poetries and Sciences* (1970) and *Beyond* (1975). In the field of **semiotics**, however, his most famous book remains his first, co-written with C. K. **Ogden**, *The Meaning of Meaning* (1923). In this volume the authors discussed an array of contemporary and near-contemporary theorists of signification including **Saussure**, **Peirce**, Russell and Frege, as well as precursors such as **William of Ockham** and **Humboldt**. They also outlined a threefold version of signification which is not far removed from Peirce's triadic theory of the **sign**. Richards might also be best remembered in literary and sign theory for his investigation of metaphor and the distinction between 'vehicle' and 'tenor' in this trope.

Richards' approach to analysis was always eclectic, drawing on linguistics, literature and science, but invariably focusing on the vicissitudes of the sign. Interestingly, this has proved problematic for literary theory which has successively tried to claim his work as an early example of, on the one hand, New Criticism and, on the other, reader-response theory. (**PC**)

Further reading

Richards, I. A. (1976) *Complementarities: Uncollected Essays*, ed. J. P. Russo, Manchester: Carcanet.

Rossi-Landi Ferruccio Rossi-Landi (Milan 1921–Trieste 1985) has contributed significantly to the development of **semiotics** and philosophy of **language**. In the early years of his intellectual formation, Rossi-Landi absorbed ideas and methodologies not only from Italian culture, but also from the cultural traditions of Austria and Germany, as well as from British–American traditions of thought. Several of his essays and books were originally published in English. For many years he lived in countries other than Italy, especially in England and the United States. He taught at the University of Michigan, Ann Arbor (1962–1963), and at the Universities of Texas, Austin (1963), which he revisited on several occasions, and acted as visiting professor at various universities in Europe as well as in America between 1964 and 1975. He also taught courses in philosophy and semiotics at the Universities of Havana and Santiago (Cuba). After a teaching appointment in Padova (1958–1962), he returned to the Italian academic world in 1975 as Professor of Philosophy of History at the University of Lecce (Southern Italy). In 1977 he became Full Professor of Theoretical Philosophy at the University of Trieste.

As an editor and translator as well as author, Rossi-Landi made significant contributions to intellectual life. He served as editor or member of the editorial board of various journals, some of which he had in fact founded: *Methodos* (1949–1952), *Occidente* (1955–1956), *Nuova corrente* (1966–1968), *Ideologie*, (1967–1974), *Dialectical Anthropology* (from 1975) and finally *Scienze umane* (1979–1981), all of which contain numerous contributions to the theory of **sign**s.

Rossi-Landi's studies may be divided into three phases (cf. Ponzio 1986, 1989b). The first phase covers the 1950s and includes the monographs: *Charles Morris* (1953, revised and enlarged in an edition of 1975; see also Rossi-Landi's correspondence with Morris, 1992a) and *Significato, comunicazione e parlare comune* (1961, but which in fact was the conclusion of his work of the 1950s, republished in 1980 and again in 1998 in a volume edited by Ponzio).

The second phase belongs to the 1960s and includes *Il linguaggio come lavoro e come mercato* (1968, English translation 1992b), which proposes a theory of linguistic production and of sign production in general which is also a theory of linguistic work and of general sign work, thereby laying the foundations to study the semiotic homology between linguistics and economics. *Semiotica e ideologia* (1972, reprinted in 1974, 1994) completes the preceding volume with the addition of important essays such as 'Ideologia della relatività linguistica'. The latter was also published as an independent volume in English under the title *Ideologies of Linguistic Relativity* (1973). Finally, *Linguistics and Economics* (1975) was written in English in 1970–1971 for the book series *Current Trends in Linguistics*, Vol. 12, and reprinted as an independent volume in 1975 and 1977.

The third period covers the 1970s and includes the book *Ideologia* (1978, 1982), where Rossi-Landi discusses the problem of the connection between ideology and language with particular reference to linguistic alienation. During this third phase he also authored various essays which were subsequently collected in the volume *Metodica filosofica e scienza dei segni* (1985).

Several essays from all three periods, including those which had originally appeared in English, were collected posthumously in the volume *Between Signs and Non-signs* (1992c, ed. S. Petrilli). This volume had been planned by Rossi-Landi himself but was among the many that remained unpublished during his lifetime. (**AP**)

Further reading

Rossi-Landi, F. (1977) *Linguistics and Economics*, The Hague: Mouton.

Rossi-Landi, F. (1990) *Marxism and Ideology*, trans. R. Griffin, Oxford: Clarendon.

Rossi-Landi, F. (1992) *Between Signs and Non-signs*, ed. S. Petrilli, Amsterdam: John Benjamins.

Rules In *logic* two types of rules have been traditionally distinguished: formation rules, determining the way in which logical formulae are built from basic expressions, and rules of inference or deduction which determine the steps by means of which one formula can be deduced from another in such a way that truth conditions are preserved. In *linguistics* the term 'rule' has been in popular use since **Chomsky** (1957), mainly in order to cope with recursiveness: rules determine how one pattern can be expanded into another one. Thus it is possible to speak of rules of **grammar**; in the area of **language** use, however, the term 'rule' is usually disfavoured and replaced, rather, by principle or strategies (e.g. Leech 1983). In *philosophy* a distinction is made between regulative rules (regulating pre-existent forms of behaviour, such as rules or etiquette) and constitutive rules (defining forms of behaviour, such as the rules of football). Searle (1969) uses this distinction and describes the rules formulated for **speech acts** as constitutive rules (thus the act of 'promising' is constituted, created or defined by the fact that under certain conditions the uttering of 'I promise to come tomorrow' counts as the undertaking of an obligation on the part of the speaker). **(JV)**

See also GRICE.

FURTHER READING

Bartsch, R. (1987) *Norms of Language*, London: Longman.

RUSSIAN FORMALISM A trend in literary theory developed in Russia between 1915 and 1925. The most important continuator of this movement in terms of originality and critique is Mikhail **Bakhtin**. With the latter's collaboration, Pavel N. Medvedev weighs up Russian Formalism in his book of 1928, *The Formal Method in Literary Scholarship* (Bakhtin and Medvedev 1985 [1928]). Formalism was condemned under Stalin as a bourgeois conception which contrasted with Marxist orthodoxy. The formalists were above all 'specifiers' who dealt with the problem of the 'specificity of the poetic text' for the first time ever. Two prominent figures in Russian Formalism are **Jakobson** and Jakubinsky. One of the inaugurating texts of this movement is V. B. Shklovsky's booklet *The Resurrection of the Word* (1973 [1914]), while the first attempt at a historical sketch of formalism is B. M. Eikhenbaum's 'Teoriia "formal" nogo metoda' (1926; English translation in Todorov 1965).

Russian Formalism developed in three phases. Its guiding theoretical principles were established in the first phase (1914–1919). 'Poetic **language**' was the specific object of research and to this problematic was dedicated the Society for the Study of Poetic Language (*Opoiaz*). Poetic language is a special linguistic system. A relation of opposition was established between the laws of *poetic* and *practical language* on the basis of specific linguistic characteristics, especially phonetic. *Poetic construction* was differentiated from practical language and considered extraneous to it through a process of 'foreignization'. In poetic construction the *plot* is central whereas the *story* (*fabula*) is only an expedient. An important contribution consists in explaining the art work in terms of literary **genre** instead of referring to the author and his/her life. The second stage (1920–1923) is characterized by a lack of unity and a failure to reconcile itself with Marxist orthodoxy. The third (1924–1925) was the time of disintegration into different theories to the point of engendering as many formalisms as there were formalists. **(AP)**

FURTHER READING

Steiner, P. (1984) *Russian Formalism: A Metapoetics*, Ithaca, NY: Cornell University Press.

S

Sapir Edward Sapir (1884–1939) was an American linguist and anthropologist. Born in Germany, his family moved to the United States when he was five. While studying at Columbia University he met the anthropologist Franz **Boas**, who encouraged Sapir to study native American languages and cultures. Sapir worked in Ottawa for fifteen years, researching the indigenous peoples of Canada. He later taught at the Universities of Chicago and Yale.

Sapir did important pioneering work in **phonology** and historical linguistics, and on the classification of the indigenous **language**s of America. His introductory textbook *Language* (1921) is an elegant and attractive book that is still often recommended as an introduction to linguistics. Sapir often made use of the notion of a grammatical process, not in the sense of a historical change over time but as a way of describing relationships between different variants of the same word or morpheme. For instance, the noun *nation* has a related adjective *national*. Thinking of this relationship as a process, one could say that the adjective is formed by adding *al* onto the end of the noun and changing the pronunciation of the first vowel from the one in *hate* to the one in *hat*. Many American structuralists were suspicious of this way of describing linguistic relationships, preferring a strictly distributional method (see **American structuralism**). **Chomsky**'s work in **generative grammar** reintroduced processes into grammatical theory.

Sapir's name is sometimes linked with that of **Whorf**, though statements rejecting the 'Whorf hypothesis' can be found in his writings. He made important contributions to anthropology, notably on the relation between culture and society, and to Jewish studies. He read widely in psychiatry and psychoanalysis, and wrote papers on the relation between culture and personality. His poems appeared in many places, and he wrote several musical works.

Although Sapir and **Bloomfield** are usually regarded as the main architects of structuralist linguistics in America, Sapir's broader range of scholarly interests meant that much of his influence was in anthropology and cultural studies, leaving Bloomfield as the more dominant figure in linguistics. As Chomsky's prestige grew in the second half of the century, however, Sapir was named more often as a major intellectual precursor, while the weaknesses of Bloomfield's work were emphasized. One reason for this was that Bloomfield avoided linking language and the mind, whereas Sapir was keen to connect linguistics and psychology. The various brands of linguistics which use 'cognitive' as a label (see **cognitive linguistics**) see themselves as continuing Sapir's work in different ways.

Sapir was a rare combination: a rigorous scholar with a broad humanist range of interests and achievements. For appreciations of his work, see Koerner (1984). (**RS**)

FURTHER READING

Koerner, K. (1984) *Edward Sapir: Appraisals of His Life and Work*, Amsterdam: John Benjamins.

Sapir, E. (1921) *Language*, London: Hart-Davis MacGibbon (reprinted 1978).

Sapir, E. (1949) *Selected Writings in Language, Culture and Personality*, ed. D. G. Mandelbaum, Berkeley, CA: University of California Press (reprinted 1985).

SAPIR–WHORF HYPOTHESIS *see* SAPIR and WHORF

SAUSSURE Ferdinand-Mongin de Saussure (1857–1913), Swiss linguist, one of the twentieth century's most influential thinkers on **language**. His posthumously published *Cours de linguistique générale* (1916), edited by colleagues on the basis of students' notes, became the Magna Carta of modern linguistics. It is a key text not only in the development of language studies but also in the establishment of '**semiology**', a more general science of signs, of which linguistics was to be one special branch and in the formation of that broader intellectual movement which came to be known as '**structuralism**'.

Saussure's revolutionary proposal was that, instead of language being seen as peripheral to an understanding of reality, our understanding of reality revolves around language. This idea later became commonplace in various areas of intellectual inquiry, from anthropology to philosophy and psychology; but in Saussure's *Cours* it is clearly articulated, and also expounded in some detail, for the first time.

The basis of Saussure's thinking is a new conception of how the speaker, by uttering certain sounds, is able to articulate ideas. How are these two activities related? In a famous comparison, Saussure likens a language to a sheet of paper. Thought is one side of the sheet and sound the reverse side. Just as it is impossible to cut the paper without cutting corresponding shapes on both sides, so it proves to be impossible in the linguistic case, he held, to isolate thought from sound or sound from thought. The two matching configurations are the back and front of a single form of experience. They are not separate things artificially brought together for purposes of linguistic expression. On the contrary, their indissoluble unity is a *precondition* for the possibility of linguistic expression.

The minimal unit of correlations between sound and thought is the linguistic **sign**, which exists in the speaker's mind as a pairing of *signifiant* (sound pattern) with *signifié* (concept). The linguistic sign is both arbitrary and linear. Arbitrariness implies that the relation between *signifiant* and *signifié* is determined by no external factors. Linearity implies the sequential concatenation of signs in linguistic messages, where they enter into '**syntagmatic**' relations with signs preceding and following.

Saussure held that each language correlates sound and thought in its own unique way. In this sense, speakers of language A do not inhabit the same mental world as speakers of a different language B, even if they live in the same physical space. He insisted on distinguishing the individual linguistic act (***parole***) from the linguistic system underlying it (***langue***), and both of these from the human language faculty in general (***langage***). *Langue* he saw as a system belonging to society, i.e. to the collectivity of its speakers, and even said that it is never complete in any individual. He also insisted that it be studied as a '**synchronic**' phenomenon (i.e. without reference to the passage of time) and relegated the study of linguistic change to '**diachronic**' linguistics. In his view the failure to distinguish synchronic from diachronic facts had vitiated large areas of nineteenth-century language studies. **(RH)**

See also *Signifiant* and *Signifié*.

Further reading

Harris, R. (1987) *Reading Saussure*, London: Duckworth.

Saussure, F. de (1972 [1916]) *Cours de linguistique générale*, ed. T. de Mauro, Paris: Payot.

Saussure, F. de (1983) *Course in General Linguistics*, trans. R. Harris, London: Duckworth.

Schaff Adam Schaff (1913, Lwów–2006, Warsaw) is a Polish philosopher. Of his numerous books, several treat problems of **semantics**, philosophy of **language**, logic, theory of knowledge and ideology. According to Schaff, language is a social product as well as a genetic phenomenon and is functional to human praxis. This is the basis of the 'active role' of the human subject both at the level of cognitive processes as well as of practical action. Language is not only an instrument for the **expression** of **meaning**, but also the material which goes to form meaning and without which meaning could not exist. Consequently Schaff criticizes the reductive innatist and biologistic interpretation of language as proposed by linguist Noam **Chomsky** and biologist Eric H. Lenneberg (see Schaff 1978).

According to Schaff, we must free ourselves from what he calls (1962) the 'fetishism of **signs**' (a direct echo of **Marx**'s 'fetishism of commodities'). The 'fetishism of signs' is reflected in the reified conception of the relations among signs as well as between **signifier** and **signified**; analysis must begin from the social processes of **communication**, and sign relations must be considered as relations among humans who use and produce signs in specific social conditions. In Schaff's opinion, by contrast with naïve materialism, we must recognize the superiority of language theories which stress the active function of language in the cognitive process; the connection between language and *Weltanschauung*; and the connection between language and the 'image of reality'. However, the human being should be considered as the result of social relations, and language as inseparable from social praxis (Ponzio 1974).

In studies of human **semiosis**, this leads us to a new vision of issues related to sign and language: the problem of the connection between language and knowledge (see Schaff 1973, 1975); language and **consciousness**; language, ideology and stereotypes; and language and responsibility. Conversely, it is apparent that theories of knowledge are theories in need of support from studies on language; in order to maintain an adequate consideration of the concepts of 'choice', 'responsibility' and 'individual freedom', and such problems as the 'tyranny of words', 'linguistic alienation' and its causes must also be taken into account. (**AP**)

Further reading

Ponzio, A. (1990) 'Humanism, language and knowledge in Adam Schaff', in A. Ponzio (ed.), *Man as a Sign*, Berlin: Mouton de Gruyter.

Schaff, A. (1973) *Language and Cognition*, New York: McGraw-Hill.

Schaff, A. (1978) *Structuralism and Marxism*, Oxford: Pergamon Press.

Scotus John Duns Scotus (*c.* 1266–1308) does more than any Latin thinker after **Aquinas** but prior to **Poinsot** to explain how and why concepts are **sign**s. He introduces the distinction between awareness of things physically present here and now, which he calls *intuitive*, and awareness of things absent or non-existent, which he calls *abstractive*, and shows that concepts are not *self*-representations but *other*-representations, necessary both for the interpretation of present things known and also for the making present in awareness of absent things as objects. The full import of this distinction for **semiotics** becomes clear in Book III of the early seventeenth-century *Tractatus de Signis* of John Poinsot. (**JD**)

Further reading

Scotus, J. D. (1999–2006) *Opera Philosophica*, 5 vols. Critical edition ed. Timothy Noone *et al.*, St Bonaventure, NY: Franciscan Institute Publications/ Washington, DC: Catholic University of America Press.

Sebeok Thomas Albert Sebeok (Budapest 1920–Bloomington, IN 2001) emigrated to the USA in 1937, where he became a citizen in 1944. He was a faculty member of Indiana University for the whole time of his academic career. He acted as Editor-in-Chief of *Semiotica*, the journal and main organ of the International Association for Semiotic Studies (**IASS**), from the time both were founded, in 1969. Sebeok has greatly contributed to the institutionalization of **semiotics** internationally, and to its configuration as 'biosemiotics', 'semiotics of life' or 'global semiotics' (*Global Semiotics* is the title of his 2001 monograph). His work was inspired by Charles S. **Peirce**, Charles **Morris** and Roman **Jakobson**. Sebeok's diversified interests broadly ranged from the natural sciences to the human sciences.

The entire universe is perfused with **sign**s, Sebeok held, after Peirce, and enters 'global semiotics'. In light of his 'holistic' approach, Sebeok's research on the 'life of signs' was closely connected with his interest in the 'signs of life': ***semiosis*** and *life* converge. Semiosis originates with the first stirrings of life, which led to Sebeok's cardinal axiom that semiosis is the criterial attribute of life. 'Global semiotics' provides a meeting point and observation post for studies on the life of signs and the signs of life.

Sebeok's global approach to semiotic theory and practice presupposes his critique of anthropocentrism and **glottocentrism**. He opened the science or 'doctrine' of signs (the term he preferred, recalling **Locke**) to include **zoosemiotics** (a term he introduced in 1963) or even more broadly **biosemiotics**, on the one hand, and endosemiotics, on the other, extending his gaze to semiosis throughout the whole living universe, to the realms of macro- and micro-oganisms. In Sebeok's conception, sign science is not only the 'science qui étude la vie des signes au sein de la vie sociale' as Saussure famously held, the study of **communication** in culture, but also of communicative behaviour from a biosemiotic perspective.

Sebeok's global approach to semiosis favours the discovery of new perspectives, interdisciplinary interconnections and interpretive practices, new cognitive fields and **language**s, which interact dialogically, as foreseen by the open and detotalized nature of his semiotics. Sebeok identifies sign relations where there only seemed to exist 'mere' facts and relations among things, independent from communication and interpretation processes. Use of the expression 'doctrine of signs' takes account of Peirce and of **Kant**ian critique. According to Sebeok, the task of semiotics is not only to observe and describe signs, but also to interrogate the conditions of possibility that characterize and specify signs for what they are and for what they must be (cf. Sebeok's Preface to his monograph of 1976).

A pivotal notion in global semiotics is '**modelling**', used to explain life and behaviour among living entities conceived in terms of semiosis. On the basis of biosemiotic research, Sebeok averred that the modelling capacity is observable in all life forms and that these subsist in species-specific worlds – living beings signify and communicate in species-specifically modelled worlds. Modelling is an a priori transcendental in the Kantian sense, the foundation of communication and signification. Modelling systems theory (cf. Sebeok and Danesi 2000) studies semiotic phenomena in terms of modelling processes. Sebeok dubs the human species-specific primary modelling device 'language' (capable of constructing multiple worlds, therefore the condition for the evolution of humanity), distinguishing it from 'speech' (the capacity for verbal communication) which appeared much later in human evolution. With speech, different historical languages arise which assume a secondary modelling function through exaptation and generate a plurality of cultural systems which constitute tertiary modelling (cf. Sebeok 1988b, 1994).

Sebeok's opening remarks to *The Sign and Its Masters* (1979a) can be extended to all his research viewed in light of current debate in philosophico-linguistic and semiotic theory. A transition is now occurring from '**code** semiotics' to 'interpretation semiotics', from semiotics centred on linguistics to one which is autonomous from it.

Sebeok privileged interpretation semiotics in his early theoretical volume *Contributions to the Doctrine of Signs* (1976), and explored semiotics as an adequate methodological tool applicable to different fields in his more discursive volume *The Play of Musement* (1981a).

Other important volumes have since followed in rapid succession: *I Think*

I Am a Verb: More Contributions to the Doctrine of Signs (1986c), *Essays in Zoosemiotics* (1990), *A Sign is Just a Sign* (1991a), *Semiotics in the United States* (1991b) and *Signs: An Introduction to Semiotics* (1994). **(SP)**

See also SEMIOTIC SELF.

FURTHER READING

Brier, S. (ed.) (2003) *Thomas Sebeok and the Biosemiotic Legacy*, Sebeok Memorial Special Issue, *Cybernetics & Human Knowing*, 10(1).

Petrilli, S. and Ponzio, A. (2001) *Thomas Sebeok and the Signs of Life*, Cambridge: Icon Books.

Sebeok, T. A. and Danesi, M. (2000) *The Forms of Meaning. Modelling Systems Theory and Semiotic Analysis*, Berlin: Mouton de Gruyter.

SECONDNESS Secondness is one of Charles S. **Peirce**'s three categories of phenomena, the other two being **firstness** and **thirdness**. The category of secondness (obsistence, over-againstness), together with firstness and thirdness, are the omnipresent categories of mind, **sign** and reality (*CP* 2.84–94).

Secondness is the category according to which something is considered relative to, or over against, something else. It involves binarity, a relation of opposition or reaction. From the viewpoint of signs, secondness is connected with the **index**. The index is a sign that signifies its object by a relation of contiguity, causality or by some other physical connection. However, this relation also depends on a **habit** or convention. For example, the relation between hearing a knock at the door and someone on the other side of the door who wants to enter. Whereas the **icon**, which is governed by firstness, presents itself as an *original* sign, and the **symbol**, which is governed by *thirdness*, as a *transuasional* sign; the index, which is governed by secondness, is an *obsistent* sign (*CP* 2.89–92).

From the viewpoint of logic, inference regulated by secondness corresponds to deduction. In fact, in the case of an Obsistent Argument or Deduction, the conclusion is *compelled* to acknowledge that the facts stated in the premises, whether in one or both, are such as could not be if the fact stated in the conclusion were not there (cf. *CP* 2.96).

From the viewpoint of ontology, that is, of being, secondness is present in the law of *anancasm* or necessity which, on Peirce's account, regulates the evolutionary development of the universe together with *agapasm* (creative love, which corresponds to firstness) and *tychasm* (causality, which corresponds to thirdness) (cf. *CP* 6.287–317; Petrilli 1999b).

Therefore, on the level of logic, firstness, secondness and thirdness correspond to **abduction**, **deduction** and **induction**; on the level of the typology of signs they correspond to the icon, index and symbol; and on the level of ontology to agapasm, anancasm and tychasm.

To secondness or obsistence, a binary category, there corresponds a relation of relative **alterity** in which the terms of the relation depend on each other. Effective alterity, the possibility of something being-on-its-own-account, *absolute per se*, autonomously, presents itself under the category of firstness, or orience, or originality, according to which something '*is what it is without reference to anything else* within it or without it, regardless of all force and of all reason' (*CP* 2.85). An effective relation of alterity would not be possible if there were only binarity, secondness, and therefore obsistence (cf. Ponzio 1990a: 197–214). Relations of alterity would not be possible in a system regulated exclusively by secondness and, therefore, by binarity, where an element exists only on the condition that it refers to another element and would not exist should this other element be negated.

> Take, for example, a husband and wife. Here there is nothing but a real twoness; but it constitutes a reaction, in the sense that the husband makes the wife a wife in fact (not merely in some comparing thought); while the wife makes the husband a husband.
>
> (*CP* 2.84) (**SP**)

FURTHER READING

Peirce, C. S. (1955) 'The principles of phenomenology', in *Philosophical Writings of Peirce*, ed. J. Buchler, New York: Dover.

Peirce, C. S. (1958) 'Letter to Lady Welby, 12 October 1904', in *Charles S. Peirce: Selected Writings*, ed. P. Wiener, New York: Dover.

Petrilli, S. (1999) 'About and beyond Peirce', *Semiotica*, 124(3/4): 299–376.

SEMANTICS In **Morris**'s theory of **semiosis**, the semantical dimension of the functioning of **sign**s pertains to 'the relation of signs to the objects to which the signs are applicable' (1938: 6) and the study of this dimension is called semantics. In linguistics, this translates into a view of semantics as the component of a linguistic theory dealing with **meaning**, whether at the word level (lexical semantics) or at the sentence or propositional level. Often, semantics is said to study meaning out of context, whereas **pragmatics** studies meaning in context (Levinson 1983). However, most sentences can only be understood against a set of background assumptions which effectively define a context (Searle 1978). A more useful distinction may be, therefore, to regard the province of semantics as the properties of the **language** system that directly enable the generation of meaning in language use, a process which is itself within the realm of pragmatics. (**JV**)

See also BRÉAL *and* GRICE.

FURTHER READING

Lyons, J. (1995) *Linguistic Semantics: An Introduction*, Cambridge: Cambridge University Press.

SEMIOLOGY Not to be confused either with **semantics** or with **semiotics**, despite the fact that the latter term is often loosely treated as synonymous with semiology. The English word is a translation of the French word *sémiologie*, coined by Ferdinand de **Saussure** in 1894 and intended as the designation for a (then non-existent) discipline devoted to studying 'the life of **sign**s as part of social life'. In Saussure's *Cours de linguistique générale* this discipline is presented as a branch of social psychology. Saussure did not conceive of semiology as a general science of signs of every kind. From his Geneva lectures, it seems clear that he excluded from semiology all signs dependent on or controlled by the decisions of individuals. Nor did he include so-called 'natural' signs (storm clouds, blushing, etc.). Semiology was apparently to be confined to the study of public institutional signs, particularly those in which the relation between form and **meaning** was 'arbitrary': of these Saussure regarded linguistic signs as constituting the most important class.

Followers of Saussure later extended the definition of the term. Buyssens equated semiology with the study of **communication** processes in general (at least when conceived of as actions intended to influence others, and recognized as such by the 'others' in question). **Barthes** reversed Saussure's view of the relations between semiology and linguistics, treating the former as part of the latter. **Lévi-Strauss** considered anthropology to be a branch of semiology. None of these later developments corresponds to Saussure's original conception. **(RH)**

See also HJELMSLEV, POSTSTRUCTURALISM *and* STRUCTURALISM.

FURTHER READING

Saussure, F. de (1983) *Course in General Linguistics*, trans. R. Harris, London: Duckworth.

SEMIOSIS Semiosis is the name given to the action of **signs**. **Semiotics** might therefore be understood as the study of semiosis or even as a 'metasemiosis', producing 'signs about signs'. Behind this simple definition lies a universe of complexity. In general parlance, and sometimes in semiotics, signs are conceived only as inanimate objects which are utilized for the purpose of sending messages. However, semiosis occurs in many different ways and in places where signs are not necessarily apparent to humans. Whereas human semiosis has been the object of the many investigations which make up **anthroposemiotics**, there is an enormous variety of semiosis which is non-human in character. Moreover, anthroposemiosis should not be considered as separate from the wider-ranging actions of signs between all kinds of cells. Instead, it should be understood as being *contained* within the latter, its vicissitudes merely being differently ordered than that of its neighbours: 'Thus, physics, biology, psychology and sociology each embodies its own peculiar level of semiosis' (Sebeok 1994: 6).

Morris famously defines semiosis as a 'process in which something is a sign to some organism' (1946: 366). Like **Peirce**, he identifies a threefold operation of semiosis consisting of the *sign vehicle*, the ***designatum*** and the ***interpretant*** (equivalent to **representamen**, **object** and interpretant), in which the first acts as a sign, the second is what is referred to and the third is the effect of, and the effector of, the relationship between the other two (Morris 1938). Morris's work is a good example of how simple sign relations entail semiosic complexity. He envisages three realms of semiosis: these are the relations between sign vehicles, to which he gives the name *syntactics* (or **syntax**); the relations between each different sign vehicle and its designatum, named **semantics**; and the relations between signs and their users – **pragmatics**. With adjustments, this triad of approaches to semiosis in general has provided the agenda for much of modern linguistics.

The relations between the terms 'semiosis' and '**communication**' should also be noted. It is well known that Peirce used the term 'semiosis' and seldom invoked concepts of 'communication' and 'intentionality' (although, see Johansen 1993: 189ff.). The latter, however, are often taken as axiomatic in anthroposemiotics. **Saussure**, for example, in his *Cours*, outlines the 'speech circuit'. A diagram of two human heads is shown, passing **code**d speech to each other and thus connecting the contents of two minds in an act of 'telementation' (1983: 11; cf. Harris 1987: 205ff.).

Such emphasis on the 'success' of human semiosis characterizes much communication theory. Much later in the twentieth century, for example, **relevance theory** questioned code models, suggesting that:

> most human communication is intentional, and it is intentional for two good reasons. The first reason is the one suggested by **Grice**: by producing direct evidence of one's informative intention, one can convey a much wider range of information than can be conveyed by producing direct evidence for the basic information itself. The second reason humans have for communicating is to modify and extend the mutual cognitive environment they share with one another.
>
> (Sperber and Wilson 1995: 64)

The code in Saussure's speech circuit and the ostension and inference in relevance theory are powerful components in the act of human communication. Both imply the manifest transaction in the verbal transmission of signs.

However, this should not be allowed to obscure the fact that communicative acts and intentionality are only a small part of the universal semiosic repertoire. For biosemioticians, especially after **Sebeok**, 'life' and 'semiosis' are sufficiently synonymous that one cannot exist without the other. For others, such as **Deely**, physiosemiosis must be considered as a possibility because before life it is possible that there were, nevertheless, the first flickerings of **thirdness** that eventually take hold when the full throttle of semiosis in life occurs. For Deely, however, this does not entail pansemiosis (see Deely 2006d); nevertheless, there are (pan)semioticians who are happy to embrace the possibility that the entirety of the universe is semiosic, for example the theoretical biologist Stanley Salthe (1999) and the sociologist/anthropologist Edwina Taborsky (2002). What is not in dispute is that semiosis is simply ineffable and many semioses, like the action of subatomic particles (Sebeok 1994: 8), can only be discerned through a **model** of their activity. (**PC**)

See also SIGNIFICATION.

FURTHER READING

Hoffmeyer, J. (2008) *Biosemiotics: An Examination into the Signs of Life and the Life of Signs*, Scranton, PA: University of Scranton Press.

Morris, C. (1938) *Foundations of the Theory of Signs*, Chicago: University of Chicago Press.

Sebeok, T. A. (2001) *Signs: An Introduction to Semiotics*, 2nd edn, Toronto: University of Toronto Press.

Semiosphere The term 'semiosphere' has at least three broad definitions in contemporary **semiotics**. Derived from Vernadsky's idea of a 'biosphere', **Lotman** (2000: 123) defines semiosphere as the 'semiotic space necessary for the existence and functioning of **languages**, not the sum total of different languages; in a sense the semiosphere has a prior existence and is in constant interaction with languages'. Lotman's idiosyncratic use of 'language', here, is to refer to 'a cluster of semiotic spaces and their boundaries'. Outside these spaces, for Lotman, there is no **communication**. As such, Lotman's idea of semiosphere contributes directly to a theory of culture compatible with **cybernetics** and **autopoiesis**: 'Every living culture has a "built-in" mechanism for multiplying its languages.' Thus, the smallest unit of **semiosis** is not a 'language' but the entire semiosphere of 'languages' in all its heterogeneity of semiosis (see also 'The logic of explosion' in Lotman 2009); the semiosphere's highest form and final act is when it is able to produce self-description.

Kull's definition of semiosphere extends Lotman's by making it more compatible with semiotics as it is to be understood after **biosemiotics**. He suggests that 'Semiosphere is the set of all interconnected **Umwelt**s. Any two Umwelts, when communicating, are a part of the same semiosphere' (Kull 1998: 301). Thus, a domestic cat and its owner share the same semiosphere when they are each eating a portion of a fish that the latter has cooked for both of them. For both, the fish is a component of what they understand as food. However, the ways that these two members of different species will relate to the food, how the food exists in their Umwelt, are very different – the cat's eating may be solely for survival, it may be totally dependent on its owner; the human might eat simply for pleasure, for specific gustatory experience, to partake of a cultural and culinary pursuit, to exercise some knowledge of the history of the fish and members of its species. In Lotman's terms, different 'languages' are at play in the consumption of this food.

A third definition of semiosphere is proposed by **Hoffmeyer**, who developed his notion initially without reference to Lotman (Hoffmeyer 1996). Later, he writes that:

> The biosemiotic idea implies that life on Earth manifests itself in a global and evolutionary *semiosphere*, a sphere of sign process and elements of meaning that constitute a frame of understanding within which biology must work. The semiosphere is a sphere like the atmosphere, hydrosphere, or biosphere. It permeates these spheres from their innermost to outermost reaches and consists of communication: sound, scent, movement, colors, forms, electrical fields, various waves, chemical signals, touch, and so forth – in short, the signs of life.
>
> (Hoffmeyer 2008a: 5)

Thus, Hoffmeyer's understanding of semiosphere is compatible with his idea of **semiotic niche**, that part of a species' existence holding all the things that are necessary for it to survive within its Umwelt, which is itself specifically placed within a larger semiosphere of Unwelten. It is also compatible with **Sebeok**'s equation of semiosis and life, although not with any notion of semiosphere that might be developed to account for physiosemiosis.

For Kull, the notion of semiosphere in Hoffmeyer suggests that it is partially independent of organisms' Umwelten. His own understanding of semiosphere entails that it is entirely created by organisms' Umwelten. (**PC**)

Further reading

Hoffmeyer, J. (2008) *Biosemiotics: An Examination into the Signs of Life and the Life of Signs*, Scranton, PA: University of Scranton Press.

Kull, K. (1998) 'On semiosis, Umwelt, and semiosphere', *Semiotica*, 120(3/4): 299–310.

Lotman, Y. M. (2000) *Universe of the Mind: A Semiotic Theory of Culture*, London: I. B. Tauris.

Semiotic niche ***see*** **Hoffmeyer and Semiosphere**

Semiotic self Fundamental formulation of subjectivity and self-hood introduced by Sebeok in 1979 and subsequently elaborated (Sebeok 1989, 1992, 1998b). Sebeok's notion of the 'semiotic self' derives from an account of anxiety, an **indexical sign** integral to the workings of the immune system of any organism, that system being the mechanism which maintains a distinction between 'self' and 'non-self'. According to Sebeok, the immune system harbours a kind of 'memory' based on biological discrimination, but also operates another kind of memory, anxiety, whose domain is patterns of behaviour. Anxiety is activated when the self is menaced and the organism identifies the behaviour of another organism in terms of its own **Umwelt**. Considering self-hood at the semiotic threshold of the humble cell, Sebeok identifies two apprehensions of the self: a) *immunologic*, or biochemical, with semiotic overtones; and b) *semiotic*, or social, with biological anchoring. The immune system responds to (the threat of) invasion somatically, but does so in an indexical fashion; anxiety develops from somatic roots but becomes almost fully autonomous in its semiotic vicissitudes. As Sebeok adds, 'In evolution, (a) is very old, whereas (b) is relatively recent' (1979c: 267). Despite the proliferation of theories of the subject since the Enlightenment and, especially, the myriad twentieth-century theories which implicate signs or discourses as nurturing factors in the constitution of self-hood, Sebeok's theory of the semiotic self goes further than any other reflection on subjectivity yet offered. Featuring some cognate implications but approaching the matter through the heritage of **Peirce**, Mead and the **pragmatic** tradition in sociology, as opposed to approaching the matter from **biosemiotics**, is Wiley's concept of the semiotic self in his 1994 book of the same name. (**PC**)

Further reading

Sebeok, T. A. (1979) 'The semiotic self', in *The Sign and Its Masters*, Austin, TX: University of Texas Press.

Semiotics Semiotics may be understood as indicating:

1 the specificity of human **semiosis**;
2 the general science of **sign**s.

Concerning (1) in the world of life which coincides with **semiosis**, human semiosis is characterized as *metasemiosis*, that is, as the possibility of reflecting on signs, of making signs not only the object of interpretation not distinguishable from the response to these signs, but also of interpretation as reflection on signs, as suspension of response and possibility of deliberation. We may call this specific human capacity for metasemiosis 'semiotics'. Developing **Aristotle**'s correct observation made at the beginning of his *Metaphysics*, that man tends by nature to knowledge, we could say that man tends by nature to semiotics. Human semiosis, **anthroposemiosis**, is characterized by its presenting itself as semiotics. Semiotics as human semiosis, or anthroposemiosis, can a) venture as far as the entire universe in search of **meaning**s and senses, considering it therefore from the viewpoint of signness; or, b) absolutize anthroposemiosis by identifying it with semiosis itself.

Concerning (2), semiotics as a discipline or science (**Saussure**) or theory (Charles **Morris**) or doctrine (**Sebeok**) presents itself in the first case (a) as 'global semiotics' (Sebeok) extensible to the whole universe insofar as it is perfused by signs (**Peirce**); whereas in the second case (b) it is limited and anthropocentric.

The origins of semiotics as a field of knowledge are identified above all in the origins of medical semiotics, or symptomatology, the study of symptoms. In truth, since man is a 'semiotic animal' all human life has always been characterized by knowledge of a semiotic order. If, therefore, medical semeiotics may be considered as the first branch of development in semiotics, this is only because, in contrast to **Hippocrates** and **Galen**, hunters, farmers, navigators, fishermen and women, with their wisdom and sign practices relative to the production and reproduction of life, have always been involved in semiotics, but without writing treatises.

Given that verbal signs, oral and written, are unique in the sense that they carry out nothing other than a sign function, reflection on verbal signs since ancient times represents another pillar in the semiotic science. Indeed, the study of verbal signs has greatly oriented the criteria for determining what may be considered as a sign.

This explains how, in very recent times (the beginning of the twentieth century), semiotics presents itself, on the basis of its linguistico-verbal interests, in the form of *sémiologie* with the task, in Saussure's view, of studying the life of signs 'dans le sein de la vie sociale'. And though linguistics was included as merely a branch of **semiology**, *sémiologie* in its totality was profoundly influenced by it. Saussure only recognized signs in entities which carry out an intentionally communicative function in a social context. From the limits of this conception, *communication semiotics*, a transition takes place to *signification semiotics* (**Barthes**) which also recognizes signs in what is not produced with the intention of functioning as such, and finally to the phase which with Barthes (1975b) may be called 'third sense semiotics', or '**text** semiotics', or *significance semiotics*. But parallel to all this, other semiotic perspectives have developed in different fields of interest as well. Without claiming to exhaust the list, consider the following perspectives together with the names of their main representatives: the psychological (Freud, **Bühler**, Vygotsky), philosophical (Peirce, **Welby**, **Ogden and Richards**, **Wittgenstein**, Morris, **Cassirer**), literary critical (**Bakhtin**), biological (Romanes, Jakob and Thure von **Uexküll**, Jacob, Monod) and mathematical–topological (René Thom). By making the 'semiosphere' (**Lotman**) consist in the 'semiobiosphere', Sebeok's 'global semiotics' has offered the most exhaustive account of signs: this perspective is the most capable of questioning the presumed totalities of semiotics and showing them up for what they really are, its parts. **(SP)**

See also ANTHROPOSEMIOTICS, BIOSEMIOTICS *and* ZOOSEMIOTICS.

FURTHER READING

Cobley, P. (2010) *Contemporary Semiotics: History and Practice*, Berlin: Mouton de Gruyter.

Deely, J. (1994) *The Human Use of Signs, or Elements of Anthroposemiosis*, Lanham, MD: Rowman and Littlefield.

Posner, R., Robering, K. and Sebeok, T. A. (eds) (1997–2004) *Semiotik/Semiotics. A Handbook on the Sign-Theoretic Foundations of Nature and Culture*, 4 vols, Berlin: Walter de Gruyter.

SHIFTER *see* DEIXIS

SIGN A sign is a factor in a process conceived either dyadically (**signifier/signified**) in accord with **Saussure** and his followers or triadically (sign [**representamen**]/**object**/ **interpretant**) in accord with **Peirce** and his.

The fundamental terms of a sign include what we may call the *interpreted* sign, on the side of the object, and the *interpretant* in a relation where the interpretant is what makes the interpreted sign possible. The interpreted becomes a sign component because it receives an interpretation, but the interpretant in turn is also a sign component with the potential to engender a new sign: therefore, where there is a sign, there are immediately two, and given that the interpretant can engender a new sign, there are immediately three, and so forth as described by Charles S. Peirce with his concept of infinite semiosis (popularized by **Eco** as **unlimited semiosis**), the chain of deferrals from one interpretant to another.

To analyse the sign beginning from the object of intepretation, that is, the interpreted, means to begin from a secondary level. In other words, to begin from the object-interpreted means to begin from a point in the chain of deferrals, or semiosic chain, which cannot be considered as the starting point. Nor can it be privileged by way of abstraction at a theoretical level to explain the workings of sign processes.

An example: a spot on the skin is a sign insofar as it may be interpreted as a symptom of sickness of the liver: this is already a secondary level in the interpretation process. At a primary level, retrospectively, the skin disorder is an interpretation enacted by the organism itself in relation to an anomaly which is disturbing it and to which it responds. The skin disorder is already in itself an interpretant response.

To say that the sign is first an interpretant means that the sign is first a response. We could also say that the sign is a reaction: but only on the condition that by 'reaction' we intend 'interpretation' (similarly to Charles **Morris**'s behaviourism, but differently from the mechanistic approach).

The expression 'solicitation–response' is preferable to 'stimulus–reaction' to the end of avoiding superficial associations between the approaches that they recall respectively. Even a 'direct' response to a stimulus, or better solicitation, is never direct but 'mediated' by an interpretation: unless it is a 'reflex action', formulation of a response involves identifying the solicitation, situating it in a context, and relating it to given behavioural parameters (whether a question of simple types of behaviour, e.g. the prey–predator model, or more complex behaviours connected to cultural values, as in the human world). Therefore, the sign is first of all an interpretant, a response beginning from which something is considered as a sign and becomes its interpreted and is further able to generate an unlimited chain of other signs.

A sign presents varying degrees of plurivocality and univocality. A signal may be defined as a univocal sign, or better as a sign with the lowest degrees of plurivocality.

(Note, also, that 'sign' is the usual shorthand term given to the formal **sign language** used by the deaf.) (**SP**)

See also SEMIOLOGY, SEMIOSIS, SEMIOTICS *and* SIGNIFICATION.

FURTHER READING

Deely, J. (2001) 'A sign is *what*? A dialogue between a semiotist and a would-be realist', *Sign Systems Studies*, 29(2): 705–743.

Peirce, C. S. (1955) 'Logic as semiotic: The theory of signs', in *Philosophical Writings of Peirce*, ed. J. Buchler, New York: Dover.

Sebeok, T. A. (2001) *Signs: An Introduction to Semiotics*, 2nd edn, Toronto: University of Toronto Press.

SIGNANS The signans is, with the signatum, a sign component. These recently revived Augustinian terms are preferable to the Saussurean *signifiant* and *signifié*, 'acoustic image' and 'concept', since they do not imply a psychologistic and phonocentric version of **sign**.

The signans is an object which, once interpreted, becomes material of the signatum. The sign is the totality and should not be confused with the signans as in the current expression 'to be a sign of', which would be better said as 'to be a signans of': something is interpreted as that which *stands for*, or *refers to*, or is a *vehicle of a signatum* – or ***designatum*** (Morris 1938), or **significatum** (Morris 1946), or **signification** (Morris 1964) – to be distinguished from **denotatum**. Instead, when a whole sign acts as a new signans of a signatum at a secondary level, we then have the case of **connotation** (Hjelmslev 1961).

The materiality of the signans (cf. Petrilli 1990: 365–401; Rossi-Landi 1992d: 271–299) is not only extrasign materiality, physical materiality (the body of the signans) and instrumental materiality (nonverbal signs, their non-sign uses and functions), but also semiotic materiality, that is, historico-social materiality at more or less high levels of complexity, elaboration and/or articulation (elaboration materiality); ideological materiality; extra-intentional materiality, that is, objectivity independent from **consciousness** and volition; and also signifying otherness materiality, that is, the possibility of other signata with respect to the signatum of any one specific interpretive path. (**SP**)

FURTHER READING

Rossi-Landi, F. (1992) 'Signs and material reality', in *Between Signs and Non-signs*, ed. and intro. S. Petrilli, Amsterdam: John Benjamins.

SIGNIFIANT The sound pattern which, through its association with the ***signifié***, forms the linguistic sign according to **Saussure**. The first English translation of Saussure's *Cours* erroneously renders the term as 'signifier' (i.e. synonymous with 'that which signifies'), while **Barthes**' much-consulted Saussurean primer *Elements of Semiology* (1967a) attempts to present the *signifiant* as a material substance (i.e. the sounds uttered by a speaker or, by extension in semiology, any material element that signifies). Both misconstruals constitute departures from Saussure's restriction of *signifiant* to the mental realm. (**PC**)

See also SIGNANS.

SIGNIFICATION/SIGNIFICANCE Charles **Morris** distinguishes between signification and significance, thereby indicating two different aspects of '**meaning**': the **semantic** and the axiological. Victoria **Welby**, instead, uses significance (see **significs**) for the third term of her meaning triad, the other two being 'sense' and 'meaning'. Both authors (in the same way as others who work on the same concepts, e.g. Barthes 1975b) relate sense to value and, therefore, semiotics to axiology. In the words of Morris (1964: vii), 'if we ask what is the meaning of life, we may be asking a question about the signification of the term "life", or asking a question about the value or significance of living – or both'. And the fact that usage of such terms as 'meaning' (with the polarity suggested) is so widespread suggests, continues Morris, that there is a fundamental relation between what he distinguishes as signification and significance. (**SP**)

SIGNIFICATUM Use of the term significatum in **semiotics** is explained by Charles **Morris** in *Signs, Language, and Behavior* (1946). The **sign**, or better, the **signans**, *signifies* its significatum. To signify, to have **signification** and to have a significatum are synonyms. In the words of Morris: 'Those conditions which are such that whatever fulfills them is a denotatum will be called a *significatum* of the sign' (1971: 94). In his description of the conditions which allow for something to be a sign, the significatum is distinct from the **denotatum**. If something satisfies the conditions such that something else functions as a sign, while this second something is a denotatum, the first something is the significatum.

All signs signify, that is, have a significatum, but not all signs denote. The significatum of the bell (sign) which attracts the attention of

Pavlov's famous dog (interpreter) is that something edible is available; the food found by the dog which enables it to respond in a certain way (**interpretant**), as provoked by the sign, is the denotatum. The latter, however, may actually not exist, to the dog's great disappointment. In *Foundations of the Theory of Signs* (1938: Ch. 2), Morris uses the term designatum instead of significatum. Every sign insofar as it is a sign has a designatum, but not every sign has a denotatum, because not every sign refers to something which actually exists: where what is referred to (significatum or designatum) actually exists as referred to, the object of reference is a denotatum. In other words, the significatum is what the sign or signans refers to, a set of qualities forming a class or type of objects or events to which the interpreter reacts independently of the fact that what is referred to actually exists (denotatum) according to the existence value attributed to it by the sign (cf. Ponzio 1981a). In *Signification and Significance* (1964) he replaces the term 'significatum' with 'signification' while the term 'denotatum' is dropped altogether. (**SP**)

FURTHER READING

Morris, C. (1971) *Writings on the General Theory of Signs*, ed. T. A. Sebeok, The Hague: Mouton.

SIGNIFICS Significs is a neologism introduced by Victoria **Welby**, after first trying *sensifics*, for her approach to the study of **signs**, **meaning** and interpretation. A provisional definition of significs was formulated by Welby in *Significs and Language* (1911): 'the study of the nature of significance in all its forms and relations' (Welby 1985a [1911]: vii), with a practical bearing 'not only on **language** but on every possible form of human expression in action, invention, and creation' (ibid.: ix). But see her own dictionary definition of 1902 and encyclopaedia entry of 1911 (now Welby 1977). In contrast to '**semantics**', 'semasiology' and '**semiotics**', 'significs' was free from technical associations, thus making it suitable to signal the connection between meaning and value in all its aspects (pragmatic, social, ethic, aesthetic, etc.) (cf. Welby 1983, 1985a; Schmitz 1985). It takes account of the everyday expression 'What does it signify?', with its focus on the sign's ultimate value and significance (see **signification/significance**) beyond semantic meaning. In addition to a theory of meaning, significs proposes a 'significal method' that transcends pure descriptivism and strictly logico-epistemological boundaries in the direction of axiology and of the study of the conditions that make meaningful behaviour possible (cf. Petrilli 1988, 1998a, 2009). Central to significs is Welby's analysis of meaning into three main levels: 'Sense' – 'the organic response to environment'; 'Meaning' – the specific sense which a word 'is intended to convey'; and 'Significance' – 'the far-reaching consequence, implication, ultimate result or outcome of some event or experience' (cf. Hardwick 1977: 169). According to Charles S. **Peirce**, the triad of sense, meaning and significance relates closely to his own triad of Immediate **Interpretant**, Dynamical Interpretant and Final Interpretant, respectively (Hardwick 1977: 109–111). (**SP**)

FURTHER READING

Petrilli, S. (ed.) (2009) *Signifying and Understanding: Reading the Works of Victoria Welby and the Significs Movement*, Berlin: Mouton de Gruyter.

SIGNIFIÉ The conceptual component of the linguistic sign according to **Saussure**. In the first English translation of Saussure's *Cours* and then in subsequent translations of broadly Saussurean commentaries, the *signifié* was called the 'signified', giving the false impression that Saussure intended 'the thing signified' (i.e. the **referent**), which was never the case. (**PC**)

SIGNIFIED ***see SIGNIFIÉ***

SIGNIFIER ***see SIGNIFIANT***

SIGN-ENVIRONMENT Sign-environment is a defined **sign-space** belonging to a given living being (**interpretant**). In **biosemiotics**, sign-environment contains partly the sign system of a living being and partly other foreign signs providing information about the other elements of this environment. At the level of **anthroposemiotics**, peoples, communities and individuals have their own sign-environments respectively. Human beings have always developed their own sign-environments which, due to their interactions, produced new development lines. In history, cities have constitued exceptionally saturated sign-environments compared to villages and have contributed to a considerable extent to the evolution of human civilization. (**MS**)

SIGN LANGUAGE Phenomena to which the term sign language has been, or might be, applied are numerous indeed. A great many species in the animal kingdom survive by interpreting and using what they see. For many of them, the most important information comes from interpreting the visible actions of conspecifics (e.g. von Frisch on the language of honey bees). The broadest views of the phenomena are taken by **semiotics** and biology. But when the behaviour is human, researchers in anthropology, linguistics, psychology and sociology also take note of portions of this behaviour. They may label their selection as **gesture**, gesticulation, **kinesics**, surrogate speech, nonverbal behaviour or something else; but sign language is the designation that frequently seems to have the most appeal to the public and the broadest scope.

The amount and variety of such phenomena cause great variation in what is covered by the terms used for them. Philosophers from ancient times regarded gesture either as a forerunner of speech or dismissed it and saw **language** as spoken only. It was only in the middle of the twentieth century that social scientists came to recognize that the signing of deaf people serves in all respects as does the speaking of hearing people, to make the primary signs of a language; in short, that a sign language; is a language. When members of a social group sign instead of speaking their first or only language, their signing expresses a language. Their manual, facial and body actions constitute language signs just as vocal actions do. This is true also of sign languages people use as alternatives to the languages they normally speak (Kendon 1988; Farnell 1995). But circumstances keep apart the groups using these 'primary' and 'alternative' sign languages (SLs) even more than they keep apart groups using spoken languages (see **sign languages (alternative)**). Different groups of people use different languages, whether they speak or sign them.

Although humans who share no common language can communicate with gestures, no common or universal sign language exists. (**WCS**)

See also BIOSEMIOTICS *and* SIGN LANGUAGES (PRIMARY).

FURTHER READING

McNeill, D. (2008) *Language and Gesture*, Cambridge: Cambridge University Press.

SIGN LANGUAGES (ALTERNATIVE) A century ago studies of alternative **sign languages** (SLs) tended to concentrate on what has come to be known as Plains Indian Sign Language. The work of Mallery (1972 [1881]) provides much otherwise unobtainable data about the signs used in various Native American tribes. However, virtually all linguistic studies of Native American languages have been focused on their spoken languages, their possible relationship and their linguistic typology. These tribes may have used (and still use: see Farnell 1995) their SLs as alternatives to the languages they normally speak, but linguists have so far failed to treat their SLs as languages too.

Apart from works by Kendon (1988) and Farnell (1995), there is a dearth of research on alternative SLs. This may result from the tendency in the social sciences to rely on Aristotelian or rigorous logic – something is either language or is not language. With such a mind set, it becomes impossible to determine whether what one is looking at in an exotic population is the gesturing everyone is likely to do while speaking or the signing that expresses a sign language. Logical categorization puts out of reach the possibility that gesturing and signing are related by evolution. (**WCS**)

See also SIGN LANGUAGES (PRIMARY) *and* STOKOE.

FURTHER READING

Farnell, B. (1995) *Do You See What I Mean? Plains Indian Sign Talk and the Embodiment of Action*, Austin, TX: University of Texas Press.

SIGN LANGUAGES (PRIMARY) Languages where signing is the primary mode of **communication**. There are many primary **sign languages** (SLs), and when a widely distributed population uses one of them, it may be marked by **dialects**. That is, deaf signers may have **signs** that differ from those used in other parts of the country, but they share a **grammar**.

Signers of the dialects still use the same key grammatical markers, like signs for 'and', 'but', 'to', 'for', 'not', 'because', etc., but usually do so differently. This variety in national SLs comes about from the same causes that make spoken languages different – separation and contact of populations. But another factor operates with deaf SLs. In the eighteenth and nineteenth centuries, changes in attitudes towards deaf people led great innovators to provide effective formal education for those who could not hear. Most notable was the institute founded in Paris (1755) by the Abbé Charles Michel de l'Epée (1712–1789).

Its success, based on the use of the pupils' own signs, led rapidly to establishment of schools for the deaf in most European capitals and as early as 1817 in Hartford, Connecticut, USA. Consequently, deaf persons educated in Paris became leaders in the arts, printing and publishing, and other fields. They carried their successes – and their sign language – to other places, where their language and that used in the national schools inevitably led local signers to adopt new signs. This process continues today: deaf signers in Asian countries are rapidly adopting signs from American Sign Language (ASL). Modern Thai SL differs greatly from that used by deaf signers of an older generation, and the difference is the use of signs from ASL.

Apart from Woodward's lexicostatistic studies of the relatedness of primary SLs, little has been done to compare primary SLs. Instead, recent attempts by linguists to find a **Universal Grammar** of language have led some sign language researchers to ignore differences and look for similarities among SLs, and between SLs and spoken languages. Much current post-Chomskyan theory has it that language comes from an organ in the human brain not from social interaction. This has turned SL research towards treating deaf signs and infants' gestures as automatic products of innate mechanisms. In this view, differences in SLs and comparative study have little to offer, as the goal is not sought for in bodies of visible data but in the intricacies of the brain. (**WCS**)

FURTHER READING

Stokoe, W. C. (1972) *Semiotics and Human Sign Languages*, The Hague: Mouton.

SIGN-SPACE Sign-space is a semiotic space in which different **sign** systems exist and function synchronously. In Jakob von **Uexküll**'s model, the living being actually experiences and uses this space as its own sign-environment due to continuous **communication**. At the level of **biosemiotics** a sign-space always offers occasions for the development of new pragmatic situations because of the changing coincidence of sign systems and **codes**. In the anthroposemiotic sense of the word, the human's sociosemiotic space contains all its sign systems, enabling their free interactions, including their partial cognition and conscious use. (**MS**)

See also SIGN-ENVIRONMENT *and* UMWELT.

SINSIGN Charles S. **Peirce**'s term for the second division of his trichotomy of the **ground**s of signs. A sinsign is a sign which, in itself, is an existent thing or event. There are different kinds of sinsigns distinguished principally by whether they represent their **referent**s **icon**ically, e.g. an individual diagram (an iconic sinsign), or **index**ically, e.g. a cry of pain or a weathervane (***dicent*** sinsigns). Iconic sinsigns inform of essences while indexical sinsigns only inform of causes or actual facts. A sinsign may be a token of a type. (**NH**)

See also LEGISIGN *and* QUALISIGN.

SITUATION Utterances, spoken or written, always occur in (social) situations. In socially oriented theories of language the assumption is that features of the situation (who is involved, in what social relations, for what purposes, in what institutional settings) will be reflected in aspects of the utterance. (**GRK**)

See also Field, Mode *and* Tenor.

Social semiotics *see* Sociosemiotics

Social structure Social theories of language (or of representation more generally) explicitly or implicitly refer to the structurings of the social environment. These may be structures of class; of 'stratification'; and of derived or dependent categories, such as power, gender or family. The type of structure assumed will affect assumptions about language (use). (**GRK**)

See also Situation.

Sociolinguistics Sociolinguistics deals with the variability of language given changes in social circumstances. Three distinct approaches are discernible: one sees language and its uses as a reflection of social factors; a second treats the social as an effect of the linguistic; and a third accounts for relations between social and linguistic structures, where both are seen as autonomous. Instances of the first describe the language (use) of professions; of social **dialect**s or '**code**s'; of **genre**s and **register**s of all kinds; or the language uses associated with gender, age and class. Instances of the second are forms of **discourse analysis** which see social organizations – the law, medicine and science – as the result of linguistic action. Here too belong studies which deal with 'language about' genders, races, classes or ethnicities, producing the social facts of gender as sexism, or of race as racism. Attempts to change the social by changing linguistic behaviours, the struggles of feminism to change naming practices, for instance, rest on this approach. The third approach treats language and society as autonomous, but sees regularities in interrelations between them: code-switching shows how changes in social circumstances lead to a switch from one language (or dialect) to another; studies in phonological variation show how speakers pronounce the same word differently in an informal and a formal environment. (**GRK**)

See also Discourse *and* Labov.

Further reading

Hudson, R. A. (1996) *Sociolinguistics*, 2nd edn, Cambridge: Cambridge University Press.

Sociosemiotics All semiotic activity is communal, available for humans as social, being produced or articulated in human communities. Sociosemiotics studies **semiosis**, **communication** and communicative situations (comprising physical, cultural and social objects) in social conglomerations and with the human semiotization of surrounding phenomena (nature, space, universe), treasuring the original foundation triplet of semiotic analysis: **semantics**, **syntactics**, **pragmatics**. Sociosemiotics shares in the constructivist view on reality filtered by sociocultural reality. Sociocultural systems are reflective systems and the overt behaviour revealed in culture traits depends on the covert behaviour directed by cognitive structures (**image schemas**, values, behavioural schemes). The aim of understanding cultures is to describe them as reflective systems of knowledge, as intersemiotic and intersemiosic systems. Human semiotic systems filter semiotic reality in communication; thus human cognition is largely defined through language and language-based sign systems. Human perceptual abilities form through sign systems; therefore 'reality' is inevitably mediated and arbitrated. The realization of the semiotic determination of the human relation to 'reality' comes from a **pragmaticist** understanding influencing various fields from linguistics to sociology. The realities in which humans live are socially, culturally and linguistically constructed, and fundamentally semiotic (sign systems structure the world, the world structures sign systems). Therefore, the metalevel must concentrate on the study of methods people use to build their sociocultural environment. Sociosemiotics focuses on processes and structures inside sign systems as described by **Saussure** (the idea of semiology as a subdivision of social psychology, all human sign systems as social). Principles of studying relations between sign systems and the environment derive from **Peirce** who equated **semiotics** with logic, while abductive logic is socioculturally contextual and habitual. Pragmaticism gave rise to ethnomethodology, *verstehen*-methodology, Conversation Analysis and **discourse analysis**, all of which bring sociocultural studies back to the notion of representation that also applies to the concept of 'self-in-society'.

Understanding the self as a product of social communication relates to the topic of socialization and the social construction of reality. Hence, sociosemiotics studies signs, representations, sign systems and sociocultural systems in their creation, maintenance and transmission of information at the level of individuals, groups, cultures and societies in intracultural and intercultural communication. Thus sociosemiotics concentrates also on processes between individuals and sociocultural systems (e.g. levels of acculturation and integration), as on intercultural relations (e.g. cultural distance). Chronotopically specific tendencies of semiotization are disclosed through the analysis of the interplay between physical, cultural and social objects in communicative situations. Likewise, sociosemiotics concentrates on linguistic, communicative, cultural and semiotic competence.

The sociosemiotic research kit contains object, subject and informant (information from users of the meaningful phenomena analysed), enabling differentiation between signs and entities interpretable as signs. This sociosemiotic analytic triplet places semiotics within the social sciences as the empirical paradigm *par excellence*. Its objects and empiricism are rooted in the 'mediatedness' of physical and sociocultural reality and its study of the mediation of these realms in communication goes as far as possible in search of 'objective empirical reality'. The contextuality of sociocultural phenomena, and the same complementarity in the organization of semiotics, requires an understanding of social and cultural entities in terms of processes and functions that vary in space and time. (**AR**)

See also HALLIDAY, KRESS, LABOV, ROSSI-LANDI *and* Randviir and Cobley.

FURTHER READING

Berger, P. L. and Luckmann, T. (1972 [1966]) *The Social Construction of Reality: A Treatise in the Sociology of Knowledge*, Harmondsworth: Penguin Books.

Parsons, T. (1952) *The Social System*, London: Tavistock.

Ruesch, J. (1972) *Semiotic Approaches to Human Relations* (Approaches to Semiotics 25), The Hague: Mouton.

SPEECH ACT The term 'speech act' was first introduced by **Austin** (1962) to draw attention to the fact that people perform actions when saying something. It was Searle's (1969) further elaboration of this idea that made 'speech act theory' into a popular domain of research not only in the philosophy of language but also in linguistics. The general form of a speech act is F(p), where 'p' stands for a **proposition** (a reference and a predication) and 'F' for the **illocutionary** *force* of the utterance. Speech acts can be described in terms of *constitutive* **rules** which bear on the *necessary and sufficient conditions* for the felicitous performance of an act of a certain type. Thus a 'propositional content condition' for a promise is that the speaker predicates a future act on his/her own part; 'preparatory conditions' for promising include that the hearer would prefer the speaker to perform this act to his/her not performing it, and that it is not obvious to both speaker and hearer that the speaker would perform this act in the normal course of events; the 'sincerity condition' for promising is that the speaker intends to do what he/she promises; and the 'essential condition' is that the speaker intends his/her utterance to place him/her under an obligation to do as promised.

An important distinction is made between direct and indirect speech acts (Searle 1975). Indirect speech acts such as 'Can you reach the salt?' have a double illocutionary force: there is a primary illocutionary act (a request to pass the salt in this case) and a secondary act (i.e. the one by means of which the primary force is indirectly obtained, in this case a question pertaining to one of the preparatory conditions for the speaker being able to make the request). (**JV**)

FURTHER READING

Searle, J. R. (1969) *Speech Acts: An Essay in the Philosophy of Language*, Cambridge: Cambridge University Press.

SPEECH COMMUNITY A **language** is not uniformly the same throughout: there are differences of geographical and social **dialect**; of specialist languages, the language of the law, of medicine, of motor mechanics; of differences in levels of formality; and others. One can assume either that these just exist ('In this part of the country this dialect is spoken, in this part that dialect is spoken'), or one can attempt to understand the causes of that difference.

The term 'speech community' locates the origins of difference in the fact that members of groups are characterized, among other things, by a greater density/frequency of interaction than others; that the occasions of their interaction within the community, the 'speech events', are marked by greater similarity than those of interaction 'outside' the community or across communities; that certain 'speech events' in the group occur frequently; and that the substance/content of interaction has relative persistence and stability. A number of factors of this kind will lead to the emergence of very similar pronunciations, of words used, of **grammar**, **syntax**, and of **genre**s. All these mark the group as a 'community', are *reinforced* by the community, and make its language uses recognizably distinct. (**GRK**)

Further reading

Gumperz, J. J. (ed.) (1982) *Language and Social Identity*, Cambridge: Cambridge University Press.

Stoics and Epicureans Zeno of Citium (*c.* 336–260 BCE) founded a movement of thought that came to be known as Stoicism, because of the location at which he originally taught, the famous *stoa poecille* or 'painted porch'. The Stoic philosophy encouraged involvement in public affairs and the performance of great deeds as fulfilling the mission of human existence. A nearly opposite view was proposed in Epicurean philosophy, the movement of thought founded at nearly the same historical moment by Epicurus of Samos (341–270 BCE).

Epicurus taught withdrawal from public notice and the 'cultivation of one's own garden' where, with like-minded friends and associates, one could explore the realm of reason (so far as wisdom is given to humankind) in the peace that only avoidance of the currents of public life can provide. Stoics and Epicureans tended to agree on the basically material nature of the world. But whereas Stoics saw the universe suffused with divine reason which they called, after the usage attributed to the poem of Heraclitus (*c.* 540/535–*c.* 480/475 BCE), the λογος, the 'fertilizing wisdom of God', and which they saw as the purpose of human reason to grasp, Epicureans saw the universe rather, after the teachings of Democritus (*c.* 460–370/362 BCE), as a dance of atoms in a void.

Reconstruction of Stoic views in particular represents a problem, because the report of their theoretical views survives for us only in the reports of their enemies, notably the sceptic Sextus Empiricus (*c.* 150–*c.* 225) and the follower of Epicurus Philodemus of Gadara (*c.* 110–40 BCE). As far as this concerns **semiotics**, by far the most important testimony concerning both the Stoics and the Epicureans is that which shows a crossing of their theoretical paths in the understanding of natural **sign**s. The main source of this testimony is the mid-first-century BCE tract *On the Sign and Inferences Therefrom*, Περὶ σημείων καί σημειώσεων, by Philodemus. Philodemus intended that his tract prove the Epicurean position correct on all matters at issue. Even so, in present hindsight, what is fundamentally interesting about the tract (variously referred to by a Latin plural title, *De Signis*, or by the English title under which it was in fact published,

On Methods of Inference, which omits the σημείον even in the singular) is the evidence it provides of a controversy rooted in the notion of sign, σημείον, toward the dawn of the Christian era, a controversy whose terms reveal that at this late period there did not exist in Greek philosophy a general notion of sign in which the two orders of nature and culture (linguistic **communication** in particular) are unified. The sign still belonged to the order of nature, language to the order of convention.

As we might expect in a controversy between Epicureans and Stoics over the subject matter of logical inference, the Epicureans view everything in a posteriori, experiential terms, the Stoics in a priori terms of rational necessity. In the Stoic and the Epicurean analysis alike the σημείον is a material object or natural event accessible to sense, a *tynchánon* (in the transliteration of Manetti, for a Stoic actual sensible **referent**). To such an **object** a linguistic expression, *sēmaínon* in the Stoic logic, *onoma* in Epicurean, is mediately related; in the former case by what the Stoics call the *sēmaínomenon* or *lekton*, in the latter case by prolepsis (προλη΄ψσις, 'preconception' or 'anticipation').

Hence, within the agreement 'about the validity of particular signs', this great theoretical difference emerges: 'while the Stoics considered an object to be a sign beginning from the consequent (or rather from what was referred to), the Epicureans considered it from the point of view of the antecedent' (Manetti 1993: 128–129). Much more than this as a firm general conclusion we have no evidence of to state particulars. All that appears definitive is that in both the Stoic and the Epicurean cases the link between any theory of linguistic expressions and signs as such remains indirect and implicit in their time.

What Manetti (1993: 98) remarks regarding the Stoics applies equally to the Epicureans, to wit, they 'do not reach the point of saying that words are signs (**Augustine** is the first to make such a statement)', and, in the particular case of the Stoics, 'there remains a lexical difference between the sēmaínon/sēmaínomenon pair and sēmeíon'. Concerning this triad of terms, **Eco** (1984: 32) had already remarked that 'the common and obvious etymological root is an indication of their relatedness'; so that perhaps (Jackson 1972: 136) we see in the sēmaínon/sēmaínomenon pairing some semantic drift in the direction Augustine will mark out as a unique path for philosophy to pursue in its Latin language development. But this suggestion seems unlikely and, in any event, exceeds actual evidence from existing texts. Much more obvious than any such imputed or implicit drift is the approximation to isomorphism between the Stoic sēmaínon/sēmaínomenon pair and the *signifiant/signifié* pair proposed by late modern **semiology** as the technical essence of 'sign'. This similarity would also, and perhaps better, explain why Mates' version of Stoic logic (e.g. Mates 1961: 20) proves so congenial to the logical theories of Frege and Carnap.

Speculations to one side, the present evidence from Greek antiquity requires us to hold that the eventual suggestion for sign as a general notion by Augustine (354–430) will mark an original Latin initiative in philosophy, the one which will most distinctively mark the speculative character of the Latin Age from its origin in Augustine's day to its culmination in the 1632 work of John **Poinsot** (1589–1644), where Augustine's general notion, for the first time, is reduced systematically to its foundations in the theory of relative being. After Poinsot, the Latin Age gives way to the development of modern times. Attention turns to the work of Galileo and Descartes, and Latin gives way to the national languages. The crossing of ways of the Stoics and Epicureans will not be of interest again till the contemporary development of semiotics makes the historical ancestry of notions of sign a matter of general interest and scholarly urgency. **(JD)**

See also SIGNANS, SIGNIFICATION, SIGNIFIED *and* SIGNIFIER.

FURTHER READING

Fisch, M. H. (1986) 'Philodemus and semeiosis (1879–1883)', section 5 (pp. 329–330) of the essay 'Peirce's general theory of signs', reprinted in M. H. Fisch, *Peirce: Semeiotics and Pragmatism*, Bloomington, IN: Indiana University Press, pp. 321–356.

Mates, B. (1949) 'Stoic logic and the text of Sextus Empiricus', *American Journal of Philology*, LXX(3): 290–298.

Philodemus (*c.* 110–*c.* 40 BCE). i.54–40 BCE. Περὶσημειώσεων (*De Signis*), trans. as *On the Methods of Inference* in the edition of P. H. De Lacy and E. Allen De Lacy, rev. with the collaboration of M. Gigante, F. Longo Auricchio and A. Tepedino Guerra, Naples: Bibliopolis, 1978; Greek text pp. 27–87, English pp. 91–131.

STOKOE

STOKOE William C. Stokoe (1919–2000) was an American educator and linguist widely recognized as the pioneer of the linguistic study of American Sign Language (ASL), which led to the international study of the world's signed **language**s of the deaf. Stokoe received his bachelor's and PhD degrees from Cornell University in the 1940s. He taught at Wells College before moving to Washington, DC in 1955 to teach English to deaf students at Gallaudet College (now Gallaudet University). It was here that he first began to study the signing used by his deaf students.

In his 1960 treatise *Sign Language Structure*, Stokoe offered the first structural analysis of ASL form, demonstrating that it exhibits duality of patterning. Stokoe analysed signs into three major phonological classes: handshape (the configuration that the hand makes when producing the sign), location (the place where the sign is produced) and movement (the movement made in producing the sign). He termed these meaningless units of formation *cheremes*, the signed equivalent of phonemes in spoken languages. Stokoe argued that signed language phonological structure is in important aspects simultaneous. While recognizing that the articulation of certain signs exhibited internal sequentiality, recording this fact in his notational system, Stokoe claimed that the major units of organization, the cheremes, are simultaneously rather than sequentially organized. Applying this linguistic approach to signs, Stokoe and his colleagues Carl Croneberg and Dorothy Casterline produced the first dictionary of American Sign Language. Previous to this work, there were no true dictionaries of the language. At most, so-called dictionaries were lists of signs ordered alphabetically by their English translation equivalent, or by **semantic** category (food, people, etc.). Stokoe's *Dictionary of American Sign Language on Linguistic Principles* (1965) introduced a writing system based on his phonological analysis of signs, using this system to list signs alphabetically.

Stokoe returned to the formational structure of signed language in a 1991 essay entitled 'Semantic phonology'. He sought to simplify what he regarded as overly complex models of sign phonology, including his own original three-part conception of handshape, location and movement. In this new view, Stokoe proposed that signs should be viewed more simply as 'something that acts together with its action'.

The term 'semantic phonology' was meant to unify two facts about signed language. First, Stokoe recognized that the phonological primes of a signed language, hands and their shapes, locations and movements – or, in his simplified view, *something that acts with its action* – possess inherent conceptual import in the same way that cognitive linguists attribute conceptual or notional import to grammatical categories such as noun and verb. Second, Stokoe believed that this archetypal conceptual structure corresponded to the nature of human vision and the difference of retinal cells receptive to detail ('something') and movement ('acts').

Stokoe was also a proponent of the gestural theory of language origin. This notion was a part of his conception of language from the start, appearing in the first few pages of *Sign Language Structure*, where he noted that '**communication** by a system of **gesture**s is not an exclusively human activity, so that in a broad sense of the term, sign language is as old as the race itself' (Stokoe 1960: 1). Seeing the gestural activity of a culture to be the raw material on which the signed languages of deaf people are built, he came to regard the essence of all human language as the ability to make and understand meaningful, visible movements.

Prior to Stokoe's work, signed languages were regarded as nothing more than pictorial gestures without internal structure, strung together without grammar. Stokoe demonstrated that signed languages are true human languages, and in so doing he revolutionized deaf education and fuelled the Deaf Pride movement. (**SW**)

Further reading

Armstrong, D. F., Karchmer, M. A. and Van Cleve, J. V. (eds) (2002) *The Study of Signed Languages: Essays in Honor of William C. Stokoe*. Washington, DC: Gallaudet University Press.

Stokoe, W. C. (1991) 'Semantic phonology', *Sign Language Studies*, 71: 107–114.

Stokoe, W. C. (2001) *Language in Hand*, Washington, DC: Gallaudet University Press.

Structuralism (Structuralist) The term 'structuralism' designates a number of things. **American structuralism** refers to tendencies in linguistics associated with the names of **Bloomfield, Sapir, Harris** and, more problematically, **Chomsky**. Structuralism also refers to a tendency in anthropology instanced by contemporary anthropologists such as **Douglas**. Then there is the 'structural linguistics' or structuralism of the **Prague School** which focused upon different functional levels in language and was carried from **Russian Formalism** through the Prague Linguistic Circle and into his later work by Roman **Jakobson** (for example, Jakobson 1960). Most often, however, structuralism is associated with a widespread movement in the human sciences whose heyday was the 1950s and 1960s in France and the late 1960s and 1970s in the Anglo-American world (see, for example, de George and de George 1972; Macksey and Donato 1972). The term 'structure' is undoubtedly latent in 'structuralism' but is not always explicit; what is quite frequently implicit is a set of semiological principles derived from **Saussure**'s notion of ***langue***.

Crudely put, structuralism entertained a common method across disciplines whereby surface manifestation of phenomena were interrogated in order that they might reveal a limited set of underlying principles. The anthropology of **Lévi-Strauss** is a good example of this, particularly his approach to myth. Essentially, his approach is akin to searching through numerous examples of ***parole*** (the various myths under study) in order to discover a universal *langue* (a master **code** which makes possible all myths). In the process, a given myth might therefore be stripped bare to reveal its own structure in relation to the master code. Famously, Lévi-Strauss took the Oedipus myth and treated it 'as an orchestra score would be if it were unwittingly considered as a unilinear series' (1977a: 213). The result was a table of columns showing the distribution of various narrative functions in a fashion almost resembling the cross-section of a cell and certainly fulfilling the **synchronic** remit set by Saussure. This was not just an abstract exercise, however; as a result of such work Lévi-Strauss was able to posit theories about the recurrent – or even universal – features of the human mind in such activities as mythmaking and storytelling.

A broadly similar approach can be seen in the work of **Greimas**, Bremond and even 'proto-structuralists' such as the Russian folklorist Vladimir Propp (about whose work Lévi-Strauss wrote an incisive critique in 1961 – see Lévi-Strauss 1977b). The early writings of Roland **Barthes** might also be said to be structuralist in their orientation. Such works as his 1957 collection *Mythologies* (1973a [1957]) have become famous for the skilful way in which they show some of the most 'obvious' and 'natural' artefacts of popular culture to have been generated by a more or less coherent system that is ideological through and through.

Even though Barthes undoubtedly harboured a critical purpose in his structuralism, what underlies his approach and that of the others mentioned above is the belief in a semiological master code governing the appearance and immediate nature of phenomena. For this reason structuralism is often associated with functionalism, a tendency in sociological thinking which is already present in Saussure's *langue*, a concept which itself is frequently thought to have been influenced by the functionalist sociology of Durkheim. In functionalism, the machinery of society works to facilitate human interaction and its different branches are largely believed to operate with a minimum of conflict. (Work deriving from **Vološinov** and the tradition of **sociolinguistics** posits virtually the opposite theory: see Vološinov 1973 [1929].) As such, humans are frequently seen in structuralism to be the 'bearers' or 'arbitrators' of systems rather than their controllers. Where **poststructuralism** breaks with structuralism is precisely on this point, seeing humans, instead, as largely the *effect* of systems and structures. However, the distinction here is subtle and it is usually difficult to immediately identify such a break between the two movements. (**PC**)

Further reading

de George, R. and de George, F. (eds) (1971) *The Structuralists: From Marx to Lévi-Strauss*, Garden City, NY: Anchor.

Lévi-Strauss, C. (1987) *The View from Afar*, Harmondsworth: Penguin.

Macksey, R. and Donato, E. (eds) (1970) *The Structuralist Controversy: The Languages of Criticism and the Sciences of Man*, Baltimore, MD: Johns Hopkins University Press.

Surface structure In early **generative grammar**, the level of analysis after transformations have applied. The basic idea was that the grammatical structure of complex sentences is best described by decomposing them into more transparent representations called **deep structure**s to which a series of operations called transformations apply. Surface structures are thus the grammatical structures that are immediately discernible in sentences: it is not quite true to say that they are 'the sentences we see or hear', since phonological rules apply to surface structures to produce actual sequences of sounds, sometimes called phonetic form.

In more recent work the role of deep structure was reduced and more work was done by surface structure. The most recent theory proposed by **Chomsky** and his associates, known as minimalism, suggests that surface structure can be dispensed with. (**RS**)

Further reading

Chomsky, N. (1965) *Aspects of the Theory of Syntax*, Cambridge, MA: MIT Press.

Syllogism A syllogism is a deductive argument consisting of two categorical premises with a conclusion resulting from the elimination of a common term, as in: All men are born of women; anything born of a woman is mortal; therefore, all men are mortal. Traditional logic focused on the study of the forms of syllogism and rules for valid inferences. The principle of transivity (if *a* then *b*, and if *b* then *c*, then if *a* then *c*) is the key to syllogistic reasoning. (**NH**)

Symbol This term is **polysemic** both in everyday discourse and in philosophical–scientific discourse including the semiotic one. We may distinguish between the following two main acceptations: symbol is

1 a synonym for **sign**; or
2 a special type of sign.

As regards (1): The notion of symbol is used by Ernst **Cassirer** in *Philosophy of Symbolic Forms* (1953–1957 [1923–1929]) to refer to signs. The human being constructs culture through signs and is an *animal symbolicum*. Symbol is connected to symbolic form which leads to Cassirer's *critique of symbolic reason* or of the diverse aspects of culture including language, myth, religion, etc.

In **Ogden** and **Richards** (1923) as well, 'symbol' stands for *sign* which presents **meaning** in terms of the interactive relation between so-called *symbol*, *thought* or *reference*, and **referent**.

As regards (2): For Freud and subsequent psychoanalytically oriented thinkers the symbol is a particular type of sign which indicates all psychic or oniric activity *insofar as it reveals the unconscious*. The unconscious, by presenting **consciousness** with the symbol of the symbolized object, exerts a screening and protective function.

The symbol is also a particular type of sign in the typology described by Charles S. **Peirce**: the symbol is the sign 'in consequence of a **habit** (which term I use as including a natural disposition)' (*CP* 4.531).

According to Charles **Morris**, it is a sign which replaces another as a guide for behaviour (cf. Morris 1946: I, 8). In John Dewey's account (1938: 'Introduction'), it is an arbitrary or conventional sign.

The symbol is a particular type of sign for **Saussure** (1916: Ch. I) as well. However, on the latter's account it is not completely arbitrary and therefore it is distinct from the verbal sign. In contrast to verbal signs, the relation between **signifier** and **signified** in the symbol is always to a degree conventional (as in the case of scales acting as a sign of justice), though not wholly arbitrarily.

With reference to the encyclopaedic entry 'Symbol' by S. S. Averincev (1971), M. **Bakhtin** (1974) describes the symbol as the sign which most requires answering comprehension, given the dialectic correlation between identity and **alterity**. The symbol includes the warmth of mystery that unites, juxtaposition of one's own to the other, the warmth of love and the coldness of extraneousness, juxtaposition and comparison: it is not circumscribable to an immediate context but relates to a remote and distant context, which accounts for its opening to alterity. (**AP**)

See also Icon *and* Index.

Further reading

Ponzio, A. (1985) 'The symbol, alterity, and abduction', *Semiotica*, 56(3/4): 261–277.

Synchrony (Synchronic) Synchrony is the Saussurean technical term for a theoretical perspective in which a (linguistic) sign system is seen as a self-contained structure not subject to change. The study of linguistic change **Saussure** relegated to '**diachronic**' linguistics. The opposition between synchronic and diachronic is often loosely but wrongly interpreted as merely contrasting relations between linguistic phenomena which happen to be contemporaneous with relations between linguistic phenomena which happen to be separated in time but phylogenetically connected. Thus 'diachronic' becomes (misleadingly) equated with 'historical'. For Saussure ***langue*** is an exclusively synchronic concept, and diachronic linguistics does not study *langue* in any sense. Saussure's alternative term for synchronic linguistics was 'static linguistics', i.e. the study of linguistic states (*états de langue*). (**RH**)

Syntagm (Syntagmatic) In **Saussure**an terminology, syntagmatic relations are those into which a linguistic unit enters in virtue of its linear concatenation in a speech chain. Thus the word *unbeatable* is a syntagm comprising three syntagmatically related signs: i) *un*, ii) *beat* and iii) *able*. The **meaning** of a syntagm is always more than the sum of its parts. Syntagmatic relations are contrasted in Saussurean theory with 'associative' relations (see **paradigm**). Syntagmatics should not be confused with **syntax**, in the sense in which that term is usually understood in traditional **grammar** or non-Saussurean linguistics. (Saussure's editors warned explicitly against this confusion, but it is commonly made.) Saussure described syntagmatic relations as holding *in praesentia*, as opposed to associative relations, which hold *in absentia*. (**RH**)

Syntax (Syntactic) Syntax is the part of a **grammar** which deals with the arrangement of words in sentences. An important part of syntax is the order of words. Compare these English and German sentences:

1 Max has read the book.
2 Max hat das Buch gelesen. (*Max has the book read.*)

The two sentences have the same **meaning**, but the two languages have different syntactic rules of word order: in English, the object normally comes after the verb (*read + the book*), whereas in this kind of German sentence the object comes before the verb (*das Buch + gelesen*).

Syntax also deals with operations on sentences. English and German have a way of turning statements like (1) and (2) into questions by moving the first auxiliary verb to the front of the sentence, giving us:

3 Has Max read the book?
4 Hat Max das Buch gelesen? (*Has Max the book read?*)

In French, however, the syntax of questions is different, since French does not allow (5) to be turned into a question like (6):

5 Max a lu le livre.
6 *A Max lu le livre?

(The asterisk in (6) indicates that this sentence is not possible in French.) Since the meaning of the sentences is the same in each language, these rules of syntax are independent of meaning. (**RS**)

Further reading

Fabb, N. (1994) *Sentence Structure*, London: Routledge.

Systemic functional grammar SFG is an approach to language which puts function first: the emphasis is on what people do with language, rather than analysing the structure of language in isolation (for this reason it is also known as functional grammar (cf. Halliday 1994)). The driving force is Michael **Halliday**, a British linguist who has worked in Australia for many years. Any single utterance or longer **text** is seen as the result of choices by speakers or writers, and systemic grammarians try to classify these choices in terms of three basic functions of language: the **ideational** function is the use of language to convey information; the **textual** function is the creation of links between different parts of a text; and the **interpersonal** function is the use of language to create and maintain social relations between people.

Systemic grammar is one of the few frameworks which analyses whole texts, identifying the words and structures which makes texts coherent (cf. Halliday and Hasan 1976). It is also distinctive in giving a central place to links between language and social processes. Because of this it has been influential in stylistics, in **sociolinguistics** and in education. (**RS**)

FURTHER READING

Halliday, M. A. K. (1994) *An Introduction to Functional Grammar*, 2nd edn, London: Arnold.

SYSTEMS THEORY ***see*** **AUTOPOIESIS, CYBERNETICS, CYBERSEMIOTICS, MODELLING SYSTEMS THEORY** ***and*** **POSTHUMANISM**

T

TARASTI Eero Tarasti (b. 1948), Finnish semiotician and musicologist, Professor at the University of Helsinki, editor of *Acta Semiotica Fennica*, Director of the International Semiotics Institute of Imatra, President of the **IASS** (2004 onwards) and, as well as the author of hundreds of articles, (like his fellow semioticians **Bouissac** and **Eco**) a novelist (e.g. *Le Secret de Professeur Amfortas*, 2000). Initially heavily influenced by **Lévi-Strauss** during a period in which he produced fertile works on myth (e.g. *Myth and Music*, 1979), Tarasti joined the seminar of **Greimas** in Paris which led to his most influential works in semiotics and musicology (e.g. *Signs of Music: A Guide to Musical Semiotics*, 2002). Later, he developed his own theory of **existential semiotics**, showcased in the 2001 book of the same name. (**PC**)

TENOR In the theory of **register**, tenor refers to the set of role relationships among participants in a speech **situation**. In a classroom, for example, the **field** or the social practices which inform the linguistic interaction will be the general ethos or process of education. The tenor will be the power relations between the teacher who might be active in imparting information and the student who might rely on the teacher for this purpose. These role relationships will take place through the **mode**: typical forms of pedagogic **communication** including lectures, seminars, brainstorming, and so on. (**PC**)

See also HALLIDAY.

TEXT As a result of the increased recognition of the importance of semiotics and linguistics to so many disciplines in the later part of the twentieth century, the term 'text' has become widely used. It is a neutral way of acknowledging that different kinds of semiotic phenomena are connected by virtue of their **sign**-based character. This includes texts such as films, speeches, novels, short stories, advertisements, drama, paintings, virtual reality environments, instruction manuals, opera, historical writing, statuary, conversation, and so on.

In the sphere of **biosemiotics**, the presence of entities classifiable as texts has not always been clear until quite recently. However, such facts as the proliferating knowledge of the properties of the DNA strand have encouraged some to consider biological processes and their results as akin to texts (Pollack 1994).

In the theory of **discourse** and **discourse analysis** text continues to have specific **meanings**. Sometimes text is considered as synonymous with that notion of discourse which simply means many signs joined together; in **Saussure**'s terms, for example, a lengthy instance of ***parole***. In these linguistic cases, text is usually conceived as more extensive than a sentence. Sometimes, in a way similar to treatments of discourse, text is conceptualized only as a collection of signs which displays definite **rules** or structures.

In **Halliday**'s social semiotics text refers to 'actualized meaning potential'. It 'represents choice. A text is "what is meant", selected from the total set of options that constitute what can be meant' (1978: 109). In this version, text is a potential for meaning which suffuses collections of signs as a result of the enabling and constraining forces of **situation** and the general culture in which those signs appear. **(PC)**

FURTHER READING

Barthes, R. (1977) 'From work to text', in *Image–Music–Text*, ed. and trans. S. Heath, Glasgow: Fontana.

TEXTUAL The textual function deals with the organization of language as message. It refers to text-internal relations, between and across sentences and paragraphs; to the relations of text to its context; and to the overall shape of the text as an effect of its social function. **(GRK)**

See also HALLIDAY, IDEATIONAL, INTERPERSONAL *and* SYSTEMIC FUNCTIONAL GRAMMAR.

THEME For **Vološinov** the theme of an utterance is contrasted to its **meaning**. An utterance such as 'What is the time?' has a general meaning which is applicable to all social situations. It is like the strict dictionary definition which might be thrown up by an investigation of the construction of the question. In this example, the definition or meaning of 'What is the time?' might be 'an inquiry into temporal passage'. The theme, on the other hand, changes from moment to moment and from situation to situation. 'What is the time?' has a different theme for a) the person with a tyrannical boss who is late for work and asks the question of a passer-by; b) his/her fellow employees who ask each other the question because they are appalled by the way that time drags in the workplace; and c) the profit-obsessed bosses who survey what they consider to be the poor production rate of their workforce and ask the question in disgust.

Theme is hence the significance of a whole utterance in relation to a specific historical situation. As such, it is traversed by a social **accent**. **(PC)**

See also DIALOGUE, ILLOCUTION, LOCUTION *and* PRAGMATICS.

FURTHER READING

Vološinov, V. N. (1973) *Marxism and the Philosophy of Language*, New York: Seminar Press.

THIRDNESS Thirdness is a category introduced by Charles S. **Peirce**, the other two being **firstness** and **secondness**. Firstness (in-itselfness, originality), secondness (over-againstness, obsistence) and thirdness (in-betweenness, transuasion) are universal categories. Together with the other two categories, thirdness guides and stimulates inquiry and therefore has a heuristic value. The inferential relation between premises and conclusion is based on mediation, that is, on thirdness. And since for Peirce all mental operations are **sign** operations, not only are his categories universal categories of the mind but also of the sign. And, furthermore, given that all of reality, in other words being itself, is perfused with signs, they are also ontological categories. A sign, says Peirce, exemplifies the category of thirdness; it embodies a triadic relation among itself, its **object** and the **interpretant**. A sign always plays the role of third party, for it mediates between the interpretant and its object.

Any sign may be taken as something *in itself*, or in relation *to something else* (its object), or as a go-between (mediating between its object and interpretant). On the basis of this threefold consideration, Peirce establishes the following correspondences between his trichotomy of the categories which includes thirdness (but all his trichotomies contain thirdness insofar as they are trichotomies) and three other important trichotomies in his semiotic system: *firstness*: **qualisign**, **icon**, **rheme**; *secondness*: **sinsign**, **index**, dicisign (or **dicent** sign); *thirdness*: **legisign**, **symbol**, **argument** (cf. *CP* 2.243).

Thirdness regulates continuity which, according to Peirce, subsists in the dialectic relation among symbolicity, indexicality and iconicity. The symbol is never pure but contains varying degrees of indexicality and iconicity; similarly, as much as a sign may be characterized as an index or icon, it will always maintain the characteristics of symbolicity, that is, a sign to subsist as such requires the mediation of an interpretant and recourse to a convention. Symbolicity is the dimension of sign most sharing in thirdness, characterized by mediation (or in-betweenness), while iconicity is characterized by firstness or immediacy (or in-itselfness), and indexicality by secondness (or over-againstness).

Peirce foresees the possibility of tracing signs in nature, intrinsically, i.e. independently from the action of an external agent. From this viewpoint, the universe is perfused with signs antecedently to the action of an interpretive will. Genuine *mediation* – irreducible thirdness – is an inherent part of the reality we encounter in experience, which imposes itself on our attention as sign reality and reveals itself in interpretive processes. Thirdness characterizes the relation (of mediation) among signs throughout the whole universe. From this viewpoint, Peirce identifies a close relation between thirdness and ‘synechism’, his term for the doctrine of *continuity* (cf. *CP* 7.565, 7.570, 7.571), which while excluding all forms of separateness does not deny the discrete unit, secondness. Therefore, while recognizing the discrete unit, the principle of continuity does not allow for irreducible distinctions between the mental and the physical, between self and other (cf. *CP* 6.268). Such distinctions may be considered as specific units articulated in existential and phenomenological semiosic streams.

Gérard Deledalle (1990) establishes a series of correspondences between the categories of firstness, secondness and thirdness, on the one hand, and transcendentalism, methodological **pragmatism** and metaphysical pragmatism, on the other. (**SP**)

FURTHER READING

Peirce, C. S. (1955) ‘The principles of phenomenology’, in *Philosophical Writings of Peirce*, ed. J. Buchler, New York: Dover.

Peirce, C. S. (1958) 'Letter to Lady Welby, 12 October 1904', in *Charles S. Peirce: Selected Writings*, ed. P. Wiener, New York: Dover.

Petrilli, S. (1999) 'About and beyond Peirce', *Semiotica*, 124(3/4): 299–376.

Thomism *see* **Aquinas**

Trajector/Landmark The concepts trajector/landmark have been developed by Ronald Langacker within his cognitive grammar. They designate a fundamental asymmetry in the sense that the trajector is the element of a cognitive representation which is foregrounded or otherwise profiled, whereas the landmark is the other element against which the trajector is highlighted. Their relation is thus cognate to the figure/ground asymmetry known from Gestalt theory.

The trajector/landmark concepts can for example be used to capture linguistic specification of distribution of attention and intentional focus in relational predications that refer to the same referent scene. In *The lamp over the table*, 'lamp' is a subject trajector, while table is the landmark. The inverse is the case in *The table under the lamp*. (**PB**)

Translation '*Strictu sensu*', translation is the transposition of a **text** from one historical language to another. However, in a semiotic perspective such authors as Victoria **Welby**, Charles S. **Peirce** and Roman **Jakobson** recognize the importance of translation in **semiosis** and in semiotic processes at large. Translation, understood as a process where one sign entity is considered as equivalent to another which it replaces, presupposes:

1 *translating*; a series of operations whereby one semiotic entity is replaced by another; and
2 *translatability*; inter-replaceability, or interchangeability among semiotic entities.

We must underline that (1) and (2) are prerogatives of *semiosis* and of the **sign**. Translation, therefore, is a phenomenon of sign reality and as such it is the object of study of **semiotics** (cf. Petrilli 1992, 1998e, f, 1999c, d; Ponzio 1981b, 1997: 158–163). With Jakobson we may distinguish between three types of translation: *interlingual* translation (between two semiotic entities from two different verbal languages); *intralingual* translation (between two semiotic entities within the same verbal language); and *intersemiosic* translation (between two semiotic entities from two different sign systems, whether one of them is verbal or not). The absence of a fourth type, *intrasemiosic* translation (that is, internal to one and the same nonverbal sign system), is justified by the lack of a metalinguistic capacity in nonverbal sign systems. (**SP**)

See also Whorf.

Further reading

Merrell, F. (1999–2000) 'Neither matrix nor redux, but reflux: Translation from within semiosis', *Athanor*, X(2): 83–101.

Truth A statement or body of knowledge that accords with or conforms to the facts. Although truth is often loosely ascribed to the facts themselves, or what is the case, it really pertains to representations of a certain kind: **propositions**. Propositions are usually expressed in sentences, which in Charles S. **Peirce**'s semeiotic are **dicent symbols**, but Peirce allows that a painted portrait with the subject's name written at the bottom is a proposition, in effect representing that so-and-so looks like this. We can also think of an article or even an entire book as 'a proposition' in an extended sense, and thus as 'a truth' if the world is satisfactorily represented. In a way, all propositions represent the world, or some part of it – their object – to be 'like this', namely as described in the predicate. So a truth is a proposition that represents its object, however complex and whether real or fictional, in the right way, namely as it really is. Thus we can say that truths accord with reality. In Peirce's view, a proposition is true if it represents its object in the way inquiry would settle on if carried on long enough. We can say that truths correspond to the facts, but for a Peircean pragmatist such correspondence means only that the set of experiential expectations associated with a truth, if they have grown out of an indefinitely long inquiry into the facts of the matter, will be met. It must be remembered that propositions are **sign**s and that significance always depends on the interrelations of signs with their **object**s and interpreters. There can be no truth that is not of something for someone.

According to Peirce, truth as that which conforms to the facts is not the highest kind of truth; a higher kind is conformed to by the facts. Such truths would be laws of nature. (**NH**)

FURTHER READING

Saatkamp, H. J. Jr (ed.) (1995) *Rorty and Pragmatism*, Nashville: Vanderbilt University Press. (See especially the exchange between Susan Haack and Richard Rorty, pp. 126–153.)

U

Uexküll, J. Jakob von Uexküll (1864, Keblaste [now Mihkli], Estonia–1944, Capri, Italy) was a biologist, and the founder of **biosemiotics**. He studied zoology at the University of Tartu (then Dorpat), Estonia, from 1884 to 1889; after that he worked at the Institute of Physiology of the University of Heidelberg in the group led by Wilhelm Kühne (1837–1900), and at the Zoological Station in Naples. In 1907 he was given an honorary doctorate from the University of Heidelberg for his studies in the field of muscular physiology and tonus. One of his results from those years became known as Uexküll's law, which is probably one of the first formulations of the principle of negative feedback occurring inside an organism. His later work was devoted to the problem of how living beings subjectively perceive their environment, how they build the inner model of the world, and how this model is linked to their behaviour. He introduced the term ***Umwelt*** (1909) to denote the subjective world of an organism. This is the notion according to which Uexküll is most frequently cited in the contemporary literature. Uexküll developed a specific method of the experimental study of behaviour which he termed '*Umwelt*-research'. Between 1927 and 1939, Uexküll was the director of the *Institut für Umweltforschung* (also founded by him) at the University of Hamburg, spending his summers with his family on Puhtu peninsula (western coast of Estonia) in his summer cottage, where he wrote many of his works (Brock 1934a, 1934b: G. v. Uexküll 1964).

Uexküll's field of research was the behaviour of living organisms and their interaction as cells and organs in the body or as subjects within families, groups and communities (T. v. Uexküll 1987). He is recognized as one of the founders of behavioural physiology and ethology, and a forerunner of biocybernetics.

Of particular interest to Uexküll was the fact that **sign**s and **meaning**s are of prime importance in all aspects of life processes. His concept of the functional cycle (*Funktionskreis*) can be interpreted as a general model of sign processes (**semiosis**).

Uexküll considered himself a follower of the biologists Johannes Müller (1801–1858) and Karl Ernst von Baer (1792–1876).

Uexküll wrote one of the first monographs on theoretical biology (1920, 1928). The fields in which he also made a remarkable contribution include comparative physiology of invertebrates, comparative psychology and philosophy of biology. He is recognized as the founder of the semiotic approach in biology (1940; translation 1982). In **semiotics**, his work became widely known after the publications of **Sebeok** (1979b) and J. v. Uexküll's son T. v. **Uexküll** (1987), followed by republications of earlier works (Uexküll 1980, 1982, 1992). Since 1993, the Uexküll Centre in Tartu, Estonia, has organized work on Uexküll's legacy. (**KK**)

See also Kull.

FURTHER READING

Kull, K. (ed.) (2001) *Jakob von Uexküll*, special issue of *Semiotica*, 134(1/4).

Mildenberger, F. (2007) *Umwelt als Vision: Leben und Werk Jakob von Uexkülls (1864–1944)*, Stuttgart: Franz Steiner Verlag.

Sebeok, T. A. (1989) 'Neglected figures in the history of semiotic inquiry: Jakob von Uexküll', in *The Sign and Its Masters*, 2nd edn, Lanham, MD: University Press of America.

UEXKÜLL, T. Thure von Uexküll (1908–2004), German physician and son of Jakob von **Uexküll**, was an early figure in the emergence of biosemiotics. His involvement in semiotics began in the 1970s with the recognition of the important semiotic implications of his father's work in biology. His contributions include pioneering work in endosemiotics, microsemiotics, **medical semiotics** and psychosomatic medicine. He criticized modern biomedicine for its failure to understand the body as a living system engaged in a **dialogue** with its environment and itself. He was an early proponent of the inclusion into semiotics of all biologically based sign-producing systems, arguing that 'even the single cell has its **semiotic self**'. For von Uexküll, the 'somebody' in **Peirce**'s definition of the sign was the living system itself which constantly engages in the transformation of inputs from its environment into meaningful signs that guide its behaviour and further structure it as a 'semiotic self'. (**KSR**)

UMWELT Umwelt is the self-centred world of an organism, the world as known, or modelled. The concept was introduced by Jakob von **Uexküll** (1909, 1928).

The basis for the existence of an Umwelt is **semiosis** (*Funktionskreis* or functional cycle, according to Uexküll) that forms the functional world in its whole. The Umwelt is the modelled part of the functional world, whereas the **modelling** process belongs to the part that Uexküll has called *Innenwelt*. The Innenwelt is like a cognitive map that relates the self to the world of objects, the Umwelt being the objective world ('objects' in the sense of **Peirce**, the aspects of the triadic **sign** relation). Umwelt can also be defined as a species-specific network of relations according to which an organism becomes *aware* of its environment (Deely 2001b).

The Umwelt is the conjunction of the perceptual world (*Merkwelt*) and the operational world (*Wirkwelt*) through the functional cycle. Umwelt as the individual (species-specific) world is opposed to the environment as the physical world, the latter being the same for different organisms. Innenwelt is the world as represented in the sign system of an organism.

One can distinguish between simple Umwelten which may consist of only a few interrelated iconic signs (e.g., in bacteria, protozoa, plants), and more complex Umwelten which include space that is built using **icon**ic and **index**ical signs, and yet more complex Umwelten, rich in symbols, which include space and time (the human *Lebenswelt*). The Umwelten that feature imaginary objects (i.e. in the case of organisms which can recognize the non-existent) existing to the subject alone and bound to no experiences, or, at most, related to one single experience, are called magic Umwelten (these may include also genetically inherited Umwelten).

The description of Umwelten is possible through the study and comparison of the sense and effector organs of living organisms. In addition to this, comparative behavioural studies and behavioural experiments can shed light on the categorization of forms in the structure of Umwelt, which it may not be possible to describe on the basis of anatomical data. The notion of Umwelt is nowadays also widely used in anthropology and comparative psychology. **(KK)**

See also BIOSEMIOTICS *and* Kull.

FURTHER READING

Kull, K. (1998) 'On semiosis, Umwelt, and semiosphere', *Semiotica*, 120(3/4): 299–310.

Uexküll, J. von (1928) *Theoretische Biologie*, 2nd edn, Berlin: Verlag von Julius Springer.

Uexküll, J. von (1982 [1940]) 'The theory of meaning', *Semiotica*, 42(1): 25–82.

UNIVERSAL GRAMMAR **Chomsky**'s term for those parts of our **competence** in a particular **language** which are innate, transmitted via our genes, apply to all languages, and therefore do not need to be learned by young people acquiring a language. Chomsky argues that it is a reasonable initial assumption that some aspects of language are genetically encoded, and that they are specific to language, i.e. not general aspects of human cognition. He proposes that linguists can formulate specific hypotheses about universal grammar by investigating parts of **grammar**s of individual languages which can be shown to be impossible to learn on the basis of the data available to young people. These hypotheses must be general enough to apply to all languages but specific enough to account for the relative ease with which young people acquire their particular first language.

Universal Grammar is seen by Chomsky as a system of principles which limit the range of hypotheses which young people have to try out in the process of acquiring a language.

For Chomsky, it is the possibility of finding out about Universal Grammar that makes linguistics interesting. If his approach is correct, then studying linguistics enables us to discover fundamental things about the human mind. **(RS)**

FURTHER READING

Salkie, R. (1990) *The Chomsky Update*, London: Unwin Hyman.

UNLIMITED SEMIOSIS Charles S. **Peirce**'s definition of '**sign**' (with its dynamic triadic relationship between sign or **representamen**, **interpretant** and **object**) contains implicitly an ongoing semiosic process that can be defined as infinite or unlimited semiosis. For Peirce:

> a sign or representamen is something which stands to somebody for something in some respect or capacity. It addresses somebody, that is, creates in the mind of that person an equivalent sign, or perhaps a more developed sign. That sign which it creates I call the interpretant.
>
> (*CP* 2.228)

It is important to note that the interpretant of the sign becomes in itself a sign or representamen and, thus, we initiate a series characterized by an 'interpretant becoming in turn a sign, and so on ad infinitum' (*CP* 2.303).

Peirce has also defined a sign as 'something by knowing which we know something more' (*CP* 8.332), implicating an endless cognitive process that develops as we follow the chain of signs/interpretants. For Peirce every act of cognition is determined by previous ones and cognition, being of the nature of a sign, must be interpreted in a subsequent cognition and so on.

In the 1980s these notions of 'infinite semiosis', combined with those of 'unlimited intertextuality', became quite popular especially with semioticians and narratologists. We recall that **Eco** in *The Name of the Rose* underlines frequently the idea that 'often texts speak of other texts'. Radical deconstructionists go as far as to maintain that there is nothing outside of a text except other words pointing to other texts, and so on. And thus, infinite semiosis, like intertextuality, often accompanies images and metaphors of libraries, labyrinths, encyclopedias, rhizomes and of the theoretically infinite 'web' of possible links on the Internet, in order to illustrate the potentially unlimited chains of definitions, explanations, quotations or allusions employed in the process of acquiring and conveying knowledge. (**RC**)

See also POSTSTRUCTURALISM.

FURTHER READING

Eco, U. (1990) 'Unlimited semiosis and drift', in *The Limits of Interpretation*, Bloomington, IN: Indiana University Press.

Merrell, F. (1995) *Peirce's Semiotics Now: A Primer*, Toronto: Canadian Scholars Press.

Peirce, C. S. (1931–1935; 1958) *Collected Papers of Charles Sanders Peirce*, Vols 1–6 ed. C. Hartshorne and P. Weiss; Vols 7 and 8 ed. A. Burks, Cambridge, MA: Harvard University Press.

V

Vailati Giovanni Vailati (1863–1909), mathematician, logician and pragmatist philosopher. A pupil of Giuseppe Peano, Vailati lectured in mathematics and physics at the University of Turin (in 1892 and 1899) and subsequently taught in various state schools. He corresponded with such thinkers as Franz Brentano and Victoria **Welby** whose **significs** he appreciated and developed. He acknowledged the importance of **Peirce**'s **pragmatism** which he introduced to Italy. In his short lifetime he distinguished himself as an innovative thinker in philosophy of language, history of science, and epistemology.

The aim of Vailati's work is to reveal expressive ambiguity and verbal fallacies. In his articles (collected in *Scritti*, 1911 and 1987) Vailati calls our attention to linguistic anarchy ensuing from the incorrect use of language, and proposes to search for 'effectual pedagogic contrivances for creating the **habit** of perceiving the ambiguities of language' (letter to Lady Welby of 12 July 1898 in Vailati 1971: 141).

In 'Sull'arte dell'interrogare' (1987 [1905]) Vailati proposes to replace questions of the 'what is it?' kind – which produce stereotyped sentences and mechanical definitions – with those of the series 'What would you do, if…' or 'in order that', which emphasize the connection between concepts or definitions and behaviours, contexts and expectations. For Vailati, as for Welby, the question 'what does it signify for you/us?' is fundamental (see Ponzio 1990d, e).

In 'I tropi della logica' (1987 [1905]) Vailati shows that metaphors are not only present in ordinary language, in **rhetoric** and in poetry, but also in logic and in mathematics (in such expressions as 'to be based', 'to descend', etc.). In 'La grammatica dell'algebra' (1987 [1908]) Vailati compares verbal language to the language of algebra from a semiotic viewpoint. Independently of Peirce, Vailati was conscious of the importance of **abduction** in discovery and in innovation.

In Italy the explicit and programmatic continuation of language studies in the direction indicated by Vailati is the work of **Rossi-Landi**. (**SP**)

Further reading

Petrilli, S. (1990) 'The critique of language in Vailati and Welby', in A. Ponzio, *Man as a Sign*, ed. S. Petrilli, Berlin: Mouton de Gruyter, pp. 339–347.

Value English translation of the Saussurean technical term *valeur*, to which an entire chapter is devoted in the *Cours de linguistique générale*. **Saussure** distinguishes between the value of a **sign** and all its other properties. The value of a sign is determined by the network of contrasts it enters into with all other signs in the system.

In the case of linguistic signs, *la* ***langue*** is itself 'a system of pure values', i.e. it confers a value on every constituent sign within it. This notion plays a key role in the whole theory of Saussurean **structuralism**, and sets it apart from the cruder versions of structuralism which became current in American linguistics during the inter-war and post-war periods. The value of a term is *not* its '**meaning**', although this equation, which Saussure explicitly rejects, is nowadays commonplace. (**RH**)

Vico Giambattista Vico (1668–1744) was an Italian philosopher considered by many today to have been far ahead of his time. His most important book was *The New Science* (1725) in which he elaborated the notion of poetic logic – a universal form of imaginative thinking that allows humans to understand the world initially in sensory and affective ways. Vico claimed that we can gain a good understanding of what poetic logic reveals about human thinking by studying one of its most basic products – **metaphor**. The ancient names of the gods, for instance, were humanity's first metaphorical models for explaining phenomenological events. *Jove* was a metaphor for the thundering sky. Once the sky was called *Jove*, all other experiences of the same phenomenon could be 'found again' in the name. *Jove* is a conscious metaphorical separation of the sky from the earth, of the divine from the human world. From these metaphorical ideas, the first conscious humans learned to make sense together. The ideas so formed were the basis for the creation of the first human institutions. (**MD**)

Vološinov Valentin Nikolaevich Vološinov (1895–1936) graduated in law from St Petersburg. He was a poet and musical critic, with interests in philosophy of language, literary criticism and psychology. He was a friend and collaborator of Mikhail M. **Bakhtin** and a member of his 'Circle' during the 1920s. His two books *Freudianism: A Critical Sketch* (1927) and *Marxism and the Philosophy of Language* (1929), and his essays published between 1925 and 1930, the most important of which is 'Discourse in life and discourse in art' (1926), were probably written with Bakhtin's collaboration.

Vološinov's texts share Bakhtin's recognition of the **alterity** relation as the fundamental character of the word. The problem of the relation between one's own word and the word of the other is a constant and unitary focus in all the former's writings. Part III of *Marxism and the Philosophy of Language* analyses this relation in its various forms as it is manifested in different **discourse genre**s and in different **natural languages**. But this problematic is also dealt with in his critique of 'Freudian philosophy' just as it is present in his conception of expression as the manifestation of autonomous interiority, independently from the interlocutor as well as from receiver-oriented intentionality. (**AP**)

FURTHER READING

Vološinov, V. N. (1987) *Freudianism: A Critical Sketch*, trans. I. R. Titunik, Bloomington, IN: Indiana University Press. (This edition also contains 'Discourse in life and discourse in art' as an appendix.)

Welby Victoria, Lady Welby (1837–1912), philosopher, originator of **significs** and founding mother of '**semiotics**', born into the highest circles of English nobility, was an independent scholar. She was not educated in any conventional sense and in her early years travelled widely with her mother (cf. Hardwick 1977: 13–14), publishing her travel diary in 1852. After her marriage to Sir William Earle Welby in 1863, she began her research fully aware of her exceptional status as an open-minded female intellectual of the Victorian era.

She introduced the neologism 'significs' for her theory of **meaning** which examines the relation among **signs**, sense in all its signifying implications and values, as well as their practical consequences for human behaviour. Initially her interest was directed towards theological questions, which led to her awareness of the problems of language, meaning and interpretation. In 1881 she published *Links and Clues*, considered unorthodox by official opinion in religious circles. In it she reflects on the inadequacies of religious discourse which, she believed, was cast in outmoded linguistic forms. In her examination of language and meaning she found a pervasive linguistic confusion which largely stemmed from a misconception of language as a system of fixed meanings, and which could be resolved only by the recognition that language must grow and change as does human experience generally. She proposed a critique of figurative language and insisted on the need to adequately develop a critical linguistic **consciousness** (cf. Welby 1891, 1892, 1893, 1897, 1898). She made a serious study of the sciences with special reference to biology and evolutionary theory which she read critically, with the conviction that important scientific discoveries supplied the new experiences in the light of which all **discourse**, including the religious, could be updated and transformed into something more significant. Her main publications on these topics include *What is Meaning?* (1983 [1903]), her most sophisticated theoretical work, *Significs and Language* (1985a [1911]), which is more of an appeal for significs, and her articles 'Meaning and metaphor' (1985b [1893]) and 'Sense, meaning and interpretation' (1985c [1896]), both included in the republished *Significs and Language* (1985a [1911]), with a selection from her other previously unpublished writings.

Besides numerous articles in newspapers, magazines and scientific journals, Welby published a long list of privately printed essays, parables, aphorisms and pamphlets on a large range of subjects addressed to diverse audiences: science, mathematics, anthropology, philosophy, education and social issues. She promoted the study of significs, announcing the Welby Prize for the best essay on significs in the journal *Mind* (1896), awarded to Ferdinand Tönnies (1899–1900) in 1898 (cf. Welby and Tönnies 1901). Important moments of official recognition for Welby's research are represented by publication of the entry 'Significs', co-authored with J. Baldwin and F. Stout (1902) for Baldwin's *Dictionary of Philosophy and Psychology* (1901–1905), followed by the entry 'Significs' in the *Encyclopaedia Britannica*, in 1911 (cf. Welby 1977).

She wrote regularly to over 450 correspondents, developing a vast epistolary network through which she developed her ideas and exerted her influence, though mostly unrecognized – as in the case of C. K. **Ogden** – over numerous intellectuals of her times. Charles S. **Peirce** reviewed *What is Meaning?* for *The Nation* in 1903 alongside Russell's *Principles of Mathematics* (cf. Peirce 1977). The correspondence thus begun lasted until 1911, influencing the focus of his research during the last decade of his life; indeed, some of his best semiotic expositions are in letters to Welby (cf. Fisch 1986b; Hardwick 1977). Part of her correspondence was edited and published by her daughter Mrs Henry (Nina) Cust (cf. Welby 1929 and 1931), including letters exchanged with B. Russell, C. K. Ogden, J. M. Baldwin, H. Spencer, T. A. Huxley, M. Müller, B. Jowett, F. Pollock, G. F. Stout, H. G. Wells, M. E. Boole, H. and W. James, H. L. Bergson, M. **Bréal**, A. Lalande, J.-H. Poincaré, F. Tönnies, R. Carnap, O. Neurath, H. Høffding, F. van Eeden, G. **Vailati** and many others.

The Significs Movement in the Netherlands originated from Welby's research through the mediation of Frederik van Eeden (1860–1932) (cf. Schmitz 1990; Heijerman and Schmitz 1991). The results of her research, including her many unpublished writings, are to be found in the Welby Collection in the Archives of Toronto's York University and the Lady Welby Library in the University of London Library (cf. Schmitz 1985; Petrilli 1998a). (**SP**)

Further reading

Hardwick, C. (1977) *Semiotic and Significs: The Correspondence Between Charles S. Peirce and Victoria Lady Welby*, Bloomington, IN: Indiana University Press.

Petrilli, S. (ed.) (2009) *Signifying and Understanding: Reading the Works of Victoria Welby and the Significs Movement*, Berlin: Mouton de Gruyter.

Welby, V. (1983 [1903]) *What is Meaning?*, ed. A. Eschbach, intro. G. Mannoury, Amsterdam: John Benjamins.

Whorf Benjamin Lee Whorf (1897–1941) was an American linguist and anthropologist. After training as a chemical engineer, Whorf worked for many years in the insurance business. His interest in language led him to study linguistics under Edward **Sapir**, and his publications were widely read. His main writings were republished posthumously as *Language, Thought, and Reality* (Carroll 1956).

Whorf is best known for his view that the language you speak influences the way you think, a view known as the linguistic relativity hypothesis or the 'Whorf hypothesis'. Since Sapir sometimes expressed similar views, it is sometimes called the '**Sapir–Whorf hypothesis**'. Whorf was struck by the enormous differences between native American languages like Hopi and European languages. He published several papers claiming that the world view encoded in each language determines the way its speakers perceive and understand the world.

This 'strong' form of the Whorf hypothesis does not seem justifiable. If it were correct, **translation** between languages would be impossible much of the time. Translation is certainly difficult on occasion, but it is clearly possible most of the time. This leaves a weaker form of the hypothesis, which asserts that the influence of language on thought is less pervasive.

It is probably true to say that Whorf's reputation is higher today outside linguistics than within it. For a more positive assessment, see Gumperz and Levinson (1996). (**RS**)

FURTHER READING

Gumperz, J. and Levinson, S. (eds) (1996) *Rethinking Linguistic Relativity*, Cambridge: Cambridge University Press.

WILLIAM OF OCKHAM Along with **Scotus** before and **Poinsot** after, though not with equal merit, Ockham (*c.* 1285–1349) is a defining figure of the later Latin Age (Deely 1994c). He was notable for applying the designation 'natural **sign**' to concepts (Ockham 1323; McCord Adams 1978). Followers, beginning with Pierre d'Ailly (a. 1396), inspired by this actually baffling designation (Gilson 1955: 491), further distinguished concepts as 'formal signs' from objects as 'instrumental signs' (Meier-Oeser 1997: 114, 119). This new terminology marked a turning point (Deely 2001a: Ch. 8) in the identification of signs as consisting essentially in or 'being' relations in precisely the sense Ockham notoriously denied, namely suprasubjective in nature independently of human thought ('ontological relation', as it came to be known after Boethius, **Aquinas** and Poinsot). Ockham himself affirmed 'but one mode of being, the being of an individual thing or fact, the being which consists in the object's crowding out a place for itself in the universe, so to speak' (Peirce 1903: *CP* 1.17) – in a word, subjectivity. This doctrine, called '**nominalism**', was viewed by **Peirce** (e.g. *c.* 1902; *CP* 2.167ff.) as incompatible alike with science and the doctrine of signs. Modern in what he anticipated, Ockham stands antiquated among the Latins by the postmodern anticipations of Scotus and Poinsot. (**JD**)

FURTHER READING

Maurer, A. (1999) *The Philosophy of William of Ockham in the Light of Its Principles*, Toronto: Pontifical Institute of Mediaeval Studies.

WITTGENSTEIN Ludwig Josef Johann Wittgenstein (1889–1951) was born into a wealthy, talented Austrian family. He spent most of his working life in England, teaching philosophy at Cambridge. The *Tractatus Logico-Philosophicus* (1922) is the only extended work published during his lifetime. His *Philosophical Investigations* appeared posthumously in 1953. Wittgenstein exerted an enormous influence on Anglo-American philosophy and is a living force in international studies on verbal **language** and **sign**s.

Wittgenstein began his work on language–thought production processes and on semiotic–cognitive procedures in his *Tractatus*. However, this aspect of his research is subsequently left aside in his *Philosophical Investigations* where attention is focused on **meaning** *as use* and on linguistic conventions (linguistic games). The importance attributed to the 'turn' operated by the *Philosophical Investigations*, especially by the analytical philosophers, must not lead one to lose sight of the importance of the *Tractatus*, particularly as regards the **icon**ic aspect of language (cf. Ponzio, 'Segno e raffigurazione in Wittgenstein', in Ponzio 1997: 309–313). In fact, in the *Tractatus*, Wittgenstein distinguishes between names and **propositions**: the relation between names or 'simple signs' used in the proposition, and their objects or meanings, is of the conventional type. The relation between whole propositions or 'propositional signs', and what they signify, is a relation of similarity. The proposition is a logical picture (cf. *CP* 4.022 and 4.026). As much as propositions are also conventional–symbolic, they are fundamentally based on the relation of representation, that is, the iconic relation; and, similarly to **Peirce**'s 'existential graphs', this relation is of the proportional or structural type. (**AP**)

Further reading

Wittgenstein, L. (1953) *Philosophical Investigations*, Oxford: Blackwell.

Z

Zoosemiotics 'Zoosemiotics' is the name for the study of animal **semiosis**, **communication** and representation. The term was proposed in 1963 by the Hungarian-American semiotician Thomas A. **Sebeok** (Sebeok 1972a: 178). He also established the framework for the new paradigm by finding and tightening connections to predecessors, developing terminology and methodology. Zoosemiotics stems from the semiotic tradition that does not limit sign processes to human species. Such an approach is developed most clearly in the pragmatic **semiotics** of Charles S. **Peirce** and Charles **Morris**. Other main sources of the zoosemiotic paradigm established by Sebeok include Jakob von **Uexküll**'s ***Umwelt*** theory that describes meanings in animals' subjective worlds, the communication semiotics of Roman **Jakobson** and Karl **Bühler**, as well as ethological studies by Konrad Lorenz, Karl von Frisch and others.

Zoosemiotics is one of several directions of semiotic research including: **anthroposemiotics** (the study of the human use of signs), phytosemiotics (the study of communicative activities in plants) and physiosemiotics (the study of semiotic relations in the material world). This classification largely follows the classical typologies of nature established already by **Aristotle** and Linnaeus. Another possibility to locate zoosemiotics in the science of semiotics is to focus on the sign process and to distinguish animal semiosis from vegetative and language-based semiosis. This approach makes it possible to include also nonverbal elements of human communication such as **gestures** and **proxemics** within the scope of zoosemiotics.

In zoosemiotics, three major directions of study can be distinguished that focus on the processes of, respectively, signification, communication and representation. The first direction studies the semiotic processes that relate organisms to their natural environment and addresses such questions as which properties of the environment are relevant to organisms and which meanings are attributed to the environment. This approach is closely related to **ecosemiotics** (Nöth 2001: 71) and *Umwelt* theory (Uexküll 1982).

The second approach studies the process of communication where the sender of the message is also involved. However, the animal sender does not always need to be active and act with intent. For instance, in some cases of biological mimicry, the sender's semiotic intentionality can be detected on the level of the species and evolutionary processes (Maran 2007: 228–230). In the communicational approach attention is paid to the specific aspects of the communication process, for example message, channel, **code**, repertoire, coding and interpretation. Sebeok combined these aspects with the terminology of Charles Morris and proposed a distinction between zoopragmatics, zoosyntactics and zoosemantics (Sebeok 1972b: 124–132). Zoopragmatics deals with the origin, propagation and effects of signs. Zoosyntactics targets the combination of signs: such questions as message composition, code and the repertoire of messages available for particular species. Zoosemantics is concerned with the meaning and context of messages, tries to identify the part of the signal that is meaningful for the animal and find out its meaning in the environment of a particular communicative situation.

The third direction of study – the representational approach (also anthropological zoosemiotics; Martinelli 2007: 34) – comes close to cultural semiotics and anthropology by studying concepts and categories used to denote animals, representations of animals in different media of human culture, and communicational, behavioural and social aspects of human–animal relationships. **(TM)**

See also BIOSEMIOTICS.

FURTHER READING

Martinelli, D. (2007) *Zoosemiotics. Proposal for a Handbook* (Acta Semiotica Fennica XXVII), Imatra: Finnish Network University of Semiotics.

Sebeok, T. A. (1972) *Perspectives in Zoosemiotics* (Janua Linguarum, Series Minor 122), The Hague: Mouton de Gruyter.

Sebeok, T. A. (1990) *Essays in Zoosemiotics* (Monograph Series of the TSC 5), Toronto: Toronto Semiotic Circle; Victoria College in the University of Toronto.

References

Ackrill, J. L. (1963) *Aristotle's 'Categories' and 'De Interpretatione'*, trans. J. L. Ackrill, Clarendon Press, Oxford.

Alter, J. (1991) *A Sociosemiotic Theory of Theatre*, Philadelphia, PA: University of Pennsylvania Press.

Althusser, L. (1975) *For Marx*, trans. B. Brewster, New York: Pantheon.

Anderson, M. and Merrell, F. (1991a) 'Grounding figures and figuring grounds in semiotic modeling', in Anderson and Merrell (eds), *On Semiotic Modeling*, Berlin: Mouton de Gruyter.

Anderson, M. and Merrell, F. (eds) (1991b) *On Semiotic Modeling*, Berlin: Mouton de Gruyter.

Andrews, E. (1990) *Markedness Theory*, Durham, NC: Duke University Press.

Aquinas, T. (1982 [*c.* 1266–1273]) 'Summa theologiae', in R. Busa (ed.), *S. Thomae Aquinatis Opera Omnia ut sunt in indice thomistico*, Vol. 2, Stuttgart: Frommann-Holzboog.

Araújo, F. de (1617) *Commentariorum in universam Aristotelis Metaphysicam tomus primus*, Burgos: J. B. Varesius.

Armstrong, D., Stokoe, W. and Wilcox, S. (1995) *Gesture and the Nature of Language*, Cambridge: Cambridge University Press.

Arrivé, M. (2002) 'La sémiologie saussurienne entre le Cours de linguistique générale et la recherché sur la légende', in A. Hénault *et al.* (eds) *Questions de sémiotique*, Paris: Presses Universitaires de France.

Arrivé, M. (2007) *A la recherche de Ferdinand de Saussure*, Paris: Presses Universitaires de France.

Ashby, W. R. (1957) *Introduction to Cybernetics*, London: Chapman and Hall.

Asmis, E. (1996) 'Epicurean semiotics', in G. Manetti (ed.), *Knowledge through signs. Ancient Semiotic Theories and Practices*, Turnhout: Brepols.

Augustyn, P. (2009) 'Uexküll, Peirce, and other affinities between biosemiotics and biolinguistics', *Biosemiotics*, 2(1): 1–17.

Austin, J. L. (1957) 'A plea for excuses', *Proceedings of the Aristotelian Society*, LVII (new series): 1–30.

Austin, J. L. (1962) *How To Do Things with Words*, ed. J. O. Urmson, Oxford: Oxford University Press.

Averincev, S. S. (1971) 'Sinvol', in *Kratkaja literaturnaja enciclopedija*, Vol. VII, Moscow.

Badmington, N. (ed.) (2007) *Posthuman Conditions*, special issue of *Subject Matters*, 3(2)/4(1).

Baer, E. (1988) *Medical Semiotics*, Lanham, MD: University Press of America.

Bain, A. (1959) *The Emotions and the Will*, London: Longmans and Green.

Bains, P. (2001) 'Umwelten', *Semiotica*, 134(1/4): 137–167.

Bakhtin, M. M. (1981) *The Dialogic Imagination: Four Essays*, trans. C. Emerson and M. Holquist, Austin, TX: University of Texas Press.

Bakhtin, M. M. (1984 [1963]) *Problems of Dostoevsky's Poetics*, trans. C. Emerson, Minneapolis, MN: University of Minnesota Press.

Bakhtin, M. M. (1986a) 'Toward a methodology for the human sciences', in *Speech Genres and other Essays*, trans. V. McGee, Austin, TX: University of Texas Press.

Bakhtin, M. M. (1986b) *Speech Genres and Other Late Essays*, trans. V. McGee, Austin, TX: University of Texas Press.

Bakhtin, M. M. (1990) *Art and Answerability. Early Philosophical Essays by M.M. Bakhtin*, ed. M. Holquist and V. Liapunov, trans. V. Liapunov, suppl. trans. K. Brostrom, Austin, TX: University of Texas Press.

Bakhtin, M. (1993 [1965]) *Rabelais and His World*, trans. H. Iswolsky, Bloomington, IN: Indiana University Press.

Bakhtin, M. M. and Medvedev, P. N. (1985 [1928]) *The Formal Method in Literary Scholarship*, trans. A. J. Werle, Cambridge, MA: Harvard University Press.

Bakhtin, N. M. (1998) *La scrittura e l'umano. Saggi, dialoghi, conversazioni*, ed. M. De Michiel and A. Ponzio, Bari: Edizioni dal Sud.

Barbieri, M. (ed.) (2007) *Introduction to Biosemiotics: The New Biological Synthesis*, Berlin: Springer.

Barnes, J. (1988) 'Epicurean signs', in J. Annas and R. H. Grimm (eds), *Oxford Studies in Ancient Philosophy*, Supplementary Volume, Clarendon: Oxford.

Barnett, D. (1987) *The Art of Gesture: The Practices and Principles of 18th Century Acting*, Heidelberg: Carl Winter.

Barthes, R. (1953) *Le degré zero de l'écriture*, Paris: Seuil.

Barthes, R. (1954) *Michelet par lui-même*, Paris: Seuil.

Barthes, R. (1957) *Mythologies*, Paris: Seuil.

Barthes, R. (1963) *Sur Racine*, Paris: Seuil.

Barthes, R. (1964a) *Éléments de sémiologie*, Paris: Seuil.

Barthes, R. (1964b) *Essais critiques*, Paris: Seuil.

Barthes, R. (1966a) 'L'introduction à l'analyse structurale des récits', *Communications*, 8: 1–27.

Barthes, R. (1966b) *Critique et vérité*, Paris: Seuil.

Barthes, R. (1967a) *Elements of Semiology*, trans. A. Lavers and C. Smith, London: Cape.

Barthes, R. (1967b) *Système de la mode*, Paris: Seuil.

Barthes, R. (1970a) *S/Z*, Paris: Seuil.

Barthes, R. (1970b) *L'Empire des signes*, Geneva: Skira.

Barthes, R. (1971) *Sade, Fourier, Loyola*, Paris: Seuil.

Barthes, R. (1973a) *Mythologies*, trans. A. Lavers, London: Paladin.

Barthes, R. (1973b) *Le plaisir du texte*, Paris: Seuil.

Barthes, R. (1975a) *The Pleasure of the Text*, trans. R. Miller, New York: Hill and Wang.

Barthes, R. (1975b) *Roland Barthes*, Paris: Seuil.

Barthes, R. (1977a) 'Change the object itself', in *Image–Music–Text*, trans. and ed. S. Heath, London: Fontana.

Barthes, R. (1977b) *Fragments d'un discours amoureux*, Paris: Seuil.

Barthes, R. (1977c) *Image–Music–Text*, trans. S. Heath, London: Fontana.

Barthes, R. (1977d) *Leçon*, Paris: Seuil.

Barthes, R. (1980) *La chambre claire*, Paris: Seuil.

Barthes, R. (1982) *L'obvie et l'obtus. Essais critiques III*, Paris: Editions du Seuil.

Barthes, R. (1998) *Scritti. Società, testo, comunicazione*, ed. G. Marrone, Turin: Einaudi.

Bateson, G. (1973) *Steps to an Ecology of Mind*, London: Paladin.

Bateson, G. (1979) *Mind and Nature. A Necessary Unity*, New York: Bantam Books.

Battistella, E. L. (1990) *Markedness: The Evaluative Superstructure of Language*, Albany, NY: State University of New York Press.

Baudrillard, J. (1973) *The Implosion of Meaning in the Media*, New York: Semiotext(e) .

Baudrillard, J. (1975) *The Mirror of Production*, trans. M. Poster, St Louis, MO: Telos.

Baudrillard, J. (1981) *For a Critique of the Political Economy of the Sign*, trans. C. Levin, St Louis, MO: Telos.

Baudrillard, J. (1983a) *Simulations*, New York: Semiotext(e).

Baudrillard, J. (1983b) *In the Shadow of the Silent Majorities*, trans. P. Foss, J. Johnston and P. Patton, New York: Semiotext(e).

Baudrillard, J. (1988) *The Ecstasy of Communication*, trans. B. Schutze and C. Schutze, New York: Semiotext(e).

Baudrillard, J. (1995) *Simulacra and Simulation*, trans. S. F. Glaser, Ann Arbor, MI: University of Michigan Press.

Benton, T. (1984) *The Rise and Fall of Structural Marxism: Louis Althusser and His Influence*, London: Macmillan.

Benveniste, E. (1946) 'Structure des relations de personne dans le verbe', *Bulletin de la Société de Linguistique de Paris*, 43: 225–236.

Benveniste, E. (1966) *Problèmes de linguistique générale*, Vol. I, Paris: Gallimard.

Benveniste, E. (1971) *Problems in General Linguistics*, trans. M. E. Meek, Coral Gables, FL: University of Miami Press.

Benveniste, E. (1974) *Problèmes de linguistique générale*, Vol. II, Paris: Gallimard.

Berger, P. L. and Luckmann, T. (1972 [1966]) *The Social Construction of Reality: A Treatise in the Sociology of Knowledge*, Harmondsworth: Penguin Books.

Bergman, M. (2004) *Fields of Signification: Explorations in Charles S. Peirce's Theory of Signs*, University of Helsinki Philosophical Studies 6, Helsinki: University of Helsinki.

Berlo, D. K. (1960) *The Process of Communication*, New York: Holt, Rinehart, and Winston.

Bickerton, D. (1995) *Language and Human Behavior*, Seattle, WA: University of Washington Press.

Bignell, J. (1997) *Media Semiotics: An Introduction*, Manchester: Manchester University Press.

Blecha, P. (2004) *Taboo Tunes: A History of Banned and Censored Songs*, San Francisco: Backbeat.

Bloomfield, L. (1933) *Language*, London: Allen and Unwin.

Boas, F. (1963 [1911]) *The Mind of Primitive Man*, rev. edn, New York: Collier.

Boden, D. and Zimmerman, D. H. (eds) (1991) *Talk and Social Structure: Studies in Ethnomethodology and Conversation Analysis*, Oxford: Polity Press.

Bonfantini, M. A. (1987) *La semiosi e l'abduzione*, Milan: Bompiani.

Bonfantini, M. A. and Ponzio, A. (1986) *Dialogo sui dialoghi*, Ravenna: Longo.

Bonfantini, M. A., Petrilli, S. and Ponzio, A. (1996) *I tre dialoghi della menzogna e della verità*, Naples: Edizioni Scientifiche Italiane.

Bouissac, P. (1973) *La mesure des gestes: Prolegomenes à la sémiotique gestuelle*, The Hague: Mouton.

Bouissac, P. (1976) *Circus and Culture: A Semiotic Approach*, Bloomington, IN: Indiana University Press.

Bouissac, P. (ed.) (1998) *Encyclopedia of Semiotics*, New York: Oxford University Press.

Bouissac, P., Herzfeld, M. and Posner, R. (eds) (1986) *Iconicity: Essays on the Nature of Culture*. Festschrift for Thomas A. Sebeok on his 65th Birthday, Tübingen: Stauffenburg.

Bréal, M. (1897) *Essai de sémantique: Science des significations*, Paris: Hachette.

Bremmer, J. and Roodenburg, H. (eds) (1992) *A Cultural History of Gesture*, Ithaca, NY: Cornell University Press.

Brent, J. (1993) *Charles Sanders Peirce: A Life*, Bloomington, IN: Indiana University Press.

Brentano, F. (1874) *Psychologie vom Empirischen Standpunkte*, Leipzig: Verlag von Duncker & Humbolt.

Brock, F. (1934a) 'Jakob Johann Baron von Uexküll: Zu seinem 70. Geburtstage am 8. September 1934', *Sudhoffs Archiv für Geschichte der Medizin und der Naturwissenschaften*, 27: 193–203.

Brock, F. (1934b) 'Verzeichnis der Schriften Jakob Johann von Uexkülls und der aus dem Institut für Umweltforschung zu Hamburg hervorgegangenen Arbeiten', *Sudhoffs Archiv für Geschichte der Medizin und der Naturwissenschaften*, 27: 204–212.

Bruin, J. and Dicke, M. (2001) 'Chemical information transfer between wounded and unwounded plants: Backing up the future', *Biochemical Systematics and Ecology*, 29: 1103–1113.

Bruni, L. E. (2007) 'Cellular semiotics and signal transduction', in M. Barbieri (ed.), *Introduction to Biosemiotics*, Dordrecht: Springer.

Bühler, K. (1933) *Ausdruckstheorie*, Jena: Fischer.

Bühler, K. (1934) *Sprachtheorie: Die Darstellungsfunktion der Sprache*, Jena: Fischer.

Bühler, K. (1990) *Theory of Language: The Representational Function of Language*, trans. D. Fraser Goodwin, Amsterdam: John Benjamins.

Cantril, H. (2005 [1940]) *The Invasion from Mars: A Study in the Psychology of Panic*, New York: Transaction.

Carroll, J. B. (ed.) (1956) *Language, Thought, and Reality: Selected Writings of Benjamin Lee Whorf*, Cambridge, MA: MIT Press.

Carson, R. (1962) *Silent Spring*, Harmondsworth: Penguin.

Cashman, T. (2008) 'What connects the map to the territory', in J. Hoffmeyer (ed.), *A Legacy for Living Systems: Gregory Bateson as Precursor to Biosemiotics*, Dordrecht: Springer.

Cassirer, E. (1916) *Freiheit und Form. Studien zur deutschen Geistesgeschichte*, Berlin: Bruno Cassirer.

Cassirer, E. (1923 [1910]) *Substance and Function and Einstein's Theory of Relativity*, trans. W. C. Swabey and M. C. Swabey, Chicago: Open Court Publishing.

Cassirer, E. (1930) 'Form und technik', in L. Kestenberg (ed.), *Kunst und Technik*, Berlin: Wegweiser Verlag.

Cassirer, E. (1944) *An Essay on Man*, New Haven, CT: Yale University Press.

Cassirer, E. (1946) *The Myth of the State*, New Haven, CT: Yale University Press.

Cassirer, E. (1953 [1923]) *Philosophy of Symbolic Forms: Vol. I, Language*, trans. R. Mannheim, New Haven, CT: Yale University Press.

Cassirer, E. (1955 [1925]) *Philosophy of Symbolic Forms: Vol. II, Mythical Thought*, trans. R. Mannheim, New Haven, CT: Yale University Press.

Cassirer, E. (1957 [1929]) *Philosophy of Symbolic Forms: Vol. III, The Phenomenology of Knowledge*, trans. R. Mannheim, New Haven, CT: Yale University Press.

Cherednichenko, I. (2000) *Teorija strukturno-semioticheckogo metoda: postroenie terminosistemy, kriticheskij analiz konceptov, interpretacija metodiki (Avtoreferat)*, Krasnodar: Troika.

Chien, J.-P. (2007) 'Umwelt, milieu(x), and environment: A survey of cross-cultural concept mutations', *Semiotica*, 167(1/4): 65–89.

Chomsky, N. (1957) *Syntactic Structures*, The Hague: Mouton.

Chomsky, N. (1959) 'Review of Skinner 1957', *Language*, 35: 26–58.

Chomsky, N. (1964) *Current Issues in Linguistic Theory*, The Hague: Mouton.

Chomsky, N. and Herman, E. S. (1988) *Manufacturing Consent: The Political Economy of Mass Media*, New York: Pantheon.

Clark, K. and Holquist, M. (1984) *Mikhail Bakhtin*, Cambridge, MA: Belknap Press.

Clifford, J. (1988) *The Predicament of Culture: Twentieth Century Ethnography, Literature and Art*, Cambridge, MA: Harvard University Press.

Cobley, P. (2006a) 'General introduction', in Cobley (ed.), *Communication Theories*, 4 vols, London: Routledge.

Cobley, P. (2006b) 'Barthes' theory of the sign', in K. Brown (ed.), *Encyclopedia of Language and Linguistics*, 2nd edn, Oxford: Elsevier Science.

Cobley, P. (2007a) 'A brief note on dialogue', in S. Petrilli (ed.), *Philosophy of Language as the Art of Listening: On Augusto Ponzio's Scientific Research*, Bari: Edizioni dal Sud.

Cobley, P. (2007b) 'Semioethics, voluntarism and antihumanism', *New Formations*, 62: 44–59.

Cobley, P. and Randviir, A. (eds) (2009) *Sociosemiotica*, special issue of *Semiotica*, 173(1/4): 134.

Cohen, S. (1972) *Folk Devils and Moral Panics: The Creation of Mods and Rockers*, London: MacGibbon and Kee.

Coleridge, S. T. (1817) *Biographia Literaria or Biographical Sketches of My Literary Life and Opinions*, New York: Kirk and Mercein.

Cooley, C. H. (1902) *Human Nature and the Social Order*, New York: Scribner's.

Cooley, C. H. (1909) *Social Organization: A Study of the Larger Mind.* New York: Scribner's.

Cooley, C. H. (1918) *Social Process*, New York: Scribner's.

Corballis, M. C. (1999) 'The gestural origins of language', *American Scientist*, 87(2): 57–61.

Corbett, G. (1991) *Gender*, Cambridge: Cambridge University Press.

Coupland, N. and Jaworski, A. (1997) 'Introduction', in Coupland and Jaworski (eds), *Sociolinguistics: A Reader and Coursebook*, London: Macmillan.

Coupland, N. and Jaworski, A. (eds) (2001) *The Discourse Reader*, London: Routledge.

Csibra, G., Biro, S., Koós, O. and Gergely, G. (2003) 'One-year-old infants use teleological representation of actions productively', *Cognitive Science*, 27: 111–133.

Culler, J. (1983) *Roland Barthes*. New York: Oxford University Press.

d'Ailly, P. (1980 [1396]) *Destructiones Modorum Significandi (secundum viam nominalium), nach Inkunabelausgaben in einer vorlaufigen Fassung neu zusammengestellt und mit Anmerkungen versehen von Ludger Kaczmarek*, Munster: Munsteraner Arbeitskreis fur Semiotik.

Damasio, A. (1994) *Descartes' Error: Emotion, Reason and the Human Brain*, New York: Putnam.

Damasio, A. (1999) *The Feeling of What Happens: Body and Emotion in the Making of Consciousness*, New York: Harcourt Brace.

Damasio, A. (2003) *Looking for Spinoza: Joy, Sorrow and the Feeling Brain*, New York: Harcourt Brace.

Danesi, M. (1998) *Sign, Thought, and Culture: A Basic Course in Semiotics*, Toronto: Canadian Scholars' Press.

Danesi, M. (2002) *Understanding Media Semiotics*, London: Arnold.

Danesi, M. (2007) *The Quest for Meaning: A Guide to Semiotic Theory and Practice*, Toronto: University of Toronto Press.

Danesi, M. and Perron, P. (1999) *Analysing Cultures: An Introduction and Handbook*, Bloomington, IN: Indiana University Press.

Davis, S. (ed.) (1991) *Pragmatics: A Reader*, Oxford: Oxford University Press.

Deacon, T. (1997) *The Symbolic Species*, New York: Norton.

Deacon, T. and Sherman, J. (2008) 'The pattern which connects pleroma to creatura: The autocell bridge from physics to life', in J. Hoffmeyer (ed.), *A Legacy for Living Systems: Gregory Bateson as Precursor to Biosemiotics*, Dordrecht: Springer.

Deely, J. (1982) *Introducing Semiotic: Its History and Doctrine*, Bloomington, IN: Indiana University Press.

Deely, J. (1985) 'Editorial afterword' to Poinsot, J. (1632) *Tractatus de Signis. The Semiotic of John Poinsot*, Berkeley: University of California Press.

Deely, J. (1986) 'Semiotic in the thought of Jacques Maritain', *Recherche Sémiotique/ Semiotic Inquiry*, 6(2): 1–30.

Deely, J. (1988) 'Historiography as a current event', in J. Deely (ed.), *Semiotics 1987*, Lanham, MD: University Press of America.

Deely, J. (1990) *Basics of Semiotics*, Bloomington, IN: Indiana University Press.

Deely, J. (1994a) *The Human Use of Signs, or Elements of Anthroposemiosis*, Lanham, MD: Rowman and Littlefield.

Deely, J. (1994b) *New Beginnings: Early Modern Philosophy and Postmodern Thought*, Toronto: University of Toronto Press.

Deely, J. (1994c) 'What happened to philosophy between Aquinas and Descartes?', *The Thomist*, 58(4): 543–568.

Deely, J. (1994d) 'A morning and evening star', Editor's Introduction to the John Poinsot Special Issue of the *American Catholic Philosophical Quarterly*, LXVIII(3): 259–277.

Deely, J. (ed.) (1995) *Thomas A. Sebeok Bibliography 1942–1995*, Bloomington, IN: Eurolingua.

Deely, J. (2001a) *Four Ages of Understanding. The First Postmodern Survey of Philosophy from Ancient Times to the Turn of the Twenty-first Century*, Toronto: University of Toronto Press.

Deely, J. (2001b) 'Umwelt', *Semiotica*, 134(1/4): 125–135.

Deely, J. (2002) *What Distinguishes Human Understanding?*, South Bend, IN: St Augustine's Press.

Deely, J. (2003a) 'The semiotic foundations of the human sciences from Augustine to Peirce', *Recherches Sémiotique/Semiotic Inquiry*, 23(1–3): 3–29.

Deely, J. (2003b) 'The quasi-error of the external world', *Cybernetics & Human Knowing*, 10(1): 25–46.

Deely, J. (2004) 'From semiotic animal to semioethical animal and back', in G. Withalm and J. Wallmannsberger (eds), *Macht der Zeichen, Zeichen der Macht/Signs of Power, Power of Signs*, Vienna: Lit. Verlag.

Deely, J. (2005a) *The Semiotic Animal: A Postmodern Definition of Human Being to Supersede the Modern Definition as 'res cogitans'*, Sofia: New Bulgarian University.

Deely, J. (2005b) 'Defining the semiotic animal: A postmodern definition of human being superseding the modern definition "Res Cogitans"', *American Catholic Philosophical Quarterly*, 79: 461–481.

Deely, J. (2006a) 'From semiotics to semioethics; or, How does responsibility arise in semiosis?', in S. Monahan, B. Smith and T. J. Prewitt (eds), *Semiotics 2004/2005*, Ottawa: Legas.

Deely, J. (2006b) 'The literal, the metaphorical, and the price of semiotics: An essay on philosophy of language and the doctrine of signs', *Semiotica*, 161(1/4): 9–74.

Deely, J. (2006c) 'Semiotics, History of', in *Encyclopedia of Language and Linguistics*, Vol. 11, 2nd edn, London: Elsevier, pp. 216–229.

Deely, J. (2006d) 'Let us not lose sight of the forest for the trees . . .' (A commentary response to Frederik Stjernfelt, 'Let us not get too far ahead of the story . . .: A history of realist semiotics?', review of John Deely's *Four Ages of Understanding* (2001) in *Cybernetics & Human Knowing* (2006), 13(1): 86–103), *Cybernetics & Human Knowing*, 13(3/4): 161–193.

Deely, J. (2007a) *Intentionality and Semiotics: A Story of Mutual Fecundation*, Scranton, PA: University of Scranton Press.

Deely, J. (2007b) 'The primary modeling system in animals', in S. Petrilli (ed.), *La Filosofia del Linguaggio come arte dell'ascolto: Sulla ricerca scientifica di Augusto Ponzio* [*Philosophy of Language as the Art of Listening: On Augusto Ponzio's Scientific Research*], Bari: Edizione dal Sud.

Deely, J. (2008) *Descartes and Poinsot: The Crossroad of Signs and Ideas*, Scranton, PA: University of Scranton Press.

Deely, J. (2009) *Augustine and Poinsot: The Protosemiotic Development*, Scranton, PA: University of Scranton Press.

Deely, J., Petrilli, S. and Ponzio, A. (2005) *The Semiotic Animal*, Ottawa: Legas.

de George, R. and de George, F. (eds) (1971) *The Structuralists: From Marx to Lévi-Strauss*, Garden City, NY: Anchor.

de Josseling de Jong, J. P. B. (ed.) (1952) *Lévi-Strauss's Theory on Kinship and Marriage. Mededelingen van het Rijksmusem voor Volkenkunde* 10, Leiden: Brill.

De Lacy, P. H. and De Lacy, E. A. (1978) *Philodemus. On Method of Inference*, Naples: Bibliopolis.

Deledalle, G. (1990) *Charles S. Peirce: An Intellectual Biography*, trans. S. Petrilli, Amsterdam: John Benjamins.

Deleuze, G. and Guattari, F. (1988) *A Thousand Plateaus: Capitalism and Schizophrenia*, trans. B. Massumi, London: Athlone Press.

Deltcheva, R. and Vlasov, E. (1996) 'Lotman's *Culture and Explosion*: A shift in the paradigm of the semiotics of culture', *Slavic and East European Journal*, 1(40): 148–152.

De Mauro, T. (1972) *Édition critique du 'Cours de linguistique générale' de F. de Saussure*, Paris: Payot.

Derrida, J. (1976) *Of Grammatology*, trans. G. C. Spivak, Baltimore, MD: Johns Hopkins Press.

Descartes, R. (1985a [1628]) *Rules for the Direction of the Mind*, trans. D. Murdoch, in J. Cottingham *et al.* (eds), *The Philosophical Writings of Descartes*, Vol. 1, Cambridge: Cambridge University Press.

Descartes, R. (1985b [1637]) *Discourse on the Method of Rightly Conducting One's Reason and Seeking Truth in the Sciences*, trans. R. Stoothoff, in J. Cottingham *et al.* (eds), *The Philosophical Writings of Descartes*, Vol. 1, Cambridge: Cambridge University Press.

Descartes, R. (1985c [1641]) *Meditations on First Philosophy*, trans. J. Cottingham, in J. Cottingham *et al.* (eds), *The Philosophical Writings of Descartes*, Vol. 2, Cambridge: Cambridge University Press.

Dewey, J. (1938) *Logic, the Theory of Inquiry*, New York: Henry Holt.

Dougherty, C. J. (1980) 'The common root of Husserl's and Peirce's phenomenologies', *The New Scholasticism*, 54: 305–325.

Douglas, M. T. (1966) *Purity and Danger: An Analysis of Concepts of Pollution and Taboo*, London: Routledge.

Douglas, M. T. (1970) *Natural Symbols: Explorations in Cosmology*, New York: Pantheon Books.

Douglas, M. T. and Isherwood, B. (1979) *The World of Goods: An Anthropological Theory of Consumption*, New York: Basic Books.

Douglas, M. T. and Wildavsky, A. (1982) *Risk and Culture*, Berkeley, CA: University of California Press.

Drew, P. and Heritage, J. (eds) (1992) *Talk at Work: Interaction in Institutional Settings*, Cambridge: Cambridge University Press.

Dummett, M. (1973) *Frege. Philosophy of Language*, New York: Harper & Row.

Dummett, M. (1978) *Truth and Other Enigmas*, Cambridge, MA: Harvard University Press.

Easthope, A. (1988) *British Post-structuralism Since 1968*, London: Routledge.

Eckman, F. R., Moravcsik, E. A. and Wirth, J. R. (eds) (1983) *Markedness*, New York: Plenum.

Eco, U. (1968) *La struttura assente*, Milan: Bompiani.

Eco, U. (1973) *Segno*, Milan: Istituto Editoriale Internazionale.

Eco, U. (1976 [1975]) *A Theory of Semiotics*, Bloomington, IN: Indiana University Press.

Eco, U. (1984) *Semiotics and the Philosophy of Language*, Bloomington, IN: Indiana University Press.

Eco, U. (1989 [1962]) *The Open Work*, trans. A. Cancogni, Cambridge, MA: Harvard University Press.

Eco, U. (1990) *The Limits of Interpretation*, Bloomington, IN: Indiana University Press.
Eco, U. (1997) *The Search for the Perfect Language*, Oxford: Blackwell.
Eco, U. (1999) *Kant and the Platypus: Essays on Language and Cognition*, trans. A. MacEwen, London: Secker and Warburg.
Eco, U. (2007) *Dall'albero al labirinto: Studi storici sul segno e l'interpretazione*, Milan: Bompiani.
Eco, U. and Chatman, S. (eds) (1979) *A Semiotic Landscape: Proceedings of the First Congress of the International Association for Semiotic Studies, Milan, June 1974*, The Hague: Mouton.
Eikhenbaum, B. M. (1926) 'Teoriia "formal" nogo metoda', in T. Todorov (ed.), *Théorie de la litterature*, Paris: Seuil.
Ekman, P. (2001) *Telling Lies: Clues to Deceit in the Marketplace, Politics & Marriage*, 3rd edn, New York: Norton.
Emmeche, C. (1994) *The Garden in the Machine*, Princeton, NJ: Princeton University Press.
Emmeche, C. (1998) 'Defining life as a semiotic phenomenon', *Cybernetics & Human Knowing*, 5(1): 3–17.
Emmeche, C. and Hoffmeyer J. (1991) 'From language to nature: The semiotic metaphor in biology', *Semiotica*, 84: 1–42.
Emmeche, C., Kull, K. and Stjernfelt, F. (2002) *Reading Hoffmeyer, Rethinking Biology*, Tartu: Tartu University Press.
Enzensberger, H. M. (1973) *Gesprache mit Marx und Engels*, Frankfurt am Main: Insel Verlag.
Farnell, B. (1995) *Do You See What I Mean? Plains Indian Sign Talk and the Embodiment of Action*, Austin, TX: University of Texas Press.
Fauconnier, G. and Turner, M. (2002) *The Way We Think*, New York: Basic Books.
Favareau, D. (2007) 'The evolutionary history of biosemiotics', in M. Barbieri (ed.), *Introduction to Biosemiotics. The New Biological Synthesis*, Dordrecht: Springer.
Ferrier, F. (1854) *Institutes of Metaphysic*, Edinburgh: Kirk.
Fillmore, C. (2006 [1982]) 'Frame semantics', in D. Geeraerts (ed.), *Cognitive Linguistics: Basic Readings*, Berlin: Mouton de Gruyter.
Fisch, M. H. (1986a) 'Philodemus and semeiosis (1879–1883)', section 5 of the essay 'Peirce's general theory of signs', in *Peirce. Semeiotics and Pragmatism*, Bloomington, IN: Indiana University Press.
Fisch, M. H. (1986b) *Peirce. Semeiotics and Pragmatism*, Bloomington, IN: Indiana University Press.
Florkin, M. (1974) 'Concepts of molecular biosemiotics and of molecular evolution', in M. Florkin and E. H. Stoltz (eds), *Comprehensive Biochemistry*, Amsterdam: Elsevier.
Flynn, P. J. (1991) *The Ethnomethodological Movement: Sociosemiotic Interpretations*, Berlin: Mouton de Gruyter.
Foerster, H. von (1974) *Cybernetics of Cybernetics*, Urbana, IL: University of Illinois Press.
Foucault, M. (1972) *The Archaeology of Knowledge*, trans. A. M. Sheridan Smith, New York: Pantheon.
Foucault, M. (1973) *The Order of Things*, New York: Vintage.
Fought, J. G. (1994) 'American structuralism', in R. Asher and J. Simpson (eds), *The Encyclopedia of Language and Linguistics*, Vol. 1, Oxford: Pergamon Press.
Gadamer, H.-G. (1994) *Truth and Method,* trans. J. Weinsheimer and D. G. Marshall, New York: Continuum.
Gannon, T. J. and Deely, J. (1991) *Shaping Psychology. How We Got Where We're Going*, Lanham, MD: University Press of America.
Garfinkel, H. (1967) *Studies in Ethnomethodology*, Englewood Cliffs, NJ: Prentice Hall.

Garfinkel, H. (1974) 'On the origins of the term "ethnomethodology"', in R. Turner (ed.), *Ethnomethodology*, Harmondsworth, Middlesex: Penguin.

Gay, P. (1966) *The Enlightenment: An Interpretation. Vol. 1, The Rise of Modern Paganism*, New York: Alfred A. Knopf.

Geertz, C. (1993) 'Thick description: Toward an interpretive theory of culture', in *The Interpretation of Cultures: Selected Essays*, London: Fontana.

Gerbner, G. (1956) 'Toward a general model of communication', *Audio-Visual Communication Review*, 4: 171–199.

Gergely, G., Nádasdy, Z., Gergely, C. and Bíró, S. (1995) 'Taking the intentional stance at 12 months of age', *Cognition*, 56: 165–193.

Gergen, K. J. (1985) 'The social constructionist movement in modern psychology', *American Psychologist*, 40: 266–275.

Gergen, M. and Gergen, K. J. (eds) (2003) *Social Construction: A Reader*, London: Sage.

Gilson, E. (1955) *History of Christian Philosophy in the Middle Ages*, New York: Random House.

Godel, R. (1957) *Les sources manuscrites du Cours de Linguistique Générale de F. de Saussure*, Geneva: Droz/Paris: Minard.

Goffman, E. (1959) *The Presentation of Self in Everyday Life*, New York: Anchor Books.

Goffman, E. (1961a) *Encounters: Two Studies in the Sociology of Interaction*, Indianapolis, IN: Bobbs-Merrill.

Goffman, E. (1961b) *Asylums: Essays on the Social Situation of Mental Patients and Other Inmates*, Garden City, NY: Anchor Books, Doubleday.

Goffman, E. (1963a) *Stigma: Notes on the Management of Spoiled Identity*, New York: Simon and Schuster.

Goffman, E. (1963b) *Behavior in Public Places: Notes on the Social Organization of Gathering*, New York: Free Press.

Goffman, E. (1967) *Interaction Ritual: Essays on Face-to-Face Behavior*, New York: Doubleday.

Goffman, E. (1969) *Strategic Interaction*, Philadelphia, PA: University of Pennsylvania Press.

Goffman, E. (1971) *Relations in Public: Microstudies of the Public Order*, New York: Harper and Row.

Goffman, E. (1974) *Frame Analysis: An Essay on the Organization of Experience*, New York: Harper and Row.

Goffman, E. (1978) *Gender Advertisements*, London: Macmillan.

Goldschmidt, W. R. (ed.) (1959) *The Anthropology of Franz Boas: Essays on the Centennial of His Birth*. American Anthropological Association, Memoirs, No. 89, Menasha, WI: American Anthropological Association.

Goodenough, W. H. (1961) 'Comment on cultural evolution', *Daedalos*, 90: 521–528.

Goodenough, W. H. (1980 [1970]) *Description and Comparison in Cultural Anthropology*, Cambridge: Cambridge University Press.

Goodenough, W. H. (1981 [1971]) *Culture, Language, and Society*, Menlo Park, CA: Benjamin/Cummings.

Gordon, T. W. (1990) 'Significs and C. K. Ogden: The influence of Lady Welby', in H. W. Schmitz (ed.), *Essays on Significs*, Amsterdam: John Benjamins.

Gordon, T. W. (1991) 'The semiotics of C. K. Ogden', in T. A. Sebeok and J. Umiker-Sebeok (eds), *Recent Developments in Theory and History. The Semiotic Web 1990*, Berlin: Mouton de Gruyter.

Gottdiener, M. (1985) *The Social Production of Urban Space*, Austin, TX: University of Texas Press.

Gottdiener, M. and Lagopoulos, A. (1986) 'Introduction', in Gottdiener and Lagopoulos (eds), *The City and the Sign: An Introduction to Urban Semiotics*, New York: Columbia University Press.

Gould, S. J. (1996) 'Triumph of the root-heads', *Natural History*, 105: 10–17.

Greimas, A. J. (1966–1986) *Sémantique structurale*, Paris: Presses Universitaires de France.

Greimas, A. J. (1987) *On Meaning: Selected Writings in Semiotic Theory*, trans. P. Perron and F. Collins, Minnesota, MN: University of Minnesota Press.

Greimas, A. J. and Courtés, J. (1979) *Sémiotique. Dictionnaire raisonné du langage*, Paris: Hachette.

Greimas, A. J. and Fontanille, J. (1993) *The Semiotics of Passion: From States of Affairs to States of Feeling*, Minneapolis, MN: University of Minnesota Press.

Grice, H. P. (1957) 'Meaning', *Philosophical Review*, 66: 377–388.

Grice, H. P. (1968) 'Utterer's meaning, sentence-meaning and word-meaning', *Foundations of Language*, 4: 1–18.

Grice, H. P. (1969) 'Utterer's meaning and intentions', *Philosophical Review*, 78: 147–177.

Grice, H. P. (1975) 'Logic and conversation', in P. Cole and J. L. Morgan (eds), *Syntax and Semantics 3: Speech Acts*, New York: Academic Press.

Grice, H. P. (1978) 'Further notes on logic and conversation', in P. Cole (ed.), *Syntax and Semantics 9: Pragmatics*, New York: Academic Press.

Grice, H. P. (1981) 'Presupposition and conversational implicature', in P. Cole (ed.), *Radical Pragmatics*, New York: Academic Press.

Guiraud, P. (1975) *Semiology*, London: Routledge and Kegan Paul.

Gumperz, J. J. and Levinson, S. C. (eds) (1996) *Rethinking Linguistic Relativity*, Cambridge: Cambridge University Press.

Haack, S. (1987) 'Realism', *Synthese*, 73: 275–299.

Haiman, J. (1980) 'Dictionaries and encyclopedias', *Lingua*, 50: 329–357.

Hall, E. T. (1969 [1966]) *The Hidden Dimension*, New York: Anchor Books.

Hall, E. T. (1973 [1959]) *The Silent Language*, New York: Anchor Books.

Hall, S. (1977) *Cultured Representations and Signifying Practice*, London: Open University Press.

Halliday, M. A. K. (1961) 'Categories of the theory of grammar', *Word*, 17(3): 241–292.

Halliday, M. A. K. (1966) 'Notes on transitivity and theme in English: Part 1', *Journal of Linguistics*, 3: 37–81.

Halliday, M. A. K. (1967) 'Notes on transitivity and theme in English: Part 2', *Journal of Linguistics*, 3: 199–244.

Halliday, M. A. K. (1968) 'Notes on transitivity and theme in English: Part 3', *Journal of Linguistics*, 4: 153–308.

Halliday, M. A. K. (1978) *Language as Social Semiotic: The Social Interpretation of Language and Meaning*, London: Edward Arnold.

Halliday, M. A. K. (1985) *An Introduction to Functional Grammar*, London: Edward Arnold.

Halliday, M. A. K. (1994) *An Introduction to Functional Grammar*, 2nd edn, London: Edward Arnold.

Halliday, M. A. K. and Hasan, R. (1976) *Cohesion in English*, London: Longman.

Hardwick, C. S. (ed.) (1977) *Semiotic and Significs. The Correspondence Between Charles S. Peirce and Victoria Lady Welby*, Bloomington, IN: Indiana University Press.

Harris, R. (1987) *Reading Saussure*, London: Duckworth.

Harris, Z. S. (1951) *Methods in Structural Linguistics*, Chicago: University of Chicago Press.

Harris, Z. S. (1952) 'Discourse analysis', *Language*, 28(1): 1–30.

Harris, Z. S. (1984 [1951]) 'Review of *Selected Writings* by Edward Sapir (Berkeley, CA: University of California Press, 1949)', *Language*, 27(3): 228–333.

Harris, Z. S. (1991) *A Theory of Language and Information*, Oxford: Clarendon Press.

Harvey, G. (1663) *Archelogia philosophica nova, or, New principles of philosophy*, London: Printed by J. H. for Samuel Thomson.

Headland, T. N., Pike, K. L. and Harris, M. (eds) (1990) *Emics and Etics: The Insider/Outsider Debate*, Newbury Park, CA: Sage.

Hediger, H. (1965) 'Man as a social partner of animals and vice-versa', *Symposia of the Zoological Society of London*, 14: 291–300.

Hediger, H. (1981) 'The Clever Hans phenomenon from an animal psychologist's point of view', *Annals of the New York Academy of Sciences*, 364: 1–17.

Heidegger, M. (1962 [1927]) *Being and Time*, trans. J. Macquarrie and E. Robinson, New York: Harper.

Heijerman, E. and Schmitz, W. H. (eds) (1991) *Significs, Mathematics and Semiotics. The Significs Movement in the Netherlands*, Proceedings of the International Conference, Bonn, 19–21 November 1986, Münster: Nodus Publikationen.

Heim, R. (1983) *Semiologie und historischer Materialismus*, Cologne: Pahl-Rugenstein.

Hénault, A. (1996) *Histoire de la sémiotique*, Paris: Presses Universitaires de France.

Henle, R. J. (1987) 'Thomas Reid's theory of signs', in J. Evans and J. Deely (eds), *Semiotics 1983*, Lanham, MD: University Press of America.

Heritage, J. (1984) *Garfinkel and Ethnomethodology*, Oxford: Blackwell.

Heuer, H. (1997) 'Der taktile Kanal', in R. Posner, K. Robering and T. A. Sebeok (eds), *Semiotik: Ein Handbuch zu den zeichentheoretischen Grundlagen von Natur und Kultur*, Vol. 1, Berlin: Mouton de Gruyter.

Hillier, B. and Hanson, J. (1993 [1984]) *The Social Logic of Space*, Cambridge: Cambridge University Press.

Hjelmslev, L. (1928) *Principes de grammaire générale*, Copenhagen: Det Kongelige Danske Videnskabernes Selskab.

Hjelmslev, L. (1932) *Études Baltiques*, Copenhagen: Munksgaard.

Hjelmslev, L. (1935–1937) *La catégorie des cas*, Vols 1–2, Aarhus: Universitetsforlaget.

Hjelmslev, L. (1939) 'Note sur les oppositions supprimables', *Travaux de Cercle Linguistique de Prague*, 8: 51–57.

Hjelmslev, L. (1959) *Essais linguistiques*, Copenhagen: Nordisk Sprog- og Kulturforlag.

Hjelmslev, L. (1961 [1943]) *Prolegomena to a Theory of Language*, rev. edn, trans. F. J. Whitfield, Madison: University of Wisconsin Press.

Hjelmslev, L. (1971) *Prolégomènes à une théorie du langage*, Paris: Minuit.

Hjelmslev, L. (1973) *Essais linguistiques II*, Copenhagen: Nordisk Sprog- og Kulturforlag.

Hjelmslev, L. (1975) *Résumé of a Theory of Language*, Copenhagen: Nordisk Sprog- og Kulturforlag.

Hodge, R. and Kress, G. (1988) *Social Semiotics*, Oxford: Polity Press.

Hoffmeyer, J. (1992) 'Some semiotic aspects of the psycho-physical relation: The endo–exosemiotic boundary', in T. A. Sebeok and J. Umiker-Sebeok (eds), *Biosemiotics: The Semiotic Web 1991*, Berlin: Mouton de Gruyter.

Hoffmeyer, J. (1994) 'The global semiosphere', in I. Rauch and G. Carr (eds), *Synthesis in Diversity: Proceeding of the 5th Congress of the International Association for Semiotic Studies*, Berlin: Mouton de Gruyter.

Hoffmeyer, J. (1996) *Signs of Meaning in the Universe*, Bloomington, IN: Indiana University Press.

Hoffmeyer, J. (1998a) 'Surfaces inside surfaces. On the origin of agency and life', *Cybernetics & Human Knowing*, 5: 33–42.

Hoffmeyer, J. (1998b) 'The unfolding semiosphere', in G. v. d. Vijver *et al.* (eds), *Evolutionary Systems. Biological and Epistemological Perspectives on Selection and Self-Organization*, Dordrecht: Kluwer.

Hoffmeyer, J. (2008a) *Biosemiotics. An Examination into the Signs of Life and the Life of Signs*, Scranton, PA: University of Scranton Press.
Hoffmeyer, J. (ed.) (2008b) *A Legacy for Living Systems: Gregory Bateson as Precursor to Biosemiotics*, Dordrecht: Springer.
Hoffmeyer, J. and Kull, K. (2003) 'Baldwin and biosemiotics: What intelligence is for', in B. H. Weber and D. Depew (eds), *Evolution and Learning: The Baldwin Effect Reconsidered*, Cambridge, MA: MIT Press.
Holquist, M. (1990) *Dialogism. Bakhtin and His World*, London: Routledge.
Houser, N. (1989) 'La structure formelle de l'expérience selon Peirce', *Études Phénoménologiques*, 9–10: 77–111.
Houser, N. (1992) 'On Peirce's theory of propositions: A response to Hilpinen', *Transactions of the Charles S. Peirce Society*, 28: 489–504.
Houser, N. and Kloesel, C. (eds) (1992) *The Essential Peirce*, Vol. 1, Bloomington, IN: Indiana University Press.
Hudson, H. (1956) 'Why we cannot witness or observe what goes on "in our heads"', *Mind*, New Series, 65(258): 218–230.
Humboldt, W. von (1903–1936) *On the Kawi Language of the Island of Java*, in VII/1 of *Gesammelte Schriften*, 17 vols, ed. K. Preussische, Berlin: Akademie der Wissenschaften.
Husserl, E. (1938) *Erfahrung und Urteil*, Prague: Akademia.
Husserl, E. (1973 [1939]) *Experience and Judgment*, trans. J. S. Churchill and K. Ameriks, London: Routledge.
Husserl, E. (2001 [1900–1901]) *Logical Investigations*, 2 Vols, trans. J. N. Findlay, London: Routledge.
Hutchby, I. and Wooffitt, R. (1998) *Conversation Analysis*, Cambridge: Polity Press.
Ingold, T. (2000) *The Perception of the Environment: Essays on Livelihood, Dwelling and Skill*, London: Routledge.
Ivanov, V. V. (1981) 'Fil'm v fil'm e', *Trudy po znakovym sistemam* [*Sign Systems Studies*], 14: 19–32.
Jablonka, E., Lamb, M. J. and Avital, E. (1998) '"Lamarckian" mechanisms in Darwinian evolution', *Trends in Ecology and Evolution*, 13(5): 206–210.
Jackson, B. D. (1969) 'The theory of signs in St Augustine's *De Doctrina Christiana*', *Revue des études augustiniennes*, 15: 9–49.
Jackson, B. D. (1972) 'The theory of signs in Augustine's *De Doctrina Christiana*', in R. A. Markus (ed.), *Augustine. A Collection of Critical Essays*, Garden City, NY: Doubleday.
Jakobson, R. (1939) 'Observations sur le classement phonologique des consonnes', *Proceedings of the Third International Congress of Phonetic Sciences 1938*, ed. E. Blancquaert and W. Pée, Ghent: Laboratory of Phonetics of the University.
Jakobson, R. (1956) 'Two aspects of language and types of aphasic disturbances', in R. Jakobson and M. Halle, *Fundamentals of Language*, The Hague: Mouton.
Jakobson, R. (1957) 'Shifters, verbal categories and the Russian verb', Cambridge, MA: Russian Language Project, Department of Slavic Languages and Literature, Harvard University.
Jakobson, R. (1960) 'Closing statement: Linguistics and poetics', in T. A. Sebeok (ed.), *Style in Language*, Cambridge, MA: MIT Press.
Jakobson, R. (1971–1985) *Selected Writings*, 8 vols, The Hague: Mouton.
Jakobson, R. (1973) *Main Trends in the Science of Language*, London: George Allen & Unwin.
James, W. (1897) *The Will to Believe and Other Essays in Popular Philosophy*, New York: Dover.
James, W. (1981 [1907]) *Pragmatism*, Indianapolis, IN: Hackett.
Jenkins, A. (1979) *The Social Theory of Claude Lévi-Strauss*, New York: St Martin's Press.
Jensen, K. B. (1995) *The Social Semiotics of Mass Communication*, London: Sage.

Johansen, J. D. (1993) *Dialogic Semiosis: An Essay on Signs and Meaning*, Bloomington, IN: Indiana University Press.

Johnson, M. (1987) *The Body in the Mind*, Chicago: University of Chicago Press.

Jonas, H. (2001 [1966]) *The Phenomenon of Life*, New York: Harper and Row.

Juarrero, A. (1999) *Dynamics in Action. Intentional Behavior as a Complex System*, Cambridge, MA: MIT Press.

Kanaev, I. I. (Bakhtin, M. M.) (1992 [1926]) 'Contemporary vitalism', trans. C. Byrd, in F. Burwick and P. Douglass (eds), *The Crisis in Modernism: Bergson and the Vitalist Controversy*, Cambridge: Cambridge University Press.

Kant, I. (1781) *Kritik der reinen Vernunft*, Riga: Johann F. Hartknoch.

Kant, I. (1787) *Kritik der reinen Vernunft*, 2nd and rev. edn, Riga: Johann F. Hartknoch.

Katz, E. and Lazarsfeld, P. F. (1956) *Personal Influence: The Part Played by People in the Flow of Mass Communications*, Glencoe: The Free Press.

Kauffman, S. (1993) *Origins of Order: Self-Organization and Selection in Evolution*, New York: Oxford University Press.

Kauffman, S. (2000) *Investigations*, Oxford: Oxford University Press.

Kauffman, S. and Clayton, P. (2005) 'On emergence, agency, and organization', *Biology and Philosophy*, 21: 501–521.

Kavolis, V. (1995) *Civilization Analysis as Sociology of Culture*, Lewiston, NY: Edwin Mellen Press.

Keesing, R. M. (1972) 'Paradigms lost: The new ethnography and the new linguistics', *Southwestern Journal of Anthropology*, 28(4): 299–332.

Keesing, R. M. (1974) 'Theories of culture', *Annual Review of Anthropology*, 3: 73–97.

Kendon, A. (1988) *Sign Languages of Aboriginal Australia*, Cambridge: Cambridge University Press.

Kilpinen, E. (2000) *The Enormous Fly-Wheel of Society: Pragmatism's Habitual Conception of Action and Social Theory*, Department of Sociology, University of Helsinki: Research Report no. 235.

Kim, S. (1993) 'La mythologie saussurienne: Une nouvelle vision sémiologique', *Semiotica*, 97(1/2): 5–78.

King, R. (1991) *Talking Gender: A Nonsexist Guide to Communication*, Toronto: Copp Clark Pitman.

Kleinpaul, R. (1972 [1888]) *Sprache ohne Worte*, The Hague: Mouton.

Klima, E. and Bellugi, U. (1979) *The Signs of Language*, Cambridge, MA: Harvard University Press.

Kluckhohn, C. (1961) *Mirror for Man: A Survey of Human Behavior and Social Attitudes*, Greenwich, CT: Fawcett.

Knowlsen, J. R. (1965) 'The idea of gesture as a universal language in the XVIIth and XVIIIth centuries', *Journal for the History of Ideas*, 26: 495–508.

Koerner, K. (1984) *Edward Sapir: Appraisals of his Life and Work*, Amsterdam: John Benjamins.

Körner, S. (1955) *Kant*, Harmondsworth: Penguin.

Krampen, M. (1997) 'Models of semiosis', in R. Posner, K. Robering and T. A. Sebeok (eds), *Semiotik: Ein Handbuch zu den zeichentheoretischen Grundlagen von Natur und Kultur*, Berlin: Walter de Gruyter.

Kress, G. and van Leeuwen, T. (1996) *Reading Images: The Grammar of Visual Design*, London: Routledge.

Kristeva, J. (1969a) *Le langage, cet inconnu*, Paris: Seuil.

Kristeva, J. (1969b) *Semeiotiké. Recherches pour une sémanalyse*, Paris: Seuil.

Kristeva, J. (1974) *La révolution du langage poétique*, Paris: Seuil.

Kristeva, J. (1979) *Les samourais*, Paris: Fayard.

Kristeva, J. (1980) *Pouvoirs de l'horreur. Essais sur l'abjection*, Paris: Seuil.

Kristeva, J. (1985) *Histoires d'amour*, Paris: Denoël.
Kristeva, J. (1987) *Soleil noir. Dépression et mélancolie*, Paris: Gallimard.
Kristeva, J. (1988) *Etrangers à nous-mêmes*, Paris: Fayard.
Kristeva, J. (1991) *Le viel homme et les loups*, Paris: Fayard.
Kristeva, J. (1994) *Le temps sensible. Proust et l'expérience littéraire*, Paris: Gallimard.
Kristeva, J. (1996) *Possessions*, Paris: Fayard.
Kristeva, J. (1999) *Le génie féminine, Tome premier: Hannah Arendt*, Paris: Fayard.
Kristeva, J. (2006) *Murder in Byzantium*, New York: Columbia University Press.
Kull, K. (1998) 'On semiosis, Umwelt, and semiosphere', *Semiotica*, 120(3/4): 299–310.
Kull, K. (2000) 'Organisms can be proud to have been their own designers', *Cybernetics & Human Knowing*, 7(1): 45–55.
Kull, K. (2001) 'Jakob von Uexküll: An introduction', *Semiotica*, 134(1/4): 1–59.
Kull, K. (2005) 'Semiotics is a theory of life', in R. Williamson, L. G. Sbrocchi and J. Deely (eds), *Semiotics 2003: 'Semiotics and National Identity'*, New York: Legas.
Kull, K. and Torop, P. (2003) 'Biotranslation: Translation between umwelten', in S. Petrilli (ed.), *Translation Translation*, Amsterdam: Rodopi.
Kull, K., Kukk, T. and Lotman, A. (2003) 'When culture supports biodiversity: The case of the wooded meadow', in A. Roepstorff *et al.* (eds), *Imagining Nature: Practices of Cosmology and Identity*, Aarhus: Aarhus University Press.
Kull, K., Emmeche, C. and Favareau, D. (2008) 'Biosemiotic questions', *Biosemiotics*, 1(1): 41–55.
Lagerspetz, K. Y. H. (2001) 'Jakob von Uexküll and the origins of cybernetics', *Semiotica*, 134(1/4): 643–651.
Lakoff, G. (1987) *Women, Fire, and Dangerous Things*, Chicago: University of Chicago Press.
Lakoff, G. (1988) 'Cognitive semantics', in U. Eco, M. Santambrogio and P. Violi (eds), *Meaning and Mental Representations*, Bloomington, IN: Indiana University Press.
Lakoff, G. and Johnson, M. (1980) *Metaphors We Live By*, Chicago: Chicago University Press.
Lalande, A. (1947) *Vocabulaire technique et critique de la philosophie*, revu par MM. les membres et correspondants de la Societe francaise de philosophie et pub. avec leurs corrections et observations, 5th edn, Paris: Presses Universitaires de France.
Landwehr, K. (1997) 'Der optische Kanan', in R. Posner, K. Robering and T. A. Sebeok (eds), *Semiotik: Ein Handbuch zu den zeichentheoretischen Grundlagen von Natur und Kultur*, Vol. 1, Berlin: Walter de Gruyter.
Langacker, R. (1987–1991) *Foundations of Cognitive Grammar*, Vols I and II, Stanford, CA: Stanford University Press.
Langer, S. K. (1953) *Feeling and Form*, London: Routledge and Kegan Paul.
Langer, S. K. (1990 [1942]) *Philosophy in a New Key: Study in the Symbolism of Reason, Rite and Art*, 3rd edn, Cambridge, MA: Harvard University Press.
Lavers, A. (1982) *Roland Barthes: Structuralism and After*, Cambridge, MA: Harvard University Press.
Lazarsfeld, P. F., Berelson, B. and Gaudet, H. (1948) *The People's Choice*, New York: Columbia University Press.
Le Grand, E. (1993) 'Lotman', in I. M. Makaryk (ed.), *Encyclopedia of Contemporary Literary Theory: Approaches, Scholars, Terms*, Toronto: University of Toronto Press.
Leach, E. (1976) *Culture and Communication: The Logic by which Symbols Are Connected*, Cambridge: Cambridge University Press.
Lee, P. (1996) *The Whorf Theory Complex: A Critical Reconstruction*, Amsterdam: John Benjamins.
Leech, G. N. (1983) *Principles of Pragmatics*, London: Longman.
Lefebvre, H. (1968 [1939]) *Dialectical Materialism*, London: Jonathan Cape.
Lefebvre, H. (1991 [1974]) *The Production of Space*, Oxford: Blackwell Publishers.

Levchenko, J. and Salupere, S. (eds) (1999) *Conceptual Dictionary of the Tartu–Moscow Semiotic School*, Tartu: Tartu University Press.

Levinas, E. (1961) *Totalité et Infini*, La Haye: Nijhoff.

Levinas, E. (1972) *Humanisme de l'autre homme*, Montpellier: Fata Morgana.

Levinas, E. (1974) *Autrement qu'être ou au-delà de l'essence*, La Haye: Nijhoff.

Levinson, S. C. (1983) *Pragmatics*, Cambridge: Cambridge University Press.

Lévi-Strauss, C. (1944) 'Reciprocity and hierarchy', *American Anthropologist*, 46(2): 266–268.

Lévi-Strauss, C. (1949) *Les Structures Élémentaires de la Parenté*, Paris: Presses Universitaires de France.

Lévi-Strauss, C. (1969) *The Raw and the Cooked*, trans. J. Weightman and D. Weightman, New York: Harper and Row.

Lévi-Strauss, C. (1973) *From Honey to Ashes*, trans. J. Weightman and D. Weightman, New York: Harper and Row.

Lévi-Strauss, C. (1977a) *Structural Anthropology 1*, trans. C. Jacobson and B. Grundfest Schoepf, Harmondsworth: Penguin.

Lévi-Strauss, C. (1977b) 'Structure and form: Reflections on a work by Vladimir Propp', in *Structural Anthropology 1*, Harmondsworth: Penguin.

Lévi-Strauss, C. (1978) *The Origin of Table Manners*, trans. J. Weightman and D. Weightman, New York: Harper and Row.

Lévi-Strauss, C. (1981) *The Naked Man*, trans. J. Weightman and D. Weightman, New York: Harper and Row.

Locke, J. (1690) *An Essay Concerning Humane Understanding*, London: Printed by Elizabeth Holt for Thomas Basset.

Long, A. A. (1971) 'Language and thought in stoicism', in A. A. Long (ed.), *Problems in Stoicism*, London: Athlone Press.

Lorenz, K. (1971) *Studies in Animal and Human Behaviour*, Cambridge, MA: Harvard University Press.

Lotman, J. (1964) 'Sur la délimitation linguistique et littéraire de la notion de structure', *Linguistics*, 6: 59–72.

Lotman, J. (1965) 'From the editors', *Trudy po znakovym sistemam* [*Sign Systems Studies*], 2: 6.

Lotman, J. (1967) 'Tezisy k probleme "iskusstvo v ryadu modeliruyuščhih sistem"', *Trudy po znakovym sistemam* [*Sign Systems Studies*], 3: 130–145.

Lotman, J. (1975) 'Notes on the structure of a literary text', *Semiotica*, 15(3): 199–205.

Lotman, J. (1976) *Analyses of the Poetic Text: Verse Structure*, Ann Arbor, MI: Ardis.

Lotman, J. (1977a) 'Primary and secondary communication-modeling systems', in D. P. Lucid (ed.), *Soviet Semiotics: An Anthology*, Baltimore, MD: Johns Hopkins University Press.

Lotman, J. (1977b) *Structure of the Artistic Text*, Ann Arbor, MI: Michigan Slavic Contributions 7.

Lotman, J. (1984) = Лотман, Юрий М., ред. (1984) О семиосфере. *Труды по знаковым системам*, 17: Структура диалога как принцип работы семиотического механизма. Тарту: Тартуский государственный университет. Ст. 5–23.

Lotman, J. (2000 [1990]) *Universe of the Mind: A Semiotic Theory of Culture*, trans. A. Shukman, Bloomington, IN: Indiana University Press.

Lotman, J. (2009) *Culture and Explosion*, Berlin: Mouton de Gruyter.

Lotman, J. M. and Uspenski, B. A. (1984) *The Semiotics of Russian Culture*, Ann Arbor, MI: Michigan Slavic Contributions 11.

Lotman, J. *et al.* (1973) 'Theses on the semiotic study of sultures (as applied to slavic texts)', in J. van Eng (ed.), *Structure of Texts and Semiotics of Culture*, The Hague: Mouton.

Lotman, J. *et al.* (1985) *The Semiotics of Russian Cultural History*, ed. A. D. Nakhimovsky and A. S. Nakhimovsky, Ithaca, NY: Cornell University Press.

Lotman, M. (2003) 'Umwelt and semiosphere', *Sign Systems Studies*, 30(1): 33–40.

Lucid, D. P. (ed.) (1977) *Soviet Semiotics: An Anthology*, Baltimore, MD: Johns Hopkins University Press.

McCord Adams, M. (1978) 'Ockham's theory of natural signification', *The Monist*, 61: 444–459.

Macksey, R. and Donato, E. (eds) (1970) *The Structuralist Controversy: The Languages of Criticism and the Sciences of Man*, Baltimore, MD: Johns Hopkins University Press.

McLuhan, M. (1951) *The Mechanical Bride: Folklore of Industrial Man*, New York: Vanguard.

McLuhan, M. (1962) *The Gutenberg Galaxy: The Making of Typographic Man*, Toronto: University of Toronto Press.

McLuhan, M. (1964) *Understanding Media: The Extensions of Man*, New York: Mentor.

McNeill, D. (1992) *Hand and Mind: What Gestures Reveal About Thoughts*, Chicago: Chicago University Press.

Malinowski, B. (1999 [1922]) *Argonauts of the Western Pacific: An Account of Native Enterprise and Adventure in the Archipelagoes of Melanesian New Guinea*, London: Routledge.

Mallery, G. (1972 [1881]) *Sign Language among the North American Indians Compared with that of Other Peoples and Deaf Mutes*, The Hague: Mouton.

Mandelker, A. (1994) 'Semiotizing the sphere: Organicist theory in Lotman, Bakhtin, and Vernadsky', *PMLA*, 3(109): 385–396.

Mandler, J. M. (1992) 'How to build a baby II: Conceptual primitives', *Psychological Review*, 99: 587–604.

Mandler, J. M. (2005) 'How to build a baby III: Image schemas and the transition to verbal thought', in B. Hampe (ed.), *From Perception to Meaning – Image Schemas in Cognitive Linguistics*, Berlin: Mouton de Gruyter.

Manetti, G. (1993) *Theories of the Sign in Classical Antiquity*, trans. C. Richardson, Bloomington, IN: Indiana University Press.

Maran, T. (2007) 'Semiotic interpretations of biological mimicry', *Semiotica*, 167(1/4): 223–248.

Marcellesi, J.-B. *et al*. (1978) *Linguaggio e classi sociali. Marrismo e stalinismo*, Bari: Dedalo.

Marcus, G. E. and Fischer, M. J. (1986) *Anthropology as Cultural Critique: An Experimental Moment in the Human Sciences*, Chicago: University of Chicago Press.

Maritain, J. (1955) Letter published as 'Preface' to *The Material Logic of John of St. Thomas*, trans. Yves R. Simon *et al*., Chicago: University of Chicago Press.

Maritain, J. (1956) 'Le Langage et la Theorie du Signe', Annexe au Chapitre II, *Quatre Essais sur l'Esprit dans sa Condition Charnelle*, Paris: Alsatia.

Martinelli, D. (2007) *Zoosemiotics. Proposals for a Handbook.* Acta Semiotica Fennica XXVI, Imatra: Finnish Network University of Semiotics.

Marx, K. (1962) *Capital*, Book I, 2 vols, trans. E. and C. Paul, London: Dent.

Marx, K. and Engels, F. (1968) *The German Ideology*, ed. S. Rayzankaya, Moscow: Progress Publishers.

Mates, B. (1961) *Stoic Logic*, Berkeley, CA: University of California Press.

Matsuno, K. and Salthe, S. (1995) 'Global idealism/local materialism', *Biology and Philosophy*, 10: 309–337.

Mauss, M. (1969) *The Gift Forms and Functions of Exchange in Archaic Societies*, London: Cohen and West.

Mazzali-Lurati, S. (2007) 'Here is the author! Hyperlinks as constitutive rules of hypertextual communication', *Semiotica*, 167: 119–134.

Mead, G. H. (1907) 'Concerning animal perception', *Psychological Review*, 14: 383–390.

Mead, G. H. (1913) 'The social self', *Journal of Philosophy, Psychology and Scientific Methods*, 10: 374–380.

Mead, G. H. (1922) 'A behavioristic account of the significant symbol', *Journal of Philosophy*, 19: 157–163.

Mead, G. H. (1930) 'Cooley's contribution to American social thought', *American Journal of Sociology*, 35: 693–706.

Mead, G. H. (1934) *Mind, Self, and Society*, ed. C. W. Morris, Chicago: University of Chicago Press.

Mead, G. H. (1938) *The Philosophy of the Act*, ed. C. W. Morris *et al.*, Chicago: University of Chicago Press.

Meier-Oeser, S. (1997) *Die Spur des Zeichens. Das Zeichen und seine Funktion in der Philosohie des Mittelalters und der frühen Neuzeit*, Berlin: Walter de Gruyter.

Merleau-Ponty, M. (1966) *Sens et non sens*, Paris: Nagel.

Merquior, J. G. (1986) *From Prague to Paris: A Critique of Structuralist and Post-Structuralist Thought*, London: Verso.

Merrell, F. (1992) *Sign, Textuality, World*. Bloomington, IN: Indiana University Press.

Michotte, A. (1963) *The Perception of Causality*, trans. T. R. and E. Miles, London: Methuen.

Mildenberger, F. (2007) *Umwelt als Vision: Leben und Werk Jakob von Uexkülls (1864–1944)* (Sudhoffs Archiv 56). Stuttgart: Franz Steiner Verlag.

Moeller, A. (1993) 'Fungus infecting domestic flies manipulates sexual behavior of its host', *Behavioral Ecology and Sociobiology*, 33: 403–407.

Moriarty, M. (1991) *Roland Barthes*, Cambridge: Polity Press.

Morris, C. (1932) *Six Theories of Mind*, Chicago: University of Chicago Press.

Morris, C. (1937) *Logical Positivism, Pragmatism and Scientific Empiricism*, Paris: Hermann.

Morris, C. (1938) *Foundations of the Theory of Signs*, Chicago: University of Chicago Press.

Morris, C. (1946) *Signs, Language and Behavior*, Englewood Cliffs, NJ: Prentice-Hall.

Morris, C. (1964) *Signification and Significance. A Study of the Relations of Signs and Values*, Cambridge, MA: MIT Press.

Morris, C. (1971) *Writings on the General Theory of Signs*, ed. T. A. Sebeok, The Hague: Mouton.

Morris, C. (1993 [1925]) *Symbolism and Reality. A Study in the Nature of Mind*, ed. A. Eschbach, Amsterdam: John Benjamins.

Morris, D. (1963) *The Biology of Art*, London: Methuen.

Morris, D. (1967) *The Naked Ape*, London: Jonathan Cape.

Morris, D. (1969) *The Human Zoo*, London: Jonathan Cape.

Morrish, J. (1999) *Frantic Semantics: Snapshots of Our Changing Language*, London: Macmillan.

Morson, G. S. and Emerson, C. (eds) (1989) *Rethinking Bakhtin: Extensions and Challenges*, Evanston, IL: Northwestern University Press.

Morson, G. S. and Emerson, C. (1990) *Mikhail Bakhtin. A Creation of a Prosaics*, Stanford, CA: Univesity of California Press.

Mukařovský, J. (1923) *Príspevek k estetice ceského verse*, Prague: Filosofická fakulta University Karlovy.

Mukařovský, J. (1948) *Kapitoly z ceské poetiky*, Prague: Nakl Svobody.

Mukařovský, J. (1982 [1940]) 'O jazyce básnickém IV. Slovo v básnictví', in *Studie z poetiky*, Prague: Nakl Svobody.

Murphy, J. P. (1990) *Pragmatism. From Peirce to Davidson*, Boulder, CO: Westview Press.

Nattiez, J.-J. (1976) *Fondements d'une sémiologie de la musique*, Paris: Union Générale d'Editions.

Negroponte, N. (1995) *Being Digital*, New York: Knopf.

Nesselroth, P. W. (2007) 'Playing doubles: Derrida's writing, *Semiotica*, 166: 427–444.

Nicholson, M. (1983) *The Scientific Analysis of Social Behaviour: A Defence of Empiricism in Social Science*, London: Pinter.

Nikolaenko, N. N. (1983) 'Funkcionaljnaja asimmetria mozga i izobrazitleljnye sposobnosti: 1. Problema risunka; 2. Vosprijatie i oboznachenia cveta'. *Trudy po znakovym sistemam*, 16: 84–98.

Nöth, W. (1985) *Handbuch der Semiotik*, Stuttgart, Verlag J. B. Metzler.

Nöth, W. (1998) 'Ecosemiotics', *Sign Systems Studies*, 26: 332–343.

Nöth, W. (ed.) (1997) *Semiotics of the Media*, Berlin: Mouton de Gruyter.

Nöth, W. (2001) 'Ecosemiotics and the semiotics of nature', *Sign Systems Studies*, 29(1): 71–82.

O'Toole, M. (1994) *The Language of Displayed Art*, London: Continuum.

Ockham, William of (1974–1988 [1323]) *Summa Logicae*, Vol. I of the *Opera Philosophica* in the 17-volume critical edition *Guillelmi de Ockham Opera Philosophica et Theologica*, St Bonaventure, NY: Editions of the Franciscan Institute of the University of St Bonaventure.

Odling-Smee, F. J., Laland, K. N. and Feldman, M. W. (2003) *Niche Construction: The Neglected Process in Evolution*, Princeton, NJ: Princeton University Press.

Ogden, C. K. (1932) *Opposition: A Linguistic and Psychological Analysis*, London: Paul, Trench, and Trubner.

Ogden, C. K. (1994) 'The progress of significs', in C. K. Ogden, *From Significs to Orthology*, Vol. 1, *C.K. Ogden and Linguistics*, 5 vols, ed. T. W. Gordon, London: Routledge–Thoemmes Press.

Ogden, C. K. and Richards, I. A. (1923) *The Meaning of Meaning: A Study of the Influence of Language upon Thought and of the Science of Symbolism*, with supplementary essays by B. Malinowski and F. G. Crookshank, London: Routledge and Kegan Paul.

Osgood, C. E., Suci, G. J. and Tannenbaum, P. H. (1957) *The Measurement of Meaning*, Urbana, IL: University of Illinois Press.

Owens, J. (1992) *Cognition: An Epistemological Inquiry*, Houston: Center for Thomistic Studies.

Pariente, J. C. (1973) *Le langage et l'individuel*, Paris: A. Colin.

Parsons, T. (1952) *The Social System*, London: Tavistock Publications.

Peirce, C. S. (1839–1914) *The Charles S. Peirce Papers*. Manuscript Collection in the Houghton Library, Cambridge, MA: Harvard University. Manuscript numbers refer to the Richard Robin arrangement.

Peirce, C. S. (*c.* 1902) *Minute Logic*, draft for a book complete consecutively only to Chapter 4. Published in *CP* in extracts scattered over six of the eight volumes, including 1.203–283, 1.575–584; 2.1–202; 4.227–323; 6.349–352; 7.279, 7.374n10, 7.362–387 except 381n19.

Peirce, C. S. (1923) *Chance. Love and Logic*, ed. M. R. Cohen, Lincoln, NE: Bison Books.

Peirce, C. S. (1931–1958) *Collected Papers of Charles Sanders Peirce*, ed. A. Burks, C. Hartshorne and P. Weiss, Cambridge, MA: Harvard University Press.

Peirce, C. S. (1966) 'Letter to Lady Welby, 23 December 1908', in *Charles S. Peirce: Selected Writings*, ed. P. Wiener, New York: Dover.

Peirce, C. S. (1975–1988) *Charles Sanders Peirce: Contributions to the Nation*, 4 vols, ed. K. L. Ketner and J. E. Cook, Lubbock, TX: Texas Tech University Press.

Peirce, C. S. (1976) *The New Elements of Mathematics*, Vol. IV, Atlantic Highlands, NJ: Humanities Press.

Peirce, C. S. (1977) '*What is Meaning?* by V. Welby. *The Principles of Mathematics* by Bertrand Russell' (1903, review article), in C. Hardwick (ed.), *Semiotic and Significs. The Correspondence Between Charles S. Peirce and Victoria Lady Welby*, Bloomington, IN: Indiana University Press.

Peirce, C. S. (1982–) *The Writings of Charles Sanders Peirce. A Chronological Edition*, ed. Peirce Edition Project, Vols 1–6, Bloomington, IN: Indiana University Press.

Peirce, C. S. (1984 [1867–1868]) 'Critique of positivism', in *Writings of Charles S. Peirce*, Vol. 2, ed. E. C. Moore, M. H. Fisch, *et al.*, Bloomington, IN: Indiana University Press.

Peirce, C. S. (1992a) *The Essential Peirce: Selected Philosophical Writings*, Vol. 1, ed. N. Houser and C. Kloesel, Bloomington, IN: Indiana University Press.

Peirce, C. S. (1992b [1868]) 'Some consequences of four incapacities', in *The Essential Peirce: Selected Philosophical Writings*, Vol. 1, ed. N. Houser and C. Kloesel, Bloomington, IN: Indiana University Press.

Peirce, C. S. (1992c [1871]) 'Review of Fraser's *The Works of George Berkeley*', in *The Essential Peirce: Selected Philosophical Writings*, Vol. 1, ed. N. Houser and C. Kloesel, Bloomington, IN: Indiana University Press.

Peirce, C. S. (1998a [1906]) 'The basis of pragmaticism in the normative sciences', in Peirce, *The Essential Peirce: Selected Philosophical Writings*, Vol. 2, ed. Peirce Edition Project, Bloomington, IN: Indiana University Press.

Peirce, C. S. (1998b) *The Essential Peirce: Selected Philosophical Writings*, Vol. 2, ed. Peirce Edition Project, Bloomington, IN: Indiana University Press.

Peirce, C. S. (1998c [1905]) 'Issues of pragmaticism', in *The Essential Peirce: Selected Philosophical Writings*, Vol. 2, ed. Peirce Edition Project, Bloomington, IN: Indiana University Press.

Peirce, C. S. (1998d [1908]) Draft of a letter dated December 24, 25, 28, 'On the Classification of Signs', in *The Essential Peirce: Selected Philosophical Writings*, Vol. 2, ed. Peirce Edition Project, Bloomington, IN: Indiana University Press.

Peirce Edition Project (ed.) (1998) *The Essential Peirce*, Vol. 2, Bloomington, IN: Indiana University Press.

Pelc, J. (1992) 'The methodological status of semiotics: Sign, semiosis, interpretation and the limits of semiotics', in Michel Balat and Janice Deledalle-Rhodes (eds), *Signs of Humanity. Proceedings of the IVth International Congress, International Association for Semiotic Studies*, Berlin: Mouton de Gruyter.

Pelc, J. (1997) 'Understanding, explanation, and action as problems of semiotics', in R. Posner, K. Robering and T. A. Sebeok (eds), *Semiotik: Ein Handbuch zu den zeichentheoretischen Grundlagen von Natur und Kultur*, Berlin: Walter de Gruyter.

Pepperell, R. (2002) *The Posthuman Condition*, London: Intellect.

Petitot, J. (1992) *Physique du sens*, Paris: Editions du CNRS.

Petitot, J. (1995) 'Morphodynamics and attractor syntax', in R. Port and T. van Gelder (eds), *Mind as Motion*, Cambridge, MA: MIT Press.

Petitot, J. (2004) *Morphogenesis of Meaning*, trans. F. Manjali, Bern: Peter Lang.

Petrilli, S. (1986) 'Introduzione', in V. Welby, *Significato, metafora, interpretazione*, trans. S. Petrilli, Bari: Adriatica.

Petrilli, S. (1988) *Significs, semiotica, significazione*, Bari: Adriatica.

Petrilli, S. (1990) 'On the materiality of signs', in A. Ponzio, *Man as a Sign*, trans. S. Petrilli, Berlin: Mouton de Gruyter.

Petrilli, S. (1992) 'Translation, semiotics and ideology', *TTR. Etudes sur le texte et ses transformations*, 5(1): 233–264.

Petrilli, S. (1995a) 'La metafora in Charles S. Peirce e Victoria Lady Welby', in Petrilli, *Materia segnica e interpretazione*, Lecce: Milella.

Petrilli, S. (1995b) 'Between semiotics and significs. C. K. Ogden and V. Welby', *Semiotica*, 105(3/4): 277–309.

Petrilli, S. (1995c) *Materia segnica e interpretazione. Figure e prospettive*, Lecce: Milella.

Petrilli, S. (1996) *Che cosa significa significare? Itinerari nello studio dei segni*, Bari: Edizioni dal Sud.

Petrilli, S. (1998a) *Su Victoria Welby. Significs e filosofia del linguaggio*, Naples: Edizioni Scientifiche Italiane.

Petrilli, S. (1998b) *Teoria dei segni e del linguaggio*, Bari: Graphis.

Petrilli, S. (1998c) 'Linguaggio figurato, processo linguistico e processi del significare',in Petrilli, *Su Victoria Welby. Significs e filosofia del linguaggio*, Naples: Edizioni Scientifiche Italiane.

Petrilli, S. (1998d) 'La significs e il significato di "significato": La corrispondenza di Welby con Charles K. Ogden', in Petrilli, *Su Victoria Welby. Significs e filosofia del linguaggio*, Napoli: Edizioni Scientifiche Italiane.

Petrilli, S. (1998e) 'Intersemiosi e traduzione', in Petrilli, *Su Victoria Welby. Significs e filosofia del linguaggio*, Naples: Edizioni Scientifiche Italiane.

Petrilli, S. (1998f) 'Translation and ideology', *Signs of Research on Signs*, *Semiotische Berichte*, 22(3/4): 127–139.

Petrilli, S. (1999a) 'Semiotic phenomenology of predicative judgement', *S: European Journal for Semiotic Studies*, Special Issue *Trajectories in Semiotic Studies from Bari*, ed. S. Petrilli.

Petrilli, S. (1999b) 'About and beyond Peirce', *Semiotica*, 124(3/4): 299–376.

Petrilli, S. (1999c) 'Traduzione e traducibilità', in S. Gensini (ed.), *Manuale di comunicazione*, Rome: Carocci.

Petrilli, S. (ed.) (1999d) 'Traduzione e semiosi: Considerazioni introduttive', special issue of *Athanor. Semiotica, Filosofia, Arte, Letteratura*, X(2).

Petrilli, S. (2004) 'Responsibility of power and the power of responsibility: From the "semiotic" to the "semioethic" animal', in G. Withalm and J. Wallmannsberger (eds), *Macht der Zeichen der Macht/Signs of Power of Signs*, Festschrift für Jeff Bernard, Vienna: Lit. Verlag.

Petrilli, S. (2009) *Signifying and Understanding: Reading the Works of Victoria Welby and the Significs Movement*, Berlin: Mouton de Gruyter.

Petrilli, S. and Ponzio, A. (2001) *Thomas Sebeok and the Signs of Life*, Cambridge: Icon Books.

Petrilli, S. and Ponzio, A. (2003) *Semioetica*, Rome: Meltemi.

Petrilli, S. and Ponzio, A. (2005) *Semiotics Unbounded. Interpretive Routes through the Open Network of Signs*, Toronto: Toronto University Press.

Petrilli, S., Ponzio, A. and Sebeok, T. A. (2001) *Semiotica dell'io*, Rome: Meltemi.

Petrus Hispanus (1972 [1230?]) *Tractatus. Called afterwards Summule logicales*, ed. L. M. De Rijk, Assen: Van Gorcum.

Philodemus (i.54–40 BCE) Περί σημειώσεων (*De Signis*), trans. as *On the Methods of Inference* in the edition of P. H. De Lacy and E. A. De Lacy, rev. with the collaboration of Marcello Gigante, F. Longo Auricchio and A. Tepedino Guerra, Naples: Bibliopolis, 1978; Greek text pp. 27–87, English text pp. 91–131.

Pike, K. L. (1954) *Language in Relation to a Unified Theory of the Structure of Human Behaviour*, Part 1, Glendale, CA: Summer Institute of Linguistics.

Pike, K. L. (1959) 'Language as particle, wave, and field', *Texas Quarterly*, 2(2): 37–54.

Pinker, S. (1994) *The Language Instinct*, New York: William Morrow.

Poinsot, J. (1632) *Tractatus de Signis*, subtitled *The Semiotic of John Poinsot*, arranged in bilingual format by J. Deely in consultation with R. A. Powell. First Edition, Berkeley, CA: University of California Press, 1985; available in electronic form as a text database, Charlottesville, VA: Intelex Corp., 1992.

Pollack, R. (1994) *Signs of Life: The Language and Meanings of DNA*, Harmondsworth: Penguin.

Pollner, M. (1987) *Mundane Reason: Reality in Everyday and Sociological Discourse*, Cambridge: Cambridge University Press.

Ponzio, A. (1974) *Persona umana, linguaggio e conoscenza in Adam Schaff*, Bari: Dedalo.

Ponzio, A. (1980a) 'Introduzione', in V. N. Vološinov and M. Bakhtin, *Il linguaggio come pratica sociale*, essays 1926–1930, ed. A. Ponzio, Bari: Dedalo.

Ponzio, A. (1980b) *Michail Bachtin. Alle origini della semiotica sovietica*, Bari: Dedalo.

Ponzio, A. (1981a) 'Das Problem der Bezeichnung bei Morris und in der zeitgenössischen Semiotik', in A. Eschbach (ed.), *Zeichen über Zeichen über Zeichen*, Tübingen: Gunter Narr.

Ponzio, A. (1981b) 'Polisemia e traduzione', in A. Ponzio, *Segni e contraddizioni. Fra Marx e Bachtin*, Verona: Bari.

Ponzio, A. (1985) 'The symbol, alterity, and abduction', *Semiotica*, 56(3/4): 261–277.

Ponzio, A. (1986) 'On the signs of Rossi-Landi's work', *Semiotica*, 62(3/4): 207–221.

Ponzio, A. (1989a) 'Semiotics and Marxism', in T. A. Sebeok and J. Umiker-Sebeok (eds), *The Semiotic Web 1988*, Berlin: Mouton de Gruyter.

Ponzio, A. (1989b) *Rossi-Landi e la filosofia del linguaggio*, Bari: Adriatica.

Ponzio, A. (1990a) *Man as a Sign*, trans. S. Petrilli, Berlin: Mouton de Gruyter.

Ponzio, A. (1990b) 'Signs to talk about signs', in *Man as a Sign*, trans. S. Petrilli, Berlin and New York: Mouton de Gruyter.

Ponzio, A. (1990c) 'Meaning and referent in Peter of Spain', in *Man as a Sign*, trans. S. Petrilli, Berlin: Mouton de Gruyter.

Ponzio, A. (1990d) 'Significs and semiotics. Victoria Welby and Giovanni Vailati', in *Man as a Sign*, trans. S. Petrilli, Berlin: Mouton de Gruyter.

Ponzio, A. (1990e) 'Theory of meaning and theory of knowledge: Vailati and Welby', in H. W. Schmitz (ed.), *Essays on Significs*, Amsterdam: John Benjamins.

Ponzio, A. (1992) *Tra semiotica e letteratura. Introduzione a Michail Bachtin*, Milan: Bompiani.

Ponzio, A. (1993) *Signs, Dialogue and Ideology*, trans. S. Petrilli, Amsterdam: John Benjamins.

Ponzio, A. (1994) *Scrittura, dialogo, alterità tra Bachtin e Lévinas*, Florence: La Nuova Italia.

Ponzio, A. (1995a) *La differenza non indifferente. Comunicazione, migrazione, guerra*, Milan: Mimesis.

Ponzio, A. (1995b) 'Nel segno di Barthes', in *I segni dell'altro. Eccedenza letteraria e prossimità*, Naples: Edizioni Scientifiche Italiane.

Ponzio, A. (1996) *Sujet et altérité. Sur Lévinas*, Paris: L'Harmattan.

Ponzio, A. (1997) *Metodologia della formazione linguistica*, Bari: Laterza.

Ponzio, A. (ed.) (1998a) *Lévinas vivant. Riflessioni sul pensiero di Emmanuel Lévinas*, Bari: Edizioni dal Sud.

Ponzio, A. (1998b) *La revolución Bajtiniana. El pensamiento de Bajtín y la ideología contemporánea*, Madrid: Ediciones Cátedra.

Ponzio, A. (2001a) 'Modelling', in P. Cobley (ed.), *The Routledge Companion to Semiotics and Linguistics*, London: Routledge.

Ponzio, A. (2001b) 'Marx', in P. Cobley (ed.), *The Routledge Companion to Semiotics and Linguistics*, London: Routledge.

Ponzio, A. (2006a) *The Dialogic Nature of Sign*, trans. S. Petrilli, Ottawa: Legas.

Ponzio, A. (2006b) *La cifrematica e l'ascolto*, Bari: Graphis.

Ponzio, A. (2006c) 'The I questioned: Emmanuel Levinas and the critique of occidental reason', *Subject Matters*, 3(1): 1–45.

Ponzio, A. (2007) *Fuori luogo. L'esorbitante nella riproduzione dell'identico*, Rome: Mimesis.

Ponzio, A. and Petrilli, S. (1996) 'Peirce and medieval semiotics', in V. M. Colapietro and T. M. Olshewsky (eds), *Peirce's Doctrine of Signs. Theory, Applications, and Connections*, Berlin: Mouton de Gruyter.

Ponzio, A. and Petrilli, S. (1998) *Signs of Research on Signs*, *Semiotische Berichte*, 22(3/4).

Ponzio, A. and Petrilli, S. (2000) *Il sentire della comunicazione globalizzata*, Rome: Meltemi.

Ponzio, A. and Petrilli, S. (2002) *I segni e la vita. La semiotica globale di Thomas A. Sebeok*, Milan: Spirali.

Ponzio, A. and Petrilli, S. (2003) *Semioetica*, Rome: Meltemi.

Ponzio, A. and Petrilli, S. (2005) *La raffigurazione letteraria*, Milan: Mimesis.
Ponzio, A. *et al.* (1985) *Per parlare dei segni/Talking about Signs*, trans. S. Petrilli, Bari: Adriatica.
Posner, R., Robering, K. and Sebeok, T. A. (eds) (1997–2004) *Semiotik/Semiotics. Ein Handbuch zu den zeichentheoretischen Grundlagen von Natur und Kultur* [*A Handbook on the Sign-Theoretic Foundations of Nature and Culture*], 4 vols, Berlin: Walter de Gruyter.
Potter, J. and Wetherell, M. (1987) *Discourse and Social Psychology: Beyond Attitudes and Behaviour*, London: Sage.
Prodi, G. (1988) *La biologia come semiotica naturale* [*Biology as Nature Semiotics*], in M. Herzfeld and L. Melazzo (eds), *Semiotic Theory and Practice*, Vol. II, Berlin: Mouton de Gruyter.
Putnam, H. (1987) *The Many Faces of Realism*, LaSalle, IL: Open Court.
Quine, W. V. O. (1961) *From a Logical Point of View*, New York: Harper and Row.
Quintilian, M. F. (1924) The *Institutio Oratoria of Quintilian*, trans. H. E. Butler, London: Heinemann.
Randviir, A. (2004) *Mapping the World: Towards a Sociosemiotic Approach to Culture*, Tartu: Tartu University Press.
Réthoré, J. (ed.) (1993) *Variations sur l'objet*, special issue of *European Journal for Semiotic Studies*, 5(1/2).
Rey, A. (1984) 'What does semiotics come from?', *Semiotica*, 52(1/2): 79–93.
Riggins, S. H. (ed.) (1994) *The Socialness of Things: Essays in the Sociosemiotics of Objects*, Berlin: Mouton de Gruyter.
Romeo, L. (1977) 'The derivation of "semiotics" through the history of the discipline', *Semiosis*, 6(2): 37–49.
Rorty, R. M. (ed.) (1967) *The Linguistic Turn: Essays in Philosophical Method with Two Retrospective Essays*, Chicago: University of Chicago Press.
Rosaldo, R. (1993) *Culture and Truth: The Remaking of Social Analysis*, London: Routledge.
Rosen, R. (1999) *Essays on Life Itself*, New York: Columbia University Press.
Rosen, R., Pattee, H. H. and Somorjai, R. L. (1979) 'A symposium in theoretical biology', in P. Buckley and F. D. Peat (eds), *A Question of Physics: Conversations in Physics and Biology*, Toronto: University of Toronto Press.
Rossi-Landi, F. (1953) *Morris e la semiotica novecentesca*, Milan: Feltrinelli.
Rossi-Landi, F. (1961) *Significato, comunicazione e parlare comune*, Venice: Marsilio.
Rossi-Landi, F. (1972) *Semiotica e ideologia*, Milan: Bompiani.
Rossi-Landi, F. (1973) *Ideologies of Linguistic Relativity*, The Hague: Mouton.
Rossi-Landi, F. (1975) *Linguistics and Economics*, The Hague: Mouton.
Rossi-Landi, F. (1985) *Metodica filosofica e scienza dei segni*, Milan: Bompiani.
Rossi-Landi, F. (1986a) 'Marx, Karl (1818–1883)', in T. A. Sebeok (ed.), *Encyclopedic Dictionary of Semiotics*, Vol. 1, Berlin: Mouton de Gruyter.
Rossi-Landi, F. (1986b) 'Materialist semiotics', in T. A. Sebeok (ed.), *Encyclopedic Dictionary of Semiotics*, Vol. 1, Berlin: Mouton de Gruyter.
Rossi-Landi, F. (1990 [1978]) *Marxism and Ideology*, trans. R. Griffin, Oxford: Clarendon.
Rossi-Landi, F. (1992a) *Social Practice. Semiotics and the Sciences of Man: The Correspondence between Charles Morris and Ferruccio Rossi-Landi*, ed. and intro. S. Petrilli, *Semiotica*, 88(1/2).
Rossi-Landi, F. (1992b [1968]) *Language as Work and Trade*, trans. M. Adams *et al.*, South Hadley: Bergin and Garvey.
Rossi-Landi, F. (1992c) *Between Signs and Non-signs*, ed. S. Petrilli, Amsterdam: John Benjamins.
Rossi-Landi, F. (1992d) 'Signs and material reality', in *Between Signs and Non-signs*, ed. S. Petrilli, Amsterdam: John Benjamins.

Rossi-Landi, F. (1998) *Significato, comunicazione e parlare comune*, rev. edn, ed. A. Ponzio, Venice: Marsilio.

Rossi-Landi, F. (2005 [1978]) *Ideologia*, new edn, ed. A. Ponzio, Rome: Meltemi.

Rossi-Landi, F. (2006 [1985]) *Metodica filosofica e scienza dei segni*, new edn, ed. A. Ponzio, Milan: Bompiani.

Ruesch, J. (1972) *Semiotic Approaches to Human Relations*, The Hague: Mouton.

Russell, B. (1948) *An Inquiry into Meaning and Truth*, London: George Allen and Unwin.

Russell, B. (1959) *My Philosophical Development*, New York: Simon and Schuster.

Russell, L. J. (1939) 'Note on the term *sēmeiōtikē* [*sic*] in Locke', *Mind*, 48: 405–406.

Rüting, T. (2004) 'History and significance of Jakob von Uexküll and his Institute in Hamburg', *Sign Systems Studies*, 32(1/2): 35–72.

Sacks, H. (1992) *Lectures on Conversation*, Vols I and II, ed. G. Jefferson, Oxford: Blackwell.

Sacks, H., Schegloff, E. and Jefferson, G. (1974) 'A simplest systematics for the organization of turn-taking for conversation', *Language*, 50: 696–735.

Said, E. (1978) *Orientalism*, New York: Pantheon.

Salthe, S. N. (1993) *Development and Evolution. Complexity and Change in Biology*, Cambridge, MA: MIT Press.

Salthe, S. N. (1999) 'A semiotic attempt to corral creativity via generativity', *Semiotica*, 127(1/4): 481–495.

Salthe, S. N. (2007) 'What is the scope of biosemiotics? Information in living systems', in M. Barbieri (ed.), *Introduction to Biosemiotics. The New Biological Synthesis*, Dordrecht: Springer.

Sapir, E. (1962 [1916]) 'Time perspective in Aboriginal American culture: A study in method', in D. G. Mandelbaum (ed.), *Selected Writings of Edward Sapir in Language Culture and Personality*, Berkeley, CA: University of California Press.

Saussure, F. de (1916) *Cours de linguistique générale*, ed. C. Bally and A. Sechehaye, Paris: Payot.

Saussure, F. de (1959) *Course in General Linguistics*, trans. W. Baskin, London: Peter Owen.

Saussure, F. de (1972 [1916]) *Cours de linguistique générale*, ed. Tullio de Mauro, Paris: Payot.

Saussure, F. de (1983) *Course in General Linguistics*, trans. R. Harris, London: Duckworth.

Saussure, F. de (1986) *Le leggende germaniche*, ed. A. Marinetti and M. Meli, Este: Zielo.

Saussure, F. de (1993) *Cours de linguistique générale. Premier et troisième cours, d'après les notes de Riedlinger et Constantin*, ed. E. Komatsu, Collection Recherches, Université Gakushuin, no. 24.

Schaff, A. (1962) *Introduction to Semantics*, Oxford: Pergamon Press.

Schaff, A. (1973) *Language and Cognition*, New York: McGraw-Hill.

Schaff, A. (1975) *Humanismus – Sprachphilosophie-Erkenntnistheorie des Marxismus*, Vienna: Europa Verlag.

Schaff, A. (1978) *Structuralism and Marxism*, Oxford: Pergamon Press.

Schank, R. C. and Abelson, R. (1977) *Scripts, Plans, Goals and Understanding*, Hillsdale, NJ: Lawrence Erlbaum Associates.

Schiller, F. C. S. (1907) *Studies in Humanism*, London: Macmillan.

Schmitz, H. W. (1985) 'Victoria Lady Welby's significs: The origin of the Signific Movement', in V. Welby, *Significs and Language (The articulate form of our expressive and interpretative resources)* (1911), with additional essays, ed. H. W. Schmitz, Amsterdam: John Benjamins.

Schmitz, H. W. (1990) 'The Signific Movement in the Netherlands', in H. W. Schmitz (ed.), *Essays on Significs. Papers Presented on the Occasion of the 150th Anniversary of the Birth of Victoria Lady Welby*, Amsterdam: John Benjamins.

Scholl, B. D. and Tremoulet, P. D. (2000) 'Perceptual causality and animacy', *Trends in Cognitive Science*, 4: 299–309.

Schramm, W. (1954) 'How communication works', in W. Schramm (ed.), *The Process and Effects of Communication*, Urbana, IL: University of Illinois Press.

Schutz, A. (1967 [1932]) *The Phenomenology of the Social World*, ed. G. Walsh and F. Lehnert, Evanston, IL: Northwestern University Press.

Searle, J. R. (1969) *Speech Acts: An Essay in the Philosophy of Language*, Cambridge: Cambridge University Press.

Searle, J. R. (1975) 'Indirect speech acts', in P. Cole and J. L. Morgan (eds), *Syntax and Semantics 3: Speech Acts*, New York: Academic Press.

Searle, J. R. (1976) 'A classification of illocutionary acts', *Language in Society*, 5: 1–23.

Searle, J. R. (1978) 'Literal meaning', *Erkenntnis*, 13: 207–224.

Searle, J. R. (1989) 'How performatives work', *Linguistics and Philosophy*, 12: 535–558.

Sebeok, T. A. (ed.) (1963) *Animal Communication. Techniques of Study and Results of Research*, Bloomington, IN: Indiana University Press.

Sebeok, T. A. (1971) '"Semiotic" and its congeners', as reprinted in J. Deely *et al.* (eds), *Frontiers in Semiotics*, Bloomington, IN: Indiana University Press, 1986.

Sebeok, T. A. (1972a) 'The word "zoosemiotics"', in *Perspectives in Zoosemiotics*, The Hague: Mouton.

Sebeok, T. A. (1972b) 'Semiotics and ecology', in *Perspectives in Zoosemiotics*, The Hague: Mouton.

Sebeok, T. A. (1975) 'The semiotic web: A chronicle of prejudices', *Bulletin of Literary Semiotics*, 2: 1–63.

Sebeok, T. A. (1976) *Contributions to the Doctrine of Signs*, Bloomington, IN: Indiana University Press.

Sebeok, T. A. (ed.) (1977) *How Animals Communicate*, Bloomington, IN: Indiana University Press.

Sebeok, T. A. (1978) 'Looking in the destination for what should have been sought in the source', *Diogenes*, 104: 112–137.

Sebeok, T. A. (1979a) *The Sign and Its Masters*, Austin, TX: University of Texas Press.

Sebeok, T. A. (1979b) 'Neglected figures in the history of semiotic inquiry: Jakob von Uexküll', in *The Sign and Its Masters*, Austin, TX: University of Texas Press.

Sebeok, T. A. (1979c) 'The semiotic self', in *The Sign and Its Masters*, Austin, TX: University of Texas Press.

Sebeok, T. A. (1981a) *The Play of Musement*, Bloomington, IN: Indiana University Press.

Sebeok, T. A. (1981b) 'Smart simians: The self-fulfilling prophecy and kindred methodological pitfalls', in *The Play of Musement*, Bloomington, IN: Indiana University Press.

Sebeok, T. A. (1982) 'Foreword' to J. Deely, *Introducing Semiotic. Its History and Doctrine*, Bloomington, IN: Indiana University Press.

Sebeok, T. A. (1984) 'The evolution of communication and the origin of language', lecture in the June 1–3 ISISSS '84 Colloquium on 'Phylogeny and Ontogeny of Communication Systems'.

Sebeok, T. A. (1985a) 'Vital signs', *The American Journal of Semiotics*, 3(3): 1–27.

Sebeok, T. A. (1985b) 'Modern man, communication and language', in C. Thomson (ed.), *The Phylogeny and Ontogeny of Communication Systems*, Monographs, Working Papers and Prepublications of the Toronto Semiotic Circle, 1: 163–169.

Sebeok, T. A. (1985c) 'On the phylogenesis of communication, language, and speech', *Recherches Sémiotiques* [*Semiotic Inquiry*], 5(4): 361–367.

Sebeok, T. A. (1986a) 'Can animals lie?', in *I Think I am a Verb*, New York: Plenum Press.

Sebeok, T. A. (1986b) 'The problem of the origin of language in an evolutionary frame', *Language Sciences*, 8(2): 168–174.

Sebeok, T. A. (1986c) *I Think I am a Verb: More Contributions to the Doctrine of Signs*, New York: Plenum Press.

Sebeok, T. A. (1988a) 'Language: How Primary a Modeling System?', in J. Deely (ed.), *Semiotics 1987*, Lanham, MD: University Press of America.

Sebeok, T. A. (1988b) 'In what sense is language a "primary modeling system"?', in H. Broms and R. Kaufmann (eds), *Semiotics of Culture*, Helsinki: Arator.

Sebeok, T. A. (1988b) 'Foreword', in B. Lee and G. Urban (eds), *Sign, Self and Society*, Berlin: Mouton.

Sebeok, T. A. (1990) *Essays in Zoosemiotics*, ed. M. Danesi, Toronto: Toronto. Semiotic Circle.

Sebeok, T. A. (1991a) *A Sign is Just a Sign*, Bloomington, IN: Indiana University Press.

Sebeok, T. A. (1991b) *Semiotics in the United States*, Bloomington, IN: Indiana University Press.

Sebeok, T. A. (1992) 'Tell me where is fancy bred? The biosemiotic self', in T. A. Sebeok and J. Umiker Sebeok (eds), *Biosemiotics: The Semiotic Web 1991*, Bloomington, IN: Indiana University Press.

Sebeok, T. A. (1994) *Signs: An Introduction to Semiotics*, Toronto: University of Toronto Press.

Sebeok, T. A. (1996) 'Signs, bridges, origins', in J. Trabant (ed.), *The Origins of Language*, Budapest: Collegium Budapest Institute for Advanced Study.

Sebeok, T. A. (1998a) *A Sign is Just a Sign* and *La semiotica globale* [*Global Semiotics*], Milan: Spirali.

Sebeok, T. A. (1998b) 'The cognitive self and the virtual self', in W. Pencak and J. R. Lindgren (eds), *New Approaches to Semiotics and the Human Sciences: Essays in Honor of Roberta Kevelson*, New York: Peter Lang.

Sebeok, T. A. (1999) 'Editor's note: Towards a prehistory of biosemiotics', *Semiotica*, 134: 1–3.

Sebeok, T. A. (2000) 'Semiotics as bridge between humanities and sciences', in P. Perron, L. G. Sbrocchi, P. Colilli and M. Danesi (eds), *Semiotics as Bridge between the Humanities and the Sciences*, New York: Legas.

Sebeok, T. A. (2001a) 'Galen in medical semiotics', in *Global Semiotics*, Bloomington, IN: Indiana University Press.

Sebeok, T. A. (2001b) *Global Semiotics*, Bloomington, IN: Indiana University Press.

Sebeok, T. A. (2001c) *Signs: An Introduction to Semiotics*, 2nd edn, Toronto: University of Toronto Press.

Sebeok, T. A. (2001d) 'Nonverbal communication', in P. Cobley (ed.), *The Routledge Companion to Semiotics and Linguistics*, London: Routledge.

Sebeok, T. A. and Danesi, M. (2000) *The Forms of Meaning: Modeling Systems Theory and Semiotic Analysis*, Berlin: Mouton de Gruyter.

Sebeok, T. A. and Ramsay, A. (eds) (1969) *Approaches to Animal Communication*, Bloomington, IN: Indiana University Press.

Sebeok, T. A. and Rosenthal, R. (eds) (1981) *The Clever Hans Phenomenon: Communication with Horses, Whales, Apes, and People*, New York: New York Academy of Sciences.

Sebeok, T. A. and Umiker-Sebeok, J. (1981) 'Clever Hans and smart simians: The self-fulfilling prophecy and kindred methodological pitfalls', *Anthropos*, 76(1/2): 89–165.

Sebeok, T. A. and Umiker-Sebeok, J. (eds) (1992) *Biosemiotics: The Semiotic Web 1991*, Berlin: Mouton de Gruyter.

Sebeok, T. A., Petrilli, S. and Ponzio, A. (2001) *Semiotica dell'io*, Rome: Meltemi.

Sedley, D. (1982) 'On signs', in J. Barnes, J. Brunschwig, M. Burnyeat and M. Schofield (eds), *Science and Speculation. Studies in Hellenistic Theory and Practice*, Cambridge: Cambridge University Press.

Seigel, J. P. (1969) 'The Enlightenment and the evolution of a language of signs in France and England', *Journal for the History of Ideas*, 30: 96–115.

Shannon, C. E. (1948) 'A mathematical theory of communication', *Bell Systems Technical Journal*, 27: 379–423.

Shannon, C. E. and Weaver, W. (1949) *The Mathematical Theory of Communication*, Urbana, IL: University of Illinois Press.

Sharov, A. (2001) 'Umwelt-theory and pragmatism', *Semiotica*, 134(3/4): 211–228.

Shklovsky, V. (1973 [1914]) 'The resurrection of the word', trans. R. Sherwood, in S. Bann and J. E. Bowlt (eds), *Russian Formalism: A Collection of Articles and Texts in Translation*, New York: Barnes and Noble.

Short, T. L. (1986) 'Life among the legisigns', in J. Deely, B. Williams and F. E. Kruse (eds), *Frontiers in Semiotics*, Bloomington, IN: Indiana University Press.

Short, T. L. (1998) 'What's the use?', *Semiotica*, 122(1/2): 1–68.

Shukman, A. (ed.) (1984) *The Semiotics of Russian Culture*, Ann Arbor, MI: University of Michigan.

Shukman, A. (1987) 'Semiotic aspects of the work of Jurij Michailoviè Lotman', in *The Semiotic Web 1987*, Berlin: Mouton de Gruyter.

Silverman, K. (1983) *The Subject of Semiotics*, Oxford: Oxford University Press.

Sinclair, J. (1991) *Corpus, concordance, collocation*, Oxford: Oxford University Press.

Singer, M. B. (1984) *Man's Glassy Essence: Explorations in Semiotic Anthropology*, Bloomington, IN: Indiana University Press.

Skinner, B. F. (1957) *Verbal Behavior*, New York: Appleton-Century-Crofts.

Smith, B. (1993) 'Putting the world back into semantics', *Grazer Philosophische Studien*, 43: 91–109.

Snow, C. P. (1993) *The Two Cultures*, Cambridge: Cambridge University Press.

Sperber, D. (1979) 'Claude Lévi-Strauss', in J. Sturrock (ed.), *Structuralism and Since*, Oxford: Oxford University Press.

Sperber, D. and Wilson, D. (1986) *Relevance: Communication and Cognition*, Oxford: Blackwell.

Sperber, D. and Wilson, D. (1995) *Relevance: Communication and Cognition*, 2nd edn, Oxford: Blackwell.

Spiegelberg, H. (1957) 'Husserl's and Peirce's phenomenologies: Coincidence or interaction?', *Philosophy and Phenomenological Research*, 17: 164–185.

Sterelny, K. and Griffiths, P. E. (1999) *Sex and Death. An Introduction to Philosophy of Biology*. Chicago: University of Chicago Press.

Stjernfelt, F. (2007) *Diagrammatology: An Investigation on the Borderlines of Phenomenology, Ontology, and Semiotics*, Dordrecht: Springer.

Stocking, G. W., Jr (1966) 'Franz Boas and the culture concept in historical perspective', *American Anthropologist*, 68: 867–882.

Stocking, G. W., Jr (ed.) (1996) Volksgeist *as Method and Ethic: Essays on Boasian Ethnography and the German Anthropological Tradition* (History of Anthropology, Vol. 8), Madison, WI: University of Wisconsin Press.

Stokoe, W. C. (1960) *Sign Language Structure*, Silver Spring, MD: Linstok Press.

Stokoe, W. C. (1991) 'Semantic phonology', *Sign Language Studies*, 71: 107–114.

Stokoe, W. C. (2001a) *Language in Hand*, Washington, DC: Gallaudet University Press.

Stokoe, W. C. (2001b) 'The origins of language', in P. Cobley (ed.), *The Routledge Companion to Semiotics and Linguistics*, London: Routledge.

Stokoe, W. C., Casterline, D. and Croneberg, C. (1965, rev'd 1976) *A Dictionary of American Sign Language on Linguistic Principles*, Washington, DC: Gallaudet College Press.

Strauss, D. F. M. (2003) 'The "Copernican turn" of biology in the 20th century', *Acta Academia*, 35(3): 49–76.

Strube, G. and Lazarus, G. (1997) 'Der akustische Kanal', in R. Posner, K. Robering and T. A. Sebeok (eds), *Semiotik: Ein Handbuch zu den zeichentheoretischen Grundlagen von Natur und Kultur*, Vol. 1, Berlin: Mouton de Gruyter.

Sturrock, J. (1991) 'Inside the Semiosphere', *TLS*, May 3.

Sutrop, U. (2001) 'Umwelt – word and concept: Two hundred years of semantic change', *Semiotica*, 134(1/4): 447–462.

Sweetser, E. (1990) *From Etymology to Pragmatics: Metap-orical and Cultural Aspects of Semantic Structure*, Cambridge, MA: Cambridge University Press.

Szasz, T. (2001) *Pharmacracy. Medicine and Politics in America*, rev. edn, New York: Syracuse University Press.

Taborsky, E. (2002) 'Energy and evolutionary semiosis', *Sign Systems Studies*, 30(1): 361–381.

Talmy, L. (2000) *Toward a Cognitive Semantics*, Vols I and II, Cambridge, MA: The MIT Press.

Talmy, L. (2005) 'The fundamental system of spatial schemas in language', in B. Hampe (ed.), *From Perception to Meaning – Image Schemas in Cognitive Linguistics*, Berlin: Mouton de Gruyter.

Tarasti, E. (1979) *Myth and Music*, Berlin: Mouton de Gruyter.

Tarasti, E. (2001) *Existential Semiotics*, Bloomington, IN: Indiana University Press.

Tarasti, E. (2002) *Signs of Music: A Guide to Musical Semiotics*, Berlin: Mouton de Gruyter.

Terras, V. (1985) 'Lotman', in V. Terras (ed.), *Handbook of Russian Literature*, New Haven, CT: Yale University Press.

Thom, R. (1972) *Structural Stability and Morphogenesis*, New York: Advanced Book Classics.

Thom, R. (1983) *Mathematical Models of Morphogenesis*, Chichester: Ellis Horwood.

Tiersma, P. M. (1982) 'Local and general markedness', *Language*, 58: 832–849.

Todorov, T. (ed.) (1965) *Théorie de la littérature*, Paris: Seuil.

Todorov, T. (1977) 'The birth of occidental semiotics', trans. D. Swabey and J. Mullen, in R. W. Bailey, L. Matejka and P. Steiner (eds), *The Sign*, Ann Arbor, MI: Michigan Slavic Publications.

Todorov, T. (1981) *Le principe dialogique, Mikhail Bakhtine*, Paris: Editions du Seuil.

Toman, J. (1995) *The Magic of a Common Language: Jakobson, Mathesius, Trubetzkoy, and the Prague Linguistic Circle*, Cambridge, MA: The MIT Press.

Trubetzkoy, N. S. (1936) 'Essaie d'une théorie des oppositions phonologiques', *Journal de Psychologie*, 33: 5–18.

Trubetzkoy, N. S. (1939) 'Grundzüge der Phonologie', special issue of *Travaux du Cercle Linguistique de Prague* 7.

Turner, R. (1974) *Ethnomethodology*, Harmondsworth: Penguin.

Tylor, E. (1865) *Researches into the Early History of Mankind*, London: John Murray.

Uexküll, G. von (1964) *Jakob von Uexküll: seine Welt und seine Umwelt*, Hamburg: C. Wegner.

Uexküll, J. von (1904) 'Die ersten Ursachen des Rhythmus in der Tierreihe', *Ergebnisse der Physiologie*, 3(2): 1–11.

Uexküll, J. von (1907) 'Die Umrisse einer kommenden Weltanschauung', *Die neue Rundschau*, 18: 641–661.

Uexküll, J. von (1909) *Umwelt und Innenwelt der Tiere*, Berlin: Verlag von Julius Springer.

Uexküll, J. von (1910) 'Die Umwelt', *Die neue Rundschau*, 21(2): 638–649.

Uexküll, J. von (1912) 'Die Merkwelten der Tiere', *Deutsche Revue* (Stuttgart), 37: 349–355.

Uexküll, J. von (1913a) *Bausteine zu einer biologischen Weltanschauung: Gesammelte Aufsätze*, Munich: F. Bruckmann A-G.

Uexküll, J. von (1913b) 'Die Aufgaben der biologischen Weltanschauung', *Die neue Rundschau*, 24: 1080–1091.

Uexküll, J. von (1919) 'Biologische Briefe an eine Dame', *Deutsche Rundschau*, 178: 309–323; 179: 132–148, 276–292, 451–468.

Uexküll, J. von (1920) *Theoretische Biologie*, Berlin: Verlag von Gebrüder Paetel.

Uexküll, J. von (1922) 'Wie sehen wir die Natur und wie sieht sie sich selber?', *Die Naturwissenschaften*, 10(12/14): 265–271, 296–301, 316–322.

Uexküll, J. von (1928) *Theoretische Biologie*, 2nd rev. edn, Berlin: Verlag von Julius Springer.

Uexküll, J. von (1940) *Bedeutungslehre*, Leipzig: Verlag von J. A. Barth.

Uexküll, J. von (1973 [1920, 1928]) *Theoretische Biologie*, Frankfurt am Main: Suhrkamp.

Uexküll, J. von (1980) *Kompositionslehre der Natur: Biologie als undogmatische Naturwissenschaft. Ausgewählte Schriften*, ed. T. von Uexküll, Frankfurt am Main: Verlag Ullstein GmbH.

Uexküll, J. von (1982) 'The theory of meaning', *Semiotica*, 42(1): 25–82.

Uexküll, J. von (1992) 'A stroll through the worlds of animals and men: A picture book of invisible worlds', *Semiotica*, 89(4): 319–391.

Uexküll, J. von (2001a) 'An introduction to Umwelt', *Semiotica*, 134(1/4): 107–110.

Uexküll, J. von (2001b) 'The new concept of Umwelt: A link between science and humanities', *Semiotica*, 134(1/4): 111–123.

Uexküll, T. von (1987) 'The sign-theory of Jakob von Uexküll', in M. Krampen *et al.* (eds), *Classics of Semiotics*, London: Plenum Press.

Ulanowicz, R. E. (2008) 'Process ecology: Creatura at large in an open universe', in J. Hoffmeyer (ed.), *A Legacy for Living Systems. Gregory Bateson as Precursor to Biosemiotics*, Dordrecht: Springer.

Ulanowicz, R. E. (2009) *A Third Window: Natural Foundations for Life*, New York: Templeton Foundation Press.

Uldall, H. J. (1957) *Outline of Glossematics*, Copenhagen: Nordisk Sprog- og Kulturforlag.

Umiker-Sebeok, J. (2003) 'T. A. Sebeok. A bibliography of his writings (1942–2001)', *Semiotica*, 147(1/4): 11–73.

Uspenskij, B. A., Ivanov, V. V., Toporov, V. N. *et al.* (1973) 'Theses on the semiotic study of cultures (as applied to Slavic texts)', in J. van Eng and M. Grygar (eds), *Structure of Texts and Semiotics of Culture*, The Hague: Mouton.

Vailati, G. (1971) *Epistolario*, Turin: Einaudi.

Vailati, G. (1987) *Scritti*, ed. M. Quaranta, Bologna: Arnaldo Forni.

Vegetti, M. (ed.) (1976) *Opere di Ippocrate*, Turin: Utet.

Verdiglione, A. (1997) *La psicanalisi, questa mia avventura*, Milan: Spirali.

Verschueren, J. (1999) *Understanding Pragmatics*, London: Edward Arnold/New York: Oxford University Press.

Verschueren, J. (2001) 'Pragmatics', in P. Cobley (ed.), *The Routledge Companion to Semiotics and Linguistics*, London: Routledge.

Vološinov, V. N. (1973 [1929]) *Marxism and the Philosophy of Language*, trans. L. Matejka and I. R. Titunik, New York: Seminar Press.

Vološinov, V. N. (1987 [1926]) 'Discourse in life and discourse in art (concerning sociological poetics)', in *Freudianism: A Critical Sketch*, trans. I. R. Titunik, Indianapolis, IN: Indiana University Press.

Vološinov, V. N. (1987 [1927]) *Freudianism: A Critical Sketch*, trans. I. R. Titunik, ed. I. R. Titunik with N. H. Bruss, Indianapolis, IN: Indiana University Press.

Volterra, V. and Iverson, J. (1995) 'When do modality factors affect the course of language acquisition?', in K. Emmorey and J. Reilly (eds), *Language, Gesture and Space*, Hillsdale, NJ: Erlbaum.

Waugh, L. and Monville-Burston, M. (1990) 'Introduction', in R. Jakobson, *On Language*, Cambridge, MA: Harvard University Press.

Welby, V. (1852) *A Young Traveller's Journal of a Tour in North and South America during the Year 1850*, London: T. Bosworth.

Welby, V. (1881) *Links and Clues*, London: Macmillan and Co.

Welby, V. (1891) *Witnesses to Ambiguity. A Collection*, Grantham: W. Clarke (Late L. Ridge).

Welby, V. (1892) *The Use of 'Inner' and 'Outer' in Psychology: Does the Metaphor Help or Hinder? A small collection of extracts bearing upon this question respectfully submitted to the International Congress of Experimental Psychology, August 1892*, Grantham: W. Clarke (Late L. Ridge).

Welby, V. (1893) *A Selection of Passages from 'Mind' (Jan. 1876, to July 1892), 'Nature' (1870 and 1888 to 1892), 'Natural Science' (1892), bearing on changes and defects in the significance of terms and in the theory and practice of logic*, Grantham: W. Clarke (Late L. Ridge).

Welby, V. (1897) *Grains of Sense*, London: J. M. Dent.

Welby, V. (1898) *The Witness of Science to Linguistic Anarchy: A collection of extracts, chiefly from 'Nature', 'Science' and 'Natural Science'*, Grantham: W. Clarke.

Welby, V. (1929) *Echoes of Larger Life: A Selection from the Early Correspondence of Victoria Lady Welby*, ed. Mrs. Henry Cust, London: Jonathan Cape.

Welby, V. (1931) *Other Dimensions: A Selection from the Later Correspondence of Victoria Lady Welby*, ed. Mrs. Henry Cust, London: Jonathan Cape.

Welby, V. (1977 [1911]) 'Significs', in *The Encyclopedia Britannica*, 11th edn, Vol. XXV. Now in C. Hardwick (ed.), *Semiotic and Significs. The Correspondence Between Charles S. Peirce and Victoria Lady Welby*, Bloomington, IN: Indiana University Press.

Welby, V. (1983 [1903]) *What is Meaning?*, ed. A. Eschbach, Amsterdam: John Benjamins.

Welby, V. (1985a [1911]) *Significs and Language (The articulate form of our expressive and interpretative resources)*, with additional essays, ed. H. W. Schmitz, Amsterdam: John Benjamins.

Welby, V. (1985b [1893]) 'Meaning and metaphor', *The Monist*, 3(4): 510–525. Now in Welby, V. *Significs and Language (The articulate form of our expressive and interpretative resources)*, with additional essays, ed. H. W. Schmitz, Amsterdam: John Benjamins.

Welby, V. (1985c [1896]) 'Sense, meaning and interpretation', *Mind*, 5(17): 24–37; 5(18): 186–202. Now in Welby, V. *Significs and Language (The articulate form of our expressive and interpretative resources)*, with additional essays, ed. H. W. Schmitz, Amsterdam: John Benjamins.

Welby, V. (1986) *Significato, metafora, interpretazione*, intro., trans. and ed. S. Petrilli, Bari: Adriatica.

Welby, V. and Tönnies, F. (1901) 'Notes on the "Welby Prize Essay"', *Mind*, 10(38): 188–209.

Welby, V., Baldwin, J. M. and Stout, G. F. (1902) 'Significs', in J. M. Baldwin (ed.), *Dictionary of Philosophy and Psychology in Three Volumes, 1901–1905*, Vol. 2, New York: Macmillan.

Wells, G. A. (1987) *The Origin of Language: Aspects of the Discussion from Condillac to Wundt*, La Salle, IL: Open Court Publishing.

Westley, B. and MacLean, M. (1957) A conceptual model for communication research, *Journalism Quarterly*, 34: 31–38.

Wiener, N. (1961 [1941]) *Cybernetics: Or Control and Communication in the Animal and the Machine*, Cambridge, MA: MIT Press.

Wiley, N. (1994) *The Semiotic Self*, Cambridge: Polity Press.

Williams, R. (1950) *Reading and Criticism*, London: Frederick Muller.

Williams, V. J., Jr (1996) *Rethinking Race: Franz Boas and his Contemporaries*, Lexington, KY: University Press of Kentucky.

Wittgenstein, L. (1922) *Tractatus Logico-Philosophicus*, trans. D. F. Pears and B. F. Guinness, London: Routledge and Kegan Paul.

Wittgenstein, L. (1953) *Philosophische Untersuchungen*, trans. G. E. M. Anscombe, Oxford: Blackwell.

Wuketis, F. M. (1997) 'Anthroposemiose', in R. Posner, K. Robering and T. A. Sebeok (eds), *Semiotik: Ein Handbuch zu den zeichentheoretischen Grundlagen von Natur and Kultur*, Vol. 1, Berlin: Mouton de Gruyter.

Yates, E. F. (1985) 'Semiotics as bridge between information (biology) and dynamics (physics)', *Recherches Sémiotiques* [*Semiotic Inquiry*], 5: 347–360.

Zeitschrift für Semiotik (1988) 10: 1–2.

Index

Note: **Bold** type indicates an entry in Part II and **bold** type number indicates its location

A library at your fingertips!

eBooks are electronic versions of printed books. You can store them on your PC/laptop or browse them online.

They have advantages for anyone needing rapid access to a wide variety of published, copyright information.

eBooks can help your research by enabling you to bookmark chapters, annotate text and use instant searches to find specific words or phrases. Several eBook files would fit on even a small laptop or PDA.

NEW: Save money by eSubscribing: cheap, online access to any eBook for as long as you need it.

Annual subscription packages

We now offer special low-cost bulk subscriptions to packages of eBooks in certain subject areas. These are available to libraries or to individuals.

For more information please contact webmaster.ebooks@tandf.co.uk

We're continually developing the eBook concept, so keep up to date by visiting the website.

www.eBookstore.tandf.co.uk

LIBRARY, UNIVERSITY OF CHESTER